Research Methodologies, Innovations and Philosophies in Software Systems Engineering and Information Systems

Manuel Mora
Autonomous University of Aguascalientes, Mexico

Ovsei Gelman
Center of Applied Sciences and Technology Development of the National Autonomous University of Mexico, Mexico

Annette Steenkamp
Lawrence Technological University, USA

Mahesh S. Raisinghani
Texas Woman's University, USA

Information Science
REFERENCE

Managing Director:	Lindsay Johnston
Senior Editorial Director:	Heather Probst
Book Production Manager:	Sean Woznicki
Development Manager:	Joel Gamon
Development Editor:	Myla Harty
Acquisitions Editor:	Erika Gallagher
Typesetter:	Deanna Jo Zombro
Cover Design:	Nick Newcomer, Lisandro Gonzalez

Published in the United States of America by
Information Science Reference (an imprint of IGI Global)
701 E. Chocolate Avenue
Hershey PA 17033
Tel: 717-533-8845
Fax: 717-533-8661
E-mail: cust@igi-global.com
Web site: http://www.igi-global.com

Library of Congress Cataloging-in-Publication Data

Research methodologies, innovations, and philosophies in software systems
engineering and information systems / Manuel Mora ... [et al.], editors.
       p. cm.
 Includes bibliographical references and index.
 ISBN 978-1-4666-0179-6 (hardcover) -- ISBN 978-1-4666-0180-2 (ebook) -- ISBN
978-1-4666-0181-9 (print & perpetual access) 1. Software engineering. 2.
System engineering. 3. Research--Methodology. 4. Information technology. I.
Mora, Manuel, 1961-
  QA76.758.R467 2012
  005.1--dc23
                          2011044987

British Cataloguing in Publication Data
A Cataloguing in Publication record for this book is available from the British Library.

All work contributed to this book is new, previously-unpublished material. The views expressed in this book are those of the authors, but not necessarily of the publisher.

List of Reviewers

Eileen M. Trauth, *The Pennsylvania State University, USA*
Phillip Dobson, *Edith Cowan University, Australia*
Dorin Andreescu, *Lawrence Technological University, USA*
Damodar Konda, *Lawrence Technological University, USA*
Gonzalo Génova, *Universidad Carlos III de Madrid , Spain*
Juan Llorens, *Universidad Carlos III, Spain*
Jan H. Kroeze, *University of South Africa, South Africa*
Lucio Biggiero, *L'Aquila University, Italy*
T. Schwartzel, *University of South Africa*
M.M. Eloff, *University of South Africa*
Theresa Edgington, *Baylor University, USA*
Jorge Morato, *Universidad Carlos III de Madrid, Spain*
José L. Roldán, *Universidad de Sevilla, Spain*
Manuel J. Sánchez-Franco, *Universidad de Sevilla, Spain*
Martha Garcia-Murillo, *Syracuse University, USA*
Theresa Kraft , *University of Michigan-Flint, USA*
Rory O'Connor, *Dublin City University, Ireland*
Doncho Petkov, *Eastern Connecticut University, USA*
MSc. Elisabeth Sørup, *IT Consultant, Denmark*
Loet Leydesdorff, *ASCoR, The Netherlands*
Esther VLieger, *ASCoR, The Netherlands*
M. R. (Ruth) De Villers, *University of South Africa, South Africa*
Jan C. Mentz, *University of South Africa, South Africa*
Miroljub Kljajic, *University of Maribor, Slovenia*
Mirjana Kljajić Borštnar, *University of Maribor, Slovenia*
Andrej Škraba, *University of Maribor, Slovenia*
Moti Frank, *HIT – Holon Institute of Technology, Israel*
Rafael González, *Pontificia Universidad Javierana, Colombia*
Henk G. Sol, *Delft University of Technology, The Netherlands*
Timothy L.J., *University of South Australia, Australia*
Manuel Mora, *Autonomous University of Aguascalientes, Mexico*
Annette L. Steenkamp, *Lawrence Technological University, USA*
Mahesh Rainsinghani, *Texas Woman's University, USA*
Ovsei Gelman, *CCADET-UNAM, Mexico*

Table of Contents

Section 2
Contemporaneous Research Methods and Techniques

Section 3
Innovative Research Methods and Techniques

Detailed Table of Contents

Section 1
Foundations of Research Methods and Paradigms

Eileen M. Trauth, The Pennsylvania State University, USA
Lee B. Erickson, The Pennsylvania State University, USA

This chapter examines the influence of philosophical framing on the way in which research is conducted and the findings that result. It does so by considering choices with respect to five dimensions of research: epistemology, theory, review of literature, stakeholder perspective, and rigor-relevance.

Damodar Konda, RGIS, LLC., USA

This chapter proposes several models to guide IS researcher to help appropriately position the research using Rigor and Relevance Quadrants Model, triangulate the research using Triangulation Model and achieve the right balance using a comprehensive IS Research Process model.

Jan H. Kroeze, University of South Africa, South Africa

This chapter investigates the relationship between postmodernism, interpretivism, and formal ontologies, which are widely used in Information Systems (IS). Interpretivism has many postmodernist traits. It acknowledges that the world is diverse and that knowledge is contextual, ever-changing, and emergent.

This chapter discusses some of the practical implications consequent from adopting critical realism in terms of philosophy, theory, and methodology.

Organizational knowledge is at the center of the debate focused on the nature of knowledge, where the perspective of knowledge as possession opposes the perspective of knowledge as practice. These two views are rooted in the radical versions of realist and constructivist epistemology, respectively, according to which knowledge is an object *or* a practice.

Qualitative (i.e. meta-methodical) reasoning plays the *directive role* in scientific activity. In this chapter the authors claim that acknowledging a plurality of research methods in software engineering will benefit the advancement of this branch of science.

In this effort, the purpose of this chapter is to provide scholars with a general understanding of process theories and a taxonomy to provide some direction about how to make contributions to the theoretical legacy, particularly through often-ignored process theories, which are also relevant to practice.

In this chapter, the authors review the landscape of research methodologies and paradigms available for Information Technology (IT) and Software Engineering (SwE). The aims are two-fold: (i) create awareness in current research communities in IT and SwE on the variety of research paradigms and methodologies, and (ii) provide an useful map for guiding new researchers on the selection of an IT or SwE research paradigm and methodology.

Section 2
Contemporaneous Research Methods and Techniques

This chapter contributes to the literature by providing an overview of important considerations in reporting results from covariance-based structural equation modeling execution and analysis. It incorporates models and other examples of EQS, one of the leading SEM software applications. While EQS is increasingly used by IS researchers, exemplars of its code and output have not been well published within the IS community, overly complicating the reviewing process for these papers.

In this chapter, the authors propose both the theory underlying PLS and a discussion of the key differences between covariance-based SEM and variance-based SEM, i.e., PLS. In particular, the authors: (a) provide an analysis of the origin, development and features of PLS; and (b) discuss analysis problems as diverse as the nature of epistemic relationships and sample size requirements. In this regard, the authors present basic guidelines for the applying of PLS as well as an explanation of the different steps implied for the assessment of the measurement model and the structural model. Finally, the authors present two examples of Information Systems models in which they have put previous recommendations into effect.

This chapter is a meta-research study that briefly explains the concepts of positivism, interpretivism, and qualitative and quantitative research, before over viewing the advent of interpretive IS research. The chapter then presents two interpretive models that can serve as research designs for postgraduate studies and ad-hoc research. Action research, which originated in the social sciences, involves longitudinal studies, in which the researcher participatively investigates products or interventions that address real-world problems over several cycles, in a reflective and responsive way.

This chapter introduces interpretive research as a background to research that is time-and context-dependent. The study presents practical, yet theoretical, research approaches that are relevant to postgraduate studies and to ad-hoc research.

Chapter 13

The primary aim of this chapter is to outline a potentially powerful framework for the combination of research approaches utilizing the Grounded Theory coding mechanism for case study, and focus groups data analysis. A secondary aim of this chapter is to provide a roadmap for such a usage by way of an example research project.

A large proportion of students who enroll for postgraduate degrees never finish their studies, with non-completion rates yielding 30% for a sample size of 2000 students. A number of empirical studies have been conducted indicating the possible factors for the non-completion rate. This chapter briefly highlights such factors and proposes a possible solution to increase the number of successful studies using relevant philosophies and problem-solving to build insight in determining IS/IT solutions and innovations.

This chapter addresses the systemic integration of conceptual and empirical methods in Software Engineering (SWE) research in terms of the systems approach, where theory, empiricism, and pragmatics are combined as required in the research phases.

Section 3
Innovative Research Methods and Techniques

Chapter 16

Esther Vlieger, University of Amsterdam, The Netherlands
Loet Leydesdorff, University of Amsterdam, The Netherlands

A step-to-step introduction is provided on how to generate a semantic map from a collection of messages (full texts, paragraphs, or statements) using freely available software and/or SPSS for the relevant statistics and the visualization. The techniques are discussed in the various theoretical contexts of (i) linguistics (e.g., Latent Semantic Analysis), (ii) sociocybernetics and social systems theory (e.g., the communication of meaning), and (iii) communication studies (e.g., framing and agenda-setting).

Chapter 17

Miroljub Kljajić, University of Maribor, Slovenia
Mirjana Kljajić Borštnar, University of Maribor, Slovenia
Andrej Škraba, University of Maribor, Slovenia
Davorin Kofjač, University of Maribor, Slovenia

In this chapter, the authors discuss system dynamics (SD) as a research methodology in Information Systems (IS). The goal is to demonstrate the usefulness of SD methodology in research and its implementation in IS and management Information Systems (MIS).

Chapter 18

D. Petkov, Eastern Connecticut State University, USA
S. Alter, University of San Francisco, USA
J. Wing, Durban University of Technology, South Africa
A. Singh, Durban University of Technology, South Africa
O. Petkova, Central Connecticut State University, USA
T. Andrew, Durban University of Technology, South Africa
K. Sewchurran, University of Cape Town, South Africa

This chapter summarizes three software development and systems approaches that are often viewed as somewhat unrelated: soft system methodology (SSM), work system method (WSM), and agile development.

Chapter 19

Moti Frank, Holon Institute of Technology, Israel

This chapter presents a method of applying the principles of the descriptive research method to studies aimed at ascertaining the data needed for making a recommendation in regard to what strategy or approach should be chosen in a certain development stage of future projects.

This chapter shows how the actual design of engineered artefacts is research because it provides knowledge of the impact of the integration of various elements of existing knowledge, which demonstrates the properties of the designs achieved through the design work and leads to discovery of solutions to the various challenges of integration discovered through the project that attempts to achieve the integration.

This chapter aims at elucidating several components of DSRIS in relation to validation. The role of theory and theorizing are an important starting point, because there is no agreement as to what types of theory should be produced. Moreover, if there is a theoretical contribution, then there needs to be clear guidance as to how the designed artifact and its evaluation are related to the theory and its validation.

Preface

Knowledge of research methodologies is critical for advancing our scientific knowledge (Popper, 2002; Bhaskar, 2008). In particular, given the increasing complexity and interaction of Systems Engineering, Software Engineering (Boehm, 2000, 2006) and Information Systems disciplines (Mora et al. 2008), and the myriad of classic research methodologies and innovative hybrid or multi-methodological approaches (Glass et al. 2004; Mingers, 2000; 2001; Valerdi & Davidz, 2009), we consider that research faculty involved in such disciplines are faced with the challenge to incorporate in their research methodological repertory, a set of updated approaches (e.g., the design vs. natural research approach (March & Smith, 1995; Hevner et al. 2004), among others).

While there are excellent and multiple research books available at present, a majority of them are focused either on a single discipline, a single approach, or on statistical or qualitative procedures and techniques. Furthermore, while some integrative studies on research approaches appear in refereed journals and conference proceedings, these are scarce.

We believe that the integrative and systemic approach -used in this book with its interdisciplinary and multi-methodological research chapters- will provide an integrated source of high-quality material with rigor and relevance on research approaches for researchers in the highly interrelated disciplines of Software Systems Engineering and Information Systems. Adopting such a systemic approach from an editorial perspective, we propose that a research approach (extended from Ackoff et al. 1962; Checkland, 1983, 2000; Jackson, 1991; Gelman & Garcia, 1989)) may be used as an answering and problem-solving system comprising: (i) philosophical paradigms (P's: an ontological, epistemological and axiological stance on the world): (ii) theoretical frameworks (F's: ideas-constructs, theories, and models); (iii) methodologies (M's: methods, techniques, and instruments), and (iv) situational domains (D's: natural, artificial or social objects, artifacts and subjects under study).

Thus, this book invited authors through an open call for chapters and through special contributions, for submitting high-quality chapters which enhance our scientific knowledge on Software Systems Engineering and Information Systems. We had a very positive academic response of the scientific community interested in the theme of research paradigms and methodologies. Finally, after a rigorous peer-review process, 21 high-quality chapters were approved for their publication. These 21 chapters are grouped in three sections. The section 1 titled "Foundations de Research Methods and Paradigms" includes 8 chapters. The section 2 titled "Contemporaneous Research Methods and Techniques" includes 7 chapters, and the section 3 titled "Innovative Research Methods and Techniques" includes 6 chapters.

Section 1 -"Foundations of Research Methods and Paradigms"- present 8 chapters that address philosophy of science themes as well as particular methodological research problems (extension of classic science methods used in SwE, development of process theories, and a survey of research methods and paradigms). In chapter 1, Eileen M. Trauth and Lee B. Erickson, both in the Pennsylvania State University, USA, highlight the relevance that researchers in the IT field can identify the philosophical framing which they are, explicitly or implicitly, endorsing through their selected research methodologies. For this aim, the authors propose a 5-dimensional framework (on epistemology, theory, review of literature, stakeholder perspective, and rigor-relevance) for reporting several research methods. Authors concludes with the defense of being methodologically plural given that while "Methodological conservatism might be in order in some areas" ... "research that endeavors to respond to real-world problems needs to employ a variety of methodological tools".

In chapter 2, Damodar Konda, Vice President, Global Business Applications at RGIS, LLC , Michigan, USA, presents a comprehensive IS research process model which highlights rigor as well relevance. The author identifies that a trade-off situation is usually accepted in IT research circles, and that such a debate for a balance between rigor and relevance must be reached. However, author also identifies that few studies from practitioner's view have been conducted. Consequently, author elaborates a research process model -based on extant literature- but strongly focused on a praxis view, given his experience as an IT consultant. This chapter, thus contributes bringing to the IT academic arena, the voice of IT users through IT consultant.

In chapter 3, Jan H. Kroeze in the School of Computing, University of South Africa, South Africa, develops the thesis of placing Interpretivism as a legitimate Potsmodernism philosophical stance for Information Systems, in contrast to other intellectual positions where Interpretivism is considered as parallel to Postmodernism (Klein & Myers, 1999, p. 68). Once he established it, the author reviews the utilization of ontologies in the ICT domain under a Postmodernism perspective. Given that "*Postmodernism accepts a plurality of ethics and lifestyles. It rejects ontological priority and allows alternative understandings*" and "*Postmodernism is skeptic about a solid basis to differentiate between truth and falsehood. It rejects traditional authorities and grand narratives*", Given the pluralistic and anti-foundational nature of Postmodernism, the deployment of formal ontologies is considered more of a hyper-multiple reality specification rather than a formal and unique one. The author concludes that despite such perils "*the marriage of ontology and information systems also creates interesting opportunities to humanize technology. Interpretivist research approaches will often be the vehicles used to facilitate this process.*"

In chapter 4, Phillip Dobson, in Edith Cowan University, Australia, elaborates a brief but substantial review on the tenets of Bhaskar's Transcendental Realism philosophy of science – also called Critical Realism- and reports a set of methodological recommendations for its better utilization in IT research. Author reports that Transcendental Realism has been few used in this domain and that additionally its utilization is not ease. Author identifies Abduction as the main innovative logical mechanism – in contrast to Deduction and Induction as classic modes of scientific inferences, as well as other core tenets of Transcendental Realism as follows: the intransitive (e.g. the ontological layer) vs the transitive layer (e.g. the epistemological layer), the empirical, actual and real layers, and the need to compare diverse competitive models before to arrive to a plausible finding. Furthermore, author proposes to rely on Hedström and Swedberg's and Archer's morphogenetic models as methodological guidelines to apply Transcendental Realism in IT research.

In chapter 5 Luccio Biggiero in the Department of Economic Systems and Institutions in the L'Aquila University, Italy, analyzes the still -in some domains- dichotomy and confrontation of Realist and Constructivist views of what is knowledge: as an object versus as a process. Author reviews the main arguments of each intellectual position and proposes to introduce a Pragmatic philosophical stance for integrating both specifications of what is knowledge. Furthermore, given that position of knowledge as process is supported mainly by social scientists which also endorses the autopoiesis theory, the author claims that exist several second-order cybernetics conceptual tools – like automata studies, complexity theory, artificial life, social network analysis, and researches in organizational cognition and learning – already available that becomes autopoiesis an unnecessary theory. Author concludes that "the development of IS/IT studies and the design of knowledge management systems would substantially benefit" of an accepted dual-view of knowledge.

In chapter 6, Gonzalo Génova, Juan Llorens and Jorge Morato, all of them in Universidad Carlos III de Madrid, Spain, review the general assumption on the sufficiency of using a classic scientific method (observation, hypotheses, and experimentation for not refutation/refutation of hypotheses). They suggest that such a process, while is totally sufficient for physical-alike sciences could be not so totally suitable for Software Engineering domain. The main reason is that Software Engineering (and other IT related disciplines) have systems as units of study comprising technology and humans, and they are affected by human social environments. Authors support their claims alerting on the risks of using the classic scientific method through a mechanical mode. Thus, authors elaborate the thesis and the supporting arguments to have a plurality of research methods in the Software Engineering domain.

In chapter 7, Martha García-Murillo and Ezgi Nur Gozen, in Syracuse University, USA, identify the relevance and lack of utilization of process theories in the domain of IT research. Authors consider that due to IT field "IS field is grounded in its applications to organizations, the challenge is to develop a coherent theoretical body of scholarly research, while also remaining relevant to the needs of the practitioner community". Under such a situation, authors consider that variance-based theories, while are useful, do not account for all research situations. Consequently, they must be complemented with process theories. Authors, thus, review the process theories tenets and provide a taxonomy for guiding new IT researchers interested in using this research view.

Section 1 ends with the chapter 8 from book guest editors (Manuel Mora from Autonomous University of Aguascalientes, Mexico; Annette Steenkamp from Lawrence Technical University, Michigan, USA; Ovsei Gelman from Universidad Nacional Autónoma de México, México; and Mahesh S. Raininghani from Texas Woman's University, USA). In this chapter, we review the landscape of research methodologies and paradigms available for Information Technology (IT) and Software Engineering (SwE). Our objectives are two-fold: (i) create awareness in current research communities in IT and SwE on the variety of research paradigms and methodologies, and (ii) provide an useful map for guiding new researchers on the selection of an IT or SwE research paradigm and methodology. To achieve this, we review the core IT and SwE research methodological literature, and based on the findings, we illustrate an updated IT and SwE research framework that comprehensively integrates findings and best practices and provides a coherent systemic (holistic) view of this research landscape.

Section 2 -"Contemporaneous Research Methods and Techniques"- present 6 chapters that are focused on current modern research methods and techniques. Statistical-based modern techniques like covariance-based SEM, variance-based structural equation modeling, action research, grounded theory, and case studies are reported. Additionally practical recommendations for organizing theories and for combining conceptual and empirical research are addressed. In chapter 9, Theresa M. Edgington in Baylor University, USA and Peter M. Bentler, in the University of California – Los Angeles -, USA, review the covariance-based structural equation modeling execution and analysis procedures. They explain that despite of the almost 15 years of being used in the IT discipline, still there are critical omissions in the statistical information reported in IT research papers. Authors report methodological guidelines illustrating them through EQS – a software platform which implements covariance-based algorithms posed by one of the authors (Bentler and Weeks, 1980). Their target users are covariance-based structural equation modeling users rather than developers of such software tools, with the final aim to reduce inconsistency in acceptance criteria for well-executed research using covariance-based SEM.

In chapter 10, José L. Roldán and Manuel J. Sánchez-Franco, both in the University of Sevilla, Spain, complement chapter 9 with a thoughtful review of the main SEM method: Partial Least Squares (PLS). PLS is variance-based SEM in contrast to most known and used covariance-based SEM implemented in LISREL, AMOS or EQS software tools. Authors recognize that studies reporting PLS limitations exist in the literature. However, as it is reported in the chapter, PLS is a correct data analysis technique for SEM when their research assumptions are respected. In particular, authors report that such conditions are less restrictive that covariance-based SEM techniques, but their purpose must be also limited to predictive.

In chapters 11 and 12, M. R. (Ruth) De Villiers, in the University of South Africa, South Africa, presents the a review of interpretative research methods. Action research and Grounded Theory research methods are presented in first part. Development research, design-science research, and design-based research (a term coined for educational technology research) are presented in second part. Author provides a well-structured descriptive review of such five research methods. Such descriptions help to new researchers to for being introduced in such methods and capturing a well-developed global perspective from an efficient release mode.

In chapter 13, Rory O'Connor in Dublin City University, Ireland, elaborates a methodological research integration of two well-known qualitative research methodologies: Case Study and Grounded Theory. The author indicates that while the former is widely used in Information Systems, the latter is less known despite its similar initial reports of use in the early 1990s. Succinctly the author distinguishes the concept of methodology (as a full set of procedures and philosophical assumptions) and from methods (as individual techniques) for elaborating a full integrated methodology. Additionally it is enhanced with a Focus Group data collection technique. The author illustrates it with a real case in the Irish software industry of VSB.

In chapter 14, T. Schwartzel and M. Eloff, in the University of South Africa, identifies an international problem of a high rate of non-completion graduate studies in developed countries. The authors suggest that a wrong research methodological preparation of such graduate students is a main cause of it. Based on the Johnstone El-Bana's Model, the authors suggest that such graduate students could select a high-difficulty problem with many included sub-problems. The authors review several research frameworks to identify shared phases and aims, and elaborate an thoughtful integration consisting of four phases: Planning, Approach, Analysis and Evaluation, and Validation. The authors provide sufficient methodological guidelines on it.

In chapter 15 Annette L. Steenkamp in Lawrence Technological University, USA, and Theresa Kraft in University of Michigan-Flint, USA, provides an integrated methodological research approach which includes conceptual and empirical methods. Authors illustrate their 4-theme based methodology with a real case in the domain of success factors for managing IT Projects. The themes are: Research Planning (Problem Analysis & Literature Review); Proposal Development; Conceptualization; and Experimentation and Research Validation.

Section 3 - "Innovative Research Methods and Techniques"- completes this book with 6 chapters that report modern and still few used research methods and techniques. These are: analysis of content (latent dimensions) through visualization of the network and vector spaces, system dynamics, soft systems and work systems, systems engineering, and engineering design. In chapter 16 Esther Vlieger and Loet Leydesdorff, in the University of Amsterdam, The Netherlands, report an innovative quantitative technique to visualize latent dimensions (called frames) enclosed in a collection of textual messages. Authors indicate that social scientists are advancing their usual analysis of latent dimensions in messages from classic factor analysis and multidimensional scale analysis to a more rich vizualization mode. Authors describes one of such innovative modes based in computer-based content analysis in the network and vector spaces of the usual word-document matrix. Final long-term aim of this research is advancing the modeling of the dynamics of knowledge in scientific discourse, under the premise of that is happens in the vector space rather in the network space.

In chapter 17, Miroljub Kljajić, Mirjana Kljajić Borštnar, Andrej Škraba and Davorin Kofjač, in the University of Maribor, in Slovenia, elaborates the case for System Dynamics as a legitimated research methodology for doing research in Information Systems. Authors report that despite of the old origin of System Dynamics (early 1960s), their utilization in Information System research is reduced. Authors describe the methodological steps used in System Dynamics and illustrate with three already reported cases of use in the literature. Authors indicate as main advantage of System Dynamics -as a part of the Systems Approach methodologies- ist ability to define in natural language a problem model, which finally can be translated in the simulation model for convenient qualitative and quantitative analysis in a computer program.

In chapter 18, Doncho Petkov in Eastern Connecticut State University, USA, and Steven Alter, in the University of San Francisco, USA, lead a chapter – written jointly with John Wing, Alan Singh, and Theo Andrew, in Durban University of Technology, South Africa, and Olga Petkova in Central Connecticut State University, USA and Koshesh Sewchurran, inUniversity of Cape Town, South Africa- on the modes of Soft Systems Methodology, Work Systems Method, and Agile System Development can be used jointly for particular system development project contexts. Authors quote a Professor Boehm's call for using a more holistic approach for developing current complex software systems. On such recommendation the authors identify and compare alternative contexts for software and system development and pose guidelines for using combinations of the aforementioned methodologies in particular project contexts. This research, then, advances on the integration of two system development methods (Work System Method and Agile Development) with a research-oriented methodology (soft systems methodology) for Software Engineering.

In chapter 19, Moti Frank in Holon Institute of Technolog, in Israel, reports an innovative combination of interpreting findings from experimentation with single case of studies (different of the usual experimentation on at least two groups with at least 20 subjects by group) as a wider descriptive research study. The author uses two date from two case studies (using experiments on single case studies) in the domain of Systems Engineering for large-scale system projects. One case is about the contrast of the system development strategy for Defense Projects, and the other one about the contrast of the system integration strategy for electronics-software embedded systems. Author contributes with an innovative research descriptive proposal for coping with real Systems Engineering problems related with the selection of development and integration strategies, which cannot be studied by normal experimentation by the cost and other organizational difficulties related with these kind of projects (time pressures, confidentiality of information, scope and size of projects, among others).

In chapter 20, Timothy L.J. Ferris, in University of South Australia, Australia, elaborates the case for Engineering Design as a legitimate research methodology. Author traces Engineering journals to identify a shared research purpose of Engineering Design. A contrast with Science oriented research is reported where a generalizable knowledge on the extant things is expected, while that in Engineering design research is about to propose satisfying solutions to current needs. Author argues that Research Design is valued by its contribution to the know-how and the knowing types of knowledge while that Science is focused in advancing the "know that" type of knowledge. Finally, author advances on usual Engineering general hypothesis from feasibility of building an artifact to feasibility of building an artifact which satisfies a particular need.

In chapter 21, Rafael A. Gonzalez in Javeriana University, in Colombia, and Henk G. Sol, in University of Groningen, in The Netherlands, elaborate a theory validation scheme for Design Research for Information Systems. The authors initially describe the theory validation problematic in Design Research, for which a variety of guidelines but not still uniquely accepted are available. Authors elaborate such a validation scheme through a thoughtful review of epistemological types, reasoning types, and theory types, which should be considered for a logical consistency and coherence in the selection and utilization of the suitable evaluation technique. Authors contribute to Design Research with a comprehensive review of the main different and conflicting tenets reported in the literature. Given the complexity of this topic, authors suggest several open questions, where the notion of insufficiency of evaluation or validation of the artifact can happen "... *because its acceptance or usefulness may not necessarily be an inherent property of the artifact and its theoretical premises, but rather the result of its configuration in a particular context (and as such, contextual factors should enter into the evaluation / validation effort). Conversely, if the artifact does not work or does not work as expected, this may suggest contextual limitations, rather than disconfirmation*"

This book was projected to pursue the following aims: (i) to advance our scientific knowledge on the diverse research approaches used in Engineering of Software Systems and Information Systems, (ii) to update and integrate disperse and valuable knowledge on research approaches isolated in each discipline, (iii) to make available to Software Systems Engineering and Information Systems faculty a repertory of such research approaches in a single source, and (iv) to serve to the following academic and research international audiences: research-oriented faculty in Engineering of Software Systems and Information Systems disciplines, PhD Students on in Engineering of Software Systems and Information Systems disciplines, and Instructors of graduate Research Methods courses on Engineering of Software Systems and Information Systems disciplines.

Hence, we believe that the 21 high-quality chapters included in this book, makes real the aforementioned objectives. We finally, thank all chapter authors, external reviewers, and the IGI Editorial staff as their collaborative work has made this book possible..

Manuel Mora
Autonomous University of Aguascalientes, Mexico

Annette Steenkamp
Lawrence Technological University, USA

Ovsei Gelman
CCADET-UNAM, Mexico

Mahesh S. Raisinghani
Texas Woman's University, USA

REFERENCES

Ackoff, R. with Gupta, S., & Minas, J. (1962). *Scientific method: Optimizing applied research decisions.* New York, NY: Wiley.

Bhaskar, R. (2008). *A realist theory of science*. London, UK: Leeds Books.

Boehm, B. (2000). Unifying software engineering and systems engineering. *Computer*, (March): 114–116. doi:10.1109/2.825714

Boehm, B. (2006). Some future trends and implications for systems and software engineering processes. *Systems Engineering*, 9(1), 1–19. doi:10.1002/sys.20044

Checkland, P. (1983). O.R. and the systems movement: mappings and conflicts. *Journal of Optical Research Society*, 34(8), 661–675.

Checkland, P. (2000). Soft systems: A 30-year retrospective . In Checkland, P. (Ed.), *Systems thinking, systems practice* (pp. A1–A65). Chichester, UK: Wiley.

Gelman, O., & Garcia, J. (1989). Formulation and axiomatization of the concept of general system. Mexican Institute of Planning and Systems Operation. *Outlet IMPOS*, 19(92), 1–81.

Glass, R., Ramesh, V., & Vessey, I. (2004). An analysis of research in computing disciplines. *Communications of the ACM*, 47(6), 89–94. doi:10.1145/990680.990686

Hevner, A., March, S., Park, J., & Ram, S. (2004). Design science in Information Systems research. *Management Information Systems Quarterly*, 21(8), 75–105.

Jackson, M. (1991). *Systems methodology for the management sciences*. New York, NY: Plenum.

March, S., & Smith, G. (1995). Design and natural science Research on Information Technology . *Decision Support Systems*, 15(4), 251–266. doi:10.1016/0167-9236(94)00041-2

Mingers, J. (2000). Variety is the spice of life: Combining soft and hard OR/MS methods. *International Transactions in Operational Research*, 7, 673–691. doi:10.1111/j.1475-3995.2000.tb00224.x

Mingers, J. (2001). Combining IS research methods: Towards a pluralist methodology. *Information Systems Research*, 12(3), 240–253. doi:10.1287/isre.12.3.240.9709

Mora, M., Gelman, O., Frank, M., Paradice, D., Cervantes, F., & Forgionne, G. (2008). Toward an interdisciplinary engineering and management of complex IT-intensive organizational systems: A systems view. *International Journal of Information Technologies and Systems Approach*, 1(1), 1–24. doi:10.4018/jitsa.2008010101

Popper, K. (2002). *The logic of scientific discovery*. London, UK: Routledge.

Valerdi, R., & Davidz, H. (2009). Empirical research in systems engineering: Challenges and opportunities of a new frontier. *Systems Engineering Journal*, 12(2), 169–181. doi:10.1002/sys.20117

Section 1
Foundations of Research Methods and Paradigms

Chapter 1
Philosophical Framing and Its Impact on Research

Eileen M. Trauth
The Pennsylvania State University, USA

Lee B. Erickson
The Pennsylvania State University, USA

ABSTRACT

The variety of lenses and openness that is brought to the research process shapes both academic research and the application of knowledge to real-world settings. Researchers who endeavor to contribute both rigor and relevance require a wide range of methodological tools and a clear understanding of how such tools frame the questions to be answered, as well as the methods used and potential outcomes. It is important that both researchers and publication gatekeepers clearly understand the impact of philosophical framing on research methods and findings. Drawing on research related to the use of social media to facilitate product innovation "crowdsourcing," the authors consider the implications of alternative research scenarios on five key dimensions of research: epistemology, theory, review of literature, stakeholder perspective, and rigor-relevance. Examples of existing and emergent topics within the research field of crowdsourcing are provided to illustrate methodological pluralism.

INTRODUCTION

This chapter examines the influence of philosophical framing on the way in which research is conducted and the findings that result. It does so by considering choices with respect to five dimensions of research: epistemology, theory, review of literature, stakeholder perspective, and rigor-relevance. Extending the work presented in Trauth (2011) that focused on the contribution of interpretivist as an alternative to positivist approaches to business research (1), this chapter draws upon research within the field of product innovation to consider the implications of alternative research scenarios that are based upon differing choices regarding these five dimensions. Arguably, the variety of lenses and openness researchers and

DOI: 10.4018/978-1-4666-0179-6.ch001

publication gatekeepers bring to the research process is indicative of the variety of approaches used in the exploration of both existing and emergent topics. This, in turn, will have a direct effect on the relevance of academic research.

Based on their collective experience in conducting academic research and in applying that knowledge in real-world settings, the authors provide examples of research related to the use of social media to leverage the "crowd" for knowledge, creativity, and productivity. The advancement of scientific knowledge requires that researchers are responsive to business trends and issues that might bring with them challenges to current research methods. Researchers who endeavor to contribute both rigor and relevance require a wide range of methodological tools and a clear understanding of how such tools frame the questions to be answered as well as the methods used and potential outcomes.

BACKGROUND

Before we begin our discussion of the impact of philosophical framing, we offer some background to help situate the reader within the context in which the discussion will progress. There is little disagreement that the widespread use of the Internet combined with new social media technologies is changing not only our personal lives, but also our workplaces, our communities, our society, and our world. We are seeing more and more examples of how individuals, organizations, and governments are leveraging the power of the Internet to bring attention to social, political, and personal issues (Morello, 2007; Magid, 2009; Webster, 2009). Budding entrepreneurs are leveraging the reach of the Internet to start new businesses (Howe, 2008; Brabham, 2008a, 2008b, 2009; Lakhani & Panetta, 2007; Trompette et al., 2008; Chanal & Caron-Fasan, 2008; Feller et al., 2010). One growing area of interest is the use of social media tools to tap into the knowledge and

creativity of the "crowd." Individuals from around the world are helping to complete tedious tasks more quickly, solve complex problems, and create new profit centers for businesses small and large (Nambisan & Sawhney, 2008; Sawhney, Verona, & Prandelli, 2005).

Turning to the crowd for their knowledge and creativity is often referred to as "crowdsourcing," a term coined by Jeff Howe a writer for *Wired* magazine (Howe, 2006). Howe noticed that more and more companies were taking advantage of the Internet to reach out to the crowd to complete a variety of tasks historically accomplished using internal resources. Each day we are seeing companies both small and large leverage crowdsourcing for problem solving (Archak, 2010; Lakhani et al., 2007), data collection (Chilton, 2009), knowledge sharing (Wasko & Faraj, 2000; Allen et al., 2008), market research (Whitla, 2009), and even new product innovation (Prandelli, Sawhney, & Verona, 2008; Jeppesen & Frederiksen, 2006; Nambisan & Sawhney, 2008).

But researchers are only just beginning to understand how organizations, governments, and individuals are leveraging crowdsourcing and new social media tools for innovation. As researchers we are hungry to unravel, dissect, and explain the growing popularity and use of these models and tools. And our approach to unraveling these new mysteries is fundamentally influenced by the philosophical framing we bring to the task. With this background in place, we now turn our attention to the impact of the philosophical framing of the researcher on the research that is conducted.

UNDERSTANDING THE IMPACTS OF PHILOSOPHICAL FRAMING ON RESEARCH

Epistemological Framing

A fundamental consideration in the philosophical framing of a research project is the decision regarding epistemology: how we will come to know what we know. Different research objectives are achieved by different epistemologies. Positivist studies are focused on accurate and replicable documentation of a phenomenon leading to valid generalizations about it. Interpretive research, on the other hand, is interested in understanding *how* an observed phenomenon has come to occur. Its goal is to understand the social and psychological processes at work. In shifting from a positivist to an interpretive examination of a research topic, the goal would change from *who*, *what*, or *how many*, to *how*. In an interpretive study the focus is on the subjective reality expressed by the participants in the research study. Critical research goes one step further by asking *why* an observed phenomenon is the way it is. In doing so, particular attention is given to systems of inequality that privilege particular interests. Hence, it endeavors to expose systems of power. The purpose of critical research is to challenge assumptions, identify contradictions, and to raise awareness about systems of power. Its goal is to raise issues of a structural and ideological nature.

Intimately bound up in the discussion of epistemology is the consideration of quantitative vs. qualitative data. Each has a particular contribution to make to our understanding of issues. Each also has its strengths and weaknesses. Quantitative research provides explicit, objective documentation of a phenomenon. It enables wider reach and population generalizations. Qualitative research, on the other hand, provides "the story behind the statistics." In some senses, it extends quantitative research by moving from observing and documenting the phenomenon to a nuanced understanding of it. Whereas quantitative research endeavors to generalize to a population, the goal of qualitative research is to generalize to theory (Lee & Baskerville, 2003). Finally, qualitative research also allows for epistemological variety by enabling not only interpretive but critical research as well.

In choosing between quantitative and qualitative data, both the strengths and weaknesses of each need to be taken into account. For example, a disadvantage of quantitative research is that there is no opportunity for the nuanced understanding that is afforded by qualitative research. But a drawback of qualitative research can be its lack of transparency about the data collection and analysis. The reader is often asked to believe without explanation the conclusions at which the author arrived. These strengths and weaknesses have led to methodological bias in some publication venues towards exclusive publication of one type of data or the other. Hence, authors wishing to publish in certain journals often attempt to "fit" their research to a publisher's methodological constraints rather than allowing the appropriate method to emanate from the nature of the research to be conducted. A related issue is the use of mixed methods. Bias towards one type of data or another will diminish the opportunity to produce rich insights through the use of multiple lenses to view a phenomenon.

An illustration of the effect of epistemological framing is provided in Trauth & Jessup's (2000) study of group decision support systems in which two different epistemologies (first positivist and then interpretive) were used to analyze transcripts from a group decision support system discussion. What emerged from the analysis were two very different conclusions. The positivist analysis concluded that effective group behavior directed at consensus around alternative solution scenarios had occurred. However, the interpretive analysis revealed a very different picture: the absence of shared consciousness about the issue at hand as well as imbalanced participation by relevant stakeholders in the decision-making process.

A shift in the framing of a research problem from positivist epistemology to interpretive or critical is a move from the "safe" research space of objective, quantification of seemingly immutable phenomenon to the "vulnerable" research space of multiple and subjective understandings of reality. This can be unsettling for some readers and publications that prefer the seeming objectivity of numbers. It is even more unsettling for those made uncomfortable by the unstable territory of power, control, resistance, and inequality. Nevertheless, for research that endeavors to address real-world questions, interpretive or critical epistemologies may be the most appropriate choice.

Epistemological Framing in Context

When it comes to understanding the impact of new social tools on individuals, organizations, and society, from the early studies of the Internet we see how epistemology and data type impacts what is studied and how. Many early researchers held the view that because the Internet and new interactive communications technologies (ICT) lacked salient verbal and behavioral cues found in face-to-face (FtF) communications, it represented a new type of communications medium that was not truly "social." The focus of many of these studies was assessing and quantifying the "communications bandwidth" of new ICTs in relation to our FtF experiences. Because the focus was on quantifying online context in relation to FtF context, those subscribing to this perspective raised concerns regarding the potential negative impacts of such a limited communications medium on our social interactions (Kraut et al., 1998). In short, using quantifiable measures online channels did not "measure up."

But this quantitative focus was not shared by all. In the other camp were researchers who brought a qualitative, interpretivist approach to the study of ICT. These researchers focused on understanding the impact of these new communication channels from the point of view of those involved in the communications. They viewed the Internet and ICTs as having the potential to extend and enrich our FtF experiences (Spears et al., 2002). Instead of focusing on quantitative or ordinal measures of bandwidth or technology richness, these researchers began examining the social contexts in which the communication

took place and the perceptions of those involved (Blanchard & Markus, 2004; Fogg et al., 2002; Green & Brock, 1998). Those subscribing to this perspective held that the level of "socialization" was not inherent in the technology but instead was directly connected to the context in which the communications took place. These researchers focused on qualitative measures and sought to interpret the perceptions of those engaged in the communications to assess the impact of these new technologies.

Today we can again see how epistemology may be impacting our knowledge and understanding of the use of crowdsourcing for product innovation. A number of scholars are attempting to quantify the value that crowdsourcing brings by measuring the economic benefits of turning to the crowd (Huston & Sakkab, 2006; Bishop, 2009). Certainly, it is natural for businesses to want to quantify such initiatives. Managers are asked to provide demonstrable results to the company's bottom line and research can help to quantify not only return on investment, but also increased profits, and decreased costs. However, such an approach only tells one part of the story. Looking solely at the value of the final product or the cost savings incurred does not shed light on which factors within the innovation process that may have accounted for those results.

An interpretive approach can be extremely valuable in unlocking the nature of crowdsourced innovation. For example, we know little regarding the motivations of participants in the crowdsourcing process. Using an interpretivist epistemology to explore participants' motivations can add greatly to our overall understanding and to practical issues about how best to encourage participation from those individuals with whom we are hoping to connect. Additionally, organizational culture related to innovation has been shown to be a critical component of a company's ability to innovate. Organizational culture has been found to both encourage and discourage open innovation (Tushman & O'Reilly, 2002;

Chesbrough, 2003a). The beliefs and values of leaders within the organization as well as their interpersonal relationships with employees can be a driving force or inhibitor of innovation. As such, organizational culture directly affects whether innovation is encouraged within an organization and the amount of innovation that is generated (Martins & Terblanche, 2003). When it comes to crowdsourcing, organizational culture will certainly continue to be important, but the public nature of crowdsourcing may require new organizational characteristics to deal with the open nature of these initiatives. A qualitative approach to examining the impact of organizational culture and motivations of participants would be beneficial in revealing *why* individuals participate and *how* organizational culture impacts the success of these initiatives.

From a critical vantage point, as researchers we may need to challenge the very definition of innovation and what it means to be an innovative company. Innovation has typically been linked to internal R&D activities of corporations where scientists, researchers, and experts in the field often work in isolated undisclosed locations in the hopes of finding breakthrough innovations. Today we may be experiencing a metamorphosis in terms of the innovation process and a company's ability to leverage new sources of knowledge for innovation potential. Early research into crowdsourcing and open innovation suggests that for certain fields, individuals with limited or no prior knowledge or experience may bring the most innovative ideas to the table (Lakhani et al., 2007). With today's networked world and the pace at which new information is generated we may need to rethink our definition of innovation and how we go about generating innovations in the marketplace.

Just as organizations can get caught up in their own proven processes and suffer from organizational inertia, researchers can also fall into comfortable and proven approaches to the study of innovation. Entertaining the idea that the very nature of innovation is changing opens up many new questions. The idea that we may need to rethink current theories and frameworks may be difficult or even painful. To think that we may have to back track and begin looking at the very nature of innovation anew is disturbing. But such openness to alternative epistemologies is necessary if we are to fully understand and explain the evolving nature of innovation in today's world.

Theoretical Framing

The relationship between theory and the phenomenon being researched can take on a variety of forms. Sometimes research, particularly in a new area, can be designated as "pre theoretical" (Trauth, 2006) insofar as the focus is exclusively on the collection and presentation of statistical data. However, the absence of a stated theory doesn't necessarily mean that no theory is in use. Rather, it might mean that an implicit theory is in use. The drawback with employing implicit theory is that it is not possible for others to critique or build on such implicit theories. Trauth has critiqued the use of implicit gender essentialist theories in the literature of gender and IT (Trauth, 2006). In much of this research the theories that are explicitly used are not those used to explain the phenomenon of gender. Rather, they are theories about technology adoption and use such as the technology acceptance model or the theory of reasoned action. Examples include Venkatesh & Morris (2000), Venkatesh, Morris & Ackerman, (2000), Gefen & Straub (1997), Webster & Martocchio (1992), and Ahuja & Thathcher (2005).

Research that employs explicit theory can do so in a number of different ways. The decision about the role of theory is a function of both the research tradition and the purpose of the research. Gregor (2006) explains that understandings of theory can range from a very narrow definition of theory as being used solely for prediction, to a more inclusive definition that defines theory as explanation. In between are the issues of causality and generalization. In our view theory is, at heart, an attempt to understand a phenomenon. As such, that understanding can range from a descriptive conceptualization to a systematic statement of rules to be tested towards the production of general principles or causes.

Some business researchers and some business journals limit their definition of the "acceptable" role of theory to theory testing. This can be limiting, particularly in settings such as crowdsourcing where the phenomenon is at the early stages of being understood. It can bring a narrowness to investigations with the potential for analytical rigor but real-world irrelevance. Taking a broader view, one that emerges from the phenomenon itself, allows for theory to take on a variety of roles that could include: theory testing, theoretically-informed research, theory development or extension, or grounded theory.

Theoretical Framing in Context

Certainly reaching outside the walls for new sources of innovation is not unique to crowdsourcing. Researchers have written extensively about "open innovation" providing a theoretical framework from which to understand how firms can extract knowledge from others to support their R&D initiatives (Chesbrough, 2003a, 2003b, 2006; von Hippel, 2005; Burt, 1992; McAfee, 2009; Lakhani & Panetta, 2007; Nambisan & Sawhney, 2008; Prandelli et al., 2008). Additionally, there is a large body of research examining the use of the crowd for programming innovation via open source software initiatives (Lakhani & Wolf, 2003; von Hippel, 2001; von Hippel & von Krogh, 2003; Hars & Ou, 2002). Within the crowdsourcing literature, most researchers cite theories of open innovation and open source software as background for understanding the characteristics, benefits of, and structure of crowdsourced product innovation (Albors et al., 2008; Archak, 2010; Di Gangi & Wasko, 2009; Dodgson, Gann, & Salter, 2006; Kleemann, Voß, & Rieder, 2008). However, only a handful of scholarly articles have

included a detailed discussion of the differences between these three innovation models (Schenk & Guittard, 2009; Trompette et al., 2008; Chanal & Caron-Fasan, 2008). While most agree open innovation, open source software, and crowdsourcing are based on an open model, not all agree on the relationship between these three models.

There are two main theoretical perspectives within the literature regarding the relationships between these three models. The first places crowdsourcing and open source software within the category of open innovation, but acknowledges there are some differences between crowdsourcing and open source initiatives (Trompette et al., 2008; Burger-Helmchen & Pénin, unpublished; Panchal & Fathianathan, 2008; Chanal & Caron-Fasan, 2008; Fantoni et al., 2008). The other views open innovation, open source software, and crowdsourcing as sharing some common characteristics, but concludes that none can be categorized as a sub-category of the other (Schenk & Guittard, 2009).

Here we see how theoretical framing may account for the difference between these two viewpoints. The researchers in the first camp (e.g., crowdsourcing as a category of open innovation) view open innovation as any initiative that includes those outside the boundary of the corporate structure. Therefore, they view crowdsourcing as a sub-category of open innovation. Additionally, these authors are attempting to explain how one unique characteristic of crowdsourcing (i.e., a company profiting from a community-generated product) may create a new dynamic not seen before within other models of open innovation. Their goal is to provide guidance to sponsoring firms on how best to manage the new environments that are created through the use of the crowd for open innovation.

Researchers in the second camp (e.g., similar but not subcategories of each other) are attempting to define crowdsourcing in relation to our understanding of other models of open innovation. These authors compare and contrast each model along a wide variety of different characteristics that include: 1) the purpose of the initiative, 2) the nature of the collaboration, 3) how participants are invited, and 4) who owns the final work product. As such, they are looking to clearly define the boundaries of this field of study in relation to similar fields. This meta level of analysis is designed to provide a description of the unique characteristics that define each of these approaches.

Because crowdsourcing is a relatively new field, we may need to walk before we run. That is, we need to create a common definition and framework from which to examine the impact of this new source of innovation. While some challenge the fact that a definition is not a theory, most would agree that it is a necessary first step. Clearly articulating the unique characteristics of crowdsourcing is a critical first step in building up a theory base related to this new phenomenon as well as providing guidance to corporations who wish to implement such initiatives.

Framing the Disciplinary Literature

A significant challenge with research that is driven by real-world problems is that the real world doesn't fit neatly into disciplinary categories (Ackoff, 1974 ch 1; Ackoff & Emery, 1972, ch 1). Hence, the research is often multidisciplinary and the research literature can be found in many places. This brings the challenge of keeping up not only with the increasing number of journals in one's own area (such as information systems) but also the relevant literature that is published in journals and conferences in the other fields.

But in doing so, a researcher can encounter another, and potentially more challenging, issue: academic politics. This issue is about what journals, conferences, and books are considered to be "legitimate" in a given discipline. The problem occurs when the definition of "legitimate literature" is too narrow. This would be manifested by a reward system that recognizes research only when it is published in certain venues or when emerging scholars are taught to look for relevant

research only when it appears in certain locations. When this occurs, there is a danger of researchers missing important research, of "reinventing the wheel" by not sufficiently building upon the full extent of cumulative knowledge.

To address a real-world problem a researcher needs to follow the research – wherever that leads her or him. Hence, the challenge is to be able to follow the relevant research literature wherever it may be found and to train students for boundaryless literature searching. In this digital age there is little excuse for not thoroughly searching for relevant literature; it would only be the construction of "legitimacy" that would limit inclusion of potentially relevant research.

Literature Framing in Context

We find within the literature on crowdsourcing, many researchers referring to crowdsourcing sites as "communities." This has sparked a growing discussion regarding our theoretical understanding of "community." These early explorations are playing an important role in raising questions regarding which theories are most appropriate and relevant to the study of crowdsourcing. Additionally, such discussions are raising questions regarding the application of theory originating in different domains.

There are a number of different viewpoints associated with the construct of community and there are a number of different perspectives on whether crowdsourcing represents one or more of these communities (Di Gangi & Wasko, 2009; West & Lakhani, 2008; Albors et al., 2008; Kozinets et al., 2008; Wiertz & de Ruyter, 2007). To some, community is an integral component of crowdsourcing (Di Gangi & Wasko, 2009; Malone, Laubacher, & Dellarocas, 2009; Trompette et al., 2008; Kozinets et al., 2008). However, others take the opposite view stating that most crowdsourcing sites do not meet the definition of community (Schenk & Guittard, 2009; Haythornthwaite, 2009a). Additionally, within the crowdsourcing literature, some use the term "community" to describe any group of people who are working on a task regardless of their relationship and interactions (Trompette et al., 2008; Whitla, 2009; Feller et al., 2009). Others believe interactions between members are necessary for a "community" to exist (Wenger & Snyder, 2000; Haythornthwaite, 2009a; Dholakia, Bagozzi & Pearo, 2003; McAfee, 2009, chap. 5; Wasko & Faraj, 2000; Lakhani & Panetta, 2007).

Here we see how philosophical framing related to a researcher's discipline impacts the very definition of community. Some researchers bring a management theory perspective to the discussion of community (Trompette et al., 2008). Within this discipline "community" is viewed as a function of who is generating the work product (i.e., a large group of individuals versus employees within a corporation). These theorists also incorporate concepts from economics to the study of crowdsourcing. Theories of "collective action," "public goods," and the tragedy of the commons are all being used to explain why individuals participate in crowdsourcing initiatives. Still others bring a sociological perspective to the study of community within crowdsourcing. In contrast to the management view, the sociological view posits that interactions between individual members are necessary for a community to exist (Wenger & Snyder, 2000; Haythornthwaite, 2009a; Dholakia et al., 2003; McAfee, 2009, chap. 5; Wasko & Faraj, 2000; Muniz & O'Guinn, 2001; Lakhani & Panetta, 2007). In this view, community is defined by the quality of the relationship between individuals not the fact that a group is working on a task. These factors are viewed as key to an individual's participation.

While there are currently many different definitions and theories related to community (West & Lakhani, 2008) even when using the broadest view, it is unclear what role community may play within crowdsourcing. What may be most interesting, however, is not that there are many different viewpoints – as researchers we have come to expect it – but instead, we may be see-

ing a merging of ideas from different disciplines to create new "hybrid" theories of community. None of these viewpoints is incorrect per se. Clear, concise definitions of key constructs are critical. We wish, however, to raise the point that by limiting our understanding of key constructs to specific disciplines, we may be missing out on the insights that can be gained by working across disciplines and bringing multiple views to the research at hand.

Framing the Stakeholder Perspective

The stakeholder perspective on the research has two dimensions: the producer of the research and the consumer of the research. The topic of researcher reflexivity relates to discussions about the perspective of the researcher on what is researched. Proponents of reflexive or "confessional" accounts of research (e.g., Kvasny, Greenhill, & Trauth, 2005; Schultze, 2000) argue for greater transparency in presenting methodological details, that includes information about the researcher and how her or his identity characteristics (e.g. gender, ethnicity, nationality, philosophical orientation, disciplinary background, etc.) has influenced the research. In the information systems field foundational work on methods such as that of Klein and Myers (1999)[1] has included the relationship between the researcher and the subjects being researched as one of the seven principles for conducting interpretive field studies (2). Another term that expresses the same methodological stance comes from feminist methodology. Feminist standpoint theory (FST) emphasizes the situated knowledge of marginalized individuals. It provides a systematic approach for theorizing the complexities of lived contexts, experiences and perspectives of women (Haraway, 1988). Harding (2004) describes standpoint theory as "an organic epistemology, methodology, and social theory that can arise whenever oppressed peoples gain public voice. The social order looks different from the perspective of our lives and our struggles" (p. 3).

While transparency about researcher standpoint is commonplace, if not ubiquitous, for interpretive and critical research a case can be made for its inclusion in positivist studies as well. The argument is that an individual's life experiences, biases, interests, and identity will shape the assumptions one makes about a phenomenon. This is true even in positivist research. Decisions about what to include and not include in a survey, what theory to use to inform the research, and how the interpretation of findings is conducted all result from human judgments made by a human researcher. Advocates of transparency about researcher standpoint believe that the claim of an "objective researcher" is a myth.

With respect to the consumers of the research, there are different stakeholders. This is not to say that one perspective is more important than another. Rather, the point is simply that multiple perspectives exist. For example, whereas there is a tendency to address business research results to executives, that might not always be the best orientation. But to the extent that a definition of legitimate "business relevance" is limited to executive perspectives then a narrowness enters the research domain. The determination of legitimate business relevance is the joint action of institutions and publication outlets. Academic institutions, by rewarding executive perspectives, can drive narrowness. On the other hand conference committees and journal editors can also drive narrowness. Doing so has implications for both the approach that is taken to study a phenomenon and how the implications of findings are considered.

Stakeholder Framing in Context

Within the study of crowdsourcing we, again, see how the perspectives of the producer of the research and the consumer of the research can have a major impact on the research itself. Stakeholder perspectives impact the very definition of the field and the characteristics by which it is defined. For example, with respect to producers of research

within the field of crowdsourcing a number of researchers are building frameworks that help to describe the defining characteristics to be studied. Frameworks range from simple one-dimensional models (Feller et al., 2009; Howe, 2008; Kleemann et al., 2008) to complex multidimensional models with detailed descriptions of sub-elements within each dimension (Nambisan & Sawhney, 2008; Reichwald, et al., 2004). A number of frameworks are general in nature and apply to any type of crowdsourcing activity (Whitla, 2009; Bonabeau, 2009; Haythornthwaite, 2009a). Others have been created specifically for the study of crowdsourced product innovation (Trompette et al., 2008; Feller et al., 2009; Chanal & Caron-Fasan, 2008; Sawhney et al., 2005; Reichwald, et al., 2004).

Within these frameworks there are a wide array of dimensions deemed relevant to the study of crowdsourcing including: the characteristics of the task to be completed, the purpose of engaging the crowd, the nature of the collaboration, governance structure, who is targeted within the crowd, and incentives/ motivations. There is no doubt that the researcher's perspective is reflected in which aspects of crowdsourcing are viewed as most pertinent. Those examining the phenomenon from an economic and business perspective tend to focus on governance practices, intellectual property issues, and the value that can be extracted. Researches interested in the social aspects of crowdsourcing tend to focus on the nature of online collaboration, the motivations of individuals who participate, and how such practices may be impacting the role of consumers in society. Even when we narrow the focus to frameworks created specifically for the study of product innovation via crowdsourcing we see variation in terms of what characteristics researchers feel are most important. This is not to say that these frameworks are not useful. Instead it merely raises the question of how one decides which key constructs are most important in unraveling this new space.

From the perspective of the consumer of the research, we again see how stakeholder perspective can have an impact on research. For those companies wishing to leverage crowdsourcing for competitive advantage (e.g., product innovation) the ability to extract value is typically foremost in one's mind. As such, interests lie in identifying the "right" crowd to approach and how best to quickly identify contributions that are most profitable. For those interested in leveraging the productivity of the crowd to outsource routine time consuming tasks (also known as Human Intelligence Tasks), key questions revolve around how best to provide incentives for individuals to participate. In these cases, research often seeks to compare the use of contest, games, and monetary payments for work completed. No doubt each of these perspectives influences researchers who wish to study this new phenomenon. Additionally, because researchers in this field are often working with companies who are currently leveraging the crowd for one or more business purposes, we again see the potential for stakeholder perspectives to drive research agendas. Certainly, there are many excellent researchers who know how to navigate potential conflicts that may arise, and managing research settings within organizations is not new to crowdsourcing. However, because crowdsourcing is only in the early stage of exploration we must be cognizant of how early adopters of this new practice may be influencing our very understanding of the phenomenon.

Framing Rigor vs. Relevance

The final dimension of philosophical framing of research to be considered here relates to the intended measure of quality. Particularly in research that is problem-oriented there is a tension between "theoretical vs. applied" orientation. This dichotomy is often presented as a conundrum: research cannot be practical and at the same time scholarly. It can be methodologically rigorous at the cost of relevance. But if it is highly relevant to real-world problems then it must not be rigorous research. This is a false dichotomy. Rather,

what is behind this argument is mistaking the use of *different research methods* for *bad research*. For example, consider a researcher who believes that theory only exists to be tested, that positivism is the only epistemology that exists and that quantitative measurement is the only valid way to conduct research. How does this person react when confronted with research employing interpretive fieldwork, that uses theory only as a sensitizing device, and from which population generalizations cannot be made?

The plain fact is that there is a tremendous need for theoretically-informed interventions in order to properly address real-world problems. Under theorized and ad hoc approaches to interventions that do not reflect a systematic and thorough theorizing of the problem run the risk of being irrelevant. Hence, a strong argument can be made that rigor and relevance go hand in hand.

Framing Rigor vs. Relevance in Context

Here, the second author will shift to the first person to enable her to bring her industry experience to the discussion of rigor vs. relevance. As a businesswomen working with high tech companies and only entering academia in my late 40's, I can't help but bring a practical viewpoint to my research studies. For some, as previously mentioned, this may seem like it would create conflict. But instead it presents a challenge. The challenge is to frame questions, select methods, and report findings in ways that contribute both to theory and to practice. In many ways attempting to do both is more difficult than only focusing on one or the other. As such it requires the ability to "live" in both worlds and an understanding that both rigor and relevance are critical to helping organizations and society benefit from new innovative processes. Additionally, because the study of crowdsourcing for product innovation is so new, I believe that without first identifying relevant theory to help direct and frame our research we may be postponing and limiting the applicability of our results to practice. However, it also requires an openness to and understanding of both sides of the equation. This is where multidisciplinary teams may be most beneficial. By bringing together researchers from diverse disciplines such as business/management, sociology, and information science we expose ourselves to differing viewpoints. We challenge ourselves to explain and justify our research questions, methods, and findings. Is this easy? Certainly not. In the same way that crowdsourcing leverages the diversity of the crowd, researchers can also leverage diversity to bring together theoretical and practical expertise to craft research that advances both theory and practice.

CONCLUSION

This consideration of philosophical framing with regard to business research is intended to highlight the ways in which such framing impacts the methods used, the theory selected, and the subsequent findings. By examining the influence of epistemology, theoretical considerations, literatures reviewed, stakeholder perspectives, and rigor-relevance within the context of the emerging study of crowdsourcing for product innovation we bring awareness to how each impacts the research to be conducted as well as potential findings. We do not argue for one particular mode of philosophical framing over another. Rather, we advocate for both researcher reflexivity in order to highlight potential biases, and methodological transparency in articulating the philosophical framing employed in the research. We believe that doing so will serve to not only broaden but also strengthen the discussion of "research limitations" that typically appears in a research paper.

Arguably, the degree to which institutions and publication outlets take these issues into account is indicative of their openness to exploring emergent topics. Methodological conservatism might be in order in some areas. But research that endeavors to respond to real-world problems needs to employ a variety of methodological tools. It must also be responsive to trends and issues that bring with them challenges to current methods of conducting research. The evolving nature of innovation in our new knowledge economy, the impact of the Internet and social media tools on innovation practices, and globalization of markets blur traditional research boundaries. We believe that in today's hyper-connected global economy, the research community at large needs to overcome resistance to different ideas, methodologies, epistemologies, and theories if we are to contribute substantively to both theory and practice.

This chapter focuses on the naïve realism reflected in the vast majority of positivist research conducted in the IT field. It does not entertain a postmodern critical realist approach which acknowledges "underlying structural and institutional mechanisms of society, including sets of ideas, which are in some respects independent of the reasoning and desires of stakeholders, but which none the less affect the IS initiative and the negotiation process" (Madon, 2005, 329-330).

ACKNOWLEDGMENT

This research has been supported by a grant from the National Science Foundation (NSF award #1039546).

REFERENCES

Ackoff, R. L. (1974). *Redesigning the future: A systems approach to societal problems*. New York, NY: John Wiley & Sons.

Ackoff, R. L., & Emery, F. E. (1972). *On purposeful systems*. Chicago, IL: Aldine Atherton, Inc.

Ahuja, M., & Thathcher, J. B. (2005). Moving beyond intentions and toward the theory of trying: Effects of work environment and gender on post-adoption Information Technology use. *Management Information Systems Quarterly, 29*(3), 427–459.

Albors, J., Ramos, J. C., & Hervas, J. L. (2008). New learning network paradigms: Communities of objectives, crowdsourcing, wikis and open source. *International Journal of Information Management, 28,* 194–202. doi:10.1016/j.ijinfomgt.2007.09.006

Allen, N., Ingham, J., Johnson, B., Merante, J., Noveck, B. S., & Stock, W. … Wong, C. (2008, June). *PeerToPatent first anniversary report.* The Center for Patent Innovations, New York Law School. Retrieved from http:// dotank.nyls.edu/ communitypatent/ P2Panniversaryreport. pdf

Archak, N. (2010). Money, glory and entry deterrence: Analyzing strategic behavior of contestants in simultaneous crowdsourcing contests on TopCoder.com. *Proceedings of the 19th International Conference on World Wide Web,* (pp. 21-30).

Bishop, M. (2009, May). *The total economic impact of InnoCentive challenges. Single company case study.* Forrester Consulting. Retrieved from http:// www.economist.com/ businessfinance/ displaystory.cfm? story_id= 14460185

Blanchard, A. L., & Markus, M. L. (2004, Winter). The experienced "sense" of a virtual community: Characteristics and processes. *The Data Base for Advances in Information Systems, 35*(1), 65–79.

Bonabeau, E. (2009, Winter). Decision 2.0: The power of collective intelligence. *MIT Sloan Management Review, 50*(2), 45–52.

Brabham, D. C. (2008a). Moving the crowd at iStockphoto: The composition of the crowd and the motivations for participation in a crowdsourcing application. *First Monday, 13*(6). Retrieved December 4, 2009, from http:// www.uic.edu/ htbin/ cgiwrap/ bin/ ojs/ index.php/ fm/ article/ view/ 2159/1969

Brabham, D. C. (2008b). Crowdsourcing as a model for problem solving: An introduction and cases. *The International. Convergence (London), 14*(1), 75–90. doi:10.1177/1354856507084420

Brabham, D. C. (2009). *Moving the crowd at Threadless: Motivations for participation in a crowdsourcing application.* Paper presented at the Annual Meeting of the Association for Education in Journalism and Mass Communication, Boston, MA.

Burger-Helmchen, T., & Pénin, J. (unpublished). *The limits of crowdsourcing inventive activities: What do transaction cost theory and the evolutionary theories of the firm teach us?* Retrieved from http:// cournot.ustrasbg.fr/ users/ osi/ program/ TBH_JP_ crowdsouring% 202010% 20ENG.pdf

Burt, R. S. (1992). *Structural holes: The social structure of competition.* Massachusetts: Harvard University Press.

Chanal, V., & Caron-Fasan, M. L. (2008, May). *How to invent a new business model based on crowdsourcing: The Crowdspirit case.* Paper presented at the Conférence de l'Association Internationale de Management Stratégique, Nice.

Chesbrough, H. W. (2003a). *Open innovation: The new imperative for creating and profiting from technology.* Boston, MA: Harvard Business School Publishing Corporation.

Chesbrough, H. W. (2003b, Spring). The era of open innovation. *MIT Sloan Management Review,* 35-41.

Chesbrough, H. W. (2006). *Open business models: How to thrive in the new innovation landscape.* Boston, MA: Harvard Business School Press.

Chilton, S. (2009). *Crowdsourcing is radically changing the geodata landscape: Case study of OpenStreetMap.* Paper presented at the 24th International Cartographic Conference.

Dholakia, U. M., Bagozzi, R. P., & Pearo, L. K. (2003). A social influence model of consumer participation in network- and small-group-based virtual communities. *International Journal of Research in Marketing, 21,* 241–263. doi:10.1016/j.ijresmar.2003.12.004

Di Gangi, P. M., & Wasko, M. (2009). Steal my idea! Organizational adoption of user innovations from a user innovation community: A case study of Dell IdeaStorm. *Decision Support Systems, 48,* 303–312. doi:10.1016/j.dss.2009.04.004

Dodgson, M., Gann, D., & Salter, A. (2006). The role of technology in the shift towards open innovation: The case of Proctor & Gamble. *R & D Management, 36*(3), 333–346. doi:10.1111/j.1467-9310.2006.00429.x

Fantoni, G., Apreda, R., Valleri, P., Bonaccorsi, A., & Manteni, M. (2008). *IPR tracking system in collaborative environments.* Retrieved from http:// 74.125.155.132/ scholar?q=cache: uPhWjfQFxXMJ: scholar.google.com/ &hl=en&as_sdt= 800000000000

Feller, J., Finnegan, P., Hayes, J., & O'Reilly, P. (2009). Institutionalizing information asymmetry: Governance structures for open innovation. *Information Technology & People, 22*(4), 297–316. doi:10.1108/09593840911002423

Feller, J., Finnegan, P., Hayes, J., & O'Reilly, P. (2010). *Sustainable crowdsourcing.* Draft Working Paper of the O3C Business Models Project, University College Cork.

Fogg, B. J., & Kameda, T. Boyd. J., Marshall, J., Seith, R., Sockol, M., & Trowbridge, T. (2002). Stanford-*Makovsky Web credibility study 2002: Investigating what makes Web sites credible today.* A research report by the Stanford Persuasive Technology Lab & Makovsky & Company. Stanford University.

Gefen, D., & Straub, D. (1997). Gender differences in the perception and use of e-mail: an extension to the technology acceptance model. *Management Information Systems Quarterly, 21*(4), 389–400. doi:10.2307/249720

Green, M. C., & Brock, T. C. (1998). Trust, mood, and outcomes of friendship determine preferences for real versus ersatz social capital. *Political Psychology, 19*(3), 527–544. doi:10.1111/0162-895X.00116

Gregor, S. (2006). The nature of theory in information systems. *Management Information Systems Quarterly, 30*(3), 611–642.

Haraway, D. (1988). Situated knowledges: The science question in feminism and the privilege of partial perspective. *Feminist Studies, 14,* 575–599. doi:10.2307/3178066

Harding, S. (2004). *The Feminist standpoint theory reader.* New York, NY: Routledge.

Hars, A., & Ou, S. (2002, Spring). Working for free? Motivations for participation in open-source projects. *International Journal of Electronic Commerce, 6*(3), 25–39.

Haythornthwaite, C. (2009a). *Online knowledge crowds and communities.* In International Conference on Knowledge Communities. Reno, NV: Center for Basque Studies.

Howe, J. (2006). The rise of crowdsourcing. *Wired, 14*(6).

Howe, J. (2008). *Crowdsourcing: Why the power of the crowd is driving the future of business.* New York, NY: Crown Business.

Huston, L., & Sakkab, N. (2006, March). Connect and develop. Inside Procter & Gamble's new model for innovation. *Harvard Business Review*. Retrieved from http:// 74.125.155.132/ scholar?q=cache: nJmmXaQ4Gj0J: scholar.google.com/ +harvard+business+ review+connect+ and+develop+P% 26G&hl=en&as_ sdt=2000

Hythornthwaite, C. (2009b). Crowds and communities: Light and heavyweight models of peer production. Proceedings from the *42nd Hawaii International Conference on System Science,* (pp. 1-10).

Jeppesen, L. B., & Frederiksen, L. (2006, January-February). Why do users contribute to firm-based user communities? *Organization Science, 17*(1), 45–63. doi:10.1287/orsc.1050.0156

Kleemann, F., Voß, G. G., & Rieder, K. (2008, July). Un(der)paid innovators: The commercial utilization of consumer work through crowdsourcing. *Science. Technology & Innovation Studies, 4*(1), 5–26.

Klein, H. K., & Myers, M. (1999). A set of principles for conducting and evaluating interpretive field studies in information systems research. *Management Information Systems Quarterly, 23*(1), 67–93. doi:10.2307/249410

Kozinets, R. F., Hemetsberger, A., & Schau, H. J. (2008, December). The wisdom of consumer crowds: Collective innovation in an age of networked marketing. *Journal of Macromarketing, 4*, 339–354. doi:10.1177/0276146708325382

Kraut, R., Patterson, M., Lundmark, V., Kiesler, S., Mukopadhyay, T., & Scherlis, W. (1998). Internet paradox: A social technology that reduces social involvement and psychological well-being? *The American Psychologist, 53*(9), 1017–1031. doi:10.1037/0003-066X.53.9.1017

Kvasny, L., Greenhill, A., & Trauth, E. M. (2005). Giving voice to Feminist projects in management information systems research. *International Journal of Technology and Human Interaction, 1*, 1–18. doi:10.4018/jthi.2005010101

Lakhani, K. R., Jeppesen, L. B., Lohse, P. A., & Panetta, J. A. (2007, October). *The value of openness in scientific problem solving.* (Harvard Business School Working Paper 07-050).

Lakhani, K. R., & Panetta, J. A. (2007, Summer). The principles of distributed innovation. *Innovations*, n.d., 97–112. doi:10.1162/itgg.2007.2.3.97

Lakhani, K. R., & Wolf, R. G. (2003, September). *Why hackers do what they do: Understanding motivation effort in free/open source software projects.* MIT Sloan School of Management. Retrieved from http:// ssrn.com/ abstract=443040

Lee, A. S., & Baskerville, R. (2003). Generalizing generalizability in information systems research. *Information Systems Research, 14*(3), 221–243. doi:10.1287/isre.14.3.221.16560

Madon, S. (2005). Evaluating e-governance projects in India: A focus on micro-level implementation. In Howcroft, D., & Trauth, E. M. (Eds.), *Handbook of critical Information Systems research: Theory and application* (pp. 325–349). Cheltenham, UK: Edward Elgar Publishing Limited.

Magid, L. (2009, February 17). Microlending: Do good, make money? In *CBSNEWS*. Retrieved September 5, 2009, from http:// www.cbsnews. com/ stories/ 2009/ 02/ 17/ scitech/ pcanswer/ main4808591.shtml

Malone, T. W., Laubacher, R., & Dellarocas, C. (2009, February). *Harnessing crowds: Mapping the genome of collective intelligence* (Working paper no. 2009-001). MIT Center for Collective Intelligence, MIT website. Retrieved from http:cci. mit.edu/ publications/ CCIwp2009-01. pdf

Martins, E. C., & Terblanche, F. (2003). Building organizational culture that stimulates creativity and innovation. *European Journal of Innovation Management, 6*(1), 64–74. doi:10.1108/14601060310456337

McAfee, A. (2009). *Enterprise 2.0: New collaborative tools for your organization's toughest challenges*. Boston, MA: Harvard Business Press.

Morello, H. J. (2007, Winter). E-(re)volution: Zapatistas and the emancipatory Internet. *A Contra Corriente, 4*(2), 54-76.

Muniz, A. M., & O'Guinn, T. C. (2001, March). Brand community. *The Journal of Consumer Research, 27*, 412–432. doi:10.1086/319618

Nambisan, S., & Sawhney, M. (2008). *The global brain. Your roadmap for innovating faster and smarter in a networked world*. New Jersey: Pearson Education.

Panchal, J. H., & Fathianathan, M. (2008). Product realization in the age of mass collaboration. In *Proceedings of ASME 2008 International Design Engineering Technical Conferences and Computers and Information in Engineering Conference*. Retrieved from http://westinghouse.marc.gatech.edu/ Members/ jpanchal/ Publications/ DETC2008_ 49865_ MassCollaboration. April.12. 08.pdf

Prandelli, E., Sawhney, M., & Verona, G. (2008). *Collaborating with customers to innovate: Conceiving and marketing products in the networking age*. United Kingdom: Edward Elgar Publishing Limited.

Reichwald, R., Seifert, S., Walcher, D., & Piller, F. (2004, January). Customers as part of value webs: Towards a framework for webbed customer innovation tools. *Proceedings from 37th Hawaii International Conference on System Sciences*. Retrieved from http:// wwwkrcmar.in. tum.de/ public/ webcoach/ wsw/ attachments/ WINserv_ Arbeitsbericht_ Value-webs. pdf

Sawhney, M., Verona, G., & Prandelli, W. (2005, Autumn). Collaborating to create: The Internet as a platform for customer engagement in product innovation. *Journal of Interactive Marketing, 19*(4), 4–17. doi:10.1002/dir.20046

Schenk, E. & Guittard, C. (2009). *Crowdsourcing: What can be outsourced to the crowd and why?* Manuscript. Retrieved from L'archive ouverte pluridiciplinaire database.

Schultze, U. (2000). A confessional account of an ethnography about knowledge work. *Management Information Systems Quarterly, 24*(1), 3–39. doi:10.2307/3250978

Spears, R., Postmes, T., Lea, M., & Wolbert, A. (2002). When are net effects gross products? The power of influence in computer-mediated communications. *The Journal of Social Issues, 58*(1), 91–107. doi:10.1111/1540-4560.00250

Trauth, E. M. (1997). Achieving the research goal with qualitative methods: Lessons learned along the way. In Lee, A. S., Liebenau, J., & DeGross, J. I. (Eds.), *Information Systems and qualitative research* (pp. 225–245). London, UK: Chapman & Hall.

Trauth, E. M. (2000). *The culture of an information economy: Influences and impacts in the Republic of Ireland*. Dordrecht, The Netherlands: Kluwer Academic Publishers.

Trauth, E. M. (2006). Theorizing gender and information technology research. In Trauth, E. M. (Ed.), *Encyclopedia of gender and Information Technology* (pp. 1154–1159). Hershey, PA: Idea Group Publishing. doi:10.4018/978-1-59140-815-4.ch182

Trauth, E. M. (2011). What can we learn from gender research? Seven lessons for business research methods. *Electronic Journal of Business Research Methods, 9*(1), 1–9.

Trauth, E. M., & Jessup, L. (2000). Understanding computer-mediated discussions: Positivist and interpretive analyses of group support system use. *Management Information Systems Quarterly*, *24*(1), 43–79. doi:10.2307/3250979

Trompette, P., Chanal, V., & Pelissier, C. (2008). Crowdsourcing as a way to access external knowledge for innovation: Control, incentive and coordination in hybrid forms of innovation. *Proceedings of the 24th EGOS Colloquium*.

Tushman, M. L., & O'Reilly, C. A. (2002). *Winning through innovation: A practical guide to leading organizational change and renewal*. Boston, MA: Harvard Business School Press.

Venkatesh, V., & Morris, M. (2000). Why don't men ever stop to ask for directions? Gender, social influence, and their role in technology acceptance and usage behavior. *Management Information Systems Quarterly*, *24*(1), 115–139. doi:10.2307/3250981

Venkatesh, V., Morris, M. G., & Ackerman, P. L. (2000). A longitudinal field investigation of gender differences in individual technology adoption decision making processes. *Organizational Behavior and Human Decision Processes*, *83*(1), 33–60. doi:10.1006/obhd.2000.2896

von Hippel, E. A. (2001, Summer). Learning from open-source software. *MIT Sloan Management Review*, 82-86.

von Hippel, E. A. (2005). *Democratizing innovation*. Cambridge, MA: MIT Press.

von Hippel, E. A., & von Krogh, G. (2003, April). Open source software and the "private collective" innovation model: Issues for organization science. *Organization Science*, *14*(2), 209–223. doi:10.1287/orsc.14.2.209.14992

Wasko, M. M., & Faraj, S. (2000). "It is what one does": Why people participate and help others in electronic communities of practice. *The Journal of Strategic Information Systems*, *9*, 155–173. doi:10.1016/S0963-8687(00)00045-7

Webster, B. (2009, May). Facebook democracy in Iran. *PoliticsOnline*. Retrieved September 5, 2009, from http://www.politicsonline.com/blog/archives/2009/05/facebook_and_de.php

Webster, J., & Martocchio, J. (1992). Microcomputer playfulness: Development of a measure with workplace implications. *Management Information Systems Quarterly*, *16*(2), 201–226. doi:10.2307/249576

Wenger, E. C., & Snyder, W. M. (2000, January-February). Communities of practice: The organizational frontier. *Harvard Business Review*, *78*(6), 139–146.

West, J., & Lakhani, K. R. (2008, April). Getting clear about communities in open innovation. *Industry and Innovation*, *15*(2), 223–231. doi:10.1080/13662710802033734

Whitla, P. (2009, March). Crowdsourcing and its application in marketing activities. *Contemporary Management Research*, *5*(1), 15–28.

Wiertz, C., & de Ruyter, K. (2007). Beyond the call of duty: Why customers contribute to firm hosted commercial online communities. *Organization Studies*, *28*(3), 347–376. doi:10.1177/0170840607076003

ADDITIONAL READING

Becker, J., & Niehaves, B. (2007). Epistemological perspectives on IS research: A framework for analysing and systematizing epistemological assumptions. *Information Systems Journal*, *17*, 197–214. doi:10.1111/j.1365-2575.2007.00234.x

DiMaggio, P. J. (1995, September). Comments on "What theory is not". *Administrative Science Quarterly, 40*(3), 391–397. doi:10.2307/2393790

Mingers, J. (2003). The paucity of multimethod research: A review of the information systems literature. *Information Systems Journal, 13*, 233–249. doi:10.1046/j.1365-2575.2003.00143.x

Orlikowski, W. J., & Baroudi, J. J. (1991). Studying information technology in organizations: Research approaches and assumptions. *Information Systems Research, 2*(1), 1–28. doi:10.1287/isre.2.1.1

Sutton, R. I., & Staw, B. M. (1995, September). What theory is not. *Administrative Science Quarterly, 40*(3), 371–384. doi:10.2307/2393788

KEY TERMS AND DEFINITIONS

Critical Approach: Challenges assumptions, identifies contradictions and seeks to raise awareness about systems of power. Asks the question *why* an observed phenomenon is the way it is.

Crowdsourcing: The use of the online social media tools by organizations to reach out to an undefined group of people (i.e., the "crowd") to complete tasks traditionally accomplished with internal resources.

Epistemology: Our beliefs about how we will come to know what we know. Epistemology impacts the methods we choose, the theories we leverage, as well as our understanding of results.

Interpretive Approach: Focuses on subjective reality expressed by participations in a research study. Asks the question *how* or *why*.

Positivist Approach: Focuses on accurate and replicable documentation of a phenomenon leading to valid generalizations about the phenomenon. Asks the question *who*, *what*, or *how many*.

ENDNOTE

[1] Klein and Myers (1999) explain *The Principle of Interaction between the Researchers and the Subjects* as one that "requires critical reflection on how the research materials (or 'data') were socially constructed through the interaction between the researchers and participants (p. 72)." The example provided is from Trauth's reflexive account of her ethnographic study of Ireland's information economy (1997, 2000) in which she reveals that her deepening understanding of Irish society enabled her to question her own assumptions.

Chapter 2
Rigor and Relevance in Information Systems Research:
A Comprehensive IS Research Process Model

Damodar Konda
RGIS, LLC., USA

ABSTRACT

There is an ongoing debate and discussion around rigor and relevance of Information Systems (IS) research. The published work so far on this subject remains largely confined to IS scholarly journals. Several models have been proposed that portray some kind of relationship between rigor and relevance with the common assumption that rigor and relevance are in some way or other related to each other and a tradeoff is needed between them for the right balance. Interestingly, much of the debate has been held within the confines of IS academic research circles without any significant participation from the practitioners. Nor did it have any overall context or framework for a meaningful and thorough discussion. This chapter proposes several models to guide IS researcher to help appropriately position the research using Rigor and Relevance Quadrants Model, triangulate the research using Triangulation Model, and achieve the right balance using a comprehensive IS Research Process model.

INTRODUCTION

Rigor versus relevance has been a burning topic among academic circles conducting research in the field of Information Systems. The ongoing debate on rigor and relevance can be traced from

DOI: 10.4018/978-1-4666-0179-6.ch002

the IS conferences and academic journals from early 1990s to till date. The initial contribution to this debate can be attributed to Peter Keen at the 1990 International Federation for Information Processing (IFIP) conference at Copenhagen (Bhattacherjee, 2001). Several articles have been published again in the late 1990s. The winter 1998 issue of *Information Resources Management*

Journal published two articles and MIS Quarterly devoted a significant portion of the March 1999 issue to the topic. Most of the discussion was around the right trade-off between rigor and relevance. The discipline of Information Systems is relatively young compared with other well-established fields of research such as physics, chemistry, and engineering. The early academic researchers in IS depended on research methodologies from other established fields. While academic research requires rigor, the applied nature of IS research requires relevance (Steinbach & Knight, 2006). The focus has always been on the rigor of research methodologies used in IS research to lend legitimacy and credibility in broader academic circles. The early researchers tended to follow empirical research in a behaviorist style similar to natural sciences. The research was based on the positivist tradition that became synonymous with the rigor in IS research. However, the domain of IS research has significantly expanded beyond early computer age into human dominated socio-technical systems that include IS development projects, and enterprise systems. Information Systems has evolved as a multi-disciplinary area primarily dealing with software engineering but with a human aspect in its business problem domain, system usage and in systems development project undertakings. The IS researchers will need to look at pluralistic tradition of research methodologies appropriate to the specific areas of IS and business problem domain. What is needed here is an appropriate set of research methodologies and tools that would provide the right level of rigor to the research process and yield credible and repeatable results. The goals and objectives of these research projects should be closely aligned with the interests of relevant academic and business stakeholders.

This chapter examines the rigor and relevance debate so far published in IS journals and proposes comprehensive set of models to guide IS research. The section on background starts with the examination of definitions of rigor and relevance of IS

research. IS rigor and relevance problem scenario is presented to provide high level business context for better understanding of the problem. It then discusses the concerns expressed on rigor and relevance and summarizes the recommended actions to improve them. The rigor and relevance relationship models are discussed in the next section. Key themes and core issues of the debate are identified and summarized to build Rigor and Relevance Quadrants Model, IS Research Triangulation Model, and IS Research Process Model to guide a more relevant and sufficiently rigorous IS research. A three step model has been proposed to appropriately *position* the research based on research goals and objectives and desired characteristics of research, and *triangulate* to determine the right alignment between the IS research, research methodology, and business practice knowledge domains. Then IS Research Process Model has been proposed at the end to *plan and control* the research project to achieve the right balance between rigor and relevance and create both academic and business value. The section on Future Research Directions discusses the limitations of the proposed models and suggests recommended enhancements as part of future research. The chapter ends with a Conclusion section summarizing the material covered in this chapter. It is hoped that the models presented in this chapter can help guide an IS research to achieve the right level of rigor and required relevance to successfully investigate into a research problem in IS domain.

BACKGROUND

Definitions of Rigor and Relevance of IS Research

The whole debate hinges around rigor and relevance of IS research. The concept of rigor of IS research comes into play while determining appropriate research methodologies for conducting IS research on a selected topic. The concept of relevance comes into play while choosing a research topic in the consideration when the topic is relevant to business practice. Several variations of definitions for both "rigor" and "relevance" have been provided. However, appropriate selection of research methodologies and the relevance of research topic to the business practice and alignment of research goals with the interests of target stakeholders is a predominant theme. The following sections examine the definitions of rigor and relevance of IS research.

Rigor of IS Research

For a good understanding of what a rigor is and to define the term "rigor", in the context of conducting research in IS domain, it is necessary to briefly describe the considerations of research design.

Research Design Considerations

In this sub-section, we provide a brief background on the research methodology and research design considerations. The quality of research outcomes depends upon the quality of research design and considerations that go into choosing appropriate research methodology. These choices in turn depend on selected research topic and predefined research goals and objectives. A good research design is based on carefully chosen research paradigmatic alternatives and takes into consideration the intent of the research, the methodological choices available, and research methods to be used. There are two very different views of research paradigms broadly categorized as "positivism" and "interpretivism" (Silverman, 2004). While positivism seeks to test correlations between variables in the world that is external and objective, interpretivism sees the world as socially constructed and subjective. Some researchers categorize these two broad approaches as "positivism" and "phenomenology." The phenomenology research paradigm is sometimes described as a

descriptive/interpretative approach and implies that every event studied is a unique incident in its own right. In this school of thought there is nothing other than phenomena and the essence of a phenomenon is understood intuitively.

Information Systems as a research discipline stretches from physical science at one end to social science at the other end presenting range of methodological choices and research methods for conducting research. A good research design and determination of appropriate methodological choice depends upon

- The research goals and objectives, purpose of study and interests of target stakeholders. The purpose and intent of research would decide the type of investigation in terms of exploratory, explanatory or predictive (Marshall & Rossman, 1999)
- The nature of research topic from paradigmatic considerations to determine the right balance between positivist or interpretivist research traditions. It could be quantitative hypothesis-testing or qualitative hypothesis-generation.
- The range of methodological choices and applicable research methods based on the selected research topic
- the method of evidence collection, analysis and interpretation of results using a combination of qualitative, quantitative or mixed-methods approach
- the type of knowledge contributions that can be legitimately claimed and verified
- validation of research design at every major step and documentation and validation of research findings
- generalization of findings that can be applicable in other contexts

An example of these research design considerations in case of a sample doctoral dissertation project on Knowledge Management can be found in chapter 3 Research Design and Procedure of

Konda's doctoral dissertation work published in the form of a book (Konda D., 2010).

Definition of Rigor

A rigorous research is research that follows a well-defined, structured, and transparent research process based on sound research design considerations and appropriate selection of research methodologies and research methods determined by the type and topic of research. Such research is more likely to produce high quality results that are dependable, repeatable, and independently verifiable. It would also effectively meet stated research goals and objectives and produce research findings that are of value to interested stakeholders. The methods and methodological choices should be explicit and transparent so that a researcher can describe them clearly and other researchers can repeat the same studies to independently arrive at similar findings and verify the results. A rigorous research is relevant if the research findings can be applied to solve critical business problems in real-world scenarios with a high level of confidence. Next we will look at the relevance of IS research.

Relevance of IS Research

The key theme in all of the published definitions is either the "Business Practice" or the interests of "Target Stakeholders." The definitions from Saunders (1998), Senn (1998), and Rollier (2001) include the applicability of IS research to business practice and serving the interests of target stakeholders. According to Saunders (1998), research is relevant if it focuses on usefulness for managers to successfully solve the critical business problems. According to Senn (1998), the research is relevant when the topic or question of investigation does pertain to the challenges faced by the targeted stakeholders and findings can be applied in practice. Benbasat & Zmud (1999) limited their study to the question of relevance of IS research in the positivist, empirical research tradition. According

to them, the most "relevant" topic to practitioners is that which is implementable and pragmatic. Rollier (2001) considers research as relevant if it leads to the solution of future problems. In other words, the research should be "leading" practice and have potential to lead to future solutions in business practice. The aspect of timing to relevance is also suggested by Cresswell (2001). Cresswell (2001) suggests a "frame of reference" for the term relevance. The frame of reference checks to see

- if research is relevant for or in the interest of that stakeholder
- if the work is intended to "advance knowledge" or
- if it is intended to "serve the public good, preferably in direct, tangible, and immediate ways"

IS research can be considered "relevant" if the research goals and objectives are aligned with the interests and needs of the business practitioners and the research results create business value by helping to solve current and future critical business problems through advancement of knowledge. Next section presents a pictorial representation of overall context for the problem scenario for a meaningful discussion the issues related to rigor and relevance of IS research.

IS Research Rigor and Relevance Problem Scenario

Although the discussion of rigor versus relevance of Information Systems (IS) research can be traced to early 90s based on the published articles in IS scholarly journals and continues till date. Most of the published work so far has been primarily driven by individual perceptions and opinions of IS researchers and in the facilitated discussions during the conferences. Several of these scholars made an attempt to piece together various concepts on rigor and relevance of IS research and these have been presented in the form of rigor

Figure 1. IS research knowledge management scenario

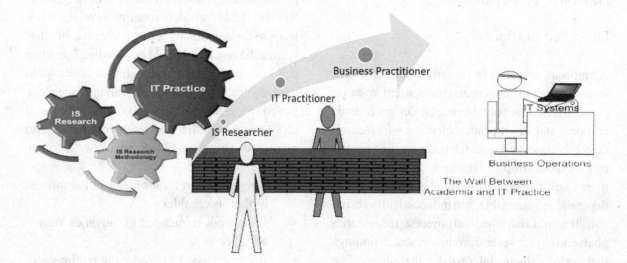

versus relevance relationship models or as overall frameworks (Fallman & Gronlund, 2002; Steinbach & Knight, 2006) claimed to address some of these concerns. A practitioner's perspective of an overall context of the discussion is needed to better understand and address the underlying issues. IS Research Knowledge Management Scenario is presented in this section to provide such an overall context for a better appreciation of the discussion.

Figure 1 depicts Information Systems Research Knowledge Management Scenario to provide a problem context and to better understand the rigor versus relevance debate of IS research and the underlying problems. IS research process can be considered as a knowledge management process with the primary purpose of creating new Information Systems knowledge to IT enable business processes and use IT Systems to solve critical business problems. The process involves three roles; IS Researcher, IT Practitioner, and Business Practitioner. IS Researcher creates new knowledge. Depending on how relevant the research topic is to business practice and how efficient and effective is the knowledge transfer process between

academics and professionals, this knowledge may remain confined within academic circles or may get transferred past the dividing "wall" between academia and practice. IT practitioner and Business Practitioner together can be called as Business Practice. If the knowledge transfer of the new IS knowledge to IT practice is successful, IT Practitioner receives and applies it to build, enhance, and support enterprise systems or IT applications. Business Practitioner uses these systems and IT applications to solve critical business problems in order to support and grow business operations. IS Researcher is typically situated in an academic or research environment while IT Practitioner and Business Practitioner are situated in business world. If this process is functioning effectively as intended, the newly created IS knowledge will result in creating business value by solving critical business problems. This process involves three knowledge domains; IS Research, IS Research Methodology and IT Practice which is part of Business Practice. The success of this process depends to a great extent on how harmoniously the three interdependent knowledge domains are orchestrated in the process of knowledge creation, transfer, and application to create business value by solving critical business problems. These knowledge domains are represented in the form of three interlocking gears that need to mesh and drive each other smoothly without any interference to support the underlying knowledge management processes. With the above understanding of the overall problem context depicted in the form of IS Research Knowledge Management Scenario, let us now review the concerns pertaining to rigor and relevance of IS research in the next section. This will help identify key themes and develop appropriate tools and approaches to study, identify and address the problem.

Concerns on Rigor and Relevance

It is important to understand the concerns expressed by various IS scholars pertaining to both rigor and relevance of IS research. This will help to better understand and appreciate the topic of rigor and relevance. Most of these issues hinge around the three interlocking knowledge domains depicted in Figure 1. These concerns can be broadly discussed under three categories: 1. Issues with IS Research Methodology, 2. Quality of IS Research, and 3. Alignment with Business Practice. Following sections discuss these concerns in detail.

Issues with IS Research Methodology

Rigor should not be confused with measurement precision or quantification or generalization. Because of this confusion, early IS researchers always tried to follow confirmatory hypothesis-driven research following positivist tradition and empirical data collection and analysis. The misconception in the minds of IS researchers has been that rigor is equivalent to following positivist inquiry paradigm that uses quantitative analysis and sophisticated statistical techniques. The notion is that the research tradition followed in physical sciences should be followed in IS research for drawing

precise and measurable conclusions. This ignores the fact that Information Systems transcends past scientifically driven computer engineering well into human-centered information systems requiring a pluralistic methodological choices appropriate for both physical and social science related subjects. There are also issues that need to be addressed while making appropriate methodological choices. The first issue is choosing a research methodology before selecting a research topic. This is partly driven by personal preference or knowledge of researcher and partly guided by one's supervisor. This is equivalent to putting the methodological cart before the philosophical horse (Brown, 2009). The second issue is lack of due consideration for range of research methodological choices and research methods available and confusion between research methodology and research method and lack of discipline in terminology with many researchers using the terms interchangeably (Brown, 2009). Research Methodology is a higher level procedural framework within which research is conducted. It is based upon ontological and epistemological considerations and research inquiry paradigms. It links methods to outcomes and governs our choice and use of methods. Research methods are techniques and procedures for data collection, analysis, documentation and validation of research findings.

Many researchers do not follow the required rigor in their research work. In a research article published in MIS Quarterly, Dubé & Paré (2003) identify a list of attributes for evaluating rigor in positivist case research based on the work of Benbasat et al. (1987), Eisenhardt (1989), Lee (1989), and Yin (1994) that would serve as an example. These attributes are divided into three main areas: 1. Research Design, 2. Data Collection, and 3. Data Analysis. The IS positivist case studies have been studied to assess the rigor in terms of these attributes and issues in each of the area have been identified and recommendations made to address them. The design issues consisted of lack of clarity in research questions, and rationale for single or multiple case selection and not considering alternative theories for increasing the validity and predictive power of case studies. There were several issues with respect to second area of data collection. These pointed to lack of detailed information with respect to data collection and analysis methods, not effectively summarizing the information in the form of tables, and not triangulating the data in order to increase the internal validity of the findings. The issues pertaining to the third area of data analysis included lack of clear description of the analytic methods and procedures and comparing findings with extant literature so as to increase the confidence in the findings. While the above findings are drawn in the context of a positivist case research, the method of assessing the rigor is equally applicable to qualitative IS research following interpretivist paradigm of inquiry as well.

There are also issues with respect to relevance of research methods and lack of appropriate style and relevant context. Often, IS research is not accepted by colleagues of the respective reference disciplines, because of insufficient quality of the research. Benbasat & Zmud (1999) relate specifically to behaviorist empirical research and provide critical assessment concerning the relevance of IS research articles. They see a tendency to emphasize rigor over relevance in journals and in promotion and tenure criteria. They state that a cumulative research tradition is needed in order to build strong theoretical models that can serve as a reliable basis for "prescriptive actions" for industry practice. However, the authors do not see such a cumulative tradition in IS. The authors criticize that the dynamism of technological innovation in combination with long publication cycles lead to outdated articles in current journals. The insufficient readability and attractiveness of research articles from the view point of practitioners also add to the problem. Specific issues of critique relate to the prerequisite knowledge assumed, the emphasis on shortcomings and future work, the time lag due to long publication cycles, the complex language, and changes in terminology (Kavan, 1998; Klein, 2002).

Quality of IS Research

The poor quality of IS research due to lack of relevance can be attributed to several reasons. It could be due to (1) lack of interesting topics, application-oriented research results and knowledge (Klein, 2002; Dennis, 2001), (2) lack of relevant research methods (Benbasat & Zmud, 1999; Keen, 1991), and (3) insufficient attractiveness of research articles and inappropriate style from the view point of the practitioners' community (Benbasat & Zmud, 1999). Some authors criticize that the IS discipline has not been successful in producing research results and knowledge of value to practitioners. Several reasons are provided: research results do not address critical problems, the topics covered are not of interest anymore and IS research rarely produces new approaches and innovations. Keen (1991) criticizes that there are many research papers that do not explicate the target audience but justify their research through the method applied rather than through the demand in business practice.

Alignment with Business Practice

Alignment of IS research with business practice is not possible without appropriate level of Interaction between Academics and Professionals. One way to assure relevance is to encourage frequent interaction and transfer of knowledge between academics and professionals. Currently, there are several concerns around the "so called" divide between academia and business practice. This is due to lack of sufficient level of interaction between academics and IT practitioners. This can be attributed to several reasons. Academics do not use the media of practice to communicate their research findings and that academics and practitioners rarely attend the same conferences (Senn, 1998; Gray, 2002). As a result, the knowledge created by IS researchers is not being disseminated to practitioners. IS professionals rarely subscribe or read academic IS journals due to lack of perceived value to them (Senn, 1998; Keen, 199; Davenport, 1997; Benbasat & Zmud, 1999). IS academics also lack sufficient experience with today's business and technology environment (Benbasat & Zmud, 1999). These can be attributed to the requirements of tenure and promotion committees that largely determine acceptable research methods and publication outlets with particular emphasis on highly ranked academic journals, which focus on theoretical, rigorous research rather than on application-oriented and relevant research. The time available for IS faculty to interact with practitioners and to stay current with technology is frequently limited by institutional circumstances and by promotion requirements. The two core issues that can be discerned form the above discussion are Research Motivation and Research Environment. While Research Motivation represents the motivating factors that positively or negatively influence both the researchers and research sponsors to pursue relevant research, Research Environment represents external environment that could provide a positive or negative working environment to pursue relevant research. The next section summarizes the published recommendations that can be gleaned from various IS journals.

Published Recommendations for Improving IS Research Relevance

Schauer (2007) summarizes various recommendations for improving relevance in IS research under two main categories; (1) recommended values and attitudes, and (2) recommended actions. A closer scrutiny behind these fragmented recommendations points to the need for alignment among three dimensions: IS Research, Business Practice, and Research Methodology.

Recommended Values or Attitudes

Following are the recommendations under the category of values and attitudes. The first recommendation pertains to more appreciating relevant

research and diversity. It is important that the peers and academia do appreciate conducting more relevant and diverse research topics that are closely aligned with the needs of business practice (Davenport & Markus, 1999; Mathieson & Ryan, 2001). The second recommendation talks about respecting consultancy research as an alternative which may lack the required standards of rigor acceptable to academia (Davenport & Markus, 1999). The most significant recommendation in this category is not to view rigor and relevance as conflicting (Robey & Markus, 1998) and dependent variables requiring a either-or or trade-off but that can be independently controlled and orchestrated in terms of relevance to business practice, appropriate research methodologies, and advancement of IS research knowledge. The question is more with regard to positioning of the research in rigor and relevance quadrant as explained in the earlier section rather than changing the acceptance criteria of consultancy research by trying to impose unnecessary standards of rigor. The other recommendation is to wait until completing the tenure before starting the relevant approach (Rockart, 2002a; Hoving, 2002). This seems to provide a plausible solution with easier route to take rather than appropriately positioning the research based on research goals and objectives and interests of stakeholders.

Recommended Actions to Improve Relevance of Research

Schauer (2007) summarizes specific recommended actions and initiatives under two categories relating to (1) improving the relevance of IS research and (2) improving the acceptance of relevant research in academia.

Following are the recommended actions to improve the relevance of research.

- Devise suitable approaches to foster the exchange between academics and practitioners to address the divide between academia and business practice (Kohli,

2001; Borchers, 2001; Benbasat & Zmud, 1999; Alter, 2001; Kavan, 1998; Watson & Huber, 2000).

- Emulate law and medical schools as suitable examples for the IS discipline on how to organize interaction between academic researchers and professionals in business practice (Davenport, 1997; Davenport & Markus 1999; Klein, 2002; Lee, 1999).
- Strive for better focus on particularly relevant types of research questions and results (Davenport, 1997; Senn, 1998; Davenport & Markus, 1999; Robey & Markus, 1998; Westfall, 1999; Westfall, 2001; Rollier, 2001; Klein, 2002; Gray, 2002).
- Emphasize the need to change priorities in selecting research questions and methods (Keen, 1991; Benbasat & Zmud, 1999).
- Produce better consumable research (Senn, 1998; Kavan, 1998; Robey & Markus 1998; Benbasat & Zmud, 1999). Improve readability from the view point of practitioners through appropriate changes in the outline and style of research articles.
- Utilize the opportunity to influence students as the future professionals to improve the future exchange between academia and practice (Davenport & Markus, 1999).

Several recommendations have been made to improve the acceptance of research as summarized below. These include

- Reward publications in practitioner outlets for promotion and tenure (Davenport & Markus, 1999; Robey & Markus, 1998; Sein, 2001; Jennex, 2001; Rockart, 2002a).
- Identify the need and establish new publication outlets that foster relevant research (Keen, 1991; Senn, 1998; Munkvold & Khazanchi, 2001; Dennis, 2001; Gray, 2002).
- Change academic journal policies in terms of standards of rigor and improving rel-

evance of IS research (Benbasat & Zmud, 1999; Westfall, 1999; Hoving, 2002).
- Broaden the acceptable research including the general requirements for acceptable criteria for dissertation research (Gray, 2002).

The rigor and relevance debate also hinged around the relationship and the right balance between them. The needed rigor of the research process and the relevance to the business practice need to be orchestrated for maximizing the business value by solving the critical business problems. The following section explores various models that depict some kind of relationship between rigor and relevance and proposes an IS Research Rigor and Relevance Quadrants Model to appropriately position IS research based on the intended business impact and academic value.

Relationship between Rigor and Relevance in IS Research

Several models depicting the relationship between rigor and relevance have been proposed and advancements identified in these models have been claimed to better represent the relationship. Three models have been depicted in Figure 2 shown below. These include rigor versus relevance as a dichotomy by Mason (1989) represented in dashed line, the Impact Frontier model by Davenport & Markus (1999) shown in chain dotted line, and the Consumable Research Model by Robey & Markus (1998) shown in solid line. All the three models portray rigor and relevance as variables dependent upon each other. Both dichotomy and impact frontier models depict rigor and relevance as reciprocal to each other whereas consumable academic research model shows them as directly proportional to each other. The dichotomy and impact frontier models assume a fundamental trade-off between rigor and relevance of research and suggest that we cannot achieve better rigor or relevance without sacrificing the other. This

Figure 2. Rigor vs. relevance relationship models

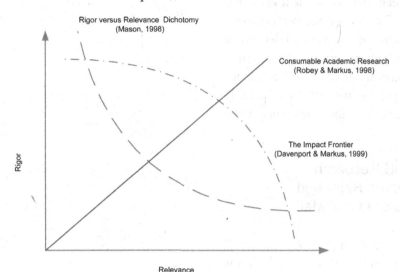

assumed relationship might be depiction of a plausible relationship based on how research-oriented academic journals and practice-oriented trade journals operate. Academic journals follow higher standards of rigor and as a result may lose sight of relevance of the published research to business practice. These research publications with high level of rigor and low level of relevance can be represented by top left portion of the graph. On the other hand, trade journals emphasize relevance to business practice in preference to the rigor and serve the interests of business practitioners. These publications display low level of rigor and high level of relevance and can be represented by bottom right portion of the graph. Davenport & Markus (1999) propose an alternative model to the relationship between rigor and relevance, called the impact frontier model.

They introduce the concept of "impact quotient" of a product of research where the researcher is intended to have the potential to contribute to both business and academic communities by having a choice of how to position a publication for the kind of impact wanted. Research published in a rigor-oriented journal may have the same, less or more impact than an article published in a relevance-oriented magazine. Al-though this model, in a way, portrays a trade-off relationship between rigor and relevance, it introduces the new concept of a third variable, "impact" being dependent upon the rigor and relevance which are not necessarily dependent upon each other. The middle portion of the curve also portrays a somewhat optimal combination of rigor and relevance for a maximum impact. The main problem with both of these models is that they are by far too simplified, and do not take into consideration the practical ability to independently choose the right level of rigor to the research process while at the same time ensuring that the research is relevant to a business practice and benefits the targeted stakeholders. The consumable research model, proposed by Robey & Markus (1998), deviates from both of the above models in that there is no longer a trade-off between rigor and relevance. It suggests that there is no "either or" relationship between rigor and relevance. The researcher should strive for increasing both rigor and relevance simultaneously in order to achieve the goal of consumable research that would benefit the practitioners.

From the above discussion of the rigor and relevance relationship models, it appears that the authors were trying to depict a non-existing relationship between two independent variables. From an IT practitioner's perspective, rigor and relevance would rather appear as two independent but equally desirable characteristics of IS research product and IS researcher should make a conscious decision to position the research appropriately in terms of rigor and relevance quadrants model proposed below.

Positioning of IS Research Using IS Research Rigor and Relevance Quadrants Model

Based on the discussion in previous section of IS Research Rigor and Relevance Models, it was argued that the implied trade-off relationship does not exist and rather rigor and relevance are two independent characteristics of IS research. Figure 3 depicts Rigor and Relevance Quadrants model with rigor and relevance of IS research depicted as two independent characteristics of IS research. This model is based on assumption that an IS research product may exhibit either High or Low values of rigor and research based on the decisions made by the researcher while establishing research goals and objectives. According to this model, IS research work can be positioned in one of the four quadrants labeled as R1, R2, R3, or R4 respectively in the counterclockwise direction. A research with high degree of rigor is expected to produce high quality research outcomes that are reliable, verifiable, and repeatable. Such research will have high standards of rigor and are typically required in academic circles. Such high standards of rigor are also required in academia for publication in IS scholarly journals and for counting towards faculty tenure and promotions or for awarding doctoral degrees. High rigor is also expected to produce high academic value to the researcher and research sponsors and academic stakeholders. If a research is conducted without required standards of rigor, the research products may not be of high quality and may not be reliable, repeatable and verifiable.

Figure 3. IS research rigor and relevance quadrants

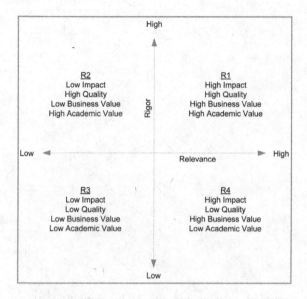

A research with high degree of relevance should be closely aligned with the needs of business practice, and research goals and interests should be aligned with the interests and communicational needs of relevant business stakeholders. As business practitioners will find such research findings readable, interesting, and directly applicable to their business practice, such research is expected to have high impact and create high business value. Lack of IS research relevance to the business practice will probably remain confined within academic circles and will probably not find good audience in business practice. This is the general concern expressed in several IS publications. Lack of such relevance will result in low impact to business practice and will create low business value. It is necessary to distinguish between business value and academic value. A highly rigorous research complying with established academic standards will have high academic value and will help in obtaining faculty tenure and promotions and students fulfilling doctoral degree requirements. Such research, if not relevant to business practice and hence not directly applicable to solve critical business problems, will not add any business value and will probably be confined within academic circles.

With the above understanding, let us now discuss the positioning of an IS research in terms of rigor and relevance quadrants. First quadrant represents high rigor and high relevance. Second quadrant represents high rigor but low relevance. Third quadrant represents low rigor and low relevance. And finally, the fourth quadrant represents high relevance and low rigor. R1 represent a research product that is an outcome of a research process with high standards of rigor and the research topic is of high relevance to business practice. High standards of rigor would ensure high quality research outcomes that are reliable, repeatable, and verifiable. Such characteristics of research product are typical of academic research. If the research topic is also of high degree of relevance to the business practice and the research results are clearly communicable to business practitioners, the research product will have the potential to provide solutions to solve current and future problems in business practice.

Such research will have high business impact and will create high business value. R1 represents such research and is the best case scenario where the interests of both academic and business community are met and the research outcomes have high impact and create high business and academic value. Thus, R1 represents positioning of IS research product that is an outcome of a highly orchestrated research process using right level of rigor appropriate for the research topic and the research goals and objectives have been closely aligned with the interests of both academic and business stakeholders. R2 represents a research product that is an outcome of a highly rigorous research process but the research topic has been selected without any due consideration of relevance to the business practice. This type of research is what has been perceived as lacking relevance to business practice and primarily geared towards faculty promotions and tenure requirements or fulfillment of doctoral degree requirements. As a result, R2 type of research may have a high quality and high academic value because of the research rigor and acceptability within academia but may suffer from low impact to business and may only add low business value due to lack of relevance or applicability to business practice. It may also suffer from lack of appropriate communication style, channel or methods for its effectiveness in knowledge transfer. R3 represents type of IS research that has not followed any structured research methodology or research design standards and the research products are not intended to be relevant to current or future business practice. This type of work can be found in opinion-based online websites or IT blog sites where the technical writings are of low quality, and have low impact to business, and add no or little value to academic and business practice. Research work represented by R4 has characteristics of low rigor but high relevance. Because of low rigor, the quality of research results may not be high and hence may not be acceptable in academia and hence add little or no value to academia unless the value system in academia is changed. Because of its high relevance to business, this kind of research work has high impact to the business practice and has the potential to create high business value. The trade journals, product vendor conferences, and white papers will belong in this category of research work.

The IS Research Rigor and Relevance Quadrant Model is a tool to help assess current positioning of the IS research based on the rigor and relevance values and appropriately reposition it in a desired quadrant to produce a research product with the associated characteristics in terms of desired business impact, academic and business value, and quality of research. This IS research positioning model is distinctly different from other rigor and relevance relationship models in that this does not assume any relationship between rigor and relevance. Rather they are treated as two independent characteristics of the IS research product that can be controlled through a well designed research process and highly and timely orchestrated communication with relevant stakeholders. This model is used as part of first step of three step process model provided to guide a research process for improving the rigor and relevance of IS research. The actual usage of this model is explained as part of the three step process elaborated in the later section of this chapter. We will now examine the key themes and core issues of IS relevance based on published recommendations and propose a three step process to address these concerns.

KEY THEMES AND CORE ISSUES OF IS RELEVANCE

Key Themes in IS Research Relevance

From the analysis of material presented in the previous sections, several key themes emerge from the definitions, concerns, and recommended actions to improve IS research relevance as summarized in Table 1. Several things always stand out in the definition of relevance. The relevance of IS research always included references to Research Goals of research project, Target Stakeholders both in academia and business practice and Business Practice as part of definitions. The other aspects of relevance included Knowledge Creation of IS Knowledge and its timely Transfer to Business Practice for its timely application in a suitable Time Frame. If we consider IS research projects in the light of a knowledge management life cycle processes, the initial IS research project can be viewed as a Knowledge Creation process and the creation of business value happens from knowledge application of newly created IS knowledge within a business practice (Steenkamp & Konda, 2003). Every IS research project should have Research Goals that are relevant to a Business Practice and are closely aligned with the interests of Target Stakeholders. Then the IS research products and newly created IS knowledge can

Table 1. Key themes on IS research relevance

Category	Key Theme
Definitions	Research Goals
	Target Stakeholders
	Knowledge Creation
	Knowledge Transfer
	Business Practice
	Knowledge Application
	Time Frame

be beneficially applied to solve current and future business problems in the targeted Business Practice domain. Business value is created from the application of newly created IS knowledge from the research. The knowledge requirements of business practice to solve current and future problems may continue to grow over a period of time and the knowledge created from IS research should stay ahead of practice in a given time frame.

In order to understand the significance of Time Frame, let us examine the knowledge requirements of business practice on IS research as shown in Figure 4. The figure shows the trend of increasing knowledge requirements of a business practice on IS knowledge domain over a period of time. This knowledge is required for solving current and future business problems. If the knowledge base is a measure of level of knowledge required to solve current and future problems of business practice, and the level of contribution of the IS Research to the existing knowledge base, the state of IS Research can be identified under one of three categories: 1. Leading Research, 2. Controlled Research, and 3. Lagging Research.

The blue line (0) labeled Practice depicts the trend line of increasing knowledge requirements of IS to support current and future business practices over a period of time. If the IS research project is done in isolation without aligning the research goals and objectives with the interests of relevant business stakeholders, the knowledge created from such research would be below the knowledge requirements of current and future business practice. Such IS research can be con-

Figure 4. Time frame: Increasing knowledge requirements of business practice

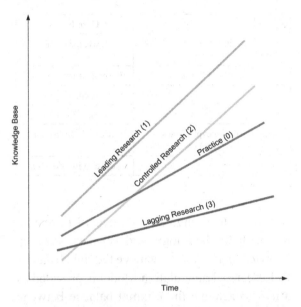

sidered as a Lagging Research and is depicted by a red line (3) in Figure 4. This kind of research may not meet the knowledge requirements of either the current or the future business practices and creates no positive business value due to lack of relevance. Such IS research project may have followed a very thorough and rigorous research methodology and may have been published in highly regarded and peer reviewed IS scholarly journals. This is likely to happen especially when the criteria for such publications do not include the relevance to a business practice as a requirement and peer reviewing scholars are out of touch with IT Practice. The Research Motivation and Research Environment are not conducive to recognize and encourage that kind of research. The predominant opinion of the publications on the IS research rigor and relevance debate allude to this state of IS research.

On the other hand, if IS research has been consciously targeting research topics whose goals and objectives are closely aligned with the interests of relevant stakeholders in the business practice, the research results have the potential

to provide solutions to current and future critical business problems. Such kind of IS research can be considered as Leading Research (1) and is shown by a green line in Figure 4.

The third scenario exists when, a current IS research that is currently identified as a lagging research undertakes appropriate course corrections and can be converted into a leading research through a controlled exploration of new technology knowledge areas that have the potential to solve critical business problems in the future. This kind of IS research trend can be called as Controlled Research (2) and is depicted by a yellow line in Figure 4. This requires a proactive knowledge management of IS research through active collaboration of relevant business stakeholders. Thus, Figure 4 clearly brings out the concept of timeframe and identifies the status of relevance of IS research with respect to time in order to ensure that the IS research does not result in obsolete and outdated knowledge and ensures that it has the potential to contribute positive business value.

Core Issues for the Lack of IS Research Relevance

Table 2 summarizes the core issues of IS research relevance, that can be gleaned from the summary of research publications. There are four core issues that can be identified from the areas of concerns expressed by various authors for the lack of IS research relevance. These issues cover the complete knowledge management life cycle of IS research project. They range from selection and usage of appropriate research methodologies for creation of IS knowledge using a research process with the right level of rigor to quality of knowledge created from the IS research, and the effectiveness of knowledge transfer from IS Research domain into Business Practice domain. The effectiveness of knowledge transfer from IS knowledge domain to business practice domain depends upon the appropriate selection and type of communication channels and level of interaction between academics and professionals. For example, publishing a summary level IS research results with right style in relevant trade journals and ensuring appropriate interaction between IS researchers and practitioners may enhance the effectiveness of the knowledge transfer process. The knowledge transfer should also happen in a timely manner for it to create positive business value. For this, the knowledge creation and application should follow the trend line of a leading IS research with levels of knowledgebase well above what is needed to solve current and future critical business problems. The approaches used to explain the lack of relevance of IS research, primarily focus on the lack of Research Motivation on the part of both researchers and research supporting institutions to pursue business practice relevant research and lack of Research Environment that rewards solving real world business problems. The core issues identified so far are listed in Table 2 below and need to be effectively addressed to achieve IS research relevance. This is accomplished through a set of concerted actions that are systematically orchestrated to align three critical dimensions. These alignment actions are collectively accomplished through IS Research Triangulation Model which supports critical step 2 of the three- step process to guide IS research for improving the relevance and rigor as explained in the next section.

MODELS TO GUIDE IS RESEARCH FOR IMPROVING RIGOR AND RELEVANCE

This section proposes a three-step model for achieving the most optimal balance between rigor and relevance in IS research. The three steps are: 1. Position, 2. Triangulate, and 3. Plan and Execute. As part of first step "position", the IS researcher will need to position his or her research on the IS Research Rigor and Relevance Quadrant model. The second step "triangulate" helps IS

Table 2. Core Issues underlying relevance of IS research

Category	Core Issues
Areas of concerns for the lack of relevance	Knowledge Creation
	Research Methodology
	Knowledge Transfer
	Time Frame
Approaches to explain lack of relevance	Research Motivation
	Research Environment

researcher to triangulate between IS Research, Research Methodology, and Business Practice knowledge domains to achieve the right balance. IS Research Triangulation Model is provided as a tool to achieve the optimal balance between rigor and relevance of IS research by consciously orchestrating the interaction among IS Research, Research Methodology, and Business Practice knowledge domains. The third step "plan and execute" is achieved by following IS Research Process Model. IS Research Process Model serves as a roadmap to guide IS research project during various life cycle stages of the research process and can be used for planning and controlling the rigor and relevance aspects of IS research.

Following sections provide the necessary details for each of the three steps along with the supporting models and underlying details for guidance.

Positioning of IS Research

The first step of the process explains proper positioning of IS research. The researcher can use IS Research Rigor and Relevance Model to determine the current positioning of the research and come up with an action plan to appropriately reposition it as R1 that has the best optimal combination of rigor and relevance. Figure 5 depicts the four quadrants along with the characteristics of research product in each of the four quadrants and appropriate reposition of research from one quadrant to another. Once researcher determines the current positioning, he or she will have to make a conscious decision about the future positioning and should come up with action plan for repositioning his or her research into one of the four quadrants of IS Rigor and Relevance Quadrants. The research goals and objectives of the research project and primary motivation of the researcher will help determine appropriate positioning of the research. If the research intent is only to obtain tenure and promotions or a doctoral degree, one can target R2 type of research and achieve all of the research goals and objectives which are most likely to be academic in nature. However, if the research is industry sponsored research in an academic setting trying to solve critical business problems, try to reposition the research as R1 by moving it from R2. On the other hand, if you are a practitioner doing research for publications in trade journals, you are probably positioned as R4 currently. But, if you like to achieve the additional goals of high quality research that is reliable, verifiable and repeatable, try to reposition your research from R4 to R1. If you don't follow any research methodologies and don't care for its relevance to business practice, you are simply wasting your time unless that is your hobby. This position is represented by R3. In that case, try to improve your research skills and work on business relevant topics so that you can either move your research position either into R2 or R4. Moving from R3 to R2 would represent a practitioner pursuing a doctoral degree and participating in early research. Alternatively, R3 to R4 would represent active collaboration with product vendors or practice consultancies to conduct high impact research with reasonably good quality. Moving from R3 to R1 will be a difficult transition given the research methodology training and business practice knowledge requirements to improve the quality of research and gain understanding of current and future business problems.

Figure 5. Positioning of IS research

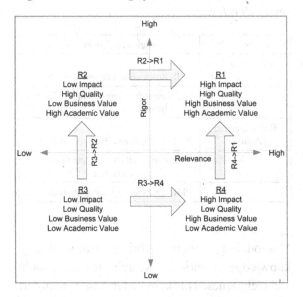

Having determined the appropriate positioning of research in terms of IS Research Rigor and Relevance Quadrants, the next step is to follow the IS Research Triangulation Model given below to appropriately align the IS Research, Research Methodology, and Business Practice knowledge domains and strive towards best case scenario positioning of research as R1.

IS Research Triangulation Model

The second step of the three step process is the IS Research Triangulation model. The recommendations to improve the IS research relevance can be summarized as an orchestrated set of actions along the alignment dimensions broadly grouped under two categories: 1. Values and Attitudes and, 2. Recommended Actions as listed in Table 3. There are three interconnected knowledge domains that come into play from the recommendations made to improve IS research relevance. These are IS Research domain creating new knowledge bases in IT, Business Practice domain consisting of IT Practice and Business Practice that consume this newly created IT knowledge for solving current and future critical business problems and Research

Table 3. Alignment dimensions to improve IS research relevance

Category	Alignment Dimensions
Values and Attitudes	IS Research and Business Practice
	IS Research Triangulation: Trade-off between rigor and relevance
Recommended Actions	IS Research and Business Practice
	Research Methodology and Business Practice
	IS Research and Research Methodology

Methodology domain that brings in the necessary knowledge of various research processes, tools and techniques. This knowledge base is required to identify and apply appropriate research methodologies to the IS research work that would yield credible, and repeatable research results creating IS knowledge bases with the characteristics of a leading research. The interplay among these three knowledge domains can be better depicted in the form of IS Research Triangulation model depicted in Figure 6. This model explains how the IS research needs to focus on three inter-connected knowledge domains: IS, Business, and Research Methodology.

Each of these three knowledge domains is represented in the form of a circle. The intersecting area between IS Research and Research Methodology domains, represented by 1, represents a rigorous IS Research that is typical of academic research that is not necessarily relevant to a business practice. The intersecting area between Business Practice and Research Methodology, denoted by 2, depicts critical business process issues that would need the application of IS Research knowledge for solving the problems.

The intersecting area between IS Research and Business Practice knowledge domains, depicted by 3, identifies the inefficient application of IS knowledge, that is not necessarily the result of a rigorous research, and hence not necessarily credible and

proven to improve the business processes in the Business Practice domain. The proper alignment of IS Research and Research Methodology will provide a rigorous IS Research with an intersecting area 1 that needs to be aligned with Business Practice domain. Similarly, the alignment between IS Research and Business Practice will provide IS Research knowledge that is not necessarily rigorous, credible, and useful and hence needs appropriate alignment with the Research Methodology domain. The alignment between Business Practice and Research Methodology domains will only identify business issues represented by intersecting area 2 and would need the application of IS knowledge to create business value. What is needed here is an optimal orchestration of alignment between each of the three interconnected IS, Business, and Research Methodology domains that would lead towards common intersection of these three knowledge domains represented by 4. IS Research Triangulation is this optimal process of orchestrating the alignment with an end goal of the comingling of each of the three knowledge domains represented by the area 4. Thus, the IS Research Triangulation Model leads to IS research that is in proper alignment with the business needs of relevant stakeholders in the target Business Practice domain and the credibility, repeatability, and usefulness of such IS Research work is ensured by utilizing appropriate Research Methodologies. The IS Research Process Model presented in the following section attempts to achieve this IS Research Triangulation with rigor and relevance as two independent variables both of which will have a significant influence on the quality of IS Research and the extent of benefits the research outcomes will bring in for the targeted stakeholders in the relevant business practice. Once the second step of research triangulation is complete, go to the third and last step of the model to plan and execute the research project using the IS Research Process Model for proactively managing the rigor and relevance aspects of the research as explained below.

Figure 6. IS research triangulation model

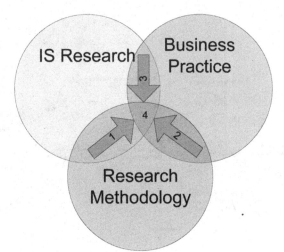

1. Academic Research (Rigor)

2. Critical Business Issues (Knowledge Gaps)

3. IS Consultancy Services (Relevance)

4. IS Research Triangulation (Relevant and Credible Research)

IS Research Process Model to Improve Rigor and Relevance of IS Research

This section introduces the IS Research Process Model which is the "plan and control" step of the three step model. It depicts an end-to-end comprehensive process view of life cycle of IS research in the form of a swim lane diagram shown in Figure 7. It presents a comprehensive view of entire gamut of research process steps covering rigor and relevance and incorporates the process steps and decision points to achieve appropriate IS Research Triangulation.

The primary objective of this model is to enable researchers to create and validate new knowledge in IS domain and empower practitioners and consumers of the knowledge through effective knowledge transfer and application mechanisms to successfully solve current and future critical business problems. The model is depicted in the form of a two swim lane diagram shown in Figure 7 with top swim lane depicting IS Research domain and bottom swim lane depicting Business Practice domain. IS Research domain creates new knowledge bases which need to be transferred to Business Practice domain for applying it to solve critical business problems. The entire process

model has 20 process steps serially numbered from 1 – 20 punctuated with a Start and Stop elliptical shapes to mark the boundary of the IS Research Process. Each process step is depicted in the form a rectangle with a number followed by action(s) performed in it. The process steps are numbered in the order in which they are executed. Some of the process steps are separated by appropriate decision points represented by diamond shaped decision boxes. A pure academic research without due regard to relevance to business practice and serving only academic community may end at step 14 when a research project is published in IS journals after completing research investigation and documenting and defending research results. This is a typical case when a student completes his or her doctoral dissertation. Much of the argument about lack of relevance in IS research is made mainly because most of the IS research work is done either to satisfy some academic tenure and promotion requirements or doctoral dissertation requirements. This is the case if the relevant stakeholders are limited only to academics and research does not involve the interests of business practice. The following paragraph provides an explanation of the IS Research Process model as it is intended

Figure 7. IS research process model

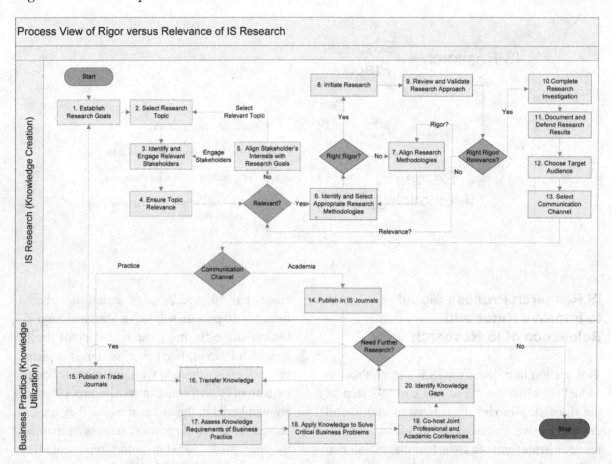

to accomplish the right combination of relevance and rigor to create positive business value.

Every IS research project should start with establishing research goals that take into consideration the interests and concerns of targeted academic and/or business stakeholders. The goals also should identify and define the scope of the research project given the resources and time available for completing the research project. The identified scope will go into the selection of research topic in step 2. Step 3 calls for the identification and engagement of relevant stakeholders that are interested in the IS research project. These may include the interested parties from both academia as well as business practice. Step 4 ensures relevance of the selected topic followed by a decision box to ensure relevance of IS re-

search by aligning the interests of the stakeholders with the research goals and scope of the research project. Once the relevance of research topic is ensured, step 6 calls for the identification and selection of appropriate research methodologies based on the topic selected, type of investigation, and the resources available at the disposal of the research project and timeframe within which the research project needs to be completed. The decision box for the right rigor ensures that the selected research methodologies provide the right level of rigor for producing credible, repeatable, verifiable, and quality research results that have characteristics of a leading research. The research project is initiated in step 8 and step 9 calls for reviewing and validating research approach to make sure that the research topic is still relevant and the research methodology chosen provides the right level of rigor for the stated research goals. Appropriate adjustments are made at this time to ensure topic relevance and research methodology rigor before lot of effort and time is invested into the research project. Process steps 10 and 11 signify the major milestones of completing the research work and documenting and defending research results. Step 12 calls for choosing target audience for communicating research results. Communication channel is selected in step 13 based on the target audience. If the intended target audience is practitioner community, the appropriate communication channel could be trade journals and practitioner forums. On the other hand, if the intended audience is academia, the communication channel could be peer reviewed IS scholarly journals and research publications. Step 14 represents the publication of research in IS journals and Step 15 represents publication in trade journals and practitioner forums. The process steps from Step 15 onwards fall within bottom swim lane of the diagram depicting the business practice domain where the knowledge transfer, assessment of knowledge requirements of business practice and application of knowledge to solve critical business problems happen. Step 16 depicts the interaction between research and practitioner communities and the knowledge transfer process that takes place through such interactions. This step addresses the issue of lack of interaction between the research and practitioner community and bridges the knowledge gaps between the two. The practitioner community then assesses this newly acquired knowledge as part of step 17 to determine the knowledge requirements of current and future business practices. If the knowledge bases represented by this knowledge are higher than the knowledge requirements of the current business practice, the practitioners apply this knowledge to solve critical business problems in step 18. With the application of IS knowledge to solve critical business problems, both practitioners and IS researchers will have a fairly good idea

of what is working and what is not working and should be able to identify the knowledge transfer issues. Step 19 provides another opportunity for both practitioner and research community to come together post deployment of newly created knowledge and be able to explore and understand the knowledge gaps. Step 20 is the final process step and identifies the knowledge gaps and provides valuable information regarding the potential IS research topics that go as a critical input into step 1. If there is no need for further research on the same topic, the knowledge management life cycle is now complete and this marks the end of the process. When the knowledge management life cycle process is complete, it creates a positive business value on an ongoing basis through systematic creation of new knowledge bases in IS knowledge domain, their effective transfer and application of this knowledge to solve critical business problems, identification of any knowledge gaps in practice and providing this input to identify potential research topics. This model provides a comprehensive view of IS Research Process from start to end representing "plan and control" step 3 of three step process. The process incorporates the control variables of IS research and relevance for their timely consideration and control for creating positive business value. It is suggested that every IS research project may be examined in the light of this model for positively addressing the issues of rigor and relevance of IS research.

This section has outlined a three-step process model to appropriately position IS research in terms of rigor and relevance quadrants, triangulate research to achieve proper alignment among IS Knowledge, Research Methodology, and Business Practice knowledge domains, and use IS Research Process Model to plan and control rigor and relevance variables using the research process model to continuously create positive business value.

FUTURE RESEARCH DIRECTIONS

This chapter proposed three models: IS Research Rigor and Relevance Quadrants Model, IS Research Triangulation Model and IS Research Process Model. IS Research Rigor and Relevance Model provides a way to determine current position of the research in order to reposition it to R1 representing most optimal positioning in terms of balancing rigor and relevance of IS research. IS Research Triangulation Model provides the recommended set of actions IS researcher has to take to strike right balance among three critical knowledge domains. IS Research Process Model provides a process view of IS research and details various steps with appropriate decision points to achieve IS Research Triangulation. These models have been developed based on the background information gleaned from various IS Journal publications on the subject of rigor and relevance of IS research and based on insights gained from several years of professional experience. These models can be tried out through case studies to test their validity, usefulness, and applicability in both IS research and business practice domains. Future research can enhance these models by developing specific criteria for establishing standards of rigor, and recommending methodological choices based on the type of investigation and nature of research topic. Specific criteria checklist may be developed for determining the relevance of IS research. These steps may go a long way to positively contributing to this debate.

CONCLUSION

The ongoing discussion and debate about rigor and relevance of IS research will continue and the IS Knowledge will continue to revolutionize our life style. Whether IS researchers or IT product vendors or practitioners are leading this change will be a difficult question to answer. The rate of product innovation is far outpacing the research

and for an IS research to be a leading research, research relevance is a critical need and right level of rigor to ensure the quality of research results is equally important.

This chapter focused on the debate of rigor and relevance of IS research and tried to provide critically needed insights for both IS researchers and practitioners as well. The background information of the chapter started out with the definitions of rigor and relevance of IS research. Concerns pertaining to rigor and relevance of IS research have been examined and recommended actions to address these issues have been summarized. Several existing models depicting the relationship between rigor and relevance of IS research have been examined. These included Rigor versus relevance as a dichotomy by Mason (1989), the Impact Frontier model by Davenport & Markus (1999), and the Consumable Research Model by Robey & Markus (1998). It has been argued that rigor and relevance are not dependent variables needing a trade-off between them and rather they are independent characteristics of research product that can be positioned in terms of IS Research Rigor and Relevance Quadrants model. Key themes and core issues have been identified based on the understanding of the issue from published research and based on the insights gained from several years of professional experience. Recommended actions by several authors have been studied in detail that point to alignment among three critical knowledge domains; (1) IS Research, (2) Business Practice, and (3) Research Methodology. The IS Research Triangulation model has been proposed as a recommended action to orchestrate the alignment among these three critical dimensions. A comprehensive IS Research Process Model has been proposed to provide a comprehensive process view of IS research in terms of knowledge management life cycle of IS research knowledge. A three step process consisting of "position", "triangulate", and "plan and control" steps have been proposed utilizing the above models to achieve the right balance between rigor and relevance and maximize the creation of business value from the application of IS research to solve critical business problems. It is hoped that the three step process and supporting models would help guide an IS researcher on a right path and would result in a leading IS research. Such research, if done right, should fully meet the interests of both academic and business stakeholders, and create positive academic and business value by advancing knowledge and solving current and future critical business problems. The IS Rigor and Relevance Model helps reposition the IS knowledge based on desired rigor and relevance characteristics, IS Research Triangulation Model identifies the critical dimensions for alignment, and IS Research Process Model lays out various steps to guide an ongoing research. While the three step process and supporting models provide guidance for conducting rigorous and relevant IS research, these models have not been tried out for their usefulness and applicability. They do not provide specific criteria for determining the IS research relevance and prescriptive research methodologies for achieving right level of rigor that can be undertaken as part of future research effort.

REFERENCES

Alter, S. (2001). Recognizing the relevance of IS research and broadening the appeal and applicability of future publications. *Communications of the Association for Information Systems, 6*(1).

Amaravadi, C. S. (2001). Improving consumption. *Communications of the Association for Information Systems, 6*(1).

Applegate, L. M., & King, J. L. (1999). Rigor and relevance: Careers on the line. *Management Information Systems Quarterly, 23*(1), 17. doi:10.2307/249404

Benbasat, I., Goldstein, D. K., & Mead, M. (1987). The case research strategy in studies of Information Systems. *Management Information Systems Quarterly, 11*(3), 369–385. doi:10.2307/248684

Benbasat, I., & Zmud, R. W. (1999). Empirical research in Information Systems: The practice of relevance. *Management Information Systems Quarterly, 23*(1), 3–16. doi:10.2307/249403

Bhattacherjee, A. (2001). Understanding and evaluating relevance in IS research. *Communications of the Association for Information Systems, 6*(1).

Borchers, A. S. (2001). Adding practitioner scholars to our faculties. *Communications of the Association for Information Systems, 6*(1).

Brown, S. F. (2009). *Naivety in systems engineering research: Are we putting the methodological cart before the philosophical horse?* 7th Annual Conference on Systems Engineering Research, Loughborough University, UK.

Cresswell, A. M. (2001). Thoughts on relevance of IS research. *Communications of the Association for Information Systems, 6*(1).

Davenport, T. (1997, April 15). Think tank – Storming the ivory tower. *CIO Magazine*.

Davenport, T. H., & Markus, M. L. (1999). Rigor vs. relevance revisited: Response to Benbasat and Zmud. *Management Information Systems Quarterly, 23*(1), 19–24. doi:10.2307/249405

Deci, E. L., & Ryan, R. M. (1991). A motivational approach to self: Integration in personality. In R. Dienstbier (Ed.), *Nebraska Symposium on Motivation: Vol. 38. Perspectives on motivation* (pp. 237-288). Lincoln, NE: University of Nebraska Press.

Dennis, A. R. (2001). Relevance in Information Systems research. *Communications of the Association for Information Systems, 6*(1).

Dubé, L., & Paré, G. (2003). Rigor in Information Systems positivist case research: Current practices, trends, and recommendations. *Management Information Systems Quarterly, 27*(4), 597–636.

Eisenhardt, K. M. (1989). Building theories from case study research. *Academy of Management Review, 4*(4), 532–550.

Fallman, D., & Gronlund, A. (2002). Rigor and relevance remodeled. *Proceedings of Information Systems Research in Scandinavia*, IRIS25, Bautahoj, Denmark, August 10-13.

Gray, P. (2002). *Relevance as an "unfulfilled promise"*. Presentation at ICIS 2001 Panel.

Hoving, R. (2002). Commments on the presentations by Klein, Gray and Myers, discussion at ICIS 2001 Panel.

Jennex, M. E. (2001). Research relevance-You get what you reward. *Communications of the Association for Information Systems, 6*(1).

Kavan, C. B. (1998). Profit through knowledge: The application of academic research to information technology. *Information Resources Management Journal, 11*(1), 17–22.

Keen, P. G. W. (1991). Relevance and rigor in Information Systems research: Improving quality, confidence, cohesion and impact. In Nissen, H. E., Heinz, K. L., & Hirschheim, R. (Eds.), *Information Systems research: Contemporary approaches and emergent traditions* (pp. 27–49). Amsterdam, The Netherlands: North-Holland.

Klein, H. (2002). *Relevance as a "subtle accomplishment"*. Presentation at ICIS 2001 Panel.

Kock, N., Gray, P., Hoving, R., Klein, H., Myers, M., & Rockart, J. (2002). IS research relevance revisited: Subtle accomplishment, unfulfilled promise, or serial hypocrisy? *Communications of the Association for Information Systems, 8,* 330–346.

Kohli, R. (2001). Industry-academia interaction: Key to IT relevance. *Communications of the Association for Information Systems, 6*(1).

Konda, D. (2010). Knowledge management framework for system development projects: Integrated knowledge management framework for knowledge enablement of Information Systems development (ISD) projects. *LAP LAMBERT Academic Publishing., ISBN-10,* 3838391004.

Lee, A. S. (1989). A scientific methodology for MIS case studies. *Management Information Systems Quarterly, 13*(1), 33–52. doi:10.2307/248698

Lee, A. S. (1999). Rigor and relevance in MIS research: Beyond the approach of positivism alone. *Management Information Systems Quarterly, 23*(1). doi:10.2307/249407

Marshall, C., & Rossman, G. B. (1999). *Designing qualitative research* (3rd ed.). Thousand Oaks, CA: Sage.

Mason, R. O. (1989). MIS experiments: A pragmatic perspective. In Benbasat, I. (Ed.), *The Information Systems research challenge: Experimental research methods* (Vol. 2, pp. 3–20). Harvard Business School Research Colloquium, Harvard Business School.

Mathieson, K., & Ryan, T. D. (2001). A broader view of relevance. *Communications of the Association for Information Systems, 6*(1).

Munkvold, B. E., & Khazanchi, D. (2001). Expanding the notion of relevance in IS research: A proposal and some recommendations. *Communications of the Association for Information Systems, 6*(1).

Olfman, L. (2001). We are doing relevant IS research: It's the truth. *Communications of the Association for Information Systems, 6*(1).

Paper, D. J. (2001). IS relevance: Are we asking the right questions? *Communications of the Association for Information Systems, 6*(1).

Robey, D., & Markus, M. L. (1998). Beyond rigor and relevance: Producing consumable research about information system. *Information Resources Management Journal, 11*(1), 7–16.

Rockart, J. (2002a). *Comments on the presentations by Klein, Gary, and Myers, discussion at ICIS 2001 panel.*

Rockart, J. (2002b). Editor's comments. *MISQ Executive, 1*(1).

Rollier, B. (2001). Information Systems research: Reversing the orientation. *Communications of the Association for Information Systems, 6*(1).

Saunders, C. S. (1998). The role of business in IT research. *Information Resources Management Journal, 11*(1), 4–6.

Schauer, C. (2007). *Relevance and success of IS teaching and research: An analysis of the "relevance debate".* ICB Research Report No. 19, University Duisburg-Essen, Institute for Computer Science and Business Information Systems.

Sein, M. K. (2001). The relevance of IS academic research: Not as good as it can get. *Communications of the Association for Information Systems, 6*(1).

Senn, J. (1998). The challenge of relating IS research to practice. *Information Resources Management Journal, 11*(1), 23–28.

Silverman, D. (2004). *Qualitative research: Theory, method and practice* (2nd ed.). Thousand Oaks, CA: Sage Publications.

Steenkamp, A. L., & Konda, D (2003). Information Technology, the key enabler for knowledge management: A methodological approach. *International Journal of Knowledge, Culture and Change Management, 3.* Article: MC03-0070-2003.

Steinbach, T. A., & Knight, L. V. (2006). The relevance of Information Systems research: Informing the IS practitioner community; informing ourselves. *Proceedings of the 2006 Informing Science and IT Education Joint Conference*, Salford, UK – June 25-28.

Valerdi, R., & Brown, S. (2010). *Towards a framework of research methodology choices in systems engineering.* 8th Conference on Systems Engineering Research March 17-19, 2010, Hoboken, NJ.

Watson, H. J., & Huber, M. W. (2000). Innovative ways to connect information systems programs to the business community. *Communications of the AIS, 3*(11).

Westfall, R. (1999). An IS research relevancy manifesto. *Communications of the Association for Information Systems, 2*(1).

Westfall, R. D. (2001). Dare to be relevant. *Communications of the Association for Information Systems, 6*(1).

Yin, R. K. (1994). *Case study research, design and methods* (2nd ed.). Beverly Hills, CA: Sage Publications.

ADDITIONAL READING

Benbasat, I., & Zmud, R. W. (1999). Empirical Research in Information Systems: The Practice of Relevance. *Management Information Systems Quarterly, 23*(1), 3–16. doi:10.2307/249403

Dubé, L., and Paré, G. "Rigor in Information Systems Positivist Case Research: Current Practices, Trends, and Recommendations," *MIS Quarterly* (27:4) 2003, pp 597-636.

Fallman, D & Gronlund, A 2002, 'Rigor and Relevance Remodeled', paper presented to *Proceedings of Information Systems Research in Scandinavia*, IRIS25, Bautahoj, Denmark, August 10-13.

Konda, D. (2010). *Knowledge Management Framework for System Development Projects: Integrated Knowledge Management Framework for Knowledge Enablement of Information Systems Development (ISD) Projects.* Publisher: LAP LAMBERT Academic Publishing (September 2, 2010) ISBN-10: 3838391004 ISBN-13: 978-3838391007

Schauer, C. (2007). Relevance and Success of IS Teaching and Research: An Analysis of the "Relevance Debate", ICB Research Report No. 19, University Duisburg-Essen, Institute for Computer Science and Business Information Systems.

Steinbach, Theresa A & Knight, Linda V. (2006) "The Relevance of Information Systems Research: Informing the IS Practitioner Community; Informing Ourselves," *Proceedings of the 2006 Informing Science and IT Education Joint Conference,* Salford, UK – June 25-28

KEY TERMS AND DEFINITIONS

IS Research Process Model: IS Research Process Model serves as a roadmap to guide IS research project during various life cycle stages of the research process and can be used for planning and controlling the rigor and relevance aspects of IS research.

IS Research Rigor and Relevance Quadrants: The IS Research Rigor and Relevance Quadrant Model is a tool to help assess current positioning of the IS research based on the rigor and relevance values and appropriately reposition it in a desired quadrant to produce a research product with the associated characteristics in terms of desired business impact, academic and business value, and quality of research.

IS Research Triangulation: IS Research Triangulation Model is a research tool that helps to achieve the optimal balance between rigor and relevance of IS research by consciously orchestrating the interaction among IS Research, Research Methodology, and Business Practice knowledge domains.

Relevance: IS research can be considered "relevant" if the research goals and objectives are aligned with the interests and needs of the business practitioners and the research results create business value by helping to solve current and future critical business problems through advancement of knowledge.

Research Method: Research methods are techniques and procedures for data collection, analysis, documentation and validation of research findings.

Research Methodology: Research Methodology is a higher level procedural framework within which research is conducted. It is based upon ontological and epistemological considerations and research inquiry paradigms. It links methods to outcomes and governs our choice and use of methods.

Rigor: A rigorous research is research that follows a well-defined, structured, and transparent research process based on sound research design considerations and appropriate selection of research methodologies and research methods determined by the type and topic of research.

Chapter 3
Postmodernism, Interpretivism, and Formal Ontologies

Jan H. Kroeze
University of South Africa, South Africa

ABSTRACT

This chapter investigates the relationship between postmodernism, interpretivism, and formal ontologies, which are widely used in Information Systems (IS). Interpretivism has many postmodernist traits. It acknowledges that the world is diverse and that knowledge is contextual, ever-changing, and emergent. The acceptance of the idea of more than one reality and multiple understandings is part and parcel of postmodernism. Interpretivism is, therefore, characterized as a postmodern research philosophy. To demonstrate this philosophical premise more concretely, the creation of the logical structure of formal ontologies is sketched as an example of typical interpretivist and postmodernist activity in IS.

INTRODUCTION

Humanities aspects and approaches are present and embedded in various branches of information and communication technology (ICT). One outstanding example is the increase in research on and use of "ontologies" in Information Systems (IS). This chapter investigates interpretivism as a postmodern research philosophy, as well as the problematic association between the philosophical concept of ontology and the notion of formal ontologies as it is used and researched in IS. The

DOI: 10.4018/978-1-4666-0179-6.ch003

chapter's objective is to show that both formal ontologies and the interpretivist paradigm used to create them show very clear postmodernist traits.[1]

Although the term ontology has been borrowed by Information Systems from philosophy, it has been given a slightly different meaning. The concept has been pluralised, but the two uses of the word are still historically and logically related. The author believes that the shift – from singular to plural – was made possible by the postmodern era that we live in. Like reality, knowledge and understanding have become fluid. Software development, too, did not escape the philosophical shift from modernism to postmodernism. Indeed, one may also regard the creation of information systems ontologies in a positive way as the endeavour of academics to embrace the multifaceted nature of reality by representing subsets of it. On the other hand, the danger of formal ontologies is that, although they are meant to mirror and capture reality, ontology-based software could create hyperrealities that become more real than reality because it is typical of postmodernism that real life phenomena are replaced by representations.

This chapter is a purely conceptual study and no empirical methodologies are used (cf. Klein & Myers, 1999, p. 70 for a seminal paper using a purely conceptual approach). The central premise is that, although the singular and plural terms are used differently, they are still semantically related, and that postmodernism underpins the divergence in meaning. Using a qualitative approach, the chapter reflects on the intimate relationship between postmodernism, interpretivism, ICT, and formal ontologies.

After the concepts of postmodernism and interpretivism are defined and discussed, general postmodernist traits in IS and IS research are discussed. Formal ontologies are then explored as the epitome of postmodernism in this field. The chapter concludes with a critical discussion of the understanding and use of ontologies, highlighting some ironies and paradoxes, as well as dangers and opportunities.

BACKGROUND ON POSTMODERNISM AND INTERPRETIVISM

Postmodernism: A Survey of the Paradigm

Origins

The idea of multiple realities and parallel or divergent understandings is essential to postmodernist thinking. Critical theory and postmodernism both

"draw attention to the social, historical, or political construction of knowledge, people, and social relations" (Mitev, 2006, p. 316). It is typical of the postmodern era that our concept of reality and knowledge is ever-changing (Tarnas, 1991, p. 395). Not only is our understanding of the world ambiguous and pluralistic, but the world itself is open and created by people: "Reality is not a solid, self-contained given but a fluid, unfolding process, an 'open universe,' continually affected and molded by one's actions and beliefs" (Tarnas, 1991, p. 396).

Since reality is not regarded as a single, concrete and objective phenomenon, postmodernists also reject an ontological priority and allow alternative readings in making sense of the world (Mitev, 2006, p. 321). Like reality, knowledge and understanding have become fluid. It is not possible to "grasp and articulate a foundational Reality" (Tarnas, 1991, p. 400). "Any alleged comprehensive, coherent outlook is at best no more than a temporarily useful fiction masking chaos, at worst an oppressive fiction masking relationships of power, violence, and subordination" (Tarnas, 1991, p. 401).

According to Harrison (2004, p. 165), postmodernism describes the current cultural and societal condition to which one could react in different ways; however, it is not a philosophical position that one could decide to accept or reject. Postmodernism may even be regarded as a new stratum in human civilisation (Siraj and Ullah, 2007, p. 1).

Postmodernism is everywhere around us, in literature, music, cinema and television (Sim, 2001a). Easthope (2001, p. 17) refers to examples in art in which the difference between the real and the apparent is cancelled, a typical example of the ambivalence inherent in postmodernism. In architecture, postmodernism comes to the fore in a "pluralistic admixture of styles" (Easthope, 2001, p. 18). In politics, groupings are fluid forming "micropolitical alliances" to promote individual issues, thus defying the traditional idea of political parties (Grant, 2001a, p. 31). The feminist movement may also be regarded as typical postmodern since it rejects traditional authorities and aims to construct a new concept of femininity and change power relations between the sexes (Thornham, 2001, pp. 41-42).

Whereas the previous era, modernism, was characterised by technology, the new era is typified by, and even embodied in, ICT: "We are hooked up, wired in to [sic] a system" (Siraj and Ullah, 2007, p. 4). Postmodernism, therefore, represents a whole paradigm, referring to a set of assumptions regarding ontology, epistemology, methodology and axiology (the study of values). A paradigm usually refers to one set of theories which is typical of a historical phase in the philosophy of science, but in social science various competing paradigms co-exist in the postmodern era (Mingers, 2008, p. 81).

The idea of scientific paradigms "highlights the constructed, conventional nature of scientific theorising" (Mingers, 2008, p. 81). "Postmodernist themes focus on the constructed nature of people and reality, concentrate on language as central to this construction process, and argues against grand narratives such as Marxism or functionalism" (Mitev, 2006, p. 314). Master narratives are suspended due to the overwhelming offering of information that causes a fragmentation of knowledge and a lack of a central principal that guides a coherent and unified understanding of the cosmos. Totalizing theories are replaced by localizing theories (Siraj and Ullah, 2007, pp. 1-3).

"We no longer unquestioningly accept the universal claims to knowledge and truth of the great stories which have organized our culture. These include religion, the progress of modernism, the progress of science, and absolute political theories like Marxism" (Watson, 2001, p. 58). In science, knowledge is replaced by knowledges and the legitimacy of empirical proofs are questioned (Easthope, 2001, pp. 18-19). The rationalist idea that science frees people was a grand narrative, and so was the positivist idea that science rep-

resents pure, authentic knowledge (Easthope, 2001, p. 19). The dissolution of tradition is one of the characterizing features of postmodernism (Watson, 2001, p. 53). This could also be true of research traditions like empiricism and positivism. One culture is not better that another, neither is any scientific paradigm superior to another.

The far-reaching shift from modernism to postmodernism, often driven by ICT, affected even the natural sciences. The objectivist divide is not that sharp anymore. "Given this unexpected convergence between the natural and the human sciences, technology, ironically, emerges as a vital component driving and shaping postmodern culture itself" (Grant, 2001b, p. 66). Usually regarded as factual, empiricist and objective, "science has had to reinvent its own rules" leading to an incredulity to its meta-narrative which has consequently been replaced by "a series of locally applicable discourses" (Harrison, 2004, p. 165). It may even be argued that it is the remarkable development of science over the past few centuries that lead to the postmodernist trend. Yet, the drift is even more clear in the humanities and social sciences, which are traditionally regarded as "soft" sciences. For example, it is now realized and acknowledged that even historical studies do not simply reflect facts, but create realities because they are written for specific purposes – "a past is nostalgically recreated as a form of substitute reality" (Watson, 2001, p. 55). Even minutes of meetings create realities – they are historical constructions aimed at specific audiences which rarely are a precise rendering of a meeting's proceedings (Oates, 2006, p. 144). IS is regarded as a social science and one may, therefore, expect to see many postmodernist traits in its practice and research.

Use of Postmodernism in IS and ICT

Various authors have indicated that ICT has played a supporting role in the advance of postmodernism. It has been causing fundamental cultural shifts in society, including a move from reality to hyperreality (Siraj and Ullah, 2007, p. 7). ICT and especially the internet has played a major part in compressing time and space and fragmentizing experience (Watson, 2001, p. 58-59). It has also served – and still does – to accelerate "postmodern phenomena such as globality and mobility" (Hohmann, 2007, p. 26).

ICT has caused an overload of information which undermines the viability of a single meta-narrative, while multimedia and hyperlinking allow users to make their own connections and sequences, all of which results in an eclectic experience of life (Watson, 2001, p. 62). This eclectic trend has even impacted research theory and philosophy to a certain extent. The one and only "scientific method" has made way to a plethora of research philosophies and approaches, from which IS researchers may pick and mix. Mixed methods and triangulation of strategies and data generation methods have become perfectly acceptable (cf. Oates, 2006; Myers, 2009).

Science plays an important role in the construction of societies; not only scientific facts, but also science in action has enormous effects on society (Grant, 2001b, p. 67). With reference to ICT, one could only reflect on how email changed the profile of the successful worker, computer literacy the profile of the successful researcher, and internet radio the connectedness of dispersed cultural groups. Action research is often used in ICT research and the interventions may have serious consequences on the research participants and their communities. Researchers should, therefore, seriously consider the ethical implications of their intercessions. While technology, including ICT, may appear to be neutral, it is actually loaded with the ideology of the culture within which it was created. To assume that research participants' groups will experience this technology as beneficial, is a new form of imperialism. According to Sim (2001b, pp. 10-11), Lyotard was even concerned about techno-science, i.e. the reduction of humanity to thought and the movement of thought (and thus humanity) from the human body to the computer.

There is, however, a flip side of the coin. Society also has an effect on science and technology, e.g. the trend that more men are ICT professionals may be related to traditional gender roles that are (still) inherent in the related societies (cf. Grant, 2001b, p. 67). The impact of ICT and postmodernism is also bi-directional. While the postmodern temperament of multiplicity has been strengthened by information and communication technology, it now lives and thrives on it (Nel, 2007, pp. 113-117). According to Wells (1996, pp. 602-604), many advances in IT are indeed a result of postmodernism. While ICTs support and speed up cultural shifts, they are simultaneously affected by these transformations (Firat & Dholakia, 2004/2005, p. 123).

The idea that ICT is an agent of postmodernism has been noticed in other academic disciplines too. Firat and Dholakia (2004/2005, p. 124), for example, identify ICT as an instrument/mediator of postmodern marketing practice and theory. According to Conlon (2000, p. 111), ICT is strongly entangled in the postmodern paradigm shift taking place in education since it facilitates globalization, automation, consumerism and virtuality.

According to Hackney & Pillay (2002, pp. 28-29), postmodernist ideas have, however, not enjoyed a lot of deliberate attention in the IS world. They apply some of the basic trends into the IT management field, believing that a more flexible approach could provide the cultural context for mission statements, a deconstructive analysis of these statements, as well as an "ethnographic empathy for further IS/IT research". The modernist goal of a mission statement is to create a shared understanding of a company's vision and strategies, but ironically, it could highlight diverse cultures within an organisation (Hackney & Pillay, 2002, pp. 32-33).

Mingers's (2008, p. 84) plea for a pluralist approach towards IS research and philosophy is a typical postmodernist stance, although he does not present it like this himself and only mentions postmodernism fleetingly. Mingers (2008, pp. 83-

Table 1. A summary of Mingers's (2008) pluralist scientific paradigm for IS research

	Ontology	Epistemology	Axiology
Different worlds and types of knowledge	Objective/material	Observation	Pragmatic
	Social/normative	Participation	Moral
	Subjective/personal	Experience	Ethical

84) may be regarded as a critical realist since he adopts both the ideas of ontological realism and epistemological relativism. He believes that there are three different types of worlds, corresponding to three ways of understanding them, different methods to study them and different value systems for each. This may be summarized in Table 1.

Mingers's suggestion of a more postmodern approach in IS is echoed by various other scholars. Greenhill and Fletcher (2007a, p. 9) say that information systems development is grounded in a typical modernist view of static information and singular meaning. They suggest a more pluralistic approach to Information Systems research and practice that allows the incorporation of multiple non-lineal texts and meanings. Even contemporary physics is challenging the modernist principles of causality, objectivity, rationality and falsification, and suggests the use of multiple views – IS research should learn from this and implement complementary views, e.g. sociological and philosophical perspectives, in order to grow the discipline (Monod & Boland, 2007, p. 139). One example of such an attempt is a collection of papers that investigate the implementation of postmodern methods in Human-Computer Interaction. Since postmodern methods have become marginalised in academic circles, Greenhill and Fletcher (2007b, pp. i-v) reintroduce postmodernism to advocate inclusiveness and a wider understanding of the world and especially of the discipline of Human-Computer Interaction. Mitev (2006, pp. 310-312) suggests that critical research in IS be enriched by postmodern concepts, especially in terms of critique. Another attempt to pluralise research approaches in IS, is to borrow

more intensely from the humanities in order to enrich IS (Kroeze, 2010; Kroeze et al., 2011).

Interpretivism: A Postmodern Research Philosophy

A research philosophy is the surrounding paradigm within and from which a school of scientists operationalizes their study and reflects on it. Myers (2009, pp. 35-44) defines a scientific paradigm as the philosophical stance that encompasses one's underlying assumptions about reality and knowledge. It influences beliefs about valid and legitimate/justifiable research. Positivism is the traditional paradigm in IS and believes in a concrete, measurable reality, which can be studied objectively. Positivist researchers try to study human and social phenomena in the same way as natural scientists study the physical world. Interpretivism, on the other hand, focuses on reality as a human construction which can only be understood subjectively. Since no researcher can distance him/herself from the social reality being studied it is important to take note of the context in order to make sense of the phenomena and to create knowledge about them. Data is interwoven with theory. The purpose of interpretivist research is to acquire meaning and understanding. In an interpretive study "[t]he generalizations derived from experience are dependent upon the researcher, his or her methods, and the interactions with the subject of study", and the validity of the research depends on its plausibility, consistency and logical reasoning (Myers, 2009, p. 40). Knowledge is much more fluid and emergent. The philosophical assumptions of critical research are similar to those of interpretivism, but it goes further than a mere description and understanding by also challenging these issues (Myers & Klein 2011, pp. 30-32). Although this three-fold classification of research philosophies in IS has been widely accepted, critical research has received less attention than positivism and interpretivism and its principles have not been discussed in the same depth (Myers & Klein, 2011, pp. 18-19). A detailed study on the postmodernist traits of both interpretivism and critical research is desirable. This article addresses the first of these two needs.

Acknowledging that science in a postmodern world cannot always objectify nature (or its research objects), but often enters into a dialogue with it (Grant, 2001b, p. 72) resonates the characterization of interpretivism as context-bound approach to knowledge creation. Even positivist, empiricist and statistical approaches may not be as value-free and objective as it hopes and pretends to be. Postmodernism is anti-foundational – it undermines the philosophical points of departure of theories (Sim, 2001b, p. 3). "[P]ostmodernism is to be regarded as a rejection of many, if not most, of the cultural certainties on which life in the West has been structured over the last couple of centuries… To move from the modern to the postmodern is to embrace skepticism about what our culture stands for and strives for…" (Sim, 2001a, p. vii).

Postmodernism is also poststructuralist in that it rejects the belief that all systems are inherently structured and discoverable (Sim, 2001b, p. 3). In addition, science is often driven by cultural and political motives; the agendas for theoretical and experimental work are determined by people and groups with their own motives and goals (Grant, 2001b, p. 66). Parallel to the postmodern possibility of choosing a lifestyle rather than to conforming to old traditions (Watson, 2001, p. 55), is the idea of choosing a research philosophy and methodology. A variety of legitimate research approaches exist which again reflects the wide variety of products available on the postmodern

market. One may also wonder if the stringent requirements by journals for the formatting of papers and articles according to very specific style requirements prior to submission could be a consequence of the postmodern emphasis on style and appearance rather than on content (cf. Watson, 2001, p. 57).

Positivist IS research assumes a single reality and truth, while interpretivist research uses the point of departure of many realities and diverse explanations of the world. Interpretivism has in fact many postmodernist traits. Not only could one look at reality either from a positivistic or interpretive stance, but even within interpretivism there are more than one strand. In addition, it acknowledges that reality is not always concrete and objectifiable, but is very often created by communities. This is true especially of social worlds, but it also often crystallizes into concrete artifacts created by these societies (Klein & Myers, 1999, pp. 68-73). The rest of this section will highlight some of these attributes.

According to Oates (2006, p. 292), interpretive studies try to understand a pluralistic world based on the principle that people assign meanings and values to their unique contexts. It should be noted that Oates herself does not typify interpretivism as postmodern, but the following traits clearly point in this direction. The acceptance of the idea of multiple subjective realities and "dynamic, socially constructed meaning" (e.g. how different IT company cultures experience truth and knowledge and methodologies) is part and parcel of the interpretivist paradigm. Researcher and research participants influence each other during their communication and create understanding, insight and knowledge in the process. The participants are also interpreters and analysts and participate in the creation of facts (Klein & Myers, 1999, pp. 74, 77). Table 2 tries to map some of the postmodern traits onto interpretivist characteristics. It uses the seven principles of interpretive research as identified by Klein & Myers (1999) as its point of departure.

Table 2. Mapping interpretivism on postmodernism (cf. Klein & Myers, 1999; Myers & Klein, 2011; Oates, 2006; Tarnas, 1991; and Easthope, 2001)

Interpretivism	Postmodernism
1. According to the principle of the hermeneutic circle shared meaning emerges in iterative cycles of interpretation. People make sense of emerging social settings and assign meanings to these complex and unfolding realities. Interpretivism provides deep insight into the contexts of organizations. Getting insight and understanding of unique situations and the people issues relating to these is the main goal of interpretivism. Interpretive field studies are 'idiographic', i.e. trying to make sense of unique phenomena.	Knowledge is constructed socially.
2. The principle of contextualization implies that, since societies create their own concrete and social worlds, these should be studied and understood in context. Interpretivism accepts that people create their own physical and social worlds.	The world is open and created by people. Localizing theories replace totalizing theories.
3. The principle of interaction between researchers and participants believes that understanding is an emergent process because researchers and research participants interact and influence each other in a bi-directional way. Therefore, interpretivism tends to use qualitative research approaches.	Postmodernism critiques the "scientific" method (that is, the natural scientific/positivistic method).
4. According to the principle of abstraction and generalization interpretivism attempts to relate unique instances to multiple scenarios. It generates concepts and theories.	Science retains its status due to its rigor and practical applications.
5. The principle of dialogical reasoning implies that researchers have to reflect on their own prejudices since it guides their understanding. However, in some forms of interpretivist IS research, pre-existing theoretical assumptions are not mandatory, e.g. in grounded theory.	Postmodernism has a fluid view of ontology and epistemology; science and technology are not believed to be value-free.
6. The principle of multiple interpretations acknowledges that understanding is not always consensual but that there may be different viewpoints of the same study objects. Meaning and understanding is created by researchers and their participants. Interpretivism accepts that researchers are subjectively involved in the phenomena that they study and that the field of study is pre-interpreted.	Postmodernism accepts a plurality of ethics and lifestyles. It rejects ontological priority and allows alternative understandings.
7. The principle of suspicion guides researchers to look deeper than the surface to identify role players' political agendas.	Postmodernism is skeptic about a solid basis to differentiate between truth and falsehood. It rejects traditional authorities and grand narratives.

The conviction that interpretivism is a typical postmodern research approach does have some serious implications. Since interpretivists believe that individuals or groups construct notions of reality, a typical postmodernist idea, triangulation (comparing the results of different research approaches and methods used to study the same phenomenon) would not always lead to converging results (Oates, 2006, p. 38). When doing group action research in ICT there is a danger of groupthink where the members tacitly create a pseudo-reality in order to prove the validity of their methods and results (Oates, 2006, p. 161). Although the underlying philosophical paradigm of action research may be either positivism, interpretivism or critical research, it has a specific affinity for interpretivism, since it reflects on

people in a specific social setting (Oates, 2006, pp. 156, 301). Case studies with its focus on unique situations and multiple interpretations also tend to occur more in the interpretive paradigm (Oates, 2006, pp. 142, 300).

Another IS research strategy that leans heavily towards postmodernism is ethnography. "Ethnographers... examine the 'webs of significance' that people in any culture weave" (Oates, 2006, p. 161). In order to be open for other cultures implies a certain amount of skepticism about the researcher's own (often Western) culture (cf. Oates, 2006, p. 300). In all of these qualititative research approaches – often underlain by interpretivism – taking into account the social context is very important. This is in line with postmodernist traits in other cultural areas, for example art. "[P] ostmodern buildings and cityscapes are characterized by sensitivity to context" (Watson, 2001, p. 61). A bigger awareness of research participants' communities and values explains the relatively recent upsurge in ethical committees and ethical clearance processes in Social Informatics research.

Software development, too, did not escape the philosophical shift from modernism to postmodernism. According to Brown et al. (2004, pp. 4136, 4141), the move from structured and object oriented approaches to agile approaches allows developers to subjectively create realities because "developers must continually question their assumptions and adopt new ways of thinking". Agile approaches represent a more holistic, relativistic and pluralistic methodology.

It should come as no surprise that design and creation research in IS also tends to be postmodernist. Website audiences are constructions of the developers. IT creates not only information, but also concrete entities. One way to see the web is as a medium that people use to create sets of meanings, communities and practices (Oates, 2006, pp. 145, 146, 180). The web, of course, is built on hypertext. Cotkin (1996, pp. 104, 113) explores the relationships between hypertext, postmodernism and history writing. He suggests that this new technology will change the way in which readers understand text and communicate since it replaces the basic characteristics of text, such as fixedness and linearity, with open-endedness and non-sequentiality. He predicts that hypertext would relativize our concepts about truth by allowing us "to consider a pluralistic universe teaming with options". Atlhough Cotkin does not investigate formal ontologies, one could extend his idea by regarding this related, but more advanced technology, as a way to represent our knowledge regarding subsets of this pluralistic universe. This idea will be discussed in depth in the following section.

From the discussion above it has become clear that postmodernism is deeply embedded in Information Systems practice and research. This

reinforces the premise of the chapter that formal ontologies – and the plural form of the word – may be regarded as a typical effect of postmodern trends in IS.

ONTOLOGIES

The IS use of the term ontologies was coined in 1967 by Mealy (Buchholz, 2006, p. 695), and, maybe, this is not by chance only five years after the publication of Kuhn's seminal work, "The structure of scientific revolutions" (Tarnas, 1991, pp. 397, 465), which may be regarded as one of the milestones in postmodern thinking. The author indeed believes that the shift from singular to plural was made possible by the postmodern era that we live in. The question about the origin of the plural form of the word ontology, therefore, necessitated an overview of postmodernism and interpretivism. In this section, formal ontologies, which often are the outcomes of interpretivist research in IS, will be discussed as a postmodernist phenomenon.

Ontology: Exploring the Concept

Ontology has traditionally been (and still is) a philosophical discipline that studies the nature of existence (Yun et al., 2011, p. 57). It has always fitted into a bigger theoretical framework (or meta-narrative), such as rationalism. In a certain time and philosophical era, there usually was, therefore, only one correct or current ontology. In the modernist era, for example, people (including scientists) believed that there was one concrete and common reality outside and independent of human constructs. While ontology is the study of being, epistemology is the theory about understanding and knowledge. Parallel to the ontological belief of a single, concrete reality, positivism with its premise of falsification was regarded as the superior epistemology and other views such as relativism were suppressed (Firat and Dholakia, 2004/2005, p. 135).

The plural of the word *ontology* did not exist.[2] Academics who were trained in philosophy are often startled when they hear the plural of the word ontology for the first time. Indeed, from a philosophical perspective, ontology is an abstract term. Some philosophers would even regard it as unacceptable to use the plural form (cf. Fonseca, 2007). Yet, in the world of IS, many practitioners use it as one of the most natural things to do.

This section investigates the philosophical move from ontology to ontologies. It tries to answer the question how it happened that the word ontology got a plural and became ontologies. It may even be regarded as an ontology of ontologies, a philosophical discussion regarding the essence of information systems taxonomies which are enriched by description logic.

Although the term ontology has been borrowed by IS from philosophy, it has been given a slightly different meaning. Zúñiga (2001, p. 194) says "the term 'ontology' in information systems circles is distinct from its original philosophical meaning". According to Zúñiga, the essential difference in meaning is due to the interdisciplinary nature of IS. Oates (2006, p. 120) defines ontology as a "set of semantic concepts relevant to a particular domain". Zúñiga (2001, p. 187) defines an information systems ontology as a "formal language designed to represent a particular domain of knowledge". "Ontologies are used to capture knowledge about some domain of interest. An ontology describes the concepts in the domain and also the relationships that hold between those concepts" (Horridge, 2009, p. 10). In this chapter, IS ontology and formal ontology are used as synonyms. While the singular term refers to a comprehensive conceptual set of terms representing one, specific domain, the plural refers to conceptual sets of different domains (Chandrasekaran et al., 1999, p. 21).

A formal ontology may be regarded as a taxonomy with added consistency and reliability. While a thesaurus is a plain list of related concepts, and a taxonomy is an enhanced form that highlights the relations between the concepts, a formal ontology adds reliability to the mixture. Adding description logics makes the system computer-processable and enables it to reason about its own consistency (Gilchrist, 2003, pp. 7, 10, 13; Lambe, 2007, p. 6). A formal ontology consists of individuals, properties and classes. Individuals identify specific instances of entities, a class (also called a concept) is a set of individuals, and properties describe the relations between two individuals, linking them together. Taxonomies that are bootstrapped into ontologies contain a hierarchy of super-classes and subclasses. The built-in reasoner of an ontology web language (such as Protégé 4) can compile these subsumption relationships automatically (Horridge, 2009, pp. 9-12).

The dual role of the word ontology is described excellently in a call for papers for FOIS2010:

Ontology began life in ancient times as a fundamental part of philosophical enquiry concerned with the analysis and categorisation of what exists. In recent years, the subject has taken a practical turn with the advent of complex computerised information systems which are reliant on robust and coherent representations of their subject matter. The systematisation and elaboration of such representations and their associated reasoning techniques constitute the modern discipline of formal ontology, which is now being applied to such diverse domains as artificial intelligence, computational linguistics, bioinformatics, GIS, knowledge engineering, information retrieval, and the Semantic Web. Researchers in all these areas are becoming increasingly aware of the need for serious engagement with ontology, understood as a general theory of the types of entities and relations making up their respective domains of enquiry, to provide a solid foundation for their work (International Association for Ontology and its Applications, 2009).

IS ontologies facilitate the building of knowledge representations and the sharing of these bodies of understanding. "An ontology can represent beliefs, goals, hypotheses, and predictions about a domain, in addition to simple facts" (Chandrasekaran et al., 1999, pp. 21-22). However, ontologies are not objective representations of reality. Creating them requires analysis of a subset of reality and reaching consensus between the role players on what aspects are chosen and how they are grouped and related. Therefore, there are often different ontologies that reflect the same general concepts. Ontologies are used, for example, in artificial intelligence to facilitate natural language understanding and knowledge-based problem solving (Chandrasekaran et al., 1999). Linguistic ontologies are used to enhance web searches (Guarino et al., 1999). In engineering, ontologies are used to create shared frameworks to overcome the lack of consensus regarding key concepts which exists due to different disciplinary backgrounds (Borgo et al., 2009). Since different technologies and approaches are used to represent knowledge, upper ontologies are used to integrate divergent domain ontologies, but integration remains one of the main challenges for the field (Schlenoff & Uschold, 2004).

However, one could not go so far as to say that the two uses of the word have become homonyms. They are still historically and logically related. The relationship between the two uses is founded in the cornerstone of classification. The work done by philosophers in trying to make sense of reality by means of classification forms the basis of ICT ontologies, which may be regarded as practical applications of these philosophical endeavours (Buchholz, 2006, p. 694).

Information Systems theory uses the concept of ontology in another, more philosophical sense, namely regional or fundamental ontologies. In this sense the concept of ontology refers to the essence of a phenomenological domain (Sewchurran et al., 2010). An in-depth discussion of its use to explicitly locate research within a philosophical ontology falls outside the scope of this chapter.

One could only hope that informaticians and philosophers will explore the interrelationships of their disciplines by building on the connections revealed by ontology and ontologies. Zúñiga (2001, pp. 187, 189) indeed says that ontology "has served as the bridge for the coming together of information systems and philosophy" and pleads for the integration of insights from philosophical ontology into IS ontologies. Hence, the next sections is an attempt to understand the philosophical, postmodernist drift that underpins the pluralisation of the ontology concept in IS.

Formal Ontologies as the Epitome of Postmodernist, Interpretivist Research Outcomes in IS

Despite the relativity of knowledge and the fluidity of understanding and wisdom in the postmodern era, scientists do not have to feel that their work is without value. It has retained its status due to its rigour and practical applications, and in fact, it has been enabled to be more creative and less restricted (Tarnas, 1991, p. 404). The validity and quality of interpretivist research may be judged against its own set of criteria, such as confirmability and plausibility (Oates, 2006, pp. 294-295).

Scientists and practitioners can choose an ontology that reflects their viewpoints and practical needs the best, and they may even adapt or build a new one, thus participating in the creation of a new reality (cf. Tarnas, 1991, p. 406). The design and implementation of a formal ontology in an information system may indeed be regarded as the construction of a reality. Formal ontologies are the concrete representations of "little narratives", i.e. fleeting realities created for specific objectives (Sim, 2001b, p. 7). They declare subsets of reality as entities and describe the relations between them in a machine programmable way.

Although it aims to reflect the tacit knowledge regarding a business or social aspect, it also freezes that knowledge and forces users to accept this version as truthful and authoritative. It is typical design and creation research because it generates a type of vocabulary or set of concepts used in a specific ICT scenario, a type of construct regarded as an IT artefact (Oates, 2006, p. 108). Oates (2006, p. 120) also refers to the creation and instantiation of an ontology in website research as a new construct. Creating an ontology does not only require technical skills, but also analytical abilities and philosophical wisdom, and, therefore, also contributes to academic knowledge, while at the same time being traceable, confirmable and based on solid theory (cf. Oates, 2006, pp. 109-110, 294-295). On the other hand, formal ontologies are also used to check/test the logical consistency of the theoretical paradigms on which they are built (Fonseca and Martin, 2007, p. 137). Formal ontologies are used in the semantic web to allow "software agents to understand, share and reason about data" (Ferdinand, Zirpins & Trastour, 2004, p. 354). This is made possible by the ontology web languages into which artificial intelligence and description logics are built to facilitate the incorporation of inference rules and axioms in the taxonomies.

Since each ontology can only be an attempt to represent knowledge of a certain subset of reality, it seems to be an unattainable goal to strive for one single overall ontology that spans the whole world. "In information science, an ontology refers to an engineering artifact, constituted by a specific vocabulary used to describe a certain reality" (Fonseca, 2007).

The divergent multiplicity of ontologies in IS itself can also be understood in the context of multiple realities that is so typical of postmodernism. An ontology may be regarded as a representation of the human knowledge of a specific group of people regarding a specific subject area, which is provisional and transitory because "[h]uman knowledge is the historically contingent product of linguistic and social practices of particular local communities of interpreters, with no as-

sured 'ever-closer' relation to an independent a-historical reality" (Tarnas, 1991, p. 399). Indeed, one may also regard the creation of IS ontologies in a positive way as the endeavours of academics to embrace the multifaceted nature of reality by representing subsets of it by means of more meaningful vocabularies and taxonomies (cf. Tarnas, 1991, p. 407).

Formal ontologies may, therefore, be regarded as a venture into postmodern analysis that acknowledges "the potential of local systems solutions" and the importance to accept "as valid a range of methodologies" (Harrison, 2004, pp. 165-166). A single (philosophical) ontology is replaced by a plurality of (formal) ontologies that reflect partial and fragmented sets of knowledge. The plural concept of ontologies, used in ICT, reflect the idea of multiple realities that is so typical of postmodernism. While IS ontologies may be regarded as one way of describing the objective/material world, the plurality of ontologies is simultaneously a witness of different embodiments of truth. It should be combined and synthesized with other methodologies to provide a holistic understanding.

Although the multiplicity of ontologies being created and used in IS mirror "the most significant characteristics of the larger postmodern intellectual situation – its pluralism, complexity, and ambiguity" (Tarnas, 1991, p. 402), this status quo may be regarded as a melting-pot of ideas that may eventually give birth to a "fundamentally new form of intellectual vision, one that might both preserve and transcend the current state of extraordinary differentiation" (Tarnas, 1991, p. 402).

An attempt to integrate various systems is an endeavour towards a synthesis of mental perceptions (Tarnas, 1991, p. 397). When one is confronted with various ontologies addressing the same subject area, one is actually dealing with the typical postmodern condition in which "[a] chaos of valuable but seemingly incompatible interpretations prevails, with no resolution in sight", but which also creates new challenges for scientists to clarify and reconcile (Tarnas, 1991, p. 409).

It is inevitable that scholars build their subjective perspectives into the software that they create; their theoretical paradigms become ingrained in the structuring and analysis of the data (Rechenmacher & Van Der Merwe, 2005, pp. 77-78; Buchholz, 2006, pp. 694-695). According to Tummarello et al. (2008, p. 468), "[a]greeing on an encoding scheme is an obvious step for interoperability...". For example, the creation of an ontology of Biblical Hebrew (BH) syntax could be an undertaking that stimulates a debate among BH grammarians to integrate various existing systems in use (Kroeze, 2009). The integration of ontologies by super (top-level) ontologies may be an attempt to reconcile deconstructed world views – deconstruction and integration are two opposite trends complementing each other (Tarnas, 1991, p. 407).

Many aspects of research on formal ontologies may also be regarded as postmodern. Since IS ontologies are cultural products, an interpretivist approach is more suitable than a positivist approach for critical analysis and research regarding them (Oates, 2006, p. 292). Above, intrepretivism has been characterised as typically postmodern.

As was suggested by the premise of the chapter, it may be concluded from the discussion above that formal ontologies are quintessential examples of postmodern deposits in ICT. Some implications of this close relationship, however, still need to be pointed out.

IMPLICATIONS AND FUTURE RESEARCH DIRECTIONS

There are some interesting paradoxes regarding the postmodern cultural state. For example, globalization stimulates a reappearance of nationalism, and wider choices for consumers created new, quite traditional mega-companies (Conlon, 2000, p. 111). Another paradox is that ICT, which

is regarded as modernist technology, is now called on to undergo a paradigm shift itself and become, via emotional digitization, postmodernist in essence (Hohmann, 2007, p. 24). The finding that ICT can both be regarded as an agent and as a result of postmodernism is also rather ironic, but understandable since postmodernism is to be regarded as the continuance of modernism and does not necessarily stand in direct opposition to it. It may be the effect of the cyclical succession of modernisms and postmodernisms, and of the deconstruction and reconstruction of grand narratives (Sim, 2001b, p. 14).

Formal ontologies reflect the typical postmodernist characteristic of both multiple truths and an attempt to integrate these. They have a dual nature since they are social constructions that may reflect divergent views or develop as disciplines evolve, while they simultaneously represent the fixed result of shared understanding and definition of the scientific vocabularies (Sicilia, 2006, p. 85). In order to create a useful ontology, some level of standardization has to be agreed upon (Sicilia, 2006, p. 83). Or in the words of Murphy (1988, p. 180), "order represents a social contract, as persons learn to read the world in a similar manner". Ontology web languages facilitate the creation of a plethora of formal ontologies, which reflects the pluralistic universe. It is, therefore, rather ironic that there is an attempt within individual formal ontologies to be very modernist by trying to incorporate strict rules by means of formal logic that describe the relationships between the entities. This seems to go against the fluidity that is typical within postmodern structures.

Besides the paradoxes of the quadruple ICT-ontologies-interpretivisim-postmodernism relationship, one also has to reflect on possible dangers regarding the hyper-reality of ontology-driven software. In a wider context, Matusitz (2008) explores ICTs as tools used by cyber-terrorists to create a chaotic scenario, which he believes is typical of the postmodern age. More relevant for the topic of this chapter is the risk that formal ontologies could become more real than reality, although they are meant to mirror and capture a slice of it (cf. Matusitz, 2008, p. 180). It is typical of postmodernism that real life phenomena are replaced by representations (simulacra) (Siraj and Ullah, 2007, p. 3). Simulations and hyper-reality developed from direct representations of the real word through an intermediate phase of emancipation into independent signs (cf. Watson's 2001, pp. 59-60 discussion of the history of simulacra). Simulacra now replace the realities that they represent resulting in a situation where people are not able to differentiate between them (Sim, 2001b, p. 11). In the twenty-first century simulacra very often are electronic simulations. Edutainment, for example, presents products in advertisements in the cloak of rigid research results. The pretention is made all that more feasible by pseudo-scientific, computer-aided graphs and statistics. Artificial intelligence is another good example of electronic simulation. The Turing test is, like postmodern science in general, more interested in signs and simulations than in reality itself. A machine or program may be regarded as intelligent if it is impossible to differentiate between a human's real intelligence and the computerized simulation thereof (Grant, 2001b, pp. 66, 73).

An implemented ontology may eventually become a technological tyrant if it enforces a new or attenuated reality on the enterprise. Such a tyranny of ontology could become a new cause of anxiety, which is similar to the phenomenon that people may feel like victims of information due to information overload and information pollution (cf. Siraj and Ullah, 2007, p. 9).

An ontology that locks people into a language system may in fact undermine human agency or free will. Rychlak (1999, p. 385) believes that traditional computer models, which are built on binary logic using Boolean algebra, cannot simulate human agency because they cannot think laterally like humans do. However, the open-world assumption of formal ontologies (the declaration of an individual entity as a member of a specific class does not imply that it cannot also be a member of another class) and the possibility to define attributes of classes and to create relationships between them (Horridge, 2009, pp. 9-12) may pave the way to a more human-type of reasoning in computing. This implies that formal ontologies also provide opportunities to free enterprises from digital despotism. Rychlak (1999, p. 388) indeed sees possibilities for the modeling of human agency in postmodernism since the postmodern outlook sustains oppositionality (the ability to link semantically related concepts), which he believes is the essence of human thinking or dialectical reasoning. If the proposition of this chapter is correct, i.e. that ontologies are a typical postmodern phenomenon, it could, therefore, substantiate the idea that formal ontologies simulate human thinking in a more natural way.

A further opportunity rendered by postmodernist technology is the integration of human-oriented qualities such as emotion and aesthetics, which would differentiate it from modernistic technologies that are experienced as cold, precise and rationalistic. Postmodernism pluralises culture and humanises technology (Hohmann, 2007, pp. 18-19). A typical trait of postmodernism is "the change from a technology that replaces people to a technology that supports people" (Hohmann, 2007, p. 19). Formal ontologies may be another way to humanize and pluralize technology. Yet, more research is needed on how formal ontologies could be used to incorporate aesthetics and emotion in software.

The postmodernization of ICT may also indicate a positive turn in the creation of bodies of knowledge. In the eighties of the previous century computerization was still seen as technology that would bring modernism to fulfilment due to its rationalistic and quantitative tendencies which would make information and knowledge context-less (Murphy, 1988, pp. 175-176). Viewed from this perspective the creation of an ontology may be regarded as an endeavour that produces the illusion of a knowledge system. "Stress is placed on massaging data and exploring their interconnections, until events are classified correctly. Once this taxonomic exercise is completed, a system of knowledge is thought to be available" (Murphy, 1988, p. 178). Ironically, ICT became an agent of postmodernism, and text-based computer languages, like HTML and XML, changed the modernistic, binary character of computing because it facilitates the incorporation of context by means of hyper-linking networks of data and knowledge.

Educational systems are also influenced by postmodernism and its changing concepts of knowledge and wisdom. According to Conlon (2000, p. 113), ICT promotes a de-schooled society, which is one of the visions of libertarianism (a postmodern view of education, the counterpart of a paternalistic vision of education). If one accepts the finding that formal ontologies reflect divergent world views, endeavours to design and select an educational taxonomy that resonates with a culture's belief systems should be regarded as a step in the direction towards a more balanced vision of paternalistic and libertarian approaches (cf. Conlon, 2000, pp. 114, 116).

A final remark pertains to the co-evolution of humans and machines. Mazlish (1993) regards this process as overcoming "the fourth discontinuity". The first discontinuity was broken when Copernicus indicated that the earth (and people) is not in the centre of the universe. The second mental barrier was crossed when Darwin showed that people are part and parcel of evolved life. Freud bridged the third discontinuity by linking humans' consciousness and sub-consciousness. In the current culture of the computer-brain revolution the difference between human and machine reasoning has become blurred (Mazlish, 1993, pp. 178-198), and formal ontologies will blur the boundaries between technology and concrete reality even further, thus facilitating the convergence even further. Since no technology is neutral, this merging of man and machine will probably have both positive and negative impacts on humanity.

One may express the wish that the incorporation of formal ontologies will humanize the products of these unions. Indeed, "technology without philosophy is blind. Unless it is harnessed to a clear vision of change then chip by chip, the technology could take us into a future that we would never willingly have chosen for ourselves" (Conlon, 2000, p. 116).

Limitations and Future Work

Since postmodernism is not directly addressed in most IS literature, many logical deductions had to be made in order to characterize interpretivism as a postmodernist research theory. Since it would be impossible to test these premises empirically, the ideas should be scrutinized by IS philosophers, well versed in philosophical theory, to judge the credibility of the reflection. No doubt a lot more could have been said, either for or against these arguments, and the author hopes to have stimulated some debate. The time has come in IS research to take note of the postmodernist era and to reflect on its consequences for the discipline. Another area which has only been touched upon, pertains to the quality assurance of interpretivist research (cf. Oates, 2006, pp. 294-295; Klein & Myers, 1999, p. 68). Grounded theory, surveys and triangulation are more IS research concepts that have not been covered in depth (see Oates, 2006, pp. 38, 93, 276, 300).

In future research, the limitations mentioned above, should be addressed. Since critical research shares a lot of interpretivism's points of departure, an in-depth study is also needed to map postmodernist traits onto the characteristics of this anti-authoritarian research philosophy that is becoming more popular in IS (cf. Oates, 2006, pp. 293-298 and Sim, 2001b, p. 7). A recent article proposing a set of principles for IS critical research may be a good starting point towards a comparison of this epistemology with postmodernism (Myers & Klein, 2011). Since the philosophy of science is the point of departure of this article, it refers exclusively to IS literature. Future work should move away from this self-referencing approach and enter into a discussion with general philosophers in order to test these ideas in the wider philosophy.

CONCLUSION

The chapter investigated the move from philosophical ontology to information systems ontologies, referring to the computer-based representation of subsets of reality and knowledge. After a discussion of basic concepts needed for the argument the idea was explored and confirmed that a postmodernist view of reality prompted the pluralization of the abstract concept of the study of being, a cultural shift that was accelerated by ICT. This conceptual development is expressed *par excellence* in interpretivist IS research and formal ontologies that both reflect and integrate multiple realities. Although the aim of a single formal ontology may be quite modernistic, since it is an attempt to formalize the terminology and attributes of a certain field, the proliferation of ontologies, often to describe the same subcultures, may paradoxically bring various beliefs and understandings to the surface. Despite some perils, the marriage of ontology and information systems also creates interesting opportunities to humanize technology. Interpretivist research approaches will often be the vehicles used to facilitate this process.

REFERENCES

Borgo, S., Carrara, M., Garbacz, P., & Vermaas, P. E. (2009). A formal ontological perspective on the behaviors and functions of technical artifacts. *Artificial Intelligence for Engineering Design, Analysis and Manufacturing*, *23*(01), 3–21. doi:10.1017/S0890060409000079

Brown, R., Nerur, S., & Slinkman, C. (2004). Philosophical shifts in software development. In *Proceedings of the Tenth Americas Conference on Information Systems (AMCIS)*, New York, NY, August 2004 (pp. 4136-4143). Retrieved August, 23, 2009, from http:// aisel.aisnet.org/ amcis2004/ 516

Buchholz, W. (2006). Ontology. In D. Schwartz (Ed.), *Encyclopedia of knowledge management* (pp. 694-702). Hershey, PA: IGI (Idea Group).

Chandrasekaran, B. B., Josephson, J. R., & Benjamins, V. (1999). What are ontologies, and why do we need them? *IEEE Intelligent Systems & Their Applications*, *14*(1), 20. doi:10.1109/5254.747902

Conlon, T. (2000). Visions of change: Information Technology, education and postmodernism. *British Journal of Educational Technology*, *31*(2), 109–116. doi:10.1111/1467-8535.00141

Cotkin, G. (1996). Hyping the text: Hypertext, postmodernism, and the historian. *American Studies (Lawrence, Kan.)*, *37*(2), 103–116.

Easthope, A. (2001). Postmodernism and critical and cultural theory. In Sim, S. (Ed.), *The Routledge companion to postmodernism* (pp. 15–27). London, UK: Routledge.

Ferdinand, M., Zirpins, C., & Trastour, D. (2004, July 26-30). Lifting XML schema to OWL. In *Proceedings of the 4th International Web Engineering Conference. Lecture Notes in Computer Science*, *3140*, 354–358. doi:10.1007/978-3-540-27834-4_44

Firat, A. F., & Dholakia, N. (2004/2005). Theoretical and philosophical implications of postmodern debates: Some challenges to modern marketing. *Marketing Theory*, *6*(2), 123-162. Retrieved May 17, 2010, from http:// mtq.sagepub.com/ cgi/ content/ abstract/ 6/ 2/ 123

Fonseca, F. (2007). The double role of ontologies in Information Science research. *Journal of the American Society for Information Science and Technology, 58*(6) 786-793. Preprint retrieved March 23, 2009, from http:// www.personal.psu. edu/ faculty/ f/ u/ fuf1/ publications/ Fonseca_ Ontologies_ double_ role_ JASIST_ 2006.pdf

Fonseca, F., & Martin, J. (2007). Learning the differences between ontologies and conceptual schemas through ontology-driven information systems. *Journal of the Association for Information Systems, 8*(2), 129-142 (Article 3). Retrieved November 24, 2009, from http:// aisel.aisnet.org/ jais/ vol8/ iss2/ 4

Gilchrist, A. (2003). Thesauri, taxonomies and ontologies – An etymological note. *The Journal of Documentation, 59*(1), 7–18. doi:10.1108/00220410310457984

Grant, I. H. (2001a). Postmodernism and politics. In S. Sim (Ed.), (2001a), *The Routledge companion to postmodernism* (pp. 28-40). London, UK: Routledge.

Grant, I. H. (2001b). Postmodernism and science and technology. In S. Sim (Ed.), (2001a), *The Routledge companion to postmodernism* (pp. 65-77). London, UK: Routledge.

Greenhill, A., & Fletcher, G. (2007a). Exploring events as an Information Systems research methodology. *International Journal of Technology and Human Interaction, 3*(1), 1–16. doi:10.4018/ jthi.2007010101

Greenhill, A., & Fletcher, G. (2007b). Postmodern methods in the context of human-computer interaction (guest editorial preface). *International Journal of Technology and Human Interaction, 3*(1), i–v.

Guarino, N., Masolo, C., & Vetere, G. (1999). OntoSeek: Content-based access to the Web. *IEEE Intelligent Systems & Their Applications, 14*(3), 70–80. doi:10.1109/5254.769887

Hackney, R., & Pillay, J. (2002). *Organisational mission statements: A postmodernist perspective on the management of the IS/IT function. Information Resources Management Journal, ITJ2204 (Jan.-Mar. 2002)*. Hershey, PA: Idea Group Publishing.

Harrison, C. (2004). Postmodern principles for responsive reading assessment. *Journal of Research in Reading, 27*(2), 163–173. doi:10.1111/j.1467-9817.2004.00224.x

Hohmann, C. (2007). Emotional digitalization as technology of the postmodern: A reflexive examination from the view of the industry. *International Journal of Technology and Human Interaction, 3*(1), 17–29. doi:10.4018/jthi.2007010102

Horridge, M. (Ed.). (2009). *A practical guide to building OWL ontologies using Protégé 4 and CO-ODE tools, edition 1.2*. The University of Manchester. Retrieved August 23, 2009, from http:// owl.cs.manchester.ac.uk/ tutorials/ protegeowltutorial/ resources/ ProtegeOWLTutorialP4_ v1_2. pdf

International Association for Ontology and its Applications. (2009). *Welcome to FOIS 2010*. Retrieved October 28, 2009, from http:// fois2010. mie. utoronto.ca/

Klein, H. K., & Myers, M. D. (1999). A set of principles for conducting and evaluating interpretive field studies in information systems. *Management Information Systems Quarterly, 23*(1), 67–93. doi:10.2307/249410

Kroeze, J. H. (2009). Bootstrapping an XML schema of syntactic functions into a skeleton ontology. *South African Journal of Information Management (SAJIM), 11*(3). Retrieved February 27, 2011, from http:// www.sajim.co.za/ index. php/ SAJIM/ article/ view/ 410/ 399 or http:// hdl. handle.net/ 10394/ 2911

Kroeze, J. H. (2010). The mutualistic relationship between Information Systems and the Humanities (full paper, edited version of inaugural lecture). In K. R. Soliman (Ed.), *Knowledge Management and Innovation: A Business Competitive Edge Perspective, Proceedings of the 15th International Business Information Management Association Conference (15th IBIMA),* November 6-7, 2010, Cairo, Egypt (pp. 915-927). Retrieved February 27, 2011, from http://hdl.handle.net/10394/3824

Kroeze, J. H., Lotriet, H. H., Mavetera, N., Pfaff, M. S., Postma, D. J. R., Sewchurran, K., & Topi, H. (2011). ECIS 2010 panel report: Humanities-enriched Information Systems. *Communications of the Association for Information Systems (CAIS), 28*(1), 373-392. Retrieved May, 26, 2011, from http:// aisel.aisnet.org/ cais/ vol28/ iss1/ 24

Lambe, P. (2007). *Organising knowledge: Taxonomies, knowledge and organisational effectiveness.* Oxford, UK: Chandos.

Matusitz, J. (2008). Cyberterrorism: Postmodern state of chaos. *Information Security Journal: A Global Perspective, 17*(4), 179-187.

Mazlish, B. (1993). *The fourth discontinuity: The co-evolution of humans and machines.* New Haven, CT: Yale University Press.

Mingers, J. (2008). Pluralism, realism, and truth: The keys to knowledge in Information Systems research. *International Journal of Information Technologies and Systems Approach, 1*(1), 79–90. doi:10.4018/jitsa.2008010106

Mitev, N. N. (2006). Postmodernism and criticality in Information Systems research: What critical management studies can contribute. *Social Science Computer Review, 24*(3), 310–325. doi:10.1177/0894439306287976

Monod, E., & Boland, R. J. (2007). Special issue on philosophy and epistemology: A Peter Pan Syndrome? *Information Systems Journal, 17,* 133–141. doi:10.1111/j.1365-2575.2007.00231.x

Murphy, J. (1988). Computerization, postmodern epistemology, and reading in the postmodern era. *Educational Theory, 38*(2), 175–182. doi:10.1111/ j.1741-5446.1988.00175.x

Myers, M. D. (2009). *Qualitative research in business & management.* Los Angeles, CA: Sage.

Myers, M. D., & Klein, H. K. (2011). A set of principles for conducting critical research in information systems. *Management Information Systems Quarterly, 35*(1), 17–36.

Nel, D. F. (2007). *IT as an agent of postmodernism.* Unpublished Master's mini-dissertation, University of Pretoria, South Africa. Retrieved September 30, 2009, from http:// upetd.up.ac.za/ thesis/ available/ etd-07032008- 130105/

Oates, B. J. (2006). *Researching Information Systems and computing.* Los Angeles, CA: Sage.

Rechenmacher, H., & Van Der Merwe, C. H. J. (2005). The contribution of Wolfgang Richter to current developments in the study of Biblical Hebrew. *Journal of Semitic Studies, 50*(1), 59–82. doi:10.1093/jss/fgi004

Rychlak, J. F. (1999). Social constructionism, postmodernism, and the computer model: Searching for human agency in the right places. *Journal of Mind and Behavior, 20*(4), 379–390.

Schlenoff, C., & Uschold, M. (2004, November 30). Knowledge engineering and ontologies for autonomous systems: 2004 AAAI Spring Symposium. *Robotics and Autonomous Systems, 49,* 1–5. doi:10.1016/j.robot.2004.08.004

Sewchurran, K., Smith, D., & Roode, D. (2010). Toward a regional ontology for Information Systems project management. *International Journal of Managing Projects in Business, 3*(4), 681–692. doi:10.1108/17538371011076118

Sicilia, M. (2006). Metadata, semantics, and ontology: Providing meaning to information resources. *International Journal of Metadata. Semantics and Ontologies, 1*(1), 83–86. doi:10.1504/IJMSO.2006.008773

Sim, S. (Ed.). (2001a). *The Routledge companion to postmodernism*. London, UK: Routledge.

Sim, S. (2001b). Postmodernism and philosophy. In Sim, S. (Ed.), *The Routledge companion to postmodernism* (pp. 3–14). London, UK: Routledge.

Siraj, S. A., & Ullah, F. (2007, Dec.). Postmodernism and its insinuations on media and society. *The Journal of Development Communication, 18*(2), 1–10.

Tarnas, R. (1991). *The passion of the western mind: Understanding the ideas that have shaped our world view*. New York, NY: Ballantine Books.

Thornham, S. (2001). Postmodernism and feminism (or: repairing our own cars). In Sim, S. (Ed.), *The Routledge companion to postmodernism* (pp. 41–52). London, UK: Routledge.

Tummarello, G., Morbidoni, C., Puliti, P., & Piazza, F. (2008). A proposal for textual encoding based on semantic web tools. *Online Information Review, 32*(4), 467-477. Retrieved August 23, 2009, from http:// www.emeraldinsight.com/1468-4527. htm

Watson, N. (2001). Postmodernism and lifestyles (or: you are what you buy). In S. Sim (Ed.), (2001a), *The Routledge companion to postmodernism* (pp. 53-64). London, UK: Routledge.

Wells, J. D. (1996). Postmoderism and Information Technology: Philosophical perspectives and pragmatic implications. In J. Carey (Ed.), *Proceedings of the Americas Conference on Information Systems,* Arizona State University, Phoenix, Arizona (pp. 602-604).

Yun, H., Xu, J., Xiong, J., & Wei, M. (2011). A knowledge engineering approach to develop domain ontology. *International Journal of Distance Education Technologies, 9*(1), 57–71. doi:10.4018/jdet.2011010104

Zúñiga, G. L. (2001). Ontology: Its transformation from philosophy to information systems. *Proceedings of the International Conference on Formal Ontology in Information Systems,* Ogunquit, Maine, US (pp. 187-197).

ADDITIONAL READING

Banville, C., & Landry, M. (1989). Can the field of MIS be disciplined? *Communications of the Association for Information Systems, 32*(1), 48–60.

Belsey, C. (2002). *Poststructuralism: A very short introduction*. Oxford: Oxford University Press.

Benbasat, I., & Zmud, R. W. (2003). The identity crisis within the IS discipline: Defining and communicating the discipline's core properties. *Management Information Systems Quarterly, 27*(2), 183–194.

Butler, C. (2002). *Postmodernism: A very short introduction*. Oxford: Oxford University Press.

Craig, E. (2005). *Philosophy: a very short introduction* Franklin, Tennessee: Nos Audiobooks.

De Villiers, R. (2005). Interpretive research models for Informatics: Action research, grounded theory, and the family of design- and development research. *Alternation, 12*(2), 10–52.

Galliers, R. D., & Whitley, E. A. (2007). Vive les differences? Developing a profile of European Information Systems research as a basis for international comparisons. *European Journal of Information Systems, 16*, 20–35. doi:10.1057/palgrave.ejis.3000662

Grassie, W. (1997). Postmodernism: What one needs to know. *Zygon: Journal of Religion and Science,* March 1997. Retrieved March 17, 2005, from http:// www.voicenet.com/ ~grassie/ Fldr. Articles/ Postmodernism.html

Grover, V., Straub, D., & Galluch, P. (2009). Turning the corner: The influence of positive thinking on the Information Systems field (Editor's comments). *Management Information Systems Quarterly, 32*(1), iii–viii.

Hill, C., & Every, P. (2001). Postmodernism and the cinema. In S. Sim (Ed.), (2001a), *The Routledge companion to postmodernism* (pp. 101-111). London: Routledge.

Hirschheim, R., & Klein, H. K. (2003). Crisis in the IS field? A critical reflection on the state of the discipline. *Journal of the Association for Information Systems, 4*(10), 273–293.

Hovorka, D. S., & Lee, A. S. (2010). Reframing interpretivism and positivism as understanding and explanation: Consequences for Information Systems research. In *ICIS 2010 Proceedings,* St. Louis, Paper 188 (pp. 1-13). Retrieved February 27, 2011, from http:// aisel.aisnet.org/ icis2010_ submissions/ 188

Klein, H. K., & Hirschheim, R. (2008). The structure of the IS discipline reconsidered: Implications and reflections from a community of practice perspective. *Information and Organization, 18,* 280–302. doi:10.1016/j.infoandorg.2008.05.001

Lewis, B. (2001). Postmodernism and literature (or: word salad days, 1960-90). In S. Sim (Ed.), (2001a), *The Routledge companion to postmodernism* (pp. 121-133). London: Routledge.

Lister, R. 2005. Mixed methods: Positivists are from Mars, constructivists are from Venus. *Inroads – The SICSCE Bulletin, 37*(4), 18-19.

Mora, M., Gelman, O., Forgionne, G., Petkov, D., & Cano, J. (2007). Integrating the fragmented pieces of IS research paradigms and frameworks: A systems approach. *Information Resources Management Journal, 20*(2), 1–22. doi:10.4018/ irmj.2007040101

Morgan, D. (2001). Postmodernism and architecture. In S. Sim (Ed.), (2001a), *The Routledge companion to postmodernism* (pp. 78-88). London: Routledge.

Mouton, J. (1985). Contemporary philosophies of science and the qualitative paradigm in the social sciences. *Die Suid-Afrikaanse Tydskrif vir Sosiologie, 16*(3), 81–89.

Northover, M., Kourie, D. G., Boake, A., Gruner, S., & Northover, A. (2008). Towards a philosophy of software development: 40 years after the birth of software engineering. *Journal for General Philosophy of Science Zeitschrift fur Allgemeine Wissenschaftstheorie, 39*(1), 85–113.

O'Day, M. 2001. Postmodernism and television. In S. Sim (Ed.), (2001a), *The Routledge companion to postmodernism* (pp. 112-120). London: Routledge.

Powers, W. (2010). *Hamlet's Blackberry: A practical philosophy for building a good life in the digital age.* Melbourne: Scribe.

Scott, D. (2001). Postmodernism and music. In S. Sim (Ed.), (2001a), *The Routledge companion to postmodernism* (pp. 134-146). London: Routledge.

Sidorova, A., Evangelopoulos, N., Valacich, J. S., & Ramakrishnan, T. (2008). Uncovering the intellectual core of the Information Systems discipline. *Management Information Systems Quarterly, 32*(3), 467–482.

Spencer, L. (2001). Postmodernism, modernity, and the tradition of dissent. In S. Sim (Ed.), (2001a), *The Routledge companion to postmodernism* (pp. 158-169). London: Routledge.

Storey, J. (2001). Postmodernism and popular culture. In S. Sim (Ed.), (2001a), *The Routledge companion to postmodernism* (pp. 147-157). London: Routledge.

Trodd, C. (2001). Postmodernism and art. In S. Sim (Ed.), (2001a), *The Routledge companion to postmodernism* (pp. 89-100). London: Routledge.

Weber, R. (2004). The rhetoric of positivism versus interpretivism: A personal review (Editor's comments). *Management Information Systems Quarterly, 28*(1), iii–xii.

Whitley, R. (1984). The development of management studies as a fragmented adhocracy. *Social Sciences Information. Information Sur les Sciences Sociales, 23*(4-5), 775–818. doi:10.1177/053901884023004007

KEY TERMS AND DEFINITIONS

Epistemology: A theory which makes explicit the underlying assumptions about understanding and knowledge.

Formal Ontology: A taxonomy of a subset of reality, which defines the relationships between the entities and ensures consistency and reliability by means of description logics.

Interpretivism: An epistemology that focuses on reality as a human construction which can only be understood subjectively.

Ontology: A theory which makes explicit the underlying assumptions about reality and the nature of existence.

Paradigm: A paradigm refers to a set of theories which is typical of a historical phase in the philosophy of science.

Positivism: An epistemology that focuses on reality as a concrete given entity which can be understood objectively.

Postmodernism: An encompassing paradigm, referring to a set of assumptions regarding ontology (realities are created), epistemology (knowledge is fluid and provisional), methodology (interpretive and critical methods are more apt to study a plural society) and axiology (the study of values: no one set of values are per definition better than another).

Qualitative Research: A research approach that aims to understand patterns and to answer how and why questions.

Quantitative Research: A research approach that aims to identify patterns by means of numerical and statistical means.

ENDNOTES

[1] This chapter is a revised and extended version of the following conference paper: Kroeze, J. H. (2010). Ontology goes postmodern in ICT. In *Fountains of Computing Research* – Proceedings of SAICSIT 2010 (Annual Research Conference of the South African Institute of Computer Scientists and Information Technologists), 11 to 13 October 2010, Bela Bela, South Africa, edited by Paula Kotzé, Aurona Gerber, Alta van der Merwe and Nicola Bidwell, CSIR Meraka Institute, A Volume in the ACM International Conference Proceedings Series, ACM Press, ACM ISBN: 978-1-60558-950-3, pp. 153-159. Available: http://portal.acm.org/.

[2] This explains the fact that the plural form, *ontologies*, is not even recognized by the spell checker of a word processor such as MS Word.

Chapter 4
Critical Realism and IS Research:
Some Methodological Implications

Philip J. Dobson
Edith Cowan University, Australia

ABSTRACT

Critical realism is seeing more application within the Information Systems field, but its application is still limited. Applying critical realism has proven to be difficult, partly because critical realism provides little practical guidance as to methodological development and even less guidance as to the role of technology within its complex arguments. This chapter discusses some of the practical implications consequent from adopting critical realism in terms of philosophy, theory, and methodology.

INTRODUCTION

This chapter briefly introduces critical realism and suggests some of the implications from adopting the philosophy to examine information systems within organizations. As Kljajic & Farr (2008) suggest information systems (IS), systems engineering (SE) and a systems approach (SA) are closely inter-related, yet their basic arguments depend on different underlying assumptions and beliefs. Systems "thinking" can be roughly separated into "soft" systems thinking and "hard"

systems thinking. For example Checkland's Soft Systems Methodology (Checkland, 1981) is often presented as a useful "soft systems" approach that regards the concept of a "system" as being purely an epistemological device having no ontological foundation. According to Checkland systems thinking is a "particular way of describing the world" (Checkland, 1983, p. 671). Checkland saw social systems as intrinsically different from natural systems – such a belief fundamentally in opposition to critical realism which argues that the methods of the sciences can be carefully (ie critically) applied to social systems.

DOI: 10.4018/978-1-4666-0179-6.ch004

In contrast cybernetics can be seen as a "hard" systems approach in that systems are seen as real objects with important cybernetic interactions. Mingers (2011b, p. 6) presents systems approaches as fundamentally depending on "The central systemic idea – that the characteristics and behaviour of entities depended on the structure of relationships between components rather than the properties of the components themselves – carries with it several other concepts – emergence, hierarchy and boundaries". Mingers (2011b) argues for a substantial correspondence between critical realism and the systems approach, questioning the reasons for critical realist neglect of the long history of systems thinking. He compares many of the systemic concepts such as emergence, boundary, and hierarchy with corresponding critical realist concepts. He calls for a much greater communication between the two groups to improve both disciplines.

Avgerou (2001) suggests many authors in the Information Systems arena separate the technological content from the social context in which the IT change ensues. This has allowed useful specialized IS knowledge to be developed largely separate from the social context. This analytical separation has been useful and can be seen to provide similar benefits to the so-called "analytical dualism" within critical realist argument. Analytical dualism is presented by Archer (1995) as an artificial, analytical separation of structure and agency, designed to assist in examining each of their different effects (see the morphogentic model explained below). Systems engineering can perhaps be argued as benefiting in a similar fashion from the separation of the technical from the social. As its name implies Systems Engineering has a strong technical focus and has grown from a basic underlying assumption that systems can be "engineered"; it tends to be focused on "what works".

Avgerou (2001) suggests a more appropriate model for today's information system combines the social and the technical in a heterogeneous network:

It suggests that what is generally called "information system" in the jargon of practitioners as well as academics cannot be meaningfully restricted to computer or communications applications within an independently delineated social environment. Technical artefacts such as hardware, software, data in paper or electronic form, carry with them engineers with the conventions of their trade, industries that sell, install and support them, "users" who understand their significance and interpret the way they should be put to action according to their circumstances and consultants who convert them from symbol manipulating machines to "competitive advantage. (p. 46)

The argument that the study of information technology in organizations requires a sociotechnical emphasis encourages the adoption of methods from the social sciences arena. One of the recent philosophical developments from within social sciences is the philosophy of critical realism. Its adoption as underlabourer for research logically requires a strong emphasis on the social aspects of the object under study. The term underlabouring is taken from Locke (1894, p. 14) as "clearing the ground a little...removing some of the rubbish that lies in the way of knowledge".

Critical realism is primarily associated with the writings of Roy Bhaskar. His first thorough description is presented in A Realist Theory of Science (1978) and then in the more approachable The Possibility of Naturalism (1979). The first book presents Bhaskar's approach to the philosophy of science addressing much of positivist criticism. The second book argues for the extension of these arguments to the social arena; the term "critical" realism developing from the suggestion that the methods of the sciences should be carefully or critically applied to social investigation.

Whilst critical realism does help in guiding research and "clearing the ground a little", it can only do this given a commitment from the researcher to understand its basic philosophical arguments. A philosophical commitment can be seen to involve rational thinking and logical argument – it encourages being specific about "things" and acknowledging foundational assumptions. As Gramsci (1971, p. 323) argues "…everyone is a philosopher, though in his own way and unconsciously, since even in the slightest manifestation of any intellectual activity whatever, in "language" there is contained a specific conception of the world" (from Collier 1994, p. 17).

The IS and SE fields, however, have a strong practical focus and, as Orlikowski and Barley (2001) argue, have much in common with engineering where the major focus is on such practical questions as "what works?". Given this heavy practical focus it is no surprise that an alternate perspective exists disparaging this involvement in philosophy and philosophical argument. Yet there are clear benefits to be gained from an approach that "goes back to basics" and a philosophical focus is not inconsistent with being practical – philosophy can provide practical direction and guidance both in terms of defining the object under study and suggesting the most appropriate means for examination. This chapter aims to indicate how some of the philosophical arguments consequent from a critical realist foundation can provide practical methodological guidance.

BACKGROUND

Bhaskar's brand of realism (referred to by Searle (1995) as a form of external realism) argues that there exists a reality totally independent of our representations of it; the reality and the "representation of reality" operating in different domains - roughly a transitive epistemological dimension and an intransitive ontological dimension – real objects within the ontological dimension are subject to value-laden observation from within the epistemological dimension (very roughly since the value-laden observations, once made, become "real" and themselves have causal effects).

Fleetword (2005) argues for the importance of ontology when he suggests:

The way we think the world is (ontology) influences: what we think can be known about it (epistemology); how we think it can be investigated (methodology and research techniques); the kinds of theories we think can be constructed about it; and the political and policy stances we are prepared to take. Although having the 'right' ontology does not guarantee that the ensuing meta-theory, theory and practice will also be 'right', having the 'wrong' ontology makes this virtually impossible—although we might be 'right' by accident. Similarly, having an unambiguous ontology does not guarantee that the ensuing meta-theory, theory and practice will also be unambiguous, but having an ambiguous ontology makes this much harder. In short, ontology matters. (p. 197).

For the realist the most important driver for decisions on methodological approach will always be the intransitive dimension - the target being to unearth the real mechanisms and structures underlying perceived events. As Reed (2009, p. 438) suggests "Critical realism presupposes that ontology precedes epistemology; ontology is prior to epistemology, because it tells us where to look and what to look for." The focus of critical realist research is the understanding of deep structures and mechanisms that lie beneath events and sense experiences. This is difficult "…because it requires that we engage in in-depth understanding and analysis of the historical contexts, structural conditions and interpretive schemes that, in their interplay, shape our lives and the opportunities that are made available to us" (p. 438). Reality is complex and examining it is a daunting and challenging task.

The change in focus from the positivist emphasis on the empirical, or events, to what produces them has significant implications as to the

Table 1. Four modes of inference (Based on Danermark et al (p. 80))

	Deduction	Induction	Abduction	Retroduction
Fundamental structure/ thought operations	To derive logically valid conclusions from given premises. To derive knowledge of individual phenomena from universal laws.	From a number of observations to draw universally valid conclusions about a whole population. To see similarities in a number of observations and draw the conclusion that these similarities also apply to non-studied cases. From observed covariants to draw conclusions about law-like relations.	To interpret and recontextualize individual phenomena within a conceptual framework or a set of ideas. To be able to understand something in a new way by observing and interpreting this something in a new conceptual framework	From a description and analysis of concrete phenomena to reconstruct the basic conditions for these phenomena to be what they are. By way of thought operations and counterfactual thinking to argue towards transfactual conditions.
The central issue	What are the logical conclusions of the premises?	What is the element common for a number of observed entities and is it true also of a larger population?	What meaning is given to something interpreted within a particular conceptual framework?	What qualities must exist for something to be possible?
Strength	Provides rules and guidance for logical derivations and investigations of the logical validity in all argument.	Provides guidance in connection with empirical generalizations, and possibilities to calculate, in part, the precision of such generalizations.	Provides guidance for the interpretative processes by which we ascribe meaning to events in relation to a larger context.	Provides knowledge of trans factual conditions, structures and mechanisms that cannot be directly observed in the domain of the empirical.
Limitations	Deduction does not say anything new about reality beyond what is already in the premises. It is strictly analytical	Inductive inference can never be either analytically or empirically certain = the internal limitations of induction. Induction is restricted to conclusions at the empirical level = the external limitations of induction	There are no fixed criteria from which it is possible to assess the validity of an abductive conclusion.	There are no fixed criteria from which it would be possible to assess in a definite way the validity of a retroductive conclusion.
Important quality on the part of the researcher	Logical reasoning ability	Ability to master statistical Analysis	Creativity and imagination	Ability to abstract
Examples	If A then B A Thus: B	From an investigation of the attitude of a representative sample of Swedes, draw the conclusion that 30% of the Swedish population is in favour of the EU.	Karl Marx: reinterpretation/redescription of the history of humankind from the historical materialist view	For a ritual to be just a ritual there must exist, inter alia, emotionally loaded symbols and common notions of inviolable/ sacred values.

progress and targets of research. The fact that a researcher must move from observed events to propose underlying, perhaps unobservable, causes requires the adoption of a differing abductive or retroductive enquiry process from the traditional deductive and inductive enquiry process. The differences between each mode of enquiry is highlighted below in Table 1.

Thus, the need for abduction and retroduction determine the methodological development within critical realist examination in that the critical realist must postulate the social structures or mechanisms that make or have made a significant causal contribution to the social phenomena that the researcher is aiming to explain. The basic research question is "under what conditions might the observed happenings occur?". The social structures or mechanisms postulated must be then demonstrated to exist and a convincing explanatory account of their impacts derived and checked against observed outcomes.

Such a process is difficult in the complex reality of organizations as Miller and Tsang (2011, p. 140) argue when discussing the testing of management theories. Organizations are diverse, complex, and changing social phenomena where it is difficult to clearly delineate all of the competing variables and their combined effects. Social reality is complex and the examination of its components requires careful handling. Multiple theories may be required to explain particular aspects of the social situation and, as Miller and Tsang argue, these theories often tend to require a complementary usage for explanation rather than the competing approach more common in the natural sciences. This makes it difficult to, firstly determine appropriate explanatory theories and, secondly to determine the relative merits of each. The initial stages of critical realist examination can be over-whelming due to the sheer weight of theories needed for explanation.

Critical realism argues for the importance of considering structure, agency and their interplay in social situations and highlights the agent as non-passive. As Miller and Tsang suggest organizational players can and do make decisions based on personal choices and creativity – these decisions determined by complex rationales from multiple layers of social reality. This means that theories of human behaviour cannot have straightforward predictive power, thus adding another layer of complexity.

Similarly the researcher themselves can act as causal sources within organizations in that the researcher unearthing of explanatory structures and mechanisms can actually lead to changes in behaviours of the persons interviewed: "A theory of, say, planetary motion will not change how planets actually move. By contrast, managers may alter their behaviours on the basis of the knowledge created by researchers (Knights, 1992). The extent to which research influences managerial practice likely varies widely depending on the theory and organization of interest." (Miller et al p. 141). This suggests that the tracing of a causal influence through a complex series of successive interactions of structures, agential decisions and mechanisms is enormously difficult but whilst difficult must be attempted.

The philosophical arguments detailed above provide examples as to how philosophy plays an integral part in defining the research object, the research question and ultimately the research process. As Bhaskar and Danermark (2006, p. 295) suggest critical realism can be used as a "meta-theory" to support research – a meta-theory being seen as "a set of presuppositions about the nature of the world and knowledge, respectively. These presuppositions are of two kinds, namely about the objects of knowledge (ontology) and about the conditions for knowledge (epistemology)…. ontology and epistemology are "guidelines" when approaching the real world in order to do science". Metatheory implicitly or explicitly directs an investigator towards "what you can/cannot do (and even see) and what kind of knowledge you can/cannot obtain if you want to do science." In this light we examine the ways that critical realism can act as an underlabourer or meta-theory for research on the organizational use of IT.

THE ATTRACTION OF CRITICAL REALISM IN IS/IT RESEARCH

Within IS research Orlikowski and Baroudi (1991) present interpretivism and critical theory as major responses to the shortcomings of the more common and traditional positivist approaches. Blaikie (1993) from within the social sciences arena suggests that contemporary responses to the dissatisfaction with positivism include critical theory, naïve realism, contemporary hermeneutics, sructuration theory and feminism. Such responses to the shortcomings of positivism have been similarly noticed in the IS field as Smith (2006), for example, points out. Giddens' structuration theory is an example of a contemporary realist response that has had a significant impact on IS research (see Rose (2000) and Jones and Karsten (2008)) yet critical realism is only recently having any impact. This was somewhat surprising given the elements of similarity between the two theories, for example their similarly rich ontological focus and their commitment to a meta-theoretical position that recognises the importance of structure and agency.

This lack of interest in critical realism within IS research has been addressed somewhat in recent years, for example, Mutch(1999), Mingers (2000), Dobson(2001), Carlsson(2003), Smith(2006) argue for its adoption. Several practical examples of its adoption have also been presented (for example Morton (2006), Volkoff et al (2007), Dobson et al (2007), Smith (2008;2010), Mutch (2010), Strong & Volkoff (2010), Bygstad (2010)). All argue for the recognition of information systems as social systems.

Smith (2006) highlights the dominance of positivism and interpretivism within IS research and argues for the adoption of critical realism to avoid some of the theory-practice inconsistencies

consequent from interpretivist and positivist foundations. He suggests that the explanatory focus and causal representation within critical realism addresses the question often neglected within positivist enquiry as to "why" things happen in IS research. It also "provides interpretivists with an ontology that strongly asserts the crucial role of meanings, interpretation and context" (p. 193).

Of course critical realism is just one of many possible meta-theoretical positions. For example, Bhaskar and Danermark (2006) compare a critical realist meta-theoretical perspective with naive realism/empiricism, social constructionism, hermeneutics and neo-Kantianism. Each perspective is seen to have particular advantages in examining disability:

Empiricism pinpoints epistemologically the role of experience and the need for empirical controls; neo-Kantianism highlights the important interpretive role of theory and hints at the non-empirical character of laws, mechanisms and the other objects of scientific understanding; hermeneutics emphasizes the already interpreted character of the social world and hence of any syndrome which could be a disability or a differential ability; and social constructionism, combining the virtues of hermeneutics and neo-Kantianism, points to the ingrained character and authoritative cognitive power of such constitutive pre-interpretations of social reality, including what are known as disabilities. (p. 287).

CRITICAL REALIST FOUNDATIONS

Critical realism argues for a so-called depth realism which suggests that beneath the level of events and the level of empirical observations there is a deeper level of reality where the mechanisms that instigate events exist. There is more to the world than that which we experience. Bhaskar(1978) distinguishes between three overlapping ontological domains: the empirical, the actual and the real. The empirical domain consists of what we experience, directly or indirectly. This domain is part of the actual domain where events happen whether we experience them or not - what happens in the world is not the same as that which is observed. The actual domain is in its turn different from the real domain, where we also find the forces, mechanisms, which can produce events in the world.

As Lawson (1997) argues transcendental (or critical) realism is developed around a scientific realist position which asserts that "the ultimate objects of scientific investigation exist for the most part quite independent of, or at least prior to, their investigation" (p. 15). This common external realist position is extended under critical realism in that it presents a philosophical argument for the nature, constitution and structure of the underlying objects of enquiry. Such a realism is heavily concerned with ontology or metaphysics, that is, the nature of *being* and *existence*. This philosophical questioning concludes a, so-called, depth realism that proposes that "the world is composed not only of events and our experience or impression of them, but also of (irreducible) structures and mechanisms, powers and tendencies, etc. that, although not directly observable, nevertheless underlie actual events that we experience and govern or produce them" (Lawson, 1997, p. 8).

An important element within critical realism is that these deep structures and mechanisms may, in fact, be only observable through their effects and thus a causal criterion for existence is accepted:

Observability may make us more confident about what we think exists, but existence itself is not dependent on it. In virtue of this, then, rather than rely purely upon a criterion of observability for making claims about what exists, realists accept a causal criterion too. According to this a plausible case for the existence of unobservable entities can be made by reference to observable effects which can only be explained as the products of such entities.... A crucial implication of this ontology

is the recognition of the possibility that powers may exist unexercised, and hence ...the nature of the real objects present at a given time constrains and enables what can happen but does not predetermine what will happen. (Sayer 2000, p. 12).

The ontological complexity assumed by critical realism is, however, matched by a conservative epistemology that leans heavily on scientific argument and development. Stones (1996) suggests that if contemporary realist research is to address post-modern criticism it needs to be more aggressive in its methodological approach. Realist methodologies need to be able to account for the underlying ontological richness they implicitly assume and also need to reflect the belief that any knowledge gains are typically provisional, fallibilist, incomplete and extendable. Realist methodologies and writings, thus, must reflect a continual commitment to caution, scepticism and reflexivity.

Critical realism presupposes ontological realism and epistemological relativism in that it suggests that reality can only be known under particular descriptions. Lawson (2003, p. 162) provides a critical realist view:

[epistemological relativism] expresses the idea that our categories, frameworks of thinking, modes of analysis, ways of seeing things, habits of thought, dispositions of every kind, motivating concerns, interests, values and so forth, are affected by our life paths and socio-cultural situations and thereby make a difference in how we can and do 'see' or know or approach things, and indeed they bear on which we seek to know. (as quoted in Al-Amoudi and Willmott (2011, p. 28)).

However despite arguing for epistemological relativism critical realism denies "judgemental relativism" – the view that one cannot judge between different discourses and decide that some accounts are better than others. As detailed below a major element within the critical realist "method" and retroductive argument is to be able to judge between alternative explanations as to the proposed mechanisms and structures that underlie events. Judgemental rationality with respect to competing explanations is an important part of critical realist argument.

Al-Amoudi et al (2011, p. 30) suggest that this belief in judgemental rationality has methodological implications in that methods used and outcomes discussed need to better support judgemental rationality by offering comparisons with alternative positions more clearly so that readers of critical realist studies are better placed to judge between rival claims. In particular they highlight the divide between realist and constructivist positions: "Scholarship located and positioned on one or other side of the divide in a way has tended to cultivate and justify a disinclination to give careful consideration to the other's claims" (p. 27). Perhaps critical realist practice needs to better reflect the accommodating nature of its epistemological position and include a more constructivist element in its examinations.

They also suggest that critical realist researchers needs to more clearly reflect the historical embeddedness of retroductive decisions: "The criteria employed for preferring one explanation rather than another is, at least in part, dependent on the historico-cultural community in which debates about competing claims are staged (Roy Bhaskar, personal communication). Retroductive judgements provide possible but historically contingent explanations of certain states of affairs" (p. 30). This view suggests that critical realist examination needs to emphasize the fallibility of explanations and the historical context of their explanatory arguments.

Critical realism has been presented as a foundation for pluralist methodology use (for example, Mingers 2001). This support for pluralism is largely founded on the critical realist underlying focus on ontology and its perception that a major role for theory is to improve our understanding of a complex separate reality. The philosophy of critical realism is compatible with a large number of different theories, yet the depth realism assumed by critical realism has implications with respect to the ongoing development of research and as such is perhaps less free with respect to the use of multiple theories and methodologies than is often implied. Critical realism argues for an intimate link between philosophy and consequent methodological and epistemological development. As Archer (1995) suggests "the nature of what exists cannot be unrelated to how it is studied...the social ontology endorsed does play a powerful regulatory role vis-à-vis the explanatory methodology for the basic reason that it conceptualises social reality in certain terms, thus identifying what there is to be explained and also ruling out explanations in terms of entities or properties which are deemed non-existent" (p. 16-17). Similarly, Craib (1992, p.656) suggests that "our methods of understanding the world and the forms of the theory we use are based on the nature of the realities we are trying to understand". Consistency is a major consequence of adopting critical realism as a foundational platform – the critical realist underpinnings affect decisions made throughout the research process. The adoption of critical realism as an underlying philosophical approach has important methodological and epistemological consequences.

As Reed (2005a, p. 1637) suggests "Critical realism does not legitimate or license any particular substantive theoretical perspective or body of social theorizing. But it is incompatible with approaches based on the assumption that 'discourse makes the world' or that material conditions and social relations have no ontological status or explanatory relevance unless and until they are discursively constituted".

Critical realism cannot support the indiscriminate use of theory since it strongly argues for an intimate linkage between all aspects of the research process. For example critical realism has important things to say about the sort of questions that can be asked and the conclusions that can be reached. The basic target of critical realist examination is causal explanation. Such causal explanation requires proposing alternative perhaps unobservable mechanisms (ie theories). Abductive questioning is a fundamental part of critical realist enquiry and as Easton (2010) suggests the "key epistemological process" (p. 124).

The Importance of Abduction in Critical Realist Study

As detailed in Table 1 below Danermark et al (2002) present the four different modes of inference used in research. Mingers (2011a) usefully uses an example provided by Peirce (2.623) to demonstrate the differences between each inference mode:

General law: All beans in this bag are white
Particular case: All these beans come from this bag
Conclusion: All these beans are white

The above being an example of deductive inference. Given a general law or rule we can deduce a particular consequence from it.

Similarly:
Context: All these beans come from this bag
Empirical observations: All these beans are white
General law: All beans in this bag are white

The above captures the logic of induction – from particular instances we induce a general conclusion. As Mingers (2011a, p. 4) suggests "In terms of pure logic it is invalid since there could still be beans in the bag that are not white but were not selected, but it obviously has utility as a practical mode of inference".

And finally:
(Unexpected) observation: All these beans are white
Possible cause: All beans in this bag are white

Explanatory hypothesis: All these beans come from this bag

This final example again is not valid in a logical sense since some other reason could explain why all the beans are white – Peirce termed this type of argument as "abduction" or "retroduction". Peirce (1960, p.117) described the formal logic of abductive reasoning as follows:

A surprising fact, C, is observed.
But if A were true, C would be a matter of course.
Hence, there is reason to expect that A is true.

As detailed in Table 1 Danermark et al (2002) distinguish between abduction and retroduction when they propose abduction as being able to "understand something in a new way by observing and interpreting this something in a new conceptual framework" and retroduction as transfactual thinking which moves from "a description and analysis of concrete phenomena to reconstruct the basic conditions for these phenomena to be what they are". The central issue respectively for abduction is "what meaning is given to something interpreted within a particular conceptual framework" and for retroduction "what qualities must exist for something to be possible" (p. 81). They comment that in both cases it is not possible in a definitive way to verify the validity of either conclusions.

Abduction must play an important role in critical realist analysis since such an approach requires transcending, or speculating, perhaps non-observable mechanisms and structures to explain perceived happenings. As Wad (2001, p. 2) suggests "If we take explanation to be the core purpose of science, critical realism seems to emphasise thinking instead of experiencing, and especially the process of abstraction from the domains of the actual and the empirical world to the transfactual mechanisms of the real world".

Such a perspective is consistent with a depth realism where explanation is not about prediction but about the steady unearthing of deeper levels of structures and mechanisms. Mechanisms are the "stuff" of research and being often non-observable depend heavily on theory to unearth. Various mechanisms and structural interactions are hypothesized to explain observed happenings – the success of the proposition determined by the extent to which observations are consistent with the proposals.

But as Wuisman (2005) argues, the critical realist "method" cannot rest on abduction alone, abduction must be used in combination with induction and deduction to complete valid scientific discovery:

The cycle of scientific discovery can be thought of as an iterative process consisting of a series of three stages. According to Peirce the cycle starts with some unexplained amazing fact, that is, a perceived gap between some sensory perception and the existing stock of knowledge. To close this gap a hypothesis is conjectured specifying a particular rule or law, which, if it were true, would explain the amazing fact as a matter of course. In the second stage, in order to determine whether the explanation based on the hypothesis conjectured by abduction is valid or not, from this hypothesized rule or law should be deduced what must be the case by necessity, assuming that the hypothesized cause is really true. In the third stage, based on detailed and carefully gathered information about what actually is the case, by way of induction, a judgment should be made as to whether the amazing fact is properly understood and explained in terms of the previously hypothesized rule or law or not. If not, the perceived gap is not closed and a new hypothesis should be conjectured based on abduction. (p. 383)

Wuisman (2005) quotes Peirce (1883) in describing the different forms of inference: Abduction is 'the process of forming an explanatory hypothesis. It is the only logical operation, which introduces any new idea; for induction does noth-

ing but determine a value, and deduction merely evolves the necessary consequences of a pure hypothesis. Deduction proves that something must be; induction shows that something actually is operative; abduction merely suggests that something may be'.

As Table 1 suggests abduction requires creativity and imagination. The guesswork required of abductive argument necessitates a creative element as Mingers (2011a) suggests

Abduction is the point where novelty, innovation and creativity enter the scientific method, as indeed they must. With deduction, we get nothing more than the consequences of the premises – but where did they come from? With induction, we just get a generalisation from the observations we have made – but how do we know they are all that matters? However, with abduction we get explanation and the possibility of new knowledge. (p. 4)

CRITICAL REALISM AND "METHOD"?

Outhwaite (1987, p. 58) suggests the critical realist method involves "the postulation of a possible [structure or] mechanism, the attempt to collect evidence for or against its existence and the elimination of possible alternatives". The realist agrees that we have a good explanation when (i) the postulated mechanism is capable of explaining the phenomenon (ii) we have good reason to believe in its existence (iii) we cannot think of any equally good alternatives.

This type of thinking is called transcendental by Bhaskar in that it gives an important role to the crossing of the divide between the empirical and speculative activities of scientific work. As Wad (2001) suggests this is necessary since often the experienced world of events is not explainable in terms of the empirical facts, but only by way of incorporating non-experienced mechanisms incorporated in objects which may be within or outside our domain of investigation. Such a perspective is consistent with a depth realism where explanation is not about prediction but about the steady unearthing of deeper levels of structures and mechanisms.

Raduescu and Vessey (2008) suggest that the most widely used explanatory frameworks within critical realism are Archer's morphogenetic framework, Danermark et al's (2002) staged model and Pawson and Tilley's (Pawson and Tilley 2007) realistic evaluation framework. They compare and contrast the ontological grounding provided by each particular framework. In this chapter we will briefly cover Archer's and Danermark et al's models.

Danermark's Staged Model

Danermark et al describe 6 stages in explanatory research moving from the concrete initial description (stage 1) to "analytical resolution" (stage 2) whereby the components of interest are identified and separated. Abduction is involved in the third stage where the components are re-interpreted using different theories and frameworks. Retroduction (stage 4) is then applied whereby the abstractions are then made "real" within a critical realist frame by hypothesizing the necessary structures and mechanisms consistent with the previous abstraction. The two stages of abduction and retroduction are in practice closely related as the theoretical re-framing is matched against consequent realist outcomes. The 5th stage examines the relative merit of each abstraction/ theory in explaining the observed happenings. The final stage termed "concretization and contextualization" involves examining "how the different structures and mechanisms manifest themselves in concrete situations". Whilst stages 2 to 5 tend to reside in the conceptual space – or the so-called transfactual domain - they continually involve reference back to the contextual situation.

An example of this general approach is provided by Smith (2010) when he uses critical realism as a foundation for his examination of the impacts of e-services on citizen's trust in government in Chile. His research question is "how, for whom, and in what circumstances do e-services impact on citizens' trust in government?" or more specific to a critical realist representation "what are the generative mechanisms that connect e-services to changes in citizens' trust perceptions of government?".

Smith (2010) provides an important example of the use of this staged model when he uses critical realism to examine the impacts of e-services on citizen's trust in government in Chile. His research question is "how, for whom, and in what circumstances do e-services impact on citizens' trust in government?" or more specific to a critical realist representation "what are the generative mechanisms that connect e-services to changes in citizens' trust perceptions of government?". This usage of the staged model to examine ICT implementation can be usefully extended to examine the usage of IS within organizations.

After first describing the situation he effectively begins with meta-theory and mid-range theory to gain the "analytical resolution" suggested by Danermaker et al. A core theory of trust is first developed based around high-level theory of sociological and psychological theories of trust and trustworthiness. This core theory is then used as a platform for subsequent more detailed theoretical development from mid-range theory to concrete testable hypotheses specific to the research context. The IT artefact is introduced at this third contextualized stage.

As Smith (2008) describes early theoretical scanning is difficult since the researcher cannot hope to determine a single dominating theory to explain the complex reality of e-services and its impact on trustworthiness:

[early theorization] was made following the assumption that (at least a priori) there is no single theory that will be sufficient to explain what may be happening in Chile with citizens, egovernment services, and trust. Perhaps after engaging in re-

search one theory will provide sufficient explanatory power through identification of a big-effect; that is, a large causal influence that overrides most of the other contextual causal mechanisms. Beforehand, however, it was not possible to know what the most influential causes might be. (p. 8)

Theoretical descriptions of mechanisms tend to operate at the middle-range theory level - middle range theory describing theories lying between minor working hypotheses, close to empirical data, and general all-inclusive (often called 'grand') theories. Mid-range theory is useful in providing an opportunity to identify high-level representation of mechanisms as relatively enduring – these mechanisms then open to better delineation by realist examination. As Pawson (2000, p. 291) describes realism provides the missing practical element in middle-range theory in that realist representations provide the "ontological skeleton on which to build explanations".

The final stage of hypothesis generation is the development of case-specific testable hypotheses. As Smith (2008) suggests the method has benefits and disadvantages:

In particular, the approach proposed here is heavy on front-end theorizing and theory-integration. This requires extensive multi-disciplinary exposure. Undoubtedly, this adds significant richness to the theoretical propositions, and potential understanding when confronting the empirical site. It also helps to prevent social scientists from reinventing the wheel. However, there is a significant risk that a jack-of-all-trades is really a master of none. Furthermore, the result of theorization for the case presented here was a very broad set of potential causes (reality is complex!) on which the author tried to gather data. The end result was breadth rather than depth, and plenty of time was spent on particular causes that in the end were not of any importance. (p. 12)

For Smith's study meta-theory and mid-range theory is used over the equivalent of stages 2 to 5 in Danermark's model. The final stage in Smith's "method" is the movement from abstract to concrete to define case-specific testable hypotheses – this equates quite closely to Danermark's stage 6 concretization and contextualization stage.

As Danermark et al (2002, p. 150) critical realism in itself is not a method – it cannot be applied unambiguously in practical research. Yet, as their staged model suggests it can be used to guide the research process in that the objects defined by critical realism frame subsequent ontological, epistemological and methodological development.

Archer's Morphogenetic Model

For the critical realist the "generative mechanism" is the stuff of research. "What happens in the world is not the same as that which is observed... Acquiring access to forces—generative mechanisms—which can produce events in the world, we must pursue our hunt in the domain of the real (by means of abstraction and analytical work). However, according to this ontology, the world is not only differentiated and structured, it is also stratified: the mechanisms in their turn belong to different layers or strata of reality, and furthermore, these strata are hierarchically organized." (Morén & Blom, 2003 p. 46). Hedström and Swedberg (1998) propose three basic mechanisms:

1. Situational Mechanisms (macro-micro level)
2. Action-Formation Mechanisms (micro-micro level)
3. Transformational Mechanisms (micro-macro level)

The typology implies that macro-level events or conditions affect the individual (step 1), the individual assimilates the impact of the macro-level events (step 2) and a number of individuals generate, through their actions and interactions, macro-level outcomes (step 3). Such a typology is in line with perhaps the most commonly used critical realist model – Archer's morphogenetic model (Archer 1995, p. 91):

every morphogenetic cycle distinguishes three broad analytical phases consisting of (a) a given structure (a complex set of relations between parts), which conditions but does not determine (b), social interaction. Here, (b) also arises in part from action orientations unconditioned by social organization but emanating from current agents, and in turn leads to (c), structural elaboration or modification—that is, to a change in the relations between parts where morphogenesis rather than morphostasis ensued. (from Mutch, 2010, p.510).

The so-called morphogenetic model is described by Carter and New (2004) as probably the major development in realist qualitative empirical research. The model reflects the fundamental critical realist assumptions:

(i) structure necessarily pre-dates the action(s) leading to its reproduction or transformation.

(ii) structural elaboration necessarily post-dates the action sequences which gave rise to it. (Archer, 1995, p.15)

The model proposes that ensuing structural elaboration can be either morphogentic (structural change) or morphostasis (structural reproduction). The model provides a useful representation of the interaction of structure and agency for social analysis, however, as Mutch (2010) suggests there is no specific recognition of the role that technology plays in the model. He attempts to address this short-coming in his article where he specifically examines the interplay between structure, agency and technology in the design and usage of data-warehousing systems. He sees structures (for example "position-practices") often being inscribed by design practices in to the software or hardware – "ICT inscribes important aspects of such position practices into material forms that make up the context for agents' conduct" (p. 512). ICT can often prove to be an ally in organizational politics as management enforces desired behaviour through technology implementations and characteristics. For example often enterprise wide ERP systems, with inbuilt common practice process models, are implemented within organizational settings specifically to force radical change. Such ERP systems have prescribed roles and practices inbuilt or embedded in to the software that significantly restrict and guide agency action (see Volkoff et al, 2007).

Similarly, Information Technologies are also presented as mediating the effects that structure have on agents actions, with this mediation open to some flexibility in that software is often open to early amendment but "those choices, once made, commit particular groups of users to something that in practical terms is given" (p. 514). The interpretive flexibility possible in adopting and using software (perhaps less so for hardware) constrains and enables future agency actions. The interactions between structure, agent and technology is complex and as Mutch (2010) describes is very much dependent on the technology being implemented and the context within which it operates.

Mutch (2010) presents the morphogenetic model as a powerful tool for examining the interactions between technology and organizations and proposes that "Three gains are seen to accrue from this approach: greater clarity about the material properties of technology, links to broader structural conditions arising from the conceptualization of the relationship between agency and structure, and the potential to explore the importance of reflexivity in contemporary organizations, especially in conditions of the widespread use of information and communication technology" (p. 507). In terms of the Danermarker model discussed above Archer's morphogenetic model can assist with the important "analytical resolution" required in stage 2 and beyond.

For the critical realist social systems depend on the relations between and within a plurality of structures, such relations having their own independent causal properties. The resulting system founded on the various relations has emergent properties which may affect agents acting within the system. The critical realist approach to structure is in marked contrast to Giddens' conception (Giddens 1979) which suggests that structure cannot be separated from agency. Archer (1995) discusses a number of issues related to Giddens' representation of structure. One issue concerns Giddens' perception of structure as virtual, only becoming real on their instantiation – Archer argues that this necessarily requires that social theory concentrate on social 'practice'. Such concentration leads to what Archer terms as the over-active agent in that it ignores the possibility that agents may have a role to play in the elaboration of structures purely through their existence as part of a collective group; under Giddens' Structuration Theory this passive role of the non-doing agent cannot be reflected. For Archer actors (non-doing agents) and (active) agents are different things and should not be 'elided' or combined as provided for in structuration theory.

Archer also argues that Structuration Theory does not allow for the separate investigation of the emergent and irreducible properties of structures and agents. In particular the collapsing of structure into agency negates the investigation of their interplay over time - how pre-existing structure may constrain action and how action reproduces or transforms existing structures. Critical realism argues for the consideration of both structure and agency and, specifically, brings time dependency into account. The central argument is that 'structure and agency can only be linked by examining the interplay between them over time, and that without the proper incorporation of time the problem of structure and agency can never be satisfactorily resolved' (Archer, 1995, p. 65). It is interesting to compare Archer's and Giddens' conception of structure and agency and their interplay (for example King (2010)) – the analysis illuminating both approaches.

The relatively simple morphogenetic model is quite powerful in that it reflects many of the underlying critical realist assumptions such as structure pre-dating agency action, the importance of time in social analysis, and the need for an analytical separation of structure and agency in order to understand their effects. The model depends heavily on the critical realist belief that it is incorrect to suggest that agents create social systems – for the critical realist social systems are already made in that the ensemble of structures, practices and conventions precede agents' actions. In other words the critical realist emphasizes ontology rather epistemology. Facts are not only derivable via our senses there is more! Archer (1995) equates a structural perspective with a macro or collectivist perspective and an agency perspective with a micro or individualist perspective. In social situations structure is assumed to precede action in that agents either reproduce or transform existing structures.

CONCLUSION

As Miller and Tsang (2011) suggest the methodological implications of critical realism remain sketchy. The creative dependence on abduction as its primary method of enquiry is challenging. How can the researcher/s ensure that the range of explanatory theories from which to postulate underlying causal structures and mechanisms is sufficiently robust to address potential criticism? Researchers need to be cognoscente of a suitable range of theories to encourage reviewer confidence in derived explanations. This is a challenging task for any researcher given the commitment required to appreciate any single theory in depth.

As Kapyla and Mikkola (2010) argue research adopting such a focus on abduction needs to be careful that it does not reinforce existing conservative examination: "…it is essential to notice that the cycle of scientific discovery is culturally-laden from the very start since we inevitably use prior, socially produced and distributed knowledge and theory-laden concepts in the formation of the abductive existential hypothesis that is meant to explain an event or phenomenon. As such, the abductive mode of inference is incapable of escaping the condition of epistemological relativism" (p. 20). They quote Patomäki (2002 p. 148) who suggests that frameworks that over-emphasize the importance of ontology may bring along, even unintentionally and by accident, conservative elements, 'the authority of dominant', to the scientific community. The pluralism required of the critical realist study is difficult for the researcher and perhaps suggests the need for experienced research teams, particularly as support for those new researchers who may not have the necessary pluralist background.

Similarly, the requirement to seek out the "best" explanation for underlying mechanisms and structures suggests a need for multiple data sources. Often it is only by interviewing the most senior people that one can hope to understand the deeper reasons and causes behind organizational happenings. The critical realist focus on explanation requires that data sources be from as wide a range of concerned parties as possible often to the most senior level (see for example Dobson 2003).

The adoption of critical realism as underlabourer for research has ongoing implications that researchers need to be clear about. Prospective adopters need to appreciate how the nature of what exists fundamentally affects the way we study it. Reality is complex and often requires complex tools and techniques. The solid foundation and the integrated nature of critical realist philosophical arguments can help to "clear the ground a little" and bypass many of the pitfalls along the research journey. However as Mutch (2010) argues this focus on philosophical issues and ontology, whilst necessary and of continuing importance, must not result in researchers getting "stuck" at the level of ontological abstraction and subsequently neglect practical and methodological development. Bhaskar proposes that philosophy

plays an important and integral role in research, its continued use conditional on its practical success, yet critical realist development has traditionally been weak on methodological development. More examples of practical usage need to be forthcoming to ensure that the approach is recognized for its practical contribution.

Researchers need also to be aware of and address criticisms of the approach. As Reed (2005b) suggests there is "an undoubted risk that CR-based explanation will overemphasize structure at the expense of agency because it gives so much explanatory weight to the manifold way in which social structures shape and constrain the opportunities for action. But this risk is very considerably reduced as long as the creative interplay between structure and agency over time and place is kept at the very centre of organizational research and analysis". The adoption of Archer's morphogenetic model can help to ensure this focus and as such is an important tool (although even Archer (2003) builds on the morphogenetic model to more fully reflect agent's reflexivity).

As Al-Amoudi and Willmott (2011) suggest, critical realist studies need to more fully reflect the fact that critical realists do not have unmediated access to reality; they need to more fully reflect the epistemological relativism that they espouse by, for example, placing their arguments more fully within a socio-historical context. They make the point that the judgemental rationality required of the critical realist when assessing rival retroductive explanations requires a recognition that "the criteria employed for preferring one explanation rather than another is, at least in part, dependent on the historico-cultural community in which debates about competing claims are staged" (p. 30). Perhaps critical realist examination needs to moderate its claims for superiority and genuinely seek the accommodation of alternative positions more completely in its analysis. Reality is complex and its analysis is, unfortunately perhaps, necessarily the same – it is a difficult path to follow and can be open to significant criticism precisely because of the complexity it is aiming to represent.

REFERENCES

Al-Amoudi, I., & Willmott, H. (2011). Where constructionism and critical realism converge: Interrogating the domain of epistemological relativism. *Organization Studies*, *32*(1), 27–46. doi:10.1177/0170840610394293

Archer, M. (1995). *Realist social theory: The morphogenetic approach*. Cambridge, UK: Cambridge University Press. doi:10.1017/CBO9780511557675

Archer, M. (2003). *Structure, agency and the internal conversation*. Cambridge, UK: Cambridge University Press.

Avgerou, C. (2001). The significance of context in information systems and organizational change. *Information Systems Journal*, *11*(1), 43–63. doi:10.1046/j.1365-2575.2001.00095.x

Bhaskar, R. (1978). *A realist theory of science*. Sussex, UK: Harvester Press.

Bhaskar, R. (1979). *The possibility of naturalism*. Harvester Wheatsheaf, Hemel Hempstead.

Bhaskar, R., & Danermark, B. (2006). Metatheory, interdisciplinarity and disability research: A critical realist perspective. *Scandinavian Journal of Disability Research*, *8*(4), 278–297. doi:10.1080/15017410600914329

Blaikie, N. (1993). *Approaches to social enquiry*. Cambridge, UK: Polity Press.

Bygstad, B. (2010). Generative mechanisms for innovation in information infrastructures. *Information and Organization*, *20*, 156–168. doi:10.1016/j.infoandorg.2010.07.001

Carlsson, S. A. (2003). Advancing information systems evaluation (research): a critical realist approach. *Electronic Journal of Information Systems Evaluation*, *6*(2), 11–20.

Carter, B., & New, C. (Eds.). (2004). *Making realism work: Realist social theory and empirical research (critical realism: interventions)*. Oxfordshire, UK: Routledge.

Checkland, P. (1981). *Systems thinking, systems practice*. Chichester, UK: Wiley.

Checkland, P. (1983). OR and the systems movement - Mappings and conflicts. *The Journal of the Operational Research Society*, *34*(8), 661–675.

Collier, A. (1994). *Critical realism: An introduction to the philosophy of Roy Bhaskar*. London, UK: Verso.

Craib, I. (1992). *Modern social theory: From Parsons to Habermas*. Hertfordshire, UK: Harvester Wheatsheaf.

Danermark, B., Ekström, M., Jakobsen, L., & Karlsson, J. (2002). *Explaining society: Critical realism in the social sciences*. London, UK: Routledge.

Dobson, P. (2001). The philosophy of critical realism - An opportunity for Information Systems research. *Information Systems Frontiers*, (July): 2001.

Dobson, P. (2003). BPR versus outsourcing – Critical perspectives. *Journal of Systemic Practice and Action Research*, *16*(3), 225–233. doi:10.1023/A:1023863906650

Dobson, P., Myles, J., & Jackson, P. (2007). Making the case for critical realism: Examining the implementation of automated performance management systems. *Information Resources Management Journal*, *20*(2), 138–152. doi:10.4018/irmj.2007040109

Easton, G. (2010). Critical realism in case study research. *Industrial Marketing Management, 39*, 118–128. doi:10.1016/j.indmarman.2008.06.004

Fleetwood, S. (2005). Ontology in organization and management studies: A critical realist perspective. *Organization, 12*, 197-222.

Giddens, A. (1979). *Central problems in social theory: Action, structure and contradiction in social analysis*. London, UK: Macmillan.

Gramsci, A. (1971). *Prison notebooks*. London: Lawrence & Wishart.

Hedström, P., & Swedberg, R. (1998). *Social mechanisms: An analytical approach to social theory*. Cambridge, UK: Cambridge University Press. doi:10.1017/CBO9780511663901

Jones, M. R., & Karsten, H. (2008). Giddens's structuration theory and Information Systems Research. *Management Information Systems Quarterly, 32*(1).

King, A. (2010). The odd couple: Margaret Archer, Anthony Giddens and British social theory. *The British Journal of Sociology, 61*(Suppl 1), 253–260. doi:10.1111/j.1468-4446.2009.01288.x

Kljajic, M., & Farr, J. (2008). The role of systems engineering in the development of Information Systems. *International Journal of Information Technologies and Systems Approach, 1*(1), 49–61. doi:10.4018/jitsa.2008010104

Knights, D. (1992). Changing space: the disruptive impact of a new epistemological location for the study of management. *Academy of Management Review, 17*, 514–536.

Lawson, T. (1997). *Economics and reality*. London, UK: Routledge.

Lawson, T. (2003). Theorizing ontology. *Feminist Economics, 9*(1), 161–169. doi:10.1080/1354570032000063038

Locke, J. (1894). *An essay concerning human understanding* (Fraser, A. C., Ed.). *Vol. 1*). Oxford, UK: Clarendon.

Kapyla, J., & Mikkola, H. (2010). A critical look at critical realism: Some observations on the problems of the metatheory. *World Political Science Review, 6*(1), 1–37. doi:10.2202/1935-6226.1088

Miller, K., & Tsang, E. (2011). Testing management theories: Critical realist philosophy and research methods. *Strategic Management Journal, 32*(2), 139–158. doi:10.1002/smj.868

Mingers, J. (2000). The contribution of critical realism as an underpinning philosophy for OR/MS and systems. *The Journal of the Operational Research Society, 51*(111), 1256–1270.

Mingers, J. (2001). Combining IS research methods: Towards a pluralist methodology. *Information Systems Research, 12*(3), 240–259. doi:10.1287/isre.12.3.240.9709

Mingers, J. (2011a). *Explanatory mechanisms: The contribution of critical realism and systems thinking/cybernetics*. Working paper, Kent Business School. Retrieved from http:// kar.kent.ac.uk/ 26306/

Mingers, J. (2011b). *The contribution of systemic thought to critical realism*. Working paper, Kent Business School. Retrieved from http:// kar.kent.ac.uk/ 26306/

Morén, S., & Blom, B. (2003). Explaining human change - On generative mechanisms in social work practice. *Journal of Critical Realism, 2*(1), 37–60.

Morton, P. (2006). Using critical realism to explain strategic information systems planning. *Journal of Information Technology Theory and Application, 8*(1), 1–20.

Mutch, A. (1999). Critical realism, managers and information. *British Journal of Management, 10*, 323–333. doi:10.1111/1467-8551.00142

Mutch, A. (2010). Technology, organization, and structure—A morphogenetic approach. *Organization Science*, *21*(2), 507–520. doi:10.1287/orsc.1090.0441

Orlikowski, W. J., & Barley, S. R. (2001). Technology and institutions: What can research on information technology and research on organizations learn from each other? *Management Information Systems Quarterly*, *25*(2), 145–165. doi:10.2307/3250927

Orlikowski, W. J., & Baroudi, J. J. (1991). Studying information technology in organizations: research approaches and assumptions. *Information Systems Research*, *2*(1), 1–28. doi:10.1287/isre.2.1.1

Outhwaite, W. (1987). *New philosophies of social science: realism, hermeneutics, and critical theory*. New York, NY: St. Martin's Press.

Patomäki, H. (2002). *After international relations: critical realism and the (re)construction of world politics*. London, UK: Routledge.

Pawson, R. (2000). Middle-range realism. *European Journal of Sociology*, *41*(02), 283–325. doi:10.1017/S0003975600007050

Pawson, R., & Tilley, N. (2007). *Realistic evaluation*. London, UK: Sage Publications.

Peirce, C. (1931-1958). *Collected papers of Charles Sanders Peirce* (8 Volumes). Cambridge, MA: Harvard University Press.

Raduescu, C., & Vessey, I. (2008). *Causality in critical realist research: An analysis of three explanatory frameworks*. Annual Conference of International Association for Critical Realism, London, United Kingdom, 1st January 2008-31st December 2008

Reed, M. (2005a). Doing the loco-motion: Response to Contu and Willmott's commentary on 'The realist turn in organization and management studies'. *Journal of Management Studies*, *42*(8), 1663–1673. doi:10.1111/j.1467-6486.2005.00561.x

Reed, M. (2005b). Reflections on the realist turn in organization and management studies. *Journal of Management Studies*, *42*(8), 1621–1644. doi:10.1111/j.1467-6486.2005.00559.x

Reed, M. (2009). Critical Realism: Philosophy, method or philosophy in search of a method. In Buchanan, D., & Bryman, A. (Eds.), *The Sage handbook of organizational research methods* (pp. 430–448). Sage Publications.

Rose, J. (2000). *Information systems development as action research - Soft systems methodology and structuration theory*. PhD thesis, Management School, Lancaster University, England.

Sayer, A. (2000). *Realism and social science*. Sage.

Searle, J. R. (1995). *The construction of social reality*. New York, NY: Free Press.

Smith, M. (2006). Overcoming theory-practice inconsistencies: Critical realism and Information Systems research. *Information and Organization*, *16*(3), 191–211. doi:10.1016/j.infoandorg.2005.10.003

Smith, M. (2008). Testable theory development for small-N studies: Critical realism and middle-range theory. *CONF-IRM 2008 Proceedings*.

Smith, M. L. (2010). Testable theory development for small-n studies: Critical realism and middle-range theory. *International Journal of Information Technologies and Systems Approach*, *3*(1), 41–56. doi:10.4018/jitsa.2010100203

Stones, R. (1996). *Sociological reasoning: Towards a past-modern sociology*. MacMillan.

Strong, D. M., & Volkoff, O. (2010). Understanding organization–enterprise system fit: A path to theorizing the Information Technology artifact. *Management Information Systems Quarterly*, *34*(4), 731–756.

Volkoff, O., Strong, D., & Elmes, M. (2007). Technological embeddedness and organizational change. *Organization Science*, 18(5), 832–848. doi:10.1287/orsc.1070.0288

Wad, P. (2001). *Critical realism and comparative sociology.* IACR conference, Roskilde University, August, 2001.

Wuisman, J. (2005). The logic of scientific discovery in critical realist social scientific research. *Journal of Critical Realism*, 4(2), 366–394. doi:10.1163/157251305774356586

KEY TERM AND DEFINITION

Critical Realism: A relatively new philosophical approach and its implications are still under review. A good glossary of some of the basic critical realist terms is available at www.raggedclaws.com.

Chapter 5
Practice vs. Possession:
Epistemological Implications on the Nature of Organizational Knowledge and Cognition

Lucio Biggiero
L'Aquila University, Italy

ABSTRACT

Organizational knowledge is at the center of the debate focused on the nature of knowledge, where the perspective of knowledge as possession opposes the perspective of knowledge as practice. These two views are rooted in the radical versions of realist and constructivist epistemology, respectively, according to which knowledge is an object or a practice. Far from being a Byzantine dispute, the adoption of one or the other has relevant and concrete consequences for the design and management of IS/IT, because as such, the two paradigms result incommensurable in both theoretical and methodological aspects. However, from a moderate and middle-ground version the following fruitful implications would stem: 1) the juxtaposition would dissolve, and a dual nature of knowledge as object and practice would emerge; 2) the epistemology of pragmatism would be able to account for all the concepts and methods employed by the two fronts, thus terminating a sterile "paradigm war"; 3) the theory of autopoiesis would become irrelevant and eventually even misleading; 4) standard scientific methodologies and simulation models would be acknowledged as useful and common tools for progressive confrontations among the supporters of both the paradigms; 5) the development of IS/IT studies and the design of knowledge management systems would substantially benefit.

DOI: 10.4018/978-1-4666-0179-6.ch005

1. INTRODUCTION

The classic view on knowledge grounds on the research program of artificial intelligence (Minsky, 1987; March & Simon, 1958; McCorduck, 1979; Newell & Simon, 1972; Simon, 1969, 1977, 1997), and dominates the scientific landscape still now. Accordingly, knowledge is a set of information, which can, more or less hardly, be stored and transferred between people and organizations. Intelligence and knowledge are obtained through symbols manipulation and basically coincide with computation. This view started with the foundation of artificial intelligence, and the shift of some developments from the strong to the weak program – that is, from the central to the distributed processing – does not change the essence very much. Accordingly, individuals and organizations are information processors, and there is no any fundamental distinction between data, information and knowledge, if not that they can be human-embodied, when possessed by people, or machine-embodied, when stored as datasets or entrapped in the meaning or usability of goods. Some types of knowledge - namely, the tacit forms - are eventually hardly transferable, because its codification consumes too many resources, so that it is transferred more effectively by imitation and cooperation. However, in this classic view it is argued that this difference between tacit and explicit knowledge is based on economic convenience (Amin & Cohendet, 2004; Cowan, 2001; Cowan *et al.*, 2000; Cowan & Foray, 1997), and not on some ontological distinctions. Within and between organizations, all these forms of knowledge are produced and transferred along with data and information, which are supposed to be the raw, sensory-shaped, and not-yet interpreted forms of knowledge[1]. In this standard perspective, cognition refers to the ability to treat information eventually (but not necessarily) through symbols. A cognitive system can be an information processor, whose objects could be knowledge and information, entities separable from its creators and transferable between the users. This classic view is still the far dominant one, and can be easily recognized – in an explicit or implicit expression – in most papers dealing with IS/IT, knowledge management systems (KMS), as well as in almost all the fields of organization and management science.

From the eighties and in various ways many scholars (Brown & Duguid, 1991, 1998, 2000; Cook & Brown, 1999; Lave, 1988; Lave & Wenger, 1992; Maturana & Varela, 1980, 1987; Mingers, 1995; Orlikowski, 2002; Tsoukas, 1996, 2005; Varela, 1979, 1992; Varela *et al.*, 1991; von Foerster, 1982; von Glasersfeld, 1995; von Krogh, Roos & Slocum, 1996; von Krogh, Roos & Kline 1998; Weick, 1969, 1995; Wenger, 1998; Winograd & Flores, 1986; Yolles, 2006; Zeleny, 2000, 2005) challenged that view by arguing that knowledge has a radically different nature with respect to data and information. Accordingly, knowledge tout-court (and not only its tacit forms) cannot be considered as a storable or transferable object, and eventually, it is not considered as an object at all, and cannot be separated from its creators, i.e., human beings. In fact, it is argued that machines can process information but not knowledge, which is produced by humans through interactions during their practices. In this view, cognition, at least in its highest sense, signifies the ability to do something, and knowledge has an unavoidable tacit dimension, eventually occurring in combination with the explicit dimension. Moreover, for practices that are performed socially, individual knowledge cannot be separated from its collective nature.

These two perspectives have been presented as an epistemology of possession vs. an epistemology of practice, respectively (Cook & Brown, 1999). According to the former, databases, routines, codebooks, and books are all forms of knowledge, and the efficiency of organizations depends to some extent on just the size, appropriateness, and management of organizational knowledge. In the most "enlightened" (recent) approaches belonging to this perspective, a great emphasis is placed on the relationships between the technical and human user's requirements. According to the other epistemology, knowledge resides in the way people concretely and collectively produce their outcomes. In this sense, databases, routines, codebooks, and books are just devices supporting the collective practices. Actually, non-codified routines could be assimilated to practices, and hence, can be categorized as knowledge. To reject any form of reification of social life, the epistemology of practice suggests a perspective shifting: from knowledge to knowing, and from organization to organizing (Chia 2003; Czarniawska, 1997, 2008; Orlikowski, 2002).

Partisans of the two epistemologies seem to consider this as a radical juxtaposition (Amin & Cohendet, 2004). Economists, engineers, theorists of distributed artificial intelligence and simulation modeling, and traditional scholars in operations or information systems management and in the various branches of natural sciences adhere mostly to the epistemology of possession. On the opposite side, the landscape of constructivism is made by two main types of social scientists: those who follow social constructivism, post-modernism, ethnography or anyway non-computational or non-quantitative approaches, and those who adopt a systems science perspective applied to social systems, as are some branches of operational research and cybernetics. The theorists of autopoiesis and a significant part of scholars in IS/IT and KMS are in this second group. There are two main reasons that push and pool these apparently very different types of social scientists into the same radical constructivist epistemology.

The first one is related to the emphasis on the tout-court identification of autopoietic systems with the living systems and vice versa. If living means acting, and if acting requires knowing - and vice versa knowing requires acting - then knowing means (refers to or even dissolves into) practice. Knowledge could not be possessed – or at least manifested – else than in action and through its

concrete outcomes. These latter appear as the trivialization and reification of the act of knowing, but should be not confused with it. The second reason is anti-representationism, which brings constructivism to its extreme consequences. In fact - it is argued that - if reality is constructed by the mind, then it is not an object independent of it (von Glasersfeld, 1995; Watzlawick, 1984; Weick, 1995, 2000). Consequently, knowledge, which is clearly a human construction, cannot be out-there as well. These two origins lead to a definition of knowledge, which is de-objectified and shifted to the activity of knowing, and distinguished from data and information (Yolles, 2006; Zeleny, 2000, 2005). So far, the two epistemologies of practice and possession seem to be totally juxtaposed and irreconcilable, and they lead to as well irreconcilable alternative views of knowledge, and consequently of organizational knowledge (Yolles, 2006).

This paper challenges such a juxtaposition and irreconcilability by raising and dealing with the following research questions:

- **RQ1:** could knowledge be not a monist but rather a dualist phenomenon, which includes both a practice and a possession nature? In other words, mimicking what holds in fundamental physics when considering light as both quanta and a wave, could we say that knowledge is practice *and* possession instead of practice or possession?

- **RQ2:** could the referred epistemologies of realism and constructivism be both wrong? In other words, could their irreconcilability be a secondary problem respect to the fact that, especially in its radical versions, they are both false?

- **RQ3:** is there any other appropriate epistemology, free from the failures and constraints affecting those two, and able to explain the dual nature of knowledge?

In this contribution a positive answer to all of these questions will be given, and it is argued that by taking both the two epistemologies outside their radical versions, they appear not so strongly juxtaposed. There are three main arguments. First, the true difference between knowledge and information should be considered in its different logical types and in the causal relationships occurring between its constitutive parts. Second, the moderate versions of the two contending paradigms can be brought together by the pragmatist epistemology. Third, in order to consider organizations as partially self-organizing cognitive systems, the autopoiesis theory is superfluous. In fact, second-order cybernetics - with its derivation in automata studies, complexity theory, artificial life, social network analysis, and researches in organizational cognition and learning - offers all the necessary concepts. Conversely, while nothing substantial is added to this aim, autopoiesis theory introduces quite disputable and ambiguous concepts, which have been seldom (if ever) submitted to empirical tests[2]. Consequently, autopoiesis theory is irrelevant and even misleading for advancements in organization (and social) science. Lastly, once acknowledged the dual nature of knowledge, scientific research on organizational knowledge and learning would be enriched and swiftly improved, and scientific research methodologies, and in particular also agent-based simulation modeling, would definitely be legitimized.

The paper proceeds by first summarizing the realist and the radical constructivist epistemologies, and then by highlighting their rationale for viewing knowledge as possession and practice, respectively. Then in Section three it will be argued that the abandonment of the radical versions of both paradigms would approach them reciprocally and would avoid some of their evident fallacies and limitations. In the next Section, the pragmatist epistemology is outlined, and its ability to support and include adequately the characteristics of the moderate versions of both realism and constructivism is pointed out. This epistemological

perspective dissolves the "paradigm war", which is still crossing either management and organization studies or sociology and economics. Further, in Section five it is showed how the pragmatist epistemology is philosophically progressive, especially into the field of IS/IT and KMS. Indeed, while at first sight (and perhaps in particular for engineers or technologists) this debate might appear nearly Byzantine or irrelevant, at a closer sight its relevance becomes more evident.

In fact, besides the obvious fact that into a field where knowledge, information and data are key concepts there shouldn't be any ambiguity or uncertainty concerning what precisely they mean, only from a deep understanding can be conceived clear ideas about what and how knowledge and information can be effectively stored, managed and transferred. And the implications for the design of KMS can be easily intuited. If constructivists were right, then KMS would result in just an activity into the field of human resource management, because knowledge would be strictly related to practices and human interactions. Knowledge transfer would be meaningless without them, and so nobody had to worry for exchanging patents, because this wouldn't imply any knowledge exchange if not associated with the mobility or interactions of the corresponding competent people. As well, the acquisition of entire databases would have nothing to do with knowledge, and the concept itself of knowledge base would be meaningless or coincide with that of competence. Nearly the whole current language and theorization about the knowledge-based society, economy, etc. would be reformulated. And so on.

Finally, if knowledge could acquire a meaning only through human interactions and if it is interpretable when contextualized and through observer-dependent descriptions, then many of the standard scientific methodologies would be inapplicable, and science would resolve in narrating single facts. Even more, the methodology of simulation modeling would be completely meaningless, because the reduction of the complexity of human interactions to computational algorithms would be far from any minimum capacity of representation. (Not to mention that one of the key-points of radical constructivism is just anti-representationism.) Therefore, it seems clear that this dispute between the classic and the new view is full of implications for both academics and practitioners.

2. THE DUAL NATURE OF KNOWLEDGE AS META-INFORMATION AND PURPOSEFUL PRACTICE

According to radical constructivism, knowledge and information are two completely different entities (Zeleny; 2000, 2005). What distinguishes organizations from other types of cognitive systems (Biggiero, 2009), like expert systems, classifier systems, and KMS, is that cognitive systems can only be information processors, while organizations are also knowledge creators (Nonaka & Nishiguchi, 2001; Nonaka & Takeuchi, 1995; Nonaka *et al.*, 1998, 2006; Tsoukas, 1996, 2005; Tsoukas & Vladimirou, 2001; von Krogh *et al.*, 1996, 1998; Yolles, 2006). KMS deal essentially with people and not with devices to store, retrieve, and transfer information. Artificial intelligence would have nothing to do with "true" intelligence, as artificial life with "true" life, and a sharp (qualitative) distinction between data, information, and knowledge is supposed to hold: "although information is an enhanced form of data, knowledge is not an enhanced form of information" (Zeleny, 2005: 3). "Knowledge is not a thing to be possessed, like information or money, but a process to be learned, mastered, and carried out, like baking and milking. One can have information, one cannot have knowledge, one only knows" (2005: 4). Knowledge can necessarily be merely tacit, human-embodied, and practice-related, because any quantity of information does not produce knowledge; for instance, a person with a good

memory of cookbooks may not necessarily be a great chef. Thus, explicit (or codified) knowledge could sound as an oxymoron.

This view evidently is in sharp contrast with both the common sense and standard computer science. People believe in learning and acquiring knowledge, and KMS are supposed to store and transfer knowledge. In this classical view there are no clear and qualitative differences between knowledge and information, the former being just a thematic aggregation of the latter, perfectly (albeit eventually very costly) codifiable and transferable. This approach is so diffused and standard in both social and natural sciences as well as in daily life that is somehow superfluous listing references. It can be just reminded that this view has been strongly reinforced by the birth and development of the so-called strong program of artificial intelligence (Casti, 1989; Guttenplan, 1994; Haugeland, 1981; Waldrop, 1987), and through some of its most famous theorists introduced into social sciences (Cyert & March, 1963; March & Simon, 1958; Simon, 1969, 1977, 1997). Accordingly, all of us possess a certain amount of data, information and knowledge, archived in our brain or in some physical support. The question of our awareness of possessing them and of our ability to explicit or transfer them is retained secondary and mostly a psychological, or technical one, or anyway depending on our cognitive capability. Questions that, though interesting, do not affect the central issue of viewing knowledge as somehow similar to information and data, as an object all of us possess to some extent.

These two seemingly irreconcilable views can indeed be reconciled if we acknowledge a dual nature of knowledge by making a distinction between knowledge as a network of causal relationships and as the ability (or disposition) to employ such knowledge in practice. Roughly speaking, the former refers to knowledge as know-what and know-why, while the latter signifies knowledge as know-how and, within collective action, as know-who (possess some information or knowledge). To the extent that practice involves abilities (actions) that are hard or impossible to be explicated or codified into formal descriptions and causal relationships, tacit knowledge (and thus, know-how) becomes crucial for successful action and effective knowledge. In this perspective, knowledge has a dual nature: a reified network of causal relationships and people's practices enacted everyday and over time.

Knowledge as (Reified) Meta-Information

To explain the world, or at least to guide purposeful and successful action (practice), knowledge should be based on causal relationships about real phenomena, which assume the form of "what … if …" links between information (nodes). Leaving aside the process of discovery of such relationships, their fixation constitutes the reified form of knowledge as a pattern of "what … if …" links. This property makes knowledge a different entity respect to information. In this form knowledge might be storable and transferable as well as information. According to graph theory (Bollobas, 1985; Dorogovtsev & Mendes, 2003; Wasserman & Faust, 1994), a network is a set of connected nodes, and hence, knowledge is a set of causally connected information. Consequently, knowledge is on a superior logical type (Bateson, 1972; Roach & Bednar, 1997) with respect to information.

However, the question still remains on how many properties are maintained while moving from the level of single elements up to the level of the class of those elements. In fact, while moving from one type to the superior logical type, from an ontological point of view we change object. In principle this different object could have completely different properties, whose individuation is "simply" an empirical issue. In this sense, it has to be empirically proved that knowledge is not an object, as there are no logical reasons why knowledge is not an object, even though it is not

information. Hence, with respect to Zeleny's view, we have only demonstrated that: 1) knowledge is indeed a different entity than information but the ontological difference is based on a different logical type; and 2) in principle it could be (also) an object. Therefore, know-what and know-why are compatible with an epistemology of possession, and can be stored and moved as objects. In this sense artificial intelligence, artificial life, artificial societies, and the standard approaches to information and communication technologies are right: knowledge is (also) an object. Here we argue that, when separated from the act of its creation – and especially when that act occurs through human interactions - knowledge is *also* an object[3].

Knowledge as an Emergent Property of Information Networks

A network is more than a set, because its nodes must be connected; and, in fact, through the logical operator of causality, knowledge emerges from a network of information. Consequently, knowledge is an emergent property of information, a meta-information characterized by a logical pattern. There is a subtle but fundamental difference between this and the standard view of knowledge—although a pattern of something is a set of something, the vice versa of this does not necessarily hold. A set of information can be just a bundle of information gathered by some criterion of pertinence. Conversely, a pattern implies connections beyond pertinence, which in the case of knowledge are logical implications ("if …, then …").

A science textbook is just a collection of "what … if …" relationships that need to be acknowledged and interpreted to make sense, and to be transformed into actions. However, these requirements hold for information too, and thus, for the possibility of living itself. Moreover, nothing prevents to consider "what … if …" relationships as beliefs rather than certainties or objective states of reality. As will be argued in Section four, pragmatist epistemology (Hack & Lane, 2006; Putnam,

1995; Rorty, 1982) is perfectly compatible with a view of cognition as the activity of building "what … if …" relationships and experiencing (proving) them in achieving the expected outcomes. In its deepest sense, the question is even subtler and broader because, besides scientific sentences, any text is a set of characters linked by an alphabet (or, more generally, a collection of symbols), by words (collection of characters), and by rules (a syntax). That is, not just a set, but a network carrying emergent meanings.

3. TACIT KNOWLEDGE AND COLLECTIVE PRACTICES

A breach into the classical view of knowledge as object has been caused by the acknowledgment that some types of knowledge result hardly or no codifiable or transferable. This is addressed to as the problem of tacit knowledge, which became a shared problem through Nonaka's SECI Model on the knowledge creating company (Nonaka *et al.*, 1998; Nonaka & Takeuchi, 1995). However, while the partisans of knowledge as possession disentangled the two aspects – of tacitness and practice – the others viewed then as two faces of the same coin. This position was then taken by the Japanese School as well (Nonaka & Nishiguchi, 2001; Nonaka *et al.*, 2006), and it joined the constructivists in organization and management science (von Krogh *et al.*, 1996, 1998; Zeleny, 2005; Yolles, 2006), and especially into the IS/IT field (Boland *et al.*, 1994; Magalhães, 2004; Mingers, 1995; Orlikowski, 2002). In this section such a connection is explored, and the positions of constructivists are distinguished between the radicals and the moderate, and further between the biology- and the sociology-based approaches.

A. fundamental aspect of knowledge is its concretization into purposeful and successful actions. When it is too difficult (too resource consuming) or even impossible to exhaust all necessary knowledge into know-what and know-

why, tacit knowledge becomes more important and a critical factor of success. Tacit knowledge gains importance in collective action, when many individuals share the same practices, i.e., they use the same language and adopt similar cognitive patterns for sense-making. This legitimizes the emphasis on individual practices and dispositions, and for collective work led to suggest the concept of epistemic communities (Haas, 1992; Håkanson, 2005).

This is the position shared in various forms by Boland *et al.* (1994), Boland & Tenkasi (1995), Brown & Duguid (1991, 1998, 2000), and Wenger (1998). Tsoukas (1996) argued that the tacit and the explicit are complementary and inseparable forms of knowledge, and that knowledge is a social and emergent phenomenon which comes from the unavoidably distributed and decentralized structure of organizations. Tsoukas (1996) merges the arguments typical of sociology-based constructivism with those typical of biology-based constructivism. For instance, the idea that knowledge acquires determined meanings only within a social context and a specific language has been developed by both streams of literature (Gergen, 1999; Mingers, 1995; Varela *et al.*, 1991; von Krogh *et al.*, 1996, 1998; Weick, 1995; Wenger, 1998; Winograd & Flores, 1986).

Here, we can find two demarcations between constructivists: for the radicals, there is no relationship between information and knowledge, which is purposeful and successful collective practice, and hence, it is forcedly tacit and not an object. For the moderates, a certain objectified and codified form of knowledge is somehow acknowledged, but only in its marginal role. The main aspect is the social and tacit nature expressed through practices. For instance, right after recognizing "knowledge and practice as reciprocally constitutive, …, [Orlikowski suggests] there may be value in a perspective that does not treat these as separate or separable, a perspective that focuses on the knowledgeability of action" (2002: 250). She explicitly refers to both Giddens's (1984) theory of structuration and to Maturana's and Varela's (1987) autopoiesis. However, if the dualist nature of knowledge is not suppressed and if the radical (and most likely ideological) extreme epistemological positions of both the biology- and sociology-based forms of constructivism are cut off, it would be clear that the two perspectives are not so irreducible.

Indeed, like radical biology-based constructivists, radical sociology-based constructivists (Lave, 1988; Lave & Wenger, 1992; Orlikowski, 2002; Weick, 1969, 1995; Wenger, 1998) suppress the reified aspect of knowledge, which is dissolved into practice and transformed into knowing. These scholars argue that: i) everything, especially human action and knowledge creation, is evolving; ii) knowledge and meaning are totally subjective and context-dependent; and iii) complex systems, especially social systems, are substantially unpredictable. Hence, it is denied that there is any objective reality out there (Watzlawick, 1984). Notice that almost always, the adjective "objective" is added to these types of sentences, because it is fundamental for constructivists to demarcate their positions. In fact, once removed, the two epistemologies of possession and practice would become much less incompatible.

Maturana and Varela (1980) radicalized the positions argued previously by von Foerster (1982) and Bateson (1980), who considered that information occurs from (and is triggered by) the ability to perceive distinct entities into the environment. Von Foerster added that this can happen only if there is movement: static systems cannot perceive anything. The eye perceives something because it is always moving, and Maturana and Varela proposed that "all doing is knowing and all knowing is doing." Arguing that knowledge is the coordination of action, Zeleny (2005) recalls just classical pragmatism, and in particular Dewey, to support the idea "that action is internal and integral to knowledge. Action is not some tool for knowledge 'acquisition' or belief 'beholding': action is integral to whatever we claim to know.

The process of knowing helps to constitute what is known: *inquiry is action*. Reciprocally, what is known by the knower is not stored as data and information, independent of the process of knowing: *action is inquiry*" (2005: 25). He underlined the social nature of action, and ultimately the shared knowledge, which can be produced only within the communities of action, because they presumably adopt the same language and make the same or similar sense of the world. Through practices, these communities are supposed to develop similar cognitive patterns, and they could be depicted as epistemic communities.

The emphasis on meanings and interpretations conveys the crucial role played by languages. It can be argued that an action cannot occur without interpretations, as action becomes dependent on languages and on subjective points of view. Thus, there is no single reality, but as many realities as there are interpreters who can produce them, where each interpreter could advance more than one interpretation and change them over time.

4. THE PRAGMATIST VIEW OF COGNITION

Classical pragmatism is a philosophical view that dates back to Peirce, James, and Dewey (Hack & Lane, 2006), and has been, in the last decades, revisited and re-proposed mainly by Putnam (1995), Rorty (1982), and less explicitly but substantially by Laudan (1990, 1996). With the varied philosophical views on pragmatism, articulated in as many varied ways, many have been reduced to relativist positions. On the contrary, in this study the reference is made to classical pragmatism, whose main traits can be briefly depicted as follows.

Realism, which states that a world exists independent of us, is accepted, but its metaphysical version, i.e., the idea that truth exists independently as well, is rejected. This oblique form of realism is proven weak in the modern forms of pragmatism

(Rorty, 1979, 1982, 1991), because many social phenomena and other types of human activity are influenced by simple observations or expectations. Self-fulfilling prophecies and the many forms of expectations, like the well known "Hawthorne effect" in organization theory (Landsberger, 1958), are clear examples of modifications induced by observations on the observed system. Indubitably, the offering of a sound scientific framework to define and face these problems has been one of the main merits of cybernetics (Ashby, 1956; Bateson, 1972), especially of second-order cybernetics (Geyer & van der Zouwen, 1986; von Foerster, 1982; von Glasersfeld, 1995). However, it should be emphasized that this theoretical framework chronologically and logically precedes the theory of autopoiesis. Moreover, constructivism, both in the biology- and sociology-based versions, insists very much on this point, and is useful to clarify another realism-related question on the supposed non-realist nature of reality when it is constructed by the observers, as in the case of social phenomena.

Indeed, social phenomena, at least to a large extent, are constructed by individuals and groups. Hence, constructivists consider that social phenomena are non-independent on its "constructors" and thus, they cannot be investigated with traditional scientific methods like theory-testing empirical research, formal or quantitative analysis. This is an absolute *non-sequitur*. If organizations are made by humans, why could they not be scientifically analyzed? Once they are constructed, they are objects, which can be studied by the well-known methodologies, either by external or internal observers, and nothing prevents it. Apparently, why nobody is skeptical on whether civil engineers can study bridges, tunnels, or buildings, which are man-made as well? Furthermore, in principle artifacts could also be interpreted in many ways, as normally happens in architecture and engineering. Thus, once scientific theories take into account cognitive processes and problems, even the observer–observed interactions can be dealt

with effective methodologies. In short, there is no doubt that organizations and social phenomena are man-made, but at the same time there should be no doubt that they can be studied by standard scientific methodologies as well.

Classical pragmatism also adopts *fallibilism*, which implies the idea of an always-changing, but improving truth and the very Popperian suggestion to challenge the existing theories as the best way to nurture scientific knowledge. Biggiero (1997) maintained that in realism, not only experiments and empirical research are possible and meaningful, but are in fact crucial activities for scientific progress. Another key point is *anti-skepticism*, which means that "complete doubt" is impossible (Peirce, 1958), and that both doubt and belief must be judged (Putnam, 1995: 20-21).

Finally, classical pragmatism is also based on *anti-apriorism*, which refers to the nature and the way we create knowledge. The need for a secure foundation in some forms of primacy of sense data or neurophysiology (like in British empiricism), or in self and subjectivity or mental states (like in idealism) reflects more of human nature than absolute requirements for a sound epistemology. This description of the basic characteristics of pragmatism places it far from relativism and epistemological foundationalism, which Rorty (1979) indicated as the chronic pathology of all other forms of realism. This perspective is even slightly different from that offered by Wicks and Freeman (1998), who pulled their anti-positivism to radical positions, for instance, stating that science is a language game and that all inquiry is fundamentally interpretive or narrative.

5. ORGANIZATIONS ARE *PARTIALLY* SELF-ORGANIZING AND COGNITIVE SYSTEMS

Many social scientists, organization and management scholars, and even operational researchers and engineers into the field of IS/IT encountered the concepts of self-organization and cognitive systems through the theory of autopoiesis. Actually, that theory puts both the issues at the core of its ideas, and for the considerable fascination exerted by that theory in organization science and KMS (Magalhães, 2004; Mingers, 1995; von Krogh *et al.*, 1996, 1998), it is necessary to go deepen into some of its fundamental tenets.

Some of the major traits of this theory can be briefly summarized as follows (Luhmann, 1984, 1986, 1990; Maturana, 1975, 1978, 1981; Maturana & Varela, 1980, 1987; Varela, 1979, 1992; von Foerster, 1982, 1984; von Glasersfeld, 1995): autopoietic systems are fully self-organizing, that is, they obey to a set of inner rules and are not determined by the external environment; they are closed in terms of the connections required to allow their self-production - the textual meaning of the word "autopoiesis"; the network of such connections determines also the identity and the way in which the autopoietic system perceives itself and the external environment. Hence, the cognitive domain of autopoietic systems is given by their inner (self-)organization and distinguishes each one, that is, generates their identity and autonomy. The questions of operational closure and system autonomy and identity are central to the theory of autopoiesis (Mingers, 1995). After an early enthusiasm with respect to the idea that social systems are autopoietic, many criticisms weakened this conviction, with Varela et., al. (1991) himself abandoning it. Currently, the most diffused approach to social systems as autopoietic systems is that advanced by Luhmann (1990), who indeed disembodied social systems from individuals and placed their communication as the constituting matter of social systems. This view is as interesting as it is disputable, but will not be discussed extensively in this paper, whose focus is wondering whether the notion of autopoiesis is necessary for that of self-organization, and whether systems autonomy is a realistic property of social systems.

In this perspective, it is argued that autopoiesis theory is: i) not necessary to show that social systems are self-organizing networks; ii) misleading when suggesting that social systems are operationally closed and autonomous; and iii) superfluous to argue that social systems are cognitive systems. In essence, these criticisms contend that organizations, and more generally social systems are autopoietic systems, and assert that the concept of autopoiesis is confusing and not clarifying what organizations are.

The view of organizations as networks is as old as social network analysis, which dates back to the fifties (among the others, Barnes, 1954, 1969; Bavelas, 1948, 1950; Bott, 1955, 1956, 1957; Cartwright & Zander, 1953), and grounds its roots even earlier in the thirties (Moreno, 1934). Hence, far before the entry of autopoiesis theory with Maturana and Varela's writings at the beginning of the 1970s. The fast and growing development of social network analysis in sociology and organization science occurred parallel and independently during the 1980s and, especially in management science, during the 1990s (Barabasi, 2003; Bornholdt & Schuster, 2003; Csemerly, 2006; Dehmer & Emmert-Streib, 2009; Lewis, 2009; Scott, 1991; Wasserman & Faust, 1994; Watts, 2003, 2004a, 2004b)[4].

One could believe that, if not the view of social systems as networks, at least that of self-organizing systems is a genuinely merit of autopoiesis theory, but it's not so. Ashby's studies of self-organizing systems were already available at the von Foerster's Biological Computer Laboratory in Urbana (ILL), where Maturana and Varela went to work, and where they presumably drew the idea of autopoiesis[5]. Moreover, those studies came from von Neumann's earlier theories on self-reproducing automata, and led to successive research on cellular automata and random Boolean networks (Bollobas, 1985), which became the basis for Kauffman's (1993) NK-models of self-organization in the biological as well as physical and social sciences (Barabasi, 2003; Dorogovtsev

& Mendes, 2003; Kauffman, 1995, 2000; Newman *et al.*, 2006). Thus, to look at organizations and social systems as self-organizing networks, autopoiesis was not necessary at all.

A peculiarity of autopoiesis theory is its distinction of system's organization and structure: the former – kept out of the imprecise definitions given by Varela *et al.* (1974) and "translated" into the formal language of graph theory - means network topology, i.e. the pattern of relationships among nodes; while the latter, as well "translated" into the language of social network analysis refers to node attributes, i.e. the physical or behavioral characteristics of network nodes. Bearing this in mind, the three key-points to define autopiesis are: 1) topological invariance that gives systems identity; 2) the independence of organization from structure, i.e., of topology from node attributes; and 3) the independence and separation of both from the external environment. Now, all these three issues had to be a matter of empirical testing rather than theoretical assumptions alone, as made by Luhmann, Maturana, Varela, and others. Though in this study, the theoretical aspects are dealt only marginally, it's the case to address a bit also the empirical evidence of autopoiesis theory. Therefore, let's wonder what does topology and node attributes really mean in (social) organizations. Clearly, organizations are multiplexes (Monge & Contractor, 2003; Wasserman & Faust, 1994), which means that its nodes (individuals, objects, and machines) can be connected by various types of connections: informative, decisional, kinship, friendship, competence-based, commercial, etc. In other words, organizations are multi-dimensional networks. Node attributes can be age, competence, gender, education level, position, etc., if they refer to people, and many others, if they refer to objects and machines.

Even a minimal experience with concrete organizations could lead one to dispute the real occurrence of all the three key-points previously addressed, because:

1) Most organizations do change its topology quite often in one or many of the multiplex dimensions. Such transformations can be endogenously or exogenously induced. In the former case, they have its rationale in the rules or the learning processes, or more generally, depend on the adjustments and conflicts owing to the individuals' change. Organizations are not static: there are career tracks, strategic or spontaneous changes, employees turn-over, etc. In the latter case, changes are triggered by the need to adapt to environmental perturbations. Topological invariance is all but plausible (Biggiero, 2001a).

2) Node attributes affect topology. For instance, a change of competencies distribution will certainly modify power and informational relationships (topology). Moreover, when nodes are individuals, they are complex systems themselves, and so they co-evolve with their meta-system in a complex interaction. The hypothesis of independence between organization (topology) and structure (node attributes) is definitely not acceptable from an empirical point of view.

3) External environment induces more or less pronounced changes in organization topology, because, for instance, the entry of a new competitor can require the modification of production or distribution processes or competencies, etc. Moreover, if organizations were independent (autonomous) from the external environment, they would not be able to react or anticipate environmental changes and thus, they would risk failing. This is a precept central in any of the text of management. Thus, it is an error to assume that social systems are operationally closed and autonomous.

Another important fact that rejects the hypothesis of system autonomy is "multiple membership" (Biggiero, 2001a). While natural/biological systems are topologically closed in its boundaries – for instance, my arm belongs only to my body – social systems are not, because all organizational members are likely to belong to many organizations at the same time: family, party, union, and many other formal and informal groups. Consequently, their multiple membership allows them to bring something (competence, personality, needs, etc.) into each organization they belong to, which is also produced within other organizations. This implies that organizations are all but operationally closed. In this sense, only the entire mankind can be seen as an organization operationally closed.

This does not mean that organizations are not closed at all, and therefore, signify that they are totally dependent on their environment. Evidently, "each" organization reacts differently to the "same" environmental perturbations. The diversity of reactions that depends on the differences between the organizations and/or perturbations is a matter of research, and the multi-decennial analysis on the determinants of system/environment form might bring contingency theory from the simple views of organizations as open (and essentially technological) systems to partially closed systems. These do not react to any of the same environmental perturbations, and it should be added that, over time, because of its evolution, the same organization is likely to react differently to the same perturbation. Indeed, the interesting questions are just "to what extent a certain (type of) organization is closed and for which type of variable it is more or less closed," "how does closure change over time," etc.

Indeed, the earlier conclusion does not prevent one to wonder and study the determinants of organizational identity and identification processes, and in reality, there is an extant and growing literature on these issues (Albert & Whetten, 1985; Ashforth & Mael, 1996; Hogg & Terry, 2000; Sammarra & Biggiero, 2001). However, they were not simply grounded on to the invariance of network topology or on its independence from structure and environment, and neither considered

something monolithic and permanent. On the contrary, it is a complex matter, where many types of variables interact and co-evolve. In any case, this subject can be effectively studied without the theory of autopoiesis.

So far, we have seen that autopoiesis theory is not necessary to argue that organizations are (self-organizing) networks, and that they are not operationally closed neither autonomous. Now, let's come to the third key-point discussing whether the notion of autopoiesis is strictly necessary at least for viewing organizations as cognitive systems. Its novelty could well reside here. In fact, some developments in the studies on the biology of cognition (Maturana & Varela, 1980; Varela, 1979, 1992; Varela *et al.*, 1991; von Krogh, Roos & Slocum, 1996; von Krogh, Roos & Kline, 1998) and on distributed artificial intelligence (Mingers, 1995; Tsoukas, 1996; Winograd & Flores, 1986) in the second half of last century have re-launched the anti-realist and anti-cognitivist perspective. Actually, the key-argument of connessionism that into the brain there is no any "locus" where the representation of reality resides is not only consistent with constructivism, but even strongly supports it's anti-representationism (Aadne *et al.*, 1996).

Indeed, organizations have long been recognized as cognitive systems (Biggiero, 2009; Carley, 1986, 1989, 1994, 1999), and socio-cognitive variables like trust, identification processes, status, norms, citizenship behaviors, etc. are acknowledged to play very important roles (Gergen, 1999; Tsoukas, 2005; Weick, 1995). There is a huge and growing literature on these issues, which does not seem to benefit in any way from the autopoiesis theory. In fact, according to some interpretations of organizational closure, the focus is on cognitive domain, i.e., each organization has its cognitive domain, which constitutes its space of possibilities, which is given once for all and determines what the organizations can do. It is the filter through which organizations select environmental perturbations that will be recognized, and constraints the working of the organizations. According to autopoiesis theory, since autopoietic systems are cognitive systems, and since they are fully self-organized and invariant, they have also a fixed and self-referential cognition, which Maturana and Varela call cognitive domain. They also add that it is inaccessible from outside the system.

This view is definitely not convincing for two reasons. One is related to the previous criticisms: if organizations do change its topology and structure, for instance, owing to its multiple-membership property, then its cognitive domain is also changed accordingly. The second reason is that a cognitive domain is such a complex entity that nobody can know in advance or theoretically in how many ways it can be instantiated and whether a certain new instantiation is just one of the many possible occurrences into the same cognitive domain or, conversely, it marks the shift to a completely new one. The assumption that cognitive domain is invariant and inaccessible would just lead to the trivial assumption that every closed and invariant system does only what it is capable of doing. Thus, it does not appear that this tautology could improve our knowledge on this subject.

Conversely, with respect to the non-autopoietic-related literature, all these aspects are currently being mixed into theories that look at organizations as socio-cognitive, partially self-organizing networks (Carley, 1999; Monge & Contractor, 2003). These approaches are converging and beneficial from the development of agent-based simulation models, which otherwise would become meaningless if knowledge were considered only a practice spreading out of a self-referential cognition. A methodological tool so powerful for the advancement of all social sciences would be this way totally meaningless. In sum, this section suggests that organizational topology is not invariant, it is influenced (albeit not determined) by its environment and components, and its cognitive domain is not invariant nor completely inaccessible.

6. IMPLICATIONS FOR KNOWLEDGE MANAGEMENT SYSTEMS

As we have seen in Section three, in the pragmatist epistemology knowledge can be complementary viewed as practice and possession. Here, the gains from this perspective of re-conciliation and integration are briefly addressed with a special reference to IS/IT and KMS. In fact, as shown by Mingers (1995) and Magalhães (2004), the field of IS/IT and a significant stream of operations research is, through the theory of autopoiesis, markedly inclined towards radical constructivism. This is partially due to the strict relationships between cybernetics, from which autopoiesis and a certain stream of operations research come from, and artificial intelligence, from which IS/IT and subsequently, KMS come from. The interest is clear: if the theory of autopoiesis proposes a revolutionary and effective approach to cognition and computer science, then it should be brought into IS/IT and subsequently to KMS. Indeed, this interest has been considerably increased by the delusion of expectations roused after early enthusiasms induced by the promises of complete emulation and substitution of human work made between 1960-1980 by the so-called strong program of artificial intelligence (Casti, 1989).

In a similar way, during last 20 years there have been several failures of KMS (Damoradan & Olphert, 2000; Gallupe, 2001; Lyytinen & Robey, 1999; Magalhães, 2004; Tsoukas & Mylonopoulos, 2003): ERP, intranet, and other tools for creating, storing, and sharing knowledge that seldom delivered the expected outcomes. Some scholars attributed the failures to the epistemology underlining those approaches (Tsoukas & Mylonopoulos, 2003, 2004). What often has been hurriedly and roughly addressed as the problems of the human side of KMS actually conceals a complex and rich phenomenology of knowledge creation and transfer. Butler (2003) suggested that only a small portion of knowledge existing in an organization can be codified and transferred through computer-based information systems. In particular, all that are tacit remain as such, and thus, non-codifiable and non-transferable without human-human interactions and interventions. Bansler and Havn (2003) illustrated a case study of a global pharmaceuticals company failing, after two and half years of effort, to promote the sharing of best practices through an intranet-based application. Consistent with a constructivist perspective, others focused on "those processes, practices and policies within organizations through which competing bodies of knowledge become established and new bodies of knowledge are created and legitimized" (Tsoukas & Mylonopoulos, 2004: S4). Yanow (2004) reported that knowledge "possessed" by workers in the operating core of large companies, which is far from its relative top management, is disregarded or neglected, because it is supposed to be too practical and probably not enough "scientific." It is interesting to contrast this narrative with that stated by Ohno (1988) and Taylor (1947) in their theories and recommendations on organization and management. They were living and interacting with shop floor workers for a long time, demonstrating their knowledge on this issue. Since those authors and their approaches were fully and deeply immersed into the epistemology of possession, it is rather doubtful that (right) claims for considering practice-based and peripheral knowledge had to be assumed as a distinctive point of constructivist epistemology.

If radical constructivism was right (Tsoukas & Vladimirou, 2001), then knowledge management would be either meaningless or dissolved into human resource management. As we have seen before, knowledge tout-court would be transferable only through practice and would require common cognitive schemas among exchangers. Interpretivists (Czarniawska, 1997, 2003; Yanow, 1995, 2004) push these arguments even further arguing that organizational knowledge (Yolles, 2006) – and, indeed, the whole organization theory – cannot employ and exploit standard scientific methodologies of (hopefully formal and quantitative) theories submitted to proof and refutation testing. What could be done would be just narratives, more or less supported by case studies. Let say, things occurred this way to the observer's eyes there and that time. Nothing more.

However, when constructivists build their theories, they base them on empirical research, far from confining their findings to episodic cases, and almost always draw generalizations from them. Exactly as empirical science-making suggests, they try to induce general theories from local and concrete cases. Moreover, most of them fully use concepts and languages belonging to the epistemology of possession: for instance, Newell *et al.* (2004) underlined how the effectiveness of ERP depends on the intentions of the corresponding implementation team, and Un and Cuervo-Cazurra (2004) pointed that knowledge creation is enhanced by the degree of heterogeneity and by the organizational members' willingness to share. However, what is more reified and routinized than the procedures defined by an ERP? Every means of standardization is feasible because the corresponding system is not indeterminate, and, recursively, the adoption of routines further reduces the system's indeterminacy.

The same concept was reported by Magalhães (2004) in reconstructing the history of IS/IT approaches: the most rationalist approaches are those related to standard cognitivism, which deny that knowledge is also practice and organizations are complex (partially self-referential and self-organizing) systems. These early approaches that have failed, usually adopt a top-down task-oriented (and not human) implementation. The rich history of IS/IT theories and implementation attempts show that these approaches have proven to be unsatisfactory, and therefore, were progressively enriched by including more and more characteristics of human behavior, adding non-technological variables, and by making more local and flexible processes.

This evolution demonstrates that the asperity of positions and the irreducibility of the two perspectives on organizational knowledge seem to dissolve when moving from the ideological dimension of "paradigm war" to scientific practice. As shown by the action-oriented perspective on organization and information systems (Magalhães, 2004), the two approaches appear far from being incompatible. There is no reason to ground the approach of organizational holism (Magalhães, 2004) or organizational learning (von Krogh & Roos, 1995) on the hypothetical autopoietic properties of social systems. The adoption and integration of concepts from social and organizational psychology as well as from social cognition and evolutionary economics should be considered to be sufficient enough.

7. CONCLUSION

Organizations are dynamic networks of non-cognitive, weakly and highly cognitive agents, like objects, information processors, and individuals who, under more or less specified and intentional rules, share or confront goal and practices, and whose action requires the creation and transfer of data, information, and knowledge (Biggiero, 2009; Carley, 1999; Monge & Contractor, 2003). Organizations are distributed knowledge systems, where individuals' stock of knowledge consists of: a) role-related normative expectations; b) dispositions, which have been formed in the course of past socializations; and c) local knowledge of particular circumstances of time and place (Tsoukas, 1996). These two definitions – that organizations are networks of agents or distributed knowledge systems - are perfectly consistent with one another, even though they have been proposed by partisans of the epistemology of possession and practices, respectively. They just stress one of the two sides of the dualistic nature of knowledge, and both are based on and benefit from the empirical researches and appreciate methodological pluralism. The juxtaposition seems to be more ideological than real, and resides more in the

radical versions of the two epistemologies than in the real practices of their supporters. The former tends to view knowledge as reified, a-historical, de-contextualized, unequivocal, mostly storable, and transferable within and between the organizations, whose behavior is rather predictable and manageable. For the others knowledge is not an object, and it is not separable from unpredictable contextualized human practices, which are not even understandable outside the context, because meanings are contextual too. However, if the logical operator "or" were replaced with the logical operator "and", then both the radical views were wrong, because knowledge would be practice *and* possession. The (only human?) interactive aspect occurs especially into the activity of creation and manifests its consequences in the tacit form. The reified aspect in related to the possibility to store and transfer networks of information under the form of "what...if" structures. The former aspect is an emergent property of interaction processes, while the latter of the information network, which is on a meta-level respect to single (or unrelated, unstructured sets of) information.

Besides being conceptually and epistemologically correct, this new view allows to escape from two alternatives that seem both rather difficult to accept and to confirm in practice. According to one, there would be no qualitative difference between information and knowledge, if not for the difficulty to store and transfer some of its forms. This is indeed what is currently taken for granted by most people. Knowledge would substantially be a bunch of thematic – and more or less consistent - information. Let say, a rather simplistic view. At the opposite extreme, there would be a quite peculiar nature of knowledge, because it would be possible to create it, but then, once created, it would be impossible to store it. Moreover, its transferability would be only limited to the inter-personal channel through interactive practice. Explicit knowledge would be an oxymoron, because knowledge would be merely tacit. Let say, a very restrictive and esoteric view.

The theory of autopoiesis does not add any value to what other theories state with respect to the understanding of the cognitive aspects of organizations. Further, its application to social systems implies properties that contradict any empirical test. Conversely, the dualist nature of knowledge and the pluralist usefulness of methodology can be well integrated under the umbrella of pragmatist epistemology. There is no reason why ethnomethodology, discourse analysis, network analysis, and simulation modeling – just to mention a few of the current methodological repertoires followed in organization theory (Tsoukas & Knudsen, 2003) – cannot be reciprocally legitimized and combined. In fact, all the progressive and enriching aspects that are characteristics of the supposed revolutionary wave of autopoiesis theory (i.e., those related to the view of organizations as complex cognitive networks of distributed knowledge) can be derived by using other research streams of the organization theory. The advantage is that they are consolidated concepts and tools, free from the many disputable and constraining (albeit often fascinating) "new visions" of autopoiesis theory. Further, the radical constructivist idea that organizations are operationally closed systems unable to represent its inner and outer worlds and that such representations are not feasible to be tested through standard scientific methodologies would not hold any more.

The IS/IT and KMS are clear examples of this apparent but false paradigm war. Although declared to be consistent with constructivist epistemology, the new approaches cannot avoid considering the knowledge also as an object, organizations as changing and (at least partially) reacting to environmental perturbations, and submitting its results to empirical tests. This latter, however, is not a defect, but rather is a proof of true problems faced by non-ideological researchers. When recognizing the crowded menu of variables and the few theoretical and empirical specifications of its connections considered in the recent action-oriented approaches to KMS, we

can realize that we really know very little about this subject. It should be not surprising when considering the complexity of human systems (Biggiero, 2001b), and the lack of a laboratory to run controlled experiments. That's why a great help can be expected from developing agent-based simulation models that provide us with research laboratories (Davis et al., 2007; Dooley, 2002; Gilbert, 2008; Gilbert & Terna, 2000; Gilbert & Troitzsch, 2005; Hegselsmann, Mueller & Troitzsch, 1996; Sichman *et al.*, 1998). Though in the virtual reality, they allow us to run controlled experiments without excluding any kind of qualitative socio-cognitive or psycho-social variables, like trust, opportunistic behavior, identification, reputation, etc. Recent developments (Biggiero, 2010a, 2010b; Biggiero & Sevi, 2009; Carley, 2009; Castelfranchi & Falcone, 2004; Conte & Paolucci, 2002; Conte & Turrini, 2006; Conte *et al.*, 2001) in the application of this methodology have proven able to effectively face with extremely complex aspects of human collective behavior, and to grasp many cues of the role of cognition, knowledge base and access, and any possible form of weak rationality. Therefore, it is further noteworthy that the pragmatist epistemology, besides reconciling the two perspectives on organizational knowledge, allows and legitimate methodological pluralism, escaping from the prison of pure quantitative studies in which people seem absent or hyper-rational, and pure qualitative studies in which a non-storable, non-transferable and even non-measurable knowledge becomes something rather esoteric.

REFERENCES

Aadne, J. H., Von Krogh, G., & Roos, J. (1996). Representationism: The traditional approach to cooperative strategies. In Von Krogh, G., & Roos, J. (Eds.), *Managing knowledge. Perspectives on cooperation and competition* (pp. 9–31). London, UK: Sage.

Albert, S., & Whetten, D. A. (1985). Organizational identity. In Cummings, L. L., & Staw, B. M. (Eds.), *Research in organizational behavior* (*Vol. 7*, pp. 263–295). Greenwich, CT: JAI Press.

Amin, A., & Cohendet, P. (2004). *Architectures of knowledge: firms, capabilities, and communities.* Oxford, UK: Oxford UP.

Ashby, R. W. (1956). *An introduction to cybernetics.* London, UK: Chapman.

Ashforth, B. E., & Mael, F. A. (1996). Organizational identity and strategy as a context for the individual. In Cummings, L. L., & Staw, B. M. (Eds.), *Research in organizational behavior* (*Vol. 13*, pp. 17–62). Greenwich, CT: JAI Press.

Bansler, J. P., & Havn, E. C. (2003). Building community knowledge systems: An empirical study of IT-support for sharing best practices among managers. *Knowledge and Process Management, 10*(3), 156–163. doi:10.1002/kpm.178

Barabasi, A.-L. (2003). *Link.* Plume, Reissue edition.

Barnes, J. A. (1954). Class and committee in a Norwegian Island Parish. *Human Relations, n.d.*, 7.

Barnes, J. A. (1969). Group theory and social networks. *Sociology, n.d.*, 3.

Bateson, G. (1972). *Steps to an ecology of mind: Collected essays in anthropology, psychiatry, evolution, and epistemology.* University of Chicago Press.

Bateson, G. (1980). *Mind and nature.* New York, NY: Bantam Books.

Bavelas, A. (1948). A mathematical model for group structure. *Applied Anthropology, 7.*

Bavelas, A. (1950). Communication patterns in task-oriented groups. *Journal of the Acoustic Society of America, 22.*

Biggiero, L. (1997). Managerial action and observation: a view of relational complexity. *Systemica, 12*, 23–37.

Biggiero, L. (2001a). Are firms autopoietic systems? In van der Zouwen, G., & Geyer, F. (Eds.), *Sociocybernetics: Complexity, autopoiesis, and observation of social systems* (pp. 125–140). Westport, CT: Greenwood.

Biggiero, L. (2001b). Sources of complexity in human systems. *Nonlinear Dynamics and Chaos in Life Sciences, 5*, 3–19. doi:10.1023/A:1009515211632

Biggiero, L. (2009). Organizations as cognitive systems: is knowledge an emergent property of information networks? In Minati, G., Pessa, E., & Abram, M. (Eds.), *Emergence in systems* (pp. 697–712). Singapore: World Scientific. doi:10.1142/9789812793478_0045

Biggiero, L. (2010a). Exploration modes and its impact on industry profitability. The differentiated effects of internal and external ways to access market knowledge. In Faggini, M., & Vinci, P. (Eds.), *Decision theory and choice: A complexity approach* (pp. 83–115). Berlin, Germany: Springer. doi:10.1007/978-88-470-1778-8_5

Biggiero, L. (2010b). Knowledge redundancy, environmental shocks, and agents' opportunism. In J. Józefczyk & D. Orski (Eds.), Knowledge-based intelligent system advancements: Systemic and cybernetic approaches (pp. 252-282). Advances in Artificial Intelligence Technologies (AAIT). Hershey, PA: IGI Global Publishers. doi:10.4018/978-1-61692-811-7.ch013

Biggiero, L., & Sevi, E. (2009). Opportunism by cheating and its effects on industry profitability. The CIOPS model. *Computational & Mathematical Organization Theory, 15*, 191–236. doi:10.1007/s10588-009-9057-3

Boland, R. J., & Tenkasi, R. V. (1995). Perspective making and perspective taking in communities of knowing. *Organization Science, 6*, 350–372. doi:10.1287/orsc.6.4.350

Boland, R. J., Tenkasi, R. V., & Te'eni, D. (1994). Designing information technology to support distributed cognition. *Organization Science, 5*, 456–475. doi:10.1287/orsc.5.3.456

Bollobas, B. (1985). *Random graphs*. London, UK: Academic.

Bornholdt, S., & Schuster, H. G. (Eds.). (2003). *Handbook of graphs and networks: From the genome to the Internet*. Weinheim, Germany: Wiley-VCH.

Bott, E. (1955). Urban families: Conjugal roles and social networks. *Human Relations, n.d.*, 8.

Bott, E. (1956). Urban families: The norms of conjugal roles. *Human Relations, n.d.*, 9.

Bott, E. (1957). *Family and social network*. London, UK: Tavistock.

Brown, J. S., & Duguid, P. (1991). Organizational learning and communities of practice: Toward a unified view of working, learning and innovation. *Organization Science, 2*(1), 40–57. doi:10.1287/orsc.2.1.40

Brown, J. S., & Duguid, P. (1998). Organizing knowledge. *California Management Review, 40*(3), 90–111.

Brown, J. S., & Duguid, P. (2000). *The social life of information*. Boston, MA: Harvard Business School Press.

Butler, T. (2003). From data to knowledge and back again: Understanding the limitations of KMS. *Knowledge and Process Management, 10*(3), 144–155. doi:10.1002/kpm.180

Carley, K. (1986). An approach for relating social structure to cognitive structure. *The Journal of Mathematical Sociology, 12*, 137–189. doi:10.1080/0022250X.1986.9990010

Carley, K. (1989). The value of cognitive foundations for dynamic social theory. *The Journal of Mathematical Sociology, 14*, 171–208. doi:10.1080/0022250X.1989.9990049

Carley, K. M. (1999). On the evolution of social and organizational networks. *Research in the Sociology of Organizations, 16*, 3–30.

Carley, K. M. (2009). Computational modeling for reasoning about the social behavior of humans. *Computational & Mathematical Organization Theory, 15*, 47–59. doi:10.1007/s10588-008-9048-9

Carley, K. M., & Newell, A. (1994). The nature of the social agent. *The Journal of Mathematical Sociology, 19*, 221–262. doi:10.1080/0022250X.1994.9990145

Carley, K. M., & Prietula, M. (Eds.). (1994). *Computational organization theory*. Hillsdale, NJ: Lawrence Erlbaum Associates.

Cartwright, D., & Zander, A. (Eds.). (1953). *Group dynamics*. London, UK: Tavistock.

Castelfranchi, C., & Falcone, R. (2004). Founding autonomy: The dialectics between (social) environment and agent's architecture and powers. *Lecture Notes on Artificial Intelligence, 2969*, 40–54.

Casti, J. L. (1989). *Paradigms lost*. New York, NY: Avon Books.

Charon, J. (1998). *Symbolic interactionism: An introduction, an interpretation, an integration*. Englewood Cliffs, NJ: Prentice Hall.

Chia, R. (2003). Organization theory as a postmodern science. In Tsoukas, H., & Knudsen, C. (Eds.), *The Oxford Handbook of organization theory: meta-theoretical perspectives* (pp. 113–142). Oxford: Oxford UP.

Conte, R., Edmonds, B., Scott, M., & Sawyer, R. K. (2001). Sociology and social theory in agent-based social simulation: a symposium. *Computational & Mathematical Organization Theory, 7*, 183–205. doi:10.1023/A:1012919018402

Conte, R., & Paolucci, M. (2002). *Reputation in artificial societies: Social beliefs for social order*. Dordrecht, The Netherlands: Kluwer Academic Publishers.

Conte, R., & Turrini, P. (2006). Argyll-feet giants: a cognitive analysis of collective autonomy. *Cognitive Systems Research, 7*, 209–219. doi:10.1016/j.cogsys.2005.11.011

Cook, S. D. N., & Brown, J. S. (1999). Bridging epistemologies: the generative dance between organizational knowledge and organizational knowing. *Organization Science, 10*(4), 381–400. doi:10.1287/orsc.10.4.381

Cowan, R. (2001). Expert systems: Aspect of and limitations to the codifiability of knowledge. *Research Policy, 30*(9), 1355–1372. doi:10.1016/S0048-7333(01)00156-1

Cowan, R., David, P., & Foray, D. (2000). The explicit economics of knowledge codification and tacitness. *Industrial and Corporate Change, n.d.*, 9.

Cowan, R., & Foray, D. (1997). The economics of codification and the diffusion of knowledge. *Industrial and Corporate Change, 6*, 592–622.

Csemerly, P. (2006). *Weak links: Stabilizers of complex systems from proteins to social networks*. Berlin, Germany: Springer.

Cyert, R. M., & March, J. G. (1963). *Behavioral theory of the firm*. Oxford, UK: Blackwell.

Czarniawska, B. (1997). *Narrating the organization*. Chicago, IL: University of Chicago Press.

Czarniawska, B. (2003). The styles and the stylists of organization theory. In Tsoukas, H., & Knudsen, C. (Eds.), *The Oxford handbook of organization theory: Meta-theoretical perspectives* (pp. 237–262). Oxford, UK: Oxford UP. doi:10.1093/oxfordhb/9780199275250.003.0009

Czarniawska, B. (2008). *A theory of organizing*. Cheltenham, UK: Edward Elgar.

Damoradan, L., & Olphert, W. (2000). Barriers and facilitators to the use of knowledge management systems. *Behaviour & Information Technology, 19*(6), 405–413. doi:10.1080/014492900750052660

Davis, J. P., Eisenhardt, K. M., & Bingham, C. B. (2007). Developing theory through virtual experiment methods. *Academy of Management Review, 32*(2), 480–499. doi:10.5465/AMR.2007.24351453

Dehmer, M., & Emmert-Streib, F. (Eds.). (2009). *Analysis of complex networks: From biology to linguistics*. Weinheim, Germany: Wiley-VCH.

Dooley, K. (2002). Virtual experiment research methods. In Baum, J. A. C. (Ed.), *Companion to organizations* (pp. 849–867). Oxford, UK: Blackwell.

Dorogovtsev, S. N., & Mendes, J. F. F. (2003). *Evolution of networks*. New York, NY: Oxford UP. doi:10.1093/acprof:oso/9780198515906.001.0001

Gallupe, B. (2001). Knowledge management systems: Surveying the landscape. *International Journal of Management Reviews, 3*(1), 61–77. doi:10.1111/1468-2370.00054

Gergen, K. (1999). *An invitation to social construction*. London, UK: Sage.

Geyer, F., & van der Zouwen, J. (Eds.). (1986). *Sociocybernetic paradoxes*. London, UK: Sage.

Giddens, A. (1984). *The constitution of society: Outline of the theory of structuration*. Cambridge, UK: Polity Press.

Gilbert, N. (2008). *Agent-based models*. London, UK: Sage.

Gilbert, N., & Terna, P. (2000). How to build and use agent-based models in social science. *Mind & Society.*, *1*, 57–72. doi:10.1007/BF02512229

Gilbert, N., & Troitzsch, K. G. (2005). *Simulation for the social scientist*. Buckingham, UK: Open University.

Guttenplan, S. (Ed.). (1994). *A companion to the philosophy of mind*. Oxford, UK: Blackwell.

Haas, P. (1992). Introduction. epistemic communities and international policy coordination. *International Organization*, *46*(01), 1–26. doi:10.1017/S0020818300001442

Hack, S., & Lane, R. (Eds.). (2006). *Pragmatism old and new: Selected writings*. Amherst, NY: Prometheus Books.

Håkanson, L. (2005). Epistemic communities and cluster dynamics: On the role of knowledge in industrial districts. *Industry and Innovation*, *12*(4), 433–463. doi:10.1080/13662710500362047

Haugeland, J. (Ed.). (1981). *Mind design. Philosophy, psychology, artificial intelligence*. Cambridge, MA: The MIT Press.

Hegselsmann, R., Mueller, U., & Troitzsch, K. G. (Eds.). (1996). *Modelling and simulation in the social sciences from the philosophy of sciences point of view*. Dordrecht, The Netherlands: Kluwer Academic.

Heims, S. J. (1981). *John von Neumann and Norbert Wiener*. Cambridge, UK: NUT Press.

Heims, S. J. (1991). *The cybernetics group*. Cambridge, UK: NHT Press.

Hogg, M. A., & Terry, D. J. (2000). Social identity and self-categorization processes in organizational contexts. *Academy of Management Review*, *25*, 121–140.

Kauffman, S. A. (1993). *The origins of order: Self-organization and selection in evolution*. New York, NY: Oxford UP.

Kauffman, S. A. (1995). *At home in the universe: the search for the laws of self-organization and complexity*. New York, NY: Oxford UP.

Kauffman, S. A. (2000). *Investigations*. New York, NY: Oxford UP.

Landsberger, H. A. (1958). *Hawthorne revisited*. Ithaca, NY: Cornell UP.

Laudan, L. (1990). *Science and relativism: Some key controversies in the philosophy of science*. Chicago, IL: University of Chicago Press.

Laudan, L. (1996). *Beyond positivism and relativism*. Boulder, CO: Westview Press.

Lave, J. (1988). *Cognition in practice*. Cambridge, UK: Cambridge UP. doi:10.1017/CBO9780511609268

Lave, J., & Wenger, E. (1992). *Situated learning: Legitimate peripheral participation*. New York, NY: Cambridge UP.

Lewis, T. G. (2009). *Network science: Theory and practice*. Hoboken, NJ: Wiley.

Luhmann, N. (1984). *Soziale Systeme*. Frankfurt, Germany: Suhrkamp.

Luhmann, N. (1986). The autopoiesis of social systems. In Geyer, F., & van der Zouwen, J. (Eds.), *Sociocybernetic paradoxes* (pp. 172–192). London, UK: Sage.

Luhmann, N. (1990). *Essays on self-reference*. New York, NY: Columbia UP.

Lyytinen, K., & Robey, D. (1999). Learning failure in Information Systems development. *Information Systems Journal, 9*(2), 85–101. doi:10.1046/j.1365-2575.1999.00051.x

Magalhães, R. (2004). *Organizational knowledge and technology. An action-oriented perspective on organization and information systems.* Cheltenham, UK: Edgar Elgar.

March, J. G., & Simon, H. A. (1958). *Organizations* (revised edition). New York, NY: Wiley.

Maturana, H., & Varela, F. (1980). *Autopoiesis and cognition.* Dordrecht, The Netherlands: Reidel.

Maturana, H. R. (1975). The organization of the living: a theory of the living organization. *International Journal of Man-Machine Studies, 7,* 313–332. doi:10.1016/S0020-7373(75)80015-0

Maturana, H. R. (1978). Biology of language: The epistemology of reality. In Miller, G. A., & Lenneberg, E. (Eds.), *Psychology and biology of language and thought* (pp. 27–63). New York, NY: Academic Press.

Maturana, H. R. (1980). Autopoiesis: Reproduction, heredity and evolution. In Zeleny, M. (Ed.), *Autopoiesis, dissipative structures, and spontaneous social orders.* Boulder, CO: Westview Press.

Maturana, H. R. (1981). Autopoiesis. In Zeleny, M. (Ed.), *Autopoiesis: A theory of living organization.* New York, NY: North Holand.

Maturana, H. R., & Varela, F. J. (1987). *El arbol del conocimiento, (The tree of knowledge).* Horticultural Hall, MA: Shambhala Pub.

McCorduck, P. (1979). *Machines who think.* San Francisco, CA: Freeman.

Mingers, J. (1995). *Self-producing systems. Implications and applications of autopoiesis.* New York, NY: Plenum Press.

Minsky, M. (1987). *The society of mind.* New York, NY: Simon & Schuster.

Monge, P. R., & Contractor, N. S. (2003). *Theories of communication networks.* Oxford, UK: Oxford UP.

Moreno, J. (1934). *Who shell survive?* New York, NY: Bacon Press.

Mylonopoulos, N., & Tsoukas, H., (2003). Technological and organizational issues in knowledge management. *Knowledge and Process Management, 10*(3), 139–143. doi:10.1002/kpm.174

Newell, A., & Simon, H. A. (1972). *Human problem solving.* Englewood Cliff, NJ: Prentice-Hall.

Newell, S., Tansley, C., & Huang, J. (2004). Social capital and knowledge integration in an ERP project team: the importance of bridging and bonding. *British Journal of Management, 15,* 43–S57. doi:10.1111/j.1467-8551.2004.00405.x

Newman, M., Barabasi, A.-L., & Watts, D. J. (2006). *The structure and dynamics of networks.* Princeton UP.

Nonaka, I., & Nishiguchi, T. (Eds.). (2001). *Knowledge emergence: Social, technical, and evolutionary dimensions of knowledge creation.* Oxford, UK: Oxford UP.

Nonaka, I., & Takeuchi, H. (1995). *The knowledge-creating company.* New York, NY: Oxford UP.

Nonaka, I., Umemoto, K., & Sasaki, K. (1998). Three tales of knowledge-creating companies. In Von Krogh, G., Roos, J., & Kline, D. (Eds.), *Knowing in firms: Understanding, managing and measuring knowledge* (pp. 146–172). London, UK: Sage.

Nonaka, I., Von Krogh, G., & Voelpel, S. (2006). Organizational knowledge creation theory: Evolutionary paths and future advances. *Organization Studies, 27*(8), 1179–1208. doi:10.1177/0170840606066312

Ohno, T. (1988). *Toyota production system: Beyond large-scale production.* Productivity Press.

Orlikowski, W. J. (2002). Knowing in practice. enacting a collective capability in distributed organizing. *Organization Science, 13*(3), 249–273. doi:10.1287/orsc.13.3.249.2776

Peirce, C. S. (1931). *Collected papers.* Cambridge, MA: Belknap Press. (reprinted 1958)

Putnam, H. (1995). *Pragmatism.* Cambridge, MA: Blackwell.

Roach, D. W., & Bednar, D. A. (1997). The theory of logical types: A tool for understanding levels and types of change in organizations. *Human Relations, 50*(6), 671–699. doi:10.1177/001872679705000603

Rorty, R. (1979). *Philosophy and the mirror of nature.* Princeton, NJ: Princeton UP.

Rorty, R. (1982). *Consequences of pragmatism.* Minneapolis, MN: University of Minnesota Press.

Rorty, R. (1991). *Objectivity, relativism and truth.* Cambridge, UK: Cambridge UP.

Sammarra, A., & Biggiero, L. (2001). Identity and Identification in Industrial Districts. *Journal of Management and Governance, 5*, 61–82. doi:10.1023/A:1017937506664

Scott, J. (1991). *Social network analysis: A Handbook.* Newbury Park, CA: Sage.

Sichman, J. S., Conte, R., & Gilbert, N. (Eds.). (1998). *Multi-agent systems and agent-based simulation.* Berlin, Germany: Springer.

Simon, H. A. (1969). *The Sciences of the artificial.* Cambridge, MA: MIT Press.

Simon, H. A. (1977). *Models of discovery.* Dordrecht: Reidel.

Simon, H. A. (1997). Models of bounded rationality: *Vol. 3. Empirically grounded economic reason.* NY: MIT Press.

Taylor, F. W. (1947). *Scientific management.* Harper & Brothers.

Tsoukas, H. (1996). The firm as a distributed knowledge system: A constructionist approach. *Strategic Management Journal, 17*, 11–25.

Tsoukas, H. (2005). *Complex knowledge. Studies in organizational epistemology.* Oxford, UK: Oxford UP.

Tsoukas, H., & Knudsen, C. (Eds.). (2003). *The Oxford handbook of organization theory.* Oxford, UK: Oxford UP.

Tsoukas, H., & Mylonopoulos, N. (2004). Introduction: Knowledge construction and creation in organizations. *British Journal of Management, 15*, S1–S8. doi:10.1111/j.1467-8551.2004.t01-2-00402.x

Tsoukas, H., & Vladimirou, E. (2001). What is organizational knowledge? *Journal of Management Studies, 38*, 973–993. doi:10.1111/1467-6486.00268

Un, C. A., & Cuervo-Cazurra, A. (2004). Strategies for knowledge creation in firms. *British Journal of Management, 15*, 27–S41. doi:10.1111/j.1467-8551.2004.00404.x

Varela, F. G., Maturana, H. R., & Uribe, R. (1974). Autopoiesis: The organization of living systems, its characterization and a model. *Bio Systems, 5*, 187–196. doi:10.1016/0303-2647(74)90031-8

Varela, F. J. (1979). *Principles of biological autonomy.* New York, NY: North Holland.

Varela, F. J. (1992). Whence perceptual meaning? A cartography of current ideas. In Varela, F., & Dupuy, J. (Eds.), *Understanding origins: Contemporary views on the origin of life, mind and society* (pp. 235–263). Dordrecht, The Netherlands: Kluwer Academic.

Varela, F. J. (1996). The early days of autopoiesis: Heinz and Chile. *Systems Research, 13*(3), 407–416. doi:10.1002/(SICI)1099-1735(199609)13:3<407::AID-SRES100>3.0.CO;2-1

Varela, F. J., Thompson, E., & Rosch, E. (1991). *The embodied mind. Cognitive science and human experience*. Cambridge, MA: MIT Press.

von Foerster, H. (1982). *Observing systems*. Seaside, CA: Intersystems Publications.

von Foerster, H. (1984). Principles of self-organization in a socio-managerial context. In Ulrich, U., & Probst, G. J. B. (Eds.), *Self-organization and management of social systems* (pp. 2–24). New York, NY: Springer. doi:10.1007/978-3-642-69762-3_1

von Glasersfeld, E. (1995). *Radical constructivism: A way of knowing and learning*. London, UK: The Falmer Press. doi:10.4324/9780203454220

Von Krogh, G., & Roos, J. (Eds.). (1995). *Managing Knowledge. Perspectives on Cooperation and Competition*. London: Sage.

von Krogh, G., Roos, J., & Kline, D. (Eds.). (1998). *Knowing in firms: understanding, managing and measuring knowledge*. London, UK: Sage.

von Krogh, G., Roos, J., & Slocum, K. (1996). An essay on corporate epistemology. In von Krogh, G., & Roos, J. (Eds.), *Managing knowledge. Perspectives on cooperation and competition* (pp. 157–183). London, UK: Sage.

Waldrop, M. (1987). *Man-made minds*. New York, NY: Walker.

Wasserman, S., & Faust, K. (1994). *Social network analysis: Methods and applications*. Cambridge, UK: Cambridge University Press.

Watts, D. J. (2003). *Small worlds: The dynamics of networks between order and randomness*. Princeton UP.

Watts, D. J. (2004a). Six degrees. Vintage, New edition.

Watts, D. J. (2004b). The "new" science of networks. *Annual Review of Sociology, 30*, 243–270. doi:10.1146/annurev.soc.30.020404.104342

Watzlawick, P. (Ed.). (1984). *The invented reality*. New York, NY: Norton.

Weick, K. E. (1969). *The social psychology of organizing*. Newberry Award Records Inc.

Weick, K. E. (1995). *Sensemaking in organizations*. London, UK: Sage.

Wenger, E. (1998). *Communities of practice: Learning, meaning, and identity*. Cambridge, UK: Cambridge UP.

Wicks, A. C., & Freeman, R. E. (1998). Organization studies and the new pragmatism: positivism, anti-positivism, and the search for ethics. *Organization Science, 9*(2), 123–140. doi:10.1287/orsc.9.2.123

Winograd, T., & Flores, F. (1986). *Understanding computers and cognition. A new foundation for design*. NJ: Ablex Publishing Co.

Yanow, D. (1995). Writing organizational tales. *Organization Science, 6*, 225. doi:10.1287/orsc.6.2.225

Yanow, D. (2004). Translating local knowledge at organizational peripheries. *British Journal of Management, 15*, 9–S25. doi:10.1111/j.1467-8551.2004.t01-1-00403.x

Yolles, M. (2006). *Organizations as complex systems. An introduction to knowledge cybernetics*. Greenwich, CT: IAP.

Zeleny, M. (2000). Knowledge vs. information. In Zeleny, M. (Ed.), *The IEBM handbook of Information Technology in business* (pp. 162–168). Padstow, UK: Thomson Learning.

Zeleny, M. (2005). *Human systems management. Integrating knowledge, management and systems*. London, UK: World Scientific. doi:10.1142/9789812703538

KEY TERMS AND DEFINITIONS

Autopoiesis: Literally, it means self-production, which should not be confused with re-production, because while this latter indicates the creation of a new "copy" of the original, the former refers to the (system's) capability to produce its own elements while maintaining the same relationships among them.

Constructivism: A stream of epistemology that emphasizes the implications coming from the fact that reality is always perceived through our senses and our imagination, which both divert it. Therefore, the world is indeed created instead of discovered.

Knowledge Management Systems: A wide set of IS/IT architectures and operating systems aimed at enhancing knowledge creation, acquisition, transfer, and sharing.

Logical Types: A field of mathematical logic related to set theory, addressing the logical, ontological and epistemological distinctions and implications of building classes, classes of classes, etc.

Ontology: That part of philosophy that deals with the following kind of questions: "what is real" and "are there different degrees of reality", etc.

Organizational Knowledge: All the types of knowledge that are created, acquired or stored into organizations by variably cognitive agents, by means of machine-machine, man-man, and machine-man interactions.

Pragmatism: A stream of philosophical thought, which started and was developed mostly in US. It follows a middle line between realism and relativism.

ENDNOTES

[1] Depending on the authors, the roles can be interchanged—some consider information as the interpreted form of data, while others reverse this relationship.

[2] It's quite doubtful whether the theory is falsifiable at all.

[3] Here I do not enter into the issue whether machines can create knowledge, even though it has many connections with this paper.

[4] It is enough to score Social Networks and the Journal of Mathematical Sociology.

[5] As Varela himself tells (1996), was indeed von Foerster who coined the word "autopoiesis" and sponsored the publication of their first paper on the journal Biosystems, in which he was into the scientific committee. Unfortunately, a complete history of cybernetics, and in particular of the second-order cybernetics with its connections with automata studies, graph theory, cellular automata on one side, and economics, sociology, management and organization science on the other has not yet been written. Some pieces can be found in many places, among which (Heims, 1981, 1991).

Chapter 6
Software Engineering Research:
The Need to Strengthen and Broaden the Classical Scientific Method

Gonzalo Génova
Universidad Carlos III de Madrid, Spain

Juan Llorens
Universidad Carlos III de Madrid, Spain

Jorge Morato
Universidad Carlos III de Madrid, Spain

ABSTRACT

The classical scientific method has been settled through the last centuries as a cyclic, iterative process of observation, hypothesis formulation, and confirmation/refutation of hypothesis through experimentation. This "experimental scientific method" was mainly developed in the context of natural sciences dealing with the physical world, such as Mechanics, Thermodynamics, Electromagnetism, Chemistry, and so on. But when trying to apply this classical view of the scientific method to the various branches of Computer Science and Computer Engineering, among which Software Engineering, there are two kinds of obstacles. First, Computer Science is rooted both in formal sciences such as Mathematics and experimental sciences such as Physics, and therefore, an excessive emphasis on the experimental side is not appropriate to give a full account of this kind of scientific activity. Second, the production of software systems has to deal not only with the behavior of complex physical systems such as computers, but also with the behavior of complex human systems (developers interacting with stakeholders, for instance, or users interacting with machines) where educational, cultural, sociological, and economical factors are essential. Therefore, empirical methods in their narrow sense, even though valuable in some respects, are rather limited to understand a reality that exceeds the mere physical world. Moreover, neither formal nor empirical methods can provide a full account of scientific activity, which relies on something that is beyond any established method. Qualitative (i.e. meta-methodical) reasoning plays the directive role in scientific activity. In this chapter, the authors claim that acknowledging a plurality of research methods in software engineering will benefit the advancement of this branch of science.

DOI: 10.4018/978-1-4666-0179-6.ch006

INTRODUCTION

In the final report of the ACM Task Force on the Core of Computer Science, Denning et al. presented an intellectual framework for the discipline of computing intended to serve as a basis for computing curricula (Denning et al., 1989). They characterized computing as a discipline that sits at the crossroads among mathematics, empirical science and engineering. Therefore, there is a *plurality of research methods* that can be applied for the advance of computing in all its branches, one of them being software engineering. The study of mathematics and empirical sciences is recommended in software engineering curricula to promote abstract thinking and the appreciation for the scientific method (IEEE, 2004).

Henri Poincaré wrote at the beginning of the 20th century about the experimental scientific method: "The man of science must work with method. Science is built up of facts, as a house is built of stones; but an accumulation of facts is no more a science than a heap of stones is a house" (Poincaré, 1952, p. 141). A good scientific work is not complete with a systematic recollection of data: it requires a *rational explanation* of their relationships. In other words, the essential ingredients of the scientific method are the description of phenomena (what happens, how it happens) and the explanation of their relationships (why it happens): "What and How describe, only Why explains" (Whetten, 1989).

Michael Polanyi, another scientist-philosopher, claimed that the scientific method is not a recipe that can yield truths mechanically (Polanyi, 1958): explaining the relationships between observed phenomena requires intelligence, imagination, and creativity. Besides, a naïve but widespread empiricist account of science forgets that *observed facts are not independent from theory* (Chalmers, 1999): on the contrary, establishing the validity of observations requires human interpretation and a good deal of previous knowledge. The application of the scientific method in software engineering

research has to take into account these warnings. Our main purpose is to show that the advance of science cannot be closed within the application of a "method", however rigorous it may be. There is no universal method in science. In particular, empirical methods are rather limited to understand a reality that exceeds the mere physical world. Each branch of science needs its own method, and selecting the most adequate method is a task that lies beyond any formal or empirical method: it is a meta-methodical task.

In this Chapter we present a brief historical background of the development of the scientific method through the centuries. Then we discuss some philosophical issues that have arisen from the consideration of how scientists work, showing that the scientific method is not fully justified, and perhaps will never be. These issues are relevant when the scientific method is applied to software engineering, as we explain in the last part of the Chapter, where we emphasize the guiding role of qualitative, speculative or conceptual reasoning in research activities.

HISTORICAL BACKGROUND

The scientific method is rooted in the Greek culture, particularly in the laws of logic first defined by Aristotle (384-322 BC). However, Greek science was almost entirely lost for Latin West during the Early Middle Ages, after the fall of the Western Roman Empire. Science was meanwhile safeguarded and cultivated in the Arab culture, with influences from China and India. The main contribution of Indian culture that arrived to Europe through Al-Khwārizmī (c.780-c.850) was the place-value numeral system, which was fundamental for the development of algebraic and arithmetic operations (Mason, 1962). Another significant milestone in the recovery and development of scientific method is the *Book of Optics* by Muslim scientist Ibn al-Haytham (Alhazen, 965-1039), with his pioneering emphasis on the role of experimentation (Saliba, 2007). Aristotelian logic was also preserved in the Arab civilization, where it was studied by Islamic and Jewish scholars such as Ibn Rushd (Averroes, 1126-1198) and Moses Maimonides (1135-1204). The whole set of Aristotelian logical works (known as *Organon*, "instrument") was not available in Western Christendom until translated to Latin in the 12th century. Then it became a major field of study and significant advancement for medieval Christian scholars, who regarded Aristotle as "The Philosopher", in large part due to the influence his works had on Thomas Aquinas. The interest in logic as the basis of rational enquiry is manifested in the many systems of logic developed hereafter, but a real advancement did not arrive until the formulation of modern predicate logic in the 19th century (Łukasiewicz, 1957).

Robert Grosseteste (1175-1253) must be counted among the first scholastic thinkers in Europe to understand Aristotle's vision of the dual nature of scientific reasoning (Crombie, 1971): a process that concludes from particular observations into universal laws, and then back again, from universal laws to prediction of particulars. Roger Bacon (1220-1292), inspired by the writings of Grosseteste, described a method consisting in a repeating cycle of observation, hypothesis, experimentation, and the need for independent verification (Hackett, 1997), surprisingly advancing what would be called much later the hypothetico-deductive method by William Whewell in his *History of the Inductive Sciences* (1837). However, the admiration for Aristotle was not universal. Francis Bacon and René Descartes were among the first thinkers to question the philosophical authority of the ancient Greeks (Cantor & Klein, 1969).

Bacon published in 1620 his *Novum Organum* ("The New Organon") intending to replace traditional logic with a new system he believed to be superior. Bacon strongly criticized Aristotle, "who made his natural philosophy a mere slave to his logic" (Book I, Aphorism 54). According to

Aristotle, scientific knowledge pursues universal truths and their causes, and this is achieved only by means of deductive reasoning in the form of syllogisms: it is deduction that allows scientists to infer new truths from those already established. On the contrary, while inductive reasoning is sufficient for discovering universal laws by generalization, it does not succeed in identifying the causes of observed phenomena. Therefore, although empirical observation has a place in the Aristotelian method, knowledge acquired by induction is not truly scientific and reliable.

In contrast, induction from the particular to the general occupies the first place in the Baconian method to investigate the cause of a certain phenomenon. In successive steps known as method of agreement, method of difference, and method of concomitant variation, Francis Bacon compares different situations where the phenomenon occurs, does not occur, or occurs in different degrees, trying to find a factor that could be hypothesized as the cause of the investigated phenomenon. The proposed hypothesis must be scrutinized and compared to other hypotheses, so that the truth of natural philosophy (i.e. the laws of nature) is approached by a gradual ascent. The method was never described in full because Bacon's work remained unfinished. In fact, this inductive method had been essentially described much earlier by Persian philosopher Avicenna (Ibn Sina) in his book *The Canon of Medicine* (1025) (Goodman, 2003). John Stuart Mill systematized and expanded the method in his book *A System of Logic* (1843).

A radically different approach to the practical and empirical method of Bacon is followed by Descartes: in his *Rules for the Direction of the Mind* (1619) and his *Discourse on the Method* (1637), he emphasizes the theoretical and rational aspects based on deduction, in order to avoid deception by the senses. Both Descartes and Bacon aim at discovering the laws of nature, either by deduction from first principles or by induction from observations. While Descartes doubts the accuracy of information provided by senses, Bacon stresses the many intellectual obfuscations that hamper the mind (his famous idols of the Tribe, the Cave, the Marketplace and the Theatre). The result is a certain fracture between two reasoning methods, deduction and induction, that should cooperate to reach the truth instead of competing as enemies to demonstrate which one is better.

Despising induction as a means to discover the laws of nature is more a doctrine of those who clung inflexibly to Aristotle's teachings than of Aristotle himself. Certainly, according to Aristotle deduction is superior to induction, but both play a role in scientific inquiry. However, what Aristotle did reject was the use of mathematical reasoning in other sciences different from mathematics: his arguments to find the natural causes of phenomena are purely qualitative, what makes his physics much poorer than his logic. The merit to combine rational thinking, observation-experimentation, quantitative measurements and mathematical demonstrations corresponds mainly to Galileo Galilei, who is attributed with the saying: "Measure what can be measured, and make measurable what is not so" (Weyl, 1959). This is perhaps the most audacious, important and innovative step taken by Galileo in terms of scientific method, since the usefulness of mathematics in obtaining scientific results was far from obvious at that time, because mathematics did not lend itself to the discovery of causes (which was the primary goal of Aristotelian science) (Feldhay, 1998).

Moreover, being the founder of the experimental scientific method, it is worth noting that Galileo did not disregard theoretical thinking in favor of empirical proofs. In fact, one of his most famous demonstrations to disprove Aristotle's theory of gravity, which states that objects fall at a speed relative to their mass, had the form of a "thought experiment". The experiment involves two free falling stones of different weight that are tied together. Galileo explains that, according to Aristotelian physics, the lighter stone should retard the heavier stone in its fall, and vice versa,

resulting in an intermediate speed. But the two stones together make a heavier object than either stone apart, so that they should fall faster than the heavier stone alone. From this contradiction Galileo concludes that objects fall at the same speed regardless of their weight. Incidentally, this purely mental proof contained in the First Day of his *Discourses and Mathematical Demonstrations Relating to Two New Sciences* (1638) demonstrates also that showing a logical contradiction in a theory makes it unnecessary to disprove the theory by experiments.

Isaac Newton consolidated the scientific method with an extraordinary development of applied mathematics, and laid the groundwork for most of classical mechanics, whose inductive-deductive approach other sciences sought to emulate. His *Mathematical Principles of Natural Philosophy* (1687), usually called the *Principia*, is probably the most important scientific book ever written. His "rules of reasoning" constitute a re-creation of Galileo's method that has never been significantly changed, and in its substance is used by scientists today. The so-called hypothetico-deductive method is characterized by successive iterations of four essential elements: observation of phenomena, formulation of explanatory hypothesis, prediction of observable consequences from the hypothesis, and experimentation to confirm or refute the predictions (and thus, indirectly, the hypothesis). To reduce the risk of biased interpretations of results and achieve objectivity, data and methodology must be shared so that they can be carefully examined by other scientists who attempt to reproduce the experiments and verify the results.

SOME PHILOSOPHICAL ISSUES

The history of scientific method we have briefly sketched leads us to the consideration of some philosophical problems that remain largely unsolved. The purpose of the following exposition is not to solve them, but to show that we must not be too naïve in explaining or using the scientific method.

The Role of Mathematics

The Baconian method intended to discover the cause of a certain phenomenon by finding regularities in observations that linked it to other phenomena, but it was still a fundamentally qualitative method. As we have said, it was Galileo who first took the significant step of giving those regularities the form of mathematical laws (in fact, other contemporary scientists share this merit, significantly Johannes Kepler with his formulation of the laws of planetary motion). Galileo was intimately convinced that the laws of universe are "written in the language of mathematics" (*The Assayer*, 1623, ch. 6). Galileo, Kepler and others believed that the universe has an underlying rational structure that is within reach of human understanding.

So, the beginning of the scientific revolution is marked by the creation of mathematical models and theories that formalize observed phenomena as measurable variables and link them to each other. Since that time the building of unifying models has been a constant effort in science. Establishing mathematical laws of behavior gives the possibility to make accurate predictions, paradigmatically demonstrated with the many discoveries in the field of astronomy. The confirmation of predictions proves the validity of the theory, and once it has been well established, the theory gives us the possibility to make new predictions we can trust. In this way, mathematical theories lay the ground for engineering all kind of devices with predictable behavior, designed for the well-being of humans.

But mathematics is not an experimental discipline in itself. Mathematics is grounded on axioms and pure reason, and its results do not require experimental verification to be valid. The fact that mathematical concepts are applicable to physical phenomena, even far beyond the context where they were originally developed, has been always a motive for perplexity. The Nobel Prize physicist Eugen Wigner invokes the example of the mathematical law of gravitation, originally used to model freely falling bodies on the surface of the earth, but then extended to describe the motion of the planets, proving accurate beyond all reasonable expectations (Wigner, 1960). He analyzes the obscure and "miraculous" connections between mathematics and physics, concluding that "fundamentally, we do not know why our theories work so well". The philosopher Hillary Putnam explained this "miracle" as a necessary consequence of a realist view of the philosophy of mathematics (Putnam, 1975). Richard Hamming, one of the founders of computer science honored with the Turing Award, further reflected on Wigner's ideas and tried to give partial explanations to this "unreasonable effectiveness" (Hamming, 1980). His tentative explanations ranged from the consideration of mathematics as a human creation to fit the observed reality, to the biological evolution as having primed mathematical thinking in humans. Hamming himself concluded that his own explanations were unsatisfactory as well. The debate is still very lively (Tegmark, 2008).

Regularity and Causality

The emphasis on building mathematical models of predictable behavior leaves open the following question: do we reach the causes of phenomena with mathematics? The mere establishing of a regularity in the connection of phenomena is insufficient to state that one phenomenon is the *cause* of another phenomenon (Pearl, 2000). This is well known in the scientific method. Even though a mathematical law suffices to make practical predictions, a serious researcher will not be content with the formulation of a so-called "empirical law": a law that lacks an underlying theoretical model, a mere distillation of the results of repeated observations. In this sense, the Baconian method (discovering causes by agreement, difference and concomitant variation) is an oversimplification of scientific inquiry.

Of course, science must distinguish between accidental conjunction and true statistical correlation of phenomena. An accidental conjunction occurs when two events happen at the same time, without having a direct relationship to each other besides the fact that they are coincident in time. For example, I open the front door of my house and it starts raining. Well designed experiments and proper use of statistical tools are essential to find true correlations between variables. The first step to find a true correlation, then, is to increase the sample size of events: I open the front door many times and in different situations, and find that there is no correlation between the *kinds of events* "opening the front door" and "starting to rain" (it would be very curious indeed, and deserving further investigation, to find a strong correlation in this case!).

But, even if a true correlation is discovered, inferring a cause-effect relationship would be a premature conclusion (Simon, 1954; Holland, 1986; Aldrich, 1995). In other words, correlation does not imply causation. The opposite belief, correlation proves causation, is a logical fallacy known as "cum hoc ergo propter hoc" (Latin for "with this, therefore because of this"). A similar fallacy is "post hoc ergo propter hoc" ("after this, therefore because of this"), which is even more tempting because temporal sequence appears to be integral to causality. In general, a correlation between two variables A and B can be explained in different ways: A causes B, B causes A (reverse causation), some unknown factor C actually causes A and B (the so-called spurious relationship), or even a combination of the former (as in self-reinforced systems with bidirectional causal relationships).

Consider the crowing of the rooster (RC) and the rising of the sun (SR). A naïve conclusion, apparently supported by time sequence, is that RC causes SR. But a careful analysis of correlation and the use of counterfactual experiments lead easily to the conclusion that the independent variable is SR and the dependent variable is RC: the sun rises anyway, the rooster crows when dawn is approaching. So we can conclude with certainty that the sun's rising *causes* the rooster's crowing.

But, can we? Even a true correlation is not enough to establish a causal relationship. Some further explanation is required by the scientific method, *a rational explanation rooted in a theoretical model that unifies concepts and observations*. Something like "the rising of the sun increases the intensity of light, this awakens the rooster, that then crows". This deeper understanding of the causal relationship is beyond the results of mathematics, beyond pure statistical correlation (in this sense we can say that Aristotle's insight that mathematics does not lead to the discovery of causes was right). What the scientific method states is that correlation is a necessary but not sufficient condition for causation. Certainly, correlation suggests causation, and ignoring it would be unintelligent, but correlation in itself is not enough. A scientific explanation is a causal explanation that requires reasoning beyond pure mathematical regularity.

The philosopher David Hume went a step further when he criticized the idea of causality in *An Enquiry Concerning Human Understanding* (1748) and other works, according to his view that we *know* only what we *perceive*. He claimed that causality is purely a mental association between constantly conjoined events that cannot be inferred from experience. The causal connection is in our minds, and we cannot tell *from experience* whether it really exists. In a few words, causality is beyond experience, only correlation can actually be perceived (i.e. known). Hume strongly influenced Immanuel Kant, who further developed the critic of causality and metaphysics in general. The influence of both in modern philosophy of science is unquestionable. In a certain sense, it can be said that the metaphysical idea of causality (one that is beyond physical experience, as the word "metaphysical" denotes) has been abandoned in modern science. Even the theoretical models that "explain" the connections between observed phenomena seem to be satisfied with purely mechanical explanations, some kind of very elaborated systems of correlations between variables. In some fields of experimental science, especially in physics, causality is hardly mentioned. Nevertheless, most non-philosopher scientists will accept, against Hume and Kant, that knowing causality (at least in the weak non-metaphysical sense) is within reach of human reason.

The Origin of Hypotheses

The scientific search for cause-effect relationships, or at least for true correlations, begins with the formulation of a hypothesis. A hypothesis is a fact or theory that, if it were true, would explain the observed phenomenon. Following the hypotetico-deductive method, the hypothesis has to be confirmed or refuted by experiments. In fact, experiments specifically designed to refute a given hypothesis have a great value in the scientific method: if they succeed, then the hypothesis is discarded; if they fail to refute, then they provide a stronger confirmation of the hypothesis. But where does the hypothesis come from? Is there any logic in the origin of a hypothesis?

The common answer is: scientific hypotheses are the product of the process of induction. But this is obviously too simple. If induction is the process of formulating general rules on the basis of particular cases, then *induction cannot provide a causal explanation that goes beyond simple generalization*. The cause is not simply a generalization of the effects, therefore inferring the cause from the effects cannot be the product of induction (Génova, 1997). From the facts that the rooster has crowed today at dawn, and yesterday, and the day before yesterday… induction (generalization) can conclude that "the rooster crows everyday at dawn", but this is not a causal explanation. In fact, it is not an explanation at all, it is a mere "regularization": making individual

occurrences to be instances of a general rule. The explanation that "the rooster crows *because* it is awakened by an increased intensity of light produced by the rising of the sun" is a very different kind of explanation that goes well further beyond generalization of the observed phenomena. It is an explanation that causally relates two different kinds of events. "By induction, we conclude that facts, similar to observed facts, are true in cases not examined. By hypothesis, we conclude the existence of a fact quite different from anything observed, from which, according to known laws, something observed would necessarily result. The former, is reasoning from particulars to the general law; the latter, from effect to cause. The former classifies, the latter explains" (Peirce, 1877).

Western philosophy, rooted in Aristotelian logic, has traditionally considered that there are two basic kinds of reasoning: *deduction* is a kind of argument that shows that a conclusion necessarily follows from a set of premises; *induction*, instead, draws a generalized but not necessary conclusion from a finite collection of specific observations. But Aristotle, in fact, acknowledged in his *Organon* a third kind of argument he called "backward reasoning", different from induction. These two latter kinds of arguments, induction and backward reasoning, had been conflated through the centuries until the philosopher Charles S. Peirce recovered the distinction for modern logic (Peirce, 1867). Peirce called this backward reasoning *abduction* or retroduction: it is the logical process by which new ideas, explanatory hypotheses and scientific theories are engendered.

The main trend in modern philosophy of science, following Karl R. Popper, has ignored the logical problem of the origin of hypotheses (Hanson, 1958). The scientific method begins once a hypothesis is at hand to be tested by experiments, but the origin of the new ideas is not an issue that can be explained in logical terms (Popper, 1959). The act of conceiving or inventing a new theory is a kind of blind conjecture or guess, the fruit of chance or intuition. From this point of view, the discovery of new ideas can only be studied from a historical, psychological or sociological perspective, but it is not important for the rational description of scientific knowledge. New ideas are there, and that is all that matters.

By contrast, according to Peirce abductive reasoning provides *a likely account* of the facts that need explanation, therefore *it is a logical operation of the mind*, not a mere blind conjecture (Peirce, 1901). Of course, abduction (like induction) is not kind of argument that yields necessary conclusions: it is fallible, even extremely fallible, it is not a direct intuition of the laws of nature (as Cartesian rationalism would like); it is fallible, but rational. In its search for an explanatory hypothesis, abduction is deliberate and critical, which are elements of rational thinking (Ayim, 1982). Peirce is concerned with a notion of logic as a "theory of human reasoning" that is broader than pure formal logic. Therefore, Peirce considers that logic has to study not only formalizable kinds of arguments (deductive, necessary syllogisms), but also other kinds of arguments that are essential to human reason and progress in knowledge (fallible induction and abduction).

These various modes of reasoning are integrated in Peirce's description of scientific method: abduction invents or proposes an explanatory hypothesis for observed facts; deduction predicts from the hypothesis testable consequences that should be observed; induction verifies the hypothesis by means of experiments, that is, the observation of particular cases that agree with the proposed hypothesis and thus confirm it (Peirce, 1901). In this sense, *induction does not provide any new ideas*, it merely corroborates or refutes the abductive conjecture. The role of generating new ideas via hypothesis or conjecture corresponds solely to abduction (Fann, 1970). Even an inductive generalization requires some kind of previous, perhaps unconscious, abduction: when the scientist concentrates on a certain set of facts in search for a general law, he or she has already made some kind of conjecture about the kind of phenomena that may be subject to a generalization. In trying to formulate the laws of movement, Galileo and Newton discarded from the start qualities such as the color, the smell or the source of moving bodies: in a not yet fully specified form, only their mass is considered relevant, which is already a kind of abduction. Perhaps the material composition of the bodies (wood, lead, stone, etc.) can be also abductively considered, to be later discarded by induction from experiments.

Therefore, the enumeration of phenomena reveals the crucial role of abduction as a preparatory step for induction. What do we enumerate? Why this enumeration, why not a different one? In order to enumerate something, we need to know already *in some way* what we want to enumerate. The general concept that should be derived by induction from particular cases has to be previously known, even though known only vaguely, to be able to enumerate those particular cases. And this is just what abduction does: it provides, via hypothesis or conjecture, the clue to the general concept the scientist has to follow to identify and enumerate singular data. Induction by enumeration is not enough to explain the formation of general concepts, since the enumeration of relevant phenomena requires a previous abduction to decide which are the relevant phenomena (Génova, 1997).

The Strength and Weakness of Induction

Radical empiricism defends the idea that a work only deserves to be qualified as "scientific" if it is supported by "empirical evidence". Indeed, it is very easy to criticize this thesis: the idea that "only those propositions that are obtained through experience are scientific, and thus acceptable as true", is not supported itself by any kind of empirical evidence. Therefore, radical empiricism must be rejected as self-contradictory. Of course, we do not want to deny the extraordinarily important role that empirical evidence has in science. We only want to show the limits of obtaining knowledge through induction from experience. (Do not confuse with "mathematical induction", which despite its name is a form of rigorous deductive reasoning.)

The big problem of induction is to determine whether it truly has a rational foundation, since the mere fact that particular experiences are repeated does not warrant the positing of a general law, as the critics of inductivism have constantly remarked since ancient times. In his *Enquiry Concerning Human Understanding* (1748), Hume argued that it is impossible to justify inductive reasoning: it certainly cannot be justified deductively, and it cannot be justified inductively (from the success of past uses of induction) since it would be a circular justification. Nonetheless, he continued, we perform it and improve from it. It has no rational justification, but it is rooted in instinctual habits; it is unreliable, but we have to rely on it.

During the 20th century two main philosophical stances have dealt with the problem of induction: Verificationism and Falsificationism. However the critics, *Verificationism* upholds an optimistic thesis: induction is possible. This optimism provides the ground for the most generalized attitude among scientists, which precisely leads them to seek the confirmation of their theories in experience. Verificationism admits *a priori* that regularities cannot be casual: there must be some kind of rationality in the universe, which human reason can discover. Bertrand Russell represents the modern sarcastic criticism to this view with his story of the "inductive chicken", which after months of repeated experiences (most regular, indeed) came to the firm conclusion that the man who fed it every morning in the farmyard would continue to do so until the end of times, with all his affection… (Russell, 1997, p. 36): "It must be conceded, to begin with, that the fact that two things have been found often together and never apart does not, by itself, suffice to *prove* demonstratively that they will be found together in the next case we examine. The most we can hope is that the oftener things are found together, the

more probable becomes that they will be found together another time, and that, if they have been found together often enough, the probability will amount *almost* to certainty. It can never quite reach certainty, because we know that in spite of frequent repetitions there sometimes is a failure at the last, as in the case of the chicken whose neck is wrung. Thus probability is all we ought to seek."

Falsificationism, as set forth mainly in the writings of Karl Popper, considers also in a rather pessimistic way, together with the critics of verificationism, that induction is not possible (Popper, 1959; Popper, 1963). He argued that induction is not a part of scientific procedure, and that inference based on many observations is a myth. We cannot aspire to prove the truth of any scientific theory. Scientific hypotheses are no more than mere conjectures that are provisionally accepted until a new experience appears to refute them (what Popper calls "falsification"). This stance is informed by a commendable skepticism which has helped to give it credit among scientists, too. But the truth is that, if taken to its ultimate consequences (beyond the point Popper himself would have taken it), Falsificationism becomes absurd: scientists do not devote themselves to formulating and provisionally accepting *whatever theory*, and then to looking for counterexamples that refute it. On the contrary, scientists strive to verify hypotheses as much as to refute them, and they only accept hypotheses which are reasonable from the start and that have a huge explanatory power (Génova, 2010).

Our point here is that neither Verificationism nor Falsificationism can give a full account of scientific activity without referring to something that is beyond factual experience. We can say that both are right in what they deny, but they are wrong in what they affirm. Verificationism is right in saying that hypotheses must be experimentally verified, but it is wrong in claiming that induction from experience can reach scientific truth with absolute certainty. Falsificationism is right in saying that induction cannot be formally justified, but it is wrong in claiming that science essentially tries to refute theories. The reality of science is that induction is constantly used (and required by the scientific community) to validate theories, even if it lacks a formal justification and yields only "probable" results. The progress of science depends on principles that do not arise solely from formally verified experience. The limitation of reason to the empirically verifiable is more a hindrance than a help in the way of science.

Now, leaving apart the philosophical problem of induction, we still have the practical problem of determining what counts as a valid experiment that verifies a given theory. How many trials are enough? What percentage of confirming results should be required to accept a theory? The absence of *a priori* answers to these questions clearly implies the impossibility to fully formalize the scientific method. In fact, the answer has to be found in the "public", "social" character of science. This does not mean, far from it, that scientific truth is established by consensus, but that research results must be demonstrable to others: science is not a private affair. The sociological and subjective aspects of science have been highlighted after the failure of previous formalistic descriptions of scientific activity (Polanyi, 1958; Kuhn, 1962; Feyerabend, 1975). What the scientist looks for is to follow a way towards knowledge that can be followed by other researchers; the goal is to "convince" the scientific community of the validity of certain research results. This implies that, besides having empirical support, scientific works must be presented with adequate reasons and interpretation of results. So, how many trials? As many as the scientific community reasonably requires…

THE SCIENTIFIC METHOD IN SOFTWARE ENGINEERING

Plurality of Research Methods

The IEEE Computer Society defines software engineering as "the application of a systematic, disciplined, quantifiable approach to the development, operation, and maintenance of software; that is, the application of engineering to software" (IEEE, 2010). The application of the scientific method to research in this field has to consider both the products and the processes of engineering. The *products* of software engineering include all pieces of information that are created by developers in the course of building a software application, the "complete set of software and documentation" (IEEE, 2010): not only the running application and the source code, of course, but also other kinds of documents that are essential to develop, operate and maintain the application, such as requirements and design specifications, models, cost estimations, correctness tests, etc. The *processes* include all different kinds of procedures followed by software professionals to reach the final goal of building a software application, "a collection of steps taking place in a prescribed manner and leading to an objective" (IEEE, 2010).

The purpose of software engineering research methods is to improve both software products and processes. But these two aspects have fundamentally different properties that cannot be ignored when choosing an adequate research method. The products of software are information pieces that are essentially immaterial, certainly requiring some kind of material basis to exist (the hardware), but they are inanimate entities without free will in the end. On the contrary, the processes of software involve humans that can reflect on themselves and change their behavior accordingly. In this sense, the scientific method applied to software products shares principles with natural sciences such as physics, chemistry or biology, whilst the consideration of human factors in software processes demands a method closer to social sciences such as economics, psychology or pedagogy. The laws of behavior discovered for software products will be, like in the natural sciences, deterministic or non-deterministic. The source of indeterminism can be an inherent characteristic of the product, even intentionally wanted, or else the multiplicity of poorly known influencing variables in complex systems (improper indeterminism). It is indeed possible to discover probabilistic laws of behavior also for large human populations, but we cannot forget that non-deterministic causation means something completely different in social sciences: the subjects of research are human beings that can change their behavior through cognition and will.

We must also consider that software engineering is rooted both in *formal and empirical methods*. The origin of computer science is mathematics, and a large part of the research performed in the field of computers and their applications follows a more or less formal method, i.e. definitions, axioms and proof of theorems. A formal system is a human creation, a closed, idealized world with its own laws of behavior, like a game and its rules. In a formal system, be it about modeling languages, cryptographic algorithms or neural networks, the laws are deduced *a priori* from principles axiomatically established; the conclusions are drawn deductively and, properly speaking, there is no need for observation and experimentation of phenomena; the behavior principles are perfectly known because they have been created by humans. Whether a formal system has anything to do with reality is important for its usefulness and applicability, but does not affect its inner consistency. In contrast, the behavior of a real system, be it composed of machines, humans, or both, usually depends on factors that are *discovered* rather than established by human will. Therefore, observation and experimentation are essential to reach inductive knowledge of the laws of behavior of a real system.

Is there a place for experimentation with formal systems? Generally speaking, a formal system (sometimes called a "model" in the context of software engineering) can be used to *analyze* an existing real system, or to *design* a real system to be built (Génova et al., 2009). Indeed, a formal system can be used to build a real system (for example, a computer running a certain algorithm) whose behavior can be observed so as to draw empirical conclusions. If the experiments contradict the predictions, it can be due to an incorrect application of the formal method, or to the fact that the formal system does not adequately represent the real system. Consider a set of dice, each one having equal probability for all faces, implemented as ivory cubes or as computer programs. One can mathematically demonstrate the probability of obtaining a particular result when throwing the dice. If repeated experiments contradict the calculated probability, then either the demonstration was faulty, or else the physical dice are bad implementations of the ideal dice. Obviously, the empirical conclusions are not so strong as the results of (correct) formal proofs, but when the formal method is difficult to follow strictly, the empirical method can greatly help to understand the formal system. A good example is artificial intelligence, where the final behavior of the system is difficult to derive only from its established principles (Cohen, 1995). Empirical conclusions can even encourage finding a formal proof of the obtained results.

In the last decades of the 20th century a growing conviction consolidated: the scientific method developed for studying and analyzing *natural phenomena* was not apt to understand the design and construction of *human artifacts*. The required method should not start with the observation of phenomena, but rather with the identification of a need, followed by artifact construction and evaluation (Hevner et al., 2004). This emerging field of construction-oriented research was called *design science*, the scientific study of design, and it was based on two assumptions: first, the design of artifacts can be a sophisticated task that contributes to the development of scientific knowledge; second, the scientific design of artifacts requires a specific research method (Frank, 2006). Note that the concept of "artifact" encompasses not only physical devices, but also conceptual and social systems: information structures, knowledge representations, methods, processes, organizations, etc. Probably the most prominent proponent of establishing research disciplines that do not follow the classical scientific model was Herbert Simon, who popularized the concepts of design sciences, as opposed to natural sciences, in his seminal work *The sciences of the artificial* (Simon, 1969). Natural sciences are aimed at "truth", i.e. at the exploration and validation of generic cause-effect relationships, whilst design sciences are aimed at "utility", i.e. at the construction and evaluation of generic means-ends relations (Winter, 2008). Design sciences are grounded on natural sciences: valid cause-effect relationships give the possibility to build useful means-ends relations. Besides, design sciences pose ethical issues about what ends are desirable and what means are legitimate and proportionate to achieve those ends, which demands a solid ethical education (Génova et al., 2007). Design science research is currently an expanding field that is on its way to achieve the same standards of rigor and relevance that is currently possessed by natural sciences.

Classification of Research Methods

In the previous reflections we have considered three different dimensions of research in software engineering: (i) the product-process dimension; (ii) the formal-empirical dimension; and (iii) the analysis-design dimension. Some authors have provided useful classifications of research methods that implicitly or explicitly consider these dimensions. We summarize here two of these classifications.

Hanenberg, who is strongly concerned by the missing consideration of human factors in the justification of new artifacts that supposedly improve the software development process (such as programming language constructs), classifies research methods in two main, partially overlapping categories: technical approaches and empirical approaches (Hanenberg, 2010). *Technical approaches* are adequate whenever the software developer or user does not play any role in the subject of research, that is, the subject of research is a formal system or a physical machine. They include:

- Pure formal methods that achieve deterministic results (the "classical approach") or non-deterministic results (the "stochastic-mathematical approach"). Examples are research on inherent properties of deterministic algorithms and data structures, and research on parallel computing and randomized algorithms.
- Empirical methods that achieve statements using statistical methods applied on measurements resulting from experiments (the "stochastic-experimental approach" and the "benchmark-based approach"). An example is the research on software performance.

Empirical approaches include, besides the technical empirical methods, other approaches where the consideration of the role of the developer or user is essential (the "socio-technical approach"), since the research is performed to study how *developers* can write better software (i.e. software that has fewer errors, is more maintainable or is more reusable), or how *users* can interact better with software systems. Examples are the invention of new programming paradigms such as object orientation or aspect orientation, the design of graphical user interfaces that bring an improvement from the cognitive point of view, etc. The formal-empirical dimension is predominant in this classification, even though the product-process dimension is also implicit: the roles of users and developers are crucial to respectively assess the quality of products and processes.

Hanenberg, following Tichy (Tichy, 1998), criticizes the lack of empirical validation in a large part of the research performed in the design of new development artifacts, especially when compared with the extensive and effective use of the socio-technical approach in the field of Human-Computer-Interaction (HCI) (Shneiderman & Plaisant, 2009). Too often only qualitative criteria are provided to justify the advantages and adequacy of a new language construct, without any empirical evidence that developers *really* become more productive by learning and using it. Therefore, Hanenberg claims, the socio-technical approach *is* currently burdened with an excess of speculative reasoning, while it *should be* enriched with the kind of empirical methods that are actually used with human subjects in HCI and other sciences like psychology.

Mora et al. are more favorable to conceptual methods, against a biased negative view of non-empirical methods (Mora et al., 2008). They perform a literature review of methodological taxonomies in information systems research and offer their own framework to classify research methods. This framework is structured by two dimensions: "conceptual vs. reality" and "natural/behavioral vs. purposeful design". These two dimensions permit to classify research methods into four quadrants: the conceptual behavioral research (CB), the conceptual design research (CD), the empirical behavioral research (EB) and the empirical design research (ED). They further identify different activities that are typically performed in each quadrant, and provide examples, published in top scientific journals, of researches performed according to the four kinds of methods:

- **CB:** Conceptual analysis of behavior in existing knowledge management systems, in a tutorial and descriptive way.
- **CD:** Conceptual design of decision support systems, building predictive models of the effects of advanced information technologies in business intelligence capabilities.
- **EB:** Empirical analysis and validation of behavior and plausible causal links between different constructs in knowledge management systems.
- **ED:** Empirical design, construction and validation of a decision support system to select an investment portfolio.

The first dimension in this framework roughly corresponds to our previously identified "formal-empirical" dimension, except that, for Mora et al., conceptual methods encompass both formal and qualitative reasoning. The second dimension is also similar to our "analysis-design" dimension: the natural/behavioral method pursues a theoretical understanding (i.e. analysis) of the behavior of a given entity, be it natural, social or artificial, conceptual or real, without modifying it; the opposed method purposefully intends the design of a new artifact or the modification of an existing one. Mora et al. do not explicitly consider the "product-process" dimension.

Research methods can also be classified, from a different perspective, according to basic beliefs about scientific inquiry: ontology–what is reality, epistemology–how we know reality, and methodology–how we plan the research accordingly (Guba & Lincoln, 1994). The possible answers to these questions classify the methods into two main alternative inquiry paradigms, either positivist (reality is something given) or interpretivist (reality is something we construe), each one having several subtypes and including a variety of methods.

Summing up, the variety of research topics and objectives of information systems research cannot be covered in a satisfactory way by one method (Frank, 2006), and the purpose of a research project (exploratory, explanatory, descriptive, predictive) should be used to identify the most adequate research strategy in each case (Marshall & Rossman, 1995).

The Role of Qualitative Reasoning

Formal methods provide strong deductive tools that greatly improve the power of human reason. A rigorous mathematical or logical demonstration offers certainty in the correctness of the result, and it can be checked by anyone who masters the technique. This publicity of the method is essential for science understood as a social enterprise. But the results of formal methods are valid only within the formal system, they depend in the end of the free choice of axioms. Formal methods suffer the risk of being correct, but irrelevant: formal correctness is not truth. How can we ultimately assure that the formal system is a good representation of a real system, that it is useful or applicable? The *adequacy* to the real world is simply beyond the capability (and purpose) of the formal method, it has to be judged from outside the method. Yet it is good that it is so: a formal method would cease to be formal, losing its main strength, if it tried to answer this question.

Some will claim that empirical methods are the answer. Modern science is inconceivable without them. The repeatability of experiments fulfills the requirement of publicity and, indeed, the combination of formal and empirical methods is the distinctive mark of modern science: building theoretical models and contrasting their predictions against observation of reality. Accepting that empirical methods achieve a lower level of certainty than formal methods (remember the problem of induction), they assure instead the correspondence between theoretical models and reality. But, again, empirical methods are limited. We have already noted that justifying the reasonability of a hypothesis prior to designing experiments, judging on causality, and choosing a valid experiment to confirm a theory, are all activities that lie beyond the empirical method in and of itself. Empirical evidence must be adequately *interpreted* with good reasons to recognize what an experiment really demonstrates.

So, neither formal nor empirical methods can provide a full account of scientific activity, which relies on something that is beyond axioms and factual experience, beyond formal proofs and rigorous statistics. In other words, scientists have to reason also outside the scientific method, which is especially manifested when they are choosing the most adequate method for a certain research project, and when they are interpreting the results (Kitchenham, 1996). Even if empirical methods are useful in some fields such as HCI, qualitative methods involving heuristics and human judgment

are also required (Nielsen & Mack, 1994). Logical evidence and empirical evidence require a work of clarification and development of concepts. This kind of meta-methodical reasoning, which we call *qualitative reasoning*, is not anecdotal; on the contrary, it is the very basis onto which the scientific method is developed, however weak be that basis. Reason uses the powerful tools of formal and empirical methods, but reason is not confined within the limits of any established method. Qualitative (i.e. meta-methodical) reasoning plays the *directive role* in scientific activity. Theorems and experiments without the guide of speculative thinking are worthless.

Improving the Methods

We think software engineering needs to improve the application of the scientific method in two main directions: empirical and conceptual/qualitative methods (formal methods are strong and widely used, so we think they do not need such an encouragement at present). As Hanenberg, Tichy and others claim, better empirical methods have to be applied to verify the advantages of a new invention for the software development process, with a special consideration of human factors. Too often a new software artifact, embedded in a certain theory of the software process, is presented with a tool that implements it and shows its applicability (think of software modeling languages "demonstrated" with accompanying software CASE tools). But we should be careful to distinguish between experimentation of a theory and its practical application: the latter is particularly important in engineering, but developing a practical application does not properly constitute an experimental verification, according to inductive criteria, of the theory that supports it. The tool can demonstrate that the artifact and the theory supporting it are *applicable*, but it does not demonstrate that current practices in software development will be *improved*, i.e. that software developers will become more productive.

Tichy enumerates eight fallacies that prevent the widespread adoption of empirical methods in software engineering (Tichy, 1998): the current level of experimentation is already good enough, experiments cost too much, tool demonstrations are enough, etc. He reports that, in a random sample of papers published in ACM software-related journals before 1995, around 50% of those with claims that needed empirical support had none at all, contrasting the fraction of 15% found in other sciences. The "socio-technical" approach, then, should be fostered in software engineering research (Juristo & Moreno, 2001). However, this approach faces some obvious difficulties, as does any kind of empirical approach where the subject of research is a human population. This is not an excuse not to perform experiments, but a warning against a too naïve design and interpretation of experiments. Empirical software engineering has to learn its methods from social sciences (a good example of success is HCI). The design of controlled experiments is particularly difficult because every human person has a different culture, education and environment that clearly will influence his or her reaction to an experiment. People are not atoms or falling bodies that behave always the same: they learn from experience, and they can change their behavior.

The repeatability of experiments, then, is compromised. Can we really *repeat* an experiment with human subjects? Can we change the value of *one single variable* in the initial conditions of the experiment, everything else being equal, so as to design a counterfactual experiment and draw valid empirical conclusions? We cannot rewind history and pretend the subjects are in the same state as they were before the first try. Another particularity of human subjects is that they behave in a different way as usual when they know that they are the subjects of an experiment (a phenomenon known as the "Hawthorne effect") (Kitchenham, 1996; Katzer et al., 1998). To minimize this effect, the subjects should be unaware of the experiment. Yet this has ethical implications: we cannot ex-

periment with humans without their consent and collaboration. The only way to escape from these limitations is to increase the population that is the subject of research, making it as heterogeneous as possible. Experiments performed on a group of students from a single university or even from a single class are of very limited value. The ideal would be extending the experiments to many software professionals from different countries and organizations. A recent and promising approach based on the Mechanical Turk platform (http://www.mturk.com) could help to overcome some of these difficulties with the potential to conduct experiments on large and varied populations (Alonso & Lease, 2011).

In any case, the researcher must be conscious that statistical conclusions drawn from a large population will have very limited predictive value in particular cases. Even if it were empirically demonstrated, say, that object orientation makes developers across the world more productive than structured programming, which is a controversial statement with defenders (Haythorn, 1994; Juristo & Moreno, 2001) and opponents (Hatton, 1998), we are not guaranteed that introducing object orientation in a particular organization would be beneficial. Developers (and so instructors and students) are intelligent beings that need to be re-educated to assume a new programming paradigm or whatever new software artifact that is presumed to improve the development process. Empirical arguments do not suffice, developers need to be rationally persuaded of the benefits, often with qualitative rather than statistical arguments. Therefore, improving conceptual methods, both formal and qualitative, is also essential for the advance of software engineering (in this respect, qualitative reasoning is "methodical", in the sense that it has to be rigorous, but it is also "meta-methodical" in the sense that it cannot be subjected to the predefined set of rules of an established formal or empirical method).

There is a widespread negative view of non-empirical approaches that considers conceptual research is based on speculations rather than systematic data collecting procedures (Mora et al., 2008). The term "speculative thinking" is often referred to something that has no scientific value in itself, as if it were a game of free dancing ideas deprived of any rational significance. Surely, this negative view is supported by the frequent abuse of non rigorous speculative thinking. Of course, conceptual, qualitative or speculative thinking cannot be reduced to such weak justifications as asserting subjective beliefs ("this approach is good because I like it", "it seems intuitively obvious", etc.). Taste and intuition are not objective enough to be shared by the scientific community: again, science is a public, not private, affair. On the contrary, qualitative reasoning must be grounded on a sound rational basis. Analytical rigor is difficult, but not impossible. The arguments must be presented in a clear, concise and objective way, pros and cons must be analyzed, opposing views must be carefully considered. But, in the end, qualitative thinking will remain a kind of non-empirical reasoning that requires a particular training to achieve evidence (non-empirical evidence) with the desirable degree of rigor in science.

CONCLUSION

Ultimately, we are seeking an appropriate balance between empirical methods and qualitative reasoning. They should not be considered exclusive ways, they are not enemies but cooperators on the road to scientific truth. Qualitative thinking is satisfactory to describe a radically new idea or a significant breakthrough in science and engineering, but it has to be complemented with validating experiments in subsequent works (Tichy, 1998). Qualitative or speculative thinking is also required to clarify concepts and to perform essential activities in science that cannot be closed within any established method, such as judging the adequacy between a theoretical model and the reality it represents, inferring causal relationships between observed phenomena, proposing reasonable explanatory hypotheses, deciding which experiments are necessary and interpreting their results. The practice of the scientific method requires to acknowledge (and overcome) its own limits; improving the scientific method is something that cannot be done from inside the method itself. Therefore, acknowledging the limits of formal and empirical methods, and opening the door to meta-methodical reasoning, is a must for software engineering. The new degree on Computer Science and Philosophy recently introduced in the University of Oxford demonstrates the interest to reach an understanding (University of Oxford, 2011).

Albert Einstein is often quoted as having said: "Not everything that can be counted counts, and not everything that counts can be counted". In fact the words must be credited to sociologist William Bruce Cameron (Cameron, 1963, p. 13). We do not intend to minimize the value and importance of empirical methods, when they are required. But we claim that empiricism is insufficient. There cannot be a complete scientific activity that consists solely of proving theories by means of experiments: first, theories must be formulated and developed, and their explanatory power must be demonstrated, so that the investment of human and material resources in the experiments, which may be very costly, can be justified; then, the experiments that will prove or refute the theories must be carried out. Moreover, experimental verification may say something about the *truth* of a theory, but it can say nothing about its *relevance*, i.e. its interest to the scientific community or society as a whole.

Not all branches of science are equal, not all kinds of research are equal. Experience and speculation must go hand in hand in the way of science. Some investigations will have a basically experimental character, while others will be primarily speculative, with a wide gradation between these two extremes. As long as all are demonstrable, we should not consider some to be more worthy of respect than others. If we are closed from the start into a radical empiricism that considers only empirical evidence is a valid support for a scientific work, then we will be unable to perceive the value of other kinds of thinking that historically have proved to be indispensable for the advancement of science (Génova, 2010). If this value is not perceived, rigorous qualitative thinking will not be taught in engineering schools. Since it is unavoidable that qualitative thinking plays the leading role in scientific activity, the result will be an impoverished application of the scientific method.

REFERENCES

Aldrich, J. (1995). Correlations genuine and spurious in Pearson and Yule. *Statistical Science*, *10*(4), 364–376.

Alonso, O., & Lease, M. (2011). Crowdsourcing 101: Putting the WSDM of crowds to work for you. In I. King, W. Nejdl & H. Li (Eds.), *Proceedings of the 4th ACM International Conference on Web Search and Data Mining (WSDM)*, (pp. 1-2). February 9-12, 2011, Hong Kong, China. Tutorial slides available, Retrieved February 14, 2011, from http://ir.ischool.utexas.edu/wsdm2011_tutorial.pdf.

Ayim, M. (1982). *Peirce's view of the roles of reason and instinct in scientific inquiry*. Meerut, India: Anu Prakasan.

Cameron, W. B. (1963). *Informal sociology: A casual introduction to sociological thinking*. New York City, NY: Random House.

Cantor, N. F., & Klein, P. L. (1969). *Seventeenth-century rationalism: Bacon and Descartes*. Waltham, MA: Blaisdell.

Chalmers, A. (1999). *What is this thing called science?* (3rd ed.). Maidenhead, UK: Open University Press.

Cohen, P. R. (1995). *Empirical methods for artificial intelligence*. Cambridge, MA: MIT Press.

Crombie, A. C. (1971). *Robert Grosseteste and the origins of experimental science, 1100-1700*. Oxford, UK: Clarendon Press.

Denning, P. J., Comer, D. E., Gries, D., Mulder, M. C., Tucker, A., Turner, A. J., & Young, P. R. (1989). Computing as discipline. *Communications of the ACM*, *32*(1), 9–23. doi:10.1145/63238.63239

Fann, K. T. (1970). *Peirce's theory of abduction*. The Hague, The Netherlands: Martinus Nijhoff. doi:10.1007/978-94-010-3163-9

Feldhay, R. (1998). The use and abuse of mathematical entities: Galileo and the Jesuits revisited. In Machamer, P. (Ed.), *The Cambridge companion to Galileo* (pp. 80–145). Cambridge, UK: Cambridge University Press. doi:10.1017/CCOL0521581788.004

Feyerabend, P. K. (1975). *Against method: Outline of an anarchistic theory of knowledge*. London, UK: New Left Books.

Frank, U. (2006). *Towards a pluralistic conception of research methods in Information Systems research*. ICB-Research Report No. 7. Institute for Computer Science and Business Information Systems, University Duisburg-Essen. Retrieved May 19, 2011, from http://www.icb.uni-due.de/fileadmin/ICB/research/research_reports/ICBReport07.pdf

Génova, G. (1997). *Charles S. Peirce: La lógica del descubrimiento*. Pamplona, Spain: Servicio de Publicaciones de la Universidad de Navarra.

Génova, G. (2010). Is computer science truly scientific? Reflections on the (experimental) scientific method in computer science. *Communications of the ACM*, *53*(7), 37–39.

Génova, G., González, M. R., & Fraga, A. (2007). Ethical education in software engineering: Responsibility in the production of complex systems. *Science and Engineering Ethics*, *13*(4), 505–522. doi:10.1007/s11948-007-9017-6

Génova, G., Valiente, M. C., & Marrero, M. (2009). On the difference between analysis and design, and why it is relevant for the interpretation of models in Model Driven Engineering. *Journal of Object Technology, 8*(1), 107–127. doi:10.5381/jot.2009.8.1.c7

Goodman, L. E. (2003). *Islamic humanism*. Oxford, UK: Oxford University Press.

Guba, E. G., & Lincoln, Y. S. (1994). Competing paradigms in qualitative research. In Denzin, N. K., & Lincoln, Y. S. (Eds.), *Handbook of qualitative research*. London, UK: SAGE Publications.

Hackett, J. (1997). Roger Bacon: His life, career, and works. In Hackett, J. (Ed.), *Roger Bacon and the sciences: Commemorative essays* (pp. 13–17). Leiden, The Netherlands: Brill.

Hamming, R. W. (1980). The unreasonable effectiveness of mathematics. *The American Mathematical Monthly, 87*(2), 81–90. doi:10.2307/2321982

Hanenberg, S. (2010). Faith, hope, and love: An essay on software science's neglect of human factors. In W. R. Cook, S. Clarke & M. C. Rinard (Eds.), *Proceedings of the 25th ACM Conference on Object-Oriented Programming, Systems, Languages, and Applications (OOPSLA)*, (pp. 933-946). October 17-21, 2010, Reno/Tahoe, Nevada, USA.

Hanson, N. R. (1958). The logic of discovery. *The Journal of Philosophy, 55*(25), 1073–1089. doi:10.2307/2022541

Hatton, L. (1998). Does OO sync with how we think? *IEEE Software, 15*(3), 46–54. doi:10.1109/52.676735

Haythorn, W. (1994). What is object-oriented design? *Journal of Object-Oriented Programming, 7*(1), 67–78.

Hevner, A. R., March, S. T., Park, J., & Ram, S. (2004). Design science in information systems research. *Management Information Systems Quarterly, 28*(1), 75–105.

Holland, P. W. (1986). Statistics and causal inference. *Journal of the American Statistical Association, 81*(396), 945–960. doi:10.2307/2289064

IEEE. (2004). *Software engineering 2004. Curriculum guidelines for undergraduate degree programs in software engineering. The Joint Task Force on Computing Curricula*. IEEE Computer Society, Association for Computing Machinery.

IEEE. (2010). *ISO/IEC/IEEE international standard 24765-2010 systems and software engineering -- Vocabulary*. Retrieved February 21, 2011, from http://www.computer.org/sevocab

Juristo, N., & Moreno, A. M. (2001). *Basics of software engineering experimentation*. Dordrecht, The Netherlands: Kluwer.

Katzer, J., Cook, K. H., & Crouch, W. W. (1998). *Evaluating information. A guide for users of social sciences research* (4th ed.). Boston, MA: McGraw-Hill.

Kitchenham, B. (1996). *DESMET: A method for evaluating software engineering methods and tools*. Technical Report TR96-09. Department of Computer Science. University of Keele, Staffordshire. Retrieved February 7, 2011 from http://www.osel.co.uk/desmet.pdf

Kuhn, T. S. (1962). *The structure of scientific revolutions* (3rd ed.). Chicago, IL: University of Chicago Press.

Łukasiewicz, J. (1957). *Aristotle's syllogistic, from the standpoint of modern formal logic* (2nd ed.). Oxford, UK: Oxford University Press.

Marshall, C., & Rossman, G. (1995). *Designing qualitative research*. London, UK: SAGE Publications.

Mason, S. F. (1962). *A history of the sciences*. New York City, NY: Collier Books.

Mora, M., Gelman, O., Paradice, D., & Cervantes, F. (2008). The case for conceptual research in Information Systems. In *Proceedings of the International Conference on Information Resources Management (CONF-IRM)*, paper 52, May 18-20, 2008, Niagara Falls, Ontario, Canada.

Nielsen, J., & Mack, R. L. (Eds.). (1994). *Usability inspection methods*. New York City, NY: John Wiley & Sons.

Pearl, J. (2000). *Causality: Models, reasoning, and inference*. Cambridge, UK: Cambridge University Press.

Peirce, C. S. (1867). On the natural classification of arguments. In C. Hartshorne, P. Weiss & A.W. Burks (Eds.), *The collected papers of Charles Sanders Peirce*, (vols. 1-8, pp. 461-516). Cambridge, MA: Harvard University Press, 1931-1958.

Peirce, C. S. (1877). Deduction, induction, hypothesis. In C. Hartshorne, P. Weiss & A. W. Burks (Eds.), *The collected papers of Charles Sanders Peirce*, (vols. 1-8, pp. 619-644). Cambridge, MA: Harvard University Press, 1931-1958.

Peirce, C. S. (1901). On the logic of drawing history from ancient documents especially from testimonies. In C. Hartshorne, P. Weiss & A.W. Burks (Eds.), *The Collected Papers of Charles Sanders Peirce*, (vols. 1-8, pp. 164-255). Cambridge, MA: Harvard University Press, 1931-1958.

Poincaré, J. H. (1952). *Science and hypothesis*. New York City, NY: Dover.

Polanyi, M. (1958). *Personal knowledge: Towards a post-critical philosophy*. Chicago, IL: University of Chicago Press.

Popper, K. R. (1959). *The logic of scientific discovery*. London, UK: Hutchinson.

Popper, K. R. (1963). *Conjectures and refutations: The growth of scientific knowledge*. London, UK: Routledge.

Putnam, H. (1975). What is mathematical truth? *Historia Mathematica*, *2*(4), 529–533. doi:10.1016/0315-0860(75)90116-0

Russell, B. A. W. (1997). *Problems of philosophy*. Oxford, UK: Oxford University Press.

Saliba, G. (2007). *Islamic science and the making of the European renaissance*. Cambridge, MA: MIT Press.

Shneiderman, B., & Plaisant, C. (2009). *Designing the user interface: Strategies for effective human-computer interaction* (5th ed.). Upper Saddle River, NJ: Pearson Addison-Wesley.

Simon, H. A. (1954). Spurious correlation: A causal interpretation. *Journal of the American Statistical Association*, *49*(267), 467–479. doi:10.2307/2281124

Simon, H. A. (1969). *The sciences of the artificial*. Cambridge, MA: MIT Press.

Tegmark, M. (2008). The mathematical universe. *Foundations of Physics*, *38*(2), 101–150. doi:10.1007/s10701-007-9186-9

Tichy, W. F. (1998). Should computer scientists experiment more? *IEEE Computer*, *31*(5), 32–40. doi:10.1109/2.675631

University of Oxford. (2011). *Bachelor and Masters Degree on Computer Science and Philosophy*. Retrieved February 7, 2011, from http://www.comlab.ox.ac.uk/admissions/ugrad/Computer_Science_and_Philosophy

Weyl, H. (1959). Mathematics and the laws of nature. In Gordon, I., & Sorkin, S. (Eds.), *The armchair science reader* (pp. 300–303). New York City, NY: Simon and Schuster.

Whetten, D. A. (1989). What constitutes a theoretical contribution? *Academy of Management Review, 14*(4), 490–495.

Wigner, E. (1960). The unreasonable effectiveness of mathematics in the natural sciences. *Communications on Pure and Applied Mathematics, 13*(1), 1–14. doi:10.1002/cpa.3160130102

Winter, R. (2008). Design science research in Europe. *European Journal of Information Systems, 17*, 470–475. doi:10.1057/ejis.2008.44

KEY TERMS AND DEFINITIONS

Causality: The relationship between an event (the cause) and a second event (the effect), where the second event is understood as a consequence of the first. Statistical correlation is a necessary but not sufficient condition to determine a causal relationship.

Empirical Method: An inductive method of reasoning that achieves fallible conclusions using statistical methods applied on measurements resulting from experiments.

Empiricism: A philosophical stance that defends the idea that a work only deserves to be qualified as scientific if it is supported by empirical evidence. It is rooted in David Hume's view that we know only what we perceive. Variants are Verificationism (induction is possible because regularities cannot be casual) and Falsificationism (induction is not possible, scientific theories are always provisional until they are refuted).

Formal Method: A deductive method of reasoning that achieves necessary conclusions from definitions, axioms and proof of theorems.

Hypothesis: A fact or theory that, if it were true, would explain the observed phenomenon. Backward reasoning from effect to cause. Following the hypotetico-deductive method, the hypothesis has to be confirmed or refuted by experiments. Hypotheses are fallibly generated by abductive reasoning.

Philosophy of Science: The branch of Philosophy that deals with the metaphysical issues arising from the study of scientific method.

Qualitative Reasoning: Reasoning outside any established formal or empirical method. It is essential to clarify concepts and to perform common scientific activities such as: justifying the reasonability of a hypothesis prior to designing experiments, determining causal relationships, judging the adequacy between a formal model and the reality it represents, deciding what statements need empirical validation, choosing a valid experiment, interpreting the experimental results, etc. Also called meta-methodical reasoning, speculative reasoning, or conceptual reasoning.

Reasoning: Inference of a conclusion from a set of premises. There are various modes of human reasoning, mainly deduction, induction and abduction (but also reasoning by analogy, and others).

Scientific Method: A cyclic, iterative process of observation, hypothesis formulation, and confirmation/refutation of hypothesis through experimentation. Also called hypothetico-deductive method. In design sciences, as opposed to natural sciences, the steps are identification of needs, artifact construction and artifact evaluation.

Socio-Technical Method: The empirical method applied in a research project where human beings play an essential role as subjects of experimentation.

Chapter 7
Process Theory:
Components and Guidelines
for Development

Martha García-Murillo
Syracuse University, USA

Ezgi Nur Gozen
Syracuse University, USA

ABSTRACT

Because the IS field is grounded in its applications to organizations, the challenge is to develop a coherent theoretical body of scholarly research, while also remaining relevant to the needs of the practitioner community. In this effort, the purpose of this chapter is to provide scholars with a general understanding of process theories and a taxonomy to provide some direction about how to make contributions to the theoretical legacy, particularly through often-ignored process theories, which are also relevant to practice.

INTRODUCTION

The purpose of this chapter is to provide scholars with a general understanding of process theories and a taxonomy of the components to take into consideration when developing this type of theory. The information systems (IS) field, like many other social activities, is filled with events involving interrelated entities, which leads to the many problems and outcomes that

we study. In this case, we consider an event to be an occurrence that can be affected by a set of circumstances ("Wordnet," 2010). Keen (1997) calculated that in a large company like IBM, there can be an excess of 300 processes. These include, for example, customer service, regulatory compliance, customer retention marketing, records management, purchasing, etc. Most, if not all, require information systems. However, while many of the issues that touch information systems also involve processes, much of the IS research analyses events as if they were static.

DOI: 10.4018/978-1-4666-0179-6.ch007

To give an example, Durmusoglu and Barczak (2011) examine the impact of IT on new product development (NPD) processes. They highlight three main phases: discovery, development and commercialization. The paper focuses on these processes, but the authors, instead of looking at the interactions that exist between them and the impact that technology has on NPD, use a survey which asked participants to indicate which tools they use in which process and to self-evaluate the impact of these technologies on the success of an NPD initiative. The study ignores the dynamic nature of this work and identifies technology like e-mail and on-line collaboration tools as factors that affect these three isolated stages of the process. The main reason for this is that it is empirically easier to test models where dependencies across relevant entities and time elements exist. As Pentland et al. (1999) indicate, processes are difficult to study because they are difficult to observe at any given point or location. They take place over days or weeks and often involve multiple parties, who may not even be in the same geographic location.

Information systems is still a young field, and academics are still debating whether or not IS should be considered a discipline. Because the IS field is grounded in its applications to organizations, it cannot be entirely theoretical. In an applied field, as Taylor, Dillon, and Van Wingen (2010) state, the challenge is to develop a coherent theoretical body of scholarly research, while also remaining relevant to the needs of the practitioner community. The strength of the IS discipline derives as much from its contributions to practice as it does from its conceptual derivations. This combination is most often found in theoretical frameworks that reflect the manner in which information systems and technologies are developed, used, misused, and implemented, and the manner in which they affect the operations of an organization.

Because of the interplay between theory and practice, the purpose of this chapter is to present a taxonomy that can provide some direction about how we can make contributions to our theoretical legacy, particularly through often-ignored process theories, which are also relevant to practice. We identify and define elements which we have identified from process studies in IS and from the contributions of scholars who have written about processes. To clarify: "Process theories explain how outcomes of interest develop through a sequence of events" (Crowston, 2003a). Similarly Keen (1997) defines process theories as "a specific ordering of work activities across time and space, with a beginning, and end, and clearly identified inputs and outputs." More modern versions also include the coordination of entities involved in a process (Keen, 1997). The next section of the chapter provides a detailed definition and explanation of process theories.

Normally, when we think of theoretical research, we tend to think of a highly abstract exercise with little relevance to practice. This chapter is much more practical in nature; the objective is to help researchers think about the elements they should consider when developing a process theory to explain phenomena. Ultimately, we hope to aid scholars to venture into the area of process theory by providing them with a taxonomy that they can use to ensure that their contributions are based on systematic thinking about process components.

Many of the references that we consulted for this chapter are highly technical, and some are highly mathematical. However, the purpose of this chapter is not to present formal proofs for techniques, but instead to provide tools that can help in the construction of process theories. From the references that are highly mathematical, we took the relevant concepts and explained them more simply.

This work differs from that done by Malone and by scholars who work at, or who have follow the lines of research from the MIT Center of Coordination Science, in that in their case the purpose is to help researchers map a process, while in this study the objective is to help generate theories from processes. There are, of course, overlaps between their work and this, which, when appropriate, are noted here.

DEFINING PROCESS THEORIES

In general terms, a theory is an explanation of a phenomenon. In a theory, the factors contributing to the phenomenon should be both necessary and sufficient. If a factor is only sufficient, it cannot be considered an explanation and is, therefore, not enough to be part of a theory. Think of the factor "lack of organizational readiness," which is a cause of enterprise resource planning (ERP) implementation failures (Gargeya & Brady, 2005); we cannot use that factor alone to theorize that a lack of organizational readiness will lead to ERP failure.

Process theory, more specifically, as Gregor (2006) defines it, is "an explanation of the temporal order in which a discrete set of events occurred." Mohr (1982) colloquially describes it as "the sort [type of theory] that consists of ingredients plus the recipe that strings them together in such a way as to tell the story of how Y occurs whenever it does occur" (p. 37) or as "one that tells a little story about how something comes about, but in order to qualify as a theoretical explanation of recorded behavior, the manner of the storytelling must conform to narrow specifications" (p. 44).

Process theories require an understanding of what a process is. A process is a set of activities that occur in a specific sequence to produce an output from the given inputs (Crowston, 2003a). Processes explain why and how a sequence of events happens, and why and how a specific outcome is reached as the result of that sequence (van de Ven & Huber, 1990). In processes, along with the inputs and the outputs, the steps that lead to the outcome, the entities that perform the specific actions, and the sequence and the timing of the events become important (Langley, 1999). That is, the focus is to find out why and how certain outcomes happened because of the inputs involved.

To characterize an explanation as a process theory, "it is not sufficient merely to name a succession of necessary stages or events…; one must also supply the external forces and provide ballistic processes constituting the means by which that sequence of events is understood to unfold" (Mohr, 1982, p. 37). The explanation must consider the causality or motivation for the events to have happened, and it has to specify the necessary conditions and the processes that could lead to, not one, but potentially to various, outcomes (Mohr, 1982).

Process theory belongs to the category of theories that Gregor (2006) calls *theories for explaining* or *theories for understanding*. This set of theories explains how and why an event or phenomenon occurs. The ability of process theories to predict is still limited because of the complexities of these processes and the still-limited tools that we have to test them and make forecasts. Structural equation modeling (SEM) techniques can provide some clues as to what entities are significant in the outcome, but they fail to tell us about the efficiencies or inefficiencies of the relationships among them. Simulation can yield scenarios, which is a step beyond statistics, but these are still imperfect, because a good part of these simulations requires major assumptions that tend to substantially limit the model. Our process theories will be able to make better predictions as more scholars apply them to other contexts and verify their accuracy.

In this chapter, we focus on theories that answer the question "How?" because they convey this notion of stages and time-dependent relationships. A process theory represents a system wherein the network of relationships constitutes what Lange (1965) calls "the structure of the system."

As in any other theory development effort, there are some important elements that need to be considered:

1) *Context*. What are the boundaries of the study? What should or should not be included?
2) *Structural questions*. How can the problem be best explained? How many entities are involved? Is the outcome the result of a series of steps or of isolated factors that contribute more or less simultaneously?

3) *Sector-related questions.* For whom is the theory being developed? How can this knowledge be applied? What are social, economic, and industry implications of this work?

4) *Epistemological questions.* How can the theory be tested? How do we know that the theory is sound? How is the theory contributing to the field?

These components provide the initial thinking behind the problem we are trying to solve, but there are also other elements to consider when developing this type of theory, which will be discussed in the following section.

Types of Process Theories

Thinking about process theory today forces us to consider its many manifestations. Because early explanations about process theory were significantly influenced by statistics, scholars tried to incorporate into their models dependencies across factors/variables, to the extent that these could still be tested using statistics. These more-limited models are what we call *infra process theories*; this term is not intended to be derogatory, but refers to lower levels of complexity. The IS field has countless examples of this type of theory, some of which are mentioned in this chapter. These are process theories that are tested statistically using SEM techniques, a method that is able to capture the notion of sequences. At higher levels of complexity, we have theories that can capture complex relationships such as loops and bidirectional dependencies, and that can be tested using simulation software. These I have named *traditional process theories*. A good example of this type is Nan's (2011) study of information technology use in particular an incident tracking support system (ITSS). Using a method known as *complex adaptive systems*, he builds a simulation to capture the behavior of users, as well as their interrelations with other users and their environ-

ment. The context of the study is the use of an incident-tracking support system and the manner in which users adopted it, learned to use it, and documented it. In particular, the simulation tracks learning, ITSS assimilation, ITSS flexibility, work performance overtime and work place flexibility. In a *traditional process theory*, the entities included can have a probabilistic status, such that their different manifestations can be modeled to represent the multiple outcomes that are possible given the many paths of a process.

The third type of process theory involves much more complex representations of reality, and this type we currently have no adequate means of testing. We call this type *supra process theories*, to indicate their higher levels of complexity.

Process theories can be highly abstract-formal, but also quite specific (what are normally know as local theories). The work that emanates from the MIT Center of Coordination Science provides the best examples of supra process theories.

Dynamic vs. Static Theories

Researchers have identified the differences between static—also known as *variance*—theories and more dynamic-type theories which, in this chapter, we call *process theories* (Gregor, 2006; Markus & Robey, 1988; Mohr, 1982). Details about process theories are scattered across many articles, so that it is often difficult to determine how or what should be considered when trying to make contributions that represent a process.

In this chapter, we make a distinction between static and dynamic theories. Markus and Robey (1988) defined *variance* or *static theories* as those in which sufficient and necessary relationships between antecedents and outcomes are invariant. *Dynamic theories*—process theories—focus on the flow of stages rather than simple cause-and-effect relationships. Similarly, Markus and Robey define *process* or *dynamic theories* as a "recipe of sufficient conditions occurring over time" (Markus & Robey, 1988, p. 584).

Figure 1. Comparison of variance and process theories (Modified from Langley, 1999)

Explaining product development through a variance type theory

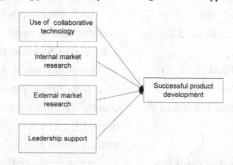

Explaining product development through a process type theory

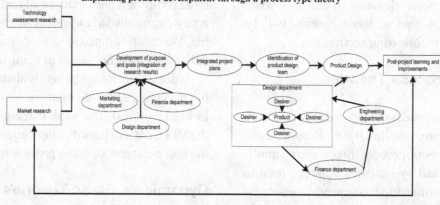

Variance theories define dependent and the independent variables, as well as the relationships between them. Crowston (2003) and Langley (1999) however, do not explain the sequence of events that take place in order for the input(s) (independent variables) to produce the output(s) (dependent variables). In a process theory along with the input, output, and the dependencies, it is important to identify the sequence of events that lead to an outcome—that is, it is important to understand how and why the inputs produce the output (Langley, 1999).

"Whereas variance theories provide explanations for phenomena in terms of relationships among dependent and independent variables (e.g., more of X and more of Y produce more of Z), process theories provide explanations in terms of the sequence of events leading to an outcome

(e.g., do A and then B to get C)" (Langley, 1999, p. 692).

Events or factors that lead to outcomes in process theories do not happen in an isolated manner. These are, in fact, related to each other sequentially, and nowadays, thanks to the Internet, simultaneously. As suggested by Mohr (1982), potential factors can lead to the outcome whenever they are combined in "a recipe that strings them together in such a way as to tell the story of how [the outcome] occurs whenever it does occur" (p. 37). More recently nonetheless, scholars have also recognized the fact that when studying processes, they find that any given outcome can happen as a result of, not one, but multiple, processes. In other words, there are points in some processes where an entity can have more than one option to move forward (Pentland, Osborn, Wyner,

& Luconi, 1999). We will discuss this notion of relationships later in the chapter.

In variance theory, time is irrelevant, meaning that factors are considered to be independent from each other, whereas in process theory, an event "tends to pick up where the other left off" (Mohr, 1982, p. 60); the order of events matters. Process theories, unlike their variance counterparts, are context-oriented and take into consideration links among the entities involved as they work together.

In variance theories, the functional relationship between the causes and the outcome is important; it may be linear or nonlinear, but the time ordering between causes and outcome is irrelevant because each cause is considered independent; even the term "holding constant," which is often used in statistics, demonstrates the irrelevance of time (Mohr, 1982). More recent statistical analyses try to capture time and sequences through lagged variables or methods such as path analysis and structural equations. These, however, are not yet able to capture the complexities associated with the dependencies that more modern process theories have identified, such as the multiple coordination types that can exist in the allocation of tasks and resources, or the sharing of resources among entities and the manner in which coordination efforts ultimately affect the outcome (Crowston, 2003b).

One significant difference between process and variance theory is the manner in which they relate causes and consequences. While in variance research the common relationship is stated as *if* x, *then* y, which means that x is necessary for y to occur, in process theory the causality is reversed; y implies x, which means that y happened *because* x happened. This is what Mohr (1982) calls *pull-type causality*.

In Table 1 the elements of static and dynamic theories are identified and distinctions between them are presented.

There are several reasons why having a clearer understanding of processes can lead to significant theoretical contributions in the IS field. First, most phenomena are affected by time, and although we normally assume that variables leading to an outcome happen simultaneously, most often factors, behaviors and entities work at different times—a feature that is not often captured by static (variance) theories. Many of the problems affecting the IS field involve human input in social settings; static theories can be quite limited in their attempts to capture the complexity of these relationships (Markus & Robey, 1988).

Variance and process theories should be seen as complementary: a variance approach can test to identify significant factors, while a variance theory can capture the manner in which the relationship, linkages, and dependencies affect the outcome.

Causality

How is causality expressed in a process theory? In this sort of theory, we do not think about binary manifestations of variables—that is, whether they are significant or not. Instead, the relationship between a string of entities is perceived within

Table 1. Comparison of elements of static and dynamic theories

	Static (variance) theory	**Dynamic (process) theory**
Time	Static/relevant	Longitudinal; the sequence of events matters
Outcome	Binary	Presented often as multiple outcomes or as scenarios
Causality	x is necessary for y to occur	y implies x
Levels of Analysis	Often one, but many are possible	Often many
Entities	Single type, normally measurable	Multiple types often not measurable
Stages	Limited, often only two	Multiple states with loops and simultaneous sequences.

Note. Modified from Markus & Robey (1988).

a range of possibilities. The likelihood that an event might happen depends on the context or the behavior of the actors of other events.

There are several tools that we can use to identify potential causal factors. One of them, as in any theory, is the regularity of patterns; we need to carefully review the context of the situation to determine if a certain entity or event happened by coincidence or if it was an element that played a role in the outcome beyond irrelevant chance. When thinking about causality in process theory, we need to collect records and attend to the regularity with which a factor that precedes another occurs.

We also need to think about spurious relationships, where a feasible factor appears to be related to another, while in fact it is hiding another relevant entity/factor. In this respect, Mohr (1982) argues that causality cannot be observed, and because of that, judgments are very much influenced by our backgrounds and beliefs. In this respect Pentland (1999) also recommend that one "cross-check (or triangulate) evidence from multiple sources to verify what is actually happening" (p. 5). The probability of events happening and the manner in which they relate to one another can change the overall course of events. Because of that, process theories often present multiple outcomes or explain a phenomenon through scenarios. Think, for example, of the selling process. When a company receives an order, it can happen through multiple channels. It can come from by phone, over the internet, or from a retail store. Depending on the product, the channel of delivery can be the internet, in the case of information, or physical delivery through postal or courier services. Each of these options will have different results, and the manner in which they are all integrated, for example, can affect the reputation and long-term profitability of a seller.

Processes matter because these complex systems work as wholes of a "higher order" that exhibit new properties and new modes of action, different from those of their individual parts (Lange, 1965). This is the *mode of action of the system* (Lange, 1965), the manner in which the states of the different elements in the system are transformed into a new set of states. Furthermore, the same entities and relationships behaving differently can lead to an entirely different outcome, and the same entities in different relationships can lead to a different outcome. In determining causality, therefore, we should think about how different behaviors and relationships, and the manner in which relationships are structured, can affect subsequent elements in the system and the outcomes.

Having said this, we need to be aware that in process theories, as Crowston (2003) indicates, instead of strict causation, we should also consider how the interaction of the multiple entities in a process theory shapes how things are used or organized and how potential problems at any given point in the process can lead to changes in the organization of work.

It should be noted that causality in our models is what differentiates a description of a process from a process theory. A description of a process simply states what entities do in a process, which leads to an outcome. In a process theory, the objective is to explain why something happened. It is assumed here that the scholar is trying to understand a phenomenon in terms of scholarly and professional interests for which a simple description is not sufficient. The task for the researcher is, thus, to move to a higher level of abstraction that extracts the essential components of a process. *Essentialism* here refers to both relationships and entities that cannot be removed without destroying the process (Pentland et al., 1999) and whose removal would make it difficult to explain the problem under study.

Figure 2. Components of process theories

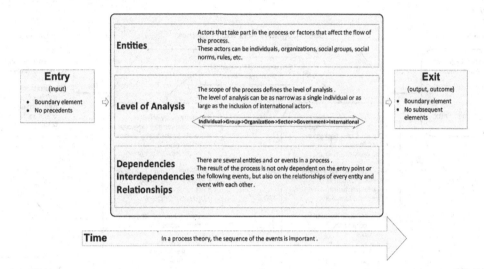

COMPONENTS OF PROCESS THEORY: A TAXONOMY

The terminology of process theory differs significantly from that of variance theory. Figure 2 presents these components.

In this section, we introduce these different components using a product development example, which features three stages of the product development process: the discovery development, and launch of a generic product.

Entities

We use Lange's (1965) definition of *entity*, which he describes as an active element that depends or acts on other elements of the system. Entities are also known as actors in more recent contributions regarding process. Pentland et al. (1999), for example, define entities as "individuals, departments, groups, or information systems"—that is, anything that performs the activities in a process (Crowston, 2003a; Pentland et al., 1999). Entities are either actors that take part in a process or factors that affect the flow of a process. Thus, entities in a process theory can include individuals, organizations, social groups, social norms, rules,

and so on. For the purpose of illustration, we will refer to the product development process, which entails multiple entities, stages, relationships and levels of analysis. Before a team engages in the development of a product they need to identify the opportunities. Generally, this entails market research. In product development, *entities* include the marketing research department, the customer service department, but also external firms that may conduct some of the customer surveys, and consumers themselves.

Entities can be categorized as tangible or intangible, as internal or external, and as actions or decisions.

In most of the papers analyzed for this chapter, we find that entities can play an active role, meaning that they can impact subsequent entities and the outcome.

Internal/External Entities

Internal entities affect the process directly. They include the entry point, the exit point and any element in between. There may also be external entities that affect the process more broadly. They affect, but are not, steps in the process, and are not impacted by its changes (Hughes, 1996).

Figure 3. Entities in a process (Vlaar, van Feneman, & Tiwari, © 2008, MIS Quarterly, Used with permission)

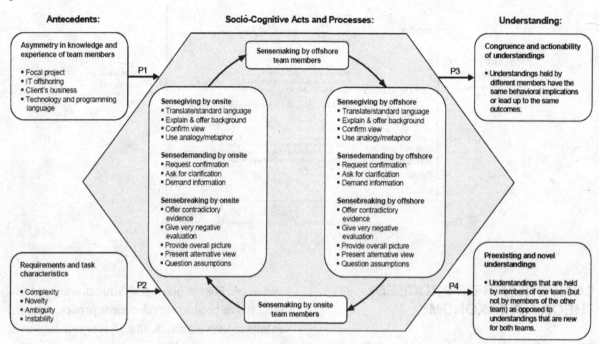

In the product development process, the internal entities would include the marketing, sales, and customer service department, while the external entities will include customers (See Figure 4).

In their paper "Co-Creating Understanding and Value in Distributed Work," Vlaar, van Fenema, and Tiwari (2008) analyze the socio-cognitive acts and communication processes that are used to understand the work of distributed teams. According to them, distributed work groups involve a wide variety of understandings, values, beliefs, cultures, norms and priorities, which may lead to different understandings of situations and/or attitudes towards goals. Communicating and creating a common understanding are very important in executing a successful project, and the process is iterative. Their framework includes sensegiving (the actions through which people influence each other and make each other understand the requirements better); sensedemanding (the act of a person asking for clarification); sensebreaking (the actions that make others change

or question the validity of their views); and sensemaking (observing, analyzing, and reasoning, so that a collective result can be reached and an understanding of the requirements can be obtained) (see Figure 3). All of these take place both onsite and offsite, and in an iterative and dynamic manner, to allow people get a better understanding of the situation. They also include background factors which affect the process and the internal entities, but which are not themselves internal. Antecedents, which the paper defines as the "asymmetry in knowledge and experience of team members" and "requirements and task characteristics," are not directly parts of the process; however, they affect it. Thus, we identify these as external entities.

Tangible/Intangible Entities

Tangible entities can be measured, seen and observed. They are less subjective, and usually have a more direct and definite impact. These can be

Figure 4. Entities in a pre-product development process

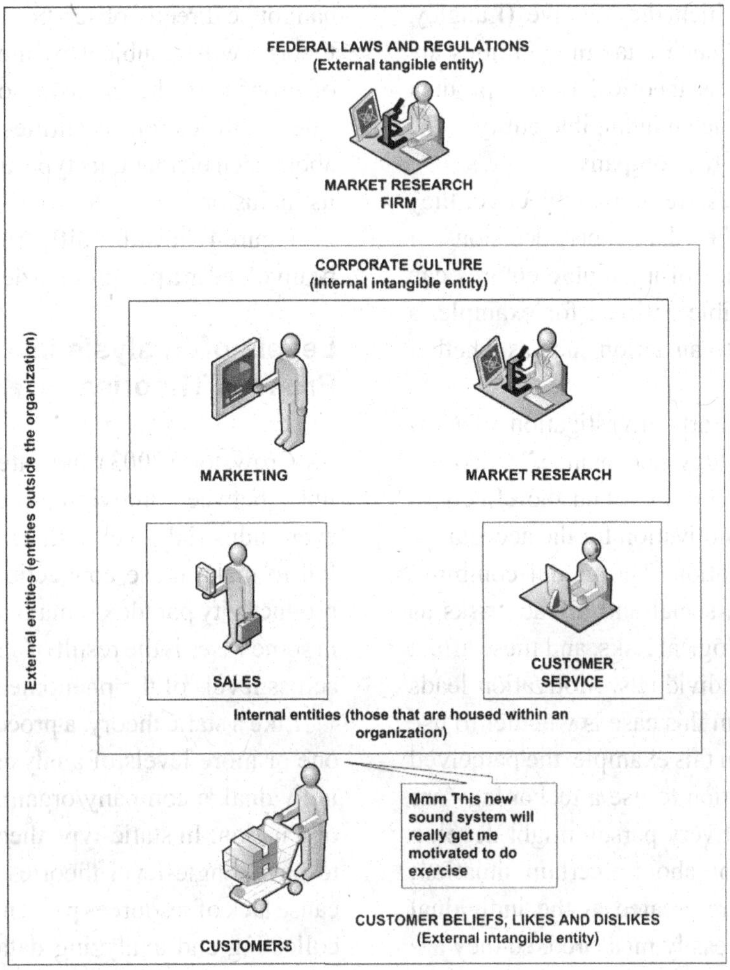

decisions, tasks, the behavior of people or the size of a market. In the product development example, tangible entities are the different departments where certain activities take place, the activities that they perform, such as the surveys that they develop, the many comments that they get from the customer support department, the reports they get from the external marketing firm and even the laws and regulations that govern the corporate sector in any given country.

Intangible entities, as the name implies, are non-material, difficult-to-measure entities, such as history (path dependency), the rules of society or the mental structure of the individuals involved in the process. Intangible internal entities include

the corporate culture that governs the activities and behavior of actors within the company and the beliefs that their customers have about the particular product the company designs (see Figure 4). Other examples of intangible entities are the interpretation and reaction of individuals to specific events, their cognition, emotions, and relationships with each other or with their environment (Isabella, 1990; Peterson, 1998). Although these are usually not testable or measurable, they may affect the flow of events by affecting the individual entities, their relationships and, ultimately, the outcome. Since process theories aim to explain why and how certain phenomena occur, they aim to explain not only individual events, but the factors that lead to them and the conditions under which they evolve (Langley, 1999). That is why such intangible entities are important for process theories. In our product development example an intangible entity is the corporate culture of the company.

Intangible entities are more subjective; they are perceptions rather than facts, decisions or actions. The behavior of intangible entities can be considered tangible entities; for example, a decision that leads to an action such as whether to buy or not.

In their paper "Early Investigation of New Information Technology Acceptance," Cocosila, Archer, and Yuan (2009) explain the effects of perceived risk and motivation for the acceptance of a new IT application. The model combines perceived financial, social and privacy risks as some of the psychological risks, and these affect the motivation of individuals. Motivation leads to behavior, which in this case is whether to use technology or not. In this example, the perceived risk and the motivation to use a technology are subjective entities. Every person might develop a different perception about a certain situation; these perceptions are created at the individual level and cannot be easily measured, so they are considered to be intangible entities. In the same example, the outcome is the behavioral intention to use the new technology, or not. That is the final decision of the individual, depending on the previous stages; this behavior is not a subjective entity. Negative or positive, the decision can be observed and tested. Thus, it is a tangible entity.

When building a process theory, we need to think about what entities to include or exclude from the process. Internal entities set the boundaries for the study, as it is not possible to include everything, while external entities help us to think about factors that may have contributed to the outcome outside of the initial context. We also need to think about the nature of the entities. Are they subjective or objective, and why? Subjective entities are much more difficult to identify because

they are often beliefs and cognitive processes that cannot be directly observed. Because of this, our theories will be subject to a more stringent burden of proof than the inclusion of tangible entities. The identification of entities forces us to think about each element, its type, and the rationale for its inclusion.

Figure 4 shows the different entities that would be involved in a pre-product development process.

Levels of Analysis in Process Theories

As Crowston (2003) indicates, processes make links between individuals, organizational and even industrial-level entities. Because we often fail to make those connections, effects like the productivity paradox remain unexplained, which in some cases is the result of a lack of connections across levels of the phenomenon of interest.

Like a static theory, a process theory can have one or more levels of analysis. These can be an individual, a company/organization, an industry or a nation. In static-type theories, it is common to have single-level theories. This happens because lack of resources prevents researchers from collecting and analyzing data at several levels. Similarly, the statistical requirements of handling more than one level are more demanding.

When we talk about levels of analysis, we refer to different aggregations of entities, be they individuals, dyads or collectives of different sizes. As Buzan, Booth & Smith (1995) indicate, the term *levels* is used because it is a simple mechanism by which the target units of analysis can be grouped according to the principle of spatial scale (small to large). As Klein et al. (1994) observe, a collective needs to have sufficiently similar attributes and express a certain cohesiveness to be able to be studied as a whole.

Generally, when we talk about levels of analysis in theory development, we want to be clear as to what level, to whom, or to what the theory applies (Rousseau, 1985). There needs to be consistency between the data collected and what we are trying to explain. In static theories, specifying the level of analysis is important, because there has to be consistency between what is being hypothesized and the data that are collected to verify it; however, with processes, the relationships can entail more than one level, and each level plays a different role in affecting how the process takes place. A process is able to encompass the links among the different levels of analysis of the different entities that contribute to the outcome (Crowston, 2003a).

In process theory, a process can relate to a single department, like in an in-house software development project, but it can also include multiple departments at different levels, as in a procurement system. Procurement for a large organization can involve all the different units of the organization, including the finance unit and the executive, each of which engages in different types of interaction with the rest of the organization. Moreover, a procurement study would have to include the different vendors and the market for each of these entities, because market dynamics can affect the quality, as well as the prices, of the items being purchased.

A good illustration of how levels are manifested in processes is Gallivan and Benbunan-Fich's (2005) paper about the use of information systems, where they try to provide a more complete picture of the problem by including multiple levels. As they note, "[S]tudying [system usage] one level at a time ultimately leads to an unnatural, incomplete, and very disjointed view of how organizations function" (p. 658). Their paper includes both individual and collective effects on system performance. This happens because of the interactions across the two levels, which create loop effects that can either positively or negatively affect performance.

In our product development example, such a process can entail several levels of analysis. Figure 5 illustrate the different levels that can be engaged in this process. The table is organized with the highest level at the top and the lowest level at the bottom

Given the richness that multiple levels can bring to a theory, when working with processes we should think about how each entity, individual or collective, is involved in the process and how its status and location within the organization or the market affects the process. Are there some collectives, for example, that affect the outcome more than others? Are there some individual entities that, because of their status, can have a much greater influence than others? What would happen to the process if we did not consider other levels? Would major pieces be missing if those other levels were not included? What would another level add to the theory?

As with any of the other components that we have identified, adding more levels adds more complexity and expands the boundaries of the study. It is for this reason that thinking critically about the value of adding levels and expanding the research is important, because there can be situations where adding another level adds complexity without significantly contributing to the main explanation of the theory.

Sequences

The reason why it is important for us to understand how entities are related when building process theories is because of the impact that a precedent has on a subsequent event. In this chapter, we use Abbot's (1995) definition of sequence: "an ordered list of elements," where time determines what goes first, second, third, etc., but not necessarily in real-time. This implies an abstract concept of time that indicates that some events happen before others. By *time*, we do not mean to say that event A happens *two hours* before event B and that event C happens *two days* after B. It should be noted that, today, technology has made it possible for people to work on a project simultaneously. The abstract element of time means that we do not care about the specific number of minutes or days

Figure 5. Levels of analysis in product development

Level	Entities involved	Description
Sector	Industry competitors 	In the development of a new product, a company needs to know about the industry trends
	External market research firms 	Market research firms are often involved in helping a company identify customer preferences .
Company	The XYZ Corporation 	A company as a whole is often the focus of a process theory, where factors such as culture and organizational patters can affect the processes of interest
Department	Marketing, product design, etc. 	Multiple departments need to be consulted and involved in the development of a new product. They help designers identify customer preferences before a project begins and later in the process help in the testing of prototype designs
Individuals	Designers, sales personnel, marketing personnel 	Each person within each department can affect a process because of the dependencies that exists in their work.

that it takes for events to happen, but simply that events happen in sequence. Sequences or stages can be simple and short linear relationships, or complex networks of events (Abbott, 1995). In this respect, Mohr (1982) criticizes the often-used approach in process theory, where only the successful outcomes are mapped. This is what he calls the *sausage machine,* "a program or a mechanism whereby one specific event follows another and a given output always results" (p. 57).

Sequencing does not preclude the presence of parallel and/or simultaneous activities. "[*S]equence* includes things like the order of steps in a manufacturing process" (Abbott, 1995, p. 95). Sequencing also implies the existence of dependencies among the different elements in the process, but this is not always necessary. There may be situations where some events are not directly linked, but their presence in the entire context can affect the outcome.

Figure 6. Product development process (Adapted from Wu & Chang, 2011)

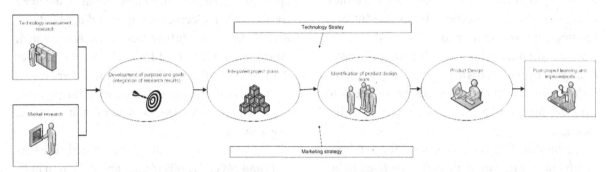

Thinking about sequence helps us determine the order of entities. The simple identification of entities is not enough for a theory to exist; how and why they occur a certain way can begin to provide an explanation, which is the purpose of theory.

It should be noted that when looking at sequences, we should pay attention to how each of them affects the phenomenon of interest. It could be, for example, that a particular entity in the sequence is no longer necessary. The Internet, for example, has made the existence of many type of intermediaries unnecessary. In our product development example, imagine for a second that what we are designing is a software package. In the past, the company may have been forced to work with retailers, who would sell their product in its packaged form. Today, with the Internet, the product can be delivered directly to the consumer either in its physical form or simply through a download. Wu and Chang (2011) present a set of sequences of the discovery phase of a product development process which nicely fits with our example. It shows how, before product development can begin, market research must be done to determine the goals and purpose for the new product. This, in turn, leads to an integrated project that includes input from both external and internal market research firms and departments. The plan incorporates the project plan, based on which a project management team is chosen to begin the design process.

Dependencies/Interdependencies/Relationships

Much can be learned from the work of Lange (1965), as well as from the *MIT Process Handbook* (2003). Lange's book on system behavior provides a basis for the conceptual understanding of processes. When depicting processes, we are inherently representing changes of events that are linked to each other. In Lange's (1965) terminology, when all the elements are connected, we have a chain of couplings. There are many ways in which processes can happen, such as loops and ramifications, which are some of the key characteristics of process theories. Similarly, more recently, Crowston (2003) gives us a taxonomy of dependencies that can help us understand the manner in which processes get organized.

In a process, entities (activities, actors, and factors) are dependent on each other. Some activities require the results of previous steps and are then impacted by these results and subsequently affect the steps that follow. Also, some activities may occur concurrently, so they may share resources (Pentland et al., 1999).

The series of configurations that is presented here represents the more traditional view of processes. Today, information technology has made it possible for some processes to happen simultaneously. In the past, when working on collaborative writing or software development, authors would go back and forth with their work, waiting for some things to be done by a collaborator before they could start their own section. Today, the Internet has made it possible for people to collaborate on a project simultaneously, which has significantly reduced the time it takes to get some projects done. So research involving processes today needs to consider the simultaneity of some events in the process.

Examples of dependencies can be found prominently in coordination theory, which explains the structure of complex processes with many interdependent activities (Malone & Crowston, 1994). Coordination theory suggests that in a process there are tasks (or events) and that there are dependencies between those, and the "process depends on the coordination mechanisms chosen to manage those dependencies" (Crowston, 1997, p. 157). In their paper, "The Interdisciplinary Study of Coordination," Crowston and Malone analyze the effects of information technology on collaboration in work settings.

The following sections examine the different representations of dependencies that can exist among entities. At the end, we present a diagram that represents all of these types within the product development example.

Loops

Chains of couplings can be open or closed. A *closed chain* is a loop where an element in the chain is coupled with an element appearing earlier in the chain. This kind of loop entails a feedback mechanism between the later and earlier elements. In contrast, a chain without feedback loops is considered an *open chain*. In some cases, the loops grow in volume over time; these are known as *spiral loops*. Battier and Girieud (2010) give an example of the development cycle that telecom operators face. Greater bandwidth allow us to have more demanding applications, which in turn require a better infrastructure that can support a bigger network load. That, in turn, provides faster speeds that allow us to have better and more demanding

applications and so on. In this scenario, the need for the higher speeds, the supported applications and the necessary infrastructure are interrelated. At every step, the need for each factor is greater than it was in the previous step. In other words, there is a amplification effect during the process, which can be visualized as a spiral that grows in every cycle.

A good example in the IS literature is Baskerville and Myers' (2009) paper about fashion in IS research. They use Abrahamson's (1996) theory of management fashion to make their argument. In their modified version, loops are at the center of the theory. In the market, supply affects demand and vice versa, and the fashion-setting process itself is dominated by loops that enforce a fashion.

In our product development example, the loop is closed after the prototype of a product has been developed and the design team needs some feedback on that initial design before the company engages in a formal launch. The company will have to go back to their marketing department, and potentially even an external marketing firm, to get feedback on the design.

Ramifications

Couplings can also have both input and output ramifications. A *ramification of outputs* is said to exist when one input can lead to multiple outcomes. A *ramification of inputs* is found when multiple inputs lead to a single output. In the product development scenario, a ramification happens right at the beginning of the process when the company decides to do market research and contracts an external marketing firm to do some of that work. Both marketing research activities are happening simultaneously. Figure 7 represents both of these types of ramification.

There are, of course, processes that include many different arrangements of couplings, which can include open and closed chains and different types of ramifications. In the product development example, there are several couplings from the

Figure 7. Graphical representation of input and output ramifications in a process. (Adapted from Lange, 1965)

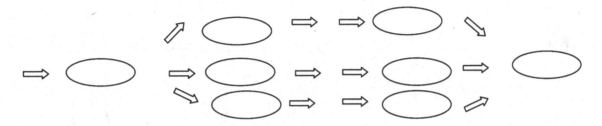

Figure 8. Representation of a network of couplings (Adapted from Lange, 1965)

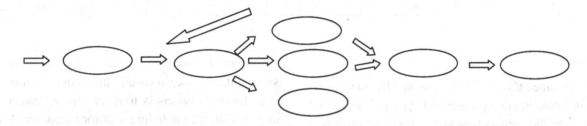

internal to the external entities, which help formulate the plan for the product. Lange (1965) calls these types of relationships a *network of couplings,* which is represented graphically in Figure 8.

The most recent work on dependencies from Crowston (2003a) makes a more sophisticated identification of dependencies. This work, in addition to identifying the entities involved in a process, includes the resources and the tasks that glue the entities together. These dependencies happen because tasks get done, and resources are allocated to accomplish them. It is this diversity of activities that need to happen along the stages of a process which generate dependencies. In his work, Crowston (2003a) finds that resources can be shared by multiple tasks, that some tasks can produce common or multiple resources, that one task can consume multiple resources, and that some resources are needed for a task which, in turn, generates a resource.

As Crowston notes, tasks can happen simultaneously and they can be organized hierarchically, where one task is composed of subtasks which all

need to be managed and where all are happening either simultaneously or sequentially and need to be integrated.

The identification of this type of sequence helps with the theorizing process because, as we think about the manner in which entities are related, we need to be aware of the many possibilities. Our brains tend to simplify things as a way of coping with the complexities of the world around us; thus, being aware of the many ways in which entities can be related to one another can help us to recognize such relationships when we encounter them in our research. Knowing that entities can relate to one another in multiple ways and having some tools to experiment as a researcher may prevent bias towards sequences that may seem obvious. In the product development example that we have presented throughout this paper, we have provided diagrams of the different components that we have identified in this taxonomy. Figure 9 is a more complete representation of the product development process, with some simple samples of the different types of relationships and dependencies that can be found across entities.

Figure 9. Representation of the software development process with its multiple relationships

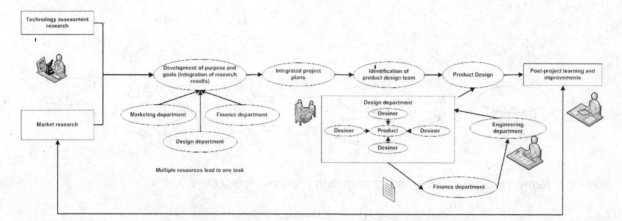

Time

In variance theories, time is generally not taken into consideration (Abbott, 1995), and it does not matter whether events happened simultaneously or sequentially. The main concern is their effect on the outcome, independent of the order. In the natural order of things, time is an ever-present element, and by taking it into consideration, we can enrich our stories as we try to explain a phenomenon.

In contrast, time is central to the development of process theories. Asking about the impact of time on any of the factors, entities, and relationships that are suspected to lead to the outcome will help us determine whether to work on a dynamic or a static theory. For example, a study about how a single person uses a new technology would benefit little from a process analysis, because not many entities are involved and thus there no need for coordination. However, a study about how an organization implements a new technology can benefit from this approach.

Monge (1990) recommends that in thinking about time, we take into consideration several dimensions of dynamic behavior, such as continuity, magnitude and the rate of change of the events involved in the process. *Continuity* means that the variable/factor/entity is always present. A *discontinuous variable* is one that manifests intermittently at regular or irregular intervals. For

discontinuous variables, the notion of *periodicity* is relevant, because it measures the amount of time that it takes for the entity to repeat. It may take a long or a short time before a factor reappears. A period can be measured from the time the entity emerges to the time it emerges again, or from the time it ends to the next time it ends. Similarly, another dimension of interest for discontinuous variables is *duration*, because the factor appears intermittently, and we may want to know how long it stays active.

Magnitude refers to the amount or degree that the variable/factor/entity manifests itself. An interesting mental experiment would be to determine, for example, the maximum, minimum and average magnitudes of the entities and to think about the implications of encountering the extremes.

The *rate of change* is the amount of time that it takes for an entity to increase or decrease, appear or disappear. A *trend* represents a pattern of change; this can be positive or negative, increasing or decreasing. An entity has no trend if it increases or decreases at random.

In variance theories, time is not considered. For example, the famous technology adoption model (TAM) relies on factors that explain why people adopt technologies. These factors will be the same for both early and late adopters, so it really doesn't matter whether you decide to buy into a technology early or later on; the factors that the theory identifies as relevant will not change. There are not many studies in IS that take time into consideration. A recent contribution by Kim (2009) provides an explanation of the logic behind the integrative framework of technology use (IFTU), where the impact of short- and long-term memory helps us explain usage after adoption. In general, both events that occur close to, and distant from, the evaluation of a technology have an effect on how a technology is evaluated after adoption. Previous research, as the authors comment, has assumed that continued use of a technology is a one-shot effort, while they argue instead that it involves interaction with the technology over time. In short, our past and recent experiences and the manner in which they get encoded in our brain can determine whether we will continue to use a technology or not.

One of the advantages of looking at single variables over time is the potential that doing so gives us to find patterns of theoretical relevance. Think about the diffusion of innovation curve through which we know how adoption happens over time. Consideration of the effects of time can uncover elements that would be impossible to identify otherwise, and taking into account how time affects the entities under study can, therefore, significantly impact our understanding of a phenomenon. The inclusion of time is, of course, not easy, because a study of this sort would normally entail potentially lengthy engagements with the entities involved.

In a product development situation, timing is crucial because it can determine, for example, the survival of a product over its competitors. Delays in the process can seriously affect its launch and ultimate success. In process research, the manner in which entities relate to each other and the efficiencies and inefficiencies of a process, often resulting in delays, are of much importance because they can represent problems that researchers may want to be able to explain.

Entry Points (Inputs) and Exit Points (Outcomes)

Entry Points (Inputs)

In a process representing a system, there are elements which Lange (1965) calls *boundary elements*. A boundary element is an entity that has no precedent (which makes it an input boundary element) or no subsequent element (which makes it an output boundary element).

The *entry point* of a process is usually the condition that starts it and shapes subsequent steps. The stages after that are thus a consequence of this first step. Moores and Chang (2006) examined individuals' decisions on whether to buy or pirate a product. The study aimed to understand how four entities—recognition, judgment, intention, and behavior—directly affected the decision to pirate (Figure 7). It also tried to understand the influence of age and gender, though indirectly. The initial recognition (entry point) was what defined whether or not a person perceived the act of piracy as wrong. Depending on that perception, a judgment was made regarding whether or not it was acceptable, and that judgment was closely tied to the next step, which was the intention to use or buy the pirated material. In this case, the whole process started with the moral recognition; thus, this was the entry point for the whole process. Not recognizing that the act is wrong led to the judgment that the behavior was acceptable, and the process proceeded from there.

In processes, subsequent steps are often inevitable responses to previous steps, including the entry point. In the case above, recognition led to judgment, which led to intention, which in the end led to behavior. In general, the entry point might be one of a variety of types, such as a problem, question, norm, perception, and so on.

In our product development example, the entry points were the technology and market research. It is assumed that the company knows that they need a new product, but we don't know the rationale for such a decision. If this were an actual research study, the question could have been, Why did the launch of the new product fail? The study could have focused only on the designed process or only on the launch process itself. These decisions and the point at which one starts the research are important because they set up the boundaries.

Exit Points (Outcomes)

Similarly, Mohr (1982) suggests that the notion of outcome differs significantly between variance and process theories. In variance theory the potential causes are conceived as discrete or discontinuous variables that affect the outcome. A process theory identifies a set of necessary conditions, such that some of them follow each other, and they may lead not to one, but to several different outcomes.

The exit, or outcome, of a process is the endpoint or end points of the entire flow. The outcome might only suggest a solution to a problem or situation, whether it is successful or not. That is the simplest form of process theory. There are other outcomes that do not propose solutions, but instead emerge as a response to a number of steps—that is, they are results shaped by the entry point and the subsequent stages. For example, in the preceding case, researchers aimed merely to find out the patterns that led to buying or using pirated material. Whether or not the user bought or used the material was manifested as a behavior, and that behavior was the outcome (exit point) of the process. The behavior, which was also a tangible entity, could be observed and tested.

There are process theories that lead to multiple outcomes, depending on how the entities behave at crucial points. It is, thus, not unusual that a process theory is presented in the form of multiple scenarios portraying different possible outcomes, depending on the form taken by the entities and their relationships along the way.

These boundary elements—entries and exits—are important because they force us to think about the initial condition we have to identify, and then the different possibilities that can emerge. Due to the fact that not everything can be included, the entry point represents a potentially arbitrary initial state. When selecting this initial step and entities, we must consider why this is a good starting point for the process. For the exit, we have to keep in mind that the outcome represents what we are trying to explain.

As scholars, we need to think carefully about the events or entities or behaviors that we believe the model should include. This is because, as the number of events and circumstances increases, so does the number of combinations of variables. The larger the number of entities and relationships, the larger the number of combinations, which can increase exponentially and lead to unmanageable results. In process theory, therefore, it is crucial to establish boundaries. We need to specify clearly the conditions under which the model can apply. As an alternative, one model can be broken into two or more models, each of which covers a smaller portion of the entire context. When a model is broken down into pieces, however, the limitations of each of the parts might make it useless. There is, thus, a trade-off between simplicity and usefulness. A theory needs to capture key events, circumstances, and factors without becoming impossible to manage.

PUTTING IT ALL TOGETHER

Up to this point, we have presented the components that should be taken into consideration when developing a process theory. We have nonetheless ignored some of the "glue" that is necessary for this type of study to work and present a viable explanation of the dynamic world around us. First, while we look at how something happens, we also need to consider how resources flow and get added or depleted as they move through the different stages. Resources need to be considered because as we work with information systems, we want to determine how technology has or has not affected resources.

The manner in which dependencies happen or develop is another issue that researchers need to consider. Sometimes the structure of a process has little to do with efficiencies and more to do with the culture and politics of the entities involved. Our understanding of processes needs, then, to explain not only how the process works, but also how factors other than sequences and tasks at any given point are affected by people's behaviors and organizational culture or rules.

The decision to develop a process theory over a variance theory depends on the problem and the resources available to the researcher. As indicated before, process theories are not easy to construct, but they can provide additional insights to our understanding of IS phenomena. The decision will also depend on whether the researcher believes that the relationships and their dependencies are more important than the factors in explaining an outcome.

EVALUATING PROCESS THEORIES

Scholars who have written about theory construction have identified several goals that they would like to achieve with their theories (Davidson-Reynolds, 1971; Dubin, 1978; Hage, 1972). These are:

(a) It should be able to organize and categorize things, a typology
(b) It should be able to explain
(c) It should be testable and replicable using the scientific method
(d) It should have some predictive value
(e) It should have the potential to control events
(f) It should be parsimonious
(g) It should be able to apply to an increasingly larger set of circumstances as it gets tested in different settings.

Within the context of process theories, goals (a), (b), and (g) can be accomplished when the theory is being developed; however, goals (c)

and (d) are more difficult because, as Crowston (Crowston, 2003b) indicates, we do not yet have appropriate methodologies to test the validity of these theoretical components. How, for example, can we test for whether the sequence is the right one to focus on? What if a process can have, not one, but several sequences—how would we know which one is better? Should time and resource efficiencies be the benchmark for evaluating them? How do we know if our theory has accurately identified all the entities involved? How can we measure the impact and weight that each of these entities has in the process? Unfortunately, this is work that still needs to be defined.

As Crowston (2003a) indicates in his article "Process as theory," we need to develop research methods that can help us operationalize the activities, sequences, and dependencies of our process theories. In this paper, we provide general guidelines about process theories. The objective is to highlight the elements that are common to this type of theory and the thinking that scholars need to consider when evaluating them. While we do not advocate the use of every one of these components, we expect scholars to think about them and make the necessary adjustments to the theory, to make sure that the scope, causality relations, entities and level of analysis are taken into consideration when developing this type of framework.

It should also be noted that the internal, external validity and effectiveness of a theory will be better assessed when scholars and practitioners begin to find similar results, or use the framework to understand a phenomenon, or make changes to an existing process, given the findings of a process explanation.

In addition to a careful consideration of these components, scholars should also consider other qualitative evaluation tools such as those proposed by Webster and Mertova (2007) whose criteria include: (a) proof of adequate access to individuals, documents and facilities, (b) honest descriptions and analyses of events, (c) avoidance of familiarity, the tendency of humans to make things routine, to the point that they become unaware of details that can be crucial to the understanding of a process, (d) inclusion of examples of similar types of processes in other settings, and (e) diligence in the identification of critical elements, but not necessarily all of the elements of a process that we are trying to explain.

These recommendations are quite limited, and that is because we have not yet developed the sophisticated tools and methods that will be necessary to test and validate the results of this type of theory.

CONCLUSION

This chapter, unlike the others in this book, aims to help researchers develop their own theories and venture into the world of process theory. It provides some basic understanding of the differences between process theory and variance theory and presents a taxonomy of its components as a tool to help scholars develop process theories.

A theory explains a phenomenon, and although many of the problems that we face in the information systems field involve processes, there are few studies focusing on them. This is the case because of the inherent bias that our research has towards static theories, which can more easily be tested using statistics. However, in favoring these, we are missing important insights that could lead to much richer explanations of the world.

In this chapter, we have outlined differences between static (variance) and dynamic theories and have explained how dynamic theories entail or treat some elements differently. We find in studying process theories that they differ in how the potential contributing factors are treated, how relationships are manifested in a process, and how time impacts outcomes.

This chapter provides a taxonomy of the different elements that scholars should take into consideration when developing process theories. We do not claim that these are the only

ones or that a process theory should include all of them, but that they should be taken into consideration because they help in the development of a theory and help to clarify the scope of the analysis, the entities, the manner in which they are related, the levels at which we want the explanation to happen, the assumptions we make about how the process begins and our expectations of how the outcomes will turn out.

We realize that these tools are unlike those of traditional research methods, because the goal is not to evaluate, but to create. We believe that, often, the enjoyable part of the research process happens when we give ourselves the opportunity to develop our own explanations, and given the limited number of process theories in the IS field, these endeavors could be a fruitful and satisfying exercise.

The greatest challenge of this type of theory is validation, for which additional work is sorely needed.

REFERENCES

Abbott, A. (1995). Sequence analysis: New methods for old ideas. *Annual Review of Sociology*, *21*, 93–113. doi:10.1146/annurev.so.21.080195.000521

Abrahamson, E. (1996). Management fashion, academic fashion, and enduring truths. *Academy of Management Review*, *21*(3), 616–618.

Baskerville, R. L., & Myers, M. D. (2009). Fashion waves in information systems research and practice. *Management Information Systems Quarterly*, *33*(4), 647–662.

Battier, M., & Girieud, S. (2010). Technical innovations. *Communications and Strategies*, *77*, 167–172.

Buzan, B., Booth, K., & Smith, S. (1995). The level of analysis problem in international relations reconsidered. In *International relations theory today* (p. 367). College Park, PA: Penn State Press.

Cocosila, M., Archer, N., & Yuan, Y. (2009). Early investigation of new information technology acceptance: A perceived risk - motivation model. *Communications of the Association for Information Systems, 25*(1).

Crowston, K. (1997). A coordination theory approach to organizational process design. *Organization Science, 8*(2), 157–175. doi:10.1287/orsc.8.2.157

Crowston, K. (2003). *Process as theory in information systems research.* Paper presented at the IFIP TC8 WG8. 2 International Working Conference on the Social and Organizational Perspective on Research and Practice in Information Technology, Aalborg, Denmark.

Crowston, K. (2003). A taxonomy of organizational dependencies and coordination mechanisms. In Malone, K. C. T. W., & Herman, G. A. (Eds.), *Organizing business knowledge: The MIT process handbook*. MIT Press.

Crowston, K. (2003a). Process as theory in information systems research. In Malone, T. W., Crowston, K., & Herman, G. A. (Eds.), *Organizing business knowledge: The MIT process handbook* (pp. 177–190). MIT Press.

Crowston, K. (2003b). A taxonomy of organizational dependencies and coordination mechanisms. In Crowston, K., Herman, G. A., & Malone, T. W. (Eds.), *Organizing business knowledge: The MIT process handbook*. MIT Press.

Davidson-Reynolds, P. (1971). *Primer in theory construction*. Indianapolis, IN: Bobbs-Merrill.

Dubin, R. (1978). *Theory building*. New York, NY: Free Press.

Durmusoglu, S. S., & Barczak, G. (2011). The use of Information Technology tools in new product development phases: Analysis of effects on new product innovativeness, quality, and market performance. *Industrial Marketing Management, 40*(2), 321–330. doi:10.1016/j.indmarman.2010.08.009

Gallivan, M., & Benbunan-Fich, R. (2005). A framework for analyzing levels of analysis issues in studies of e-collaboration. *IEEE Transactions on Professional Communication, 48*(1), 87–104.

Gargeya, V. B., & Brady, C. (2005). Success and failure factors of adopting SAP in ERP system implementation. *Business Process Management Journal, 11*(5), 501–516. doi:10.1108/14637150510619858

Gregor, S. (2006). The nature of theory in Information Systems. *Management Information Systems Quarterly, 30*(3), 611–642.

Hage, J. (1972). *Techniques and problems of theory construction in sociology*. New York, NY: John Wiley & Sons.

Hughes, T. P. (1996). Technological momentum. In M. R. Smith & L. Marx (Eds.), Does technology drive history? The dilemma of technological determinism (pp. 101-113). The Massachusetts Institute of Technology Press.

Isabella, L. A. (1990). Evolving interpretations as a change unfolds: How managers construe key organizational events. *Academy of Management Journal, 33*(1), 7–41. doi:10.2307/256350

Keen, P. G. W. (1997). *The process edge: Creating value when it counts*. Harvard Business School Press.

Kim, S. S. (2009). The integrative framework of technology use: An extension and test. *Management Information Systems Quarterly, 33*(3), 513–537.

Klein, K. J., Dansereau, F., & Hall, R. J. (1994). Levels issues in theory development, data collection, and analysis. *Academy of Management Review, 19*(2), 195–229.

Lange, O. (1965). *Wholes and parts: A general theory of system behaviour*. New York, NY: Pergamon.

Langley, A. (1999). Strategies for theorizing from process data. *Academy of Management Review, 24*(4), 691–710.

Malone, T. W., & Crowston, K. (1994). The interdisciplinary study of coordination. *ACM Computing Surveys, 26*(1), 87–119. doi:10.1145/174666.174668

Markus, M. L., & Robey, D. (1988). Information technology and organizational change: Causal structure in theory and research. *Management Science, 34*(5), 583–598. doi:10.1287/mnsc.34.5.583

Mohr, L. B. (1982). *Explaining organizational behavior*. San Francisco, CA: Jossey-Bass.

Monge, P. R. (1990). Theoretical and analytical issues in studying organizational processes. *Organization Science, 1*(4), 406–430. doi:10.1287/orsc.1.4.406

Moores, T. T., & Chang, J. C. J. (2006). Ethical decision making in software piracy: Initial development and test of four-component model. *Management Information Systems Quarterly, 30*(1), 167–180.

Nan, N. (2011). Capturing bottom-up information technology use processes: A complex adaptive systems model. *Management Information Systems Quarterly, 35*(2), 505–507.

Pentland, B. T., Osborn, C. S., Wyner, G., & Luconi, F. (1999). *Useful descriptions of organizational processes: Collecting data for the process handbook*. Retrieved from http:// ccs.mit.edu/ papers/ pdf/ wp208.pdf

Pentland, O. C. S., Wyner, G., & Luconi, F. (1999). *Useful descriptions of organizational processes: Collecting data for the process handbook*. Retrieved from http:// ccs.mit.edu/ papers/ pdf/ wp208.pdf

Pentland. (1999). Building process theory with narrative: From description to explanation. *The Academy of Management Review, 24*(4), 711-724.

Peterson, M. F. (1998). Embedded organizational events: The units of process in organization science. *Organization Science, 9*(1), 16–33. doi:10.1287/orsc.9.1.16

Rousseau, D. M. (1985). Issues of level in organizational research: Multi-level and cross-level perspectives. *Research in Organizational Behavior, 7*(1), 1–37.

Taylor, H., Dillon, S., & Van Wingen, M. (2010). Focus and diversity in information systems research: Meeting the dual demands of a healthy applied discipline. *Management Information Systems Quarterly, 34*(4), 647–667.

van de Ven, A. H., & Huber, G. P. (1990). Longitudinal field research methods for studying processes of organizational change. *Organization Science, 1*(3), 213–219. doi:10.1287/orsc.1.3.213

Vlaar, P. W. L., van Fenema, P. C., & Tiwari, V. (2008). Cocreating understanding and value in distributed work: How members of onsite and offshore vendor teams give, make, demand, and break sense. *Management Information Systems Quarterly, 32*(2), 227–255.

Webster, L., & Mertova, P. (2007). *Using narrative inquiry as a research method: An introduction to using critical event narrative analysis in research on learning and teaching*. New York, NY: Routledge.

Wordnet. (2010). *WordNet search 3.1*. Princeton University.

Wu, M. F., & Chang, P. L. (2011). Assessing mechanism for pre-development stage of new product development by stage-gate model. *African Journal of Business Management, 5*(6), 2445–2454.

Chapter 8
On IT and SwE Research Methodologies and Paradigms:
A Systemic Landscape Review

Manuel Mora
Autonomous University of Aguascalientes, Mexico

Annette L. Steenkamp
Lawrence Technological University, USA

Ovsei Gelman
CCADET-UNAM, Mexico

Mahesh S. Raisinghani
TWU School of Management, USA

ABSTRACT

In this chapter, the authors review the landscape of research methodologies and paradigms available for Information Technology (IT) and Software Engineering (SwE). The aims of the chapter are two-fold: (i) create awareness in current research communities in IT and SwE on the variety of research paradigms and methodologies, and (ii) provide an useful map for guiding new researchers on the selection of an IT or SwE research paradigm and methodology. To achieve this, the chapter reviews the core IT and SwE research methodological literature, and based on the findings, the authors illustrate an updated IT and SwE research framework that comprehensively integrates findings and best practices and provides a coherent systemic (holistic) view of this research landscape.

1. INTRODUCTION

In the context of Information Technology (IT) and Software Engineering (SwE) research a research methodology may be defined as the application of the modern scientific method (which can or not including empirical experimentation). In turn, the modern scientific method (Ackoff, Gupta & Minas, 1962; Popper, 2002; Checkland, 2000), is a systematic, rational, verifiable/falsifiable process for: (i) answering questions on a natural, artificial or social situation, (ii)a) solving the problem (an

DOI: 10.4018/978-1-4666-0179-6.ch008

optimized solution) or (ii) b) resolving a problematic well-structured natural, artificial or social situation (a satisfactory solution), or (ii)) c) gaining a better understanding of a complex natural, artificial or social situation; and (iii) developing better methods and physical or conceptual instruments for doing (i) and (ii).

Research methods are key conceptual knowledge devices for gaining and applying scientific knowledge. Thus, the final quality of the gained and applied knowledge on a natural, artificial or social situation relies strongly on the adequacy of the research method/s used.

Given that the landscape of available IT and SwE research methodologies has been expanded in the last decade, we believe a holistic summary and synthesis is required. The basic set of 5 to 7 main research methods (Straub, Ang & Evaristo, 1994), including survey, case study, laboratory experiment, conceptual, classic simulation, and engineering methods (Alavi & Carlson, 1992) has been increased by research methods, adopted from other disciplines, such as action research, grounded data theory, historical, ethnography, hybrid simulation, robust design, and mathematical proofs, among others. Furthermore, new research paradigms, defined as a set of philosophical assumptions about the objects of study and their related meta-methods, have emerged from classic positivism, classic interpretative, and classic systemic to modernism, transcendental realism (also known as critical realism), and modern systems approach. Consequently, the expansion of research paradigms and methodologies available for IT and SwE research is providing new opportunities for gaining and applying scientific knowledge. However, as with any set of techniques and tools, the method/s that is/are selected should be used correctly and for the appropriate situations.

In this chapter we review the landscape of research paradigms and methodologies available for IT and SwE from a systemic view. Our aims are two-fold: (i) create awareness in IT and SwE current research communities on the variety of research paradigms and methodologies, and (ii) provide an useful map for guiding new researchers on the selection of an IT or SwE research paradigm and methodology. To attain these aims, we firstly review the core IT and SwE research methodological literature. Secondly, we report the main findings of the literature review. Thirdly, we illustrate an updated IT and SwE research framework based on the findings. Finally, we report the implications, recommendations and limitations of our study.

2. BACKGROUND ON RESEARCH METHODOLOGIES AND PARADIGMS IN IT AND SWE

We can define a systemic research approach (extended from Ackoff *et al.*, 1962; Checkland, 2000; and Jackson, 1990) as an answering and problem-solving system comprised of the following components: (i) research paradigms (P's: a set of philosophical ontological, epistemological and axiological assumptions on the world); (ii) research purposes (S's: observe a situation (explore, describe or measure, predict, explain), or modify a situation of study (control, intervene or evaluate)); (iii) theoretical frameworks (F's: ideas-constructs, theories, and models); and (iv) research methodologies (M's: methods, techniques, and instruments), used for gaining or applying scientific knowledge; (v) the situational areas (A's: natural, artificial, social or hybrid objects of study) on which the M's are applied.

The first component of a research approach (P's: the research paradigms) accounts for the essential underlying assumptions on the constitution of the domain under study (i.e. ontology), the available modes of access to knowledge based on the set of previous knowledge, valid methods used, and interactions of the researchers with such elements (i.e. epistemology), and the human values pursued or affected by a research process (i.e., axiology) (Mingers, 2003). The second component (S's: research purposes) accounts for the feasible aims pursued by a researcher in a situation of study. Such aims may be classified as non-modifying (observation without intervention) and modifying (with intervention) aims. For the non-modifying case the purposes are: explore (gather initial insights useful for recognizing a complex or new situation under study); describe (establish a profile of quantitative or qualitative attributes of a situation under study), measure (develop a new instrument or apply one already existent for measuring a particular construct under study); predict (to establish a quantitative or qualitative relationships between at least two constructs (predictor and prediction), or explain (to formulate a set of causal-effect quantitative or qualitative relationships between several constructs). For the modifying case the purposes are: control (to identify the set of constructs and their degree of influence that permit assertion of control (an expected range of values) to one or several constructs of interest, or intervene (to identify a part of a social situation which may be modified for achieving final changes to such social situation), or evaluate (to identify the impacts of the application of social actions to a social situation). The third component (F's: theoretical frameworks) accounts for the set of known ideas-constructs, theories, and models. Constructs are conceptual denominations for entities of study that can be considered units. Theories reflect quantitative or qualitative functional relationships between constructs. Models are particular sub-sets of one or several theories, for generating or testing a new theory. The fourth component (M's: research methodologies) includes methods, techniques, and instruments. A method is one of a set of procedures used in research methodologies for generating a particular deliverable (for example a method for gathering and reporting demographic data). Techniques are particular statistical, mathematical, simulation or conceptual formulations to collect and analyze data. Instruments (physical or con-

ceptual) are tool used for measuring attributes of a construct of interest under study.

Such components of a systemic research approach facilitates that a researcher gain or apply scientific knowledge on situational areas, the fifth component (A's: natural, artificial, social or hybrid objects of study). We define natural situations as those where the main units of study are living entities (but not human beings) as a system. Artificial situations are defined as those where the main units of study are man-made physical or conceptual artifacts that are part of a system. Social situations are defined as those where the main units of study are individual or sets of human beings as systems. There is also the possibility of a hybrid situation that occurs when at least two of the previous ones are considered. Several taxonomies of IT and SwE research methodologies have been previously developed. Table 1 presents the main Information Systems (IS) research methodological taxonomies found in the literature, and Table 2 reports, the five main research methodologies used by researchers based on such taxonomies, (from Mora, Gelman, Paradice & Cervantes, 2008). In Table 2, each number represents the percentage identified of utilization in such a particular study. For instance, in Orlikowski and Baroudi's study (1991), the main research methodology was a survey methodology with a 49% usage, and the less used case study methodology with a 13.5% usage, of the total of research articles consulted

Taxonomies for IT and SwE research methodologies have been developed either directly, i.e., the focus was a classificatory scheme (Galliers & Land, 1987; March & Smith, 1995; Järvinen, 2000; Hevner, March, Park & Ram, 2004; Gonzalez & Dahanayake, 2007), or indirectly, i.e., the taxonomy was developed for reviewing IS research that was conducted during a period, introducing a new research method or explaining the discipline of study (Denning *et al.*, 1989; Nunamaker, Chen & Purdin, 1991; Orlikowski & Baroudi, 1991; Lending & Wheterbe,

Table 1. Classification criteria for main IS research methodological taxonomies

Taxonomy	Real vs. conceptual unit of study	Level of unit of analysis	Type of research outcome	Underlying philosophy
Galliers & Land (1987)	√	√	not considered	implicit use
Denning *et al.* (1989)	√	not considered	not considered	implicit use
Nunamaker at al. (1991)	implicit use	not considered	not considered	implicit use
Orlikowski & Baroudi (1991)	√	√	not considered	√
Lending & Wheterbe (1992)	√	not considered	not considered	not considered
Alavi & Carlson (1992)	√	√	not considered	not considered
March & Smith (1995)	implicit use	not considered	√	√
Jarvinen (2000)	√	not considered	not considered	not considered
Hevner *et al.* (2004)	implicit use	√	√	implicit use
Glass *et al.* (2004)	implicit use	√	implicit use	not considered
Gonzalez & Dahanayake (2007).	√	not considered	not considered	√

1992 ; Alavi & Carlson, 1992; Glass, Ramesh & Vessey, 2004).

The taxonomies on research methodologies represented in Table 1 have used the following main classification criteria: (i) the real or conceptual existence of the unit of study (e.g. empirical method vs non-empirical methods), (ii) the hierarchical analysis level of the object of study (society, organization, group/project, individual, system, or component), (iii) the type of research outcome (construct, model, method/process or instantiation) and/or (iv) the underlying philosophy of the research method (positivist, interpretative, or critical).

We can infer from Table 1 that a comprehensive and updated taxonomy of research methodologies is missing when a systemic framework is considered, i.e., one where the five components ((i) research paradigms, (ii) research purposes, (iii) theoretical frameworks, (iv) research methodologies and (v) the situational areas) are reported. From Table 2, we also can infer that there has been a preferential bias toward one or two research methodologies in a particular period. Given that

Table 2. Utilization percentages or acknowledgments of IS and SwE research methods

Study	Survey	Conceptual Studies	Case study	Engineering (proof of concept)	Experiments	Mathematical methods	Others
Studies in IS							
Orlikowski & Baroudi (1991)	49.1	-	13.5	-	29.7	-	7.7
Lending & Wheterbe (1992)	28.9	21.1	16.0	14.1	10.9	4.8	4.2
Alavi & Carlson (1992)	16.0	49.0	4.0	-	9.0	-	21.0
Vessey *et al.* (2002)	26.8	14.8	13.7	-	19.1	12.3	13.3
Glass *et al.* (2004)	24.5	14.7	12.5	-	17.8	12.3	18.2
Studies in SwE							
Glass *et al.* (2002)	1.6	43.5	2.2	17.1	3.0	10.6	22.0
Shaw (2003)	-	14.0	2.0	56.0		26.0	2.0

these studies were published in top journals, the preferential bias may be due to this fact (e.g. researchers try to use the research methodologies more used and this process is reinforced). Hence, we postulate that a systemic research approach proposed in this section (and extended from Ackoff *et al.*, 1962; Checkland, 2000; and Jackson, 1990) represents a more comprehensive set of components that may be used for developing a comparative review of IT and SwE research methodologies and paradigms, and advance the insights of previous studies. We develop it in more detail in the next section.

3. A LANDSCAPE OF RESEARCH METHODOLOGIES AND PARADIGMS USING THE SYSTEMIC RESEARCH APPROACH

3.1 Inventory of Research Methodologies

Table 3 summarizes an updated inventory of research methodologies from the main IT and SwE studies that we have reviewed. These research methodologies are classified as Empirical and Conceptual ones. Empirical studies are conducted directly on real objects/settings. Conceptual studies, in contrast, addresses research abstract objects that may or may not be associated with real objects. The symbols (•, X) are used respectively for reported and omitted research methodology by particular study. The list of research methodologies is ordered from most cited to less cited methodologies in the reviewed IT and SwE studies. From Table 3, it can be seen that IT and SwE researchers have available a powerful repository of research methodologies at present. Furthermore, for complex research problems, such methodologies can be combined (e.g. through a multi-methodology approach, Mingers, 2001) from the available repository.

The *Laboratory and Field Experiment* categories correspond to the empirically controlled study of subjects in a laboratory or the field setting. The *Case Study* category corresponds to the qualitative empirical examination of organizations. The *Survey* category corresponds to the quantitative empirical studies of a population sample (examination) - analysis? - by using statistical techniques. The *Conceptual Study* and *Conceptual Design* categories correspond to the non-empirical study of ideas related to real objects, including scholastic studies (reviews, tutorials and normative writing (Gonzalez & Dahanayake, 2007) as well as original conceptual studies (designing a new conceptual artifact: a construct, a framework/model, a method/process, or a system/component).

Mathematical Analysis and Proofs are non-empirical studies on mathematical structures using formal mathematical procedures (e.g., theorem proving, mathematical analysis). *Simulation* accounts for studying real or potentially real situations through virtual computer-based models where analytic models are usually not yet available. *Field Studies* correspond typically to data collection on a real (non-controlled) setting and their respective qualitative analysis. In the case of quantitative analysis such studies are classified as *Survey*. The *Engineering Design* category corresponds to the study of purposeful design of physical artifacts (including its proof of concept).

Action Research seeks to modify part of a real social situation through a theory, data collection, using an iterative action cycle. It differs from *Experimental* studies because in *Action Research* changes are pursued by social acceptance rather by invariable physical or social laws. *Analysis of Texts* (including Analysis of Protocols) is a research methodology which studies data embedded in textual documents (historical or presently recorded). *Meta Analysis* studies previously reported quantitative findings through statistical techniques for data evidence consolidations. *Bibliographic methods* range from simple to advanced quantitative techniques of accounting for occurrences

Table 3. *Updated inventory of research methodologies*

ID	Research Method	Comprehensive Studies on IT and SwE Research Methods												
		IT Research						SwE Research						
		Galliers & Land (1987)	Numa-maker at al. (1991)	Or-likows-ki & Baroudi (1991)	Alavi & Carlson (1992)	Hevner et al. (2004)	Vessey at al. (2002)	Den-ning et al. (1989)	Pfleeger (1994, 1995)	Mor-rison & George (1995)	Zel-kowitz & Wal-lace (1998)	Glass et al. (2002)	Shaw (2003)	Glass at al. (2004)
	Empirical Research Methods													
1	Lab. Experiment	•	•	•	•	•	•	X	•	•	•	•	•	•
2	Field Experiment	•	•	•	•	•	•	X	•	•	•	•	•	•
3	Case Study	•	•	•	•	•	•	X	•	•	•	•	•	•
4	Survey	•	•	•	•	•	•	X	X	•	X	•	•	•
9	Field Study	X	•	X	•	•	•	X	X	X	•	•	•	•
10	Engineering	X	X	X	X	X	X	•	X	X	•	•	•	•
11	Action Research	•	X	•	X	•	•	X	X	X	X	•	•	•
16	Empirical Description/Evaluation	X	X	X	X	X	•	X	X	•	•	X	X	X
17	Ethnography	X	X	X	X	•	•	X	X	X	X	•	X	•
18	Grounded Theory	X	X	X	X	•	X	X	X	X	X	•	X	•
19	Historical - Legacy	X	X	•	X	X	X	X	X	X	X	•	X	•
20	Phenomenology	X	X	X	X	X	X	X	X	X	X	•	X	•
	Conceptual Research Methods													
5	Conceptual Study	•	•	•	•	X	•	•	X	X	•	•	•	•
6	Conceptual Design	X	•	•	•	X	•	•	X	X	•	•	•	•
7	Mat. Analysis	X	X	X	•	X	•	•	X	X	X	•	•	•
8	Simulation	•	•	X	X	•	X	•	•	X	•	•	X	•
12	Mat. Proofs	•	X	X	X	X	X	X	X	X	X	•	X	•
13	Analysis of Text	X	X	•	X	X	•	X	X	X	X	•	X	•
14	Meta Analysis	X	X	X	X	X	•	X	X	•	X	•	X	•
15	Bibliographic Met.	X	X	X	•	X	•	X	X	•	X	•	X	•

of data and their quantitative interrelationships of interest. *Empirical Descriptive or Evaluative* research methods study implemented systems in real settings for description or evaluation purposes. *Ethnography* accounts for the qualitative investigation in a real social setting and the main stakeholders (benefiters and victims) who create such social settings. *Grounded Theory* pursues theory-building goals through an iterative data-collection, data-analysis, and theorization cycle. *Historical* research methods study the empirical objects and their related settings in their particular temporal context. *Phenomenology (including Hermeneutics)* accounts for research methods focusing on the plausible and diverse interpretations of meanings in a social setting of physical or conceptual objects.

3.2 Inventory of Research Paradigms

In Table 4 we provide an updated inventory of research paradigms. The symbols (•, ⊙, X) are used respectively for reported, implicitly reported, and omitted research paradigm.

The *positivist* research paradigm assumes an *ontology* of empirical-researchable objects that may be equally sensed by observers or instruments; an *epistemology* of quantitative-based or logical-mathematical modes of discovering or generating knowledge; and an *axiology* of gaining knowledge for a better prediction, or a better control of the situation of study (Habermas, 1972; Orlikowski & Baroudi, 1991). The *interpretative* research paradigm assumes an *ontology* of empirically-researchable living and non-living objects differently sensed by observers and instruments; an *epistemology* of qualitative-based or logic-argumentation modes of formulating plausible and shared knowledge; and an *axiology* of gaining knowledge for a better understanding of the human-being interrelationships of interest in the situation of study (Habermas, 1972; Orlikowski & Baroudi, 1991).

Table 4. Updated inventory of research paradigms

#ID	Research Paradigm	Comprehensive Studies on Research Methodologies											
		IT Research					SwE Research						
		Galliers & Land (1987)	Numamaker at al. (1991)	Orlikowski & Baroudi (1991)	Alavi & Carlson (1992)	Hevner et al. (2004)	Vessey at al. (2002)	Denning et al. (1989)	Pfleeger (1994, 1995)	Morrison & George (1995)	Zelkowitz & Wallace (1998)	Glass et al. (2002)	Glass at al (2004)
1	Positivism	•	⊙	•	⊙	•	⊙	⊙	⊙	⊙	⊙	⊙	⊙
2	Interpretivism	•	⊙	•	⊙	•	⊙	X	⊙	⊙	⊙	⊙	⊙
3	Critical	X	X	•	X	X	⊙	X	X	X	X	X	⊙
4	Transcendental Realism	X	X	X	X	X	X	X	X	X	X	X	X
5	Post-Modernism	X	X	X	X	X	X	X	X	X	X	X	X

A *critical* research paradigm assumes an *ontology* of empirical-researchable living and non-living objects differently sensed by observers and instruments according to their social status-quo; an *epistemology* of qualitative-based or logic-argumentation modes of formulating a plausible and shared knowledge; and an *axiology* of gaining knowledge for fair (without social alienation relationships) and truth-based human-being inter-relationships of interest on the situation of study (Habermas, 1972; Orlikowski & Baroudi, 1991; Flood, R., & Room, 1996).

Additionally, for complementing the Table 4, we consider the emergent paradigms reported in IT literature on Realism Transcendental (Mingers, 2000; Bhaskar, 2008) and Post-Modernism (Dobson & Love, 2004;. Feyeraben, 2000). The *transcendental realism* research paradigm assumes an *ontology* of empirically-observable real living and non-living objects generated by real underlying structures and mechanisms organized in layers; an *epistemology* of both quantitative-based or logical-mathematical, and qualitative-based or logic-argumentation modes of formulating plausible and shared knowledge; and an *axiology* of gaining knowledge for any of the three previous valued purposes of controlling, mutual understanding and freedom of aliened human relationships (Habermas, 1972: Mingers, 2000; Mora *et al.* 2008). The *post-modern* research paradigm assumes an *ontology* of complex object-subjects but feasible of be studied; an *epistemology* of multiple modes of inquiry based on the researcher's style; and an *axiology* of gaining knowledge of the singular, non-usual and the original (Dobson & Love, 2004) situations. The post-modern research paradigm challenges the single-mode and well-structured utilization of a research paradigm and claims that the scientific progress can only be generated by advancing the current status quo or dominant research paradigm from a anarchical process (but founded in the variety of methodological foundations) (Feyeraben, 2000).

Findings in the Table 4 suggest that Positivism and Interpretative modes are the main dominant research paradigms. The Critical paradigm is only reported by one study and implicitly by two from the 12 studies that were consulted. The last two research paradigms are not reported in previous studies, but we consider them relevant for this comprehensive study.

3.3 Taxonomy of Research Methodologies and Paradigms Using a Systems Approach

According to these systems pioneers (Bertalanffy, 1950, 1968; Boulding, 1956), and modern systems thinkers (Ackoff, 1960; 1971; Forrester, 1991; Checkland, 2000), the systems approach complements the reductionism, analytic, and mechanic worldview with an expansionist, synthetic, and teleological view. While the reductionism view in research implies that the phenomenon is isolated from wider systems and investigated as a closed-system, the expansionist view demands for a dual view: investigate the phenomenon taking account with their sub and macro systems, as well as considerate it as a closed (lab view) and open system (real view). Thus, in this section we propose an updated systemic (not reductionist) taxonomy of research methodologies based on Transcendental Realism (Bhaskar, 1975, 2008; Mingers, 2000). Transcendental Realism Philosophy is a post-modernist philosophical stance developed by Roy Bhaskar (1975; 2008) as an alternative, and update, to Hume's Empiricism and Kant's Idealism. Bhaskar (1975, p. 24) establishes the philosophical differences between Transcendental Realism and the others as follows: *" [transcendental realism] regards the objects of knowledge as the structures and mechanisms that generate phenomena; and the knowledge as produced in the social activity of science. These objects are neither phenomena (empiricism) nor human constructs imposed upon the phenomena (idealism), but real structures which endure and operate independently of our knowledge, our experience and the conditions which allow us access to them*". Using these key main premises, Bhaskar's philosophical thesis can be summarized as follows:

a) Reality exists and is structured, i.e., law-governed and stratified, independent of the existence of human beings (Bhaskar 1975, p. 26).

b) Knowledge of reality has an intransitive and other transitive dimensions. The former accounts for the invariant and enduring objects of knowledge (real things, structures, mechanisms, process and events), and the latter accounts for the dynamic social and historically dependent facts, theories, models, paradigms, methods and techniques for registering and generating knowledge. (Bhaskar 1975, p. 1).

c) Reality can be stratified in three layers: (a) real domain; (b) actual domain and (c) empirical domain. The real domain, which can be stratified in an infinite number of stratums, (Bhaskar 1975, 46; Mingers 2000, 1266;

Dickens, 2003, 99), includes the intransitive real things, structures and generative mechanisms (and the other two domains in a an extended interpretation). The actual domain accounts for the total flux of events generated by the acting of the intransitive objects, irrespective of humans' perceptions. The empirical dimension includes uniquely the observed or experienced events.

d) The stratification of the natural reality, which is done by nature and the social reality, is constructed by human beings. The real domain differs from the others in two key ways: (i) the existence and shape of natural or physical structures is independent of, and cannot be modified by, humans beings and (ii) social structures occur and can be can be created, transformed or destroyed in a space-time context (Mingers 2000, p. 1266)

Figure 1 illustrates these concepts graphically. Arrows in both directions from events to structures mean that for social reality, the structures and mechanisms can be altered.

Figure 1. A graphic representation of Bhaskar's transcendental realism structure

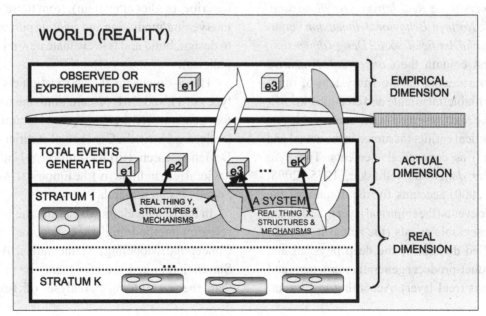

Table 5. Updated taxonomy of research methodologies

	Natural and Behavioral oriented Research Methods	Purposeful Artificial and Social Design oriented Research Methods
Conceptual Transitive Dimension of Changing Interpretations, Models, Schemes	• Conceptual Study • Conceptual Modeling • Mathematical Analysis • Simulation • Analysis Of Text • Meta Analysis • Bibliographic Method	• Conceptual Design • Mathematical Proof • Simulation
Real Intransitive Dimension of Enduring Underlying Structures and Mechanisms to be Studied	• Case Study • Survey • Field Study • Empirical Description/Evaluation • Ethnography • Grounded Theory • Historical - Legacy • Phenomenology	• Laboratory Experiment • Field Experiment • Engineering Study • Action Research

It is not possible for natural or physical structures or mechanisms, i.e., natural laws, to be altered. From previous arguments and Figure 1, our proposal adapts Mingers' (2000, p. 17) and Bhaskar's concepts to elaborate an updated framework on research methodologies. Is also extended from Mora *et al.* (2008) (see Table 5), and the findings of our literature review, which we organized as shown in the Table 3 and Table 4.

Four core dimensions are used to elaborate this taxonomy: (i) the *Conceptual Transitive dimension* versus the *Real Intransitive dimension,* and (ii) the *Natural/Behavioral dimension* versus the *Purposeful Artificial/Social Design dimension.* In the first column the *Conceptual Transitive dimension* accounts for the subsystem of organized, verifiable/falsifiable and changing knowledge on the real (observed in the empirical layer) or hypothetical entities (assumed in the actual and real layers) as conceptual elements. The *Real Intransitive dimension* (Bhaskar, 1975, 2008; Mingers, 2000) accounts for the domain of the observable events (the empirical layer), the domain of non-observable events (the actual layer) and the stratified domain of the deep physical and social product-producer generative structures and mechanisms (real layer). According to Bhaskar

(1975, 2008), such real, actual and empirical layers exist independent of the human beings. However, the scientific knowledge –e.g. in the Conceptual Transitive domain- are socially generated or co-generated by human beings in concordance with the reality (i.e., the truth criteria) and are space-temporally related. The second column - based on work by Hevner *et al.* (2004)- contrasts the study of events and things generated by nature and social structures and mechanisms, without an intervening/modifying purpose (e.g. to explore, describe, predict or explain), from those with the intervening/modifying and creating purposes (e.g. to design, build and test/evaluate new artifacts or policies).

This 4-dimensional classification divides the types of IT and SwE research into the following four quadrants: (i) the Conceptual-Natural/Behavioral research, (ii) the Conceptual-Artificial/Social Design research, (iii) the Empirical-Natural/Behavioral research and (iv) the Empirical-Artificial/Social Design research.

In the first quadrant we classify the following research methodologies: Conceptual Studies, Conceptual Modeling, Mathematical Analysis, Simulation (when used for theory testing rather than theory building), Analysis of Texts, and

Meta-analysis (while it uses empirical data they come from other studies, so the researcher does not interact with the real entities as sources of data). In the second quadrant to the right, we classify the following research methodologies: Conceptual Design, Mathematical Proofs (as new conceptual artifacts), and Simulation (when it is used for theory building). In the third quadrant bottom left, we classify the following research methodologies: Case Studies, Surveys, Field Studies, Empirical Descriptions-Evaluations, Ethnography, Grounded Theory, Historical, and Phenomenology. In the fourth quadrant bottom right, we classify the following research methodologies: Laboratory Experiments, Field Experiments, Engineering Studies, and Action Research methodologies.

Hence, we consider that Table 5 and previous ones are useful to develop an integrated and more comprehensive scheme of research paradigms and methodologies. It is presented in the Table 6. This scheme summarizes and integrates the vast literature on IT and SwE research methodologies and paradigms, and can be useful to: (i) identify the available philosophical paradigms with their main assumptions; (ii) associate such philosophical paradigms with adopted research methodologies; and (iii) investigate advanced knowledge about conducting research (the axiological axis).

4. DISCUSSION AND FUTURE RESEARCH DIRECTIONS

Why research methodologies and paradigms are needed? According to Locke *et al.*, 2004), the key issues with performing a high quality research arise from the following six perceptions: complexity of results, conflicting results, trivial topics, impractical studies, absence of commitment and caring, and conflict with other sources of truth. Thus, a cumulative tradition in the literature that is guided by typologies about multi-methodological approaches to research design is pertinent. As

Trauth (2001) and Mingers (2001, 2003) suggest, the dimensions that must be considered to enhance rigor and relevance in research are:

- Philosophical Dimension: identifying the assumed ontology, epistemology and axiological (i.e. philosophical underpinnings) for research methodologies.
- Social and Critical Dimension: including social and critical social theories; exploring the relationships among social and critical theories, research questions and empirical methods; embracing a socio-technical perspective when required; and acknowledging the social and critical construction of research and knowledge.
- Methodological Dimension: embracing multi-methodological approaches, being engaged in the research setting when possible; working with the data by using different data analysis techniques; and maintaining an adaptive and critical stance (e.g. Is there sufficient free collected evidence for reporting such results?).
- Political Dimension: developing an emerging and accurate understanding of the achievement and failures of the research community (as recommended identified by Kuhn's paradigms (1974)); coping with risks involved; and surviving academic politics and dominant or imperative methodological issues; and challenging status quo positions in research for the sake of the free knowledge and society progress rather for serving to particular research interests.

We consider also relevant to advance on the classic debate between Positivist vs Interpretative paradigms and their main associated research methodologies. According to our findings, in contrast, the debate on the need of utilization of multiple methodologies and selecting a research paradigm which can accommodate disparate assumptions is needed for advancing research in

Table 6. Research paradigms and research methodologies framework

Research Paradigm	Philosophical Assumptions			Preferred Research Methodologies
	Ontology	Epistemology	Axiology	
Positivism	Real entities with measurable attributes	Quantitative and Mathematical methods	Prediction or control	• **Laboratory Experiment** • **Field Experiment** • **Survey** • **Field Study** • **Engineering Study** • **Empirical Description/Evaluation** • **Mathematical Analysis** • **Mathematical Proof** • **Meta Analysis** • **Bibliographic Methods**
Interpretivism	Social entities with non-unique qualitative attributes	Qualitative methods (but can include quantitative data)	Shared social understanding	• **Case Study** • **Field Study** • **Ethnography** • **Grounded Theory** • **Historical - Legacy** • **Phenomenology** • **Analysis Of Text**
Critical	Social entities with aliened qualitative attributes	Qualitative methods (but can include quantitative data)	Emancipation of conflictive and aliened social relationships	• **Action Research** • **Ethnography** • **Historical - Legacy** • **Phenomenology** • **Analysis Of Text**
Realism Transcendental	Real and social entities with measurable and interpretable attributes	Quantitative and Qualitative methods	Improving real and social reality	• **All Methods**
Post-Modernism	Complex entities with complex attributes	Hybrid Methods on demand	Increase human-being freedom	• **All Methods**

complex IT and SwE topics (e.g. hybrid artificial and social systems, and now involved with natural systems by the Green IT movement as example). Whether a holistic paradigm is not totally accepted by IT and SwE research community, however, we claim that a multiple research methodological view must be pursued at least (as classic triangulation approach).

Hence, under such general research methodological recommendations, we consider that our updated research framework based on the systemic research approach of five components (paradigm, purpose, methodology, theoretical basis, and situation) is congruent with such aforementioned core recommendations.

CONCLUSION

We have also reported the findings of a comprehensive literature review on IT and SwE research methodologies and paradigms. We have identified that while there a rich variety of research methodologies and paradigms at present, still there are a set of preferred research methodologies (and paradigms) in IT and SwE research. By reported findings reported it can inferred a strong influence of top journals, on the reduced subset of them. However, it is ethic to report that emergent and few used research methodologies and paradigms have been also reported (with few instances) in top journals. In this updated taxonomy –Table 5- we distinguish the four main domains for research methodologies. These dimensions are *Conceptual Transitive, Real Intransitive, Natural/Behavioral, and Purposeful Artificial/Social Design*. In each dimension, we have identified also the main research methodologies (despite some of them could be combined for addressing multiple domains). In Table 6, we report a summary of the main research paradigms which identified of this intensive review. For each paradigm, the main philosophical assumptions are described, and their main associated research methods are listed (despite some of them can be performed from different philosophical paradigms). These findings have informed the revision of the Research Paradigms and Research Methodologies Framework of Mora *et al.* (2008), as shown in the Table 6.

Hence, we can conclude that: (i) there is a diverse number of research paradigms and methodologies used in research published in the literature; (ii) some of them have dominant utilization; (iii) some of them are used rarely despite their inherent usefulness in particular research studies; (iv) there is a greater variety of research methodologies and paradigms more used in the IT domain than in the SwE domain; (v) the positivist and interpretative paradigms are still the dominant philosophical paradigms in the IT and SwE domains at present; and (vi) this framework is helpful to IT and SwE researchers to determine an appropriate research design that is based on sound philosophical assumptions for a selected research paradigm.

This study is limited in its scope since the detailed research process models for each research methodology are not reported. However, we encourage for future research studies that show how the methodologies of the framework can be used specifically (e.g. phases, activities, and deliverables). Of particular interest are the activities for supporting the validation of research studies. Researchers can consider conceptual or empirical activities from the available methodologies to validate their hypotheses or propositions and to provide answers to the research questions that prompted the research during the initiation phase.

Finally like any scientific knowledge –e.g. in the transitive domain of science-, this framework must be considered provisional, testable, and improvable knowledge. We encourage to IT and SwE researchers and Faculty teaching research methodologies to review it and consider its potential utilization. Such application will improve the body of knowledge of IT and SwE paradigms and research methodologies.

ACKNOWLEDGMENT

The authors express their appreciation to our many MSc and PhD students who have conducted research thesis under our supervision, for the refinement of our insight in research paradigms methodologies, and for making our scholarship so meaningful, as well as to our Institutions (Autonomous University of Aguascalientes, Lawrence Technological University, Universidad Nacional Autónoma de México, and Texas Woman University) for all support provided for doing international research.

REFERENCES

Ackoff, R. (1960). Systems, organizations and interdisciplinary research. *General System Yearbook, 5*, 1–8.

Ackoff, R. (1971). Towards a system of systems concepts. *Management Science, 17*(11), 661–671. doi:10.1287/mnsc.17.11.661

Ackoff, R., Gupta, S., & Minas, J. (1962). *Scientific method: Optimizing applied research decisions.* New York, NY: Wiley.

Alavi, M., & Carlson, P. (1992). A review of MIS research and disciplinary development. *Journal of Management Information Systems, 8*(4), 45–52.

Bhaskar, R. (2008). *A realist theory of science.* London, UK: Leeds Books.

Boulding, K. (1956). General systems theory – The skeleton of the science. *Management Science, 2*(3), 197–208. doi:10.1287/mnsc.2.3.197

Checkland, P. (2000). Soft systems methodology: A thirty year retrospective. *Systems Research and Behavioral Science, 17*, S11–S58. doi:10.1002/1099-1743(200011)17:1+<::AID-SRES374>3.0.CO;2-O

Denning, P., Comer, D. E., Gries, D., Mulder, M. C., Tucker, A., Turner, A. J., & Young, P. R. (1989). Computing as discipline. *Communications of the ACM, 32*(1), 9–23. doi:10.1145/63238.63239

Feyerabend, P. (1993). *Against the method: An outline of an anarchistic theory of perception.* London, UK: Verso.

Flood, R., & Room, N. (Eds.). (1996). *Critical systems thinking.* New York, NY: Plenum Press. doi:10.1007/b102400

Forrester, J. (1991). *Systems dynamics and the lessons of 35 years.* Technical Report D-4224-4. Retrieved from http://sysdyn.mit.edu/sd-group/home.html

Galliers, R., & Land, F. (1987). Choosing an appropriate Information Systems research methodology. *Communications of the ACM, 30*(11), 900–902. doi:10.1145/32206.315753

Gelman, O., & Garcia, J. (1989). Formulation and axiomatization of the concept of general system. Mexican Institute of Planning and Systems Operation. *Outlet IMPOS, 19*(92), 1–81.

Glass, R., Ramesh, V., & Vessey, I. (2004). An analysis of research in computing disciplines. *Communications of the ACM, 47*(6), 89–94. doi:10.1145/990680.990686

Glass, R., Vessey, I., & Ramesh, V. (2002). Research in software engineering: An analysis of the literature. *Information and Software Technology, 44*, 491–506. doi:10.1016/S0950-5849(02)00049-6

Gonzalez, R., & Dahanayake, A. (2007). A concept map of Information Systems research approaches. In M. Khosrow-Pour (Ed.), *Proceedings of the 2007 IRMA International Conference*, Vancouver, Canada, May 11-14, (pp. 845-848).

Habermas, J. (1972). *Knowledge and human interests.* London, UK: Heinenmann.

Hevner, A., March, S., Park, J., & Ram, S. (2004). Design science in Information Systems research. *Management Information Systems Quarterly*, *21*(8), 75–105.

Jackson, M. (1990). *Systems approaches to management*. New York, NY: Kluwer Academic.

Järvinen, P. (2000). Research questions guiding selection of an appropriate research method. In *Proceedings of the 8th European Conference on Information Systems*, Vienna, Austria, July 2-5, (pp. 124-131).

Kuhn, T. (1974). *The structure of the scientific theories*. Chicago, IL: University of Chicago Press.

Lending, D., & Wetherbe, J. (1992). Update on MIS research: A profile of leading journals and U.S. universities. *ACM SIGMIS Database*, *23*(3), 5–11. doi:10.1145/146548.146549

Locke, L., Silverman, S., & Spirduso, W. (2004). *Reading and understanding research*. New York, NY: Sage Publications.

March, S., & Smith, G. (1995). Design and natural science research on Information Technology. *Decision Support Systems*, *15*(4), 251–266. doi:10.1016/0167-9236(94)00041-2

Mingers, J. (2000). The contributions of critical realism as an underpinning philosophy for OR/MS and systems. *The Journal of the Operational Research Society*, *51*, 1256–1270.

Mingers, J. (2001). Combining IS research methods: Towards a pluralist methodology. *Information Systems Research*, *12*(3), 240–253. doi:10.1287/isre.12.3.240.9709

Mingers, J. (2003). A classification of the philosophical assumptions of management science methodologies. *The Journal of the Operational Research Society*, *54*(6), 559–570. doi:10.1057/palgrave.jors.2601436

Mora, M., Gelman, O., Paradice, D., & Cervantes, F. (2008). The case for conceptual research in Information Systems. In G. Grant & T. Felix (Eds.), *Electronic Proceedings of the 2008 International Conference on Information Resources Management (Conf-IRM)*, May 18-20, 2008, Niagara Falls, Ontario, Canada, (pp. 1-10).

Nunamaker, J., Chen, M., & Purdin, T. (1991). Systems development in Information Systems research. *Journal of Management Information Systems*, *7*(3), 89–106.

Orlikowski, W., & Baroudi, J. (1991). Studying Information Technology in organizations: Research approaches and assumptions. *Information Systems Research*, *2*(1), 1–28. doi:10.1287/isre.2.1.1

Popper, K. (2002). *The logic of scientific discovery*. London, UK: Routledge.

Shaw, M. (2003). Writing good software engineering research papers. In *Proceedings of the 25th International Conference on Software Engineering*, (pp. 726-736). IEEE Computer Society.

Straub, D., Ang, S., & Evaristo, R. (1994). Normative standards for IS research. *Database*, *25*(1), 21–34.

Trauth, E. (2001). *Qualitative research in IS: Issues and trends*. Hershey, PA: Idea Group Publishing.

von Bertalanffy, L. (1950). An outline of general systems theory. (reprinted in Bertalanffy (1968)). *The British Journal for the Philosophy of Science*, *1*, 134–164. doi:10.1093/bjps/I.2.134

von Bertalanffy, L. (1968). *General systems theory – Foundations, developments, applications*. New York, NY: G. Brazillier.

KEY TERMS AND DEFINITIONS

Conceptual Transitve Dimension: Dimension which accounts for the subsystem of organized, verifiable/falsifiable and changing knowledge on the real (observed in the empirical layer) or hypothetical entities (assumed in the actual and real layers) as conceptual elements.

Natural/Behavioral Dimension: Dimension which contains concrete and abstract artifacts which are created or intervened/modified (e.g. designing, building and testing/evaluating purposes).

Purposeful Artificial/Social Design Dimension: Dimension which contains conceptual and empirical events and things generated by nature and social structures and mechanisms, without an intervening/modifying purpose (e.g. exploring, describing, predicting, or explaining).

Real Intransitive Dimension: Dimension which accounts for the domain of observable events (the empirical layer), the domain of non-observable events (the actual layer) and the stratified domain of the deep physical and social product-producer generative structures and mechanisms (real layer).

Research Methodology: A systematic, rational, verifiable/falsifiable process for: (i) answering questions on a natural, artificial or social situation, (ii) a) solving the problem (an optimized solution) or (ii) b) resolving a problematic well-structured natural, artificial or social situation (a satisfactory solution), or (ii)) c) gaining a better understanding of a complex natural, artificial or social situation; and (iii) developing better methods and physical or conceptual instruments for doing (i) and (ii).

Research Paradigm: A set of philosophical ontological, epistemological and axiological assumptions on the world.

Systemic Research Approach: An answering and problem-solving system comprised of the following components: (i) research paradigms (P's: a set of philosophical ontological, epistemological and axiological assumptions on the world); (ii) research purposes (S's: observe a situation (explore, describe or measure, predict, explain), or modify a situation of study (control, intervene or evaluate)); (iii) theoretical frameworks (F's: ideas-constructs, theories, and models); and (iv) research methodologies (M's: methods, techniques, and instruments), used for gaining or applying scientific knowledge; (v) the situational areas (A's: natural, artificial, social or hybrid objects of study) on which the M's are applied.

ENDNOTE

[1] Types of research methods were interpreted from Shaw (2003) based on the reported evaluation methods.

Section 2
Contemporaneous Research Methods and Techniques

Chapter 9
Contemporary Reporting Practices Regarding Covariance–Based SEM with a Lens on EQS

Theresa M. Edgington
Baylor University, USA

Peter M. Bentler
University of California – Los Angeles, USA

ABSTRACT

Structural Equation Modeling (SEM) continues to grow in use as an important research analysis tool in Information Systems research. While evaluating SEM results and interpreting them depends on a variety of reported details, SEM results continue to be reported in an inconsistent manner. Key reporting elements are discussed with regard to contemporary practices which can serve as a guide for future submissions and reviewing. This chapter contributes to the literature by providing an overview of important considerations in reporting results from covariance-based structural equation modeling execution and analysis. It incorporates models and other examples of EQS, one of the leading SEM software applications. While EQS is increasingly used by IS researchers, exemplars of its code and output have not been well published within the IS community, overly complicating the reviewing process for these papers.

INTRODUCTION

"By the end of the 1990s, [covariance-based] SEM had ascended to the ranks of the most commonly used multivariate techniques within the social sciences," (Hancock and Mueller 2006, p. 2). This

interest in structural equation modeling (SEM) extended into the Information Systems discipline, but not without reporting deficiencies. As early as 1998, at the request of the editor-in-chief of MIS Quarterly, Wynne Chin was invited to submit a paper (Chin 1998) relating to the appropriate use of structural equation modeling. While the paper made a few references to Partial Least Squares

DOI: 10.4018/978-1-4666-0179-6.ch009

(PLS), the paper itself was focused on what the IS field often refers to as covariance-based SEM. In 2000, Gefen, Straub, and Boudreau (2000) compared PLS, LISREL, and regression techniques, but positioned EQS and AMOS as a different type of analysis method from LISREL (ibid, p. 7). AMOS, EQS, and LISREL all belong to the same family of covariance-based structural equation modeling programs. LISREL (Joreskog and Sorbom 1984) began with the modeling of eight unique matrices. AMOS (Arbuckle 1989) extended this type of computational approach, but added visualization to improve modeling ease of use. While EQS and LISREL have added visualization modeling improvements, EQS (Bentler 1985) architected its SEM computational abilities along the equations-based modeling orientation already utilized by behavioral researchers.

Gefen et al. (2000) continued the no longer valid assumption (Treiblmaier et al. 2010) that covariance-based SEM cannot support formative constructs (ibid, p. 10 & p. 31). We now see formative measures used in a number of contemporary SEM studies (Diamantopoulos and Windlhofer 2001; Edwards and Bagozzi 2000; Kline 2006; Mackenzie et al. 2005; Qureshi and Compeau 2009). Unlike PLS (an analytical alternative to covariance-based SEM), EQS, AMOS, and LISREL share the factor analytic measurement model computation approach versus PLS' principal components computation (Rigdon 1996).

Even in well written and received IS research, omissions from good covariance-based reporting practice can be found. For instance, Gefen et al. (2003) do not report the p-value along with chi-square and degrees of freedom. Additionally, instead of emphasizing the model as a unified hypothesis as recommended for SEM models (Chin 1998; McDonald and Ho 2002), they emphasize the practice of reporting each path as a separate hypothesis, implying that each path can stand alone for support or rejection. Bessellier, et al. (2003) utilize a common practice in IS research of omitting the covariance matrix,

which constrains the ability to replicate results. While traditional journal articles may desire fewer pages, online journals or those whose practice is to utilize online storage for appendices' access, should not be constraining a practice that allows for one to test the model or even to suggest superior alternative models that could advance theoretical contributions. In Datta et al. (2002), neither the factor loadings nor the chi-square, degrees of freedom, and p-value are reported for the confirmatory factor model utilized with the SEM program, AMOS. Proper reporting practices for covariance-based SEM have been discussed in the SEM literature (Jackson et al. 2009; Brown 2006; McDonald and Ho 2002; Boomsma 2002; Chin 1998); however, these same sources note that proper SEM reporting is often lacking and inconsistent. By limiting the reporting of important SEM detail, submitted papers reduce their probability of acceptance by ineffectively interpreting the papers' findings. It is not apparent that authors have applied the SEM technique incorrectly as was inferred in 1998 (Chin), but it is more likely that they have not submitted sufficient detail of their methodology and results. This paper largely draws on reporting practices and guidelines of SEM methodologists and comments on why more contemporary guidelines should be followed. In doing so, we also draw on theoretical advances in Information Systems. The advances in structural equation modeling are arguably dependent upon the technological advances in SEM software, and contemporary SEM practice in this regard is often quite compatible with theoretical contributions from IS theories.

The purpose of this chapter is to aid the submission process in addressing important elements that authors need to include and that reviewers can verify are included and properly interpreted in SEM research papers. The target audience is for those who use SEM software applications in their research, rather than those who design such applications and the mathematical basis for SEM. The paper also contributes by providing examples utilizing EQS (Bentler 2006), a well-respected SEM application that addresses covariance-based SEM in a different, yet compatible, manner than presented with LISREL (Joreskog and Sorbom 1984). The examples are specific to EQS and the nomenclature aligned closely to Bentler-Weeks (1980) modeling; however, the conceptual value applies to all SEM research. Further, EQS with its deep incorporation of Bentler-Weeks modeling for enhanced ease of use is well-suited for the IS discipline where one of its main contributions is arguably the dedication to ease of use considerations in technology adoption. As noted recently in a meta-analysis of IS research, "The most written about MIS subject is IS Usage" (Palvia et al. 2004, p. 4227).

While standard use of LISREL requires the input of at least eight distinct matrices, EQS implements all conceivable models as a simple extension of single equation regression -- with which the field is well acquainted -- to multiple equations (Bentler and Weeks 1980). Within American Psychological Association journals from 1998 to 2006, EQS was second in most frequently acknowledged SEM applications in research: LISREL (28.9%), EQS (23.2%), Amos (17.0%), MPlus (7.2%), SAS PROC CALIS (3.6%), and RAMONA (0.5%) (Jackson et al. 2009, p. 14). EQS is noted as the first SEM software application to offer non-matrix based syntax (Hancock and Mueller 2006). As is common with most software applications, limitations of the software application previously documented are frequently overcome, and EQS ranks as one of the leading software applications for SEM researchers, cited frequently in textbooks on SEM (Kline 2004; Thompson 2004; Byrne 2006; Brown 2006; Hancock and Mueller 2006; Raykov and Marcoulides 2006). The utilization of EQS and its modeling orientation assist in explaining why certain IS practices with regard to SEM reporting are ill-advised. In addition, the examples should be helpful to SEM researchers in IS who have not directly utilized EQS but have been requested to review EQS papers.

The focus of this paper is to discuss the use of covariance-based SEM in IS research with regard to salient details to be addressed in journal submissions. It pays particular attention to the development of the underlying measurement model, frequently identified from confirmatory factor analysis (CFA), which is often lightly addressed in submissions, but which provides the foundation on which the validity and reliability of any subsequent structural model must stand.

MODEL DEVELOPMENT AND SPECIFICATION

As is well known, in regression the dependent variable as well as the predictor variables are observed variables found in a data file. Sets of such equations are called a path analysis model, and also extend regressions because a dependent variable in one equation can be a predictor in another equation, and vice-versa. Such flexibility is also maintained with two main other equation types that are typical of covariance-based SEM. (1) Equations in which the dependent variable is observed, but its predictors are hypothetical latent variables. For example: $V1 = *F1 + E1$; where V1 is a specific observed measure, F1 is a specific latent construct called a factor in EQS (the asterisk, *, indicates F1 will be freely estimated), and E1 is the residual error term[1]. The set of such equations is called a measurement model. The standard measurement model is basically a factor analysis model, so we may as well call the latent variables "factors." (2) Equations in which the dependent variables are factors and the predictors also are factors. For example: $F4 = *F1 + *F2 + *F3 + D4$; where F1, F2, F3, and F4 are all latent constructs (factors), the effects of F1 through F3 are freely estimated (using the asterisk), and D4 is the disturbance term for the equation. The EQS model actually allows other equation types, such as variants of (1) and (2) where some predictors are observed variables. For example: $V1 = *F1$

Figure 1. Simple example of two latent constructs as CFA factors with eight reflective indicators

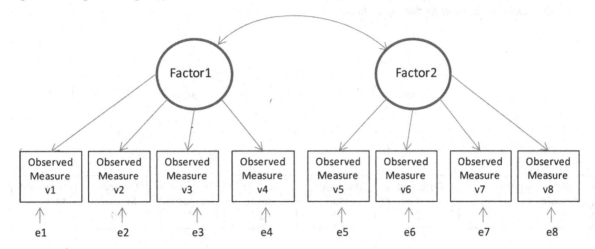

+ *V2 + E1. Any SEM model is thus a set of equations, and there will be as many equations as there are "dependent" variables. In a path diagram, every variable that has at least one one-way arrow aiming at it will be a dependent variable and will have its own equation. A model also will contain variance/covariance specifications. These variance and covariance specifications are declared separately from the equations; for example: F1 = *; if the factor variance is to be freely estimated or F1 = 1; if the factor variance is to be fixed to the value of 1. Examples of freely estimating covariance relationships include F1,F2 = *; -- for latent constructs, or E1,E2 = *; -- for covariance between two error terms.

Although we do not want to be overly technical, for completeness we note that all of the equation types above, and those discussed throughout this chapter, can be represented in the Bentler-Weeks model via the matrix simultaneous equation $\eta = \beta\eta + \Upsilon\xi$, which expresses all of the dependent variables in vector η as a weighted (β) function of other dependent variables and a weighted (Υ) function of the independent variables in vector ξ. This equation encompasses all covariance-based SEM modeling. It can address one or all of three types of standard models: measurement, path, or combined structural model. A complex model is

called the structural (or hybrid) model (Brown 2006; Kline 2004). This model includes both of the two other SEM models: the measurement model and the latent variable path model. The measurement model is normally a confirmatory factor analysis (CFA) model. In such a model, each observed variable typically is influenced by only one or a few latent factors, reflecting prior knowledge. The validity of the structural model is dependent on the validity of its associated measurement model. As noted above, even more complex models may have observed variables as predictors of factors or variables.

In the simplest example of one construct, indicators (i.e., measured observations) for the construct (factor) may be reflective (Figure 1) or formative (Figure 2). Reflective indicators are standard in covariance-based SEM research. When they are reflective, we are saying that variation in the latent construct directly influences variation in the indicators, and an arrow points from the construct to the reflective indicator. Although in reality, a construct is likely to cause effects in many reflective indicators, it is sufficient to accurately measure a few of these. To clarify, we only need three reflective indicators to just-identify a latent construct (four are required to provide over-identification); the latent construct does

Figure 2. Simple example of two emergent constructs with eight formative indicators. Covariances among predictors and residuals in factors not shown

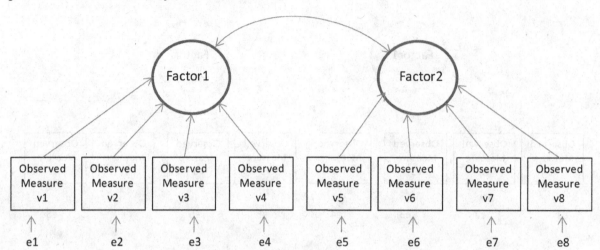

not change because it exists before the observed measure in theory.

In a formative construct, one specifies that the construct cannot be fully identified until all the necessary formative indicators are present; the latent construct exists in theory as a composition of the substantive characteristics of the indicators. If one of the formative indicators can be broken down into other indicators, we likely have a higher-order model, which should also be supported by theory. The management literature (Wong et al. 2008; Law et al. 1998) advises that the consideration of theory into higher order constructs is complex. They consider a higher-order, formative model as a muliti-dimensional construct. The manner in which the formative factors identify the higher-order factor can be via intersection (which they term as 'latent model'), via union (termed 'aggregate model'), and a third taxonomy which relies more on categorical membership than algebraic formation (termed 'profile model'). The literature reinforces the responsibility to consider the nature of how relationships form from a theoretical perspective.

Notice that both reflective and formative covariance-based models differ from component-based (e.g., PLS) models by predicting a

precise relationship between an indicator and its construct(s)[2] (Figure 3). In covariance-based SEM, an indicator does not have a loading on more than one factor unless the theory specifies that it will. In PLS, an indicator often loads on more than one component based on the principal components analysis computation approach that it employs. While cov-SEM considers the model as a unified hypothesis (McDonald and Ho 2002), whereby, all aspects of the model are estimated and evaluated as a unified whole, this does make it sensitive to misspecification. The p-value from the Chi-square test assists in understanding if the sampled data is consistent with the model as a whole and hence is liable to be externally generalizable to other settings. In PLS, the focus is on the latent constructs and there is a diminished concern on the structure of the measured observations (Schneeweiss 1990).

An SEM model must be statistically and empirically identified (ideally over-identified) to produce consistent results (Brown 2006; Kline 2004). If a model is under-identified, its parameters are to some extent arbitrary as "an unidentified parameter computed by an SEM program is arbitrary and should not be relied on" (Raykov and Marcoulides 2006, p. 34). Methodologically, if there are many constructs it will be useful to

Figure 3. Two components identified from the variances and covariances (not shown) of eight indica-tors. [Note that "PLS path analysis does not focus on accounting for measurement item covariances. Rather, depending on the particular model specified by the researcher, only the variances of dependent variables (item or construct level) variances are considered" (Chin 2010).]

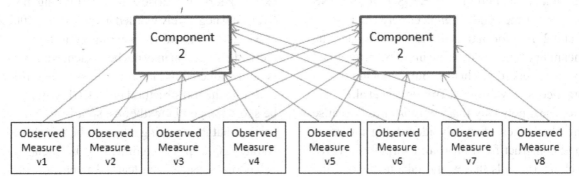

validate each construct (factor plus its indicators) before validating the full measurement or path model(s). As a rule of thumb typically at least three indicators per construct should permit model identification when constructs are uncor-related and each indicator loads on only one fac-tor (McDonald and Ho 2002), but such a recom-mendation does not mean that one should only use three indicators. Three are sufficient to avoid a statistically under-identified model. An under-identified model contributes to software execution problems with the SEM application due to model indeterminacy. A just identified model provides a solution uniquely suited to one set of data and is less likely to have generalizable value to other settings as it is tightly constrained to the specific sample. An over-identified model is the actual goal in SEM research. It can consist of SEM constructs that are just-identified individu-ally, but the overall model should support the over-identification criteria (see Brown 2006 p. 62-72 for a detailed discussion of SEM identifica-tion criteria including both statistical and em-pirical identification). Identification of the model is the sum of identifications of all its parts, and then it is closely related to degrees of freedom (df). An overidentified model has positive df and can be tested and potentially rejected; a just iden-tified model has zero df and does not test anything;

an underidentified model has negative df and an infinite number of solutions.

Formative models exist when an emergent construct is the dependent variable and when its indicators represent unique aspects of the identi-fied emergent construct. Although identification of formative constructs is difficult, covariance-based SEM (cov-SEM) can support the identification of these models (Edwards and Bagozzi 2000; Kline 2006; Hardin et al. 2011). The challenges of for-mative model identification go beyond the type of statistical analysis or any particular SEM software

Table 1. EQS /Equations section differences between reflective and formative indicators. The formative equations alone are not identified.

```
REFLECTIVE MODEL – EQS EQUATIONS SECTION
EXAMPLE
/EQUATIONS
V1 = *F1 + E1;
V2 = *F1 + E2;
V3 = *F1 + E3;
V4 = *F1 + E4;
V5 = *F2 + E5;
V6 = *F2 + E6;
V7 = *F2 + E7;
V8 = *F2 + E8;
FORMATIVE MODEL EXAMPLE – EQS EQUATIONS
SECTION EXAMPLE
/EQUATIONS
F1 = *V1 + *V2 + *V3 + *V4 + D1;
F2 = *V5 + *V6 + *V7 + *V8 + D2;
```

application. Instead of a measured variable being the dependent variable (as it is for a reflective model), the construct (or factor) is the dependent variable. Table 1 provides the EQS/EQUATIONS section for the code differences between Figures 1 and 2. In a formative measurement model, the meaning of the factor is meant to be determined by its observed predictors, but achieving this in practice is very difficult. Treiblmaier et al. (2011) propose a new way to accomplish this. Because the challenges of clearly identifying an emergent construct from measured variables involve technical details that would take us beyond the limited goals of this paper, we do not pursue this topic further.

While it is common that SEM research may focus solely on CFA and the identification of novel measurement models, it is rare to see SEM analysis focus strictly on path models. In (Kenny 2006, p. ix), "SEM always involves a measurement model and very often the best way to test that model is with CFA." In the absence of distinct, measured indicators, a single measure, such as the mean score across a set of variables, can be used to represent the construct, but this presumes the unlikely idea that this measure is perfectly reliable. Sometimes the reliability of such a measure is known, and can be used to specify an error variance for it; to do this with an estimated error variance, see Oberski (2011). As summarized by Kenny (2006, p. x): "construct validity, instrument development and validation, reduction of the number of variables, and sources of bias in measurement, to name just a few, are subjects supported by high-quality CFA." CFA is often applied to confirm the results of an exploratory factor analysis (EFA) investigation, identifying and confirming the proper data reduction and construct alignment to indicators. In addition, however, CFA can verify existence of a large number of theoretically justified factors with few indicators per factor, while an EFA applied to the same data would never recover the theoretical structure. An excellent example is the multitrait-multimethod

matrix that will have trait and method factors (e.g., Bentler, 2007). Examples of method effects are self-reporting biases such as acquiescence, or extra factors that arise when combining positively and negatively worded items (Brown 2006, p. 3). CFA is useful for isolating (confounding) method effects that may not be evident when CFA is not conducted in the proper manner and prior to testing the full structural model. CFA often can be shortchanged in textbooks, so it is not unsurprising that its reporting may also be minimized. Kenny (2006, p. ix) comments: "the social and behavioral sciences have learned much more from CFA than from SEM."

When CFA is applied, whether as the focus of the analysis or as support to testing a structural model, certain reporting criteria are expected. The methodology needs to confirm how each construct was tested, and contain some discussion of the fit of each analysis. In the interest of page limitations in today's journals, merely noting that all constructs were individually and successfully tested, achieving excellent fit may be sufficient. If a complete CFA model is run with all indicators and factors, and factors are allowed to freely correlate (with no regressions among factors), and the model fits well, the separate factors with their indicators also can be presumed to be acceptable. Of course, if one or more individual models did not achieve these goals, such as due to just-identified models, this should be noted, as well as when individual construct identification produced less than excellent fit. Ideally all standardized factor loadings will be high so that the factor structure is stable. Occasionally a composite variable is created from a set of indicators for use in other non-SEM research; such a composite will have high reliability if the factor loadings are large.

SEM MODEL AS THEORY

Sometimes, an author will depict a conceptual model traditionally in an SEM paper, ignoring the need for the psychometric details. Such an attempt depicts the model as a path model where only latent constructs and their direct and indirect paths are noted. Typically, these relationships among the latent factors represent the heart of the investigator's theory, and while the path model may be useful to introduce a complex, theoretical model, it does not remove the need to describe the psychometric details (i.e., the measurement model and its relation within the structural model) (Hancock and Mueller 2007). In a large model, this can be done with separate diagrams or tables and discussions of the measurement and structural models.

In SEM research, one is typically testing a complex theory. The SEM model, whether CFA, path, or structural is a composite hypothesis (McDonald and Ho 2002). The goodness-of-fit chi-square statistic and associated fit indices describe the fit of the overall model. The 'fit' of a model relates to how well the hypothesized model describes the behavioral patterns and relationships of the actual data. Labeling separate hypotheses for paths is to be avoided (Chin 1998) as it confounds the SEM intent. This is another area of difference between covariance-based SEM and PLS. Let's address the PLS case first. In PLS, variance is extracted on a component-by-component basis taking into account the variance among a component's direct effects. The PLS literature acknowledges that loadings are overestimated and path coefficients are underestimated (Fornell and Cha 1994). In covariance-based SEM, using a factor-analytic computation, not principal components, the model-reproduced covariances represent a unified model.

Although certain parameters may represent important substantive hypotheses, and hence will require elaboration, one seldom sees SEM methodologists employ the convention of enumerating a large set of specific hypotheses. Of course, some paths in a model may have a huge impact on model fit while others may be removed without much or any degradation of fit. There is

general agreement that simplifying a model, by removing unnecessary, i.e., nonsignificant, paths from it, is a useful way to create a final more parsimonious model. The importance of specific paths or sets of paths can be evaluated in a formal way using chi-square difference tests, in which the more general model as well as the more restricted model (with some paths set to zero) are separately fitted. The difference between the two chi-square tests from these models, evaluated relative to the difference in degrees of freedom, gives the necessary chi-square difference test to evaluate whether the restriction is reasonable. Alternative tests are the Wald test (Chou and Bentler 2002), which requires estimating only the general model, and the Lagrange Multiplier test, which requires estimating only the restricted model.[3] EQS provides these tests in multivariate versions, allowing sets of parameters to be evaluated simultaneously (Savalei and Bentler 2006). New ways of quantifying the importance of such model differences via RMSEA have recently been developed (MacCallum, Browne, and Cai 2006; Li and Bentler 2011).

When CFA is utilized for the measurement model, each construct is identified by a set of indicators that are declared in the conceptual (theoretical) model (see Figure 4). This entire psychometric model is labeled to identify which variances, covariances, and loadings are constrained or freely estimated using a standard convention. This labeling allows for ease of reference when discussing a particular path in the model. While Figure 4 depicts a sophisticated formalization for declaring these estimations, less sophisticated models will treat unlabeled estimations as free, but will, at a minimum, declare when parameters are fixed (generally to the value of '1') or freely estimated (using an '*'). In a CFA measurement model, either the factor variances (Figure 4 constrains the factor variances) or one of each factor's loadings must always be constrained for proper identification. In the absence of such notational clarity, the entire input code needs to be supplied;

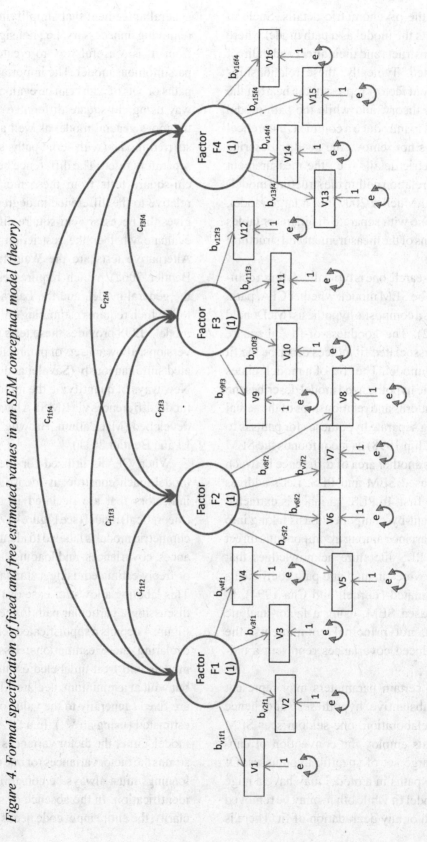

Figure 4. Formal specification of fixed and free estimated values in an SEM conceptual model (theory)

however, this is a substandard choice. While any SEM reviewer can understand a well-documented recommended model, only SEM reviewers with expertise in the author's chosen technology (AMOS, EQS, LISREL, Mplus, etc.) can easily interpret the specific code.

A typical approach is to provide one figure for the a priori hypothesized model. If the figure is very complex, it can, of course, be presented in clearly labeled parts. A figure with the final model's parameter estimates, or standardized estimates, typically helps to clarify and summarize results of the analysis.

DEPENDENT VARIABLES IN CFA

The parameters of any model are the coefficients in the equations as well as the variances and covariances of the independent (non-dependent) variables, and in the CFA model of Figure 4 the variances are shown as numbers within parentheses (factors) or a two-way arrow of a variable to itself (errors). In this model, the factors are simply correlated, i.e., there are no directional arrows among factors. In a CFA reflective model, the dependent variables are the indicators In EQS, this interpretation follows directly from Table 2. In the /EQUATIONS section, the code declares each indicator (using EQS notation, it is a numbered variable, such as V1) is the weighted sum (either freely estimated or constrained in the input code) of one or more factors plus residual error. A factor represents the commonality among its indicators, while residual or measurement error represents unknown additional influences on the indicator that are not strong enough to be independently identified. In the EQS notation, in the /EQUATIONS section, you can see that the theory specifies a *set* of linear equations, i.e., *simultaneous* equations, occurring together. The equations are executed, not in isolation of each other but, as a unified set that frames the theory. Then there are /VARIANCES and possibly /COVARIANCES

Table 2. Sample EQS code corresponding to Figure 4's theoretical model (presuming four indicators per construct)

```
/TITLE
Sample EQS program with 3 factors each with 4 reflective
indicators
/SPECIFICATIONS
DATA='C:\EQS61\EQS example v1-16.ESS';
VARIABLES=16; CASES=246; METHOD=ML,ROBUST;
ANALYSIS=COVARIANCE; MATRIX=RAW;
/LABELS !Meaningful variable names can be declared as
applicable
/EQUATIONS
V1 = *F1 + E1; !Factor loadings are all freely estimated;
V2 = *F1 + E2;
V3 = *F1 + E3;
V4 = *F1 + E4;
V5 = *F2 + E5;
V6 = *F2 + E6;
V7 = *F2 + E7;
V8 = *F2 + E8;
V9 = *F3 + E9;
V10 = *F3 + E10;
V11 = *F3 + E11;
V12 = *F3 + E12;
V13 = *F4 + E13;
V14 = *F4 + E14;
V15 = *F4 + E15;
V16 = *F4 + E16;
/VARIANCES
F1 to F4 = 1; !Factor variances are constrained to 1;
E1 to E16= *; !Residuals are freely estimated;
/COVARIANCES
F1,F2 = *; !Factors covary with each other;
F1,F3 = *;
F2,F3 = *;
/PRINT
FIT=ALL; !Prints fit indices; other options for output can be
found in Bentler (2006).
/END
```

V = measured variable; F = factor; E = residual error. Please see EQS Manual (Bentler 2006) for descriptions of the EQS code syntax.

for the independent variables – here, the factors and errors.

This unified modeling orientation is a contribution of the Bentler-Weeks model (1980). It aligns the design directly to the visual representation of the theorized model without compromising computation results. Any SEM model that can be diagrammed can be specified in the same way.

REPLICATION OF RESULTS

Correct modeling allows for the theoretical model to be duplicated in any SEM software application, but that alone is insufficient for replication of the reported modeling results. One of SEM's advantages over other statistical analysis is for reasonable duplication of the results without having to require the original data set. Many data sources, particularly empirical work in information systems, come from industry partners who regard the explicit data as proprietary. SEM generates a sample covariance matrix, and its submission, perhaps as an appendix, provides the other necessary input to support replicability. A correlation matrix with standard deviations is equivalent. Correlation matrices are riskier to analyze in that most estimation procedures in SEM presume unstandardized variables (Kline 2004, p. 70); however, EQS does provide fully acceptable statistical results for analysis of correlation matrices when variances are not important, or when categorical variables are involved[4]. SEM methodologists (Jackson et al. 2009; Brown 2006; McDonald and Ho 2002) advocate supplying the covariance matrix for their journal submissions and this requirement is becoming better recognized in the IS field; Chin (1998) highlights this requirement in IS research. The Journal of the Association for Information Systems notes the requirement explicitly on its web site with other submission requirements for authors. As more IS journals, as well as other disciplines, provide various attachments to be included online, SEM submissions extend their value to others, especially to PhD students who can replicate the study and its results as part of their own education.

A separate aspect of replicability is the researcher's own cross-validation of results to a confirmatory sample. This is especially useful when model modification is done to make the fit of a model statistically acceptable. If a study has available a large sample (say, more than a thousand cases), it may be desirable to build the model on 2/3 of all cases, and use the remaining 1/3 as a validation sample to assure that key results remain strong in the validation sample, or validated using a different sample.

In summary, since implications of a model must be visible in the covariance matrix, its inclusion helps advance our field and ensure scientific integrity. We have seen examples of models proposing a latent factor to underlie a set of variables that are essentially uncorrelated – an easily seen mismatch between theory and data. Similarly survey research has been submitted where questions were omitted based on non-significant results, and an adjusted model was presented as the final conceptual model. Yet, inspection of the covariance matrix indicated that the questions as measured observations had not been removed from the executed model. Additionally, inclusion of the covariance matrix elevates the ability to discuss preferred models on the basis of rigor, not speculation.

REPORTING RESULTS AND ANALYSIS

Each paper should note the software application used to perform the analysis as well as the appropriate delineation to note the exact version of software used. In EQS, there is a release version and a build version, so if we employed the most current version, we would report "EQS6.1, build 94 was used."

The estimation procedure is also necessary. The most common estimation procedure is *maximum likelihood* (ML in EQS), but if the data significantly violates normal distribution patterns, *robust* methods (ML, Robust in EQS), or asymptotic distribution free (AGLS in EQS; also known as weighted-least squares), or another estimation procedure will be more appropriate. We recommend that a test for multivariate normality always be reported when ML or another normal theory method like least squares is used. EQS provides Mardia's normalized multivariate kurtosis coefficient, which acts like a z-statistic. So if kurtosis is much larger than 3, the ML chi-squared test and standard errors generally are misleading. For an extended discussion of the differences in estimation methods see (Brown 2006, p. 76-77 or Kline 2004, p. 111-115, 176-180, 196.).

SUCCESSFUL EXECUTION ACHIEVED

Since SEM software checks for error-free execution and supplies meaningful error messages, the researcher should report that the specific SEM software executed free of these error messages. In EQS, execution completely free of all fatal (under-identification is a type of fatal error) and non fatal (i.e., messages where the results may be applied under limited instances that are fully described by the researcher) messages. An example of a critical fatal message is

NOTE: DO NOT TRUST THIS OUTPUT. IT-ERATIVE PROCESS HAS NOT CONVERGED. MAXIMUM NUMBER OF ITERATIONS WAS REACHED.

This requires changing the maximum number of iterations, or the start values, or as a last resort, the model itself, and rerunning the model. The ideal output includes the following two lines:

PARAMETER ESTIMATES APPEAR IN ORDER, NO SPECIAL PROBLEMS WERE ENCOUNTERED DURING OPTIMIZATION.

A few error messages may be nonfatal and arguments may be put forward with regard to why the output is interpretable and reliable. An example is when a variance is tending towards a negative estimate and is held at the boundary of zero. For example, if the variance of E1 has this problem, the program will print

E1,E1 CONSTRAINED AT LOWER BOUND.

While a zero or negative error variance estimate is not ideal, it may occur when a factor has only two indicators, and can be acceptable providing the author has verified that both indicators have large enough standardized factor loadings and that no meaningful alternative model without such a problem can be obtained. Any error messages produced in the output should be disclosed and discussed. Ideally, output free of error messages reduces the complexity of getting a paper approved based on its results.

DATA SAMPLING AND POWER

Sample size and derivation of the data must be reported. "Although there is universal agreement among researchers that the larger the sample relative to the population the more stable the parameter estimates, there is no agreement as to what constitutes large" (Raykov and Marcoulides 2006, p. 30). A small sample can be considered less than 100 (Bentler 2006; Qureshi and Compeau 2009). A rule of thumb was suggested that good sample size should be more than ten times the number of free model parameters (Raykov and Marcoulides 2006; Bentler 2006; Hu et al. 1992). While some have questioned this guideline (Marsh et al. 1998; Velicer and Fava 1998), no validated alternative has been able to replace it. Currently, there appears to be no consensus on a specific number for 'large' mainly due to the need to take into account model complexity; however, large appears to be associated with sample sizes approximating 200 or more (Jackson et al. 2009, p. 8; Saris et al. 2009, p. 9). With non-normal data, even larger samples may be needed (Hau and Marsh 2004), especially when the model includes more than 20 or so variables. The literature observes that some attempt to circumvent power issues by limiting the number of indicators, thus manipulating the degrees of freedom; however, this manipulation is not considered appropriate without theoretical basis (Marsh et al. 1998; McQuitty 2004).

This lack of consensus extends into the discussion of power. While the need to address what is known as a Type II error (accepting a predicted model as valid when it is significantly misspecified) is well-accepted, a generally agreed upon method for deriving a power value is not. The literature highlights that models can be manipulated, i.e., changed without theoretical basis, to achieve reasonable results (Marsh et al. 1998; McQuitty 2004). Modifying either sample size or degrees of freedom is likely to produce adequate power and model fit. Power is most significantly improved by increasing sample size when the initial N (number of subjects) is small (ibid). Sample size is often manipulated more frequently as modifying degrees of freedom has theoretical implications. In actuality, power is an outcome of the association of number of indicators, samples size, and degrees of freedom (ibid). Most models can be assessed as adequate when degrees of freedom are very low, in which case, the model risks being more a representation of the data sampled (i.e., a just identified model), than in being an externally generalizable model in its exact form to other settings.

One aspect of the problem is how to define the alternative model against which power is to be evaluated. One approach avoids this by using a specified value of a fit index as an alternative (MacCallum, Browne, and Sugawara 1996; Kim 2005; MacCallum, Lee and Browne 2010). A more practically useful approach with small samples is to test a meaningful but very restricted alternative model, such as a one-factor model. If such a model is rejected, evidently power is high enough to distinguish some models. Determining a general model for sample size and statistical power continues to need more research: "The extant literature provides little guidance on this issue" (Brown 2006, p. 412). Brown goes on to note that Monte Carlo studies on this have been few and often do not generalize into applied research.

REPORTING FIT FOR ALTERNATIVE MODELS

As noted, SEM models should be over-identified, meaning that more than one theoretical explanation of the data may be possible. The most informative publications also test and report alternative models (alternative theoretical explanations). Fit indices for the preferred model and for at least one or two reasonable alternatives should be reported if at all possible.

The fit of a model pertains to how well the theorized model (including constraints and freely estimated parameters) reproduce the covariance matrix of the actual data. The chi-square goodness of fit test statistic is an important statistic for evaluating this; it, and the associated probability value, should always be reported. On the other hand, it is a weakness when authors (and reviewers) rely on the chi-squared alone to accept or to reject a model's fit. The chi-squared value and its probability test how the predicted model compares to a just-identified model and in this measurement, low and nonsignificant values are sought (Kline 2004). That is, we want to accept the null hypothesis. While this goal is technically correct, there is a wealth of literature identifying the problems of chi-square nonsignificance and chi-square used solely as a determinant of fit particularly under conditions of large sample size (Bentler 2007; Brown 2006; Raykov and Marcoulides 2006a; Wood and Zhu 2006; Yuan 2005; Yuan and Bentler 2004; Kline 2004; Mac-Callum et al. 1996). "In practice, many reported chi-square statistics are significant even when sample sizes are not large, and in the context of nested models, the chi-square difference test is often not significant" (Yuan and Bentler 2004, p. 738). Most standard chi-square values are based on a sample size multiplier, and hence any model will be rejected with a large enough sample[5]. Such a paradox suggests that no determination can be made of the chi-square significance result in isolation, given that it is sensitive to large sample sizes and empirical data, against the reality that SEM is a large sample method targeted ideally to assist in statistical analysis of empirical data.

Chi-square is not to be abandoned, but merely used with caution and in the proper context. As noted previously, when performing nested model comparisons, chi-square difference tests remain valid (Brown 2006; Bentler and Satorra 2010) although not without challenges and the need for careful interpretation (Rigdon 1999; Bentler 2000). When robust statistics are used, computing correct difference tests actually can be quite complicated because several algebraic steps are required based on output from two model runs (Satorra and Bentler, 2010).[6]

Another contemporary error is the use of chi-square divided by the degrees of freedom. Earlier research suggested that chi-square divided by the degrees of freedom represents a good metric for model evaluation. While the initial paper (Wheaton, et al. 1977) introducing this evaluation criteria had become popular, Wheaton (1987) subsequently recommended that it no longer be used. Unfortunately, this statistic is quite sensitive to sample size (Brown 2006); it has not been demonstrated to withstand the scrutiny of simulation research (Hu and Bentler 1998, 1999); and it lacks consistent standards with regard to what values represent good or bad model fit (Brown 2006).

REPORTING FIT INDICES

It always makes good sense to augment the chi-square model fit statistic with other fit indices that address different orientations toward fit (Bolen 1989; Hu and Bentler 1998, 1999; Kline 2004; McQuitty 2004; Brown 2006; Raykov and Marcoulides 2006a; Hancock and Mueller 2007; Wu and West 2010). SEM methodologists recommend that several fit indices be reported. These indices can be explained along three dimensions: absolute fit, parsimony correction, and comparative fit. SEM software applications, such as AMOS, EQS,

Mplus, and LISREL, provide several commonly used fit indices.

In absolute fit, we are comparing how closely our proposed model predicts the variance-covariance matrix of the sample data. The model takes the final parameter estimates (e.g., factor loadings, factor variances and covariances, error variances) and algebraically computes all implied variances and covariances. Path tracing would yield the same results. A small discrepancy between model-based and data covariances implies a good model. Chi-square, standardized root mean square residual (SRMR), and root mean squared error of approximation (RMSEA) are included in the set of recommended absolute fit indices. The standardized root mean square residual (SRMR) provides a good measure of this discrepancy in the metric of correlation coefficients, that is, after transforming covariances to correlations (Hu and Bentler 1998). Hence it is intrinsically interpretable and always should be reported, as it is a valid measure of fit even when chi-squared test cannot be relied upon (Brown 2006). SRMR produces values between 0.0 and 1.0; the closer to 0.0, the better the fit. (Cutoff values will be addressed in the next section).

If we suppose two models where the first has more parameters freely estimated than the second, the fit of the two models are identical by chi-square or SRMR, and both models are equally meaningful theoretically, parsimony considerations would favor the model with fewer parameters. It is possible to make a parsimony correction to fit indices, in which a penalty is added for a larger number of free parameters, but fit indices corrected for parsimony are not good at selecting a true model from among several models (Williams and Holahan 1994).

The root mean squared error of approximation (RMSEA) is a widely used index of absolute fit (Steiger 1990; MacCallum et al. 1996). As a transformation of the chi-square test and degrees of freedom, it measures the quality of fit per degree of freedom. Like SRMR, perfect fit for RMSEA is 0.0. While it is unusual for RMSEA to exceed 1.0, technically it is unbounded in its upper range. One benefit of RMSEA is the that they "permit a broader interpretation of the degree of model fit than the [chi-square] test, because they recognize that sample size plays a role by affecting the confidence interval associated with an estimate of model fit" (McQuitty 2004, p. 176).

Comparative fit indices (also called incremental fit) —measure the fit of the predicted model against the fit of a similar one with no covariances among the indicators. The model of interest presumably exhibits many nonzero correlations or covariances, and comparative fit measures are designed to evaluate how well these correlations are accounted for by comparing the substantive model to the worst possible model. It is hard to think of a worse model than that of uncorrelated variables, where no variables influence or are influenced by, or correlated with, any other variables. These indices have been found to perform well under a variety of data conditions (sensitivity to sample size, modest violation of normality, categorical data, etc.) (Brown 2006). The normed-fit index (NFI) is a comparative index that is somewhat sensitive to sample size and it ignores parsimony (differences in degrees of freedom), but both comparative fit index (CFI) and the non-normed fit index (NNFI, also called the Tucker-Lewis Index or TLI) are less sensitive to sample size and do consider parsimony (Bentler 1990; Fan et al. 1999; Kline 2004; Marsh et al. 1998; McQuitty 2004). The closer the comparative model fit index is to 1.0, the better the fit of the predicted model. CFI can range from 0.0 to 1.0, but while generally falling within this range, NNFI may exceed the upper or lower bound.

These are not the only fit indices possible, but appear to be those with continued popularity in empirical studies as well as performing well in Monte Carlo research (Brown 2006). Other indices, such as goodness-of-fit (GFI) and adjusted goodness-of-fit (AGFI) have been shown to perform poorly in rigorous simulation investigations (Hu and Bentler 1995, 1998; Marsh, et al. 1988; MacCallum and Hong 1997). Selecting the 'best' one or two fit indices is a subject of ongoing discussion and debate. The accepted practice among SEM methodologists is to include a variety of fit indices, offering results from each aspect of fit. We recommend reporting chi-square, SRMR, RMSEA, NNFI, and CFI, at a minimum, for the descriptive power of this set of indices for misspecification assessment. If a model performs reasonably well according to these different types of fit indices, in the absence of a better performing model, a study's results should be considered useful.

While a model's fit are not the only indicators to consider (other dimensions are discussed in the next section), fit and reliability do provide a mechanism to assist comparing models produced by other covariance-based SEM software packages. All SEM packages will produce identical values for chi-square and fit indices when they estimate the same model with the same statistical method accounting for possible rounding error). Any differences will reflect convergence or other anomalies that might be handled differently.

The fit indices just discussed reflect the fit of the entire model, which is important to document. On the other hand, it is possible that an overall model is approximately well specified but that within it, small but serious misspecifications exist. These may be reflected in a few large standardized residuals, and if these exist, they should be removed by improving model fit or at least mentioned in the report. A misfit of the latent path model can be evaluated by comparing the final model to a CFA model where factors simply correlate. Fit indices have recently been developed to isolate the extent to which the latent path model adequately describes the unstructured covariances among factors (O'Boyle and Williams 2011).

VALIDITY BEYOND FIT INDICES: FACTOR LOADINGS, PARAMETERS, AND R-SQUARED

In addition to model fit, a number of other indices need to be reported. First, of course, the significance or nonsignificance of all freely estimated parameters should be indicated with some standard notation.[7] This information can be given in a table, or as part of a diagram.

With regard to the measurement model, factor loadings must be reported. Ideally, they will be incorporated into a visual representation of the model results (the discussion on graphical representation occurs later in the paper). Factor loadings signify the strength of the factor-indicator relationship (Brown 2006, p 2), and are usually presented from the standardized solution to assure interpretability. A standardized factor loading is a beta weight for predicting a variable from a factor. Certainly such a loading should be substantial, although the interpretation of "substantial" has some flexibility. Much of the literature normally cited on cutoff values for cov-SEM reporting (McDonald and Ho 2002; Boomsma 2000; Hu and Bentler 1999; Anderson and Gerbing 1988) does not specify a cutoff for factor loadings. A lack of specification on an actual cutoff should not be interpreted as unimportant, but rather as an indication that a specific appropriate cutoff will be influenced by what is known of the domain of interest and how well theory has been established. Chin (1998 recommends that factor loadings be .6 or above and also recommends that standardized paths equal or exceed 0.20 and ideally 0.30. As one can see, there is some flexibility and that is to consider what we may already know about the theoretical area. Lower values may be acceptable if little to no quantitative analysis exists in extant literature, but a well-developed theory and closely-tied data may imply stronger relationships.

Key parameters of the equations in the structural model also need to be reported, not only for significance, but also for meaning and substantive

significance. For example, in the theory of planned behavior (e.g., Venkatesh et al. 2003), attitude towards a behavior is presumed not to affect the behavior directly, but rather to influence intention to engage in the behavior, which in turn affects actual behavior. If the standardized effect of attitude on intention is small, its indirect influence on subsequent behavior will be small as well and hence one could surmise that programs to influence attitude are unlikely to influence behavior. As in regression, when unstandardized coefficients have no intrinsic interpretation, coefficients from the standardized solution are recommended to be presented and interpreted.

As in single equation regression, R-squared (or squared multiple correlation) is a measure of the proportion of explained variance in the dependent variable of an equation. In EQS, the standardized regression table provides the R-squared statistic adjacent to each dependent variable's linear equation. These may be optionally reported in most instances but may be critical and hence necessary information in studies where prediction has a special role. In EQS, an R-squared is the explained variance for any dependent variable (measured observation or factor) by all of its predictors (whether measured variable or factor) associated for any dependent variable, whether the model is a measurement model, latent path model, or combined structural model. Table 3 provides examples of how the R-squared applies to a dependent variable from various model equation options. Note that in typical models, R-squared equals one minus the squared coefficient of the residual variable. [It may be useful to mention that the R-squared in EQS differs from the R-squared in PLS. While explained variance in the dependent variable is represented by one measure, in PLS, there are several. The PLS R-squared represents the amount of variance in a component (as a dependent variable) that is explained by the path model; for the variance explained in the component (as a dependent variable) by its reflective indicators, a separate measure, Average Variance Explained,

Table 3. Model equation options and R-squared

Model option	Standardized Regression Result Example	R-squared Example
Reflective	V1 =.862*F1 +.507 E1;	.743
Formative	F1 =.993*V1 +.118 D1;	.986
Latent Path	F4 =.569*F1 -.206*F2 +.708 D4;	.499
Mixed option	F3 =.351*F2 +.413*V12 +.788 D3;	.379

*(values are for illustrative purposes only)

is provided (Chin 2010). Communality is another variance concept provided by PLS applications, which explains the shared variance among the indicators to a component.]

An R-squared less than .50, for example, would indicate that the majority of variance in the dependent (predicted) variable or factor has not been explained; therefore, the major influence on this variable is not accounted for in the model. Low R-square values for latent factors imply that the factor is not well explained by its predictors, and low R-square values in observed variables indicate that the indicator is not well explained by its generating factor(s). Where one's theory predicts high or low values of R-square, but the results are inconsistent with this expectation, it would be valuable to provide some reasonable explanation. The R-square need not be reported when an indicator is simple, i.e., it measures only one common factor; then, R-square is simply the square of the standardized factor loading.

CUTOFF VALUES FOR FIT

There are a number of papers addressing cutoff values for fit (Hu and Bentler 1998; McDonald and Ho 2002). These are the evaluation guidelines for assessing what values of the fit indices mentioned above represent an acceptable model fit. To some extent this is an arbitrary exercise, since it is something akin to asking what values of R-square are "large" or "large enough" to represent good prediction. But just as it is desirable to categorize effect size, it is desirable to have categories that represent whether the indices are excellent, acceptable, marginal, or poor. Excellent fit is preferred and under certain circumstances acceptable fit can be valuable. If fit cannot meet acceptable thresholds, clearly the model does not explain the data, and hence it most likely would be a waste of journal space to publish it. Table 4 provides cutoff values for the various fit indices based on Hu and Bentler (1998; 1999) and McDonald and Ho (2002) recommendations.

Table 4. Fit and reliability indices cutoff criteria

	Hu and Bentler 1998		McDonald and Ho 2002	
FIT INDICES	**Close Fit**	**Acceptable**	**Very Good**	**Acceptable**
Chi-square	Nonsignificant p-value	Significant when sample size is large or model is complex	Of 41 published papers studied, only 5 had nonsignificant chi-square	
SRMR	Close to 0.08 or less		No cutoff values reported	
RMSEA	Close to 0.06 or less	Notes (Brown and Cudek 1993) 0.05 to 0.08 = fair; >0.10 is poor fit	<0.05	<0.08
CFI, NFI, NNFI	Close to 0.95 or greater	Not specified. Bentler and Bonnett (1980) indicated >0.90	Not reported	>0.90

Underlying covariance-based SEM research is the presumption of alternative models. In SEM research, fit cutoff criteria tend to be more restrictive the more an area is researched and better alternative models are identified. Less researched areas, using SEM, are allowed less rigid criteria. It would seem then that if we find that a theory, for instance, in technology acceptance that has produced a theoretical model with an NNFI fit of .96, an alternative theoretical model with an NNFI of .90 would be less interesting and useful (all other results held equal). In an IS study suggesting a new theoretical perspective, for which there is no alternative model, an NNFI of .90 would be quite interesting. As more research on the theoretical area progressed, subsequent research would 'raise the bar.' Poorly fitting models, however, are seldom useful and imply an unknown source of serious model misspecification.

RELIABILITY INDICES

There are times when a set of variables are intended to be combined by simple summation into a total score, e.g., when one is developing a scale. Reliability is a measure of the internal consistency of the scale and is a necessary but insufficient measurement of scale validity (Nunnally and Bernstein 1994). Specifically, it is an assessment of proportion of true variance in the total scale score over its total variance, and hence it varies from 0-1 (Tabachnick and Fidell 2001). Cronbach's alpha seems to be the gold standard of reliability indices and there are few papers that do not report on it. Cronbach's alpha, though, includes an assumption that may not be part of the actual theoretical model, that is, tau level equivalence. In tau level equivalence, the factor loadings are assumed to be equivalent. If this is not an explicit part of the theory, the less restrictive Reliability Coefficient Rho (RCR), may be preferred. RCR is similar to Cronbach's alpha in that it measures the proportion of true to total variance in the composite, but

the tau level equivalence assumption is removed (Bentler, 2009). EQS reports both Cronbach's alpha and RCR for the composite based on any SEM model (Bentler 2006). As in reporting fit indices, and especially when tau level equivalence is not addressed on a theoretical level, reporting both reliability measures is appropriate. EQS also provides other reliability indices such as the greatest lower bound to reliability.

GRAPHICAL MODEL REPRESENTATION AND RESULTS

Unlike SEM methodologists who typically use graphical representation of CFA and SEM results (see Figure 5 as an example), IS researchers too often submit only lists of numerical values. Visualization is an IS field of research. Cognitive understanding, particularly as models become more complex, are better represented visually than when using other forms (Vessey and Galletta 1991; Speier and Morris 2003; Baker et al. 2009). Compare Figure 5 to Table 5, which represent the same information. In the case of highly complex models, where one model cannot be displayed on a page easily, the font of factor loadings and variances may be too small to read. In such a case, a combination of visual and tabular reporting is more useful, although there should be no duplication. In EQS, the graphical result can be supplemented by the standardized regression equations that include factor loadings, correlations between factors, and R-squared values for each equation, all of which are required for thorough reporting. Results not shown in a diagram may be organized into matrices of similar quantities, as in Table 5. Contemporary SEM reporting favors graphical models, and when one considers that a reviewer is more easily able to interpret graphical findings correctly when the results are not simple, it is counterproductive not to favor visual modeling not only of the initially hypothesized model, but, as noted previously, also of the results. Numerical results have been

Figure 5. CFA graphical results adapted from (Devaraj et al. 2002) technology acceptance model

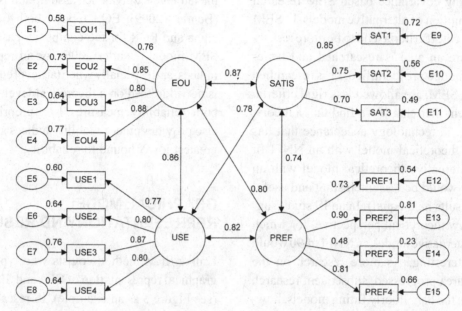

Table 5. Numerical list presentation of (Davaraj, et al. 2002) CFA of technology acceptance model

FACTOR LOADING	EOU	USE	SATIS	PREF	RESIDUAL ERROR
EOU1	0.78				0.56
EOU2	0.85				0.73
EOU3	0.80				0.64
EOU4	0.88				0.77
USE1		0.77			0.60
USE2		0.80			0.64
USE3		0.87			0.76
USE4		0.80			0.64
SAT1			0.85		0.72
SAT2			0.75		0.56
SAT3			0.70		0.49
PREF1				0.73	0.54
PREF2				0.90	0.82
PREF3				0.48	0.23
PREF4				0.81	0.66
FACTOR CORRELATIONS					
	EOU	USE	SATIS	PREF	
EOU	1.00				
USE	0.86	1.00			
SATIS	0.87	0.78	1.00		
PREF	0.80	0.82	0.74	1.00	

recommended to be reported to the third-digit (Chin 1998); however, many IS journal submissions fail to do so, probably reasonably so when sample size is less than 1000.

GREEK NOTATION

There is a trend with SEM researchers recommending the avoidance of Greek notation in specifying or reporting SEM results to allow for SEM research to appeal to a wider audience (Bentler and Weeks 1980; Hancock and Mueller 2006, 2007), although admittedly it does appear in the SEM literature and certainly is appropriate when technical statistical issues are addressed. When employed, SEM methodologists indicate its value corresponds, not to increasing the understanding of current research, but as a link to SEM's seminal origin. The seminal computational software for CFA and SEM was LISREL which required SEM researchers not only to understand matrix algebra but both the upper and lower case Greek alphabet (Thompson 2004). Maintaining this requirement is analogous to IS applications being required to transcribe program coding into assembly language, or perhaps COBOL for business applications to maintain their seminal root(s).

In SEM, competing software applications, including AMOS, EQS, and Mplus avoid the use of Greek notation. Additionally, while SEM journal papers may continue to use Greek notation for extending the SEM statistical capabilities, it is quite interesting to see that SEM textbooks (Kline 2004; Brown 2006; Hancock and Mueller 2006; Thompson 2004) greatly reduce or eliminate such notation. As the purpose of the texts is to be instructive, the trend away from Greek notation cannot be dismissed.

The continued use of Greek notation is an exclusionary choice, i.e., it reduces the readership of SEM research, certainly from those in practice for whom our research results are often intended. As an example, quickly define each of the following in SEM: Φ, Ψ, Θ, δ, φ, ψ, θ, and Γ. If you did not hesitate and are highly confident of your answers, you are likely a happy LISREL user. Others may have experienced moments of discomfort. In Information Systems, part of our culture is to be more inclusive and notation, such as that used in EQS allows more readers to follow the results of SEM research than is enabled by Greek notation. With adoption and diffusion theories (Davis 1986; Rogers 1962) emphasizing the importance of ease of use, and of reappropriation when technical designs do not follow users organizational goals and norms (DeSanctis and Poole 1994) addressed in IS research, these fundamental IS admonitions should be embraced in our own research. Unlike some of the earlier reporting guidelines and requirements, continued use of Greek notation in a discipline that cites ease of use and understanding so extensively seems to violate major core principles in IS research. If we believe that IS should continue as a unique discipline, IS researchers should adopt the major theoretical recommendations that are so frequently cited in our own field.

CONCLUSION

A summary of covariance-based SEM reporting guidelines is given in Table 6. While the traditional publication process itself may have influenced authors previously due to a 'lack of knowledge of standards, space limitations, journal focus, and editorial demand' (Jackson et al. 2009, p. 8), with online supplements becoming popular and the growth of CFA and SEM in behavioral research, these impediments should be removed.

In light of the opportunities afforded research by the use of structural equation modeling based on covariance analysis and its growing popularity (Hershberger 2003), many papers submitted to Information Systems journals are inconsistent in reporting key criteria leading to proper support and validation of the SEM results. Similarly,

Table 6. Covariance-based SEM reporting guidelines

Model Specification	Required	Preferred	Comments
Introductory Material			
Theoretical foundation	☑		Introductory sections (Background/Model Development) explain the theoretical basis for the model including if fully confirmatory (theory testing) or partially exploratory (theory development)
Model Specification			
Predicted model is over-identified	☑		A just-identified model does not generalize to other settings; an under-identified model is un-interpretable. Each construct must be ideally over-identified or, at a minimum, just-identified
Graphical model representation of psychometric research model	☑		Visualization of the relationships among constructs and measured observations
Constrained and freely estimated parameters clearly identified	☑		Theoretical model must identify which parameters are constrained (specify value) or freely estimated
Structural model (if applicable) includes measurement model specification	☑		Display latent path model ; the psychometric detail of the measurement model also needs to be specified
Unified Hypothesis Model; No separate hypotheses for paths		☑	There is one main question: does the predicted model reasonably explain the sample set of data? Use of separate hypotheses need theoretical justification
Methodological Description			
Data sampling and scale	☑		Sample size and how data was collected must be reported; the scale of observed variables must be explained clearly; scale of latent variables noted
Data distribution	☑		Discussion of data distribution is needed, including multivariate normality, missing data treatment, data transformation if utilized
Cutoff criteria for fit indices rationalized	☑		Explain the source or justification of cutoff values utilized
Power		☑	Power should not be summarily dismissed yet strict guidelines for applied research appear to need further research; N<100 should be explained
Results			
Estimation procedure and type of matrix	☑		The estimation procedure (ML, robust, ADF, other) must be declared. The type of matrix (covariance, correlation) analyzed is noted
Software application/version	☑		EQS also includes a build # w/ version; be precise
Start values		☑	Need to be reported if convergence failed without them
Model Testing Methodology	☑		Measurement model validated before structural model. Errors or limitations reported; just identified constructs should be noted
Model Testing Methodology		☑	Constructs (over) identified individually prior to the full model for complex models; just-identified constructs avoided
Modeling results are free of execution errors or unexpected results		☑	Ideally, model estimation does not have software execution errors. All non-fatal error messages should be reported and explained
Replication support: covariance matrix supplied		☑	Covariance matrix is preferred; if a correlation matrix is substituted, standard deviations must also be supplied; mean values are required when a means analysis is undertaken; journals should accommodate web access
Model modification/respecification	☑		Model modification (respecification) must always be declared and explained when utilized

continues on following page

Table 1. Continued

Model Specification	Required	Preferred	Comments
Fit Indices address absolute, parsimony, and comparative fit	☑		A set of fit indices are required to address several aspects of fit; chi-square is insufficient under certain conditions, such as large sample size
Reliability indices provided		☑	High loadings imply reliable items. If total scale scores are recommended, Cronbach's alpha and one or more others are appropriate.
Model output detailed	☑		Values for all parameter values: paths and factor loadings, variances, and covariances and their significance must be reported
Graphical representation of output		☑	Graphical output is preferred for better interpretability
Greek notation minimized		☑	Alternative notation expands interested audience when audience is intended to include readers from practice, such as managers and C-level executives
Factor loadings	☑		Can be reported in the graphical model results and/or in standardized regression format for complex models
R-squared		☑	Indicates the amount of explained variance for each equation. An $R2 < 0.5$ indicates most of the dependent variable's variance has not been explained. In latent variable regressions at the structural level, R-squares may be important and should be reported. That is, if F5 is a factor predicted by many others, it is helpful to say how well it is predicted by them
Values reported to third-digit		☑	To the second-digit is mandatory; third-digit reporting good in large samples

other submissions cling to practices better suited to linear regression analysis, ignoring contemporary practices adopted by SEM methodologists. These behaviors weaken both the persuasiveness of the paper's contributions as well as weaken the reputation of IS researchers within the broader research community. The IS field is rich in theoretical guidance dealing with acceptance, use, and understanding of technological advances. In providing recommended guidelines for proper SEM reporting, this paper borrows not merely from SEM methodologists and contemporary SEM reporting, but borrows implications, advice, and recommendations from several of our own IS theories to suggest improved adoption of more contemporary SEM reporting practices within the IS community.

REFERENCES

Arbuckle, J. L. (1989). AMOS: Analysis of moment structures. *The American Statistician, 43*, 66. doi:10.2307/2685178

Baker, J., Burkman, J., & Jones, D. (2009). Using visual representations of data to enhance sensemaking in data exploration tasks. *Journal of the Association for Information Systems, 10*(7), 533–559.

Bentler, P. M. (1985). *Theory and implementation of EQS, a structural equations program.* Los Angeles, CA: BMDP Statistical Software.

Bentler, P. M. (2000). Rites, wrong, and gold in model testing. *Structural Equation Modeling, 7*(1), 82–91. doi:10.1207/S15328007SEM0701_04

Bentler, P. M. (2006). *EQS 6 structural equations program manual.* Encino, CA: Multivariate Software. Retrieved from www.mvsoft.com

Bentler, P. M. (2007). Can scientifically useful hypotheses be tested with correlations? *The American Psychologist, 62*, 772–782. doi:10.1037/0003-066X.62.8.772

Bentler, P. M. (2009). Alpha, dimension-free, and model-based internal consistency reliability. *Psychometrika, 74*, 137–143. doi:10.1007/s11336-008-9100-1

Bentler, P. M., & deLeeuw, J. (2011). (in press). Factor analysis via components analysis. *Psychometrika*. doi:10.1007/s11336-011-9217-5

Bentler, P. M., & Satorra, A. (2010). Testing model nesting and equivalence. *Psychological Methods, 15*(2), 111–123. doi:10.1037/a0019625

Bentler, P. M., & Weeks, D. G. (1980). Linear structural equations with latent variables. *Psychometrika, 45*, 289–308. doi:10.1007/BF02293905

Bentler, P. M., & Wu, E. J. C. (2002). *EQS 6 for Windows user's guide*. Encino, CA: Multivariate Software.

Brown, T. (2006). *Confirmatory factor analysis for applied research*. New York, NY: Guilford Press.

Byrne, B. M. (2006). *Structural equation modeling with EQS*. Mahwah, NJ: Lawrence Erlbaum Associates.

Chin, W. W. (1998). Issues and opinion on structural equation modeling. *Management Information Systems Quarterly, 22*(1), vii–xvi.

Chin, W. W. (2010). How to write up and report PLS analyses. In Esposito Vinzi, V., Chin, W. W., Henseler, J., & Wang, H. (Eds.), *Handbook of partial least squares* (pp. 655–690). Berlin, Germany: Springer-Verlag. doi:10.1007/978-3-540-32827-8_29

Datta, P., Walsh, K. R., & Terrell, D. (2002). The impact of demographics on choice of survey modes: Demographic distinctiveness between Web-based and telephone-based survey respondents. *Communications of the Association for Information System, 9*, article 13.

Davis, F. D. (1989). Perceived usefulness, perceived ease of use, and user acceptance of Information Technology. *Management Information Systems Quarterly, 13*(3), 319–340. doi:10.2307/249008

DeSanctis, G., & Poole, M. S. (1994). Capturing the complexity in advanced Technology Use: Adaptive structuration theory. *Organization Science, 5*(2), 121–147. doi:10.1287/orsc.5.2.121

Devaraj, S., Fan, M., & Kohli, R. (2002). Antecedents of B2C channel satisfaction and preference: Validating e-commerce metrics. *Information Systems Research, 13*(3), 316–333. doi:10.1287/isre.13.3.316.77

Diamanthopoulos, A., & Winklhofer, H. M. (2001). Index construction with formative indicators: An alternative to scale development. *JMR, Journal of Marketing Research, 38*(2), 269–277. doi:10.1509/jmkr.38.2.269.18845

Edwards, J. R., & Bagozzi, R. P. (2000). On the nature and direction of relationships between constructs and their measures. *Psychological Methods, 5*, 155–174. doi:10.1037/1082-989X.5.2.155

Fornell, C., & Cha, J. (1994). Partial least squares. In Bagozzi, R. (Ed.), *Advanced methods of marketing* (pp. 52–78). Cambridge, UK: Blackwell.

Gefen, D., Straub, D. W., & Boudreau, M. (2000). Structural equation modeling techniques and regression: Guidelines for research practice. *Communications of AIS, 4*(7), 1–77.

Hancock, G. R., & Mueller, R. O. (2006). *Structural equation modeling*. Greenwich, CT: Information Age Publishing.

Hardin, A. M., Chang, J. C., & Fuller, M. A. (2011). Formative measurement and academic research: In search of measurement theory. *Educational and Psychological Measurement, 71*(2), 270–284. doi:10.1177/0013164410370208

Hau, K.-T., & Marsh, H. W. (2004). The use of item parcels in structural equation modeling: Non-normal data and small sample size. *The British Journal of Mathematical and Statistical Psychology, 57*, 327–351. doi:10.1111/j.2044-8317.2004.tb00142.x

Hershberger, S. (2003). The growth of structural equation modeling. *Structural Equation Modeling, 10*(1), 35–46. doi:10.1207/S15328007SEM1001_2

Hu, L., & Bentler, P. M. (1999). Cutoff criteria for fit indexes in covariance structure analysis: Conventional criteria versus new alternatives. *Structural Equation Modeling, 6*(1), 1–55. doi:10.1080/10705519909540118

Hu, L., Bentler, P. M., & Kano, Y. (1992). Can test statistics in covariance structure analysis be trusted? *Psychological Bulletin, 112*, 351–362. doi:10.1037/0033-2909.112.2.351

Hu, L. T., & Bentler, P. M. (1998). Fit indices in covariance structure modeling. *Psychological Methods, 3*, 424–453. doi:10.1037/1082-989X.3.4.424

Jackson, D., Gillaspy, J., & Purc-Stephenson, R. (2009). Reporting practices in confirmatory factor analysis: An overview and some recommendations. *Psychological Methods, 14*(1), 6–23. doi:10.1037/a0014694

Joreskog, J., & Sorbom, D. (1984). *Lisrel VI: Analysis of linear structural relationships by maximum likelihood, instrument variables, and least squares methods*. Mooreville, IN: Scientific Software.

Kenny, D. (2006). Series Editor's note. In Brown, T. (Ed.), *Confirmatory factor analysis for applied research*. New York, NY: Guilford Press.

Kim, K. H. (2005). The relation among fit indexes, power, and sample size in structural equation modeling. *Structural Equation Modeling, 12*(3), 368–390. doi:10.1207/s15328007sem1203_2

Kline, R. B. (1998). *Principles and practice of structural equation modeling* (2nd ed.). New York, NY: Guilford Press.

Kline, R. B. (2006). Formative measurement and feedback loops. In Hancock, G. R., & Mueller, R. O. (Eds.), *Structural equation modeling* (pp. 43–68). Greenwich, CT: Information Age Publishing Inc.

Law, K. S., Wong, C. S., & Mobley, W. H. (1998). Toward a taxonomy of multidimensional constructs. *Academy of Management Review, 23*(4), 741–755.

Li, L., & Bentler, P. M. (2011). (in press). Quantified choice of root-mean-square errors of approximation for evaluation and power analysis of small differences between structural equation models. *Psychological Methods*. doi:10.1037/a0022657

MacCallum, R., Browne, M., & Sugawara, H. (1996). Power analysis and determination of sample size for covariance structure modeling. *Psychological Methods, 3*(2), 131–149.

MacCallum, R. C., & Browne, M. W. (1993). The use of causal indicators in covariance structure models: Some practical issues. *Psychological Bulletin, 114*(3), 533–541. doi:10.1037/0033-2909.114.3.533

MacCallum, R. C., Browne, M. W., & Cai, L. (2006). Testing differences between nested covariance structure models: Power analysis and null hypotheses. *Psychological Methods, 11*, 19–35. doi:10.1037/1082-989X.11.1.19

MacCallum, R. C., Lee, T., & Browne, M. W. (2010). The issue of isopower in power analysis for tests of structural equation models. *Structural Equation Modeling*, *17*, 23–41. doi:10.1080/10705510903438906

MacKenzie, S., Podsakoff, P., & Jarvis, C. (2005). The problem of measurement model misspecification in behavioral and organizational research and some recommended solutions. *The Journal of Applied Psychology*, *90*(4), 710–730. doi:10.1037/0021-9010.90.4.710

Marsh, H. W., Hau, K.-T., Balla, J. R., & Grayson, D. (1998). Is more ever too much? The number of indicators per factor in confirmatory factor analysis. *Multivariate Behavioral Research*, *33*, 181–220. doi:10.1207/s15327906mbr3302_1

McDonald, R. P., & Ho, R. M. (2002). Principles and practice in reporting structural equation analysis. *Psychological Methods*, *7*, 64–82. doi:10.1037/1082-989X.7.1.64

Nunnally, J., & Bernstein, I. (1994). *Psychometric theory* (3rd ed.). New York, NY: McGraw-Hill.

O'Boyle, E. H. Jr, & Williams, L. J. (2011). Decomposing model fit: Measurement vs. theory in organizational research using latent variables. *The Journal of Applied Psychology*, *96*(1), 1–12. doi:10.1037/a0020539

Oberski, D. L. (2011). *Measurement error in comparative surveys*. Ph.D. Dissertation, Tilburg University.

Palvia, P., Leary, T., Pinjani, P., & Midha, V. (2004). A meta analysis of MIS research. *Americas Conference of Information Systems, AMCIS 2004 Proceedings*. Paper 527. Retrieved from tp://aisel.aisnet.org/amcis2004/527

Qureshi, I., & Compeau, D. (2009). Assessing between-group differences in Information Systems research: A comparison of covariance- and component-based SEM. *Management Information Systems Quarterly*, *33*(1), 197–214.

Raykov, T., & Marcoulides, G. A. (2006). Estimation of generalizability coefficients via a structural equation modeling approach to scale reliability evaluation. *International Journal of Testing*, *6*(1), 81–95. doi:10.1207/s15327574ijt0601_5

Raykov, T., & Marcoulides, G. A. (2006). *A first course in structural modeling*. Mahwah, NJ: Lawrence Erlbaum Associates.

Rigdon, E. (1995). A necessary and sufficient identification rule for structural models estimated in practice. *Multivariate Behavioral Research*, *30*(3), 359–383. doi:10.1207/s15327906mbr3003_4

Rigdon, E. (1996). *Methodological alternatives to SEM/CFA, from Ed Rigdon's structural equation modeling*. Retrieved on February 12, 2011, from http://www2.gsu.edu/~mkteer/relmeth.html

Rogers, E. M. (1962). *Diffusion of innovations*. Glencoe, IL: Free Press.

Saris, W. E., Satorra, A., & van der Veld, W. (2009). Testing structural equation models or detection of misspecifications? *Structural Equation Modeling*, *16*(4), 1–24. doi:10.1080/10705510903203433

Satorra, A., & Bentler, P. M. (2010). Ensuring positiveness of the scaled difference chi-square test statistic. *Psychometrika*, *75*, 243–248. doi:10.1007/s11336-009-9135-y

Savalei, V., & Bentler, P. M. (2006). Structural equation modeling. In Grover, R., & Vriens, M. (Eds.), *The handbook of marketing research: Uses, misuses, and future advances* (pp. 330–364). Thousand Oaks, CA: Sage Publications.

Schneeweiss, H. (1990). Models with latent variables. In Brown, P. J., & Fuller, W. A. (Eds.), *Contemporary mathematics* (*Vol. 112*, pp. 33–39). Providence, RI: American Mathematical Society.

Speier, C., & Morris, M. (2003). The influence of query interface design on decision making performance. *Management Information Systems Quarterly, 27*(3), 397–423.

Thompson, B. (2004). *Exploratory and confirmatory factor analysis*. Washington, DC: American Psychological Association. doi:10.1037/10694-000

Treiblmaier, H., Bentler, P. M., & Mair, P. (2011). Formative constructs implemented via common factors. *Structural Equation Modeling, 18*, 1–17. doi:10.1080/10705511.2011.532693

Venkatesh, V., Morris, M. G., Davis, G. B., & Davis, F. D. (2003). User acceptance of Information Technology: Toward a unified view. *Management Information Systems Quarterly, 27*(3), 425–478.

Vessey, I., & Galletta, D. (1991). Cognitive fit: An empirical study of information acquisition. *Information Systems Research, 2*(1), 63–84. doi:10.1287/isre.2.1.63

Wheaton, B. (1987). Assessment of fit in overidentified models with latent variables. *Sociological Methods & Research, 16*, 118–154. doi:10.1177/0049124187016001005

Wheaton, B., Muthén, B., Alwin, D., & Summers, G. (1977). Assessing reliability and stability in panel models. *Sociological Methodology, 8*, 84–136. doi:10.2307/270754

Williams, L. J., & Holahan, P. J. (1994). Parsimony-based fit indices for multiple-indicator models: Do they work? *Structural Equation Modeling, 1*(2), 161–189. doi:10.1080/10705519409539970

Wong, C. S., Law, K. S., & Huang, G. H. (2008). On the importance of conducting construct-level analysis for multidimensional constructs in theory development and testing. *Journal of Management, 34*, 744–764. doi:10.1177/0149206307312506

Wood, T. M., & Zhu, W. (2006). *Measurement theory and practice in kinesiology*. Champaign, IL: Human Kinetics Publisher.

Wu, W., & West, S. G. (2010). Sensitivity of fit indices to misspecification in growth curve models. *Multivariate Behavioral Research, 45*, 420–452. doi:10.1080/00273171.2010.483378

Yuan, K. H. (2005). Fit indices versus test statistics. *Multivariate Behavioral Research, 40*(1), 115–148. doi:10.1207/s15327906mbr4001_5

Yuan, K.-H., & Bentler, P. M. (2004). On chi-square difference and Z-tests in mean and covariance structure analysis when the base model is misspecified. *Educational and Psychological Measurement, 64*, 737–757. doi:10.1177/0013164404264853

ADDITIONAL READING

Bentler, P. M. 2006. EQS 6 Structural Equations Program Manual. Multivariate Software, Encino, CA (www.mvsoft.com).

Brown, T. A. (2006). *Confirmatory Factor Analysis for Applied Research*. New York: Guilford Press.

Byrne, B. M. (2006). *Structural Equation Modeling with EQS* (2nd ed.). New York: Taylor and Francis.

Hancock, G. R., & Mueller, R. O. (2006). *Structural Equation Modeling: A Second Course*. Greenwich, CT: Information Age Publishing.

Kline, R. B. (2010). *Principles and Practice of Structural Equation Modeling*. New York: Guilford Press.

ENDNOTES

[1]   Note that we are introducing SEM following the Bentler-Weeks (1980) notation: V (variables) for observed measures, sometimes called manifest variables; F (factors) for latent constructs; E (error) for residual errors in variables ; and D (disturbance) for the residual errors in factors.

[2]   For more on the relations between latent factors and components, see Bentler and (2011).In LISREL, the Lagrange Multiplier test is called the modification index. For more on the relations between latent factors and components, see Bentler and deLeeuw (2011).

[3]   In LISREL, the Lagrange Multiplier test is called the modification index. For more on the relations between latent factors and components, see Bentler and deLeeuw (2011).The statement ANALYSIS=CORRELATION; is all that is needed.

[4]   The statement ANALYSIS = CORRELATION; is all that is needed.

[5]   In general, most SEM applications calculate chi-square as the value of the maximum likelihood fit function at the solution multiplied by the sample size minus one, or FML*(N-1). In Mplus, instead of N-1, only N (sample size) is used.

[6]   An upcoming version of EQS will automate this process.

[7]   Although, as noted, if a parameter is not statistically different from zero, there may not be much point to keeping it in the model.

Chapter 10
Variance–Based Structural Equation Modeling:
Guidelines for Using Partial Least Squares in Information Systems Research

José L. Roldán
Universidad de Sevilla, Spain

Manuel J. Sánchez-Franco
Universidad de Sevilla, Spain

ABSTRACT

Partial Least Squares (PLS) is an efficient statistical technique that is highly suited for Information Systems research. In this chapter, the authors propose both the theory underlying PLS and a discussion of the key differences between covariance-based SEM and variance-based SEM, i.e., PLS. In particular, authors: (a) provide an analysis of the origin, development, and features of PLS, and (b) discuss analysis problems as diverse as the nature of epistemic relationships and sample size requirements. In this regard, the authors present basic guidelines for the applying of PLS as well as an explanation of the different steps implied for the assessment of the measurement model and the structural model. Finally, the authors present two examples of Information Systems models in which they have put previous recommendations into effect.

INTRODUCTION

During the last twenty-five years, the use of structural equation modeling (SEM) with latent variables has become widespread in information

systems (IS) research (Gerow et al., 2010; Urbach & Ahlemann, 2010). In a single, systematic, and comprehensive analysis, SEM allows assessing measurement and structural models, taking measurement error into account. The holistic analysis that SEM is capable of performing can

DOI: 10.4018/978-1-4666-0179-6.ch010

be carried out via one of two distinct statistical techniques: On the one hand, covariance-based SEM (CBSEM), as represented by software such us LISREL, EQS and AMOS; on the other hand, variance-based (or components-based) SEM, i.e., partial least squares (PLS). Although CBSEM has until recently been the most well-known SEM approach, PLS has also been gaining increasing interest among IS researchers (Gefen, Strabu, & Boudreau, 2000). In fact, compared with other scientific disciplines, the information systems area has been the object of a significant number of studies using PLS, the article by Rivard and Huff (1988) being the first study to ever use PLS for data analysis. This outstanding situation is due to, among other factors, the contributions of researchers such as Wynne Chin (University of Houston), who developed PLS-Graph, the first graphical software for PLS path modeling. In addition, much of IS research is constrained by either small sample sizes and/or nascent theoretical development, which encourage the use of PLS.

However, some limitations of this approach have recently been the cause of concern among scholars (Marcoulides & Saunders, 2006; Marcoulides, Chin, & Saunders, 2009). Our position is that PLS is an appropriate approach to SEM when the research problem presents certain conditions and this methodology is properly applied. Thus, the aim of this contribution is to shed light on the use of partial least squares (PLS) as a variance-based SEM approach. Consequently, we provide a discussion of the key differences between CBSEM and variance-based SEM, indicating the rationale upon which researchers can base their use of PLS. We present basic guidelines for the applying of PLS, as well as an explanation of the different steps implied for the assessment of the measurement model and the structural model. We describe our recommendations using two examples from the discipline of information systems.

STRUCTURAL EQUATION MODELING IN INFORMATION SYSTEMS RESEARCH

From a philosophical position, research that applies Structural equation modeling (SEM) usually follows a positivist epistemological belief (Urbach & Ahlemann, 2010). In this vein, SEM emerges as a result of the conjunction of two traditions (Chin 1998a). On the one hand, an econometric perspective (linear regression models), on the other hand, a psychometric approach (factor analysis). SEM thus combines the usage of latent (unobserved) variables that represent the concepts of theory, and data from measures (indicators or manifest variables) that are used as input for statistical analysis that provides evidence about the relationships among latent variables (Williams, Vandeberg, & Edwards, 2009). SEM is particularly useful in IS research, where many if not most of the key concepts are not directly observable. Indeed, a large portion of IS research during recent years has mainly applied SEM as an analytical methodology for theory testing (Gefen, et al., 2000; Gerow et al., 2010). In turn, an expansion to the breadth of application of SEM methods can be also noted, including exploratory, confirmatory and predictive analysis, as well as the generating of an increasing diversity of *ad hoc* topics and models (Westland, 2010).

In a single, systematic, and comprehensive analysis, SEM evaluates (Gefen et al., 2000) (Figure 1): (1) The measurement model. That is, the relationships between the latent variables and their indicators. (2) The structural model. I.e., the part of the overall model that proposes relationships among the latent variables. Such relationships reflect substantive hypotheses based on theoretical considerations.

The holistic analysis that SEM is capable of performing is carried out via one of two distinct statistical techniques (Barroso, Cepeda, & Roldán, 2010): (1) Covariance-based SEM (CBSEM) and (2) a variance-based (or components-based)

Figure 1. Graphic example of SEM

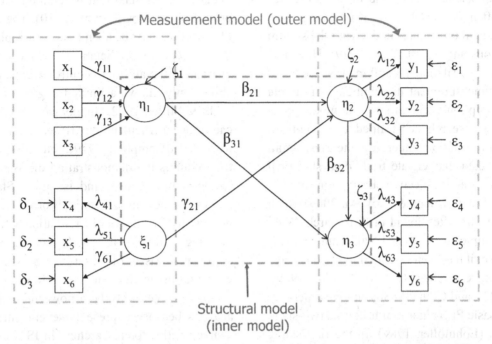

method, i.e., Partial Least Squares (PLS). Both approaches have been designed to achieve different objectives. CBSEM focuses on estimating a set of model parameters so that the theoretical covariance matrix implied by the system of structural equations is as close as possible to the empirical covariance matrix observed within the estimation sample (Reinartz, Haenlein, & Henseler, 2009). PLS works with blocks of variables and estimates model parameters via maximizing the explained variables of all dependent variables (both latent and observed) (Chin, 1998b). CBSEM hence emphasizes the overall model fit. That is, this approach is oriented towards testing a strong theory. Therefore, CBSEM is best suited for confirmatory research (Gefen et al., 2000), whereas PLS is more suited for predictive applications and theory building (exploratory analysis), although it can be also used for theory confirmation (confirmatory analysis) (Chin, 2010).

VARIANCE-BASED SEM (PLS): BASIC CHARACTERISTICS

Origin, Development and Features of PLS

According to Falk and Miller (1992), the goal of CBSEM, especially under maximum-likelihood (ML) estimation, is to provide a statement of causality, that is, a description of causal mechanisms in a closed system. However, a properly defined and estimated closed system requires a restrictive set of theoretical, measurement and distributional conditions to be met. In this respect, given those limitative requirements, Herman Wold questioned the general applicability of CBSEM to the social sciences field (Fornell & Cha, 1994), where, in practice, distributions are often unknown or far from normal, and there are nascent theories and scarce knowledge. For these situations, Wold developed an alternative methodology, Partial Least Squares, with the aim of reflecting the theoretical and empirical conditions present in the behavioral and social sciences. This kind of modeling was called soft modeling (Wold, 1980). Mathematical and statistical procedures underlying the system are rigorous and robust (Wold 1979). However, the mathematical model is soft in the sense that it makes no measurement, distributional, or sample size assumptions. Therefore, soft modeling is suited for research constrained by conditions of low information, emerging theories, small samples, data that violate traditional statistical assumptions and subjective observations of phenomena (Sosik, Kahai, & Piovoso, 2009). Such conditions are often found in IS research. Wold (1982) completed the basic PLS algorithm in 1977. Since then, it has been extended in various ways by different researchers, such as Lohmöller (1989), Hui (1982), and Chin (1998b), among others.

The basic PLS algorithm follows a two-stage approach (Lohmöller, 1989). In the first stage, the latent constructs' scores are iteratively estimated via a four-step process. The second stage calculates the final estimates of coefficients (outer weights, loadings, and path coefficients) using the ordinary least squares method for each partial regression in the model (Hair, Ringle, & Sarstedt, 2011). Applying both processes, the PLS algorithm aims to minimize the residual variances of dependent variables (Chin, 1998b). Accordingly, PLS rests on a main assumption, that is, the predictor specification, which forms the basis for PLS modeling (Chin & Newsted, 1999). Hence, the cause-and-effect directions between all the variables need to be specifically defined (Urbach & Ahlemann, 2010). Besides, PLS follows a segmentation process, so its estimates for a particular construct are limited to the immediate blocks, to which it is structurally tied. This is why Chin (2010) qualifies this approach as a limited-information procedure as opposed to the full-information process of CBSEM. A detailed description of the PLS algorithm is described by Tenenhaus et al. (2005).

The goal to be achieved in soft modeling is milder than in hard modeling (i.e., CBSEM, particularly using maximum-likelihood estimation procedures) (Barroso et al., 2010). The concept of causation must be abandoned and replaced by the concept for predictability. While causation guarantees the ability to control events, predictability only allows a limited degree of control (Falk & Miller, 1992). In any case, establishing causation is difficult in social research. According to Cook and Campbell (1979), determining causation requires the demonstrating of: association, temporal precedence, and isolation. Statistical analysis alone cannot tentatively prove causation, because it does not establish isolation or temporal ordering (Bullock, Harlow, & Mulaik, 1994). In any event, the issue of causation in SEM currently continues being challenging (cf. Markus, 2010).

PLS can certainly be a powerful method of analysis because it presents several interesting characteristics for researchers in IS. First, PLS does not impose any distributional assumption for measured variables and there is no need for independent observations (Chin, 2010). Second, compared to CBSEM, PLS avoids two serious problems (Fornell & Bookstein, 1982): inadmissible solutions (e.g., negative variances and standardized loadings greater than 1), and factor indeterminacy (Steiger, 1979), given that PLS allows the obtaining of case values (scores) for latent variables, these scores being actually immediately interpretable from a predictive perspective (Chin, 2010). Third, PLS establishes minimal demands on measurement scales. Thus, nominal, ordinal, and interval-scaled variables are permissible in soft modeling (Wold, 1985). Consequently, PLS does not require variable metric uniformity (Sosik et al, 2009). Fourth, PLS can estimate path models with small samples (Chin & Newsted, 1999; Reinartz et al., 2009). Fifth, PLS can manage complex models (i.e., with many latent variables, indicators, and paths) without leading to estimation problems (Chin & Newsted, 1999) thanks to its limited-information procedure characteristic (Barclay, Higgins, & Thompson, 1995). Sixth, PLS can estimate models with reflective and formative measurements without any problem of identification (Chin, 2010) because PLS works with weighted composites rather than factors (Gefen, Rigdon, & Straub, 2011). Finally, PLS has proven to be quite robust with respect to the following inadequacies (Cassel, Hackl, & Westlund, 1999): (1) skew instead of symmetric distributions of manifest variables, (2) multi-collinearity within blocks of manifest variables and between latent variables; and (3) misspecification of the structural model (omission of regressors).

On the other hand, we should take into account that PLS generates a certain inconsistency. Indeed, the case values of the constructs are estimated as weighted aggregates of the corresponding blocks of indicators, that is, PLS uses defined constructs. These case values are inconsistent (Fornell & Cha, 1994): loadings are overestimated and path coefficients are underestimated. However, such a bias can be minimized from the principle of consistency at large: "The PLS estimates are consistent at large in the sense that they tend to the true values when there is indefinite increase not only in the number of observed cases, but also in the number of indicators for each latent variable" (Wold, 1985, p. 231). In addition, compared to CBSEM, PLS does not allow the explicit modeling of the measurement error variance/covariance structure, does not incorporate overidentifying constraints, lacks an overall inferential test statistic (Gefen et al., 2011), and there is not an adequate global measure of goodness of model fit (Hair et al., 2011).

PLS and the Nature of Epistemic Relationships

An epistemic relationship, also known as measurement model, describes the link between theory (latent variables) and data (manifest variables or indicators). Basically, there are two types of epistemic relationships (Jarvis, Mackenzie, & Podsakoff, 2003) that influence the choice of analysis method. On the one hand, the principal factor model or common latent construct model postulates that covariation among measures is explained by the variation in an underlying common latent factor. In this case, indicators are reflective of the unobserved theoretical construct and, hence, covary with the level of that latent variable. On the other hand, the composite latent (emergent) construct model posits that the measures jointly influence the composite latent construct. Manifest variables, called formative indicators, give rise to the latent variable. Therefore, formative indicators produce or contribute to the construct, which means that the indicators are not necessarily correlated (Diamantopoulos & Winklhofer, 2001). Besides, formative items are not interchangeable. For this reason, removing a formative indicator implies omitting a theoretically meaningful part of the construct (Bollen & Lennox, 1991). The choice between both types of measurement models should be based on theoretical considerations regarding the relationship between the indicators and the constructs under examination. In this vein, four primary criteria to support this decision can be consulted in Jarvis et al. (2003). Recently, formative measurement models have received a greater attention in IS research (Cenfetelli & Bassellier, 2009; Kim, Shin, & Grover, 2010; Petter, Straub, & Rai, 2007; Roberts & Thatcher, 2009). The most recent discussion on the use of formative scales can be found in a special issue in MIS Quarterly on advanced methodological thinking for quantitative research (cf. Bagozzi, 2011; Bollen, 2011; Diamantopoulos, 2011).

PLS permits the use of both types of measurement models (Fornell & Cha, 1994). Next, we show how a latent variable can be modeled either with reflective or formative indicators. We have chosen the "perceived resources" (R) construct, which is defined as the extent to which an individual believes that he or she has the personal and organizational resources needed to use an IS (Mathieson, Peacock & Chin, 2001). Whether R is modeled via reflective items, these do not identify any specific resource, but, rather, they try to assess the general feeling of having enough

Figure 2. Perceived resources construct modeled as a common latent construct and as a composite latent construct. Source: Adapted from Mathieson, Peacock & Chin (2001).

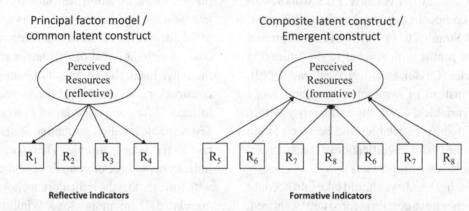

Reflective indicators

R1: I have the resources, opportunities and knowledge I would need to use a database package in my job.
R2: There are no barriers to my using a database package in my job.
R3: I would be able to use a database package in my job if I wanted to.
R4: I have access to the resources I would need to use a database package in my job.

Formative indicators

R5: I have access to the **hardware** and **software** I would need to use a database package in my job.
R6: I have the **knowledge** I would need to use a database package in my job.
R7: I would be able to find the **time** I would need to use a database package in my job.
R8: **Financial resources** (e.g., to pay for computer time) are not a barrier for me in using a database package in my job.
R9: If I needed **someone's help** in using a database package in my job, I could get it easily.
R10: I have the **documentation** (manuals, books etc.) I would need to use a database package in my job.
R11: I have access to the **data** (on customers, products, etc.) I would need to use a database package in my job.

resources. However, when R is operationalized through formative items, these represent a census of potential specific resources needed to use an IS (in that study, a database package) (Figure 2). This group of formative indicators thus contributes to creating that perception.

Sample Size Requirements

The sample size issue has traditionally been one of the main attractive characteristics of PLS compared to CBSEM. While CBSEM establishes strong sample size requirements that are often beyond the range of IS researchers, the demands of PLS are generally much smaller (Chin & Newsted, 1999; Reinartz et al., 2009). Such a capability comes from the segmentation process followed by the PLS algorithm that allows the dividing of complex models into subsets. For an initial idea of the sample required, we should find the most

complex multiple regression in the model proposed (Barclay et al., 1995). Consequently, we have to select the larger of the following alternatives: (1) the block with the largest number of formative indicators or (2) the largest number of structural paths directed at a particular dependent latent variable. Next, we should apply a rule of thumb to determine the sample size requirement. Recently, the use of such a "rule of thumb" has been one of the most controversial issues concerning PLS. Initially, Barclay et al. (1995) indicated "[s]ample size requirements, using the 'rule of thumb' of ten cases per predictor, become ten times the number of predictors from (1) or (2), whichever is greater" (p. 292). However, this regression heuristic of 10 cases per predictor has generated a claim from different scholars requesting an alternative view of sample size requirements (cf. Goodhue, Lewis, & Thompson, 2006). Even statements such as: "PLS is not a silver bullet to be used with samples of any size!" (Marcoulides & Saunders, 2006, p. viii), or "we feel a need to reiterate is the reification of the 10 cases per indicator rule of thumb" (Marcoulides, Chin, & Saunders, 2009, p. 174) can be read. Indeed, Chin and Newsted (1999) already noticed that such a rule of thumb just provided an "initial sense of the sample size required" (p. 326). However, the estimation of the sample size for a PLS model requires a statistical power analysis based on the portion of the model with the largest number of predictors. They accordingly concluded: "For a more accurate assessment, one needs to specify the effect size for each regression analysis and look up the power tables provided by Cohen (1988) or Green's (1991) approximation to these tables" (Chin & Newsted, 1999, p. 327). Following this suggestion and using Green's (1991) approximation (Table 1), we could determinate the sample size requirement for the model of Figure 1. There is only one block with formative indicators, this is ξ_1 with three manifest variables. The dependent latent variable that receives the largest number of structural paths is both η_1 and η_2, with two relationships. Thus, the largest regression consists of three predictors (x_1, x_2 and x_3). Assuming a medium effect size as defined by Cohen (1988), we would initially need a minimum sample of 76 cases with the aim of obtaining a power of .80 and an alpha level of 0.05. If we pay attention to the conclusions from the Monte Carlo simulations developed by Reinartz et al. (2009), we would then suggest increasing the sample to at least 100 cases, given that 100 observations can be sufficient to achieve acceptable levels of statistical power, given a certain quality of the measurement model.

The former calculation of 76 cases represents, in any case, a starting point for determining an appropriate sample size with an adequate level of accuracy and statistical power. Indeed, Chin (2010) has recently recommended that "[i]deally, if one wishes to customize the sample size estimation with specific effect sizes for the structural paths and include a certain amount of measurement

Table 1. Initial sample size requirements for a Power =.80 and Alpha =.05. Source: Adapted from Green (1991, p. 503)

Number of predictors	Sample sizes based on power analysis		
		Effect size	
	Small	Medium	Large
1	390	53	24
2	481	66	30
3	547	76	35
4	599	84	39
5	645	91	42
6	686	97	46
7	726	102	48
8	757	108	51
9	788	113	54
10	844	117	56
15	952	138	67
20	1066	156	77
30	1247	187	94
40	1407	213	110

error (normal or nonnormal), running a Monte Carlo simulation would be a better approach (e.g., Majchrak et al., 2005)" (p. 662).

PLS Path Modeling Software

There is no doubt that one of the reasons of the greater diffusion of the covariance-based SEM (CBSEM) approach compared to PLS has traditionally been a wider development and availability of software to perform CBSEM analysis. In this respect, the offer of this kind of software began with the introduction in the early 1970s of the first version of LISREL and has continued with the advance of programs such as EQS, AMOS, MPLUS, SEPATH, MX, PROC CALIS, and so on. With regards to PLS, the first program to carry out variance-based SEM was LVPLS developed by Lohmöller (1981). However, the first graphical and ease-of-use PLS software did not appear until

Table 2. PLS path modeling software tools

Software	Developer	Web-site
Coheris SPAD data mining	Coheris	http://www.coheris.fr/en/page/produits/SPAD-data-mining/SPAD-modelisation.html
LVPLS 1.8	Jan-Bernd Lohmöller	
PLS-Graph	Wynne Chin Soft Modeling, Inc.	http://www.plsgraph.com/
plspm	Gastón Sánchez; Laura Trinchera	http://cran.r-project.org/web/packages/plspm/plspm.pdf
PLS-GUI	Y. Li University of South Carolina	
semPLS	Armin Monecke Ludwig-Maximilian Universität München	http://cran.r-project.org/web/packages/semPLS/index.html
SmartPLS 2.0	Christian Marc Ringle; Sven Wende; Alexander Will University of Hamburg	http://www.smartpls.de/
VisualPLS	Jen-Ruei Fu National Central University in Taiwan	http://fs.mis.kuas.edu.tw/~fred/vpls/index.html
WarpPLS 2.0	Ned Kock ScriptWarp Systems	http://www.scriptwarp.com/warppls/
XLSTAT-PLSPM	XLSTAT	http://www.xlstat.com/en/products/xlstat-plspm/

the mid-90s. We are referring to the PLS-Graph program, developed by Wynne Chin (2001). Later, two graphical interfaces to LVPLS were introduced: PLS-GUI (Li, 2005) and VisualPLS (Fu, 2006). SmartPLS (Ringle, Wende, & Will, 2005) came on stage in 2005. Among other advanced capabilities, this software allows the treating of unobserved heterogeneity via the finite mixture PLS (FIMIX-PLS) (Rigdon, Ringle & Sarstedt, 2010). In addition, commercial initiatives for PLS were introduced in the market during the new millennium: Coheris SPAD data mining and XLSTAT-PLSPM. Other interesting options are two PLS tools that are part of the open source project R (R Development Core Team, 2007), which allows the modification of the PLS algorithm. We refer to the plspm (Sánchez & Trinchera, 2010) and semPLS (Monecke, 2010) packages. Finally, as a last entry in this category of PLS path modeling software, there is a software tool that permits analyzing nonlinear relationships: WarpPLS 2.0 (Kock, 2011). A detailed comparison of different PLS software packages can be consulted in Temme,

Kreis, and Hildebrandt (2010). Next, we present in Table 2 a relation of the PLS path modeling software tools, developers, and web-sites.

VARIANCE (PLS) OR COVARIANCE-BASED SEM?

The choice of SEM approach, variance *vs* covariance-based SEM, "should depend on the objectives and assumptions of the chosen SEM tool, and should be explained as such to the reader" (Gefen et al., 2011, p. vii). This is the aim of this section providing guidelines to help researchers to have a basis for their methodological decision. In this vein, we would like to initiate our line of argument highlighting that CBSEM and PLS should be considered as complementary rather than competitive methods, and both have a rigorous rationale of their own (Wold, 1985). As Jöreskog and Wold (1982) – fathers of LISREL and PLS, respectively – state: ML is theory-oriented, and emphasizes the transition from exploratory to confirmatory analysis. PLS is primarily intended for causal-predictive analysis in situations of high complexity but low theoretical information. Subsequently, Wold distinguished a division of labor between LISREL and PLS: "LISREL is at a premium in small models where each parameter has operative significance, and accurate parameter estimation is important. PLS comes to the fore in larger models, where the importance shifts from individual variables and parameters to packages of variables and aggregate parameters" (Wold, 1985).

PLS and Covariance-Based SEM (CBSEM) have been designed to achieve different aims. CBSEM tries to estimate the parameters of the model in order to minimize the difference between the sample covariances and those predicted by the theoretical model. It emphasizes the overall model fit. That is, this approach is oriented towards testing a strong theory. Therefore, it is best suited for confirmatory research (Gefen et al., 2000).

PLS path modeling focuses on the prediction of the dependent variables (both latent and manifest). This objective is achieved by maximizing the explained variance of the dependent variables. Thus, parameter estimates are obtained based on the ability to minimize the residual variances of dependent variables. Compared to CBSEM, PLS is more suited for predictive applications and theory building (exploratory analysis), although PLS can be also used for theory confirmation (confirmatory analysis) (Chin, 2010).

The decision between these approaches is whether to use SEM for theory testing and development or for predictive applications (Anderson & Gerbing, 1988). In situations where prior theory is strong and further testing and development are the goal, covariance-based full-information estimation methods are more appropriate. However, for application and prediction, when the phenomenon under research is relatively new or changing, or when the theoretical model or measures are not well formed, a PLS approach is often more suitable (Chin & Newsted, 1999). In addition, Chin (2010) states "there are other instances beyond initial exploratory stages that PLS is well suited"

(p. 660). For example, when the research has an interactive character. This is the case of an incremental study, which is initially based on a prior model but new measures and structural paths are then introduced into it. In this respect, these statements have been confirmed by the study of Reinartz et al. (2009): "PLS is the preferable approach when researchers focus on prediction and theory development, as our simulations show that PLS requires only about half as many observations to reach a given level of statistical power as does ML-based CBSEM" (p. 334).

Another situation where the use of PLS would be preferable is when the model is complex, with large numbers of indicators and/or latent variables (Chin, 2010; Hair et al., 2011). In CBSEM, complex models can be problematic relative to fit indices and computation (Chin & Newsted, 1999). Indeed, "[e]mphasis on model fit tends to restrict researchers to testing relatively elementary models representing either a simplistic theory or a narrow slice of a more complex theoretical domain" (Chin, Peterson, & Brown, 2008, p. 661). It is in this environment of high complexity where PLS would stand out with regards to CBSEM, "regardless of whether applied under a strong substantive and theoretical context or limited/exploratory conditions" (Chin, 2010, p. 661).

Historically, if CBSEM data requirements, that is, independence and normal data distribution, cannot be satisfied, PLS is posited as a good methodological alternative for theory testing (Chin, 2010; Chin & Newsted, 1999; Hair et al. 2011). However, this argument is currently considered as an obsolete reasoning (Gefen et al., 2011). On the one hand, Reinartz et al. (2009) indicate that, according to their simulations, justifying the selection of PLS due to a lack of assumptions concerning indicator distribution is often inappropriate because "ML-based CBSEM behaves robustly if those assumptions are violated" (p. 334). On the other hand, Gefen et al. (2011) argue that leading-edge CBSEM software includes estimator options which produce correct results using a broad range of data distributions. However for Reinartz et al.

(2009), "choosing PLS over ML-based CBSEM when the sample size is limited appears sensible. The absolute relative error of parameters increases less quickly with a decrease in sample size for PLS than it does for ML-based CBSEM" (p. 334). Reinartz et al. (2009) state that 100 cases can be enough to achieve acceptable levels of statistical power, given a certain quality of the measurement model. In addition, they conclude that "PLS should be the method of choice for all situations in which the number of observations is lower than 250 (400 observations in the case of less reliable measurement models, i.e., low loadings and/or few indicators), while ML-based CBSEM should be chosen otherwise" (p. 342).

When a model has formative indicators, PLS presents advantages concerning CBSEM. Although the inclusion of formative items in CBSEM has been documented (cf. Williams et al., 2009), it is also true that attempts to model formative indicators in CBSEM present problems of identification (MacCallum & Browne, 1993; Treiblmaier, Bentler, & Mair, 2011). In contrast, such problems do not arise in PLS path modeling (Chin, 2010; Gefen et al., 2011; Henseler, Ringle, & Sinkovics, 2009). In this respect, PLS has demonstrated robustness and accuracy with formative models, independent of the quality of data distribution (Ringle et al., 2009).

Finally, PLS would be the best option if the researcher needs to use latent variables scores in subsequent analysis for a predictive relevance (Chin, 2010; Hair et al., 2011). Constructs are modeled in CBSEM as indeterminate (Fornell, 1982). Consequently, scores or case values for latent variables cannot be obtained in CBSEM (Chin & Newsted, 1999). However, PLS provides such scores given that constructs are modeled as defined or determinate (Fornell, 1982). Therefore, such scores can be used, for instance, to build higher order or multidimensional constructs (cf. Calvo-Mora, Leal, & Roldán, 2005).

EVALUATION OF VARIANCE-BASED SEM (PLS) MODELS

The specific literature indicates two stages of the SEM analysis (Gefen et al., 2000): the assessment of the measurement model (outer model) and the structural model (inner model). The measurement model defines the latent variables that the model will use, and assigns manifest variables (indicators) to each. It attempts to analyze whether the theoretical constructs are correctly gauged by the measures. In reflective measurement models, this analysis is carried out with reference to reliability and validity attributes. Formative measurement models examine, among other issues, the potential multicollinearity of indicators and assess each measure's weights. On the other hand, the structural model defines the relationships between latent variables. The structural model is basically assessed according to the meaningfulness and significance of the relationships hypothesized between the constructs. This sequence ensures that we have adequate indicators of constructs before attempting to reach conclusions concerning the relationships included in the inner or structural model (Hair et al., 2011).

The main terms used are the following (Falk & Miller 1992; Wold 1985; Barclay et al., 1995; Williams et al., 2009): (1) The theoretical construct or latent variable (graphically represented by a circle), which makes a distinction between the exogenous constructs (ξ) that act as predictor or causal variables of the endogenous constructs (η). (2) Indicators, measures, manifest or observable variables (graphically symbolized by squares). Figure 3 shows a graphical example of a PLS model together with a description of the principal terminology used in soft modeling.

Figure 3. An example of a PLS model

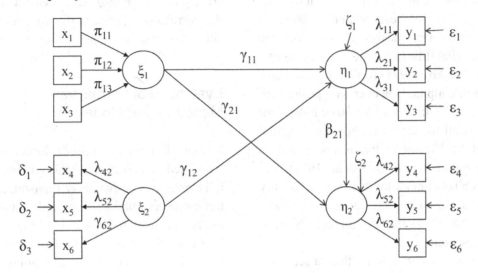

ξ : Exogenous construct
η : Endogenous construct
x : Manifest variable, measure, or indicator
y : Manifest variable, measure or indicator
π : Regression weight
λ : Loading

δ : Error term for an exogenous construct
ε : Error term for an exogenous construct
ζ : Residual in the structural model
γ : Path or regression coefficient
β : Path or regression coefficient

Measurement Model Assessment

Evaluation of Reflective Measurement Models

Reflective measurement models are evaluated with regards to reliability and validity. Individual item reliability is assessed by analyzing the standardized loadings (λ), or simple correlations of the indicators with their respective latent variable. Carmines and Zeller (1979) suggest that to accept an indicator as a constituent of a construct, the manifest variable should have a loading of 0.707 or more. This implies more shared variance between the construct and its measures (i.e., λ^2) than error variance. Nonetheless, several researchers think this rule of thumb should not be as rigid in the early stages of scale development (Chin 1998b) and when scales are applied across different contexts (Barclay et al. 1995). In addition, whereas including poor indicators will lead to a worse fit

in covariance-based SEM analysis, in the case of PLS, the inclusion of weak items will help to extract what useful information is available in the indicator to create a better construct score. It should be borne in mind that PLS works with determinate or defined constructs. Consequently, worse indicators are factored in by lower weights (Chin 2002). Besides, taking into account PLS' characteristic of consistency at large, we should be careful when eliminating indicators (Henseler et al, 2009). In this line, Hair et al. (2011) indicate that weaker indicators can be sometimes retained on the basis of their contribution to content validity. However, they simultaneously maintain that manifest variables with very low loadings (i.e., ≤ 0.4) should be removed. In such a case, "the measurement model needs to be adjusted and the PLS algorithm initiated once more in order to obtain new results" (Urbach & Ahlemann, 2010).

Construct reliability assessment allows the evaluation of the extent to which a variable or set of variables is consistent in what it intends to measure (Straub, Boudreau, & Gefen, 2004). As a measure of internal consistency reliability, the composite reliability (ρ_c) developed by Werts, Linn, and Jöreskog (1974) fulfills the same task as Cronbach's alpha. However, composite reliability is more suitable for PLS since it does not assume that all indicators are equally weighted (Chin, 1998b). The interpretation of both indexes is similar. Nunnally and Bernstein (1994) suggest 0.7 as a benchmark for "modest" reliability applicable in the early stages of research, and a more strict 0.8 or 0.9 value for the more advanced stages of research.

Convergent validity implies that "a set of indicators represents one and the same underlying construct, which can be demonstrated through their unidimensionality" (Henseler et al., 2009). Convergent validity is usually assessed by the average variance extracted (AVE) (Fornell & Larcker 1981). This measure quantifies the amount of variance that a construct captures from its manifest variables or indicators relative to the amount due to measurement error. This ratio tends to be more conservative than composite reliability (ρ_c). AVE values should be greater than 0.50. This means that 50% or more of the indicator variance should be accounted for.

Finally, discriminant validity indicates the extent to which a given construct differs from other constructs. There are two approaches to assess discriminant validity in PLS. On the one hand, Fornell and Larcker (1981) suggest that the AVE should be greater than the variance between the construct and other constructs in the model (i.e., the squared correlation between two constructs). With the aim of facilitating this assessment, the square root of the AVE of each latent variable should be greater than its correlations with any other LV. On the other hand, the second approach suggests that no item should load more highly on another construct than it does on the construct it intends to measure (Barclay et al. 1995). In addition, each construct should load higher with its assigned indicators than other items. This

cross-loadings analysis is carried out calculating the correlations between the constructs' scores and the standardized data of indicators (Gefen & Straub, 2005).

Evaluation of Formative Measurement Models

Because formative measures do not need to be correlated (Jarvis et al., 2003) and are assumed to be error free (Edwards & Bagozzi, 2000), the traditional evaluation of reliability and validity has been considered unsuitable (Bagozzi, 1994). However, the examination of the validity via a theoretical rationale and expert opinion plays a key role in well-known procedures for building composite latent constructs with formative indicators (cf. Diamantopoulos & Winkholfer, 2001). Following Henseler et al. (2009), Chin (2010), and Urbach and Ahlemann (2010), we suggest assessing formative measurement models on two levels: the construct (external, nomological and discriminant validity) and the indicator level (multicollinearity and weight assessment).

At the construct level, we should ask whether the composite latent construct carries the intended meaning (Henseler et al., 2009). This is a validation question. Accordingly, the first step of the validation process of a set of formative indicators depends on whether there is a validated group of reflective items for the focal construct. We refer to external validity and this evaluation is done via a two-block redundancy model (Chin, 2010). Thus, for the same theoretical concept, we have, on the one hand, a set of previously-validated reflective measures, and, on the other hand, a group of formative measures. A structural path would then connect both blocks. It has been suggested that such a path should be of 0.80 or above for external validity (Mathieson et al., 2001). A path of 0.90 would mean that the composite latent construct explains more that 80% of the intended meaning. In the case of a researcher only having formative measures of the focal construct, he or she should go the next step.

The second stage, nomological validity, implies placing the composite latent construct in a theoretical model in which the alternative reflective measurement model has been used in past studies (Chin, 2010). Consequently, we expect that the relationships between the composite latent construct and other model's constructs, which have been sufficiently referred to in past research, should be strong and significant (Chin, 2010; Henseler et al., 2009).

In addition to external and nomological validity, as a third step, Urbach and Ahlemann (2010) propose a straightforward assessment of discriminant validity by means of interconstruct correlations. Thus, if correlations between the composite latent construct and all other constructs are less than 0.7, then the constructs differ sufficiently from one another.

At the indicator level, a key concern deals with potential multicollinearity among items (Diamantopoulos & Winklhofer, 2001). A high collinearity among dimensions would produce unstable estimates and would make it difficult to separate the distinct effect of the individual dimensions on the construct (Petter et al., 2007). With this in mind, as a fourth step we suggest several collinearity tests. A first check is to use the variance inflation factor (VIF) statistic. According to Kleinbaum, Kupper and Muller (1988) a VIF over 5 is problematic. However, Roberts and Thatcher (2009) have recently indicated that a VIF greater than 3.3 signals a high multicollinearity. We also recommend carrying out more advanced diagnostics of collinearity, such as the analysis of condition indices and variance proportions (Belsley, 1991) using, for instance, the IBM SPSS Statistics program (cf. Díaz-Casero, Hernández-Mogollón, & Roldán, 2011).

The final step implies the assessment of the weights of the formative indicators. Weights measure the contribution of each formative item to the variance of the latent variable (Roberts & Thatcher, 2009). As with the canonical correlation analysis, the weights allow us to understand the make-up of each variable. That is to say, these provide information about how each formative indicator contributes to the respective composite construct (Chin, 1998b). Hence, it allows us to rank indicators according to their contribution. Also, a significance level of at least .05 suggests that a formative measure is relevant for the construction of the composite latent construct (Urbach & Ahlemann, 2010). However, with the exception of indicators with a high multicollinearity, we agree with Roberts and Thatcher (2009) that "even if an item contributes little to the explained variance in a formative construct, it should be included in the measurement model" (p. 30) because dropping a formative indicator implies dropping a part of the composite latent construct.

Structural Model Assessment

Once we have achieved a satisfactory assessment of the measurement model, we can evaluate the structural (inner) model estimates. Taking into account that PLS is focused on prediction and its goal is the maximizing of the variance of the dependent variables, the first criterion in order to evaluate a PLS model is the assessment of the coefficient of determination (R^2) of the endogenous constructs (Chin, 2010). The R^2 value represents a measure of the predictive power and indicates the amount of variance in the construct in question, which is explained by its antecedent variables in the model. The R^2 values should be high enough for the model to achieve a minimum level of explanatory power (Urbach & Ahlemann, 2010). For instance, Falk and Miller (1992) recommend that R^2 should be at least greater than 0.10, whereas Chin (1998b) considers R^2 values of 0.67, 0.33, and 0.19 as substantial, moderate, and weak respectively.

Next, we can analyze the individual path estimates or standardized regression coefficients. In this respect, we assess the algebraic sign, magnitude, and significance of the path coefficients. Those paths whose signs are contrary to the postulated algebraic signs, do not support the hypotheses proposed (Urbach & Ahlemann, 2010). In order to estimate the precision of the PLS estimates, a nonparametric technique of re-sampling is commonly used. We refer to bootstrapping (Efron & Tibshirani, 1993), which entails repeated random sampling with replacement from the original sample to create a bootstrap sample (Hair et al., 2011). As a result of this process, standard errors and t-statistics of the parameters are provided which allow hypothesis testing. We usually suggest a minimum of 500 samples and the number of cases should be equal to the number of observations in the original sample. Nevertheless, some scholars have recently suggested increasing the number of samples to 5,000 (cf. Hair et al., 2011; Henseler et al., 2009). Several approaches have been developed for estimating confidence intervals (cf. Efron & Tibshirani, 1993). The simplest approach implies using the bootstrap t-statistic with n-1 degrees of freedom (where n is the number of subsamples) to test the H_0: w = 0 (w being, for instance, a path coefficient) against the alternative hypothesis H_1: w ≠ 0. If we postulate a hypothesis with a direction, e.g., "H_i: Variable A is positively associated with variable B", we can apply a one-tailed test for a t Student distribution. In this way, for 500 subsamples, critical t-values for a one-tailed test are:

n = 500 subsamples: * p <.05; ** p <.01; ***p <.001 (one-tailed t Student)

t(0.05; 499) = 1.64791345; t(0.01; 499) = 2.333843952; t(0.001; 499) = 3.106644601

On the other hand, if we propose a non-directional hypothesis, e.g., "H_j: Variable C is associated with variable D", we should use a two-tailed test. For 500 subsamples, critical t-values for a two-tailed test are:

n = 500 subsamples: * p <.05; ** p <.01; ***p <.001 (two-tailed t Student)

t(0.05; 499) = 1.964726835; t(0.01; 499) = 2.585711627; t (0.001; 499) = 3.310124157

In recent times, some scholars have proposed reporting the confidence interval instead of reporting the significance of a parameter, such as a path coefficient (Henseler et al., 2009): "If a confidence interval for an estimated path coefficient w does not include zero, the hypothesis that w equals zero is rejected" (p. 306). On this subject, Chin (2010) states that both the percentile and the bias-corrected and accelerated (BCA) approaches have the advantage of being completely distribution free.

We can also evaluate whether the impact of a particular antecedent variable on a dependent construct has a substantive impact. This can be assessed by means of Cohen's f^2 (Cohen, 1988). The effect size f^2 can be calculated as $f^2 = (R^2_{included} - R^2_{excluded})/(1 - R^2_{included})$, $R^2_{included}$ and $R^2_{excluded}$ being the R-squares provided on the dependent construct when the predictor construct is used or omitted in the structural model respectively. Values of 0.02, 0.15 and 0.35 indicate the predictor variable has a low, medium, or large effect on the criterion variable.

If we wish to know the precise amount of variance that a specific antecedent variable explains on a dependent construct, we should multiply the path coefficient by the corresponding correlation coefficient and take the absolute value (Falk & Miller, 1992). For instance, if a path coefficient from "perceived ease of use" to "perceived usefulness" is 0.40 and the correlation between both constructs is 0.60, this means that 24% of the variance in "perceived usefulness" is accounted by "perceived ease of use" (0.40 × 0.60 = 0.24).

Finally, Stone-Geisser's Q^2 test is used to assess the predictive relevance of the endogenous constructs with a reflective measurement model. This test is an indicator of how well observed values are reproduced by the model and its parameter estimates. Two types of Q^2 can be obtained, depending on the form of prediction: cross-validated communality and cross-validated redundancy (Fornell & Cha 1994). Chin (1998b) suggests using the latter to examine the predictive relevance of the theoretical/structural model. A Q^2 greater than 0 implies that the model has predictive relevance, whereas a Q^2 less than 0 suggests that the model lacks predictive relevance. We can also assess the relative impact of the predictive relevance by means of the q^2 index, $q^2 = (Q^2_{included} - Q^2_{excluded})/(1 - Q^2_{included})$. As in the case of f^2, values of 0.02, 0.15, and 0.35 indicate a small, medium, or large predictive relevance of a predictor variable on the explanation of a dependent construct.

ILLUSTRATIVE EXAMPLES OF PLS

Having covered the main guidelines for a precise use of PLS, we next present two examples of IS models in which we apply the previous recommendations. The first model represents a case of a reflective measurement model, whereas the second one illustrates the use of formative indicators.

The Technology Acceptance Model (TAM), Enjoyment, and Social Site Networks (SNS)

In this first example, we study the technology acceptance model (TAM) in the context of a computer-mediated social site network. Social network sites (SNSs) are online settings that allow users to register and connect with each other in order to communicate or share resources. The Technology Acceptance Model (TAM) explains the determinants of technology acceptance over a wide range of end-user computing technologies and user populations (cf. Davis, 1989; Davis, Bagozzi, & Warshaw, 1992; Venkatesh & Davis, 2000, among others). Specifically, perceived usefulness and ease of use are hypothesized and empirically supported as fundamental determinants of user acceptance of information and communication technologies, in our case an SNS.

Perceived usefulness and ease of use are hypothesized and empirically supported as fundamental beliefs of users' attitudes towards employing a given SNS. Particularly, perceived usefulness, an extrinsic source of motivation, and defined as the degree to which users believe that a particular SNS would enhance their social life, influences SNS usage indirectly through attitude and directly through intent. Perceived usefulness is a relevant determinant of behavioral intention (or behavior), noting that users willingly use a system that has a critically-useful functionality. Perceived ease of use, a second source of motivation, defined as the degree to which a person believes that using a particular SNS would be effort free, influences the SNS attitude towards using it, and has an inverse relationship with the perceived complexity of use of the technology. An SNS that is difficult to use is less likely to be perceived as useful. Finally, behavioral intentions are a key factor influencing actual SNS usage.

Based on the above research, we assume the following hypotheses in the baseline research model:

H1: Attitude towards usage will positively influence intention to use an SNS.

H2: Perceived usefulness will positively influence intention to use an SNS.

H3: Perceived usefulness will positively influence attitude towards usage.

H4: Perceived ease of use will positively influence attitude towards usage.

H5: Perceived ease of use will positively influence perceived usefulness.

H6: Intention to use will positively influence frequency of use of an SNS.

This study was carried out on a sample of 278 users of the most popular computer-mediated SNS among the Spanish college student population, Tuenti.

Table 3. Outer model loadings and cross loadings

	PEOU	PU	Attitude	Intention	Usage
eou1	**0.828**	0.261	0.170	0.394	0.307
eou2	**0.743**	0.196	0.156	0.222	0.174
eou3	**0.826**	0.278	0.167	0.328	0.274
eou4	**0.859**	0.219	0.131	0.286	0.243
eou5	**0.871**	0.252	0.183	0.309	0.259
eou6	**0.803**	0.245	0.132	0.305	0.161
eou7	**0.810**	0.309	0.225	0.337	0.234
pu1	0.289	**0.872**	0.310	0.445	0.291
pu2	0.275	**0.868**	0.319	0.424	0.251
pu3	0.251	**0.895**	0.337	0.417	0.265
pu4	0.278	**0.873**	0.363	0.430	0.259
a1	0.228	0.398	**0.952**	0.440	0.186
a2	0.147	0.297	**0.911**	0.331	0.111
i1	0.360	0.495	0.433	**0.952**	0.417
i2	0.369	0.427	0.358	**0.939**	0.401
u1	0.181	0.226	0.136	0.336	**0.887**
u2	0.331	0.318	0.162	0.442	**0.936**

Measurement Model

According to our results, the measurement model is completely satisfactory. First, all standardized loadings (λ) are greater than .707 (Table 3). Consequently, the individual item reliability is adequate. Second, the five constructs meet the requirement of construct reliability since their composite reliabilities (ρ_c) are greater than 0.7 (Table 4). In addition, such latent variables achieve convergent validity because their average variance extracted (AVE) measures surpass the 0.5 level (Table 4). Finally, we can observe that the five constructs reach discriminant validity. This is achieved both via the comparison of the square root of AVE *vs* correlations (Table 4) and the cross-loadings table (Table 3).

Structural Model

Figure 4 and Table 5 show the variance explained (R^2) in the dependent constructs and the path coefficients for the model. Consistent with Chin (1998b), bootstrapping (500 resamples) was used to generate standard errors and t-statistics. All hypotheses have been supported since they surpass the minimum level indicated by a student's t-distribution with one tail and n-1 (n = number of resamples) degrees of freedom. Nonetheless, when we apply percentile bootstrap in order to generate a 95% confidence interval using 5,000 resamples, H1 is not supported because its confidence interval includes zero (Table 6). Figures of R^2 are not excessively outstanding (Table 7). Only intention ($R^2 = 0.304$) achieves a level near to moderate. In spite of this, cross-validated redundancy measures show that the theoretical/structural model has a predictive relevance ($Q^2 > 0$). Finally, Table 7 shows the amount of variance

Table 4. Construct reliability, convergent validity and discriminant validity

Composite reliability	AVE		PEOU	PU	Attitude	Intention	Usage
0.935	0.674	PEOU	**0.821**				
0.930	0.769	PU	0.312	**0.877**			
0.929	0.868	Attitude	0.207	0.379	**0.932**		
0.944	0.893	Intention	0.385	0.489	0.421	**0.945**	
0.908	0.831	Usage	0.291	0.304	0.165	0.433	**0.912**
		Diagonal elements (bold) are the square root of variance shared between the constructs and their measures (AVE). Off-diagonal elements are the correlations among constructs. For discriminant validity, the diagonal elements should be larger than the off-diagonal elements					

Figure 4. Structural model results (baseline model)

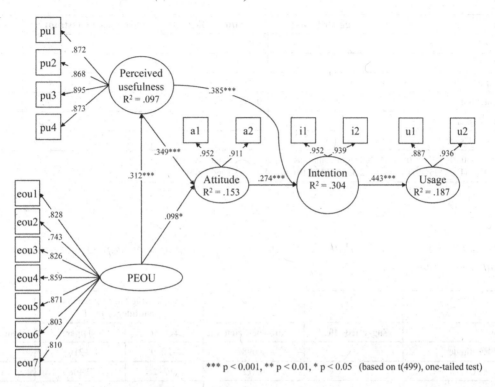

*** p < 0.001, ** p < 0.01, * p < 0.05 (based on t(499), one-tailed test)

that each antecedent variable explains on each endogenous construct.

Interactive Research: An Incremental Study

Original TAM antecedents cannot fully reflect motives. In this regard, Human-Computer Interaction (HCI) research proposes the need for incorporating intrinsic human factors to improve its particular and explanatory TAM value. Indeed, intrinsically perceived enjoyment has been identified as an important intrinsic-motivational factor in web acceptance and usage (cf. Sánchez-Franco & Roldán, 2005). It is here where this research begins to have an interactive character, prompting an incremental study. In this vein, perceived enjoyment associated by individuals with a particular act could thus have a major impact on an individuals' response to the SNS, their attitudes and behaviors. Therefore, we postulate new hypotheses:

H7: Perceived ease of use will positively influence perceived enjoyment.

H8: Perceived enjoyment will positively influence perceived usefulness

H9: Perceived enjoyment will positively influence attitude towards usage.

H10: Perceived enjoyment will positively influence intention to use an SNS.

The measurement model of the extended model satisfies all requirements described for the outer model analysis (see Tables 8 and 9).

Given our goal in this incremental study, we will focus on the analysis of the structural model (Figure 5). As can be observed in Table 10 and Table 11, all paths from perceived enjoyment are significant. Consequently, we find support for hypotheses 8 to 10. In addition, according to Table 12, perceived enjoyment now plays a key role in the explanation of both perceived usefulness and, above all, attitude. Indeed, perceived

Table 5. Structural model results (baseline model)

Hypothesis	Suggested effect	Path coefficients	t-value (bootstrap)	Support
H1: PEOU > Attitude	+	0.098*	1.713	Yes
H2: PEOU > PU	+	0.312***	6.365	Yes
H3: PU > Attitude	+	0.349***	6.146	Yes
H4: PU > Intention	+	0.385***	7.229	Yes
H5: Attitude > Intention	+	0.274***	5.363	Yes
H6: Intention > Usage	+	0.433***	10.896	Yes

*p < 0.05; **p < 0.01; ***p < 0.001; ns: not significant (based on t(499), one-tailed test)
t(0.05; 499) = 1.64791345; t(0.01; 499) = 2.333843952; t(0.001; 499) = 3.106644601

Table 6. Structural model results. Path significance using percentile bootstrap 95% confidence interval (n = 5,000 subsamples) (baseline model)

Hypothesis	Suggested effect	Path coefficients	Percentile bootstrap 95% confidence level		Support
			Lower	Upper	
H1: PEOU > Attitude	+	0.098	-0.009	0.210	No
H2: PEOU > PU	+	0.312	0.222	0.408	Yes
H3: PU > Attitude	+	0.349	0.226	0.461	Yes
H4: PU > Intention	+	0.385	0.279	0.486	Yes
H5: Attitude > Intention	+	0.274	0.171	0.380	Yes
H6: Intention > Usage	+	0.433	0.356	0.512	Yes

Table 7. Effects on endogenous variables (baseline model)

	R^2	Q^2	Direct effect	Correlation	Variance explained
PU	**0.097**	**0.072**			
H2: PEOU			0.312	0.312	9.7%
Attitude	**0.153**	**0.117**			
H1: EOU			0.098	0.207	2.0%
H3: PU			0.349	0.379	13.2%
Intention	**0.304**	**0.266**			
H4: PU			0.385	0.489	18.9%
H5: Attitude			0.274	0.421	11.5%
Usage	**0.187**	**0.145**			
H6: Intention			0.433	0.433	18.7%

Table 8. Outer model loadings and cross loadings (extended model)

	PEOU	Enjoyment	PU	Attitude	Intention	Usage
eou1	**0.828**	0.188	0.261	0.170	0.395	0.307
eou2	**0.745**	0.158	0.196	0.156	0.222	0.174
eou3	**0.824**	0.179	0.278	0.167	0.328	0.274
eou4	**0.864**	0.208	0.219	0.131	0.286	0.243
eou5	**0.875**	0.239	0.251	0.183	0.309	0.259
eou6	**0.799**	0.149	0.245	0.133	0.305	0.161
eou7	**0.805**	0.212	0.309	0.225	0.337	0.234
e1	0.191	**0.894**	0.335	0.513	0.322	0.243
e2	0.200	**0.941**	0.369	0.548	0.376	0.236
e3	0.252	**0.915**	0.329	0.576	0.398	0.259
pu1	0.288	0.322	**0.871**	0.310	0.445	0.291
pu2	0.273	0.349	**0.870**	0.320	0.424	0.251
pu3	0.251	0.305	**0.894**	0.338	0.416	0.265
pu4	0.276	0.340	**0.873**	0.364	0.429	0.259
a1	0.228	0.631	0.398	**0.953**	0.439	0.186
a2	0.146	0.457	0.297	**0.910**	0.330	0.111
i1	0.358	0.382	0.495	0.434	**0.951**	0.417
i2	0.368	0.375	0.427	0.358	**0.940**	0.401
u1	0.181	0.235	0.226	0.136	0.336	**0.887**
u2	0.331	0.254	0.318	0.162	0.442	**0.936**

enjoyment explains 12.0% and 31.2% of both variables respectively. Besides, playing attention to the f^2 index, perceived enjoyment has a medium effect on attitude above and beyond the contribution provided by perceived usefulness and PEOU. Such an effect is also corroborated by a q^2 of 0.238. The contribution of perceived enjoyment to predicting perceived usefulness reflects only a small to moderate effect. Finally, the 0.019 effect of perceived enjoyment on inten-

Table 9. Construct reliability, convergent validity and discriminant validity (extended model)

Composite reliability	AVE		PEOU	Enjoyment	PU	Attitude	Intention	Usage
0.935	0.674	PEOU	**0.821**					
0.941	0.841	Enjoyment	0.235	**0.917**				
0.930	0.769	PU	0.311	0.376	**0.877**			
0.929	0.868	Attitude	0.207	0.596	0.380	**0.932**		
0.944	0.893	Intention	0.384	0.400	0.489	0.421	**0.945**	
0.908	0.831	Usage	0.291	0.269	0.304	0.165	0.433	**0.912**
		Diagonal elements (bold) are the square root of variance shared between the constructs and their measures (AVE). Off-diagonal elements are the correlations among constructs. For discriminant validity, the diagonal elements should be larger than the off-diagonal elements						

Figure 5. Structural model results (extended model)

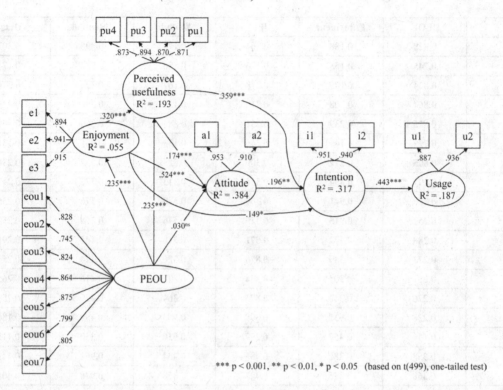

*** p < 0.001, ** p < 0.01, * p < 0.05   (based on t(499), one-tailed test)

tion is low. Altogether, we find support to include perceived enjoyment as an important intrinsic-motivational factor in SNS acceptance.

Information Quality and User Satisfaction in Executive Information Systems (EIS)

The aim of the second illustrative example is to

Table 10. Structural model results (extended model)

Hypothesis	Suggested effect	Path coefficients	t-value (bootstrap)	Support
H1: PEOU > Attitude	+	0.030ns	0.635	No
H2: PEOU > PU	+	0.235***	4.182	Yes
H3: PU > Attitude	+	0.174***	3.474	Yes
H4: PU > Intention	+	0.359***	5.886	Yes
H5: Attitude > Intention	+	0.196**	3.093	Yes
H6: Intention > Usage	+	0.433***	10.450	Yes
H7: PEOU > Enjoyment	+	0.235***	4.232	Yes
H8: Enjoyment > PU	+	0.320***	5.404	Yes
H9: Enjoyment > Attitude	+	0.524***	9.115	Yes
H10: Enjoyment > Intention	+	0.149*	2.125	Yes
*p < 0.05; **p < 0.01; ***p < 0.001; ns: not significant (based on t(499), one-tailed test) t(0.05; 499) = 1.64791345; t(0.01; 499) = 2.333843952; t(0.001; 499) = 3.106644601				

Table 11. Structural model results. Path significance using percentile bootstrap 95% confidence interval (n = 5,000 subsamples) (extended model)

Hypothesis	Suggested effect	Path coefficients	Percentile bootstrap 95% confidence level		Support
			Lower	Upper	
H1: PEOU > Attitude	+	0.030	-0.060	0.125	No
H2: PEOU > PU	+	0.235	0.135	0.339	Yes
H3: PU > Attitude	+	0.174	0.083	0.271	Yes
H4: PU > Intention	+	0.359	0.237	0.472	Yes
H5: Attitude > Intention	+	0.196	0.065	0.312	Yes
H6: Intention > Usage	+	0.433	0.355	0.514	Yes
H7: PEOU > Enjoyment	+	0.235	0.131	0.346	Yes
H8: Enjoyment > PU	+	0.320	0.200	0.434	Yes
H9: Enjoyment > Attitude	+	0.524	0.407	0.630	Yes
H10: Enjoyment > Intention	+	0.149	0.002	0.286	Yes

Table 12. Effects on endogenous variables (extended model)

	R^2	Q^2	Direct effect	Correlation	Variance explained	f^2	q^2
Enjoyment	**0.055**	**0.044**					
H7: PEOU			0.235	0.235	5.5%		
PU	**0.193**	**0.147**					
H2: PEOU			0.235	0.311	7.3%		
H8: Enjoyment			0.320	0.376	12.0%	0.119	0.063
Attitude	**0.384**	**0.287**					
H1: PEOU			0.030	0.207	0.6%		
H3: PU			0.174	0.380	6.6%		
H9: Enjoyment			0.524	0.596	31.2%	0.136	0.238
Intention	**0.317**	**0.273**					
H4: PU			0.359	0.489	17.6%		
H5: Attitude			0.196	0.421	8.2%		
H10: Enjoyment			0.149	0.400	6.0%	0.019	0.010
Usage	**0.187**	**0.145**					
H6: Intention			0.433	0.433	18.7%		

Table 13. Formative indicators of information quality index

	(Information quality). To what extent has EIS helped you?
iq1	Obtain more current and timely information
iq2	Get more factual, non-biased information
iq3	Have more relevant, useful and significant information
iq4	Enjoy more accurate information
iq5	Get more sufficient and complete information
iq6	Have more reliable information
iq7	Obtain more orderly and clear information
iq8	Obtain more reasonable and logical information

Table 14. Variance inflation factor (VIF) of formative indicators of information quality (IQ)

Indicator	Variance inflation factor (VIF)
iq1	2.396
iq2	1.980
iq3	2.593
iq4	2.350
iq5	1.848
iq6	2.073
iq7	3.439
iq8	3.684

show the use of formative indicators. We will particularly focus on the measurement model analysis. The research model corresponds to a segment of the DeLone and McLean (1992) model of information systems success. We especially test the relationship between information quality (IQ) and user satisfaction (US). According to this framework we postulate the following hypothesis:

H1: Information quality will be positively related to user satisfaction

The information quality variable has been modeled as an emergent or composite latent construct. We have built an index of 8 formative indicators based on the dimensions of the information concept (Zmud, 1978) (Table 13). User satisfaction was measured by five reflective items developed by Sanders and Courtney (1985). This study was carried out on a sample of 100 users of executive information systems in Spain.

Due to the constraint of the chapter size, we directly start our analysis testing potential multicollinearity among formative indicators using the IBM SPSS Statistics program. The variance inflation factor (VIF) indicates a problem with iq7 and iq8, since they are above 3.3 (Table 14). Additionally, we proceed to develop an advanced collinearity diagnostic, particularly, the condition index and the variance proportions. Belsley proposes

using both measures jointly. Hence, when a dimension presents a condition index above 30 and two or more indicators have a high variance proportion on this dimension (> 0.50), these indicators present multicollinearity. Our results confirm the existence of collinearity between iq7 and iq8 because there is a dimension with a high condition index (37.122), and iq7 and iq8 also show high variance proportions on this dimension: 0.91 and 0.72 respectively. Accordingly, we decide to remove iq8 because it presents the highest VIF.

Next, we proceed to test the model in PLS (Figure 6). Due to size limitations, we will simply focus on the analysis of the IQ indicator's weights (Table 15). Among the formative items, only iq3 and iq5 are significant, which means that such measures explain a significant portion of the variance in the IQ construct. Items iq3 and iq5 present weights of 0.495 and 0.338 respectively. Thus, we find that relevant information (iq3) and complete information (iq5) are the most important facets in forming an overall information quality perception. In addition, we should highlight it is necessary to understand this result within the nomological net proposed in the structural model, where IQ is an antecedent of US. If we place IQ in another context, linking it with other diverse constructs, we would obtain different results for the weights (Chin, 2010) (cf. also Hardin, Chang, & Fuller, 2008). Also, in a descending order of importance, we locate reason-

Figure 6. Structural model results

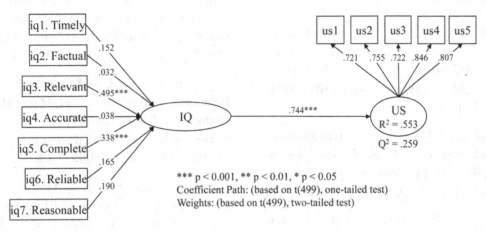

Table 15. Outer model weights

Indicator	Weight	T-Statistic
iq1	0.152	0.983
iq2	0.032	0.243
iq3	0.495***	4.454
iq4	0.038	0.264
iq5	0.338***	3.926
iq6	0.165	1.182
iq7	0.190	1.539

*p < 0.05; **p < 0.01; ***p < 0.001; (based on t(499), two-tailed test)
t(0.05; 499) = 1.964726835; t(0.01; 499) = 2.585711627; t (0.001; 499) = 3.310124157

able (iq7), reliable (iq6) and timely (iq1) information indicators, although these items are not significant. In spite of five of the seven measures not being significant, we do not drop such manifest variables because they contribute conceptually to the IQ construct.

CONCLUSION

There is currently a consolidated use of structural equation modeling (SEM) tools in the information systems research. Such development has been observed both for covariance-based SEM and for the variance-based SEM or PLS. In this chapter,

we have aimed to focus on PLS, showing its basic and key characteristics. In this vein, we have outlined why PLS can be a powerful and attractive tool for IS researchers. Indeed, the research in the IS field is usually characterized by some (if not many) of the following elements: nascent theories, small sample sizes, complex models, less well-developed measures, formative and reflective measurement models, and an interest in predicting a dependent variable. These conditions encourage the use of PLS. On the other hand, we call for a proper and well-founded use of the PLS methodology. This chapter offers guidelines to knowing when the use of PLS is appropriate. Furthermore, we have offered specific indications to determine the appropriate sample for PLS, which is perhaps, one of the most controversial issues regarding PLS. In addition, our objective has been to compile and integrate the most relevant PLS literature in order to present a detailed guidance for assessing variance-based models, both the measure and the structural model. Ultimately, we hold that PLS is an appropriate research methodology for the IS area, provided that the research problem presents certain conditions and this technique is properly applied.

REFERENCES

Anderson, J. C., & Gerbing, D. W. (1988). Structural equation modeling in practice: a review and recommended two-step approach. *Psychological Bulletin*, *103*, 411–423. doi:10.1037/0033-2909.103.3.411

Bagozzi, R. P. (1994). Structural equation models in marketing research: Basic principles. In Bagozzi, R. P. (Ed.), *Principles of marketing research* (pp. 317–385). Oxford, UK: Blackwell.

Bagozzi, R. P. (2011). Measurement and meaning in information systems and organizational research: Methodological and philosophical foundations. *Management Information Systems Quarterly*, *35*(2), 261–292.

Barclay, D., Higgins, C., & Thompson, R. (1995). The partial least squares (PLS) approach to causal modelling: Personal computer adoption and use as an illustration. (Special Issue on Research Methodology). *Technology Studies*, *2*(2), 285–309.

Barroso, C., Cepeda, G., & Roldán, J. L. (2010). Applying maximum likelihood and PLS on different sample sizes: Studies on SERVQUAL model and employee behaviour model. In Esposito Vinzi, V., Chin, W. W., Henseler, J., & Wang, H. (Eds.), *Handbook of partial least squares: Concepts, methods and applications* (pp. 427–447). Berlin, Germany: Springer-Verlag. doi:10.1007/978-3-540-32827-8_20

Belsley, D. A. (1991). *Conditioning diagnostics: Collinearity and weak data in regression*. New York, NY: John Wiley & Sons.

Bollen, K., & Lennox, R. (1991). Conventional wisdom on measurement: A structural equation perspective. *Psychological Bulletin*, *110*(2), 305–314. doi:10.1037/0033-2909.110.2.305

Bollen, K. A. (2011). Evaluating effect, composite, and causal indicators in structural equation models. *Management Information Systems Quarterly*, *35*(2), 359–372.

Bullock, H. E., Harlow, L. L., & Mulaik, S. A. (1994). Causation issues in structural equation modeling research. *Structured Equation Modeling*, *1*(3), 253–267. doi:10.1080/10705519409539977

Calvo-Mora, A., Leal, A., & Roldán, J. L. (2005). Relationships between the EFQM model criteria: A study in Spanish universities. *Total Quality Management & Business Excellence*, *16*, 741–770. doi:10.1080/14783360500077708

Carmines, E. G., & Zeller, R. A. (1979). *Reliability and validity assessment*. N. 07-017, Sage University Paper Series on Quantitative Applications in the Social Sciences. Beverly Hills, CA: Sage.

Cassel, C., Hackl, P., & Westlund, A. H. (1999). Robustness of partial least-squares method for estimating latent variable quality structures. *Journal of Applied Statistics*, *26*(4), 435–446. doi:10.1080/02664769922322

Cenfetelli, R. T., & Bassellier, G. (2009). Interpretation of formative measurement in information systems research. *Management Information Systems Quarterly*, *33*(4), 689–707.

Chin, W. W. (1998a). Issues and opinion on structural equation modelling. *Management Information Systems Quarterly*, *22*(1), 7–15.

Chin, W. W. (1998b). The partial least squares approach to structural equation modelling. In Marcoulides, G. A. (Ed.), *Modern methods for business research* (pp. 295–336). Mahwah, NJ: Lawrence Erlbaum.

Chin, W. W. (2001). *PLS-graph user's guide*, version 3.0. University of Houston, 2001

Chin, W. W. (2002). *Exploring some FAQs regarding PLS including to report results*. I Workshop on partial least squares methodology. Seville, Spain: University of Seville.

Chin, W. W. (2010). How to write up and report PLS analyses. In Esposito Vinzi, V., Chin, W. W., Henseler, J., & Wang, H. (Eds.), *Handbook of partial least squares: Concepts, methods and applications* (pp. 655–690). Berlin, Germany: Springer-Verlag. doi:10.1007/978-3-540-32827-8_29

Chin, W. W., & Newsted, P. R. (1999). Structural equation modeling analysis with small samples using partial least squares. In Hoyle, R. (Ed.), *Statistical strategies for small samples research* (pp. 307–341). Thousand Oaks, CA: Sage.

Chin, W. W., Peterson, R. A., & Brown, S. P. (2008). Structural equation modeling in marketing: Some practical reminders. *Journal of Marketing Theory and Practice, 16*(4), 287–298. doi:10.2753/MTP1069-6679160402

Cohen, J. (1988). *Statistical power analysis for the behavioral sciences* (2nd ed.). Hillsdale, NJ: Erlbaum.

Cook, T. D., & Campbell, D. T. (1979). *Quasi experimentation: Design and analytical issues for field settings*. Chicago, IL: Rand McNally College.

Davis, F. D. (1989). Perceived usefulness, perceived ease of use and user acceptance of Information Technology. *Management Information Systems Quarterly, 13*(3), 319–342. doi:10.2307/249008

Davis, F. D., Bagozzi, R. P., & Warshaw, P. R. (1992). Extrinsic and intrinsic motivation to use computers in the workplace. *Journal of Applied Social Psychology, 22*, 1111–1132. doi:10.1111/j.1559-1816.1992.tb00945.x

DeLone, W. H., & McLean, E. R. (1992). Information systems success: The quest for the dependent variable. *Information Systems Research, 3*, 60–95. doi:10.1287/isre.3.1.60

Diamantopoulos, A. (2011). Incorporating formative measures into covariance-based structural equation models. *Management Information Systems Quarterly, 35*(2), 335–358.

Diamantopoulos, A., & Winklhofer, H. (2001). Index construction with formative indicators: An alternative to scale development. *JMR, Journal of Marketing Research, 38*(2), 269–277. doi:10.1509/jmkr.38.2.269.18845

Díaz-Casero, J. C., Hernández-Mogollón, R. M., & Roldán, J. L. (2011). (in press). A structural model of the antecedents to entrepreneurial capacity. *International Small Business Journal, 29*.

Edwards, J. R., & Bagozzi, R. P. (2000). On the nature and direction of relationships between constructs and measures. *Psychological Methods, 5*(2), 155–174. doi:10.1037/1082-989X.5.2.155

Efron, B., & Tibshirani, R. J. (1993). *An introduction to the bootstrap. Monographs on Statistics and Applied Probability, no. 57*. New York, NY: Chapman and Hall.

Falk, R. F., & Miller, N. B. (1992). *A primer for soft modeling*. Akron, OH: The University of Akron.

Fornell, C. (1982). A second generation of multivariate analysis: an overview. In Fornell, C. (Ed.), *A second generation of multivariate analysis (Vol. 1*, pp. 1–21). New York, NY: Praeger.

Fornell, C., & Bookstein, F. L. (1982). A comparative analysis of two structural equation models: Lisrel and PLS applied to market data. In Fornell, C. (Ed.), *A second generation of multivariate analysis (Vol. 1*, pp. 289–324). New York, NY: Praeger.

Fornell, C., & Cha, J. (1994). Partial least squares. In Bagozzi, R. (Ed.), *Advanced methods of marketing* (pp. 52–78). Cambridge, UK: Blackwell.

Fornell, C., & Larcker, D. F. (1981). Evaluating structural equation models with unobservable variables and measurement error. *JMR, Journal of Marketing Research*, *18*, 39–50. doi:10.2307/3151312

Fu, J. R. (2006). *VisualPLS – Partial least square (PLS) Regression – An enhanced GUI for Lvpls (PLS 1.8 PC) Version 1.04*. Taiwan, ROC: National Kaohsiung University of Applied Sciences.

Gefen, D., Rigdon, E. E., & Straub, D. (2011). An updated and extension to SEM guidelines for administrative and social science research. *Management Information Systems Quarterly*, *35*(2), iii–xiv.

Gefen, D., & Straub, D. (2005). A practical guide to factorial validity using PLS-Graph: Tutorial and annotated example. *Communications of the AIS*, *16*, 91–109.

Gefen, D., Straub, D., & Boudreau, M. (2000). Structural equation modeling and regression: Guidelines for research practice. *Communications of the Association for Information Systems*, *7*(7), 1–78.

Gerow, J. E., Grover, V., Roberts, N., & Thatcher, J. B. (2010). The diffusion of second generation statistical techniques in Information Systems research from 1990–2008. (JITTA). *Journal of Information Technology Theory and Application*, *11*(4), 5–28.

Goodhue, D., Lewis, W., & Thompson, R. (2006). PLS, small sample size, and statistical power in MIS research. In *HICSS '06: Proceedings of the 39th Annual Hawaii International Conference on System Sciences*, (pp. 202.2). Washington, DC: IEEE Computer Society, CD-ROM, 10 pages.

Green, S. B. (1991). How many subjects does it take to do a regression analysis. *Multivariate Behavioral Research*, *26*, 499–510. doi:10.1207/s15327906mbr2603_7

Hair, J. F., Ringle, C. M., & Sarstedt, M. (2011). PLS-SEM: Indeed a silver bullet. *Journal of Marketing Theory and Practice*, *19*(2), 137–149. doi:10.2753/MTP1069-6679190202

Hardin, A. M., Chang, J. C.-J., & Fuller, M. A. (2008). Formative vs. reflective measurement: Comment on Marakas, Johnson, and Clay (2007). *Journal of the Association for Information Systems*, *9*(9), 519–534.

Henseler, J., Ringle, C. M., & Sinkovics, R. R. (2009). The use of partial least squares path modeling in international marketing. *Advances in International Marketing*, *20*, 277–320.

Hui, B. S. (1982). On building partial least squares models with interdependent inner relations. In K. G. Jöreskog & H. Wold (Eds.), Systems under indirect observations: Causality, structure, prediction (Part 2, pp. 249-272). Amsterdam, The Netherlands: North-Holland.

Jarvis, C. B., Mackenzie, S. B., & Podsakoff, P. M. (2003). A critical review of construct indicators and measurement model misspecification in marketing and consumer research. *The Journal of Consumer Research*, *30*(2), 199–218. doi:10.1086/376806

Jöreskog, K. G., & Wold, H. (1982). *Systems under indirect observation - Causality structure prediction*. Amsterdam, The Netherlands: North Holland.

Kim, G., Shin, B., & Grover, V. (2010). Investigating two contradictory views of formative measurement in information systems research. *Management Information Systems Quarterly*, *34*(2), 345–365.

Kleinbaum, D. G., Kupper, L. L., & Muller, K. E. (1988). *Applied regression analysis and other multivariate analysis methods*. Boston, MA: PWS-Kent Publishing.

Kock, N. (2011). *WarpPLS 2.0 user manual*. Script-Warp Systems™. Laredo, Texas USA. Retrieved May 27, 2011, from http://www.scriptwarp.com/warppls/UserManual_WarpPLS_V2.pdf

Li, Y. (2005). *PLS-GUI – Graphic user interface for partial least squares (PLS-PC 1.8) – Version 2.0.1 beta.* Columbia, SC: University of South Carolina.

Lohmöller, J. B. (1984). *LVPLS 1.6 program manual: Latent variables path analysis with partial least-squares estimation.* Munich, Germany: University of the Federal Armed Forces.

Lohmöller, J. B. (1989). *Latent variables path modeling with partial least squares.* Heidelberg, Germany: Physica.

MacCallum, R. C., & Browne, M. W. (1993). The use of causal indicators in covariance structure models: Some practical issues. *Psychological Bulletin, 114*(3), 533–541. doi:10.1037/0033-2909.114.3.533

Majchrak, A., Beath, C., Lim, R., & Chin, W. W. (2005). Managing client dialogues during information systems design to facilitate client learning. *Management Information Systems Quarterly, 29*(4), 653–672.

Marcoulides, G. A., Chin, W. W., & Saunders, C. (2009). A critical look at partial least squares modeling. *Management Information Systems Quarterly, 33*(1), 171–175.

Marcoulides, G. A., & Saunders, C. (2006). PLS: A silver bullet? *Management Information Systems Quarterly, 30*(2), iii–ix.

Markus, K. A. (2010). Structural equations and causal explanations: Some challenges for causal SEM. *Structural Equation Modeling, 17,* 654–676. doi:10.1080/10705511.2010.510068

Mathieson, K., Peacock, E., & Chin, W. W. (2001). Extending the technology acceptance model: The influence of perceived user resources. *The Data Base for Advances in Information Systems, 32,* 86–112.

Monecke, A. (2010). *semPLS - Structural equation modeling using partial least squares.* Retrieved May 27, 2011, from http://cran.r-project.org/web/packages/semPLS/semPLS.pdf

Nunnally, J. C., & Bernstein, I. H. (1994). *Psychometric theory* (3rd ed.). New York, NY: McGraw-Hill.

Petter, S., Straub, D. W., & Rai, A. (2007). Specifying formative constructs in information systems research. *Management Information Systems Quarterly, 31*(4), 623–656.

R Development Core Team. (2007). *R: A language and environment for statistical computing.* Vienna, Austria: R Foundation for Statistical Computing. Retrieved May 27, 2011, from http://www.R-project.org

Reinartz, W., Haenlein, M., & Henseler, J. (2009). An empirical comparison of the efficacy of covariance-based and variance-based (SEM). *International Journal of Research in Marketing, 26*(4), 332–344. doi:10.1016/j.ijresmar.2009.08.001

Rigdon, E. E., Ringle, C. M., & Sarstedt, M. (2010). Structural modeling of heterogeneous data with partial least squares. *Review of Marketing Research, 7,* 255–296. doi:10.1108/S1548-6435(2010)0000007011

Ringle, C.M., Götz, O., Wetzels, M., & Wilson, B. (2009). *On the use of formative measurement specifications in structural equation modeling: A Monte Carlo simulation study to compare covariance– based and partial least squares model estimation methodologies.* Maastricht University, METEOR Research Memoranda RM/09/014.

Ringle, C. M., Wende, S., & Will, A. (2005). *SmartPLS 2.0 (M3) beta.* Hamburg, Germany.

Rivard, S., & Huff, S. L. (1988). Factors of success for end user computing. *Communications of the ACM, 29*(5), 486–501.

Roberts, N., & Thatcher, J. B. (2009). Conceptualizing and testing formative constructs: Tutorial and annotated example. *The Data Base for Advances in Information Systems, 40*(3), 9–39.

Sánchez, G., & Trinchera, L. (2010). *PLSPM – Partial least squares data analysis methods.* Retrieved May 27, 2011, from http://cran.r-project.org/web/packages/plspm/plspm.pdf

Sánchez-Franco, M. J., & Roldán, J. L. (2005). Web acceptance and usage model: A comparison between goal-directed and experiential Web users. *Internet Research, 15*(1), 21–48. doi:10.1108/10662240510577059

Sanders, G. L., & Courtney, J. F. (1985). A field study of organizational factors influencing DSS success. *Management Information Systems Quarterly, 9,* 77–93. doi:10.2307/249275

Sosik, J. J., Kahai, S. S., & Piovoso, M. J. (2009). Silver bullet or voodoo statistics? A primer for using the partial least squares data analytic technique in group and organization research. *Group & Organization Management, 34*(1), 5–36. doi:10.1177/1059601108329198

Steiger, J. H. (1979). Factor indeterminacy in the 1930's and the 1970's – Some interesting parallels. *Psychometrika, 44,* 157–167. doi:10.1007/BF02293967

Straub, D., Boudreau, M. C., & Gefen, D. (2004). Validation guidelines for IS positivist research. *Communications of the Association for Information Systems, 14,* 380–426.

Temme, D., Kreis, H., & Hildebrandt, L. (2010). A comparison of current PLS path modeling software: Features, ease-of-use, and performance. In Esposito Vinzi, V., Chin, W. W., Henseler, J., & Wang, H. (Eds.), *Handbook of partial least squares: Concepts, methods and applications* (pp. 737–756). Berlin, Germany: Springer-Verlag. doi:10.1007/978-3-540-32827-8_32

Tenenhaus, M., Vinzi, V. E., Chatelin, Y.-M., & Lauro, C. (2005). PLS path modeling. *Computational Statistics & Data Analysis, 48*(1), 159–205. doi:10.1016/j.csda.2004.03.005

Treiblmaier, H., Bentler, P. M., & Mair, P. (2011). Formative constructs implemented via common factors. *Structural Equation Modeling, 18,* 1–17. doi:10.1080/10705511.2011.532693

Urbach, N., & Ahlemann, F. (2010). Structural equation modeling in information systems research using partial least squares. *Journal of Information Technology Theory and Application, 11*(2), 5–40.

Venkatesh, V., & Davis, F. D. (2000). Theoretical extension of the technology acceptance model: Four longitudinal field studies. *Management Science, 46*(2), 186–204. doi:10.1287/mnsc.46.2.186.11926

Werts, C. E., Linn, R. L., & Jöreskog, K. G. (1974). Interclass reliability estimates: testing structural assumptions. *Educational and Psychological Measurement, 34,* 25–33. doi:10.1177/001316447403400104

Westland, J. C. (2010). Lower bounds on sample size in structural equation modeling. *Electronic Commerce Research and Applications, 9,* 476–487. doi:10.1016/j.elerap.2010.07.003

Williams, L., Vandenberg, R. J., & Edwards, R. J. (2009). Structural equation modeling in management research: A guide for improved analysis. *The Academy of Management Annals, 3*(1), 543–604. doi:10.1080/19416520903065683

Wold, H. (1979). *Model construction and evaluation when theoretical knowledge is scarce: An example of the use of partial least squares. Cahiers du Département D'Économétrie.* Genève: Faculté des Sciences Économiques et Sociales, Université de Genève.

Wold, H. (1980). Soft modeling: intermediate between traditional model building and data analysis. *Mathematical Statistics*, *6*, 333–346.

Wold, H. (1982). Soft modeling: The basic design and some extensions. In K. G. Jöreskog & H. Wold (Eds.) *Systems under indirect observations: Causality, structure, prediction* (Part 2, pp. 1-54). Amsterdam, The Netherlands: North-Holland.

Wold, H. (1985). Systems analysis by partial least squares. In Nijkamp, P., Leitner, H., & Wrigley, N. (Eds.), *Measuring the unmeasurable* (pp. 221–251). Dordrecht, The Netherlands: Martinus Nijhoff.

Zmud, R. W. (1978). An empirical investigation of the dimensionality of the concept of information. *Decision Sciences*, *9*, 187–195. doi:10.1111/j.1540-5915.1978.tb01378.x

KEY TERMS AND DEFINITIONS

Average Variance Extracted (AVE): This quantifies the amount of variance that a construct captures from its manifest variables or indicators relative to the amount due to measurement error. Convergent validity is usually assessed by the AVE. AVE values should be greater than 0.50.

Bootstrapping: A nonparametric technique of re-sampling commonly used in PLS, which provides standard errors and t-statistics of the parameters.

Coefficient of Determination (R^2): This represents a measure of the predictive power and indicates the amount of variance in a dependent construct that is explained by its antecedent variables in the model.

Composite Reliability (ρ_c): This is a measure of internal consistency reliability that allows the assessment of the construct reliability, that is, the evaluation of the extent to which a variable or set of variables is consistent in what it intends to measure. 0.7 has been suggested as a benchmark for "modest" reliability applicable in the early stages of research, and a more strict 0.8 or 0.9 value for the more advanced stages of research.

Discriminant Validity: This indicates the extent to which a given construct differs from other constructs.

Measurement Model: It is also known as epistemic relationship or outer model in the PLS sphere, and describes the relationships between the latent variables (theory) and their indicators or manifest variables (data). The measurement model defines the latent variables that the model will use, and assigns manifest variables (indicators) to each.

Path Coefficient: This is also known as standardized regression coefficient and represents the direct effect of an antecedent latent variable on a dependent construct. Path coefficients are assessed with regard to algebraic sign, magnitude, and statistical significance.

Standardized Loading (λ): This shows the simple correlation of an indicator with its respective latent variable. Individual item reliability is assessed by analyzing the standardized loadings (λ) of manifest variables.

Stone-Geisser's Q^2: Test that is used to assess the predictive relevance of the endogenous constructs with a reflective measurement model. Two types of Q^2 can be obtained, depending on the form of prediction: cross-validated communality and cross-validated redundancy. The latter is used to examine the predictive relevance of the theoretical/structural model. A Q^2 greater than 0 implies that the model has predictive relevance.

Structural Model: This is also known as inner model in the PLS literature, and refers to the part of the overall model that proposes relationships among the latent variables.

Weights: These measure the contribution of each formative item to the variance of the composite latent construct.

Chapter 11
Models for Interpretive Information Systems Research, Part 1:
IS Research, Action Research, Grounded Theory – A Meta–Study and Examples

M. R. (Ruth) De Villiers
University of South Africa, South Africa

ABSTRACT

Interpretive research designs are increasingly being applied in Information Systems (IS). This chapter is a meta-research study that briefly explains the concepts of positivism, interpretivism, and qualitative and quantitative research, before overviewing the advent of interpretive IS research. The chapter then presents two interpretive models that can serve as research designs for postgraduate studies and ad-hoc research. Action research, which originated in the social sciences, involves longitudinal studies, in which the researcher participatively investigates products or interventions that address real-world problems over several cycles, in a reflective and responsive way. Grounded theory can serve as a research method, as well as a full research design, since it can be integrated into other models as an analysis approach. Grounded theory is applied to generate themes, patterns, and theories from continuous collection, coding, and analysis of contextual data. The patterns and grounded theories emerge inductively, and are expanded and refined as further data is gathered.

INTRODUCTION

Research designs based on the interpretive paradigm, can serve well as approaches for the design and development of artifacts within the discipline of Information Systems (IS). This chapter overviews research paradigms, then introduces two approaches applicable to interpretive IS research. In the current computing milieu – with its emphasis on interactivity, user-centricity, and usability – inquiry processes originating from the human

DOI: 10.4018/978-1-4666-0179-6.ch011

sciences are relevant to IS. Interpretive research is also used in educational-technology research, where interpretive goals investigate how artifacts function by addressing and interpreting phenomena of domain processes, human performances, and innovations in complex contexts. This chapter relates particularly to research on human and contextual aspects of computing, and highlights research designs appropriate for the subset of IS that incorporates e-learning systems, which users must be able to use easily before they can even begin to learn.

Different research designs have varying structures and procedures to guide the research process, and are appropriate for different kinds of computing applications. This chapter forms Part 1 of a discourse entitled 'Models for Interpretive Information Systems research'. It discusses and graphically illustrates two approaches, *action research* and *grounded theory*, explaining how they can be used as research designs and giving examples of studies where they were applied. Part 2 of the discourse, in Chapter I.7b, considers three models from the family of design- and development research, namely: *development research*, *design-science research* (so called in IS), and *design-based research* (so termed for educational technology research).

Interpretive research, which originated in the behavioural social sciences, is increasingly applied in Information Systems (IS). Research design and -paradigms in IS have been receiving focused attention over the past two decades (Baskerville, 1999; Baskerville and Wood-Harper, 1996, Cockton, 2002; De Villiers, 2005b; Glass, Ramesh and Vessey, 2004; Klein and Myers, 1999; Myers, 2004; Pather and Remenyi, 2004; Roode, 2003; Walsham 1995a; 1995b; Wood-Harper, 1985). This meta-research study suggests various underlying theoretical frameworks to guide the research and development process, providing cohesion and internal consistency. It is not focused primarily on major business systems, but more on small-scale systems for personal computing.

The fact that researchers and practitioners are taking cognizance of social responsibility (Du Plooy, 2003); human factors, and behavioural aspects, is in line with the current emphasis on the human-computer interaction (HCI) concepts of user-centricity and usability. This study outlines the positivist and interpretivist research paradigms and suggests models to operationalise interpretive research. Influences from positivism cannot be excluded, as research methodology continues to evolve and develop, and 'mixed methods is another step forward, utilizing the strengths of both qualitative and quantitative research' (Creswell, 2009: 203).

Examples are given to illustrate each research model/design, several of which come from the domain of e-learning. The chapter should be useful to postgraduate students undertaking research in IS or e-learning for their masters or doctoral studies, as well as to faculty who facilitate teaching and learning processes.

Research Paradigms: Positivist and Interpretivist

Different research paradigms are based on different philosophical foundations and conceptions of reality (Cohen, Manion and Morrison, 2005; du Poy and Gitlin, 1998; Lincoln and Guba, 1985; Olivier 2004). Each paradigm is implemented by distinctive methodological strategies.

The *positivist* paradigm holds that knowledge is absolute and objective and that a single objective reality exists external to human beings. Positivism is equated with the scientific method, whereby knowledge is discovered by controlled empirical means, such as experiments. Positivist research aims for an exact, value-free representation of reality. Research results should be reliable, consistent, unbiased, and replicable by other researchers. Positivist research is operationalised mainly (yet not exclusively) by quantitative methods, where data comprises numbers and measures, analysed by statistical methods. Studies are usually hypothesis-driven and results can be used for prediction.

Interpretivism aims to find new interpretations or underlying meanings and permits the accommodation of multiple correct approaches and findings, mediated by time, context and researcher. Related terms are naturalistic and ethnographic (Cohen, Manion and Morrison, 2005; Lincoln and Guba, 1985). Inquiry is value-related, leading to subjective findings that may vary between researchers. It is an appropriate view for studies of complex human behaviour, documents, and social phenomena.

Interpretive approaches and methods have become accepted in IS (Klein and Myers, 1999; Roode, 2003; Walsham, 1995a; 1995b; Vannoy and Salam, 2010). Klein and Myers believe that interpretive studies provide deep insight into IS phenomena, helping the IS research community to understand human thought and action in social and organizational contexts. In the context of educational technology, Reeves (2000) explains that interpretive goals determine how things work by describing and interpreting phenomena regarding domain processes, performances and innovations. Interpretivism lends itself mainly to qualitative studies. Where positivism tests hypotheses, interpretivism investigates research questions focused on understanding phenomena in natural settings using verbal data. Qualitative data collection and analysis produce findings related to intricate details where values and human experiences are relevant. The ability to interpret data is important and 'the researcher is an instrument' (Leedy and Ormrod, 2001:147). Reliability is a fit between the findings recorded and occurrences in natural settings. Research methods are often triangulated by using multiple methods of data collection.

Research Methods: Qualitative and Quantitative

Mertens (1998) describes qualitative research as a naturalistic, interpretive, multi-method science.

It involves case studies, interviews, observation, textual analysis and ethnographic data, which provide insights into organizational practices and human interactions. Creswell (2009) recommends that qualitative researchers should consider applying strategies such as narrative analysis, phenomenology, ethnography, case studies and grounded theory.

Quantitative methods include survey designs and experiments. A survey can capture numeric descriptions of trends or opinions from a sample of a population. Experiments are controlled studies that test the effect of a treatment or intervention on a group (Creswell, 2009). Statistical analysis can be undertaken on quantitative data. Cohen, Manion and Morrison (2005) caution researchers that when statistical processing is intended, it impacts on the layout and structure of the raw data. For example, the design of a questionnaire should support data entry and subsequent analysis by computer, therefore decisions should be taken upfront with regard to which statistical tests will be used for analysis.

Qualitative and quantitative methods are not mutually exclusive. Many studies require eclectic inquiry methods, i.e. mixed methods research (Creswell, 2009) to cover the terrain and triangulate. Qualitative research can be exploratory, with its findings used to formulate hypotheses for subsequent quantitative analysis and verification. Conversely, when quantitative studies precede qualitative components, their findings can be extended in the subsequent qualitative research, for example, interviews.

Figure 1 shows common research methods on a Positivist—Interpretivist axis, tending from quantitative to qualitative, yet with an overlap.

INTERPRETIVE INFORMATION SYSTEMS RESEARCH

IS is a multi-perspective discipline with scientific, technological, engineering, organizational,

Figure 1. Research methods/strategies (de Villiers, 2005a)

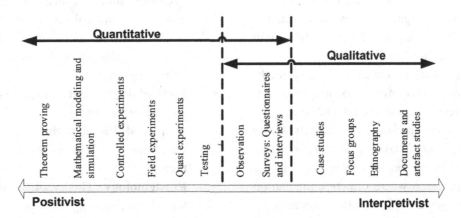

managerial, and societal aspects, which requires plural research methods (Wood-Harper, 1985). The subdiscipline of human-computer interaction (HCI) (Preece, Rogers and Sharpe, 2007) has become prominent, highlighting the end user, and adding dimensions of psychology, culture, linguistics, ergonomics, graphical design, and marketing. The increasing power and stability of technology has pushed information systems into multiple domains, requiring reflective practices and reorientation (Pather and Remenyi, 2004).

Since the 1990s, there has been a tendency in IS to take cognizance of human behaviour and to use evaluative approaches. Walsham (1995b) examined IS research journals from 1992 onwards, four each from the UK and USA, and noted the advent of interpretive studies. In an analysis of computing research from leading journals, Glass, Ramesh and Vessey (2004) coded 628 papers from Computer Science (CS), 369 from Software Engineering (SE), and 488 from Information Systems. Sixty seven percent of the IS papers used evaluative approaches. The research methods applied in IS were field studies (27%), laboratory research involving humans (16%), and case studies (13%). Sixty three percent of the IS work related to behavioural aspects, versus only 2% and 8% of the CS and SE cases, respectively. The editorial policy of the MIS Quarterly has shifted, calling explicitly for interpretive or integrated, as

well as positivist, approaches (O'Donovan and Roode, 2002; Walsham, 1995b;). In an editorial for the South African Computer Journal, Roode, (2003:1) personally requested acknowledgement of 'interpretivist research on a semi-equal footing with positivist research', thus supplementing the accepted scientific method with relevant non-positivist forms of scholarly research

Hirschheim and Klein (2000) discuss the internal and external views of IS research. The internal view identifies fragmentation, primarily due to the paradigm tension between interpretivists and positivists. The external view relates to the gap between IS research and external expectations, suggesting that the research, at that time, was not sufficiently relevant to practice. Research outputs represented *ad hoc* findings, yet lacked generality and did not broaden theoretical constructs. Where possible, IS research should be based on underlying, yet explicit, theoretical frameworks or conceptual models to provide internal continuity and cohesion. Pather and Remenyi (2004) propose critical realism as a bridge to the gap between positivist and interpretivist paradigms, using both qualitative and quantitative techniques. De Villiers (2005b) suggests approaches and methods that primarily implement the ethos of the interpretive school, such as design research, action research and grounded theory. In recent work, Vannoy and Salam (2010) applied grounded theory as an interpretive research approach to investigate how top managers used organisation-wide information systems in their competitive actions to sustain their companies' leading positions.

This chapter suggests two practical, yet methodologically- and theoretically sound approaches, which are relevant to postgraduate studies, as well as to basic-, *ad hoc-* and contract research. *Action research* and *grounded theory* both originated in the social sciences, yet are relevant to current computing research where effective interaction design is important in societies increasingly geared to the end-user. There is recognition of the 'human-factors' aim of HCI to generate interactive user-centric computing, sound usability, and empowerment of domains beyond business systems, for example, applications for e-learning/e-training and for bridging the digital divide. Acknowledging that computing has human and sociological, as well as technological and computational dimensions, research methods from the interpretive paradigm have a definitive role to play. Du Plooy (2003) stresses the importance of acknowledging human and social factors in the development of information systems. Preece, Rogers and Sharpe (2007) distinguish between the usability and the user experience (UX) of software. User experience, in particular, requires interpretive and qualitative analysis, and approaches are being proposed to measure it (Schulze and Krömker, 2010).

Research terminology includes overlapping, interrelated or exclusive terms, some of which are listed to explain how they are used in this study:

- **Paradigm:** The underlying philosophy and assumptions that form the foundation to one's approach and methodology (in this study: the *interpretive*, rather than positivist, stance).
- **Model:** the underlying research approach used to guide and operationalise a study: the approaches suggested here being *action research* and *grounded theory*.

- **Methods:** practical means/strategies/techniques for data collection: each approach has its own set of methods and instruments, usually multiple methods and/or hybrid methods.
- **Methodology:** A set of methods used in a process of inquiry.
- **Empirical:** Based on the results of experiments and/or observations; not based on theory.
- **Epistemology:** Theory of the grounds of knowledge, relating to how knowledge is produced; basis of claims to knowledge.
- **Ontology:** The science of the essence of being; closely related to one's view of reality.
- **Substantive:** Having a separate and independent existence, not merely inferential or implicit.

The next sections describe, discuss and illustrate two approaches/models and their application in interpretive IS research. Each research design has associated methods and techniques to operationalise it and is illustrated by real-world examples, some of which relate to research by the author, her colleagues, and postgraduate students.

ACTION RESEARCH

Definition and Origins

The action research (AR) approach (Baskerville, 1999; Baskerville and Wood-Harper, 1996; Cohen, Manion and Morrison, 2005; Zuber-Skerrit, 1992) emanates from action-based social psychology and encompasses various research and intervention methods. Its founder, Kurt Lewin, contended that complex societal phenomena could not be investigated under laboratory conditions and used AR to study post-World War 2 social disorders among veterans (Baskerville, 1999; du Poy and Gitlin, 1998; Wood-Harper, 1985). Zuber-Skerrit

(1992) defines AR in higher-education as inquiry into issues encountered when students learn. Its participative, practitioner-researcher approach lends itself to research in educational technology, where an evolving intervention or product is investigated over several cycles.

Commencing with the identification of a problem or situation that calls for action, AR functions as an agent for change. Based on features compiled from publications by Baskerville, 1999; Dick, Passfield and Wildman, 1995; du Poy and Gitlin, 1998; McIntosh, 2010, and Zuber-Skerrit, 1992; action research is:

- *Cyclic*: Systematic, action-oriented, iterative stages recur in a longitudinal time frame, generating knowledge for further action.
- *Participative*: Clients, end users, participants and researcher collaborate closely as co-researchers or as practitioner-researchers examine their own work.
- *Qualitative*: Operates more via verbal aspects than by numbers; emphasizes transformation in social settings.
- *Reflective*: Observation followed by critical reflection on the process and outcomes of each cycle, and is used in designing subsequent steps and events with a view to improvement.
- *Responsive*: It reacts and adapts flexibly to findings from previous cycles.

In a seminal parallel from the professional disciplines, Schön (1987) defines reflective practice, or reflection-in-action, as the professional artistry that occurs when skilled practitioners tackle work-related activities, going beyond rigid rules of inquiry, and generating new rules in uncertain situations. Furthermore, the reflective practitioner is both a participant in the process and a critic who observes and analyses. Similarly, AR aims to improve practice and advance knowledge.

Epistemology and Philosophy of AR

Action research has an interpretive ethos, incorporating social and ethnographic enquiry based on views and actions of participants, making it emancipatory research. It is a holistic approach, which includes ideographic enquiry, acknowledging the uniqueness of each setting (Baskerville, 1999). When AR originated, the collection of precise quantitative data was emphasized, yet it was recognised that AR operated under a differing qualitative epistemology and, although it can be less rigorous than other approaches, it is acknowledged as a human-focused process that generates reliable knowledge.

Distinctive characteristics of AR are its longitudinal time framework and the in-depth involvement of researcher as participant. Moreover, it focuses more on refinement of existing processes or products than on new developments. Furthermore, in many cases there is no attempt to construct theory or models.

Action research has been applied in IS since the 1980's and 1990's (Wood-Harper, 1985; Baskerville and Wood-Harper, 1996; Baskerville, 1999). With reference to the use of AR in educational- technology systems, publications have been appearing since the 1990s (Zuber-Skerrit, 1992; Dick, Passfield and Wildman, 1995). The trend continues and AR has become an accepted form of research for studies on e-learning. For example, Wang and Chen (2009) describe the use of action research methods in the development of an e-learning masters degree programme in Taiwan, comprising six courses and associated curricular. Their AR approach involved five stages and the developed courses/curricular were modified in the light of the findings. Moreover in Australia, Russell (2009) used action research for her research methodology and methods as she investigated strategies applied by university lecturers who adopted e-learning in their professional roles. Russell developed a conceptual framework for analysing university teaching and learning as a complex adaptive system. The application area of the study was the Innovative Teaching and Educational Technology (ITET) Fellowship Programme, which ran over a 5-year period and gave her the opportunity to undertake an AR study in four phases, using a variety of data collection methods.

Research Processes and Methods

The process comprises a series of cycles that feed into each other and employ a variety of research methods. The methods can be repeated from one iteration to the next or, alternatively, different methods can be used in different iterations. Du Poy and Gitlin (1998) state that although AR integrates methods from both the experimental and interpretive traditions, all AR research must be conducted within the natural context.

For Kock (2004) AR holds threats that may reduce rigour and validity. One is the complexity of analyzing broad bodies of data, where rich contexts make it difficult to separate distinct constructs. As an antidote, he advocates the integration of action research with grounded theory (next section) where the coding process identifies categories, relationships between them, and supports grouping. Another threat results from the natural context, which – though an advantage – reduces the researcher's control over the environment and

subjects. Third, the close researcher involvement can result in subjective bias in interpretation. These threats, however, can be countered by multiple cyclic iterations.

The action research process is graphically depicted in Figure 2 as a series of cycles which close in as a solution is attained. The researcher occupies a central, participative, and influential position. This model forms a useful framework to guide and monitor the progress of a research project.

Application and Example

AR is increasingly used for scholarly research in IS, and is a valid approach for applied fields (Myers, 2004). Baskerville (1999) asserts that it generates research relevant to the complex and multivariate nature of IS, due to its basis in practical action and potential for solving practical computing problems. In the 1980s, AR techniques were applied by Peter Checkland in systems analysis, as he developed soft systems methodology (Baskerville, 1999). Trevor Wood-Harper addressed the tensions between theory and practice and between traditional scientific research and the sociological approaches, by introducing AR to the IS community with his seminal paper, Research Methods in Information Systems: Using Action Research (Wood-Harper, 1985).

Figure 2. Action research model (de Villiers, 2007)

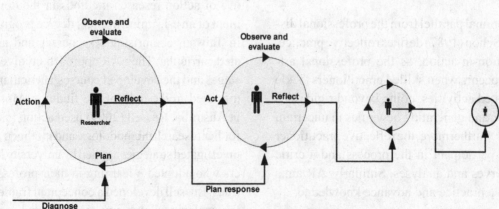

Baskerville lists forms of IS action research: prototyping, soft systems methodology, action science, participant observation, fieldwork, and process consultation. To this list, the present author adds investigation of evolving solutions in their context of use, e.g. e-learning systems and customised interfaces, where designers conduct research into their own products. Derntl and Motschnig-Pitrik (2004) also advocate AR for producing e-learning solutions.

A participative action research approach was used to design, develop, evaluate and refine an e-learning tutorial called *Relations* over a longitudinal time frame in the School of Computing at the University of South Africa (UNISA). The teaching and learning of a complex section in theoretical computer science in a distance-education context was supplemented with *Relations,* which interactively teaches mathematical skills relevant to computing, by alternating instructional and practice functionality (de Villiers, 2004; de Villiers, 2007). *Relations* offers support in a complex cognitive domain, in which learners must acquire specialized skills. It required particular expertise on the part of the system designer to interactively present computational learning content in a creative, yet effective, way that motivates and engages learners. Animated development is used to demonstrate complex concepts and learners are challenged in exercises. Students' answers are judged and diagnostic feedback is provided.

In line with Figure 2, the system was formatively and summatively evaluated by various usability evaluation methods (UEMs) and improved in successive studies by complementary use of various evaluation techniques and triangulated data (de Villiers, 2004; de Villiers, 2007). The initial UEMs were: questionnaire surveys, interviews, heuristic evaluation and a post-test, each of which had particular strengths. The designer reflected on the findings and responded with iterative refinements to *Relations*' functionality, learning content and usability. Heuristic evaluations by experts were valuable sources of critique and innovative suggestions. For optimal evaluation, an HE team should include experts with subject matter skills and experts with usability expertise. Questionnaire surveys among end-users, i.e. students, were particularly useful with regard to educational aspects. They confirmed the value of the detailed feedback to exercises, showing that the time spent in developing it, was worthwhile. The first questionnaire survey provided particularly useful information, as it identified problems that were fixed immediately. Open-ended questions elicited qualitative responses to supplement information from Likert options. Unanticipated aspects that emerged were probed further in semi-structured interviews, following up on problems and identifying features that fostered learning and engagement. Finally, in a mixed methods approach, post-tests gave quantitative measures that could be statistically analysed.

When UNISA obtained a usability laboratory with sophisticated monitoring and recording technology, *Relations* underwent usability testing sessions (Masemola and de Villiers, 2006; de Villiers, 2009). The aim was more to investigate students' actual learning experiences with the e-learning tutorial, than to evaluate the target system itself. Nevertheless, as a secondary outcome, further problems were identified in *Relations*, indicating the value of formal usability testing as a cycle in the action research process. As a user-based method, usability testing is comprehensive and focused, allowing researchers to observe intricate and detailed aspects of users' interaction with the system, whereas surveys, another user-based method, provide more general information.

The participative action research process of designing, developing, evaluating and refining the e-learning tutorial resulted in improvements to its functionality, learning content and usability. The designer and developers of *Relations* used technology, not for its own sake, but rather to motivate learners and to illustrate concepts in ways that enhance cognition. Technology was the medium and not the message (de Villiers, 2005a).

The AR approach required reflection and taught the designer and development team a great deal – not just about *Relations*. They also learned generic principles for designing e-learning and grasped the complementary roles of different evaluation methods used iteratively. The action research design thus led to a dual outcome as, in subsequent ventures, the generic lessons learned and the principles that emerged, were transferred by School of Computing researchers to a series of studies of a different e-learning system, called *Karnaugh* (Becker and De Villiers, 2008; Adebesin, De Villiers and Ssemugabi, 2009; de Villiers, 2009).

GROUNDED THEORY

Definition and Origins

In the grounded theory (GT) approach (Cockton, 2002; Glaser and Strauss, 1967; Glaser, 1992; Leedy and Ormrod, 2001), theory and models are generated inductively from the analysis of contextual data, as themes and patterns emerge. There is no testing of *a-priori* theories. GT originated from sociology, where attitudes to phenomena (initially, the phenomenon of death) were investigated by Glaser and Strauss. GT was extended to research in education, medicine, economics, and anthropology (Strauss and Corbin, 1990), while Cockton (2002; 2004) applied it in the design of computing interactions. By the definition of categories, properties and relationships, GT can account for variation in behaviour. It provides a conceptual grasp of substantive areas, which evolves and is modified to fit as findings and new data emerge. Patterns are detected and interpreted within activities and events. The data may be quantitative, qualitative or both, but for qualitative studies, it is vital that data collection, coding, analysis and interpretation are systematic. Mobility occurs between data collection and analysis. A grounded theory emerges inductively through ongoing co-

variant collection and analysis, and is adjusted, expanded and refined, (Lincoln and Guba, 1985).

As with AR, there is a parallel in the professions. 'Emerging patterns' have an analogy in Christopher Alexander's classic patterns in architecture and town planning, which form practical architectural languages, as physical and social relationships articulate themselves (Alexander, Ishikawa and Silverstein, 1977). Within a pattern language, it is possible to densify, i.e. to find added meaning by integrating overlapping patterns.

Epistemology of GT

Researcher bias and subjectivity may influence conceptualization and interpretations. However, grounded theory has mechanisms to counteract this, such as constant comparison, saturation and core relevance (Glaser, 1992). Furthermore, data collection, analysis and presentation should be linked at each step, adjusting naturally to one another.

The Glaser model posits contentiously that, to avoid preconceptions and forcing, there is little initial need to review literature. Once the emerging theory is sufficiently grounded, literature reviews in the field can commence and be related to the new work. In new fields, Glaser views the researcher as a pre-empting pioneer, producing general theories to be integrated with the literature. According to Urquhart (2002), however, the originator's actual position on avoiding existing literature is not rigid.

As an analysis method, GT can be combined with other research approaches. Kock (2004) proposes integrating grounded theory with action research. A model proposed by van Merwe and de Villiers (2011) articulates and motivates an integrated research framework that combines elements of the grounded theory method with activity theory in a partial grounded theory approach. The framework is relevant for the study of online collaborative interactions and discussion forums.

Over the past ten years interest has increased in the use of GT in IS research. As a qualitative, inductive method based on the systematic collection and analysis of data, GT supports the development of theory grounded in empirical observation (Urquhart, Lehmann and Myers, 2010). Cathy Urquhart, Hans Lehmann and Michael Myers overview the evolution of GT from 1967 to the 21st century, with a view to leveraging the grounded theory method to build theory in IS research. They synthesize a framework of five guidelines for conducting and evaluating GT studies in IS. The first three address ways of achieving adequate conceptualization for the emerging theory, while the fourth and fifth help to establish the scope of the theory by providing guidance on its level and how it could be integrated with existing literature. The five, respectively, are;

1. Constant comparison;
2. Iterative conceptualization;
3. Theoretical sampling;
4. Scaling up; and
5. Theoretical integration.

Research Processes and Methods

Urquhart (2002) refers to the grounded theory method' (GTM) to distinguish the methododology from the emergent theory. GTM literature provides guidance on how to code qualitative data. Covariant data collection and analysis (from social science) entail initial interviews and fieldwork, which after transcription, coding, and analysis delimit the field and prompt theoretical sampling and densifying (Glaser, 1992). Other methods are observation, document analysis, and videotaping to reflect perspectives of the object of study (Strauss and Corbin, 1990). Back-and-forth mobility occurs between data collection and analysis, with analysis driving further collection. Patterns are identified as the researcher systematically codes, compares, analyses and records. Constant comparative coding (Glaser and Strauss, 1967;

Glaser, 1992) is the validation process whereby observations and behaviours are compared with core categories and properties, then coded into categories. The conceptual model is reviewed, modified and expanded in the light of the new data, and new concepts are integrated into the emerging theory. When multiple behaviours indicate similar patterns and properties, saturation has occurred. When disconfirming evidence occurs, revisions are required. In this way the emerging theory is inductively discovered, bounded and confirmed. As the researcher encounters confirming cases, negative cases, and discrepancies, the theory with the most confirming cases emerges as robust (Lincoln and Guba, 1985).

Figure 3 portrays the processes and concepts of GT, serving as an underlying framework for research processes which investigate phenomena to determine their underlying theory.

Application and Example

Orlikowski's (1993) landmark paper in the MISQ describes a project in which a GT research approach was used to study organizational experience in the adoption and use of CASE tools. Findings were used to develop a theoretical framework conceptualizing organisational change and social issues for cases where installation involves both new technologies and inherent change. GT was a relevant approach, because of its emphasis on contextual elements, process management, and human actions. Urquhart (2002) proposes GTM for the analysis of qualitative data in IS research and highlights its use in interpretive studies.

Cockton (2002; 2004) discusses the applicability of grounded theory to computable interactions, and explains how, as theories and themes emerge, corresponding models can be defined and implemented using an HCI contextual approach. Such models could include personas, scenarios and sequence models, where the persona represents a stereotypical user and the scenario a stereotypical usage. It is a rich and relevant context-centered

Figure 3. Model of grounded theory emergence (de Villiers, 2005b)

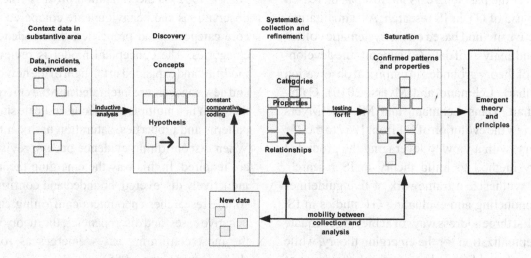

approach, which takes users' goals and aspirations into account, aiming for higher relevance. The models are used in design to generate prototypes on which the fit between context of use and interaction surfaces can be tested. Thus grounded theory research in IS investigates data, resulting in theory, which leads to models, which lead in turn to innovative grounded designs or design models, which satisfy fit-to-context (Cockton, 2004).

GT has been applied beyond information systems and management systems, and has been used in investigating web-based systems. In a study to establish factors that influence the adoption and diffusion of semantic web technology, Joo (2011) used a grounded theory approach for research into the usage of semantic web approaches within organizations. Transcripts of interviews were analysed by open coding and five factors were identified with relation to the adoption and diffusson of the Semantic Web.

The GT process can be applied in studies that focus on the extraction of design guidelines and evaluation criteria by analysis of practice in substantive areas, synthesizing them into theoretical proposals, which are further refined, tested and ratified by use. Glaser's (1992) concept of pre-emption is appropriate in the emerging Southern African technological domains where

innovative work is underway in, for example, the design of non-standard interactive environments, such as development software for the formerly disadvantaged, emergent information systems or communities of practice, culturally-sensitive environments, accessibility for both the physically challenged and indigenous peoples, and contextualized e-learning and e-training. In an innovative approach focusing on context, UNISA academics, Van der Merwe, Van der Merwe and Venter (2010), combined selected aspects of grounded theory with activity theory and applied the approach in content analysis of online discussion forums for mathematics teachers from both advantaged and formerly disadvantaged backgrounds. The data of the advantaged situation was treated as a case and the data of the disadvantaged as a case. The cases were analysed separately, after which the results were compared.

Standard GTM techniques of open- and axial coding, respectively, were used to open the data for further analysis through application of activity theory (AT) techniques. In the first phases, open coding was employed to identify concepts, while in the second, axial coding was used to discover categories from similar concepts in each case. In the next stage, Van der Merwe *et al* (2010) used AT-techniques to reconstruct the opened data in new ways, grouping concepts in categories of best-fit, with the relevant categories used to identify sub-cases or 'activity systems' within each case. Instead of using the GT-technique of selective coding to identify the core category, they applied a variant of GT and grouped related categories into classes, which defined distinct units for activity theory analysis. The classic AT framework of subjects, rules, community, division of labour, objects and goals, provided the necessary scaffolding to decompose class data in context, by way of a chronological report in rich narrative format. With each additional class-decomposition-and-comparison exercise, further

insight was gained into previous classes and categories. Within-case data was interpreted and put together in new data views by mapping it to relevant theoretical frameworks and/or quantitative inputs. This forced them to regularly revisit the raw data in order to confirm and/or expand the evolving holistic view. In back-and-forth mobility between data collection and analysis, they adopted a cyclic process of GT open coding, axial coding and decomposition within activity systems. Connections between class categories, concepts and activity systems were integrated as part of their interpretation phase – bringing meaning, coherence and saturation to the categories, and

Table 1. Summary of action research and grounded theory

Properties	Action research	Grounded theory
Goals	Development of interventions to solve practical problems; Practical, contextual and locally relevant. Advancement of local knowledge without necessarily constructing generalisable theory or principles (though theory maybe an outcome).	Theory that emerges from the data; Inductive generation of grounded theories and models, as themes and patterns emerge through ongoing covariant collection and analysis of contextual data.
Distinct features	Evolving products/interventions investigated over several cycles in longitudinal time frames; Reflective and responsive to findings of previous cycles. In-depth central involvement of researcher-practitioner (researcher and practitioner are often the same person). Analysis of varied data in natural contexts (not lab settings) using various research methods. *Limitations*: Due to the natural setting and limited control, there is a threat of low rigour and validity. Close researcher involvement can lead to subjective bias. *Counteraction*: Multiple cyclic iterations aim to overcome the limitations.	Identification of categories, properties, relationships, which are expanded and refined through constant comparison as new data emerges in further sampling. Saturation occurs when multiple behaviours indicate similar patterns and properties; and new themes no longer emerge. Data may be quantitative, qualitative or mixed. *Limitations*: Researcher bias and subjectivity may influence conceptualization and interpretation. The Glaser variant of grounded theory excludes initial literature reviews, suggesting rather that reviews should commence after the new theory is sufficiently grounded. *Counteraction*: Validation by constant comparative coding; inductive bounding and confirmation of emerging theory.
Processes	Cyclical phases: plan, act, observe and reflect. Phases feed into each other. Participative: collaboration between researcher, practitioners and end-users. Use of a variety of research methods, e.g. different ones in different cycles; Emancipatory: AR as a change agent.	Term 'grounded theory method' (GTM) used to distinguish methodology from the emerging theory. Covariant data collection and analysis, e.g of interviews, textual data, and video data. Patterns identified via systematic coding, comparison, analysis and recording. Electronic tools, e.g. Atlas-ti can assist in coding. Mobility between data collection and analysis, as analysis drives further collection.
	Both AR and GT have iterative phases	
Application	Development of new technologies, materials or products in naturalistic contexts (in this study, in the context of education).	A data analysis technique that can be synergistically integrated with various research models, e.g. action research, activity theory, etc.

developing linkages between the destabilizing tensions discovered within each activity system (i.e. when an activity system was out of balance). The above process was repeated for each polar case. Apart from the novel insertion of activity theory to maintain a situation of balance in the system, the research processes are in line with those shown in Figure 3.

Finally, to consolidate the reconstruction process in line with Glaser (1992), Van der Merwe *et al* (2010) undertook a literature study after the research to strengthen the theoretical grounding of the findings. This also served to avoid an over-emphasis on inductive reasoning, whereby theoretical sensitivity could be ignored in favour of 'creativity' that leads to 'alternative shaping of observation and explanation, rather than an *ex post facto* discovery of explanatory ideas' (Katz, 1983: 133-134).

CONCLUSION

This chapter formed Part 1 of a study of models for interpretive information systems research. After considering positivism, interpretivism, and interpretive IS research, the study moved on to a discourse on the research designs of action research and grounded theory. The two differ in their nature and purpose, in that AR is a holistic research design, incorporating various research methods, while GT is a comprehensive and iterative approach for data analysis that can be used in the context of other models. AR and GT can be synergistically combined, by using GT for analysis within one or more of the AR cycles. Table 2 summarises their main features. Their limitations/disadvantages were reported in the course of the chapter, but are repeated in the table.

Both of these models have underlying theoretical and methodological frameworks, as well as repertoires of strategies to guide the research process, offering structure and cohesion in a research venture. Part 2 of this study is a separate

chapter, which addresses development research, design-science research, and design-based research. The contribution to knowledge of the two chapters lies in their articulation of five interpretive research designs, and in the presentation of examples to illustrate application of research models in practice. Future research could be conducted on implementation of the models, with a view to further application in IS studies and in the domain of e-learning systems. Such studies could confirm, refine or extend the work reported in these two chapters.

NOTE

An earlier version of part of this chapter appeared as an article "Interpretive Research Models for Informatics: Action Research, Grounded Theory, and the Family of Design- and Development Research", *Alternation* 12,2 (2005) 10 - 52, and is re-used here with the permission of the publisher, CSSALL (© 2005 by CSSALL, P.O. Box 1734, Wandsbeck, Durban 3631, RSA). All rights reserved.

The present version is based on a reduced form of the article in *Alternation*, augmented with new content.

REFERENCES

Adebesin, T. F., De Villiers, M. R., & Ssemugabi, S. (2009). Usability testing of e-learning: An approach incorporating co-discovery and think-aloud. *Proceedings of the 2009 Conference of the South African Computer Lecturers' Association, SACLA 2009* (pp. 6-15). ACM International Conference Proceedings Series, Eastern Cape, SA, June 2009.

Alexander, C., Ishikawa, S., & Silverstein, M. (1977). *A pattern language*. New York, NY: Oxford University Press.

Baskerville, R. L. (1999). Investigating Information Systems with action research. *Communications of the Association for Information Systems, 2*(Article 19). Retrieved May 2006 from http://cais.isworld.org/articles/2-19/

Baskerville, R. L., & Wood-Harper, A. T. (1996). A critical perspective on action research as a method for Information Systems research. *Journal of Information Technology, 11*, 235–246. doi:10.1080/026839696345289

Becker, D., & De Villiers, M. R. (2008). Iterative design and evaluation of an e-learning tutorial: A research-based approach. *South African Computer Journal, Special Edition, 42*, 38-46.

Cockton, G. (2002). *My grounded design page.* Retrieved May 2006 from http://www.cet.sunderland.ac.uk/~cs0gco/grounded.htm

Cockton, G. (2004). *A tutorial: Grounded design and HCI. September 2004.* Pretoria, South Africa: University of South Africa.

Cohen, L., Manion, L., & Morrison, K. (2005). *Research methods in education* (5th ed.). Abingdon, UK: Routledge Falmer.

Creswell, J. W. (2009). *Research design: Qualitative, quantitative, and mixed methods approaches.* Los Angeles, CA: Sage.

De Villiers, M. R. (2004). Usability evaluation of an e-learning tutorial: Criteria, questions and case study. In: G. Marsden, P. Kotze, & A. Adesina-Ojo (Eds.), *Fulfilling the promise of ICT. Proceedings of SAICSIT 2004* (pp. 284-291). ACM International Conference Proceedings Series.

De Villiers, M. R. (2005a). e-Learning artifacts: Are they based on learning theory? *Alternation, 12*(1b), 345–371.

De Villiers, M. R. (2005b). Interpretive research models for informatics: Action research, grounded theory, and the family of design- and development research. *Alternation, 12*(2), 10–52.

De Villiers, M. R. (2007). An action research approach to the design, development and evaluation of an interactive e-learning tutorial in a cognitive domain. *Journal of Information Technology Education, 6*, 455–479. Retrieved from http://jite.org/documents/Vol6/JITEv6p455-479deVilliers225.pdf

De Villiers, M. R. (2009). Applying controlled usability-testing technology to investigate learning behaviours of users interacting with e-learning tutorials. In T. Bastiaens *et al.* (Eds.), *Proceedings of World Conference on E-Learning in Corporate, Government, Healthcare, and Higher Education 2009* (pp. 2512-2521). Chesapeake, VA: AACE. Canada.

Derntl, M., & Motschnig-Pitrik, R. (2004). A pattern approach to person-centered e-learning based on theory-guided action research. *Proceedings of the Networked Learning Conference* 2004.

Dick, B., Passfield, R., & Wildman, P. (1995). *A beginner's guide to action research.* Retrieved September 2006 from http://www.scu.edu.au/schools/gcm/ar/arp/guide.html

du Plooy, N. F. (2003). *The social responsibility of information systems developers.* IGI Publishing.

Du Poy, E., & Gitlin, L. N. (1998). *Introduction to research: Understanding and applying multiple strategies* (2nd ed.). St Louis, MO: Mosby Inc.

Glaser, B. G. (1992). *Basics of Grounded Theory Analysis.* Mill Valley, CA: Sociology Press.

Glaser, B. G., & Strauss, A. L. (1967). *The discovery of grounded theory.* Chicago, IL: Aldine.

Glass, R. L., Ramesh, V., & Vessey, I. (2004). An analysis of research in computing disciplines. *Communications of the ACM, 47*(6), 89–94. doi:10.1145/990680.990686

Hirschheim, R., & Klein, H. K. (2000). Information Systems research at the crossroads: External versus internal views. In R. Baskerville, J. Stage & J De Gross (Eds.), *Proceedings of the IFIP TC8 WG 8.2 International Working Conference on the Social and Organizational Perspective on Research and Practice in Information Technology*. Boston, MA: Kluwer Academic Publishers.

Joo, J. (2011). Adoption of Semantic Web from the perspective of technology innovation: A grounded theory approach. *International Journal of Human-Computer Studies*, *69*, 139–154. doi:10.1016/j.ijhcs.2010.11.002

Katz, J. (1983). A theory of qualitative methodology: The social system of analytical fieldwork. In Emerson, R. (Ed.), *Contemporary field research: A collection of readings*. Boston, MA: Little Brown Company.

Klein, H. K., & Myers, M. D. (1999). A set of principles for conducting and evaluating interpretive field studies in Information Systems. *Management Information Systems Quarterly*, *23*(12), 67–93. doi:10.2307/249410

Kock, N. (2004). The three threats of action research: a discussion of methodological antidotes in the context of an information systems study. *Decision Support Systems*, *37*, 265–286. doi:10.1016/S0167-9236(03)00022-8

Leedy, P. D., & Ormrod, J. E. (2001). *Practical research: Planning and design. Upper Saddle River, NJ: Merrill Prentice Hall. Lincoln, Y. S., & Guba, E. G. (1985). Naturalistic inquiry*. Newbury Park, CA: Sage Publications.

Masemola, S. S., & De Villiers, M. R. (2006). Towards a framework for usability testing of interactive e-learning applications in cognitive domains, illustrated by a case study. In J. Bishop & D. Kourie (Eds.), *Service-Oriented Software and Systems: Proceedings of SAICSIT 2006* (pp. 187-197). ACM International Conference Proceedings Series.

McIntosh, P. (2010). *Action research and reflective practice*. London, UK: Routledge.

Mertens, D. M. (1998). *Research methods in education and psychology: Integrating diversity with quantitative and qualitative approaches*. Thousand Oaks, CA: Sage Publications.

Myers, M. D. (2004). Qualitative research in Information Systems. *MIS Quarterly*, *21*(2), 241-242. Retrieved May 2006 from http://www.qual.auckland.ac.nz/

O'Donovan, B., & Roode, D. (2002). A framework for understanding the emerging discipline of Information Systems. *Information Technology & People*, *15*(1), 26–41. doi:10.1108/09593840210423217

Olivier, M. S. (2004). *Information Technology research: A practical guide for computer science and informatics* (2nd ed.). Pretoria, South Africa: Van Schaik Publishers.

Orlikowski, W. J. (1993). CASE tools as organizational change: Investigating incremental and radical changes in systems development. *Management Information Systems Quarterly*, *17*(3). doi:10.2307/249774

Pather, S., & Remenyi, D. (2004). Some of the philosophical issues underpinning realism in Information Systems: From positivsim to critical realism. In G. Marsden, P. Kotzé & A. Adessina-Ojo (Eds.), *Fulfilling the Promise of ICT - Proceedings of SAICSIT 2004*. Pretoria.

Preece, J., Rogers, Y., & Sharp, H. (2007). *Interaction design: Beyond human-computer interaction*. John Wiley and Sons, Inc.

Reeves, T. C. (2000). Socially responsible educational technology research. *Educational Technology*, *40*(6), 19–28.

Roode, D. (2003). Information Systems research: A matter of choice? *Editorial in South African Computer Journal*, *30*, 1–2.

Russell, C. (2009). A systemic framework for managing e-learning adoption in campus universities: Individual strategies in context. *Association for Learning Technology Journal, (ALT-J). Research in Learning Technology, 17*(1), 3–19. doi:10.1080/09687760802649871

Schön, D. A. (1987). *Educating the reflective practitioner*. San Francisco, CA: Jossey-Bass Publishers.

Schulze, K., & Krömker, H. (2010). A framework to measure user experience of interactive online products. In Spink, A. J., Grieco, F., Krips, O. E., Loijens, L. W. S., Noldus, L. P. J. J., & Zimmerman, P. H. (Eds.), *Proceedings of Measuring Behaviour 2010*. Eindhoven, The Netherlands. doi:10.1145/1931344.1931358

Strauss, A. L., & Corbin, J. (1990). *Basics of qualitative research: Grounded theory procedures and techniques*. Newbury Park, CA: Sage.

Urquhart, C. (2002). Regrounding grounded theory – Or reinforcing old prejudices? A brief reply to Bryant. *The Journal of Information Technology Theory and Application, 4*(3), 43–54.

Urquhart, C., Lehmann, H., & Myers, M. D. (2010). Putting the 'theory' back into grounded theory: Guidelines for grounded theory studies in information systems. *Information Systems Journal, 20*, 357–381. doi:10.1111/j.1365-2575.2009.00328.x

Van der Merwe, T. M., & de Villiers, M. R. (2011). The partial approach to grounded theory integrated with activity theory: A generic framework illustrated by a base study in an e-learning context. *Alternation, 18*, 2.

Van der Merwe, T. M., van der Merwe, A. J., & Venter, L. M. (2010). A model to direct online continuous professional development opportunities for mathematics teachers in the South African context of disparities. *African Journal of Mathematics. Science and Technology Education, 14*(3), 65–80.

Vannoy, S. A., & Salam, A. F. (2010). Managerial interpretations of the role of Information Systems in competitive actions and firm performance: A grounded theory investigation. *Information Systems Research, 21*(3), 496–515. doi:10.1287/isre.1100.0301

Walsham, G. (1995a). Interpretive case studies in IS research: Nature and method. *European Journal of Information Systems, 4*(2), 74–81. doi:10.1057/ejis.1995.9

Walsham, G. (1995b). The emergence of interpretivism in IS research. *Information Systems Research, 6*(4), 376–394. doi:10.1287/isre.6.4.376

Wang, M.-L., & Chen, C.-L. (2009). Action research into e-learning curriculum development for library and Information Science in Taiwan. *Proceedings of the Asia-Pacific Conference on Library and Information Education and Practice, 2009* (pp. 437-449).

Wood-Harper, T. (1985). Research methods in Information Systems: Using action research. In Mumford, E. (Eds.), *Research methods in Information Systems*. North-Holland: Elsevier Science Publishers B.V.

Zuber-Skerrit, O. (1992). *Action research in higher education*. London, UK: Kogan Page.

Chapter 12
Models for Interpretive Information Systems Research, Part 2:
Design Research, Development Research, Design–Science Research, and Design–Based Research – A Meta–Study and Examples

M. R. (Ruth) De Villiers
University of South Africa, South Africa

ABSTRACT

This chapter introduces interpretive research as a background to research that is time-and context-depen-dent. The study presents practical, yet theoretical research approaches that are relevant to postgraduate studies and to ad-hoc research. The models proposed as interpretive research designs are development research, design-science research, and design-based research. Systems development, in and of itself, is not research, but when integrated with evaluation and applied both to solve real-world problems and to propose general design principles, it gives rise to development research. Design research – termed design-science research in the domain of information systems (where it has roots in software engineer-ing) and design-based research in educational technology (where the approaches are more pragmatic) – has clearly defined features and methods in each domain respectively. The common attributes are the generation of creative and innovative artifacts to serve in complex situations, and the joint advancement of theory and practice. The three research designs are described, and each is illustrated by an example of a study where the model was applied.

DOI: 10.4018/978-1-4666-0179-6.ch012

INTRODUCTION AND BACKGROUND

Interpretive research, which originated in the behavioural social sciences, is increasingly applied in Information Systems (IS). In line with the current emphasis within IS on the social dimensions of computing, researchers and practitioners are taking cognizance of human factors and behavioural aspects. This chapter forms Part 2 of a discourse on models for interpretive information systems research. It follows on Part 1, which is a separate chapter in the book, Chapter I.7a. This meta-research study is not aimed at major systems for business, but more at small-scale systems for personal computing, in particular user-centered educational software systems. It suggests various underlying theoretical models to guide the research and development process, providing cohesion and internal consistency.

For overviews of the positivist and interpretive research paradigms, qualitative and quantitative research methods, and relevant terminology, the reader is referred to Part 1 (Chapter I.7a). Part 1 discusses interpretive IS research, then describes and graphically illustrates two interpretive approaches: *action research* and *grounded theory*, explaining their operation as research designs and giving examples of situations where they were applied as the underlying research model. This chapter, Part 2, has a similar approach and structure, and presents three models from the family of design- and development research – *development research, design-science research* (so-called in IS), and *design-based research* (in the educational technology context). In three respective sections, descriptions are given of their features and processes, and examples are provided of studies where these research designs were applied.

We briefly re-visit some key concepts from Part 1. Research paradigms are based on varying philosophical foundations and conceptions of reality (Cohen, Manion & Morrison, 2005; du Poy & Gitlin, 1998; Olivier 2004). Each paradigm, in turn, is implemented by associated methodological strategies.

The positivist paradigm holds that knowledge is absolute and objective, and that a single objective reality exists. Positivism is implemented by the scientific method, in which knowledge is discovered by controlled means, such as experiments and other quantitative methods based on numeric data and measurements. Results should be value-free, consistent, unbiased, and replicable.

Interpretivism, by contrast, aims to find new interpretations or underlying meanings and permits the accommodation of multiple correct approaches and findings, mediated by time, context and researcher. Inquiry is value-related, influenced by context and by researchers' subjective interpretations. Interpretivism is associated mainly with qualitative studies that address research questions relating to phenomena in naturalistic, human-based social settings. Data is mainly verbal and research is often triangulated by multiple methods of data collection.

Hybrid approaches, combining interpretivism and positivism, are also used. Mixed-methods research capitalizes on applying both qualitative and quantitative methods, which are not mutually exclusive, although one is usually predominant, e.g., QUAL + quant (Creswell, 2009). Many studies require eclectic inquiry to cover the terrain and to apply methodological triangulation and data triangulation. Qualitative research can be exploratory, with its findings used to formulate hypotheses for subsequent quantitative analysis and verification. Conversely, the findings of quantitative studies can be tested and extended by using qualitative research, e.g., interviews, to enrich the data.

Research designs and paradigms used in Information Systems, are under the spotlight (Baskerville, 1999; Cockton, 2002; De Villiers, 2005; Glass, Ramesh & Vessey, 2004; Myers, 2004; Pather & Remenyi, 2004). Interpretive and evaluative approaches have become accepted (Klein & Myers, 1999; Roode, 2003; Walsham,

1995a; 1995b). Klein and Myers claim that interpretive studies provide deep insight and help the IS research community understand human thought and behavior in social and organizational contexts.

The present study suggests practical, yet theoretical, approaches, which are applicable to postgraduate studies, basic research, and *ad hoc-* research. Over and above technological and computational dimensions, attention is paid to human and contextual factors. The human-computer interaction (HCI) aims of generating usable, interactive, user-centric computing applications, are acknowledged and applied in domains beyond business systems, for example, systems for e-learning/e-training and for bridging the digital divide.

The next sections discuss and illustrate the selected models and their use as research designs. Each approach has associated methods and techniques and is illustrated by practical examples, some of which relate to research by the author, her colleagues, and postgraduate students.

DEVELOPMENT RESEARCH

Introduction to Design and Development Research

The family of design research and development research comprises various research models. Terminology varies, but the concepts of innovation, design, constructed artifacts and/or interventions are common characteristics. The variants considered are *development research* (an early term) and two forms: of *design research* (current term). In Information Systems (IS) and Information Technology (IT), design research is called *design-science research*, and in Educational Technology, the prevalent term is *design-based research*. Educational systems, i.e. e-learning applications, form a subset of IS at its intersection with the learning sciences, and are common topics for postgraduate studies.

Definition and Origins

Development research (DR) has a dual focus:

* It develops practical and innovative ways of *solving real problems.*
* It proposes general design principles to *inform future development decisions.*

A classic seminal publication by Nunamaker, Chen and Purdin (1991:89) sets the original foundations for DR, referring to 'systems development as a research methodology' and advocating a systems development research process, based on software engineering methods. Nunamaker *et al* point out that a developed system can serve both as a proof-of-concept of the research, and as a real artifact that becomes the object of further, extended research. They advocate an integrated and cyclic systems development approach to research, including theory building (conceptual frameworks and mathematical models); experimentation (simulations, fieldwork and lab experiments); and observation (case studies and surveys). The outcomes of this multi-methodological approach are prototypes, product development and, ultimately, transfer of technology, as the results contribute to the body of knowledge. The outcomes evolve due to performance testing and evaluative research. The subsequent DR approaches of Reeves (2000) and van den Akker (1999; 2002), which originated in educational technology research, aim for practical and scientific contributions, supporting graduate students and researchers in pursuing development goals after a tradition of research based on the scientific-method. DR is problem-oriented, searching for new and innovative solutions, while striving for findings that are transferable, practical, and socially responsible. The complex and dynamic relationship between theory and application is acknowledged, as DR guides practice by generating design principles and methods that are both theoretically underpinned and empirically tested.

Epistemology of DR

Development research has a pragmatic epistemology as it acknowledges collaborative shaping by researchers and practitioners. Describing the knowledge acquired from DR, Van den Akker (1999) distinguishes between substantive design principles, relating to characteristics of suitable *products* and methodological aspects, with a procedural emphasis for optimal development *processes*.

In formative research, knowledge is inductively extracted from the experience of using and evaluating a prototype developed for the study. This connects the two branches of the dual focus, namely the developing solution to a specific problem and the evolution of generalisable design principles. The experiential evidence obtained from iteratively studying a prototype in use, is enhanced when integrated with theoretical arguments.

Research Process and Methods

Development research generates different kinds of research questions. *Descriptive* questions examine the nature and extent of a problem, while *development* questions investigate an intervention or new product to address the need. A *principial* question aims for generalisable principles and guidelines for use in an application domain.

The process commences with the analysis, design and development of an artifact or intervention as a solution for a real-world problem. This, in and of itself, is not yet research. It becomes research when the design-and-develop project is conducted from the perspective of a researcher striving to understand issues of the application domain and its target users, such as the required characteristics of products and reasons for such. Research is based on iterative analysis, design, development, implementation and formative evaluation (ADDIE model of instructional technology), which feeds into redevelopment and improvement. Van den Akker (2002) terms the

process 'successive approximation of the ideals'. Evaluations can be done by one or more usability evaluation methods, such as surveys among end users, observation, formal usability testing in a laboratory, logging, etc.

There are various models of DR. The approach used by van den Akker and his co-researcher, Plomp, (van den Akker, 1999; 2002) refers to outcomes of an intervention. *Immediate outcomes* relate to results of using an intervention or product within the cyclic process, and *distant outcomes* emerge when the immediate outcomes lead to generalisable principles. Reeves' (2000) model emphasizes iterative interaction between researchers and practitioners to clarify the problems and refine potential solutions in a process of evolutionary prototyping and evaluation. Figure 4 is a generic DR representation. Its iterative phases can be effectively used to structure an IS research process, providing continuity and cohesion.

Application and Example

Many IS studies involve the generation of software artifacts or web applications. These vary from simple prototypes, through interactive web sites with backend databases, through to virtual reality simulations. Design, implementation and testing comprise the focus area of development but are not research. The introduction of evaluation, which entails more than testing of functionality, constitutes a meaningful contribution to the body of knowledge. As previously stated, dual-focused research producing both an effective solution and generalisable principles for the domain, further enriches the research.

A product – often a prototype – can be custom-built to solve a problem, then iteratively evaluated and refined. For example, Conradie and de Villiers (2004) of the School of Computing at the University of South Africa (UNISA) describe the design and evaluation of an educational software tool to solve a real-world assessment problem by electronically assessing open-ended textual input, termed 'free text'. Many Web-based learning environments tend to become repositories for course materials and students' deliverables. There is a lack of interactive, dynamic pages that respond diagnostically to their academic contributions. The situation is mitigated by Web 2.0 technologies and online discussion forums but, in general, educational WWW environments present multi-media content and share information, but fall short in assessment. Most electronic assessment is in the form of multiple-choice testing. Conradie set out to address the need and improve the effectiveness of e-learning by developing, implementing, testing and analysing a prototype tool for automated assessment of textual inputs.

The tool used keyword searches and pattern-matching techniques (not artificial intelligence) to assign grades to short-answer free-text responses on course content. In line with the iterations in Figure 1, two variants of the prototype were designed and used as interventions with third-year Computer Science students. The first variant demonstrated feasibility of the e-assessment, while the second was an interactive web-based extension, the *CyberClassroom*, which provided interactive support by supplementing the scoring mechanism with instant feedback (related to the input) and animations and by recording scores. Students participated in evaluation, giving qualitative evaluation data in different ways – posting messages on the *CyberClassroom's* notice board

and communicating directly with the instructor-developer. Further empirical evaluation compared the scores with those of manual grading by an expert human assessor. Following evaluation and identification of problems and usability issues in the prototype, the intervention was refined. Use of the electronic tool achieved dual outcomes: an immediate outcome by reducing the tedious processes of manual marking (grading) and recording results for a course in the BSc programme; and it also provided a generic system for cross-domain application, since it could be exported, context-free, to databases containing questions, solution patterns and grading algorithms for other content.

As well as being used for research and development for software solutions, DR which is relevant to computer science and engineering, can be used to generate hardware solutions and associated generic principles.

DESIGN-SCIENCE RESEARCH IN INFORMATION SYSTEMS

The first few paragraphs serve as an introduction to both design-science research and design-based research.

Design research is increasingly undertaken in disciplines such as information systems, the learning sciences, and educational technology. Due to differences between the ways it is applied

Figure 1. Development research model (synthesized by de Villiers, 2005; influenced by Reeves, 2000)

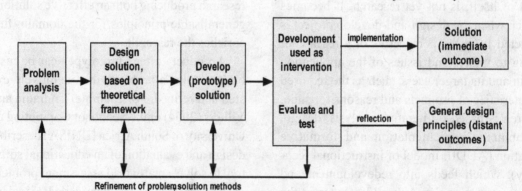

in different areas, terminologies, methodologies, and practices vary. For this reason, the so-called *design-science research* in information systems (IS) and information technology (IT) is treated separately from the *design-based research* of educational technology (ET).

Definition and Origins

Design research owes its origin to the Nobel laureate, Herbert Simon (Simon, 1981), who distinguishes between the *natural sciences* and the so-called *design sciences*. Natural sciences relate to natural phenomena such as those described in physics, astronomy, anatomy, etc. Associated descriptive theories explain how phenomena occur, discovering underlying laws and relationships. Design sciences, by contrast, are 'sciences of the artificial' and relate to man-made objects and artificial phenomena, generated in applied sciences such as medical technology, engineering, architecture, product design, and instruction. Associated prescriptive theories and models set out goals to be achieved and procedures to accomplish ends. For Simon, design science achieves its potential when innovative artifacts are created that solve real-world problems. Applied design sciences are characterized by problem-solving processes, invention, and the construction and evaluation of artifacts or interventions. Design science led, in turn, to design research, which:

- In information systems (IS) and IT, is called *design-science research* (DSR) and relates mainly, but not exclusively, to business artifacts. It is discussed in this section.
- In educational technology and e-learning, is termed *design-based research* (DBR) and is discussed in the next section.

DSR and DBR are not primarily development models. Instead, they model the research involved in the design and development of innovative prod-

ucts and environments, particularly in complex domains.

This section overviews the general IS approach of design-science research (DSR). The literature relates more to ISs in the workplace than to personal computing. According to the *Design Research in Information Systems Group* (Design Research in Information Systems (DRIS), 2006), design research changes the state of the world by introducing novel, performance-improving artifacts. DSR is a problem-solving activity involving invention, evaluation, measurement of artifacts, and investigation of their impact. Hevner, March, Park & Ram (2004) describe design science research as a problem-solving approach, rooted in engineering and Simon's sciences of the artificial. DSR aims to create innovative and effective technological artifacts as solutions to problems in ill-defined environments characterized by complex interactions and flexibility. Human cognition, creativity and teamwork are required to generate solutions. Existing foundational and methodological knowledge help to achieve rigour but, where there is no pre-existing knowledge base, designers use intuition, experience, and even trial-and-error. Prototypes are particularly valuable for proof-of-concept purposes.

Epistemology of DSR

Design research changes real-world states by introducing novel artifacts. In contrast to positivist ontologies, it acknowledges multiple world states, but does not view these states as identical to the multiple realities of interpretivism. DRIS (2006) suggests that DSR is neither positivist nor interpretive research, but in between as a philosophical perspective with a pragmatic, problem-solving approach that tolerates ambiguity. DSR has aspects of interpretivism, since its cycles of observation and interventions are similar to action research, but with shorter time frames.

The basis of DSR's knowledge claims can be termed knowing-through-making'. Hevner *et al*

(2004) explain that knowledge emanating from DSR is obtained via construction in context, and its meaning is iteratively revealed through cyclic study of the constructed object.

Research Process and Methods

Design has double connotations. As a verb, it relates to processes and, as a noun, to products. When design research is applied to classic ISs (business applications in organizations), its outputs are not only the complete systems, but also their building blocks. March and Smith (1995) and Hevner, March, Park and Ram (2004) describe the artifacts and activities of DSR. The output artifacts of DSR are not restricted to functional computing systems. Rather, they are defined as constructs, models, methods and instantiations: *Constructs* or *concepts* are the domain vocabulary that describe problems and specify solutions. They may be formal notations for data modeling or informal text. *Models* are forms or representations where constructs are combined to show relationships, e.g. entity-relationship diagrams. Models are useful in the process of designing an application. *Methods* are ways of performing goal-directed activities, often involving a set of steps, e.g. an algorithm. They build on constructs and models in the problem-solving process of systems analysis and development. An *instantiation* is an actual implementation that performs a task in a particular environment. It may be an IS itself, a prototype, or a tool for designing ISs. Instantiations are the final link in the research chain, as they operationalise constructs, models and methods. Citing Rossi & Sein (2003) and Purao (2002), DRIS (2006) suggested a fifth output, construction of *better theory*. Theories emerge as methods are studied and as construction and evaluation elaborate existing theories.

The two main complementary activities in generating DSR outputs are building and evaluation (March & Smith, 1995; Hevner, March, Park, & Ram, 2004). Constructs, models, methods, and instantiations are *designed and built* to meet identified needs within the user community, usually a business context. Foundational knowledge is required for building theories, frameworks and tools from prior research, although when completely new artifacts are created, they are experimental, and often done with little prior knowledge. *Evaluation* determines how well the artifacts function in their environments and feeds back into building. Criteria and metrics are established to judge performance in context or to compare versions. IS evaluation uses mathematical modeling and computational techniques, as well as empirical and qualitative methods to identify problems and strengths. Efficiency, effectiveness, and impact on environment should be considered, as well as human issues as subjects interact with artifacts in context, which requires qualitative study.

DRIS describes design research as: awareness of problem; suggestion of new, creative functionality in an area of complexity; design and development of an artifact with novelty in the design; evaluation feeding an iterative loop back to design and development; concluding the research with a 'satisficing' end, which means finding satisfactory solutions while sacrificing an exhaustive search through all possibilities.

The artifacts and activities are combined in the *Information technology design-research framework* (March & Smith, 1995), which maps the activities of building and evaluation against the four artifacts: constructs, models, methods, and instantiations. Hevner *et al* (2004) extended the framework, presenting a comprehensive *Information systems research framework* in the context of Simon's (1981) problem space containing organizations, people, and technology. This integrated framework shows the contributions of design research and behavioural research to IS research. Hevner *et al* also compiled guidelines for design-science research in IS:

i.   **Design:** An innovative, viable artifact must be designed and produced (construct, model, method, or instantiation) to address a particular organisational problem. The artifact is unlikely to be a full-scale operational product for use in practice.

ii. **Relevance:** A technology-based solution must have utility in addressing the problem.

iii. **Evaluation:** Utility, quality and efficacy must be demonstrated by appropriate evaluation methods. Integration of the artifact into its environment should be investigated. Evaluation methods include observational, analytical, experimental, testing, and descriptive techniques.

iv. **Research contributions:** These should be clear and verifiable in terms of the artifact's design foundations, as well as new, innovative and interesting.

v. **Rigour:** Rigorous methods should be used in construction and evaluation, but rigour should not reduce relevance in the application domains. Metrics should be related to the evaluation criteria. Furthermore, the human aspects should be addressed appropriately.

vi. **Design as a search process:** Suitable methods are iteration, heuristic search, and generate-and-test cycles. The problem can initially be simplified and decomposed, followed by expansion, i.e. a 'satisficing' approach.

vii. **Communication:** Results should be presented both to technological and user-oriented audiences. The former require construction and evaluation details, while the latter are concerned about the impact, novelty and effectiveness of the artifact.

Finally, Hevner and Chatterjee (2010) acknowledge that the progress of design research in IS has not been rapid.

Application and Example

Artifacts generated by DSR are not restricted to the design of full computing systems; the artifacts can be models, methods, and instantiations. The example that follows, relates to a model and methods for a procedure in the HCI subdiscipline of IS, namely procedures for formal usability testing of interactive e-learning systems (Masemola and de Villiers, 2006). Research has been conducted at UNISA's School of Computing to generate frameworks and methods for usability testing of e-learning applications for teaching, learning, and hands-on practicing of cognitive subject matter.

Usability testing (UT) data is obtained from real-time monitoring, logging, video and audio recordings, as well as eye-tracking. Procedures for controlled evaluation of conventional task-based information processing systems in usability laboratories are well established. The usual goal of UT is to identify problems in conventional software interfaces by measuring participants' performance in terms of: time spent, errors made, recall, and subjective response. The present example, by contrast, investigates interaction with CD-based e-learning tutorials for teaching and learning theoretical computer science. As well as applying performance metrics that test the interface and interaction design (Preece, Rogers & Sharp, 2007), the actual learning of cognitive content and the associated computational skills must be studied. The approach differs from conventional usability testing, since the distinctive characteristics of human perception and learning processes require a different framework. Differences occur in terms of:

Time spent: Efficiency cannot be judged by low times spent on learning tasks. Users have different learning styles and approaches.

View of errors: It is not always desirable to minimise errors. Usability errors should be considered as errors, but cognitive errors can be viewed as learning activities.

What is investigated: Use of the learning content is analysed, as well as interaction at the interface.

This pioneering research contributes to a generic UT framework and metrics for investigating e-learning applications and human learning behaviours, as the researchers used the sophisticated technology of a controlled usability lab in novel and interesting ways to study students' actual learning experiences with e-learning tutorials. This is in line with DSR's aim of creating innovative technological artifacts to address problems in ill-defined environments characterized by complex interactions. Masemola and de Villiers (2006) developed an initial model, a set of methods, processes, measurements and documents for investigating UT of interactive e-learning applications. To achieve rigour and to base the methodology and test plan on accepted methodological knowledge, HCI literature was studied. Features relating to learning behaviour and cognitive processing were also incorporated. Participants were actual students, who were requested to verbalise out loud as they did the specified learning tasks, expressing their expectations, reasoning, and interpretations. By recording 'think out loud' protocols over and above visual observation, the monitoring technology provides added value, informing researchers how learners use their time when apparently not engaged in active interaction, or doing exercises. It distinguishes between time spent on the interfaces and navigation, and time spent on cognitive activities as learners engage with the instructional content. The different types of errors made, were of great significance in the framework. Furthermore, a best-case scenario was acquired for benchmarking learner performance.

This research continued as Adebesin, de Villiers and Ssemugabi (2009) refined and modified the model and methodologies. The initial study had showed that think aloud was unnatural for some participants and distracted them from learning. In the follow-up study, verbalisation was combined with co-discovery to address this reticence. Participants were paired and tackled tasks collaboratively. Conversation and peer teaching occurred naturally and they were less inhibited about expressing opinions. Co-discovery also identified causes of learning problems. Re-

search is ongoing, extending the methodology by qualitative investigation of types of errors. In this regard, De Villiers (2009) presented early work on analysis of usability errors and cognitive errors as a pilot study for the in-depth research currently underway. Since 2008, the research has been triangulated with eye tracking studies, increasing the validity and reliability of the studies. To repeat, the artifact undergoing DSR is not the e-learning system being evaluated; rather, it is *the methodological model* for usability testing of interactive e-learning in cognitive domains. In line with DSR principles, the research provides pragmatic findings and shows how the evolving artifact functions in contributing to knowledge about learning with technology. Synergistically, the model proposes generic methodological approaches for usability testing in the domain of interactive e-learning.

Findings are presented to research communities, achieving the DSR requirement that results should be communicated both to technological and user-oriented audiences.

DESIGN-BASED RESEARCH IN EDUCATIONAL TECHNOLOGY

The first few paragraphs of the preceding section on design research and design science, also serve as an introduction to this section.

Design research is also undertaken in the learning sciences and educational technology (ET), where the prevailing term is *design-based research* (DBR). It is a maturing extension of DR and is increasingly used as the model for studies on *development of e-learning materials* and environments. It is widely discussed in current literature, involving meta-analyses as well as reported research.

DBR is a paradigm for educational inquiry where the goal of using technology to solve problems and design learning environments in complex ill-structured situations, is related to the goal of developing prototypical theories (Design-Based Research Collective, 2003; Wang & Hannafin, 2005). With regard to the first goal, the success or failure of a design in its setting should be documented and explained. With reference to the second, research should result in contextually-sensitive, sharable design theories, communicated to practitioners and designers. The process by which this occurs is development and research through continuous cycles of analysis, design, development, enactment, evaluation, and redesign. Amiel and Reeves (2008) argue that technology itself should be viewed not as an artifact, but as a process, producing a continuous cycle of design-reflection-design.

Definition and Origins

Design science relates to man-made objects/phenomena, including instruction with its prescriptive theories and procedures. Education is characterized by complex problems, which are addressed by the invention of solutions, and the construction and evaluation of artifacts. It is a suitable domain for the application of design-based research as a paradigm for educational inquiry. The terminology evolved from the 'design experiments' of educational practice conducted by Brown (1992) and Collins (1992) through 'development research' (Reeves, 2000; van den Akker, 1999), as addressed earlier in this chapter, and consolidated at 'design-based research'. To clarify terminology, Wang and Hannafin (2005:7) compiled a useful table of terms and methods.

Barab and Squire (2004) define design-based research as a series of approaches which aim to produce new theories, artifacts, and practices related to teaching/learning in natural settings. In the specific context of ET, DBR is characterized by:

- *Pragmatic and theoretical approaches*: generating and extending prototypical theories; producing principles to inform and improve practice.

- *Grounding*: design of learning environments in real-world settings, based on appropriate learning/instructional theories.

- *Problem-focused ethos*: addressing complex problems in real contexts.

- *Interactivity, iteration and flexibility*: designer-researcher-practitioner-participant teamwork; continuous cycles of analysis, design, prototypes, development, enactment, formative evaluation, and usability analysis; and revision and improved-design.

- *Transparent communication*: research should result in contextually-sensitive, sharable design theories, communicated to practitioners and designers.

- *Integration*: hybrid research methods; data from multiple sources; integration of design principles with new technologies to solve complex problems.

- *Rigorous and reflective inquiry*: testing and refining innovative e-learning environments and defining new design principles.

- *Contextualision*: success or failure of a design should be documented with relation to its setting.

- *Extension of existing methodologies:* such as action research, which sets out to change situations.

(Wang and Hannafin, 2005; Design-Based Research Collective, 2003; Reeves, 2006)

Epistemology and Ethos of DBR

Reeves (2000) cites Stokes' (1997) call for use-inspired basic research, where new knowledge advances new types of research, producing a reverse model that moves from applied research to basic research. The experimental generation of new prototypes highlights the roles of cognition, intuition, creativity and teamwork in solving problems and generating knowledge. The philosophical foundation of DBR is not positivism, but pragmatic enquiry, where judgement is based on the ability of a theory to work in the real world (Barab & Squire, 2004). Evidence-based claims demonstrate that a particular design works, relating it to contemporary theoretical issues. This enquiry occurs in naturalistic settings, rather than laboratory environments, as knowledge about artifacts such as e-learning systems evolves in context, and even by trial and error. Contextual investigations lead to a minimal ontology, in that researchers cannot return to the laboratory to test their claims further. Moreover, the research is not replicable due to the role of context.

Validation occurs when results regarding the designed object are validated by actual use. Validity in DBR can be achieved by iteration, as the iterative evaluation processes confirm findings and align theory, design and practice (Design-Based Research Collective, 2003).

Dede (2005:6) expresses concerns about combining designs from the 'skills of creative designers' and research by 'rigorous scholars'. When *designers* have free reign, there may be 'design creep' as exploratory sweeping interventions evolve into full-scale initiatives instead of being bounded research. A technological innovator might champion a particular technological solutions and search for situations in which to apply it. Pure *researchers* have contrasting weaknesses, aiming for designs where the variables are suitable for straightforward data collection and analysis. Some such scholars have 'design constipation' (Dede, 2005:6), as they apply analytic and methodological frameworks at the expense of effective, scalable and sustainable innovations.

Kelly (2003), by contrast, lauds DBR's convergence of research and design. First, it is innovative and acknowledges the expertise of true designers. It plays an exploratory role in novel environments, where it addresses relevant research questions, yet solves problems in pragmatic ways. Second, it contributes to contextualised theory development as well as the advancement of cumulative design knowledge. Kelly's third point is that DBR fosters cross-disciplinary exchange of expertise

and leads to insights when interventions occur in so-called 'messy' settings. In complex and ill-structured environments with real-world messiness, the design of artifacts and the development of appropriate theories proceed concurrently, each mutually informing the other.

Design research in e-learning has different methodologies and frameworks from the design research of pure IS with its software engineering roots (previous section). DBR research has methodologies and frameworks based on a strong interpretive paradigm, qualitative studies and mixed methods (Creswell, 2009). This contrasts with its traditional positivist stances and quantitative studies.

Research Process and Methods

The advent of design research in applied computing disciplines, such as information and communication technology in e-learning, owes much to design experiments, which occurred not only in the context of educational technology, but also in the general learning sciences, where 'design' may refer to the design of experiments or learning configurations, not just to the design of artifacts. Brown (1992) engineered innovative educational environments and did experimental studies in natural settings, teaching children to read, self-reflect, and retain content. The dual goal was to inform practice and work towards theoretical models. Collins (1992) conducted design experiments on educational technology in the classroom, investigating, evaluating and comparing the use of various technologies and computing tools for learning about geographical phenomena. The idea was to construct a systematic methodology, a design science of education, to support educators in exploring the problem space of designs for teaching and learning with technology.

Collins, Joseph and Bielaczyc (2004), using the term 'design research', reflectively outline the emerging theoretical and methodological issues. Generic research findings are required, but the fundamental emphasis is on studying learning in context and using methods that situate research in real-world settings, not in controlled laboratories. Real-world classroom situations present challenges due to the lack of control and large amounts of data from triangulated ethnographic and quantitative studies (Collins *et al*, 2004). Studies should be managed with systematic adjustments, so that each adaptation provides further experimentation. Collins *et al* also raise the issue that an implemented design may differ from the intended design. This is in line with 'incorporated subversion' (Squires, 1999), where users configure, or subvert, an environment or system to their own needs and use it in ways not intended by the original designer. This can have positive or negative repercussions.

Barab and Squire's (2004) view highlights the generation and testing of theories to support understanding and prediction of learning, along with the development of technological tools. Other research methods also generate theory, but DBR's defining features are its goals of influencing practice with real changes at local level and developing tangible applications with the potential for adoption elsewhere. However, Barab and Squire express a word of caution regarding the transfer of context-specific research claims to inform broad practice.

DBR features have been extracted from the extensive meta-analyses and reflective studies of Amiel and Reeves (2008), Barab and Squire (2004), Cobb, Confrey, diSessa, Lehrer, and Schauble (2003), the Design-Based Research Collective (2003), Kelly (2003) and Wang and Hannafin (2005). The present author synthesized and classified them into Table 1, which summarises the main features of DBR in e-learning systems.

Table 1. Summary of features of design-based research models (synthesized by the author)

Features of DBR models	Elaboration
Real-world complex problems	Design theory addresses complex problems in collaboration with practitioners/educators.
Problem solutions grounded in pre-existing theories	Where appropriate theories/principles pre-exist, design should be theory-driven, along with technological affordances, to propose solutions to the problems. In non-standard cases, novel pragmatic solutions are sought.
Innovation	Underlying innovative approach: DBR should investigate less-common practices and generate technological support; design of innovations, novelty, and interventionist approaches.
Engineering	Systematic methodology that involves designing and studying means or artifacts of learning.
Iterative design	Cycles of design, enactment, analysis, redesign.
Context	Research studies in context, i.e. in naturalistic settings; use of artifacts/interventions in the real-world; theories also to be contextualized; responsive to emergent features of the setting (Kelly, 2003).
Empirical research	Studying tangible, real-world products, which ideally, should be usable elsewhere, i.e. influence on teaching, learning and training practice.
Refining the artifact /system	Using formative evaluation to derive research findings; design and explore artifacts, environments, etc. to refine them and define new design principles.
Output products: 1. Useful real-world products 2. Development of theory	Real-world products: technical and methodological tools; frameworks; interventions; even curricula. These offer immediate value in the environment of use. Theories that are generated, evaluated and refined in a reflective cycle: they provide a set of theoretical constructs that be transferred and adapted beyond the initial environment.
Pragmatic	The theories developed should do real work and be supported by evidence-based claims.
Synergy	Design and research are advanced concurrently. Theory and practice are advanced concurrently.
Rigorous and reflective inquiry	To test and refine innovative learning environments and to define new design principles.

Figure 2. Model of design-based research (synthesized by the author)

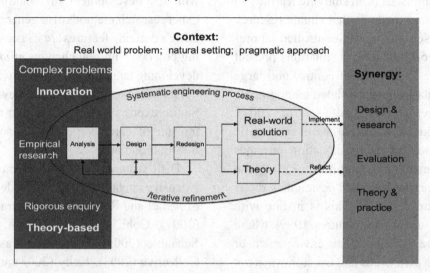

The present author adds that evaluation should consider human-factors, such as learner-centricity and the usability of artifacts.

Figure 2 complements Table 1 by depicting the concepts and processes of DBR. The central model represents its predecessor, development research (Figure 1) with its iterations and evaluative feedback loops. The surrounding infrastructure, which represents the context of real-world settings with complex problems, indicates DBR's evolution. The left side shows the approaches of innovation, rigorous empirical research, and a theoretical basis. The right side lists synergistic consequences of the reflective processes, as design and research are advanced jointly impacting on practice and on theory.

Application and Example

DBR is an approach for generating technological tools and e-learning environments in the complex intersection of learning and technology. In a bold venture, the Digital Doorway (DD) Project of the Meraka Institute at the Council for Scientific and Industrial Research (CSIR) in South Africa installed rugged computer terminals in schools, colleges and public community facilities in low-income areas (Gush, De Villiers, Smith, & Cambridge, 2011). DDs offer unassisted learning and peer-teaching of basic computer skills, as well as the use of software applications ranging from entertainment, through education and information, to reference systems for research. The DD product and processes illustrate DBR in action, implementing many of the concepts and processes in Table 1 and Figure 2, as design and research, and theory and practice; are advanced concurrently in a real-world situation of complexity, where low-income, technologically-disadvantaged communities live beyond the digital divide. Infrastructure is lacking and, in many cases, not even school teachers are computer literate.

Following the success of the *Hole-in-the-Wall* experiment in India, which offered minimally invasive education and unassisted learning at computer terminals, DDs were implemented as a pragmatic and innovative solution to an African problem. Open-source software is used; usage is free and available to the entire community, although secondary school students are the greatest user group. Learning is motivated by children's natural curiosity and cooperative approach, both of which are evidenced in use of DDs. This ICT for Development (ICT4D) venture is customized to the context. Since most DD terminals are located in easily accessible public venues, their rugged and robust, vandal-proof computer housing contrasts with typical lab-based computers. Lively, often noisy, social interaction occurs alongside learning activities.

Since the project commenced in 2002, iterative development and evaluation have occurred. The project has synergistic deployment and research phases, mutually feeding into each other. Empirical research employs various research- and data gathering methods. In an engineering approach, tracking tools record usage and collect quantitative data by automated on-site logging (Gush & de Villiers, 2010). Subjective qualitative data is accumulated via interviews, observation and video of user interaction, and surveys. Rigorous and reflective enquiry has led to refinements and enhancements. From an initial single prototype, the hardware housing evolved to a multi-terminal configuration, and rollouts have occurred at over 200 sites. Poor electricity supply at some sites has led to solar-powered systems. A version has been produced for disabled users. Software is upgraded and content has been increased to better meet the needs of the users. Certain games, edutainment,

Table 2. Summary of the three models and their use as research designs

Properties	Development research (DR)	Design Research	
		Design sciences are 'sciences of the artificial', relating to man-made artifacts (Simon, 1981). Design science gave rise to design research.	
		Design-science research (DSR)	**Design-based research (DBR)**
Goals	1) Development of practical and innovative solutions to real-world problems (immediate outcomes). 2) Transferable and generalisable design principles to inform future decisions (distant outcomes).	1) Introduction of novel artifacts to enhance performance. Problem-solving via invention, evaluation, measurement, and impact studies. 2) Theories emerge; existing theories are elaborated.	1) Implementation of novel educational technology solutions in complex situations. New products and practices in real-world settings. 2) Development/extension of models and contextual design theories, shared with practitioners and designers.
	All three have a dual focus: developing products and contributing to the body of knowledge.		
Distinct features	Pragmatic epistemology, based on collaboration between researchers and practitioners. Problem-solving orientation. Acknowledges complex and dynamic relationship between theory, principles, practice and application.	Rooted in engineering. Use of novel artifacts to change real-world states. Solutions generated by human cognition, creativity and teamwork in ill-defined, complex areas. 'Satisficing' findings, obtaining satisfactory solutions but sacrificing exhaustive search.	Rigorous and reflective inquiry into real problems in education or training Contextually-sensitive. Design experiments to find both practical outputs (innovative designs and prototypes) and theoretical outputs (contextualized theories)
Processes	Integrated and iterative analysis, design, development, implementation and evaluation processes. Problems clarified and solutions refined during the above processes. The developed system serves as proof-of-concept.	'Design' relating to both products and processes. *Products:* complete systems and building blocks, i.e. constructs, models, methods and instantiations. *Processes:* complementary activities of construction-in-context and cyclic evaluation studies, involving mathematical modeling and empirical studies.	Convergence of research, design and feedback. Continuous cycles of analysis, design, development, enactment, evaluation and redesign. Pragmatic inquiry, evidence-based claims, validation by use. Multi-disciplinary expertise. Interpretive paradigm, qualitative studies and mixed methods.
	All three have iterative/cyclic design processes		
Application	Information systems (origin); Educational technology	Information Systems	Educational Technology / e-Learning

and information packages have been uniquely developed for the South African context. With further improvements in view, current studies are investigating usability issues and content usage.

Participants can be collaborators, as a feedback mechanism gives them the opportunity to type in comments and requests, which have contributed to extensions to DD features. Community leaders and other stakeholders have joined Meraka researchers at workshops on implementation and usage aspects.

Finally, there are dual output products: the useful real-world systems which have contributed to basic ICT literacy and, second, to the development of theories regarding effective and ineffective systems, deployment strategies, and the design of technology for rural contexts. Knowledge obtained from the systems is transferable to similar installations elsewhere.

CONCLUSION

Table 2 summarises the main features of the three research designs discussed in this chapter, namely: development research, design-science research (so termed in the discipline of information systems) and design-based research (term used in educational technology). The table shows the similarities and common origins of the models, yet highlights their distinctive features.

This chapter comprised Part 2 of a study of models for interpretive information systems research. The three research designs considered – development research, design-science research, and design-based research – were influenced by design science and the associated design research. They all have undergirding theoretical frameworks and processes, as well as repertoires of methodological and reflective strategies to model and guide a cohesive research process. Outcomes are the production of effective artifacts with real-world utility and transferability to other settings.

NOTE

An earlier version of part of this chapter appeared as an article "Interpretive Research Models for Informatics: Action Research, Grounded Theory, and the Family of Design- and Development Research", *Alternation* 12,2 (2005): 10 - 52, and is re-used here with the permission of the publisher, CSSALL (© 2005 by CSSALL, P.O. Box 1734, Wandsbeck, Durban 3631, RSA). All rights reserved. The present version is based on a reduced form of the article in *Alternation*, augmented with new content.

REFERENCES

Adebesin, T. F., De Villiers, M. R., & Ssemugabi, S. (2009). Usability testing of e-learning: An approach incorporating co-discovery and think-aloud. *Proceedings of the 2009 Conference of the South African Computer Lecturers' Association, SACLA 2009* (pp. 6-15). ACM International Conference Proceedings Series.

Amiel, T., & Reeves, T. C. (2008). Design-based research and educational technology: Rethinking technology and the research agenda. *Journal of Educational Technology & Society, 11*(4), 29–40.

Barab, S., & Squire, K. (2004). Design-based research: Putting a stake in the ground. *Journal of the Learning Sciences, 13*(1), 1–14. doi:10.1207/s15327809jls1301_1

Baskerville, R. L. (1999). Investigating Information Systems with action research. *Communications of the Association for Information Systems, 2*(3), Article 4.

Brown, A. L. (1992). Design experiments: Theoretical and methodological challenges in creating complex interventions in classroom settings. *Journal of the Learning Sciences, 2*(2), 141–178. doi:10.1207/s15327809jls0202_2

Cobb, P., Confrey, J., Disessa, A., Lehrer, R., & Schauble, L. (2003). Design experiments in educational research. *Educational Researcher, 32*(1), 9–13. doi:10.3102/0013189X032001009

Cockton, G. (2002). *My grounded design page.* Retrieved March 2011 from http://www.cet.sunderland.ac.uk/~cs0gco/grounded.htm

Cohen, L., Manion, L., & Morrison, K. (2005). *Research methods in education* (5th ed.). London, UK: RoutledgeFalmer.

Collins, A. (1992). Toward a design science of education. In Scanlon, E., & O'Shea, T. (Eds.), *New directions in educational technology.* Berlin, Germany: Springer-Verlag. doi:10.1007/978-3-642-77750-9_2

Collins, A., Joseph, D., & Bielaczyc, K. (2004). Design research: Theoretical and methodological issues. *Journal of the Learning Sciences, 13*(1), 15–42. doi:10.1207/s15327809jls1301_2

Conradie, M. M., & de Villiers, M. R. (2004). Electronic assessment of free-text: a development research initiative. *South African Journal of Higher Education, 18*(2), 172–188. doi:10.4314/sajhe.v18i2.25462

Creswell, J. W. (2009). *Research design: Qualitative, quantitative, and mixed methods approaches.* Los Angeles, CA: Sage.

De Villiers, M. R. (2005). Interpretive research models for informatics: Action research, grounded theory, and the family of design- and development research. *Alternation, 12*(2), 10–52.

De Villiers, M. R. (2009). Applying controlled usability-testing technology to investigate learning behaviours of users interacting with e-learning tutorials. In T. Bastiaens *et al.* (Eds.), *Proceedings of World Conference on E-Learning in Corporate, Government, Healthcare, and Higher Education 2009* (pp. 2512-2521). Chesapeake, VA: AACE. Canada.

Dede, C. (2005). Why design-based research is both important and difficult. *Educational Technology, 45*(1), 5–8.

Design-Based Research Collective. (2003). Design-based research: An emerging paradigm for educational enquiry. *Educational Researcher, 32*(1), 5–8. doi:10.3102/0013189X032001005

Design Research in Information Systems (DRIS). (2006). Retrieved September 2006 from http://www.isworld.org/Researchdesign/drisISworld.htm

Du Poy, E., & Gitlin, L. N. (1998). *Introduction to research: Understanding and applying multiple strategies* (2nd ed.). St. Louis, MO: Mosby Inc.

Glass, R. L., Ramesh, V., & Vessey, I. (2004). An analysis of research in computing disciplines. *Communications of the ACM, 47*(6), 89–94. doi:10.1145/990680.990686

Gush, K., & de Villiers, M. R. (2010). Application usage of unsupervised Digital Doorway computer kiosks in remote locations in South Africa. In P. Kotze, A. Gerber, A. van der Merwe, & N. Bidwell (Eds.), *Fountains of Computing Research, Proceedings of SAICSIT 2010 Annual Research Conference of the South African Institute of Computer Scientists and Information Technologists.* ACM International Conference Proceedings Series.

Gush, K., De Villiers, R., Smith, R., & Cambridge, G. (2011). Digital Doorways. In Steyn, J., van Belle, J.-P., & Mansilla, E. V. (Eds.), *ICTs for global development and sustainability: Practice and applications* (pp. 96–126). Hershey, PA: IGI Global.

Hevner, A., & Chatterjee, S. (2010). Design science research in Information Systems. *Integrated Series in Information Systems, 22,* 9–22. doi:10.1007/978-1-4419-5653-8_2

Hevner, E. R., March, S. T., Park, A. R., & Ram, S. (2004). Design science in Information Systems research. *Management Information Systems Quarterly*, *28*(1), 75–105.

Kelly, A. E. (2003). Research as design. *Educational Researcher, 32*(1), 3–4. doi:10.3102/0013189X032001003

Klein, H. K., & Myers, M. D. (1999). A set of principles for conducting and evaluating interpretive field studies in Information Systems. *Management Information Systems Quarterly, 23*(12), 67–93. doi:10.2307/249410

March, S. T., & Smith, G. F. (1995). Design and natural science research on information technology. *Decision Support Systems, 15*, 251–266. doi:10.1016/0167-9236(94)00041-2

Masemola, S. S., & De Villiers, M. R. (2006). Towards a framework for usability testing of interactive e-learning applications in cognitive domains, illustrated by a case study. In J. Bishop & D. Kourie (Eds.), *Service-Oriented Software and Systems: Proceedings of SAICSIT 2006* (pp. 187-197). ACM International Conference Proceedings Series.

Myers, M. D. (2004). Qualitative research in Information Systems. *MIS Quarterly, 21*(2), 241-242. Retrieved March 2011 from http://www.qual.auckland.ac.nz/

Nunamaker, J. F., Chen, M., & Purdin, T. D. M. (1991). Systems development in Information Systems research. *Journal of Management Information Systems, 7*(3), 89–106.

Olivier, M. S. (2004). *Information Technology research: A practical guide for computer science and informatics* (2nd ed.). Pretoria, South Africa: Van Schaik Publishers.

Pather, S., & Remenyi, D. (2004). Some of the philosophical issues underpinning realism in Information Systems: From positivism to critical realism. In G. Marsden, P. Kotzé & A. Adessina-Ojo (Eds.), *Fulfilling the Promise of ICT - Proceedings of SAICSIT 2004*. Pretoria.

Preece, J., Rogers, Y., & Sharp, H. (2007). *Interaction design: Beyond human-computer interaction*. John Wiley & Sons, Inc.

Reeves, T. C. (2000). Socially responsible educational technology research. *Educational Technology, 40*(6), 19–28.

Reeves, T. C. (2006). Design research from a technology perspective. In Van Den Akker, J., Graemeijer, K., McKenney, S., & Nieveen, N. (Eds.), *Educational design research* (pp. 52–66). New York, NY: Routledge.

Roode, D. (2003). Information Systems research: A matter of choice? Editorial. *South African Computer Journal, 30*, 1–2.

Simon, H. A. (1981). *The sciences of the artificial* (2nd ed.). Cambridge, MA: MIT Press.

Squires, D. (1999). Educational software for constructivist learning environments: Subversive use and volatile design. *Educational Technology, 39*(3), 48–53.

Van Den Akker, J. (1999). Principles and methods of development research. In van den Akker, J., Branch, R. M., Gustafson, K. L., Nieveen, N., & Plomp, T. (Eds.), *Design approaches and tools in education and training*. Dordrecht, The Netherlands: Kluwer Academic Publishers. doi:10.1007/978-94-011-4255-7_1

Van Den Akker, J. (2002). The added value of development research for educational development in developing countries. In K. Osaki, W. Ottevanger C. Uiso & J. van den Akker (Eds.), *Science education research and teacher development in Tanzania*. Amsterdam, The Netherlands: Vrije Universiteit, International Cooperation Center.

Walsham, G. (1995a). Interpretive case studies in IS research: Nature and method. *European Journal of Information Systems, 4*(2), 74–81. doi:10.1057/ejis.1995.9

Walsham, G. (1995b). The emergence of interpretivism in IS research. *Information Systems Research, 6*(4), 376–394. doi:10.1287/isre.6.4.376

Wang, F., & Hannafin, M. J. (2005). Design-based research and technology-enhanced learning environments. *Educational Technology Research and Development, 53*(4), 5–23. doi:10.1007/BF02504682

Chapter 13
Using Grounded Theory Coding Mechanisms to Analyze Case Study and Focus Group Data in the Context of Software Process Research

Rory V. O'Connor
Dublin City University, Ireland

ABSTRACT

The primary aim of this chapter is to outline a potentially powerful framework for the combination of research approaches utilizing the Grounded Theory coding mechanism for Case Study, and Focus Groups data analysis. A secondary aim of this chapter is to provide a roadmap for such a usage by way of an example research project. The context for this project is the need to study and evaluate the actual practice of software development processes in real world commercial settings of software companies, which utilized both case study and focus group techniques. This research found that grounded theory coding strategies are a suitable and powerful data analysis mechanism to explore case study and focus group data.

INTRODUCTION

While both the case study and focus group methods have become widely accepted in information systems (IS) research over the last two decades, Grounded Theory research is still a distinct minor-

DOI: 10.4018/978-1-4666-0179-6.ch013

ity method for IS research. Grounded theory has been used by IS researchers since the mid-1990s (Orlikowski 1993; Hansen & Kautz 2005; Coleman & O'Connor 2007). It is becoming increasingly popular in IS research, as there is a widely held belief that it is a reliable method for investigating social and organisational phenomena.

The general goal of grounded theory is to generate theories derived from data in order to understand the social context. It is a "qualitative research method that uses a systematic set of procedures to develop an inductively derived grounded theory about a phenomenon" (Strauss 1990, p.24). Hekkala (2007) indicates that grounded theory has been used in IS research as a method (by, among others, Urquhart 2002; Jones and Hughes 2004) but that it has also been sometimes used as a methodology (by researchers including Orlikowski 1993; Goulding 2002; Goede and de Villiers 2003). Hekkala (2007) states that those who use it either as method or as a methodology do not soundly and logically demonstrate and justify their use of this theory for either of those purposes.

A methodology refers to the entire research process, from the identification of one or more research questions and the selection of a research strategy through to the formulation of the findings and results, in which the entire process is based on philosophical assumptions (ontology and epistemology). This view of the two terms coincides with Avison and Fitzgerald's (1995) definitions: a methodology is a collection of procedures, techniques, tools and documentation which is based on some philosophical view; otherwise it is merely a method, like a recipe. A case study strategy which includes grounded theory analysis under interpretative assumptions would therefore be classed as a methodology. The aim of this chapter is to argue that grounded theory can be combined with case study and focus groups to construct a compatible research methodology.

CASE STUDY

According to Yin (2003) case study is "an empirical inquiry that investigates a contemporary phenomenon within its real-life context, especially when the boundaries between phenomenon and context are not clear" (p. 23). Case study is usually seen as a specific research strategy (Eisenhardt, 1989; Yin, 2003). The underlying idea for case research is said to be the many-sided view it can provide of a situation in its context. "The intense observation made in case studies gives opportunities to study different aspects and put these in relation to each other, to put objects in relation to the environment where they operate" (Halinen and Törnroos, 2005). Instead of statistical representativeness, case studies offer depth and comprehensiveness for understanding the specific phenomenon (Easton, 1995, p. 475). They give a possibility to be close to the studied objects (firms), enabling inductive and rich description. Case research is particularly welcome in new situations where only little is known about the phenomenon and in situations where current theories seem inadequate (Eisenhardt, 1989; Yin, 2003). It is also a strong method in the study of change processes as it allows the study of contextual factors and process elements in the same real-life situation.

Case studies can be used to accomplish various aims. Yin (1989, p. 16) separates exploratory, descriptive and explanatory cases. Eisenhardt (1989, p. 535) acknowledges description but stresses the role of cases in generating and, also, testing a theory. Stake (1994) defends the value of intrinsic cases, where a rich description of a single case, in all its particularity and ordinariness, is seen valuable as such. In the management and marketing literature, theory generation from case study evidence has been the most discussed type of case research. Its basis can be found from Glaser and Strauss (1967) and the ideas of later writers (e.g., Eisenhardt, 1989; Yin, 1989; Miles and Huberman, 1994).

Feagin et al., (1991) pointed out that case studies are multi-perspective analyses. This means that the researcher considers not just the voice and perspective of the actors, but also of the relevant groups of actors and the interaction between them. This aspect is a salient point in the characteristic that case studies possess. They also added that case study is also known as a triangulated research strategy where the triangulation can occur with data, investigators, theories, and even methodologies. Moreover, case studies could generate a detailed insight of the case, its complex relationship and processes (Yin, 2003). Furthermore, Oates (2006) claimed that a case study will help the researcher produce data in a situation where the researcher has little control over the events compared to action research and ethnography.

According to Tashakkori and Teddie (1998), the case study research method helps researchers in understanding in more detail the phenomenon associated with topic under investigation. They stated that this is due to the investigation being done in many stages and that it indirectly helps researcher acquired a richer understanding of the case.

Alison and Merali (2007) added that the case studies method is suitable to capture the knowledge and views of the practitioners. Yin (2003) reported that case study design is suitable with a research question that start with 'how' and 'why' question is being asked about a contemporary set of event over which the investigator has little or no control. Because 'how' and 'why' question are explanatory and usually should be studied over time in replicated case studies or experiments.

FOCUS GROUPS

Focus groups emerged as a research method in the 1950's in the social research as researchers expanded the open ended interview format to a group discussion (Templeton, 1994). A focus group may be defined as "a group of individuals selected by researchers to discuss and comment on, from personal experience, the topic that has been a subject of the research" (Powell and Single, 1996 p. 499). In addition this method could activate forgotten details of experiences and also generate data better through a wide range of responses. Focus group interviews are also a method to

study attitudes and experiences; to explore how opinion were constructed (Kitzinger, 1995) and to understand behaviors, values and feelings, (Patton, 2002). According to Powell and Single (1996), the advantage of focus groups is the ability to help the researcher in identifying quickly a full range of perspectives held by respondents.

Focus groups are carefully planned discussion, designed to obtain the perceptions of the group members on a defined area of interest. There are typically between 3 and 12 participants and the discussion is guided and facilitated by a moderator who follows a predefined structure so that the discussion stays focused. The members are selected based on their individual characteristics as related to the session topic. The group setting enables the participants to build on the responses and ideas of the others, which increases the richness of the information gained.

Focus groups are a form of group interview that capitalizes on communication between research participants in order to generate data. Although group interviews are often used simply as a quick and convenient way to collect data from several people simultaneously, focus groups explicitly use group interaction as part of the method. This means that instead of the researcher asking each person to respond to a question in turn, people are encouraged to talk to one another: asking questions, exchanging anecdotes and commenting on each other's experiences and points of view. The method is particularly useful for exploring people's knowledge and experiences and can be used to examine not only what people think but how they think and why they think that way.

The benefits of focus group are that they produce candid, sometimes insightful, information and the method is fairly inexpensive and fast to perform (Widdows, et al 1994). However, the method shares the weaknesses of many other qualitative methods - biases may be caused by group dynamics and sample sizes are often small – and, therefore, it may be difficult to generalize the results (Judd et al, 1991). According to Powell and Single (1996), the advantage of focus group is the ability to help the researcher in identifying quickly a full range of perspectives held by respondents. They added that focus groups expand the details that might have been left out in an in-depth interview. Kruger and Casey (2000) support that the focus group technique is a proper way to understand and explore how people think and feel about the issues. They also added that focus groups elicit data that allows a better understanding of the differences between groups of people.

DATA ANALYSIS IN CASE STUDY AND FOCUS GROUPS

Case study data analysis generally involves an iterative, spiraling or cyclical process that proceeds from more general to more specific observations (Creswell, 1994). Data analysis may begin informally during interviews or observations and continue during transcription, when recurring themes, patterns, and categories become evident. The challenges of analyzing interview and focus group interview data lies in making sense of the substantial amount of data, identifying significant patterns and construction of a framework to communicate the essence of what the data reveals (Denzin et al., 2000). Elo and Kyngas (2008) claim that content analysis is a method that is suitable to analyze the written verbal or visual communication transcripts. Hsieh and Shanon, (2005) in their explanation regarding qualitative contents analysis have defined qualitative content analysis as "the subjective interpretation of the content of the text data through the classification process of coding and identifying themes or patterns" (p. 1278). Therefore a major challenge for the researcher is the choice of a suitable and justifiable mechanism to analyze case study data.

Focus group sessions produce mainly qualitative information – transcripts of structured or freeform discussions and debate amongst participants. The data analysis and reporting of focus group studies can use the methods used in qualitative data analysis (Miles and Huberman, 1984) (Patton, 1990) (Taylor and Bogdan, 1984) (Myers, 2004).

The challenges of analyzing the interview and focus group interview data lies in making sense of the substantial amount of data, identifying significant patterns and construction of a framework to communicate the essence of what the data reveals (Denzin et al., 2000). Therefore, in order to analyze these data, researchers have applied a quantitative content analysis approach (Elo and Kyngas, 2008). Elo and Kyngas (2008) claimed that content analysis is a method that is suitable to analyze the written, verbal or visual communication transcripts. Hsieh and Shanon, (2005) in their explanation regarding qualitative contents analysis have defined qualitative content analysis as the subjective interpretation of the content of the text data through the classification process of coding and identifying themes or patterns.

GROUNDED THEORY

A grounded theory design is a "systematic, qualitative procedure used to generate a theory that explains, at a broad conceptual level, a process, an action, or interaction about a substantive topic." (Creswell, 2011). Grounded Theory was first established by Glaser and Strauss (1967). The theoretical foundations of grounded theory stem from Symbolic Interactionism, which sees humans as key participants and 'shapers' of the world they inhabit. Grounded theory was created from the 'constant comparative' method, developed by Glaser and Strauss, which alternated theory building with comparison of theory to the reality unveiled through data collection and analysis. The emphasis in grounded theory is on new theory generation. A theory, according to Strauss and Corbin (1990), is "a set of well-developed categories (e.g. themes, concepts) that are systematically interrelated through statements of relationship to form a theoretical framework that explains some relevant social, psychological, educational, nursing or other phenomenon". This manifests itself in such a way that, rather than beginning with a pre-conceived theory in mind, the theory evolves during the research process itself and is a product of continuous interplay between data collection and analysis of that data (Goulding, 2002). According to Strauss and Corbin (1998), the theory that is derived from the data is more likely to resemble what is actually going on than if it were assembled from putting together a series of concepts based on experience or through speculation.

As the objective of the methodology is to uncover theory rather than have it pre-conceived, grounded theory incorporates a number of steps to ensure good theory development. The analytical process involves coding strategies: the process of breaking down interviews, observation, and other forms of appropriate data into distinct units of meaning which are labeled to generate concepts. These concepts are initially clustered into descriptive categories. They are then re-evaluated for their interrelationships and, through a series of analytical steps, are gradually subsumed into higher-order categories, or one underlying core category, which suggests an emergent theory.

Because of its interpretivist emphasis and its ability to explain socio-cultural phenomena, grounded theory has been primarily used in the fields of sociology, nursing and psychology from the time of its establishment in the late 1960s. Since then, however, it has widened its reach into the business sector and latterly into the IS field, where it has been used to explain intentions, actions, and opinions regarding management, change and professional interactions. Silva and Backhouse (1997) support its use, arguing that, "qualitative research in information systems should be led by theories grounded in interpretive and phenomenological premises to make sense and to be consistent". Myers (2004) believes that grounded theory has gained growing acceptance in IS research because it is a very effective way

of developing context-based, process-oriented explanations of the phenomena being studied.

Probably the best example of the use of grounded theory in the IS field is (Orlikowski, 1993). This study showed how grounded theory could be used to explain the impact on two organisations that implemented CASE tools to support their software development activity. The use of grounded theory in Orlikowski's study enabled a focus on the contextual issues surrounding the introduction of CASE tools as well as the role of the key actors instigating, and at the receiving end of, their adoption.

A number of researchers have used grounded theory to look at a diverse range of socio-cultural activities in IS. Baskerville and Pries-Heje (1999) used a novel combination of action research and grounded theory to produce a grounded action research methodology for studying how IT is practiced. Others have used the methodology to examine the use of 'systems thinking' practices (Goede and de Villiers, 2003), software inspections (Carver and Basili, 2003) (Seaman and Basili, 1997), process modelling (Carvalho, et al, 2005), requirements documentation (Power, 2002) and virtual team development (Sarker et al, 2002). Hansen and Kautz (2005) used grounded theory to study the use of development practices in a Danish software company and concluded that it was a methodology well suited for use in the IS sector.

Coding is the key process in grounded theory (Strauss and Corbin 1990). It begins in the early stages after the first interviews for data collection. Strauss and Corbin (1990) assert that the coding procedures in grounded theory are neither automatic nor algorithmic - "we do not at all wish to imply rigid adherence to them" (Strauss and Corbin 1990, p.59). In other words, flexibility may be necessary in certain circumstances. This process comprises three coding steps:

Open Coding and Analysis

From the interview transcripts the researchers analyse the data line-by-line and allocate codes to the text. The analytical process involves coding strategies: the process of breaking down interviews and observations into distinct units of meaning which are labelled to generate concepts. The codes represent concepts that will later become part of the theory. The codes themselves provide meaning to the text and may be created by the researchers, or may be taken from the text itself. A code allocated in this way is known as an in-vivo code. In-vivo codes are especially important in that they come directly from the interviewees, do not require interpretation by the researche, and provide additional ontological clarification or context-description. From the initial interviews, a list of codes emerges and this list is then used to code subsequent interviews. At the end of the sampling process a large number of codes should have emerged.

Axial Coding

Axial coding is the process of relating categories to their subcategories (and) termed axial because coding occurs around the axis of a category linking categories to subcategories at the level of properties and dimensions. This involves documenting category properties and dimensions from the open coding phase; Identifying the conditions, actions and interactions associated with a phenomenon and relating categories to subcategories.

Selective Coding

Selective coding is the process of integrating and refining the theory. Because categories are merely descriptions of the data they must be further developed to form the theory, the first step is to identify the central, or 'core' category around which the theory will be built. As the core category acts as the hub for all other identified categories, it must

be central in that all other categories must relate to it and it must appear frequently in the data.

GROUNDED THEORY CODING IN CASE STUDY AND FOCUS GROUPS ANALYSIS

A variety of data generation methods can be used in case study methodologies such as interviewing, questionnaires, observation or/and document analysis. The aim of case studies is to generate a detailed insight of the case, its complex relationship and processes. Given our desire to determine what is happening in actual practice in relation to software process in companies, we promote the usage of multiple case studies utilizing in-depth interviews in order to ascertain process practices which should reveal both direct and indirect data (Kvale, 2007). However, given the potential limitations and bias of the multiple single interview perspective and the fact that software development is a team based activity, we promote the usage of Focus Groups as a complimentary data acquisition mechanism to the interview approach.

In order to analyze both interview and focus group data we promote the usage of the three coding techniques of Grounded Theory methodology: open coding, axial coding and selective coding (Straus and Corbin, 1998). These data analysis methods also have been recommended in qualitative data research (Patton, 2002) in order to guide researchers in analyzing the qualitative method more systematically. We argue that there is a need for a systematic approach to analyzing case study data from interviews and focus groups and that the grounded theory coding approach is a suitable approach and one that adds value in terms of academic rigor of approach and provides for validity in terms of traceability from initial data coding to final result. In defense of this approach it is worth noting that Halaweh et al (2008) comments that a major difference between the case study and grounded theory is that the latter details the procedure of data analysis, while the analysis process proposed by Yin (1994) including pattern matching and explanation building is not as rigorous for analyzing an interpretive case study data as the procedures and techniques provided by Strauss and Corbin (1990). One of the main criticisms of the case study is related to the analysis of huge qualitative data where there is no standard analysis approach (Darke et al. 1998).

In such a mechanism the qualitative data from the interview and focus group was transformed into transcripts and organized according to the pattern which emerge during the analysis. This data was used as an input to the coding procedure in order to refine the abstract constructs and define the concept and categories. In order to assist researchers in analyzing qualitative data, three coding techniques proposed by GT methodology: open coding, axial coding and selective coding (Straus and Corbin, 1998) have been applied. These data analysis methods also have been recommended in qualitative data research (Denzin et al 2000; Patton, 2002) in order to guide researchers in analyzing the qualitative method more systematically. Social scientists (Miles et al., 1994; Patton, 2002) acknowledge that data collecting and analysis in qualitative inquiry are integrative, iterative, synergistic and interactive in nature.

Based on the prior experience (Coleman and O'Connor, 2007) of the researchers in applying grounded theory coding, we utilized the Atlas.Ti software tool (Muhr, 1997). This is a tool designed specifically for use with grounded theory and allows for the linking, searching and sorting of data. It enables the researchers to keep track of interview transcripts, manage a list of codes and related memos, generate families of related codes and create graphical support for codes, concepts and categories. It also supports the axial and selective coding process as proposed by Strauss and Corbin (1998), which is used in this study. Having installed the software, the interview transcripts from the preliminary study stage were entered into the Atlas database. Having the ability to assign

Table 1. Sample codes as assigned using Atlas TI

Autonomous work	Work independently
Self-Learning	Open Environment
Open Communication	Informal Communication

and allocate codes with quotations from multiple interviews speeded up the process dramatically and eased data management significantly. It also created an easier 'visual plane', which enabled clearer reflection and energized proposition development. A sample list of codes from this stage is contained in Table 1.

The next section describes a study combining multiple case studies, utilizing both interview and focus groups to describe the actual practice of software development processes in the real commercial setting of software companies Basri and O'Connor, (2010a, 2010b), where the three coding techniques of grounded theory methodology were integrated as part of the data analysis phase.

EXAMPLE APPLICATION OF APPROACH

This section presents an example of applying the methodology proposed above to a research project that was conducted in the domain of software process, software process improvement (SPI) and software process maintenance and evolution.

Software Process Improvement and Knowledge Management

Software Process Improvement (SPI) aims to understand the software process as it is used within an organisation and thus drive the implementation of changes to that process to achieve specific goals such as increasing development speed, achieving higher product quality or reducing costs.

A software process essentially describes the way an organization develops its software products and supporting services, such as documentation. Processes define what steps the development organizations should take at each stage of production and provide assistance in making estimates, developing plans and measuring quality. There is a widely held belief that a better software process results in a better software product, which has led to a focus on SPI to help companies realize the potential benefit. SPI models (Chrissis et al, 2003) developed to assist companies in this regard, purport to represent beacons of best practice. Contained within the scope of these models, according to their supporters, lies the road to budgetary and schedule adherence, better product quality and improved customer satisfaction. Translating these benefits into practice has, however, proved challenging. Opponents believe that these models operate primarily at a theoretical level, are too prescriptive and bureaucratic to implement in practice and require a subscribing company to adapt to the models rather than having the models easily adapt to them. Although commercial SPI models have been highly publicized and marketed, they are not being widely adopted and their influence in the software industry therefore remains more at a theoretical than practical level.

In the modern business environment where software development is becoming more complex, increased reliance upon knowledge processes to resolve problems is very important. Several researchers reported that software development processes have always been knowledge intensive (Dingdoyr et al., 2005). Bjornson and Dingsoyr (2005) stated in their review that proper management of organizational knowledge is important in SPI efforts and it is a major factor for success. Mathiassen and Pourkomeylian (2003) in their survey on practical usage of Knowledge Management (KM) to support innovation in a software organization claims that KM and SPI are very closely related. Mathiassen et al., (2002) and Bjornson and Dingsoyr (2008) emphasized that knowledge creation and sharing are among the

important principles that must be adopted by an organization in order to succeed in SPI.

In addition, in terms of managing project team knowledge, Kettunen (2003) in his study emphasized that with appropriate KM methods, problems that could impact process improvement such as possible lack of competencies, missing work instructions and others imperfect processes could be identify. Therefore it can be seen that KM and SPI have a strong relationship and one that can potentially influence the success of software projects.

The SPI KM Study

For this study the focus is on how software process and SPI is practiced within the Very Small Entities (VSEs) (Laporte et al, 2008). In particular the research is concerned with the process of software development knowledge management and team issues in supporting the software process and process improvement. We set out to answer two major research questions:

- RQ1: What is the current status of Software Process Improvement among Irish software VSEs?
- RQ2: How software knowledge in Irish Software VSEs should be managed in order to maintain and evolve software process?

Since the present research aim is to study and evaluate the research situation rather than being involved in providing a specific solution to the situation, the case study method was chosen as the most suitable for this situation. According to Tashakkori and Teddie (1998), the case study research method helped researchers in the understanding of the research study phenomenon. They stated that the research investigation can be done in many stages and indirectly helps the researcher acquire a richer understanding.

The present research used a multiple case studies research method. Yin (1994) points out that multiple case studies will help researchers prevent the possibility of misrepresentation and also ensures validity and reliability of data collection. There are two main methods in the data collection process that have been used; face to face interview and focus group interviews.

The face to face interview approach was used in this study in order to discuss topics in depth, to get respondents' candid discussion on the topic and to be able to get the depth of information required for the research context. According to Kvale (2007), interview reveals both direct and indirect data. Direct data are responses that subjects provide to direct questions, they are spoken responses. For this data collection phase, the researchers have interviewed 11 respondents from 4 identified software companies which fall under the VSEs category. The focus group interview approached was used in this study because team members develop the software and the existing team interactions helped to release inhibitions amongst the team members. In addition this method could activate forgotten details of experiences and also generate data better through a wide range of responses. Focus group interviews were also chosen because it was the most appropriate method to study attitudes and experiences; to explore how opinion were constructed (Kitzinger, 1995) and to understand behaviours, values and feelings, (Patton, 2002). According to Powell and Single (1996), the advantage of focus group is the ability to help the researcher in identifying quickly a full range of perspectives held by respondents

For the interviews and focus groups, respondents have been divided into 2 categories; the managers and the software development team. For the manager's we applied a face to face interview method and for the software development team we adopted the focus group interview method. All interview sessions were approximately 40-90 minutes in duration and were recorded with the respondents' permission. Furthermore, in order to guide the interviewer to gather specific data during an interview session, an interview guide

(Taylor and Bodgan, 1984) (for both individual and focus groups) was developed. The interview guide included closed and open-ended questions and some related notes about the direction in which to drive the interview under difference circumstances.

The data analysis process consisted of having all the individual interviews and focus group interviews analyzed and coded as per the grounded theory coding mechanism discussed previously. This process involves the development of the codes, code-categories and inter-relationship of categories which is based on the GT process and coding strategy.

The challenge of analyzing the interview and focus group data lies in making sense of the substantial amount of data, identifying significant patterns and constructing a framework to communicate the essence of what the data reveals (Denzin et al., 2000). Therefore in order to analyze this data, the researchers a applied quantitative analysis approach (Elo and Kyngas, 2008). Hsieh and Shanon, (2005) in their explanation regarding qualitative contents analysis have defined qualitative content analysis as "the subjective interpretation of the content of the text data through the classification process of coding and identifying themes or pattern". Therefore for the current research, the qualitative data from the interview and focus group were transformed into transcripts and organized according to the pattern emerging during the analysis. These data were used as an input to the coding procedure in order to refine the abstract constructs and define the concept and categories. In order to assist researchers in analyzing qualitative data, three coding techniques proposed by GT methodology: open coding, axial coding and selective coding (Straus and Corbin, 1998) have been applied. These data analysis methods also have been recommended in qualitative data research (Denzin et al 2000; Patton, 2002) in order to guide researchers in analyzing the qualitative method more systematically. The Atlas.Ti software also was used to help in coding the interview text and linking this code on the semantic network.

We applied the coding processes for the data collection as follows:

Open Coding

From each transcribed interview transcript, researchers have analysed the text using line by line or incident by incident coding before allocating open or initial code to the text. For this activity researchers have followed Charmaz (2006) initial codes approached which was done by using gerunds as this process will help the researcher to detect the process and stick to the data. She also recommended to consider the following questions in order to guide researchers to create an open code:

- What is the data a study of?
- What does the data suggest?
- From whose point of view?

After open code have been assigned and created, lists of open code then are sorted into categories based on how different codes are related and linked. These emergent categories are used to organize and group initial codes into a meaningful cluster. This process involved the breaking down of interview data and focus group data into discreet parts, closely examined and compared for similarities and differences. Open codes that were found to be conceptually similar or related were grouped under more abstract categories based on their ability to explain the SPI, knowledge, team and standard issues which are the main unit of analysis (Elo and Kyngas, 2008). Then all these open codes were linked and grouped based on similar issues on the broad categories that represent the unit of analysis. Some of the open codes allocated in this way are known as an "in vivo" code. In-vivo codes are especially important in that they come directly from the interviewees, do not require interpretation by the researcher

and provide additional ontological clarification or context-description.

Axial Coding

Axial coding is the process of relating codes (including categories and properties) to each other into subcategories (Strauss and Corbin, 1998). In this process all the general categories in open coding process were grouped under higher ordering headings. The purpose of grouping data were to reduce the number of categories by merging those similar into broader higher categories. In addition the merging process provides a mean for describing the situation to increase researcher understanding and to generate more knowledge. The process was continued with the abstraction process (Kohlbacher, 2006). The purpose of the abstraction process is to detail the categories by identifying the subcategories and how they link to one another. Subcategories with similar occurrence and incidents are grouped together as categories and categories are grouped as core categories. The abstraction process is an iterative process and continues as far as it is reasonable. In general this activity is termed axial because coding occurs around the axis of a category linking categories to subcategories at the level of properties and dimensions. This involves documenting category properties and dimensions from the initial coding phase; identifying the conditions, actions and interactions associated with a phenomenon and relating categories to subcategories.

Selective Coding

The third coding process in the analysis of qualitative data is the selective process. Selective coding is the process of selecting the core category, systematically relating it to other categories, validating those relationships and filling in categories that need further refinement and development. In this process, the first step is to identify the main or 'core' category that relates to the collected data.

The core category acts as the hub for all other identified categories. In this part, the researcher using the Atlas.Ti tool is creating a network diagram based on the abstraction process result as in the axial coding phase. The network diagrams were isolated in the beginning and merged at the end of the process. The merging network diagram helped researchers to produce inter-related network diagrams that present as a theoretical network diagram for the current research study.

Based on the detailed analysis process as described above and using an Atlas.Ti tool, we produced and identified 11 main related categories that shape the software process improvement environment in VSEs. Figure 1 illustrates the categories which consist of: staff background, business operation, working style, management style, team structure and process, learning and sharing process, communication process, documentation process, development process, technology and development method and software quality standard. Based on the analysis, these categories are the main categories and variables that have an influence on the software development process environments in VSEs.

DISCUSSION

The overall main data analysis process of this research has adopted the qualitative contents analysis approach which involved several data coding approaches. In order to ensure the systematic data coding process, researchers adopted the GT coding approach which involved open, axial and selective coding. These processes are vague in the beginning and become more specific and focused at the end. In addition, GT method helps researchers to gather detailed results, produce the resulting pattern and enhance researchers understanding on the whole research situation. Moreover uses of the systematic coding process has assisted the researchers in producing a result pattern which has helped to answer the research questions and hypothesis. Overall the processes have supported researcher in producing and validating the research theoretical diagrams as identified in the early stages of the present research.

This chapter has made both theoretical and practical contributions. In particular this chapter has provided theoretical development in methodology. In particular, it has explained and justified

Figure 1. The overall main category diagram

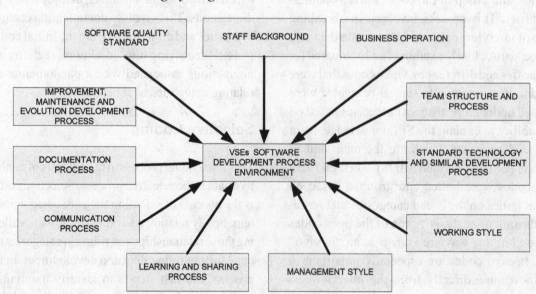

the use of grounded theory coding mechanisms in conjunction with case study research. Secondly, this chapter provides an example of applying this approach to research that has been conducted in the area of software process.

REFERENCES

Avison, D., & Fitzgerald, D. G. (1995). *Information Systems development*. London, UK: McGraw-Hill.

Allison, I., & Merali, Y. (2007). Software process improvement as emergent change: A structural analysis. *Information and Software Technology, 49*(6), 668–681. doi:10.1016/j.infsof.2007.02.003

Baskerville, R., & Pries-Heje, J. (1999). Grounded action research: A method for understanding IT in practice. *Accounting. Management and Information Technologies, 9*, 1–23. doi:10.1016/S0959-8022(98)00017-4

Basri, S., & O'Connor, R. (2010a). Understanding the perception of very small software companies towards the adoption of process standards. In Riel, A. (Eds.), *Systems, Software and Services Process Improvement, CCIS* (*Vol. 99*, pp. 153–164). Springer-Verlag. doi:10.1007/978-3-642-15666-3_14

Basri, S., & O'Connor, R. (2010b). *Organizational commitment towards software process improvement: An Irish Software VSEs case study*. 4th International Symposium on Information Technology 2010 (ITSim 2010), Kuala Lumpur, Malaysia.

Bjornson, F. O., & Dingsoyr, T. (2005). Lecture Notes in Computer Science: *Vol. 3547. A study of a mentoring program for knowledge transfer in a small software consultancy company*. Berlin, Germany: Springer.

Chrissis, M. B., Konrad, M., & Shrum, S. (2003). *CMMI: Guidelines for process integration and product improvement*. Addison Wesley.

Charmaz, K. (2006). *Constructing grounded theory: A practical guide through qualitative analysis*. Thousand Oaks, CA: Sage Publication.

Coleman, G., & O'Connor, R. (1997). Using grounded theory to understand software process improvement: A study of Irish software product companies. *Journal of Information and Software Technology, 49*(6), 531–694.

Carver, J., & Basili, V. (2003). Identifying implicit process variables to support future empirical work. *Journal of the Brazilian Computer Society, November*.

Carvalho, L., Scott, L., & Jeffery, R. (2005). An exploratory study into the use of qualitative research methods in descriptive process modeling. *Information and Software Technology, 47*, 113–127. doi:10.1016/j.infsof.2004.06.005

Creswell, J. (1994). *Research design: Qualitative and quantitative approaches*. Thousand Oaks, CA: Sage Publication.

Creswell, J. W. (2011). *Educational research: Planning, conducting, and evaluating quantitative and qualitative research* (4th ed.). Sage Publishers.

Darke, P., Shanks, G., & Broadbent, M. (1998). Successfully completing case study research. *Information Systems Journal, 8*(4), 273–289. doi:10.1046/j.1365-2575.1998.00040.x

Denzin, N. K., & Lincoln, Y. S. (2000). The discipline and practice of qualitative research. In *Handbook of qualitative research*. London, UK: Sage Publication.

Dingsøyr, T., Djarraya, H. K., & Royrvik, E. (2005). Practical knowledge management tool use in a software consulting company. *Communications of the ACM, 48*(12), 97–103. doi:10.1145/1101779.1101783

Elo, S., & Kyngäs, H. (2008). The qualitative content analysis process. *Journal of Advanced Nursing, 62*(1), 107–115. doi:10.1111/j.1365-2648.2007.04569.x

Easton, G. (1995). Methodology and industrial networks. In Moller, K., & Wilson, D. T. (Eds.), *Business marketing: An interaction and network perspective* (pp. 411–491). Norwell, MA: Kluwer Academic Publishing. doi:10.1007/978-94-011-0645-0_15

Eisenhardt, K. M. (1989). Building theories from case study research. *Academy of Management Review, 14*(4), 532–550.

Feagin, J., Orum, A., & Sjoberg, G. (Eds.). (1991). *A case for case study.* Chapel Hill, NC: University of North Carolina Press.

Glaser, B., & Strauss, A. (1967). *The discovery of grounded theory: Strategies for qualitative research.* Chicago, IL: Aldine.

Goede, R., & de Villiers, C. (2003). The applicability of grounded theory as research methodology in studies on the use of methodologies in IS practices. *Proceedings of SAICSIT,* (pp. 208-217). South Africa.

Goulding, C. (2002). *Grounded theory: A practical guide for management, business and market researchers.* Sage Publications.

Hansen, B., & Kautz, K. (2005). Grounded theory applied – Studying Information Systems development methodologies in practice. In *Proceedings of 38th Annual Hawaiian International Conference on Systems Sciences,* Big Island, HI.

Hekkala, R. (2007). Grounded theory – The two faces of the methodology and their manifestation in IS research. *Proceedings of the 30th Information Systems Research Seminar in Scandinavia IRIS,* 11-14 August, Tampere, Finland.

Halaweh, M., Fidler, C., & McRobb, S. (2008). *Integrating the grounded theory method and case study research methodology within IS research: A possible road map.* ICIS 2008.

Seaman, C., & Basili, V. (1997). An empirical study of communication in code inspections. In *Proceedings of the 19th International Conference on Software Engineering,* May, Boston, MA (pp. 17-23).

Halinen, A., & Törnroos, J.-Å. (2005). Using case methods in the study of contemporary business networks. *Journal of Business Research, 58*(9), 2006. doi:10.1016/j.jbusres.2004.02.001

Hsieh, H. F., & Shannon, S. E. (2005). Three approaches to qualitative content analysis. *Qualitative Health Research, 18*(6), 51–59.

Judd, C. M., Smith, E. R., & Kidder, L. H. (1991). *Research methods in social relations.* Harcourt Brace Jovanovich College Publishers, 1991.

Jones, S., & Hughes, J. (2004). An exploration of the use of grounded theory as a research approach in the field of IS evaluation. *Electronic Journal of Information System Evaluation, 6*(1).

Kettunen, P. (2003). Managing embedded software project team knowledge. *Software. IEEE Proceedings, 150*(6), 359–366.

Kvale, S. (2007). *Doing interviews; The Sage qualitative research kit.* Thousand Oaks, CA: Sage.

Kohlbacher, F. (2006). *The use of qualitative content analysis in case study research.* IN: Forum Qualitative Sozialforschung/Forum: Qualitative Social Research.

Krueger, R. A., & Casey, M. A. (2000). *Focus groups: A practical guide for applied research.* Sage Publications, 2000.

Kitzinger, J. (1995). Introducing focus groups. *British Medical Journal, 311,* 299–302. doi:10.1136/bmj.311.7000.299

Kvale, S. (2007). *Doing interviews: The Sage qualitative research kit.* Thousand Oaks, CA: Sage.

Laporte, C. Y., Alexandre, S., & O'Connor, R. (2008). A software engineering lifecycle standard for very small enterprises. In O'Connor, R. V. (Eds.), *Proceedings of EuroSPI, CCIS* (*Vol. 16*, pp. 129–141). Springer-Verlag. doi:10.1007/978-3-540-85936-9_12

Mathiassen, L., & Pourkomeylian, P. (2003). Managing knowledge in a software organization. *Journal of Knowledge Management, 7*(2), 63–80. doi:10.1108/13673270310477298

Mathiassen, L., Ngwenyama, O. K., & Aaen, I. (2005). Managing change in software process improvement. *Software IEEE, 22*(6), 84–91. doi:10.1109/MS.2005.159

Miles, M. B., & Huberman, A. M. (1984). *Qualitative data analysis: A sourcebook of new methods.* Sage Publications.

Miles, M. B., & Huberman, A. M. (1994). *Qualitative data analysis: An expanded sourcebook.* London, UK: Sage Publications.

Myers, M. (2004). *Qualitative research in Information Systems.* ISWorld 2004.

Muhr, T. (1997). *Atlas TI user's manual.* Berlin, Germany: Scientific Software Development.

Orlikowski, W. (1993). CASE tools as organizational change: Investigating incremental and radical changes in systems development. *Management Information Systems Quarterly, 17*(3), 309–340. doi:10.2307/249774

Oates, B. J. (2006). *Researching Information Systems and competing.* London, UK: Sage Publication.

O'Connor, R., & Coleman, G. (2009). Ignoring 'best practice': Why Irish software SMEs are rejecting CMMI and ISO 9000. *Australasian Journal of Information Systems, 16*(1).

Power, N. (2002). *A grounded theory of requirements documentation in the practice of software development.* PhD Thesis, Dublin City University, Ireland

Patton, M. Q. (2002). *Qualitative evaluation and research methods* (3rd ed.). Newbury Park, CA: Sage Publications, Inc.

Patton, M. Q. (1990). *Qualitative evaluation and research methods.* SAGE Publications.

Powell, R. A., & Single, H. M. (1996). Focus groups. *International Journal for Quality in Health Care, 8*, 499–504. doi:10.1093/intqhc/8.5.499

Urquhart, C. (2001). An encounter with grounded theory: Tackling the practical and philosophical issues. In Trauth, E. M. (Ed.), *Qualitative research in Information Systems: Issues and trends* (pp. 104–140). Hershey, PA: Idea Group Publishing. doi:10.4018/978-1-930708-06-8.ch005

Silva, L., & Backhouse, J. (1997). Becoming part of the furniture: The institutionalisation of Information Systems. In Lee, A., Liebenau, J., & DeGross, J. I. (Eds.), *Proceedings of Information Systems and Qualitative Research.* Chapman and Hall.

Sarker, S., Lau, F., & Sahay, S. (2001). Using an adapted grounded theory approach for inductive theory building about virtual team development. *The Data Base for Advances in Information Systems, 32*(1), 38–56.

Strauss, A., & Corbin, J. (1990). *Basics of qualitative research: Grounded theory procedures and techniques.* London, UK: SAGE Publication.

Strauss, A., & Corbin, J. (1998). *Basics of qualitative research techniques and procedures for developing grounded theory.* USA: Sage.

Tashakkori, A., & Teddies, C. (1998). *Mix methodology: Combining quantitative and qualitative approaches. Applied Social Research Methods, 46.* Thousand Oaks, CA: Sage Publication.

Templeton, T. F. (1994). *The focus group: A strategic guide to organizing, conducting and analyzing the focus group interview.* McGraw-Hill Professional Publishing, 1994.

Taylor, S. J., & Bordan, R. (1984). *Introduction to qualitative research method.* John Wiley & Sons.

Widdows, R., Hensler, T. A., & Wyncott, M. H. (1991). The focus group interview: A method for assessing user's evaluation of library service. *College & Research Libraries, 52*(4).

Yin, R. K. (1994). *Case study research: Design and methods.* London, UK: Sage.

Yin, R. K. (2003). *Case study research: Design and methods* (3rd ed.). Thousand Oaks, CA: Sage.

KEY TERMS AND DEFINITIONS

Case Study: An empirical inquiry that investigates a contemporary phenomenon within its real-life context, especially when the boundaries between phenomenon and context are not clear.

Focus Group: A group of individuals selected by researchers to discuss and comment on, from personal experience, the topic that has been a subject of the research.

Grounded Theory: A systematic, qualitative procedure used to generate a theory that explains, at a broad conceptual level, a process, an action, or interaction about a substantive topic.

Knowledge Management: Set of the interdependent activities aimed at developing and properly managing organization knowledge.

Software Process: Defined as "A set of activities, methods, practices and transformations that people use to develop and maintain software and the associated products.

Software Process Improvement: Analyzing a software process as it is used within an organization and thus drive the implementation of changes to that process to achieve specific goals such as increasing development speed, achieving higher product quality or reducing costs.

Chapter 14

A Practical Approach to Theory Structuring and Analysis:
A way to Structure Research and Perform Sub-Problem Solving in a Changing IS Landscape

T. Schwartzel
University of South Africa, South Africa

M. M. Eloff
University of South Africa, South Africa

ABSTRACT

A large proportion of students who enroll for postgraduate degrees never finish their studies, with non-completion rates yielding 30% for a sample size of 2000 students. A number of empirical studies have been conducted indicating the possible factors for the non-completion rate. This chapter briefly highlights such factors and proposes a possible solution to increase the number of successful studies using relevant philosophies and problem-solving to build insight in determining IS/IT solutions and innovations. A research methodology is suggested to enable data capturing aligned to research objectives and organise sub-problem solving effectively. The process of finding information, determining if it is relevant, and then relating it to existing keywords and topics can be facilitated by using a spreadsheet as a data generation method. The outcome may lead to a research proposal and study to investigate the problem identified, search for possible solutions, and prove/disprove the validity of the suggested solutions.

INTRODUCTION

A large proportion of students who enroll for postgraduate degrees never finish their studies (Mouton, 2001). For instance, the non-completion rate for sample size of 2000 doctoral students yields 30% (Rudd and Hatch, 1968). Among Canadian postgraduates, 7% had a master's degree and only 1% had a doctorate (Statistics Canada, 2000). In the United States, doctoral student attrition rates

DOI: 10.4018/978-1-4666-0179-6.ch014

have been measured at 57% across disciplines (Council of Graduate Schools 2008).

The purpose of this chapter is to briefly highlight possible reasons for postgraduate non-completion rates and discuss a possible solution in the following sections.

In science and technology for instance there are many examples of both theoretical and fundamental research conducted as well as radically new innovations that solve practical problems and contribute to creating new knowledge. These two types of research differ regarding their fundamental goals (understanding vs. use), nature (theoretical vs. industrial), and timing (long-term oriented vs. immediately applicable) but both have a place in science and technology (Mulkay, 1977).

Science and technology, though distinguishable, are linked, not by the scope or nature of the investigative activities (basic vs. applied research) but, rather by the problem-solving nature of research and in the procedural rationality which drives both (Franzoni, 2006).

The Johnstone El-Bana Model highlights the fact that if a problem has many sub-problems, the more difficult it will be for the researcher to solve it. "The researcher must use working memory to simultaneously recall needed knowledge from long-term memory and to process demands of each sub-problem." (Johnstone, 1977). The difficulty creates an overwhelmed researcher with a high likelihood of failure. This is a major hindrance in solving any research problem and may cause the researcher to end the research project prematurely.

There are a number of research methodologies that describe the steps in conducting research. For this chapter the Johnstone and El-Bana model was used to glean an alternative research methodology, i.e. structuring one's research to focus on problem management, sub-problem-linkage and resolution to ensure focus on research objectives.

The purpose of the exploratory research methodology is, therefore, to illustrate a new approach that can be used by novice researchers in performing research, conducting problem solving

and developing research topics, title, objectives, problem statement, significance of study, literature study and ultimately gearing towards a theoretical solution or concept that can be further explored or validated. The research methodology or approach caters for discovering information through journals, articles and conference papers, linking information to existing facts, and then making sense of it so as to gain new insights or identify gaps that require further investigation.

The objectives of this chapter are to outline possible philosophies and methods for students conducting sub-problem solving thereby building insight and determining IT/IS solutions and innovations.

The remainder of the chapter is structured as follows:

- Section 2 gives an overview and brief explanation of some of the existing research approaches and research terminology;
- Section 3 is a high-level overview of the proposed methodology and approach;
- Section 4 proposes a detailed method; and
- Section 5 concludes the chapter.

2. BACKGROUND

This section provides background on the basic research terms and concepts as the foundation of any research methodology in setting direction for a research project.

There are various definitions for research, with Redman & Mory (1923) defining it as the "systemized search for new knowledge" or an investigation to establish new facts using a scientific method. The term "method" leads to the term "methodology". Many people use the terms methodology, design and strategy and method interchangeably (Buchanan & Bryman, 2009).

"The purpose of conducting research is to discover new answers to questions by applying scientific procedures to find out new hidden truths which have not been discovered as yet." Kothari (2006). He states the following examples of research objectives. These are to

- comprehend a known phenomenon or achieve new insights (exploratory or formulate studies);
- represent the characteristics of an individual, situation or group (descriptive studies);
- establish and understand the frequency in which something occurs or its associations with other areas (diagnostic studies); and
- test the hypothesis of a fundamental and underlying relationship between different variables (hypothesis-testing studies).

Research methodology refers to the different ways in which research is undertaken and involves activities such as identifying problems, reviewing literature, formulating hypotheses, procedures for testing hypotheses, measurement, data collection and analysis, interpreting results and drawing conclusions. Thus, research methodology consists of all general and specific activities of research. Mastery of the research methodology invariably enhances the understanding of the research activities. Thus, it seems that research design and methodology have the same meaning i.e. mapping a strategy for undertaking research (Singh & Bajpai, 2008).

Jonker & Pennink (2010) describe research methodology as the way in which the researcher conducts research and the way in which he/she deals with a particular question and solves the problem with a certain goal in mind. Sharma (2004) describes it as the way in which one scientifically studies a research problem. This includes the research method, previous work undertaken, and the hypothesis, analysis and data collection sources.

Research methods, on the other hand, are ways to extrapolate new knowledge. In social sciences the research methods that are commonly used are qualitative research (understanding human behaviour which is more subjective in nature) or quan-

titative research (empirical investigation which is more objective). Mixed methods as a research approach gained momentum in the 1980s, while in the 1990s mixed model studies of combining quantitative and qualitative approaches within different stages of the research process emerged as a new way to conduct research. These two methods can be distinguished as follows: "realism vs. idealism, objective vs. subjective, impersonal vs. personal, deductive reasoning vs. inductive reasoning, logistic vs. dialectic, rationalism vs. naturalism, reductionist vs. holistic, generalization vs. uniqueness, causal vs. causal, macro vs. micro, quantifiers vs. describers, and numbers vs. words" (Onwuegbuzie & Leech, 2005).

Research methods, according to Kasi (2009), are the tools that a researcher uses for gathering information to find answers for the research question. Research methodology is the manner or approach which the researcher uses to answer the research question.

According to Crotty (2003), research methods are the activities researchers use to gather and analyse data while the research methodology is the explanation of the research strategy or action plan. "Methods are the techniques or procedures used to gather and analyse data related to a hypothesis or research question. Methodology is the strategy, plan of action, processor design that one uses behind the research methods to ensure the desired outcomes. Theoretical perspective is the philosophical stance informing the methodology which provides the context for the process and grounding its logic."

Ultimately the goal of research and the research process is to produce new knowledge (Oates, 2006).

There are a number of ways to conduct research in a research process with the steps typically being: selecting a topic, conducting the literature review, writing the research proposal, collecting and analysing data and then reporting on it.

The National Institute for Health Research (2009) identified the following steps when undertaking research:

- Determine a topic: this may come from a supervisor or an idea that the researcher has.
- Turn the idea into a research question.
- Review literature.
- Design study and develop methods.
- Write a research proposal.
- Find funding.
- Obtain approval.
- Collect and collate data.
- Analyse the data and interpret findings.
- Identify impact of research.
- Write a report and disseminate it.

The Cambridge Rindge and Latin Research Guide (2011), lists the basic research process having the following steps:

- Select a topic of interest.
- List topic keywords.
- Use keywords to get an overview of the topic.
- Make source cards for sources you will use for information.
- Begin to focus the topic.
- Write a statement of purpose about the topic.
- Brainstorm questions about the focused topic.
- Group questions into similar groupings.
- Add any new questions.
- Repeat step 2, listing more key words.
- Make a list of possible sources that can answer your questions.
- Find sources in the library, and/or on the computer. Make a source card for each.
- Make note cards and brainstorm questions.
- Change your statement of purpose into a thesis statement.
- Make an outline of your headings.

- Refocus your thesis statement if required.
- Write the body of your paper from notes.
- Cite any necessary information with parenthetical citations.
- Write an introduction and conclusion.
- Write a bibliography.
- Create a title page.
- Evaluate the paper.

These steps focus on "what" needs to be done to complete a research project. For the purposes of this chapter and the proposed research methodology, the focus on problem-solving, developing a solution and validating it in an effective manner will focus on "how" the research may be conducted.

According to Mingers (2006), a framework has been developed for Habermas's theory of communicative action in which the multi-dimensional world depicts that there are three different worlds namely, the objective, social and subjective. For the purpose of the proposed new research methodology to be discussed in the following section, it is important to note the significance of these world views to understand the way in which the researcher may tackle his or her research project.

As per Figure 1, the material world is outside and independent of humans. It can be shaped through our actions but this is subject to its constraints. Our relationship or perspective of this world is through observing, rather than being a participator. Through communication and self reflection, the social and personal worlds are evident as other forms of viewing the world. The personal world represents our thoughts, belief system, emotions and experiences, be it life or research experiences bringing about subjectivity into this world. In this world we are not simply observers: we experience the world with all senses. In the social world we play a participative and sharing role acting outwardly through rules, meaning, language and social practices (Mingers, 2006).

When developing a theory, theory building is based on a number of building blocks of scientific knowledge. A scientific study develops theories

Figure 1. Three worlds relevant to research methods – Mingers (2006)work developed from Habermas

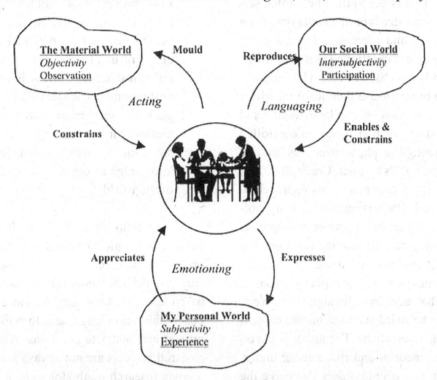

that explain how and why certain phenomena occur in order to allow for predictions to be made (Gregor, 2006).

According to Creswell (2009), there are four dominant philosophical notions and the one used affects which methods the researcher determines satisfactory to support the research questions. If the notion is understood and evident, this may assist the researcher when expressing his/her research in a verbal and written manner which supports the reason(s) for the choice of research method.

For the purpose of this chapter, the four dominant notions discussed will determine possibilities for researchers to choose a research project, title, questions and objectives based on his/her own research style. The term "horizon" (Garrett, 1978), which is used in phenomenological/interpretative literature, refers to the limits of a human's "world", that is the limit of the complex activities in which he or she is familiar. This could be certain prejudgements which change the expectation of what the truth is.

The proposed research methodology might stretch the researcher's horizon by sharing other perspectives which remove typical thinking patterns and preconceived assumptions.

The four notions include Positivism, Constructivism or Interpretivism, Critical Theory and Pragmatism. These perspectives differ on how knowledge, science and solutions work in conjunction to build a theory (Myers, 2009).

- The characteristic of Positivism, according to Oates (2006), is the objectivity in which the researcher becomes an impartial observer. In this way the researcher's worldview or notion is that there is a physical and social world to be studied and measured. The researcher's knowledge is based on logical assumptions from a set of evident facts. One of the basic techniques is through reductionism, in that they study things by breaking them into simpler components. This is due to their belief that scientific knowledge is built up over time from observations and inferences. The reliability of this notion is questioned as it is based on a researcher's observations. The methods used are more precise theories from which verifiable hypotheses can be extracted and are tested in isolation such as a controlled experiment. The phenomenon is studied in isolation of its context. Creswell (2009) states that the post positivists approach to research is by beginning with a theory, collecting data that either proves or disproves the theory, and then making revisions before additional tests are made.

- **Constructivism or Interpretivism** is a notion that does not distinguish between scientific knowledge and its human context and social interactions. The stance is less on verifying theories and more about understanding how people observe/perceive the world and make sense of it. Constructivists prefer methods that collect rich qualitative data about human activities from which local theories might emerge. This notion uses exploratory case studies and survey research. (Klein & Myers, 1999),

- **Critical Theory** focuses on scientific knowledge for its ability to free people from restraining systems of thought (Calhoun, 1995). These types of theorists have the view that research is a political act as knowledge empowers different groups within society or within existing structures. The research is then based on who it helps therefore participatory approaches and action research are used to engage people in the research. Furthermore case studies are used to point out trends and changes.

- **Pragmatism** acknowledges that all knowledge is incomplete and the value and extent of knowledge is dependent on the methods in which it was obtained (Menand, 1997). Knowledge is criticized for how useful it is

in solving practical problems. This is more relative as what may be practical for one person may not be practical for someone else. For this reason, truth is uncovered in rational discourse and it is judged by the best arguments. As this stance is less stringent, the researcher uses mixed research methods in a "free format" in order to solve the research problem from practical knowledge as opposed to an abstract view of the world.

The notions differ from each other in the perspective/angle in which the research is approached; the level of detail of the research; the way in which the theory is constructed from fact-based scientific knowledge to more abstract and observable knowledge; and to build a research project and adapt to solutions. Although IS/IT research projects are not always based on social science research methodologies, it is important to note the different angles and perspectives of research which will focus ones research in the long run. Furthermore, this will enable the researcher to solve problems and sub-problems in a structured approach with an understanding of personal research style preference or a suitable style based on what the researcher would like to research (Cornford & Smithson, 2006).

Creswell (2009) suggests that researchers embarking on a new research proposal understand their notion as this highlights the general orientation of the world and the nature of research that the researcher holds. These are shaped by discipline, belief systems and past research experience.

The following section highlights problems experienced by researchers in conducting or completing their studies and introduces the research methodology and approach.

3. PROPOSED NEW RESEARCH METHODOLOGY AND METHOD: IT/IS RESEARCH AND PROBLEM SOLVING IN A CHANGING LANDSCAPE

3.1 Issues, Controversies, Problems

As mentioned by Mouton (2001), large proportions of students who enrol for postgraduate degrees never finish their studies. With the non-completion rate for 2000 doctoral studies yielding 30% (Rudd and Hatch, 1968), a number of empirical studies have been conducted to understand the factors for low postgraduate completion rates. The most common findings or factors include: poor planning and management, methodological difficulties, writing up, isolation, personal problems and inadequate or negligent supervision (Noble, 1992; Phillips & Pugh, 1987; Rudd, 1985).

For the focus of this chapter, poor planning and management will be addressed to understand the underlying issues and to propose an alternative solution.

According to Mouton (2001), the reasons deduced through empirical studies for poor planning and management of students' research projects are as follows:

- Spending too much time in one area of the research project while neglecting other areas.
- Unfocused problem formulations that lead to inappropriate research designs.
- The collection of irrelevant data or inappropriate data analysis.
- The habit of side-tracking and getting too involved in one area of the study instead of sticking to the research objectives (Mouton, 2001).

In relation to unfocused problem formulations, the Johnstone El-Bana Model highlights that if a problem has many sub-problems, the more difficult it will be for the researcher to solve the problem. "The researcher must use working memory to simultaneously recall needed knowledge from long-term memory and to process demands of each sub-problem." (Johnstone, 1977). The outcome of this would possibly be an overwhelmed researcher who is likely to fail to solve the problem. This is a major hindrance which may cause the researcher to end the research project prematurely.

Plausible reasons for problem-solving issues include:

- Students have difficulty with problems in the absence of basic low-level facts (Frazer & Sleet, 1984).
- Students have an easier time with familiar problems which allow them to "chunk" several steps into a smaller number of steps (Newell & Simon, 1972).
- Students find problems which require conceptual understanding more difficult than problems which simply require application of an algorithm (Nakhleh & Mitchell, 1993).

Successful problem-solvers, therefore, differ from unsuccessful (or novice) problem-solvers in the following ways:

- Experts have more highly connected cognitive structure (Shavelson, 1972).
- "Novices have trouble categorising problems according to deep principles, but rather categorise according to surface features". (Chi, Feltovich, & Glaser, 1981).

To add to the complexity of IS research, the IS/IT industry, in general, is dynamic and experiences a changing IT/IS landscape on an almost daily basis.

Further research methodologies are required to enable research students to come up with research topics and to structure their research in such a way as to capture the essence of research. Furthermore, it is important that the level of detail is relevant to the solution and the completion timelines to ensure that the topic or solution is not obsolete at the end of the IS research project.

This calls for IS research to involve rapid research and IS problem-setting and problem-solving in order to analyze problems, set the right questions to solve problems and determine solutions within a shorter timeline without hampering the research quality.

For the purposes of developing new IS/IT research and innovations, this chapter will focus on achieving new insights for a conceptual IS research as opposed to a statistical project.

The following research questions will assist in understanding how the proposed solution will take shape:

- Does it ensure an understanding of basic concepts for research project?

- Does it determine how a student can keep track of sub-problems?
- Does it determine methods of conceptual thinking through cognitive structures?
- Does it propose a methodology for students to do quicker and effective problem-solving in a shorter timeline?

Some research has been conducted and the following taxonomies of IS/IT research methodologies and IS theory types will be discussed. The following tables have been extracted for discussion:

- A taxonomy of IS/IT Research Methodologies by Steenkamp & McCord (2007).
- A taxonomy of theory types in IS research by Gregor (2006).
- A Cognitive Structure for critical thinking.

Table 1. A taxonomy of IS/IT research methodologies by Steenkamp and McCord (2007)

Method	Nature	Applicability	Example Philosophical Notion
Quantitative	Relies on the collection of quantitative data resulting from formal controlled experiments.	Appropriate to replicate or build upon existing quantitative research, or to test candidate independent and dependent variables identified from qualitative studies.	Positivism
Qualitative	Relies on the collection of qualitative data from interviews, questionnaires, surveys, observations and inference.	Appropriate to understand the behaviours of systems or people in specific social and cultural contexts, and to validate findings by interpretations of the data.	Positivism, Constructivism or Interpretivism
Case Study	An empirical study which relies on observations made during or following a real world project.	Appropriate to discover potential behaviours of systems or people and to identify candidate independent and dependent variables.	Constructivism or Interpretivism; Critical Theory
Positivist	An empirical study which is based on observation and interventions using several methods.	Appropriate for research in IS/IT, business and management where phenomena, behaviours, process and objects form as part of the domain.	Positivism
Non-Positivist	Derives from phenomenology where human behaviours and organizations are studied and interpreted from individual perspectives.	Appropriate when the context within which the research is performed has social or cultural significance for the research problem	Constructivism or Interpretivism; Critical Theory
Mixed	Uses a pluristic approach and relies on several methods, known as pluralism and triangulation	Appropriate for situations where some phenomena are well understood, while others are less understood. Enables researcher to support/disagree or confirm/refute hypothesis or proposition.	Pragmatism

The Table 1 from the Taxonomy of IS/IT Research Methodologies of Steenkamp and McCord (2007) maps each of the research methodologies typically used in an IS/IT research project against one or more of the philosophical notions that were previously discussed. It should be noted that there are pure theory- and fact-based research approaches against more social and observable research. The purpose of the research methodology, discussed later in this chapter, outlines a way in which either approach or notions can be taken in order to prove/disprove a fact-based research or social/human factors using one or more of the research methods and philosophical notions.

Table 2 by Gregor (2006) shows the components of theories allowing IS researchers to identify: (i) what theory is composed of in general; and (ii) to analyse the components of their own theory and the theory of others. This framework is used in the following section for the analysis of examples of theories.

The authors found the taxonomies to be suitable as ways in addressing IS research challenges and developing predictive IS/IT solutions.

Table 3 specifies a number of ways in which to one can organize information for more effective understanding and recalling information as part of cognitive structuring (*The Basics of Effective Learning*, 2011).

The following section addresses the issues as was discussed pertaining to non-completion rates issues, problem solving issues, conceptual research issues and a dynamic and changing IS landscape through a proposed research methodology which creates a knowledge management base in which the student conducts problem setting and solving for a conceptual solution.

3.2 Solutions and Recommendations

To propose an alternative methodology addressing the non-completion of post-graduate studies the authors have linked the problem of IS research and IS/IT changing landscape to IS strategy planning where similar challenges of changing IT landscape are experienced and continuous improvements are required.

Since strategy links issue-based problem-solving for an array of challenges, the aim would therefore be to determine how an IS/IT student can make use of the Knowledge Management concept in tracking and documenting his/her train of thoughts to link it to problems and sub-problems.

Table 4, by Salmelaa and Spilb (2002), highlights comprehensive and incremental approaches

Table 2. A taxonomy of theory types in IS research byGregor (2006)

Theory Type	Attributes
Analysis	Says "what is". The theory does not extend beyond analysis and description. No causal relationships among phenomena are specified and no predictions are made.
Explanation	Says "what is", "how", "why", "when", "where". The theory provides explanations but does not aim to predict with any precision. There are no testable propositions.
Prediction	Says "what is" and "what will be". The theory provides predictions and has testable propositions but does not have well-developed justificatory causal explanations.
Explanation and prediction	Says "what is", "how", "why", "when", "where" and "what will be". Provides predictions and have both testable propositions and causal explanations.
Design and action	Says "how to do something". The theory gives explicit prescriptions (e.g., methods, techniques, principles of form and function) for constructing an artefact.

Table 3. Cognitive structures: Ways to organize information for more effectively understanding and remembering bythe basics of effective learning (2011)

Knowledge structures and critical thinking skills	Questions for review and key words found in essay questions	Ways to organize ideas visually
Knowledge: Recalling facts or observation; description.	Who, what, when, where, why? Key words: define, identify, label, list, locate, name, describe steps, process, or sequence.	List, definition, formula, illustration, diagram, map, plans, table, graph, chart, timeline, or flowchart.
Comprehension: Providing evidence of understanding by describing and/or clarifying concepts, events, or relationships between ideas.	Why, how? Key words: explain, clarify, discuss, illustrate, summarize, restate, infer, give an example, provide an analogy, classify, categorize, explain the importance or significance of...	Summary, example, analogy, web, tree, classification table, feature analysis grid, graph, matrix, index, outline.
Application: Demonstrating use for information, concepts, or techniques.	If...then? What is...? How would you apply...? Key words: demonstrate, apply.	Describe procedure or process using: algorithm, chronology, flow chart, plan, procedure, action chart, cycle chart, parts-function table.
Analysis: Examining in detail, identifying motives or causes, making inferences, finding evidence to support generalizations, decision making.	Why...? What can you conclude? What evidence can you find to support...? Key words: select, propose, sort, analyze, compare/contrast, explain, identify, prove, categorize, deduct, substantiate.	Break down into parts: Venn diagram, flow chart, fishbone diagram, troubleshooting chart, decision tree, parts-function table, stage table.
Synthesis: Solving problems, making predictions and/or producing original. representations, decision making.	Can you give an example of...? How will we solve...? What will happen...? How can we improve...? Key words: interpret, predict, hypothesize,.apply.	Troubleshooting chart, line graph, cycles, Venn diagram, illustration, decision tree.
Evaluation: Giving opinions about issues, judging the validity of ideas, judging the quality of art and other products; justifying opinions and ideas.	Do you agree...? Do you believe...? What is your opinion...? Do you think...? Why? Would it be better if...? Which...did you like? Why? Key words: evaluate, rank, rate, judge, criticize, debate, conclude.	Grid, rating chart, table.

Table 4. Comprehensive and incremental approaches for IS strategy planning by Salmelaa and Spilb (2002)

	Planning	Comprehensive practices	Incremental practices
1	Plan comprehensiveness	Plans are complicated and highly integrated with overall strategy	Plans are simple and loosely integrated with overall strategy
2	Approach to analysis	Formal, multiple analyses are used to derive plans	Personal experiences and judgment are used to derive plans
3	Planning organisation	Planning is based on formal representation from many different organizational groups	Planning is based on an informal network of a few key individuals
4	Basis for decisions	Formal methods and criteria are the basis for decisions	Shared group understanding of a few key individuals is the basis for decisions
5	Plan control	IS plans are periodically reviewed to adapt to changed circumstances	IS plans are continuously reviewed to adapt to changed circumstances

Table 5. IS Strategy planning linked to proposed methodology

	IS Planning - Comprehensive and Incremental Practices (Salmelaa and Spilb, 2002)	Research method	Philosophical notion	Theory type (Gregor, 2006)	Cognitive structure	*Post-Positivism methodology / Method (new)*
1	Plan comprehensiveness (complicated vs. simple).	Quantitative Qualitative Mixed		**Explanation:** Says "what is", "how", "why", "when", "where". The theory provides explanations but does not aim to predict with any precision. There are no testable propositions.	**Comprehension:** Providing evidence of understanding by describing and/or clarifying concepts, events, or relationships between ideas.	***Process Step:****Research Plan* ***Approach:****Gather and Capture Data* ***Method:*** *Data gathering and Analysis (Research mapping worksheet)*
2	Approach to analysis (Formal, multiple analyses vs. Personal experiences and judgement).	Quantitative Qualitative Mixed		**Analysis:** Says "what is". The theory does not extend beyond analysis and description. No causal relationships among phenomena are specified and no predictions are made.	**Application:** Demonstrating use for information, concepts, or techniques. **Analysis:** Examining in detail, identifying motives or causes, making inferences, finding evidence to support generalizations, decision making.	***Process Step:****Research Approach* ***Approach:****Analyze data* ***Method:*** *Research mapping used in conjunction with other methods*
3	Planning organisation (Large representation vs. informal network of a few key individuals).	Quantitative Qualitative Mixed	Pragmatism	**Prediction:** Says "what is" and "what will be". The theory provides predictions and has testable propositions but does not have well-developed justificatory causal explanations.	**Evaluation:** Giving opinions about issues, judging the validity of ideas, judging the quality of art and other products; justifying opinions and ideas.	***Process step:****Research analysis and evaluation* ***Approach:****Data validation* ***Method:*** *Objectives worksheet*
4	Basis for decisions (Formal methods vs. Shared group understanding).	Quantitative Qualitative Mixed	Critical Theory	**Explanation and prediction:** Says "what is", "how", "why", "when", "where" and "what will be". Provides predictions and have both testable propositions and causal explanations.	**Synthesis:** Solving problems, making predictions and/ or producing original representations, decision making.	***Process step:****Research Validation* ***Approach:****Interpret data and build associations* ***Method:*** *Idea generation worksheet*

continues on following page

Table 5. Continued

	IS Planning - Comprehensive and Incremental Practices (Salmelaa and Spilb, 2002)	Research method	Philosophical notion	Theory type (Gregor, 2006)	Cognitive structure	*Post-Positivism methodology / Method (new)*
5	Plan control (IS plans are periodically reviewed to adapt to changed circumstances vs. continuously reviewed to adapt to changed circumstances).	Quantitative Qualitative Mixed	Positivism Interpretivism	Design and action: Says "how to do something". The theory gives explicit prescriptions (e.g., methods, techniques, principles of form and function) for constructing an artefact.	Knowledge: Recalling facts or observation; description.	*Build Insight (Solution/ Interpretation worksheet)*

for IS Strategy Planning varying from complicated and loosely integrated plans with overall strategy, formal and personal experiences and judgement used to derive plans, organisational groups and personal experiences, formal methods and criteria vs. Informal basis for decisions and periodically reviewed plans to adapt to changed circumstance vs. IS plans being reviewed.

The IS strategy planning is adapted to include a theory type, cognitive structure to form a post-positivism methodology, approach and method to enable a conceptual IS research project.

Table 5 is a mapping between the different research methods, taxonomies, notions, theory types and cognitive structures as an adaption or leading to the new proposed post-positivism methodology and method proposed by the authors.

The following section provides an overview of the IS research proposition.

3.3 Approach to IS Research and Problem Solving

The proposed new research methodology combines the four philosophical notions and three worlds in a dynamic manner by using personal, social and material worldviews to validate each step of the research project. To do this it uses the strengths of each view and in doing so, manoeuvres past the weaknesses to aim for an innovative and validated research IT/IS outcome/solution that is practical and relevant now or in the future.

From this, a solution can be adapted as the best possible outcome for the research objectives and therefore the outcome of the research solution. Although IS/IT research projects are not always based on social science research methodologies, it is important to note the different angles and perspectives in which to strategically approach IS/IT research given the number of changes experienced in the field and the high level of innovation it presents on a daily basis.

Furthermore, this will enable the researcher to solve problems and sub-problems in a structured way with an understanding of personal research style preference or a suitable prescribed style that is required to get to the desired research outcome.

A knowledgebase will be created by the researcher as part of this methodology to enable information linkage as part of data gathering and literature review process such as linkage to similar information, to same or different authors talking on a similar topic, to existing facts and then making sense of it so as to gain new insights or identify gaps that require further investigation.

The objectives of the research methodology and approach are to aid a postgraduate student to:

- Develop awareness of research style and notion appropriate for the researcher in terms of personality and what is suitable for the research project.
- Determine research style in how the researcher best performs research.
- Structure research for effective problem-solving purposes.
- Focus the scope of research and research objectives by clearly stating and mapping each area to an objective.
- Create linkages in research and literature found to start building on scientific knowledge.
- Create a knowledgebase for literature study purposes and problem construction and resolution.
- Ensure that a large set of literature has been investigated and read for an overall

view for the topic and a detailed view required in writing the research proposal and beginning the research project.

- Build and track associations with the existing knowledgebase whether it is topics, authors, opinions or arguments to create the big picture for the researcher in a controlled manner.

The assumption for using the research methodology is that the researcher either has a possible solution in mind, or vaguely knows the topic that he or she would like to research.

The following sections provide an overview of the research methodology and approach from research project commencement and validation to the conclusion of a research project.

Table 6. New research process, approach and data generation mapping

Research process	• Research planning (Phase 1)	• Research approach (Phase 2)	• Research analysis and evaluation (Phase 3)	• Research validation (Phase 4)
Research activities	• Determine dominant research notion • Gather and capture data for basic understanding of concepts for a possible research topic or area of study	• Determine top-down or bottom-up approach or combination (Refer to Figure 3 and 4 in upcoming section)	• Validate data • Interpret data • Outcome and Solution	• Perform research validation using research methods (interviews, surveys etc) • Determine relevancy • Determine cost • Determine interest • Determine time frame • Test Practicality
Research approach	• Gather and capture data	• Analyze data	• Data validation	• Interpret data and build associations
Research method	• Data gathering and analysis (Research mapping worksheet)	• Research mapping used in conjunction with other methods such as creative thinking or cognitive structures	• Objectives worksheet	• Idea generation worksheet • Build insight (Solution/Interpretation worksheet)
Outcome	• Literature Study	• Research mapping • Mind mapping	• Research Proposal (topic, objectives, problem statement, significance of study) • Possible solution or point of view	Validated: • Solution • Theory • Concept • Model • Methodology • Strategy

Figure 2. Proposed research styles based on philosophical notions adapted fromCreswell (2009)

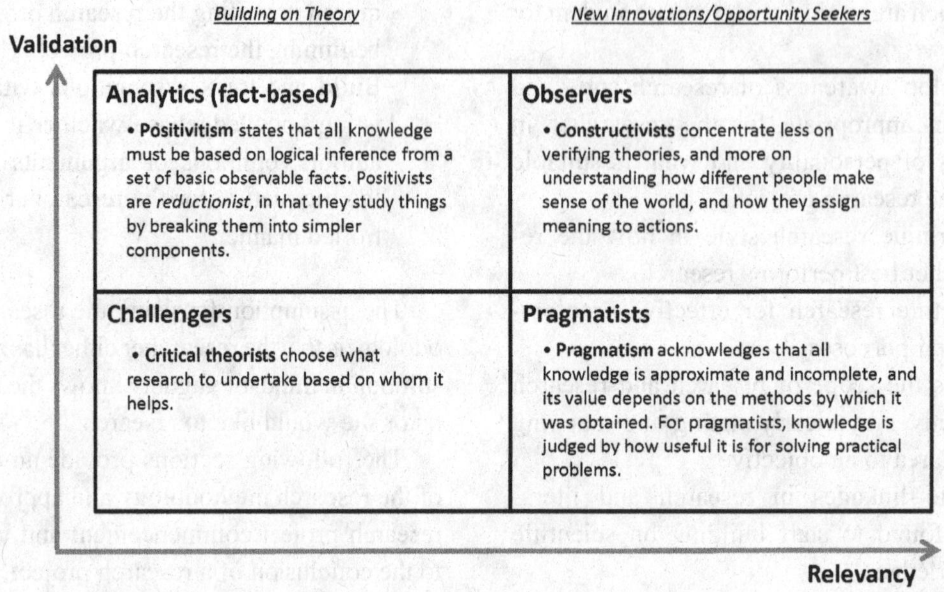

3.4 IS Research Methodology and Approach

Research projects typically use a planning, analysis and validation process against the literature review. For the purposes of this research methodology, the notions and theory styles are used in conjunction with a structured approach in interpreting, building insight and predicting possible scenarios and problem solving in determining IS solutions.

The research methodology has four areas of planning, approach, analysis and evaluation and research validation to conduct research and build relevant knowledge. Refer to Table 6 for the proposed new research process, approach and data generation mapping as part of the new methodology.

The tool used to support the process as outlined in the following section as a Microsoft Excel Spreadsheet with a number of worksheets to capture data for analysis purposes. This information would be used by the researcher to determine a method of proving or disproving the solution that was deduced from the phase 1, 2 and 3 of research.

3.4.1 Phase 1: Research Planning

The objective of this phase is for the researcher to determine his or hers dominant notion and gather data for basic understanding and comprehension of a topic.

In the previous section the philosophical notions were noted as differing in views on how knowledge, science and solutions work in conjunction to build a theory. From these notions and for the purposes of illustrating the research methodology as part of this section, the notions will be used as a starting point of a research project. They will be used in the perspective or angle in which the research is approached, the level of detail of in which the research will be targeted, and the way in which the theory is constructed or built up to form a research project. This may be from fact-based scientific knowledge to more abstract and observable knowledge.

Figure 2 has been adapted from Creswell (2009) philosophical worldviews.

Based on an adaption of Creswell (2009) philosophical worldviews, the following research styles are suggested in order for the researcher to validate and build on existing theory or, venture into seeking opportunity or new innovations that are relevant currently or in the r future.

- **Analytics** break things into simpler components and for the purposes of this research methodology, they tend to lean towards fact-based research projects whereby existing models and facts are broken down and built up again in a new way.
- **Challengers** choose research based on whom it helps or benefits. This may be a certain organisation or a government agency. For the purposes of this methodology, challengers literally test how things are currently done in the real world and focus on how a research project will help a certain organisation.
- **Pragmatist's** knowledge is judged by how useful it is for solving practical problems. Within Phase 4 of this research methodology, this research style is most appropriate in validating the proposed solution and determining its applicability or relevance in the real world.
- **Observers** concentrate less on verifying theories but more on understanding human behaviour and what drives that behaviour. For the purposes of this methodology, observers are the "bystanders" and daydreamers of the research styles by analysing "body language" for the purposes of their research projects. This research style is also important to use for Phase 4 of the methodology as the style has an underlying way of analysing the practical fit of a potential solution.

Data gathering and comprehension is to discover information through reading journals and conference papers as per literature studies. In other words, to start linking information in a structured way to support the research project, whether the outcome be a proposal, paper, conference

presentation or the actual thesis. Each possible resource, such as a journal paper, is evaluated against a number of different criteria in order to determine its relevance to the main topic at hand and capturing knowledge in the process while doing so. The research methodology can be used to determine research questions, objectives, scope and possible solutions in a post graduate research study. It outlines a structured process that was used to search for information as part of a literature study and interpret that information according to different criteria and requirements.

3.4.2 Phase 2: Research Approach

The objective of this phase is to determine whether a top-down or bottom-up approach will be used for the research project.

The following guidelines can be used to determine the most relevant approach:

- For a vague idea of a topic or field of study the researcher would use a top-down approach (Figure 3).
- For an upfront solution the researcher would use the bottom-up approach (Figure 4).

Top-Down Approach: Building Insight from Data

The Top-down approach assumes that the researcher has a vague idea of a topic or field of study to begin the research topic. The approach stems from the idea that the more data or information that is gathered and analysed, the greater or richer the insight that is built over time. As per the diagram below, the top section of the hourglass focuses on validating and interpreting data while the second half of the hourglass is where the insight development comes into play associating ideas and ultimately developing the bigpicture view upon which to narrow or focus an appropriate solution.

Figure 3. Proposed research approach: Top-down view

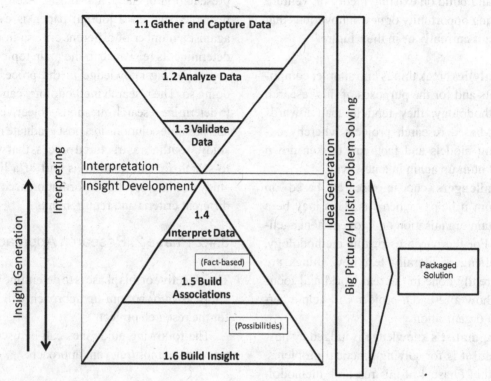

Top-Down Approach: Activities and Tasks/ Data Collection and Interpretation Techniques

As part of interpretation, the research approach suggests that as with typical research process steps, the researcher begins with gathering and capturing data. For this methodology, the data is captured in a tool as an aid in problem solving. This tool is outlined in the next section as an Excel Spreadsheet. Secondly, the researcher would analyze data that is captured in the excel tool. This data is initially raw data and re-analyzed to be processed into the researcher's own information, knowledge and insights. The researcher would then validate the data across existing journals, authors and other information.

For insight development purposes, the next step for the researcher is to interpret data that is processed in order to build associations and identify gaps that are fact based. In order to identify gaps, the spreadsheet can be used to gather and capture information as raw data, then to analyze

and create the associations through imagination, associations and layered perception-building. Once the gaps are identified they can be further researched to determine whether they are valid gaps or whether they can be positioned at another angle. For example, a researcher may identify a gap in a IS process however, after some research the gap has been closed by another researcher but there is a further opportunity to tackle it from another angle or perspective.

Once these gaps have been identified or closed and the scope of work becomes clearer, the researcher is in the position to make sense of the information based on objective, subjective and social worlds to build insight.

As the researcher is interpreting data, so does he/she build insight and generate ideas in a big picture / problem solving manner to formulate a packaged solution.

Figure 4. Proposed research approach: Bottom-up view

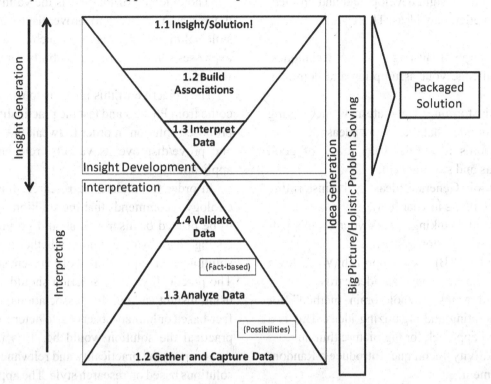

Bottom-Up Approach: Validating Insight with Data

The Bottom-up approach assumes that the researcher already has insight or a solution to an already identified problem. For this reason the approach works the other way round, with the insight or solution as the starting point that is required for interpretation. The second half of the hourglass focuses on the data gathering and analysis to support initial thinking or idea of the solution.

In the bottom-up approach the hourglass is flipped upside down as the insight development and interpretation areas are merged and take place at the same time as depicted in Figure 4 above. In step 1.1 the researcher begins the research project with specific insight (whether this be through previous perception or experience) or a solution that he/she would like to prove. Secondly, build associations would take place in reverse from the top-down approach. Building associations would

take place in conjunction with data gathering and capturing to build the associations within the literature as opposed to building associations with the outer world. Thirdly the data analysis is then interpreted as part of steps 1.3 for both interpretation and insight development. And lastly, the initial solution or insight is validated against this theory and the scientific knowledge base that the researcher has maintained through the use of the spreadsheet.

In order to gain new insights, the following may be useful to use against pre-conceived ideas, many of which are adapted from problem-solving and creative-thinking techniques as highlighted in the Squido Education Topics (2011) website.

"Creativity involves breaking out of established patterns in order to look at things in a different way." - Edward de Bono (as cited in Squid Education Topics, 2011).

The set of creative thinking techniques as per Squid Education Topics (2011), can be used as the part of the insight development and problem solving to elicit new ideas. These are:

- Assumption-Busting techniques: Challenge your assumption and dominant ideas.
- Brainstorming: Generate new ideas using techniques that create new ideas.
- Edison's Idea File: Keep track of good ideas and storing them.
- Konini: Generate ideas by brainstorming with others in your field
- Lateral Thinking: Break your brain's pattern recognition system.
- The Lotus Blossom Approach: Write down problems and generate idea cards
- Mind Maps: "Whole-brain method" for generating and organizing ideas. This is a good approach for big picture thinking.
- Creativity Technique: Introduce a Random Element.
- Reverse brainstorming: State your problem in reverse, create a positive statement.
- SCAMPER: Substitute/Simplify, Combine, Adapt, Modify/Distort, Put to other purposes, Eliminate, Rearrange.

3.4.3 Phase 3: Research Analysis and Evaluation

The objective of research analysis and evaluation is to validate data and interpret data for synthesis purposes. The outcome is a Research Proposal (topic, objectives, problem statement, significance of study) or possible solution or point of view. The step is important to link back to the research objectives to ensure focus of the research.

3.4.4 Phase 4: Research Validation

Research validation, once a possible solution or a number of solutions have been identified; the practicality of the solution is tested or validated in order to determine its relevance and practical-

ity. The outcome of Phase 4 is the validation of the research in order to prove/disprove a possible solution to package it in such a way that it expresses some type of applicability for which it was intended.

The objective of this phase is to use the outcome from Phase 3 and test the practicality of the proposed solution in order to tweak the solution and prove/disprove its validity, relevancy and applicability.

In order to validate the research, this methodology recommends that the solution or model to be proved or disproved should go through a testing phase by determining whether it is a new solution or an improvement of a current solution. The practicality of the solution should is tested using insight and building associations, whether fact-based or human-observed, to determine how practical the solution would be. This includes determining the practicality and relevancy of the solutions based on research style. The applicability should be estimated in terms of technology and resources required. For example, does the technology or resources required to build the solution exist? What is the "roadmap" for the required technology to exist? What is the price of the technology currently? Is the solution feasible?

In this section, the proposed new research methodology, approach and research guideline processes were discussed as an alternative research methodology for predictive problem solving and innovative creations as part of IS/IT research projects. The following section gives an example of how the Excel Spreadsheet is used as a supporting tool for data generation and analysis.

4. PROPOSED RESEARCH METHOD FOR DATA GENERATION AND ANALYSIS

"Methods are the techniques or procedures used to gather and analyse data related to a hypothesis or research question." Redman and Mory (1923) define research as "the systemized search for new knowledge" or an investigation to establish new Hb facts using a scientific method.

In investigating literature or the field of study for a research project the following method can be applied to systematically gather and analyze data related to a hypothesis or research question:

- Use the Microsoft Excel Spreadsheet as a tool to support the proposed new methodology with a number of worksheets to capture data for analysis and solution purposes.
- Use the spreadsheet called "IS Research Project - Problem Solving" as a data generation tool in the development of a literature review.

The benefits of using the spreadsheet are to capture and interpret information and to track which research information is useful, discover the linkage and similarities between articles/journals and authors and create associations from the knowledgebase that is created from using this spreadsheet.

The researcher can use the structured spreadsheet in capturing research information as part of a literature review. The spreadsheet is made up of a number of worksheets namely:

- Research mapping worksheet.
- "What if?" scenarios worksheet.
- Idea generation worksheet.
- Research objectives worksheet.
- Solution worksheet.
- References worksheet.

The output of the spreadsheet can be used to start the research proposal, structuring papers, or writing an actual research thesis. Together with a mind map and other creative techniques as indicated in the previous section, the researcher can use both outputs in determining a way in order to prove/disprove the initial solution. For instance,

deciding whether a simulation is suitable in proving a model.

The spreadsheet provides a practical, structured and scalable way to produce information flow in which one can build other worksheets as required and break down existing worksheets as required.

4.1 Worksheet 1: Research Mapping

The purpose of this worksheet is to capture information based on research via journals, articles and other literature. It can be used as a way to structure information in such a way as to handle the researcher's study in a "database"/knowledgebase manner. The purpose is to determine "What research has been done?"

The worksheet includes the following sections/columns to capture information. Each sub-column and description is pre-populated. The example column as per Table 7 is where the researcher would capture information.

The benefits of this worksheet include capturing information in a "database", linear structure for the researcher to maintain the control of keeping information in a consolidated place and to build on a knowledgebase.

The outcome of the worksheet forms the foundation of the research project. It will inform the outcome/solution and in developing research outcomes such as a paper, article, journal or the actual thesis. The depth of information determines how the researcher can use the information to answer the following questions:

- Will it inform the structure of the thesis?
- Will it form the storyline of the thesis?
- Will it inform a possible research solution?
- Or will it merely focus the research topic?

Note: The solution may come before you have defined your list of research questions, objectives, and topic of which the researcher may capture in the spreadsheet.

Table 7. Research mapping worksheet

Column name	Sub-column name	Description/Purpose	Example
Linkage		Linkage between topic and concept. Chaining the research through topics, authors, current research, linkages within articles	
	Area		Social Networking
	Topic	What is the research topic?	Social Networking
	Sub-topic	Is there a sub-topic?	Are people changing the way they interact?
	Topic/ Sub-topic Description	What is the description of the topic and/or sub-topic?	
	New concept	How often has this topic come up? Is it a new concept? Are there potentially any gaps that you can see at this stage	No
	Research title	What is the research title?	"People are changing the way they socialise"
	Research description	What is the research description? Summarised version.	This paper is about how young people do not use conventional means to communicate
What research has been done?		What research has been done in this area?	Not known as yet, to investigate.
Argument		What is the argument and concept, What is the topic about?	
	Argument	What is the argument?	Does social networking impact people's communication skills?
	For/Against	Are they for or against the topic? Do you support this argument? Why so?	A and B say that this is the case.
	Counter argument	Is there a counter argument by the same or another author? Do you have your own counter argument? What is it?	X and Y say that this is not the case.
	Significance / How to use it in research	What is the significance of the argument? How can you use it in your research?	Relevance for human behaviour.
	Limitations/Purpose	What are the limitations or purpose?	Unknown what the foreseen impact will be therefore there will be a prediction.
	Usefulness	What is the usefulness for this topic? Does it spurt on other topics?	Highly useful.
	Research string	What was the research string that you used to get this research?	"impact of social networking".
	Title	What is the title of the research?	
Research Information		List of the research information that will assist in building your bibliography	
	Source	Where did you source this information?	Internet – web site.
	Type?	What is the type? Journal, article, conference, newspaper article, book, web site?	Newspaper article.
	Require Access	Do you require access to the information if not acquired?	No
	Link	What is the link?	www.impactofSN.com

continues on following page

Table 7. Continued

Column name	Sub-column name	Description/Purpose	Example
	Date of access	What is the date of access?	11/01/2011
	Date published	When was the research published?	09/05/2010
	Author	Who is the author?	John Smith
	Bibliography	What will the reference be?	Reference
Paper / Thesis		Of what research objective or chapter it can form a basis? The researcher may not have an idea of what the objectives, thesis structures, storyline may be at this point, however this section will assist in formulating this.	
	Objective	What are the research objectives to which it is applicable? Can be applicable to more than one or build on it.	Does social networking impact people's communication skills and what will happen over time?
	Chapter	To what chapter is this research topic applicable? Is there any other topic to which this can link?	Chapter 2: Social interactions are changing.
To be		How this information starts informing the model or strategy (basically a possible outcome of your research project that you are trying to solve). The researcher may not have an idea of this as yet, however, this section will start forming that model/strategy/solution to some extent.	Identify new ways of socializing.
	Model	Can you see a possible model being formed? Is it a concept? Can you physically build it? Or is it theory-based only?	
	Strategy	Can this support or be a stand-alone strategy? For whom: government, company, individuals. This will start informing your scope of research and (people to interview)	

The output of this worksheet can be used to mind map ideas and research.

4.2 Worksheet 2: "What if?" Scenarios

The purpose of this worksheet is to determine the "What if?" scenarios and may lead to the development of the research question(s). From capturing the information, the researcher can start analyzing the summarised version and deduce some scenarios and interpretation. The purpose is to see how the research links to each other and real world examples or situations. This takes the theory one step forward in terms of making it real world and practical. The scenarios may be based on more than just the information read. It can be deduced by both the information and real-world facts such as the current news affairs. This begins informing the purpose of the research, significance and possible limitations. Not all research found may have significance and this is when the researcher can start highlighting the "not-so-useful" articles. These articles can be kept on a new worksheet to keep track in case the information is required at a later date or perhaps it becomes a counter-argument.

The example column, as per the Table 8, is where the researcher would capture information.

The benefits of this worksheet are to determine and interpret possible scenarios of what may occur in relation to the research and/or real life situations (historical, current affairs etc). This forms the basis of building research questions and research objectives. It also begins defining the scope and story line of the research which is

Table 8. "What if?" scenarios worksheet

Column name	Description/Purpose	Example
No.	This purpose is to keep track and show the linkage between ideas/thoughts and research	1
Problem statement	Could be linked to "What If" scenario	What if no one could communicate verbally or in person anymore?
Area	What area in the research mapping?	Social networking
Scope	This determines the scope of the scenario	Human race
Scenario	This is a sentence or short description of the actual scenario that has been deduced by research, real life (historical, current affairs, philosophical ideas)	People cannot communicate anymore?
Key Question / Statement	This becomes the research question. One of the questions will become the first or key question on which the basis of the research is formed.	What if no one could communicate verbally or in person anymore?
Description		
Link to Literature	Link back to literature in research mapping	John Smith said xyz.
Link to Research Objectives	Link to research objectives	1
Impact	Impact of the scenario	High
Effort	Effort of preventing the scenario from taking place	High
Risk	Risk of it happening? Is it likely to happen or is it purely philosophical at this stage?	Medium
Quantitative Valuation	How is this valuated in a quantitative form?	Unknown
Maturity	What is the maturity?	Medium
Type of benefit	Does it link to or have a benefit?	Yes, in future generations.
Qualitative Valuation	How is this valuated in a qualitative form?	Subjective, will be based on interviews.
Final Valuation	What is the final valuation?	Unknown at this stage.
Comments/Issues/Considerations	Any comments, issues, or considerations within scenario or against another	Consider different generations and their expectations in terms of technology.
Where (Chapter, Solution)	Where in the thesis and in which chapter it can be used, or within the solution.	Chapter 2: Social Interactions are changing.

beneficial when writing a paper or the actual thesis.

The outcome of this worksheet will lead to the development of the research questions. The output of this worksheet can be used to mind map ideas, research etc.

4.3 Worksheet 3: Idea Generation

The purpose of this worksheet is to capture ideas forming part of the problem-solving effort and solution development.

The example column as per Table 9 is where the researcher would capture information.

The benefit of idea generation is to start translating and interpreting the research and scenarios into possible solution ideas.

The outcome of the worksheet includes possible solutions to the problem such as a Solution, Model, Strategy or Methodology which may form part of your research or be a starting point for future validation. The output of this worksheet can be used to mind-map ideas and research.

Table 9. Idea generation worksheet

Column name	Description/Purpose	Example
No.	This purpose is to keep track and show the linkage between ideas/thoughts and research.	1
Problem statement	Linking back to the problem statement in the scenario.	Same as above
Area	What area in the research mapping?	
Scope	Scope of the idea?	
Idea title	Title of the idea.?	
Key question/Statement	Key question or statement which forms research question?	
Description	Description of the idea?	
Link to literature	Link back to literature in research mapping.	
Link to research objectives	Link to research objectives.	
Impact	Impact of the idea?	
Effort	Effort of implementing the idea?	
Risk	Risk of it happening? Is it likely to happen or is it purely philosophical at this stage?	
Quantitative valuation	How is this valuated in a quantitative form?	
Maturity	What is the maturity?	
Type of benefit	Does it link to or have a benefit?	
Qualitative valuation	How is this valuated in a quantitative form?	
Final valuation	What is the final valuation?	
Comments/issues/considerations	Any comments, issues, or considerations within scenario or against another?	
Where (chapter, solution)	Where in the thesis and in which chapter it can be used, or within the solution?	

Table 10. Research objectives worksheet

Column name	Description/Purpose	Example
Research objectives	Built from the scenarios and ideas as per previous worksheets	1
Building the story	Start building the story in words and "see" the outline of the paper, thesis and what you are trying to communicate	TBD

4.4 Worksheet 4: Research Objectives

The purpose of this worksheet is to create research objectives.

The example column as per Table 10 is where the researcher would capture information.

The benefit of the worksheet is to link the research, scenarios and ideas to form the research questions, objectives and to begin building the research story.

The outcomes of the worksheet include: Research questions, Research objectives, Research title

The output of this worksheet can be used to mind-map ideas and research. The mind-map may change or a second one built to show a view against research objectives.

Table 11. Solution (interpretation) worksheet

Column name	Description/Purpose	Example
Concept	Can a new concept be built from the analysis?	TBD
Model	Can a new model be built from the analysis or can an existing model be improved if the gaps are less than a certain percentage?	TBD
Strategy	Can a new strategy be built or can a framework in which a strategy be customised? To whom is this applicable?	TBD

4.5 Worksheet 5: Solution (Interpretation)

The purpose of this worksheet is to capture any thought of solution or interpretation.

The worksheet includes the following sections/columns to capture solutions, concepts, models, strategies:

The example column as per Table 11 is where the researcher would capture information.

The solution could contain one or all three (concept, model, strategy)

The benefit of this worksheet is to combine all the information, knowledge, ideas etc. into possible solutions as part of problem-solving and finalising the knowledgebase. The outcome is an initial Concept, Model, and Strategy that the researcher is striving to prove or disprove as part of his/her research.

4.6 Worksheet 6: References

The purpose of this worksheet is to capture literature references to keep a working record or list as the student researches for a literature review. The student can also use existing referencing tools.

4.7 Assumptions

Facts assumed to be true, but not verified, include that IS/IT new innovations can be identified through this process and methodology.

The research methodology assumes that the research project is conceptual in nature and does not require algorithms or statistical data analysis to determine outcomes. Furthermore, the methodology assumes that a great level of creativity is involved in the research project.

4.8 Significance of Study

The research methodology fills the gap in literature in that a post-positivism methodology is outlined for studies in which the applicability or relevancy level is high.

The professional application would be to link studies with real life applications and to ensure their relevancy. It therefore aims to improve the IT/IS industry in ensuring that research is current, applicable and practical in its application in industry.

4.9 Limitations

The limitations of the research methodology is that it is structured in nature and relies on the research student to use other preferred methods of critical thinking and analysis using methods such as Web, Troubleshooting Chart or Decision Trees to enhance the process. The proposed research methodology makes use of the spreadsheet for data-capture and analysis purposes and insight/idea generation in the form that the research student prefers.

4.10 Scope and Delimitations

The bounds of the study include cognitive structures for conceptual studies. The research methodology does not attempt to replace or enhance existing methodologies but to provide as a filter for conceptual type studies.

The weaknesses of the study are that it assumes a large percentage of the critical/creative thinking techniques and knowledge-sorting takes place and that the researcher is able to sort through this information.

5. FUTURE RESEARCH DIRECTIONS

Future research directions include linking the methodology to creative thinking and traditional methodologies for Philosophies, Methods and Innovations.

6. CONCLUSION

The IT/IS landscape and industry changes on an almost daily basis with a high level of innovations coming through. A typical five- year research study may yield to a result that is no longer applicable or relevant when the student finishes his/her research project. For this reason research in this field requires a higher level of innovation and a quicker turnaround time to keep up with the exponential revolution in the IT field.

REFERENCES

Buchanan, D. A., & Bryman, A. (Eds.). (2009). *The SAGE handbook of organizational research methods*. London, UK: SAGE Publications.

Calhoun, C. (1995). *Critical social theory: Culture, history, and the challenge of difference*. Oxford, UK: Blackwell.

Chi, M. T. H., Feltovich, P. J., & Glaser, R. (1981). Categorization and representation of physics problems by experts and novices. Pittsburgh, PA: Lawrence Erlbaum Associates. *Cognitive Science*, *5*(2), 121–152. doi:10.1207/s15516709cog0502_2

Cornford, T., & Smithson, S. (2006). *Project research in information systems: A student's guide* (2nd ed.). London, UK: Palgrave.

Council of Graduate Schools. (2008). *Ph.D. completion and attrition: Analysis of baseline program data from the Ph.D. completion project*. Washington, DC: Author.

Creswell, J. W. (2009). *Research design: Qualitative, quantitative, and mixed method approaches* (3rd ed.). Los Angeles, CA: SAGE publications.

Crotty, M. (1998). *The foundations of social research: Meaning and perspective in the research process*. St Leonards, Australia: Allen & Unwin.

Franzoni, C. (2006). *Do scientists get fundamental research ideas by solving practical problems?* Paper presented at the 11th International J. A. Schumpeter Society Conference: Innovation, Competition and Growth: Schumpeterian Perspectives, Sophia-Antipolis. France.

Frazer, M. J., & Sleet, R. J. (1984). A study of students' attempts to solve chemical problems. *European Journal of Science Education*, *6*(2), 141–152. doi:10.1080/0140528840060204

Garrett, J. E. (1978). Hans-Georg Gadamer on "fusion of horizons". *Man and World*, *11*(3), 392–400. doi:10.1007/BF01251946

Gregor, S. (2006). The nature of theories in Information Systems. *Management Information Systems Quarterly*, *30*(3), 611–642.

Johnstone, A. H. (1997). Chemistry teaching: Science or alchemy? *Journal of Chemical Education*, *74*(3), 262–268. doi:10.1021/ed074p262

Jonker, J., & Pennink, B. (2010). *The essence of research methodology. A precise guide for Masters and PhD students in Management Sciences*. Heidelberg, Germany: Springer.

Kasi, P. M. (2009). *Research what why and how? A treatise from researchers to researchers*. Indiana, USA: AuthorHouse.

Klein, H. K., & Myers, M. D. (1999). A set of principles for conducting and evaluating interpretative field studies in Information Systems. *Management Information Systems Quarterly, 23*(1), 67–93. doi:10.2307/249410

Kothari, C. R. (2006). *Research methodology: Methods and techniques.* Delhi, India: New Age International Publishers.

Leech, N. L., & Onwuegbuzie, A. J. (Eds.). (2005). *Taking the "Q" out of research: Teaching research methodology courses without the divide between quantitative and qualitative paradigms.* Florida, USA: Springer.

Menand, L. (1997). *Pragmatism: A reader.* Vintage Press.

Merriam Webster Dictionary. (n.d.). *Definition of methodology.* Retrieved February 23, 2011, from http://www.merriam-webster.com/dictionary/methodology

Meyers, M. D., & Klein, H. K. (2011). A set of principles for conducting critical research in Information Systems. *Management Information Systems Quarterly, 35*(1), 1–21.

Mingers, J. (2001). Combining IS research methods: Towards a pluralist methodology. Coventry, UK. *Information Systems Research, 12*(3), 240–259. doi:10.1287/isre.12.3.240.9709

Mouton, J. (2001). *How to succeed in your Masters and Doctoral studies – A South African guide and resource book.* Pretoria, South Africa: Van Schaik Publishers.

Mulkay, M. J. (1977). Sociology of the scientific research community. In Spiegel-Rosing, I., & de Solla Price, D. (Eds.), *Science, technology and society. A cross-disciplinary perspective* (pp. 93–148). Sage Publications.

Myers, D. M. (2009). *Qualitative research in business & management.* Los Angeles, CA: Sage.

Nakhleh, M. B., & Mitchell, R. C. (1993). Concept-learning versus problem-solving: There is a difference. *Journal of Chemical Education, 70*(3), 190–192. doi:10.1021/ed070p190

National Institute for Health Research. (2009). *University of Leeds.* Leeds Teaching Hospital Trusts. Retrieved February 15, 2011, from http://www.rdinfo.org.uk/flowchart/flowchart.html

Newell, A., & Simon, H. A. (1972). *Human problem solving.* Englewood Cliffs, NJ: Prentice Hall.

Noble, K. A. (1992). *An international prognostic study, based on an acquisition model, of the degree Philosophise Doctor (PhD).* Ottawa, Canada: University of Ottawa.

Oates, B. J. (2006). *Researching Information Systems and computing.* Los Angeles, CA: Sage.

Phillips, E., & Pugh, D. S. (1994). *How to get a PhD: A handbook for students and their supervisors* (2nd ed.). Buckingham, UK: Open University Press.

RealInnovation.com. (2011). *Innovation - What is innovation?* Retrieved 10 June, 2011, from http://www.realinnovation.com/content/what_is_innovation.asp

Redman, L. V., & Mory, A. V. H. (1923). *The romance of research, 10.*

Rudd, E. (1985). *A new look at post-graduate failure.* Guildford Surrey, UK: Society for Research into Higher Education.

Rudd, E., & Hatch, S. (1968). *Graduate study and after.* London, UK: Weidenfeld & Nicolson.

Samuels, H. (2011). Basic steps in the research process. *Cambridge Rindge and Latin School Research Guide.* Retrieved February 15, 2011, from http://www.crlsresearchguide.org/

Sharma, M. (2004). *Research methodology.* New Delhi, India: Anmol Publications.

Shavelson, R. J. (1972). Some aspects of the correspondence between content structure and cognitive structure in physics instruction. *Journal of Educational Psychology, 63*(3), 225–234. doi:10.1037/h0032652

Singh, Y. K., & Bajpai, R. B. (2008). *Research methodology: Techniques and trends*. New Delhi, India: A P H Publishing Corporation.

Squido Education Topics. (2011). *Creative thinking techniques - Enhance your creativity*. Retrieved February 1, 2011, from http://www.squidoo.com/creative-techniques

Statistics Canada. (2000). Brain drain and brain gain: The migration of knowledge workers from and to Canada. *Education Quarterly Review, 6*, 8–35.

Steenkamp, A. L., & McCord, S. A. (2007). Approach to teaching research methodology for Information Technology. *Journal of Information Systems Education; ABI/INFORM Global, 255*.

The Basics of Effective Learning. (2011). *Cognitive structures: Ways to organize information for more effectively understanding and remembering*. Retrieved 8 June, 2011, from http://www.bucks.edu/~specpop/Elabqst.htm

KEY TERMS AND DEFINITIONS

Cognitive Structures: Knowledge and critical thinking structures.

Constructivism or Interpretivism: Is a notion that does not distinguish between scientific knowledge and its human context and social interactions.

Creative Thinking Techniques: Techniques used to spur creativity.

Critical Theory: Focuses on scientific knowledge for its ability to free people from restraining systems of thought.

Idea Generation: Generating ideas.

Linkage: Creating a link between data and ideas.

Mapping: Map literature against research objectives, questions and ideas.

Philosophical Notions/Stances: The four notions include Positivism, Constructivism or Interpretivism, Critical Theory and Pragmatism. These perspectives differ on how knowledge, science and solutions work in conjunction to build a theory.

Positivism: Is the objectivity in which the researcher becomes an impartial observer.

Pragmatism: Acknowledges that all knowledge is incomplete and the value and extent of knowledge is dependent on the methods in which it was obtained.

Problem Solving: Solving problems in systematic why.

What if Scenarios: Building scenarios in the likelihood that certain events happen.

Chapter 15

Integrating Conceptual and Empirical Approaches for Software Engineering Research

Annette L. Steenkamp
Lawrence Technological University, USA

Theresa Kraft
University of Michigan-Flint, USA

ABSTRACT

This chapter addresses the systemic integration of conceptual and empirical methods in Software Engineering (SWE) research in terms of the systems approach, where theory, empiricism, and pragmatics are combined as required in the research phases. The following themes form the framework of systemic integration during SWE research processes: Theme 1 - Research Planning (Problem Analysis & Literature Review); Theme 2 – Proposal Development; Theme 3 – Conceptualization; Theme 4 – Experimentation and Research Validation. An illustrative research example is provided in terms of the four themes. The purpose of this research example was to provide a way to uncover potential causes of Information Technology (IT) project failures by employing a systemic and holistic approach to identify critical success factors for Project Management (PM). This has enabled the development of an Information Technology Project Management approach, which provides a method to evaluate the critical success factors of a given project, and the alignment of these factors with each other. The systemic methodology and its implementation proposed in this research increase the potential for IT project success by alerting project leaders of potential problems throughout the life of the project.

INTRODUCTION

Software engineering (SWE) may be defined as the "disciplined application of theories and techniques from computer science to define, develop, deliver, and maintain, on time and within budget, software products that meet customer's needs and expectations" (Melhart, 2000). This definition means that the issues of software quality, sound principles of software development, and efficiency of the software development process should be part of

DOI: 10.4018/978-1-4666-0179-6.ch015

the research context, while focusing on a particular topic within the field. An analysis done by De Villiers (2005) found that SWE research has focused in great part on systems/software (55%) and systems/software management (12%). Research has been done within the category of developing information technology (IT) systems, where the goal is to develop practical, innovative ways to solve real problems. Design research, originally espoused by Simon (1981), on the other hand is described as a problem-solving, performance improving approach. This approach in the greater area of IT systems focuses on IT enablement, and involves the creation of innovative IT artifacts and products that explain and motivate their functions (Hevner, March, Park and Ram, 2004).

General research topic categories may be considered, for example the software development process (improving the efficiency), SWE methodologies, SWE technologies, quality assurance, SWE management, management of software complexity, and business and software process integration. Conceptual research in SWE, also known as non-empirical research, is being performed in the areas of conceptual behavioral research and conceptual design research as well as philosophical issues underpinning such research (Pather & Remenyi, 2005) and dichotomies of information systems (IS) research (Brinkkemper & Falkenberg, 1991).

More common are empirical behavioral research and empirical design research. Mora, Gelman, O'Connor, Alvarez & Macia-Luevano (2008) have studied the models and standards adopted in the fields of Systems Engineering, SWE and IT using the theory of systems. Applied research in the field of SWE involves conceptual and empirical analysis and formulation during the development of original and innovative solutions to problems. The authors are promoting the adoption of systems thinking in SWE research as a sound way to understanding and solving complexities of IT enablement in business and industry (Kraft & Steenkamp, 2010).

This chapter addresses the systemic integration of conceptual and empirical methods in SWE research in terms of the systems approach, where theory, empiricism and pragmatics are combined as required in the research phases. The following themes form the framework of systemic integration during SWE research processes: Theme 1 - Research Planning (Problem Analysis & Literature Review); Theme 2 – Proposal Development; Theme 3 – Conceptualization; Theme 4 – Experimentation and Research Validation. The rest of the chapter provides an illustrative research example in terms of the four themes.

The authors describe an approach to SWE research which is grounded in the systems approach, with systemic integration of conceptual and empirical methods adopted in an investigation. The chapter has two parts, namely Part I which describes the conceptual and empirical aspects of the approach to SWE research in terms of four themes. Part II contains an illustration of the approach in a doctoral research project.

Part I. Theoretical Content. The theoretical aspects of an approach to SWE research is presented in terms of the following main themes: Theme 1 - Research Planning (Problem Analysis & Literature Review); Theme 2 – Proposal Development; Theme 3 – Conceptualization; Theme 4 – Experimentation and Research Validation.

Part II. Illustrative Example Content. An actual research project illustrating the application of the approach in terms of the four themes presented in Part I.

PART I. THEORETICAL CONTENT

Following on work by a number of researchers, the systems approach has emphasized the characteristics of a system as: teleological; has a determined performance; has users; has components, each with a purpose; is embedded within an environment; includes a decision-maker; and there is a designer (Churchman, 1979). The designer is concerned with conceptualizing the system to meet requirements specifications with purpose to create the system that maximizes the value to the user, and ensures that the system is stable. Over more than the last 50 years the main hallmarks of the general systems theory of open systems, applicable to SWE may be summarized as:

- Interdependence of objects and their attributes: Independent elements can never constitute a system.
- Holism: Emergent properties, which are not possible to detect by analysis, should be possible to define by a holistic approach.
- Goal seeking: System interaction must result in some goal or final state.
- İnputs and outputs: In a closed system, inputs are determined once and remain constant. In an open system, additional inputs are admitted from the environment.
- Transformation of inputs into outputs: This is the process by which the goals are obtained.
- Entropy: The amount of disorder or randomness present in the system.
- Regulation: A method of feedback is necessary for the system to operate predictably.
- Hierarchy: Complex wholes, which are made up of smaller subsystems.
- Differentiation: Specialized units perform specialized functions.
- Equifinality: Alternative ways of attaining the same objectives (converge).
- Multifinality: Attaining alternative objectives from the same inputs (diverge) (Skyttner, L., 2006).

The approach followed in a SWE research project is driven by the type of problem being researched. Adopting a systems approach in SWE enables researchers to acquire a holistic view of the research domain of discourse (Mora et al., 2008). These authors illustrated the useful-

ness of a systemic model with a description and comparison of two main models for the domains of business process performance complexity in organizations and engineering and managerial business process understanding complexity in the practice, namely CMMI/SE/SwE:2002 (SEI, 2002) and ITIL V.3:2007 (OGC, 2007), as well as four main ISO standards including ISO/IEC 15288:2002 Systems Engineering – System Life Cycle Processes (ISO, 2002) which has been revised in 2008, and ISO/IEC 12207:2008 (ISO, 2008) which has been revised in 2008 to cover Systems and Software Engineering - Software Life Cycle Processes (ISO, 2008).

Soft Systems Thinking may also be considered since it is best suited to ill-structured problems and can be applied to situations in which interconnections are cultural, and dominated by the meanings attributed to their perceptions by autonomous observers (Stainton, 1984). This author stated that "The aim of the Soft System Approach is to structure a systemic process of inquiry rather than to provide a means of optimizing" (Stainton, 1984, p. 149). Furthermore the Soft Systems Methodology (SSM) entails finding out about the problems situation in the real world, building relevant models of purposeful activity, use the models to question the real world in order to define purposeful actions, and then implement the agreed action (Checkland & Winter, 2006).

A research approach may be mainly empirical, or theoretical without any attempt to consider the research outcomes in actual practical terms. In empirical research the researcher participates in research activities such as observations, measurements, experiments and development. The outcomes of this type of approach helps the investigator to draw conclusions, confirm that something of value has been added to the body of knowledge, and possibly make generalizations through induction (Remenyi, Williams, Money, & Swartz, 1998). Theoretical research deals with concepts, frameworks theories and similar mental models reflecting insight, without any direct involvement in observation of behavior, experimentation, development, and collection of actual evidence.

The research strategy serves as an overarching guide for conducting the research processes as aligned with the research philosophy and approach. It is usually supported by a research process model that structures the research phases. For example, the Inductive-Hypothetic research strategy model (Graaff, 2001; Meel, 1994; Sol, 1982; Vreede, 1995) has five main research phases supported by four models.

The research design describes the methods that are followed in support of the research phases. A technique for matching the research questions

with the strategy is useful, such as proposed by Marshall and Rossman (1995).

The authors have also found that a sustainable research program requires that one follows some process towards a declared research agenda. The research process model shown in Figure 1 (Steenkamp and McCord, 2007) has been successfully in a doctoral program, and has the following phases:

1. Research Planning - Problem Identification during which problem analysis and identification are done
2. Research Planning - Proposal Development, including preliminary literature review
3. Research - Literature Review of focal theory and applications

Figure 1. Research process model (Steenkamp & McCord, 2007, p.255 – 264)

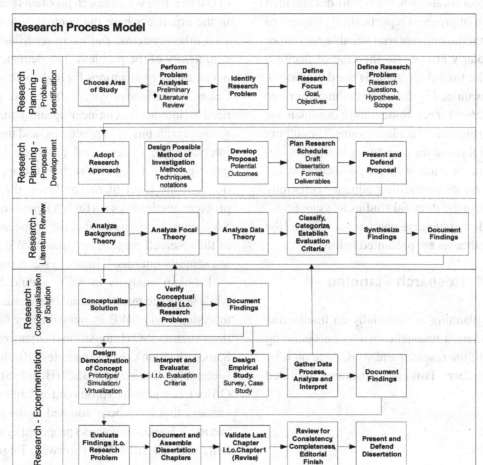

4. Research – Conceptualization of Solution
5. Research – Experimentation
6. Research Validation

The processes in these phases are typically sequential with some iteration and feedback loops as insights are gained during the investigation, and is described in this part of the chapter. The conceptualization of the solution varies in form and representation, and may be a graphic model or a mathematical formula that represents the insight of the researcher of a potential way to solve the research problem. It should be followed by applying research methods in support of the Research Experimentation Phase, which enables the researcher to validate the conceptual solution, the propositions or hypotheses, and answer the research questions. Throughout the research project outcomes and deliverables are documented in the form of progress reports, draft chapters of the dissertation, and material suitable for one or more scholarly articles. In the case of doctoral research the final deliverable is the dissertation, which is examined by the dissertation committee and is the basis for recommending a candidate for promotion to doctoral graduate status. The authors have used three main milestones in doctoral research projects, namely the proposal defense, the dissertation defense and the graduation ceremony which brings the doctoral studies to a close.

Considering such a research process model the four main themes are presented below.

Theme 1: Research Planning

Research planning is essentially an intellectual process where a researcher works on obtaining the focus of the research and work done on it by other researchers. Two sub-themes are elaborated as follows.

Theme 1.1 Problem Analysis

The research process begins with identifying the research area, identifying the specific problem to investigate, and based on such determination planning the research. One should determine the purpose of the research, and what value may be expected by solving it. In some investigations the intent is to understand a phenomenon, a process, the functional capabilities and behavior that are not well understood. Or, the purpose might be to improve an existing system, a design structure or process.

Problem analysis of potential topics within a research area involves developing some key questions (relating to the topic) that are in need of answers, and determining how researchable each questions is by evaluating them in terms of a set of criteria. In SWE research problems may reside in the practice where the context, relationships with other systems, and users contribute to the complexity of the problem. The demand in high performing organizations for high quality and efficient, cost effective systems has emphasized the need for interacting engineering and management systems with business processes, and the area of integration of systems and processes has been gaining interest. Aspects such as the application domain, the level of the problem, the type of problem, methodologies for SWE are considered. Such considerations impact the scope and focus of the research project, and many SWE projects are actually interdisciplinary systems projects.

Problem analysis in SWE should be done while informed by international standards relating to systems and SWE as published by organizations such as ISO (International Organization for Standardization), IEEE (Institute of Electrical and Electronics Engineers), BSO (British Standards Office), best practices promoted by large software vendors that have been adopted in the practice, and models and frameworks proposed by research units such as SEI-CMU (Software Engineering

Institute, Carnegie Mellon University) and the Project Management Institute (PMI).

Theme 1.2 Literature Review

The literature review provides insight about research that has been conducted by others and the arguments advanced by them; it must be logically structured, up to date, and provide a sound analysis and interpretation of contributions, issues, concerns and constraints. The standard way to start a comprehensive literature review of relevant sources, including data and informational documentation related to the focal theory (and applications), is to use keywords to access library sources and online databases. The contributions and shortcomings of the subject area should be critically evaluated. It is important to consider available data about the subject or phenomenon under study, and the need for collecting and analyzing such data to promote the research argument. Data may be collected from available sources that may provide insight into the issues of concern to the problem domain. In SWE the literature review typically follows the mapping studies approach as described in Kitchenham, Pretorius, Budgen et al. (2010) where one has coarsely grained research questions to identify available literature for searching for primary studies in specific categories. The search process of using different digital libraries and indexing services is where insight regarding the research problem starts.

Research norms relevant to this phase include analyzing the background theory, the focal theory, and the data theory. In the theory and practice paradigm the applications of the background and focal theories should also be examined. Background theory refers to the context within which the research takes place, and has relevance for research decisions regarding the scope, and potential grounded theories. The researcher must be aware of the current status of the field, namely the developments, controversies, breakthroughs and applications that are currently regarded as important, on the forefront and lead thinking in the subject area. The focal theory (and applications) indicate precisely and in detail what the researcher will investigate as well as the rationale, i.e. why. The nature of the problem must be established and the key issues that are being addressed identified. Part of understanding the focal theory is obtained during the development of the research proposal. The management of the research project, including the research strategy, the time dispensation and financial aspects are addressed during proposal development.

Theme 2: Proposal Development

Proposal development is based on the problem analysis outcome and preliminary literature review. It is a pragmatic process borrowing some techniques from PM. During the research process the researcher focuses on the activities in a research phase while remaining flexible to revisit earlier deliverables and decisions. In other words, research does not flow in a sequential fashion as shown by many research process models, but requires iteration, feedback and verification of findings.

A typical proposal format includes sections on the research area and research problem to be investigated; the purpose and goals of the research project; the research questions; the research focus of the intended research project; the propositions and/or hypotheses of the research; the literature review; the research approach, research strategy and research design of the research project; an outcomes analysis; and the research schedule or time table. In academic research the research proposal should contain a clear idea of the intent and motivation of the research project, and is reviewed and defended to the appointed dissertation committee. The format of a typical proposal is as follows:

- **Research area and research problem:** A statement of the area of research and the problem that is to be investigated.

- **Purpose and goals of the research project**: A statement of the intent of the research project and identified goals to be achieved.
- **Research questions and focus:** The heart and soul of any investigation is the research questions. The purpose of study and the research question drive the other parts of the research process, such as research design, conceptualization, data collection, data analysis, evidence collection and research validation.
- **Propositions or hypotheses**. Where possible the researcher will start with a primary narrative, based on all evidence from the reviewed literature and empirical domain. In IT and SWE research creative ideas about understanding the problem being studied results in the conceptualization about concerns, principles or rules, objects, processes, persons, behaviors, or other relevant aspect that form part of the domain of discourse, in terms of modeling constructs and their relationships. This model, a conceptual one, represents insight and enables the researcher to formulate proposition(s) or hypothesis(es) for the project that are to be validated.
- **Literature review**. A preliminary review of literature representing research that others have done on the research topic.
- **Research approach, strategy and design.** The application of the systems approach to problems in the field of SWE has been productive. This requires that all relevant aspects of the problem and its context be addressed together in a rational and systematic way.
- **Research experimentation and validation.** Validation to assure that a theoretical conjecture (or constructs of the conceptual model) contains the features that are legitimate and justifiable.
- **Outcome analysis**. Potential alternatives resulting from the research that would

improve the understanding of a research problem or provide a new solution to the problem, for example.
- **Research schedule**. The intended time table for conducting the investigation.

Theme 3: Conceptualization

The SWE research process involves developing the researcher's conceptual insight regarding the problem domain and domain of discourse using a chosen method and representation scheme. This is a theoretical endeavor which also involves the development of a conceptual solution to the research problem being investigated. The researcher may develop a grounded theory, following a deductive and an inductive, theory discovery approach (which is qualitative in nature) that represents the researcher's theoretical account of the general features of the research topic, while at the same time grounding the account in empirical observations or evidence as identified in the review. A systematic way is to examine the research field through multi-levels to develop the grounded theory in the form of a framework, constructs and/or propositions that at some later point can be validated. It is important to remain as objective as possible in generating some theory or conceptualization since it is influenced by the researcher's analysis of the literature, knowledge about the phenomenon(na) under study, and interaction with others in the research field. Once the conceptual solution is available it should be validated in terms of the research problem and research questions.

Theme 4: Experimentation and Research Validation

Theme 4.1 Experimentation

Here the conceptual solution is demonstrated by means of empirical methods. A number of empirical methods and techniques, such as prototyping, simulation, and virtualization experiments are employed. Criteria for evaluating such experimental demonstrations include feasibility, effectiveness and efficiency, cost/benefit to implement, and ease of use/ adoption. There is also the option of doing field studies or case studies to collect evidence as part of the research strategy (Yin, 2009).

Other approaches of evidence gathering are to collect data from a large population using a survey instrument to obtain quantitative support, or by interviewing experts in the research field to obtain qualitative support for the conceptual solution.

In conceptual research, methods such as numerical mathematical analysis, mathematical/ theorem proof, logical argumentation, may be used as instruments of evidence.

The data theory adopted for the research design provides the motivation for the relevance of the material that is to be used to support the hypothesis or proposition. The content of the data theory differs from topic to topic in SWE, but the form should always be relevant to the appropriateness and trustworthiness of the data resources.

Theme 4.2 Research Validation

A research project must be validated at the end in terms of the research problem, the research questions, the research propositions/ hypotheses, the conceptual solution, and is an intellectual process. Conceptual models must also be validated to be convincing, but validating concepts and conceptual models is problematic in most disciplines. Validation assures that a concept (or constructs of a conceptual model) contains the features that are legitimate and justifiable. In the absence of the ability to experiment with, or demonstrate, the conceptual models in some empirical way, face validation of the conceptual models is a viable option (Khazanchi, 1996). Face validation may be performed by a panel of experts to establish the plausibility, feasibility, effectiveness, whether pragmatic and empirically testable of the conceptual solution, and whether the concepts and

conceptual model explain a phenomenon that is expected to occur (i.e. is predictive). In addition one should establish whether the outcomes are inter-subjectively and inter-methodologically certifiable.

When a quantitative research strategy is adopted the collected data is processed statistically using a range of techniques to provide evidence in support or negation of the hypothesis(ses). In some research projects it may be deemed desirable to perform triangulation which is regarded as a validity procedure to obtain convergence among multiple and different sources of evidence. The purpose is to remove bias and increase the level of confidence in the hypothesis or proposition about some phenomenon.

With the theoretical context for how research in the fields of SWE may be perceived, Part II provides an application of this research framework.

PART II. CONTENT: ILLUSTRATIVE RESEARCH EXAMPLE

This part of the chapter presents an example of the systems approach adopted in a research project towards a doctoral dissertation in IT systems. It illustrates the systemic integration of conceptual and empirical methods used in the project. The themes described in Part I are addressed and the same format is used.

Introduction to Research Example

Despite the numerous methods and techniques for PM that have been defined and documented, and maintains that project management remains a highly problematic endeavor (White & Fortune, 2002). In efforts to reduce the risks associated with the failure of software projects, many enterprises have opted to replace existing legacy systems with packaged solutions. Some use commercial-off-the-shelf (COTS) software, rather than incurring the costs and risks involved in software development. COTS purchases now represent about 70 percent of all corporate business software expenditures, and recent estimates are that the annual market for COTS is almost US $200 Billion worldwide (Keil & Tiwana 2005). These authors go on to state that industry is attempting to leverage COTS applications as an economic necessity to shorten the implementation timeline, lower software costs, and lessen the unpredictability associated with developing custom applications.

The primary purpose of the research project described in Part II was to expand the body of knowledge of IT-PM specific to COTS software procurement and implementation, with focus on factors contributing to the successes and failures of managing such projects. The research has uncovered potential causes for project failures and identified additional critical success factors for COTS projects. The case studies utilized in the project are derived from real-world projects in a large automotive enterprise.

Theme 1:Research Planning

An empirical research approach was followed in the research project based on involvement in, and observations and related evidence available from the software project documentation repository about, COTS case studies that were conducted in the automotive industry. One of the authors was actively engaged as a project manager for several different COTS software projects. A selection of these COTS projects are discussed throughout the rest of this chapter. Case study research is appropriate and useful when the phenomenon cannot be easily quantified, which is the case here, and where multiple contextual variables influence organizational behavior (Johnson, Leach & Liu., 1999). Furthermore, case studies are useful to investigate research questions that are exploratory, confirmatory or explanatory in nature, and require detailed investigation and analysis of the context and processes involved (Yin, 2009). Research planning involving case study analysis was justi-

fied in this research, as found by Eisenhardt (1989) who motivated case studies as research units of analysis when little is known about a phenomenon, and current perspectives seem inadequate because they have little empirical substantiation. In the research project discussed in this chapter the main intent of using several case studies was to analyze the differences across the cases, and to determine if the project data provide sufficient evidence to support the stated research hypothesis (refer Theme 2). The case studies allowed the researchers to gain an enhanced understanding of the interactions among IT-PM processes, IT governance and standards, and the impact on the organization when implementing IT projects that satisfy given business requirements.

A systems approach was adopted for the research project supported by reasoning of Stainton (1984), and the notions of systemic (and holistic) were interpreted that the systems under investigation must be evaluated in their entirety, and that "the wholes must be taken at face value, understood by themselves" (Stainton, 1984, p.147). Since software PM falls within the IS field and includes many disparate disciplines, it is suited to analysis using a systemic and holistic approach (Kraft & Steenkamp, 2010).

Theme 1.1 Problem Analysis

The research project was motivated by clear evidence that there is insufficient understanding of the high rate of failure in COTS projects, and that complying with the traditional IT-PM methodology may not be enough to ensure successful procurement and implementation of COTS based IT projects. Statistical analysis of IT project data has revealed that between fifty (50%) and eighty (80%) of IT projects are unsuccessful (Desouza & Evaristo, 2006). It was also found that PM metrics of cost, schedule, resources, and scope were originally based upon traditional software development projects. Traditional approaches need to be revised if the industry is to improve the success rate of IT projects. IT alignment planning is seen as a necessary task of senior managers and was included within the scope of the research. Commercial IT research organizations such as Gartner list IT alignment as a top issue of American companies (Peak et al., 2005).

As part of Project Analysis a number of questions were considered during the initiation of the research project. The research questions are presented under Theme 2 - Proposal Development.

Theme 1.2 Literature Review

Driven by the questions above, the purpose of the initial literature review was to understand the existing subject matter on PM, and determine the gaps in the body of knowledge pertaining to COTS application, software procurement and implementation, which was the focus of the research project. This was followed with an extensive literature review to understand the background theory and focal theory of PM, and PM techniques for COTS software applications, as well as other PM factors beyond the traditional techniques that focus on project costs and timing issues.

The following on-line library search engines were used for the literature review: ACM Digital Library, EBSCOhost, EngNet DataBase, First-Search (OCLC), Forrester Research, IEEE Electronic Library Online, InfoTrac, Inspec, ProQuest, Science Direct, Scirus and Web of Science – ISI.

Table 1 shows the specific areas and sub-topics that were reviewed for the PM background theory, PM applications, and the focal theories related to the impact of organizational dynamics on PM. In addition articles on IT alignment to business processes and strategies were also included in the review.

Despite the extensive PM body of knowledge there are a number of diverse critical success factors beyond those of the "iron triangle" (cost, scope, schedule) that can impact the project outcome. Project success factors found in the literature include measures such as on-time project

delivery to the customer, adherence to the project schedule, project cost and budget control, quality of the PM process and customer satisfaction (Jugdev & Muller, 2005). "Measures of project success need to include the diversity of shareholder interests" (Milosevic & Patankul, 2005, p. 183).

The project estimation process, requirements tracking, resource allocation, and project budget and schedule must not be planned only once. Rather, they should be constantly adjusted and updated to respond to project dynamics. In 2003 Tesch and his co-authors found that current IT-PM literature and research topics are lacking relevance to real-life practical applications, and do not closely relate to everyday project issues and demands (Tesch, Kloppenborg & Stemmer, 2003). It appears that PM at the organizational level should shift attention away from performance and effectiveness metrics, and reflect a more systemic and holistic view of the value of PM as a core and strategic value to attain success. Jugdev and Muller declared as follows: "Few publications discuss PM in the context of strategic planning, company mission, and the importance of corporate management performance" (Jugdev & Muller, 2005).

Theme 2: Proposal Development

Following on the extensive literature review the proposal for this research project was developed and refined along the lines presented in Theme 1 – Proposal Development in Part I.

Research area and research problem. PM of COTS software applications was the focal research area, and the problems of poor PM success rates and lack of IT alignment with business goals and strategies were investigated.

Purpose and goals of the research project. Determine how critical success factors and key project performance criteria affect the probability of project success.

Table 1. Literature map

Topic	Classification	Literature Citation
Project Management Industry Trends	Project Management Terminology	Keil M., Ra A., Mann J. E. C., Zhang G. P. (2003) Project Management Institute PMBOK (2000) Ross M. (2006)
	Project Escalation and Abandonment Factors	Keil M., Rai A., Mann J. E. C., Zhang G. P. (2003) Pan G. S. C. (2005)
	Leadership and Vision	Christenson D., Walker D. H. T., (2004) GumÜnden H. G., Salomo S., Krieger A. (2005) Strang K. D. (2007)
	Project Control	Rozenes S., Vitner G., Spragget S. (2006)
	Project Performance Measures	Bryde D. J. (2005) Finch P. (2003) Kappelrman L., McKeeman R., Zhang L. (2006) Kendra K., Taplin L., (2004) Milosevic D., Patankal P. (2004)
	Literature Trends	Tesch D., Kloppenborg T. J., Stemmer J.K. (2003)
Organizational Dynamics	Organizational Climate	Ives M. (2005) Tan B. C. Y, Smith H. J., Keil M., Montealegre R. (2003)
	Corporate Change Management	Solomon E. (2001)
	Organizational Change Management	Collyer M. (2000) Ives M. (2005)
	Human Resource Factors	Vandapalli A., Mone M. (2000)
IT Alignment	Corporate Strategy	Morris P., Jamieson A. (2005)
	Business Process Management and Reengineering	Agrawal V., Haleem A. (2002) Arora S., Kumar S. (2000) DiBona Jr. A. (2000) Paper D., Chang R. (2005) Voelker M. (2006)
	Project Management Office	Desouza K. C., Evaristo J. R. (2006) Srivannaboon S., Milosevic D. Z. (2006)
	Business IT Alignment	Chen H. M., Kazman R., Garg A. (2006) Peak D., Guynes D., Kroon V. (2005)

Research questions and focus. The key drivers of this investigation were the research questions. The purpose of study and the research questions drive the other phases of the research process.

The research questions considered in this research project are:

1. What business processes should be redesigned to align with the overall system design of the IT application, thereby improving the outcomes of the IT project?

2. What is the relationship between business requirements and the overall system architecture?

3. How should business requirements and business processes be shaped and/or formulated so that the performance and functionality of the overall system might be enhanced?

4. How could consistency be achieved between a newly proposed system architecture and IT Governance in an enterprise?

5. How are IT standards effectively implemented in IT projects?

6. What roles might IT project managers and software vendors play in order to influence changes to IT standards that promote the success of projects within an enterprise?

7. How might the organizational dynamics be managed to advance the success rate of IT projects?

8. What might be the ideal (and potentially optimal) relationship between IT Project Managers and the business community in order to improve project success?

As indicated earlier the research focus was on PM in COTS software application implementation.

Research hypothesis. Where possible the researcher will start with a primary narrative, based on all evidence from the reviewed literature and empirical domain. Based on the insights gained from the literature review and on professional experience in the application domain, and with consideration of the research questions the following hypothesis was formulated: *The adoption of a systematic and holistic approach to COTS IT projects improves the potential for the successful implementation of COTS solutions.*

This hypothesis emerged after applying systems thinking in the form of reflective engagement in and with the problem situation, so that the conscious reflection could be carried out related to the real world situation under study. With this background a systemic and holistic approach was adopted to identify critical success factors for PM, and thus to determine a way to uncover potential causes of IT project failures in IT-PM of COTS software procurement and implementation. The research strategy included a research process model supported by mixed methods that would enable the development of a conceptual solution to the research problem, and validation of the research. A multi-method research approach was necessary to deal effectively with software PM issues of the real world. The research problem considered in this research project was inherently complex and multidimensional, and benefited from a range of

methods, in line with recommendations of Mingers (2001).

Literature review. The literature search explores research that other researchers have done on the topic. Findings of the literature review in this research project summarized in the Theme 1.2 - Literature Review confirmed that there is an obvious need to improve PM success rates. Also, that there is an ever increasing need to align IT project objectives with the business goals and strategies in order to enable companies to achieve their competitive advantage. "Increased alignment will improve IT's value to the business, but only if the company is flexible enough to react to sudden business changes" (Chen, Kazman & Garg, 2006). Companies that understand and leverage the business-IT partnership utilize IT as a business strategy enabler, and do so effectively. It is clear that when planning IT alignment a strategic view across the entire organization should be taken, and adequate IT resources must be allocated to meet the organization's business needs.

Research approach, strategy and design. As indicated in the Research Planning section an empirical research approach was followed. The strategy was to analyze real world PM case studies in which one of the authors had been engaged, supported by mixed methods. Four IT COTS case studies were analyzed using quantitative and qualitative methods. Qualitative modeling allowed the researchers to view the organization's synergistic existence as a whole entity (versus the sum of its parts) in supporting the overall organization's objectives. Adapting the research process model shown in Figure 1, the main phases of the research design called steps in this research project are shown in Figure 2.

Conceptualization was done in Step 2. The initial conceptual model was formulated in terms of variables and factors that impact the PM failures and successes, based on an analysis of two of the case studies. This conceptual model was informed by the literature analysis as well as professional experience. Analytical generalization was pos-

Figure 2. Main steps of the research design

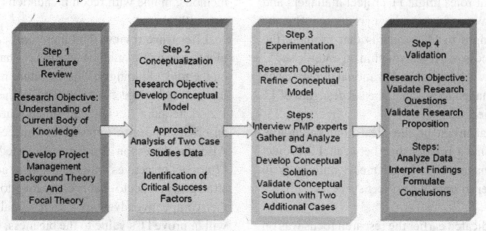

sible as a "previously developed theory is used as a template with which to compare the empirical results of the case study. If two or more cases are shown to support the same theory, replication may be claimed" (Yin, 2009).

Instead of experimentation, interviews and a survey method were employed in Step 3 of the research design. Input was solicited regarding the draft conceptual model from PM experts during interviews, and this model formed the basis of a survey which was conducted with PM professionals. The purpose was to gain insight that would aid in transforming the conceptual model of the research problem into a conceptual solution.

Validation of the research questions and hypothesis was done based on the analysis and findings of the interview and survey data.

Theme 3: Conceptualization

This section presents the conceptualization performed in the illustrative research project, and includes the development of the draft conceptual model and the conceptual solution. In developing the conceptual model the application of a systemic and holistic approach facilitated consideration of the various disparate disciplines encompassed in SWE, PM and IS. Conceptualization required a sound understanding of the complexity and

diversity of different elements pertaining to PM, including PM practices, organization dynamics, IT governance, interaction with vendors and business processes.

An analysis was performed to investigate the historical documentation of the first two case studies in order to identify key variables, and to formulate an initial draft conceptualization in terms of critical success factors and the potential dependencies among them. The draft conceptual model contains the variables and factors that impact the PM failures and successes in these cases. The authors opted to depict this draft conceptual model in terms of the cause and effect diagram shown in Figure 3. This is aligned with Yin (2009), who has stated that: "The events are staged in repeated cause and effect patterns, whereby a dependent variable (event) at an earlier stage becomes the independent variable (casual event) at a later stage". The conceptual model illustrates the events taking place in the IT-PM Office, and how critical success factors and key project performance criteria affect the probability of project success. This conceptualization was informed by insights gained from the literature review and the researchers' experience and expertise in the field.

Data was collected for each case study from the following historical documents:

Figure 3. Draft conceptual model of IS project success

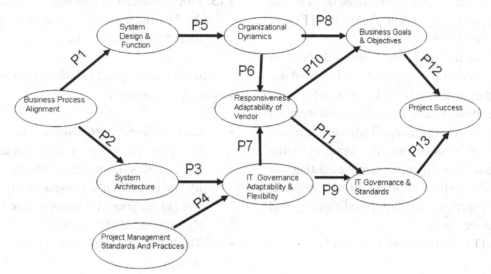

- Actual Business Requirements and System Requirements
- User Acceptance Testing
- Software Evaluations
- Business Process Models and Gap Analysis
- PM Historical Documentation
- Interviews with Project Team members.

The quantitative historical data came from business users who had completed the User Acceptance Testing, the Software Evaluations, and other data collected from the business user community by means of surveys and questionnaires. Data such as the architecture designs, the compatibility of IT architecture with IT governance and standards, are qualitative. The PM methods and practices used by each case study project team were also considered.

The conceptual model, defining the critical success factors for IT PM, is grounded in a model of Gowan and Mathieu (2005). That research had proposed a conceptual model for large scale IS PM which examined the relationships between the project characteristics of technical complexity and project size, formal PM practices (project methodology and outsourcing), and meeting the target date for completion. Their aim was to

determine factors that contribute to the success or failure of an IT Systems Project. They found that project failure or success may be traced to a combination of technical, PM and business decisions. Charette (2005) has also found that each dimension interacts with the others in complicated ways that exacerbate project risks and problems.

Figure 3 defines the draft conceptual model of this research project in terms of cause and effect relationships of critical success factors, that include both the business and the IT domains, due to a complex chain of events that took place over time (i.e. changes to customer requirements, project team members positions, corporate standards for IT governance, new software releases and hardware industry trends, and others).

From the draft conceptual model, the interdependence between the critical success performance criteria is given in terms of the following propositions:

P1: Business Processes of tasks and requirements must be aligned and satisfied with the overall System Design and Functionality.

P2: Business Requirements for Performance and Functionality must be aligned with the overall System and Infrastructure Architecture.

P3: The System Architecture must be in agreement and aligned with the overall IT Governance and Standards.

P4: PM Standards and Practices for the System Delivery Life Cycle must be followed according to the existing IT Standards.

P5: The System design and functionality must be aligned with the organizational dynamics.

P6: The business community, based upon the organizational dynamics and the existing system design functionality, will make requests to the software vendor for modifications and enhancements.

P7: The IT Governance and Standards committee.

P8: As the organization project team works together, knowledge and experience of the project will increase. Project team members will develop improved understanding of each users requirements and what is and is not feasible as possible enhancements and limitations of the software design functionality. This will result in refinements and updates to the overall business goals and objectives.

P9: Lessons learned from the project improvements and changes made to the IT standards will be included the overall company IT governance and Standards for future projects. The IT governance and standards must be dynamic and evolving based upon the project experiences.

P10: The response of the software vendor to the business organizational dynamics will impact the degree to which the business requirements and objectives will be satisfied.

P11: The degree of responsiveness and flexibility of the software vendor to accept changes recommended by the IT standards committee will result in updated status and re-evaluation of the software vendor rankings by the IT standard group.

P12: Project success is contingent upon satisfying the Business Goals and Objectives.

P13: Project success is contingent on satisfying the IT Standards and governance policies set at the corporate level.

The final conceptual solution is based on the following assumptions:

- Each alignment proposition, such as P1 - the alignment of the business processes to the overall system design and functionality can be evaluated using a Likert scale of one (1) for poor alignment to five (5) for a high degree of alignment.

- The Likert ranking for each of the propositions given above and in Figure 3 is evaluated to determine if it is less than or equal 3. If there is a poor alignment between the critical success areas, project remediation is required.

- The sooner the project remediation is begun, the higher the likelihood that the project success rate will improve.

The conceptual solution has also been refined by dividing it into two separate domains. The first domain examines the critical success areas for the business domain including the business processes, business goals and objectives, and the overall organizational dynamics (refer Figure 4). The second domain examines the critical success areas for the IT domain including IT governance, PM standards and practices, adaptability and flexibility of IT governance, and the responsiveness and adaptability of the software vendor (refer Figure 5).

Theme 4: Experimentation and Research Validation

The approach to research validation for this research project, the role of the interviews, the survey, and the case studies in the validation are explained and discussed in this section. Instead of experimentation, analysis and findings from the

Figure 4. Conceptual solution implementation for business domain

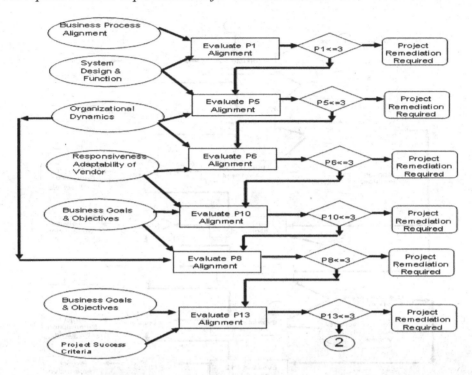

structured interviews and the survey were used to validate the draft conceptual model. As summarized in Theme 3 certified PM professionals were interviewed using a structured questionnaire, and a survey. The purpose of the interviews was to refine the draft conceptual model and to develop a conceptual solution to the research problem. The interviews were designed to solicit and identify additional critical success factors, based on the insights of the industry experts. The quantitative data consists of the survey results and the qualitative data of the critique of the conceptual model and interview process.

Additionally data for PM best practices relating to industry IT projects were collected from the survey and interviews with PM professionals. The survey questions were designed based on literature sources, the research hypothesis, the propositions given in under Theme 3, and research questions derived from the researcher's experience. The survey questions were categorized in the following categories:

1. PM Practices
2. Business Process Alignment
3. System Design and Architecture Alignment
4. Organizational Dynamics
5. IT Governance and Standards
6. IT Governance and PM
7. Software Vendor/Supplier Responsiveness

Each survey participant was asked to record the importance of project critical success factors for the categories listed above utilizing the Likert Scale. The structured interviews were done to collect informed opinions about the conceptual model that was developed as described in Theme 3. This feedback was analyzed and refined into the final conceptual solution. This final conceptual model was used to analyze two additional case studies, and served to validate the conceptual solution, the ITPM model, in terms the proposed systematic approach to improve COTS application implementation success rates in industry. It also provided answers to the research questions given in Part II,

Figure 5. Conceptual solution implementation for IT domain

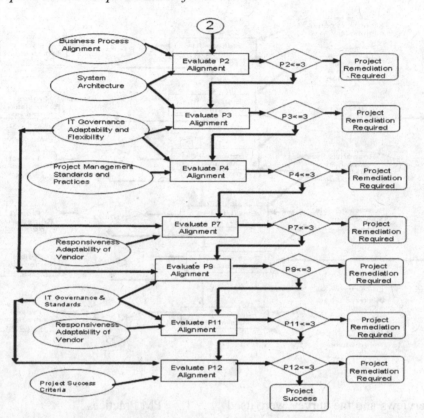

Theme 2. The findings obtained from the research deliverables support the stated propositions, and lead us to conclude that we have strong support for the research hypothesis, namely: *The adoption of a systematic and holistic approach to COTS IT projects improves the potential for the successful implementation of COTS solutions.*

DISCUSSION

The systemic integration of conceptual and empirical methods presented in Part I of the chapter was followed with the illustrative research example in Part II, highlighting some key aspects and decisions regarding the research design and methodology. Case studies have in the past been viewed as a less desirable form of research and inquiry when compared to the traditional meth-

ods of either experiments or surveys. Concerns with case study research strategy have been over the lack of rigor in case study research. This is in part due to the fact that often times the case study investigator has not been rigorous, has not followed systematic procedures, or has allowed equivocal evidence of biased views to influence the direction of the findings and conclusions (Yin, 2009). The case study relies on many of the same techniques as historical analysis, but adds two new sources of evidence, namely direct observation of events being studied, and interviews of the persons involved in the system or environment being analyzed. It is important that researchers be cautious in their role as both a participant and observer in case studies so that informal manipulation and bias do not occur. An additional concern about case study research has been that case studies provide little basis for scientific generalization

(Yin, 2009). To address this concern multiple case studies have been selected and analyzed in this research, allowing for analytical generalization to be derived.

This research has culminated in the development of an ITPM conceptual solution, which serves as a diagnostic method to predict those projects that are likely to become challenged, and require immediate attention and potential project remediation. The key findings and recommendations are:

- Implementing a systematic and holistic IT-PM approach has the benefit of including several additional critical success factors beyond those of the traditional PM body of knowledge.
- When implementing COTS software applications one must consider additional factors such as the software vendor's responsiveness, the alignment of the software functionality to the business objectives, organizational dynamics and the success factors presented in the IT-PM model.
- The utilization of factors presented in the IT-PM model has the potential to improve the overall success rate of COTS software applications, and improve predictability of those projects which will be a success or failure.
- Overall, the consideration of additional critical success factors and their interdependencies' is critical to improve the PM of future COTS software applications.

These research findings clearly indicate that applying the IT-PM model to the four case studies yielded a significant business benefit in understanding those factors that contributed to the success or failure of each case study. It was concluded that the holistic approach to PM of IT applications using the IT-PM model provides a useful diagnostic tool and PM method for estimating the likelihood of project success or failure. Also, that the adoption of a holistic approach in

IT projects improves the potential for the successful implementation of IT solutions. The findings further suggest that COTS IT projects will be successful if the business goals and objectives are satisfied, and the delivered system satisfies the IT Governance and Standards.

Future research could apply the conceptual solution in additional application domains other than the automotive industry, as well as in enterprises of small to medium sizes. More detail is available in Kraft (2008).

The approach to systemic integration of conceptual and empirical methods presented in this chapter has been successfully adopted in a number of research projects in a doctoral program since 2003.

REFERENCES

Agrawal, V., & Haleem, A. (2002). Culture, environmental pressures, and the factors for successful implementation of business process engineering and computer based Information Systems. *Global Journal of Flexible Systems Management*, *4*, 27–47.

Arora, S., & Kumar, S. (2000). Reengineering: A focus on enterprise integration. *Interfaces*, *30*(5), 54–71. doi:10.1287/inte.30.5.54.11641

Balk, L. D., & Kedia, A. (2000). PPT: A COTS integration case study. *Proceeding of the 22nd International Conference on Software Engineering*, 2000, (pp. 42 – 49). ACM Press.

Brinkkemper, S., & Falkenberg, E. D. (1991). Three dichotomies in the Information System methodology. Informatiesystemen in beweging. *Some Reflections on the Namur Conference on Information Systems*, (p. 4). Namur University, Belgium.

Bryde, D. (2005). Methods for managing different perspectives of project success. *British Journal of Management, 16*, 119–131. doi:10.1111/j.1467-8551.2005.00438.x

Charette, R. N. (2005). Why software project fails. *IEEE Spectrum*, 42–49. Retrieved from www.spectrum.ieee.orgdoi:10.1109/MSPEC.2005.1502528

Checkland, P., & Winter, M. (2006). Process and content: Two ways of using SSM. *The Journal of the Operational Research Society, 57*, 1435–1441. doi:10.1057/palgrave.jors.2602118

Chen, H. M., Kazman, R., & Garg, A. (2006). BITAM: An engineering principled method for managing misalignments between business and IT architectures. *Science of Computer Programming, 56*, 5–26.

Christenson, D., & Walker, D. (2004). Understanding the role of "vision" in project success. *Project Management Journal, 35*(3), 39–52.

Churchman, W. (1979). *Design of inquiring systems: Basic concepts of systems and organizations*. New York, NY: Basic Books.

Churchman, W. (1979). *Design of inquiring systems: Basic concepts of systems and organizations*. New York, NY: Basic Books.

Collyer, M. (2000). Communication – The route to successful change management: Lessons from Guinness integrated business programme. *Supply Chain Management: an International Journal, 5*(5), 222–225. doi:10.1108/13598540010350556

De Villiers, M. R. (2005). Interpretive research models for informatics: Action research, grounded theory, and the family of design and development research. *Alternation, 12*(2), 10–52.

Desouza, K. C., & Evaristo, J. R. (2006). Project management offices: A case of knowledge-based archetypes. *International Journal of Information Management, 26*, 414–423. doi:10.1016/j.ijinfomgt.2006.07.002

DiBona, A. Jr. (2000). Avoiding low-hanging fruit. *Knowledge and Process Management, 7*(1), 60–62. doi:10.1002/(SICI)1099-1441(200001/03)7:1<60::AID-KPM69>3.0.CO;2-9

Eisenhardt, K. M. (1989). Building theories from case study research. *Academy of Management Review, 14*, 532–550.

Finch, P. (2003). Applying the Sleving-Pinto project implementation profile to an Information System project. *Project Management Journal, 34*(3), 32–39.

Gowan, J. A. Jr, & Mathieu, R. G. (2005). The importance of management practices in IS project performance - An empirical study. *Journal of Enterprise Information Management, 18*(2), 235–255. doi:10.1108/17410390510579936

Graaff, H. (2001). *Developing interactive systems - A perspective on supporting ill-structured work*. *PhD*. Delft University of Technology.

Gumünden, H. G., Salomo, S., & Krieger, A. (2005). The influence of project autonomy on project success. *International Journal of Project Management, 23*, 366–373. doi:10.1016/j.ijproman.2005.03.004

Hevner, A. R., March, S. T., Park, J., & Ram, S. (2004). Design science in Information Systems research. *Management Information Systems Quarterly, 28*(1), 75–105.

International Standards Organization. (2002). *ISO/IEC 15288:2002 Information Technology – Systems life cycle processes*. Geneva, Switzerland: ISO/IEC.

International Standards Organization /IEC15288. (2008). *Systems engineering – System life cycle processes*. Geneva, Switzerland: ISO/IEC.

International Standards Organization/IEEE. (2008). *ISO/IEC 12207 Std 12207-2008 Systems and software engineering - Software life cycle processes*. Geneva, Switzerland: ISO/IEC.

Ives, M. (2005). Identifying the contextual elements of project management within organizations and their impact on project success. *Project Management Journal, 36*(1), 37–50.

Johnson, W. J., Leach, M. K., & Liu, A. H. (1999). Theory testing using case studies in business to business research. *Industrial Marketing Management, 28*(3), 201–213. doi:10.1016/S0019-8501(98)00040-6

Jugdev, K., & Muller, R. (2005). A retrospective look at our evolving understanding of project success. *Project Management Journal, 36*(4), 19–31.

Kappleman, L. A., McKeeman, R., & Zhang, L. (2006). Early warning signs of IT project failure: The dominant dozen. *Information Systems Management, 23*(4), 31–36. doi:10.1201/1078.10580530/46352.23.4.20060901/95110.4

Keil, M., Rai, A., Mann, J. E. C., & Zhang, G. P. (2003). Why software projects escalate: The importance of project management constructs. *IEEE Transactions on Engineering Management, 50*(3), 251–261. doi:10.1109/TEM.2003.817312

Keil, M., & Tiwana, A. (2005). *Beyond cost: The driver of COTS application value. IEEE Software, May/June.* IEEE Computer Society.

Kendra, K., & Taplin, L. (2004). Project success a cultural framework. *Project Management Journal, 35*(1), 30–45.

Khazanchi, D. (1996). A framework for the validation of IS concepts. *Proceedings of the 2nd Annual Association for Information Systems Americas Conference,* Phoenix, Arizona, (August 16-18) (pp. 755-757).

Kitchenham, B., Pretorius, R., Budgen, D., Brereton, O. P., Turner, M., Niazi, M., & Linkman, S. (2010). Systematic literature reviews in software engineering - A tertiary study. *Information and Software Technology, 52,* 792–805. doi:10.1016/j.infsof.2010.03.006

Kraft, T. (2008). *Systematic and holistic IT project management approach for commercial software with case studies.* Doctoral Dissertation, Lawrence Technological University, Southfield, Michigan, USA.

Kraft, T., & Steenkamp, A. L. (2010). A holistic approach for understanding project management. *International Journal of Information Technologies and Systems Approach, 3*(2), 17–31. doi:10.4018/jitsa.2010070102

Marshall, C., & Rossman, G. (1995). *Designing qualitative research.* CA, USA: Sage Publications.

Meel, J. W. (1994). *The dynamics of business engineering. PhD.* Delft University of Technology.

Melhart, B. (2000). Software engineering. In Ralston, A., Reilly, E. D., & Hemmendinger, D. (Eds.), *Encyclopedia of computer science.* New York, NY: Grove's Dictionaries, Inc.

Milosevic, D., & Patanakul, P. (2004). Standard project management may increase development project success. *International Journal of Project Management, 23,* 181–192. doi:10.1016/j.ijproman.2004.11.002

Mingers, J. (2001). Combining IS research methods: Towards a pluralist methodology. *Information Systems Research, 12*(3), 240–259. doi:10.1287/isre.12.3.240.9709

Mora, M., Gelman, O., O'Connor, R., Alvarez, F., & Macías-Lúevano, J. (2008). A conceptual descriptive-comparative study of models and standards of processes in SE, SWE and IT disciplines using the theory of systems. *International Journal of Information Technologies and Systems Approach, 1*(2), 57–85. doi:10.4018/jitsa.2008070104

Morris, P. W., & Jamieson, A. (2005). Moving from a corporate strategy to project strategy. *Project Management Journal, 36*(4), 5–18.

OGC. (2007). *The official introduction to the ITIL service lifecycle.* London, UK: TSO.

Pan, G. S. C. (2005). Case study: Information Systems project abandonment: A stakeholder analysis. *International Journal of Information Management, 25*, 173–184. doi:10.1016/j.ijinfomgt.2004.12.003

Paper, D., & Chang, R. D. (2005). The state of business process reengineering: A search for success factors. *Total Quality Management, 16*(1), 121–133. doi:10.1080/1478336042000309907

Pather, S., & Remenyi, D. (2005). Some of the philosophical issues underpinning research in Information Systems. *Proceedings of the 2004 Annual Research Conference of the South African Institute of Computer Scientists and Information Technologists on IT Research in Developing Countries.*

Peak, D., Guynes, & C. S., & Kroon, V. (2005). Information Technology alignment planning – A case study. *Information & Management, 42*, 635–649. doi:10.1016/j.im.2004.02.009

PMI. (2000). *A guide to the project management body of knowledge PMBOK*. Newtown Square, PA: Project Management Institute (PMI).

Remenyi, D., Williams, B., Money, A., & Swartz, E. (1998). *Doing research in business and management*. Sage Publications.

Ross, M. (2006). Integrating three level 2 CMMI process areas: Closing the loop on software project management. *Proceedings of the IEEE Aerospace Conference*, Paper 1410, (pp. 1-17).

Rozenes, S., Vitner, G., & Spraggett, S. (2006). Project control: Literature review. *Project Management Journal, 37*(4), 5–14.

Simon, H. A. (1981). *The sciences of the artificial* (2nd ed.). MIT Press.

Skyttner, L. (2006). *General systems theory: Problems, perspective, practice*. Hackensack, NJ: World Scientific Publishing Company. doi:10.1142/9789812774750

Software Engineering Institute. (2002). *CMMI for systems engineering and software engineering*. (CMU/SEI-2002-TR-001). Retrieved from www.sei.edu

Sol, H. G. (1982). *Simulation in Information Systems development*. Doctoral dissertation, University of Groningen, Holland.

Solomon, E. (2001). The dynamics of corporate change: Managements evaluation of stakeholder characteristics. *Human Systems Management, 20*, 257–365.

Srivannaboon, S., & Milosevic, D. Z. (2006). A two-way influence between business strategy and project management. *International Journal of Project Management, 24*, 493–505. doi:10.1016/j.ijproman.2006.03.006

Stainton, R. S. (1984). Applicable systems thinking. *European Journal of Operational Research, 18*, 145–154. doi:10.1016/0377-2217(84)90180-2

Steenkamp, A. L., & McCord, S. A. (2007). Teaching research methodology for Information Technology. *Journal of Information Systems Education, 18*(2).

Strang, K. D. (2007). Examining effective technology leadership traits and behaviors. *Computers in Human Behavior, 23*, 424–462. doi:10.1016/j.chb.2004.10.041

Tan, B. C. Y., Smith, H. J., Keil, M., & Montealegre, R. (2003). Reporting bad news about software projects: Impact of organizational climate and information asymmetry in an individualistic and collectivistic culture. *IEEE Transactions on Engineering Management, 50*(1), 64–77. doi:10.1109/TEM.2002.808292

Tesch, D., Kloppenborg, T. J., & Stemmer, J. K. (2003). Project management learning - What the literature has to say. *Project Management Journal, 34*(4), 33–39.

Vandapalli, V., & Mone, M. A. (2000). Information Technology project outcomes: User participation structures and the impact of organizational behavior and human resource management issues. *Journal of Engineering and Technology Management, 17*, 127–151. doi:10.1016/S0923-4748(00)00018-7

Voelker, M. (2006). Targeting excellence. *Tech-Decisions, 8*(3), 18–22.

Vreede, G. J. (1995). *Facilitating organizational change: The participative application of dynamic modeling*. Delft University of Technology.

White, D., & Fortune, J. (2002). Current practice in project management – An empirical study. *International Journal of Project Management, 20*.

Yin, R. (2009). *Case study research: Design and methods*, 4th ed. Applied Social Research Methods Series, vol. 5.

KEY TERMS AND DEFINITIONS

Business Process Alignment: Business Processes must be compatible to the functionality and design intent of the IT application.

Business Process Management: Method of efficiently aligning an organization with the wants and needs of clients. It is a holistic management approach that promotes business effectiveness and efficiency while striving for innovation, flexibility and integration with technology.

Capability Maturity Model Integrated (CMMI): A process improvement approach that provides organizations with the essential elements of effective processes.

Commercial-off-the-Shelf (COTS): Software or hardware products, which are ready-made and available for sale to the general public

Critical Success Factors: Those items which are is a business term for an element which are

necessary for an organization or project to achieve its mission.

Grounded Theory: Systematic qualitative research methodology in the social sciences emphasizing generation of theory from data in the process of conducting research.

Holistic: The properties of a given system cannot be determined or explained by its component parts alone.

Iron Triangle: The three properties of a software project of time, cost and quality are shown in each corner of the triangle.

ISO 9001: Quality management systems and requirements is a document of approximately 30 pages which is available from the national standards organization in each country.

ISO/IEC 12207: This standard defines a comprehensive set of processes that cover the entire life-cycle of a software system — from the time a concept is made to the retirement of the system. The standard defines a set of processes, which are in turn defined in terms of activities.

ISO/IEC 15504: Refer to SPICE (Software Process Improvement and Capability Determination) Model.

IT Alignment: an ongoing process that will optimize the relational mechanisms between the business and IT organization by working on the IT effectiveness of the organization in order to maximise the business value from IT.

IT Governance: A subset discipline of Corporate Governance focused on information technology (IT) systems and their performance and risk management.

Key Performance Indicators (KPIs): Financial and non-financial metrics used to help an organization define and measure progress toward organizational goals.

Section 3
Innovative Research Methods and Techniques

Chapter 16
Visualization and Analysis of Frames in Collections of Messages:
Content Analysis and the Measurement of Meaning

Esther Vlieger
University of Amsterdam, The Netherlands

Loet Leydesdorff[1]
University of Amsterdam, The Netherlands

ABSTRACT

A step-by-step introduction is provided on how to generate a semantic map from a collection of messages (full texts, paragraphs, or statements) using freely available software and/or SPSS for the relevant statistics and the visualization. The techniques are discussed in the various theoretical contexts of (i) linguistics (e.g., Latent Semantic Analysis), (ii) sociocybernetics and social systems theory (e.g., the communication of meaning), and (iii) communication studies (e.g., framing and agenda-setting). The authors distinguish between the communication of information in the network space (social network analysis) and the communication of meaning in the vector space. The vector space can be considered a generated as an architecture by the network of relations in the network space; words are then not only related, but also positioned. These positions are expected rather than observed, and therefore one can communicate meaning. Knowledge can be generated when these meanings can recursively be communicated and therefore also further codified.

DOI: 10.4018/978-1-4666-0179-6.ch016

1. INTRODUCTION

The study of latent dimensions in a corpus of electronic messages has been part of the research agenda from different disciplinary perspectives. In linguistics, for example, these efforts have been focused under the label of "latent semantic analysis" (LSA; Landauer *et al.*, 1998); in communication studies, "framing" is a leading theoretical concept for studying the latent meanings of observable messages in their contexts (e.g., Scheuffele, 1999); and in social-systems theory and socio-cybernetics, codes of communication which can be symbolically generalized (Parsons, 1963a and b; 1968; Luhmann, 1995 and 2002; Leydesdorff, 2007) are expected to operate latently or virtually as "a duality of structure" (Giddens, 1984; Leydesdorff, 2010). These efforts have in common that the analyst shifts his/her attention from the communication of information in observable networks to the communication of meaning in latent dimensions.

Latent dimensions can be operationalized as the "eigenvectors" of a matrix representing the network under study. Eigenvectors, however, operate in a vector space that can be considered as the architecture spanned by the variables (vectors) in observable networks. Statistical techniques for analyzing latent dimensions such as factor analysis and multi-dimensional scaling (MDS) are well-known to the social scientist—and where further developed for the purpose of analyzing communication (Lazarsfeld & Henry, 1968)—but the current enthusiasm for network analysis and graph theory has tended to push aside these older techniques in favour of a focus on observable networks and their structures. Spring-embedded algorithms that operate on networks such as Kamada & Kawai (1989) or Fruchterman & Reingold (1991) are integrated in software packages freely available at the internet such as Pajek and Gephi. These newer visualization capacities far outreach the traditional ones such as MDS.[2]

In this introduction, we show how one can use these newer visualization techniques with the older factor-analytic approach for distinguishing main dimensions in order to visualize the communication of meaning as different from the communication of information. The communication of information can be considered as the domain of social network analysis and its semantic pendant in traditional co-word analysis (Callon *et al.*, 1983; 1986). Words and co-words, however, cannot map the development of the sciences (Leydesdorff, 1997). The architectures of the discourse have first to be analyzed and can then also be visualized. Using an example, we walk the user through the different steps which lead to a so-called Pajek-file which can be made input to a variety of visualization programs.

In other words, we provide a step-by-step introduction that enables the user to generate and optimize network visualizations in the vector space, that is, the space in which meaning is communicated as different from the communication of information in the network. Meaning can be generated when informations are related at a systems level. In cybernetics, one often invokes an "observer" to this end (Edelman, 1989; Von Foerster, 1982), but a discourse can also be considered as a relevant system of reference. Note that meaning is provided in terms of expectations and can be informed and updated by observations. The various bits of informations can be positioned in a vector space in addition to being related or not in terms of network relations (Burt, 1982). The absence of relations can then be as informative as their presence (Burt, 1995; Granovetter, 1973).

The software for the visualization and animation of the vector space uses the cosine values of the angles between the vectors (variables) of word occurrences in distributions. We explain below how the word-document matrix can additionally be used as input to the factor analysis; for example, in SPSS. Unlike "single value decomposition" (SVD) which has been the preferred method in latent semantic analysis, factor analysis is available in most social-science statistics programs. We developed software so that one can move from a set of textual messages (either short messages or full texts) to these different software packages and take it further from there.

2. THE FRAMING CONCEPT

The concept of framing was introduced by Goffman (1974). He explained that messages in the mass media are "framed," which means that a description is provided from a certain perspective and with a specific interpretation. McCombs (1997) described framing as "the selection of a restricted number of thematically related attributes for inclusion on the media agenda when a particular object is discussed" (pp. 297-298). Van Gorp (2007) indicated that this process of selection is inevitable, as journalists are unable to provide an objective image of reality. McQuail (2005, at p. 379) agreed on this inevitability, which results in the inclusion of a specific way of thinking into the process of communication. Entman (1993) also argues that this process of selection can either be conscious or unconscious. A certain way of thinking is transmitted through the text. As Entman (1993, at p. 52) argued:

Framing essentially involves selection and salience. To frame is to select some aspects of a perceived reality and make them more salient in a communicating text, in such a way as to promote a particular problem, definition, causal interpretation, moral evaluation, and/or treatment recommendation for the item described. (p. 52)

A fact never has a meaning in itself, but it is formed by the frame in which it is used (Gamson, 1989). This latent meaning is implied by focusing on certain facts and by ignoring others. Frames appear in four different locations in the communication process: at the sender, within the text itself, with the receiver, and within culture (Entman, 1993).

When studying frames through the methods described below, one focuses on the frames that are embedded within the texts. These frames are often powerful, as changing a specific frame by a source might be interpreted by relevant audiences as inconsistent or unreliable (since dissonant). Textual frames are formed, among other things, by the use of certain key words and their relations. The relations among keywords provide the basis for this methodology.

Matthes and Kohring (2008) distinguished five methodological approaches to the measurement of media frames. First, in the qualitative *Hermeneutic approach*, frames are identified by providing an interpretative account of media texts linking up frames with broader cultural elements. Secondly in the *Linguistic approach*, one analyzes the selection, placement, and structure of specific words and sentences in a media text. A third model is provided by the *Manual holistic approach*. Frames are generated through a qualitative analysis of texts, after which they are coded in a manual quantitative content analysis. In the *Deductive approach*, fourthly, frames are theoretically derived from the literature and then coded in a standard content analysis. Lastly, the authors identify a fifth and methodological approach: the *Computer-assisted approach*. An example of this latter approach is elaborated in this study. In this approach, frame mapping can be used as a method of finding particular words that occur together. As frames then are generated by computer programs, instead of being "discovered" by the researcher(s), this method has the advantage of being a more objective tool for frame extraction than the other methods.

3. THE DYNAMICS OF FRAMES

Through the research methods described in this study, one is able to study differences or changes in frames within different discourses, not only statically, but also dynamically. Danowski (2007) studied changes in frames from the perspective of language. He indicated that frames relate to the way that facts are characterized, which is based on cultural and social backgrounds. This is consistent with the vision of Scheufele (1999), who stated that the influence of media on the public mainly works through transferring the importance of specific aspects about a certain issue. Framing is considered by Danowski (2007, 2009) as a way of shaping the process of agenda setting. He also states that framing is mainly applied to provide a positive or negative view on an issue. Unlike Entman (1993), Danowski (2007) argued that frames change relatively rapidly in the media. Discourse in the public domain would have a character more versatile and volatile than scholarly discourse. This contrast makes it interesting to study changing frames within specific discourses.

Our research method provides also a way of studying these possible differences in the dynamics. The existing network visualization and analysis program Visone was further developed for this purpose with a dynamic extension (at http://www.leydesdorff.net/visone). The network files for the different years can be assembled with a routine mtrx2paj.exe which is available with some instruction from http://www.leydesdorff.net/visone/lesson8.htm. An in-between file (named "pajek.net") can be harvested and also be read by other network animators such as SoNIA: Social Network Image Animator or PajekToSVGAnim. Exe (Leydesdorff *et al.*, 2008). In this study, however, we limit ourselves to the multi-variate decomposition of a semantic network in a static design (including comparative statics). An example of the potential of the dynamic extension to Visone showing heterogeneous networks in terms of their textual representations ("actants") can be found at http://www.leydesdorff.net/callon/animation/ which was made for a *Liber Amicorum* at the occasion of the 65th birthday of Michel Callon (Leydesdorff, 2010b).

When analyzing frames, one can make a distinction between restricted and elaborated discourses. Graff (2002) indicates that this distiction is mostly related to the audience of the communication. In restricted discourse, one single and specific meaning is constructed and reproduced. This is, for example, important in scholarly communication, when the audience in a particular field of studies has specific knowledge on the topics of communication. In elaborated discourse, communication is aimed at a wider audience. In this case, multiple meanings are created and translated into one another. The visualization of the frames in the collection of messages to be analyzed can reveal a more elaborated versus a more restricted type of discourse (Leydesdorff & Hellsten, 2005).

4. USING SEMANTIC MAPS FOR THE STUDY OF FRAMES

The research method presented in this section deals with content analysis of collections of messages. In addition to manual content analysis (Krippendorff, 1980; Krippendorff & Bock, 2009), one can use computer programs to generate semantic maps on the basis of large sets of messages. A properly normalized semantic map can be helpful in detecting latent dimensions in sets of texts. By using statistical techniques, it is possible to analyze the structure in semantic networks and to color them accordingly.

Content can be contained in a set of documents, a sample of sentences, or any other textual units of analysis. In our design, the textual units of analysis will be considered as the cases, and the words in these messages—after proper filtering of the stopwords—as the variables. Thus, we operate with matrices. Matrices which contain words as the variables in the columns and textual units of analysis as cases in the rows (following the convention of SPSS) are called word/document matrices. In co-word analysis and social network analysis, one often proceeds to the symmetrical co-occurrence matrix, but this latter matrix contains less information than the asymmetrical word/document matrix (Leydesdorff & Vaughan, 2006).

When visualizing a word/document matrix, a network appears, containing the interrelationships among the words and the textual units. In order to generate this network, one needs to go through various stages using different programs. In this section we explain how to generate, analyze, and visualize semantic maps from a collection of messages using the various programs available at http://www.leydesdorff.net/indicators and standard software such as SPSS and Pajek.

4.1. Generating the Word/Document Occurrence Matrix

In order to generate the word/document occurrences matrix, one first needs to save a set of messages in such a format that the various programs to be used below are able to use them as input files. If the messages are short (less than 1000 characters), we can save them as separate lines in a single file using Notepad or another text editor.[3] This file has to be called "text.txt". In this case one can use the program Ti.exe (available at http://www.leydesdorff.net/software/ti) that analyzes title-like phrases. If the messages are longer, the messages need to be saved as separate text-files, named text1.txt, text2.txt, etc.[4] These files can be read by the program FullText.exe (at http://www.leydesdorff.net/software/fulltext/).

4.1.1. Frequency List

The text-file text.txt can directly serve as input for the program Frequency List (FrqList.exe at http://www.leydesdorff.net/software/ti). This program produces a word frequency list from the file text.txt, needed for assessing which words the analyst wishes to include in the word/document occurrences matrix. As a rule of thumb, more than 75 words are difficult to visualize on a single map, and more than 255 variables may be difficult to analyze because of systems limitations in SPSS and Excel 2003.

Together with the text-file, one can use a standard list of stopwords in order to remove the irrelevant words directly from the frequency list. It can be useful to check the frequency list manually, to remove potentially remaining stopwords. If we begin with long texts in different files (text1.txt, text2.txt, … etc.),[5] these files have first to be combined into a single file text.txt that can be read by FrqList, for the purpose of obtaining a cumulative word frequency list across these files.[6] The use of FrqList is otherwise strictly analogous.

To be able to run FrqList, one needs to install the program in a single folder with the Text-file

Figure 1. Example of using FrqList

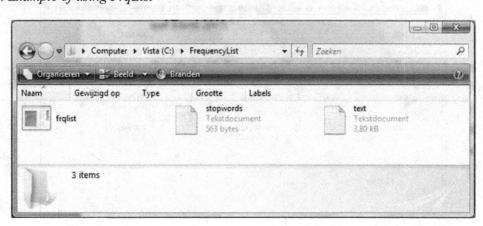

with all the messages (text.txt) and the list of stopwords, as shown in Figure 1.

After running, the program FrqList produces a frequency list: the combined word frequency list is made available as WRDFRQ.txt in the same folder, as can be seen in Figure 2. This file can be read into Excel in a next step so that, for example, the single occurrences of words can be discarded from further analysis.

4.1.2. Full Text

The next step is to import the frequency list—one can use wrdfrq.dbf or wrdfrq.txt—into an Excel file in order to separate the words from the frequencies as numerical values. At this stage, the list of words may be too long to use efficiently. To be able to visually interpret the data at a later stage, it can be advised to use a maximum of approximately 75 words. The first 75 words from the frequency list (without the frequencies) need to be saved as a Text-file by the name of words.txt. (Use Notepad for saving or obey the conventions for a plain DOS text as above.) This file "words.txt" can serve as input for the programs Ti.exe or FullText.exe.

One can use ti.exe for the case that the texts are short (< 1000 characters) and organized as separate lines in a single file text.txt, but fulltext. exe is used in the case of a series of longer text files named text1.txt, text2.txt, text3.txt, …, etc. Both programs need in addition to the information in the textual units, an input file named words.txt (in the same folder) with the information about the words to be included as variables. Prepare this file carefully using the instructions about removing stopwords and making selections specified above. You may wish to run FrqList.exe a second time with a manually revised file stopword.txt. (Save this file as a DOS file!)

As can be seen in Figure 3, the separately saved messages (text1.txt, text2.txt, etc.), together with the file words.txt, form the input for FullText. (Analogously, for Ti.exe one needs the files text. txt and words.txt.) The program produces data files, which can be used as input for the statistical program SPSS and the network visualization program Pajek. By installing the program FullText in the same folder containing the saved messages and words.text, the program can be run. The output of FullText can also be found in this same folder, as can be seen in Figure 4.

Figure 2. Output FrqList

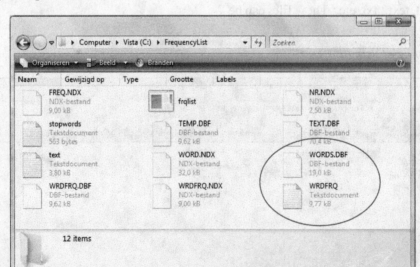

Figure 3. Example FullText

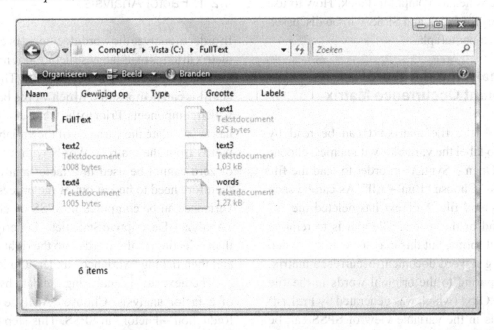

Prior to running FullText, the program demands to insert the file name ("words") and the number of texts. After running FullText (or Ti.exe), one can use the files matrix.txt[7] and labels.sps to statistically analyze the word/document occur-rence matrix by using SPSS. (The file matrix.txt contains the data and can be read by SPSS. The file labels.sps is an SPSS syntax file for labelling the variables with names.) In order to generate a visualization of the semantic map, one can use

Figure 4. Output FullText

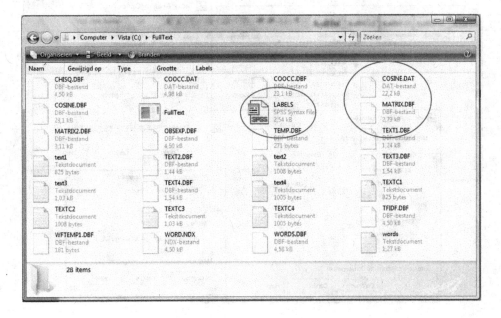

the file cosine.dat as input to Pajek. How to use these files for Pajek and SPSS will be discussed in the next paragraph.

4.2. Analyzing the Word/ Document Occurrence Matrix

As noted, the file matrix.txt can be read by SPSS. To label the variables with names, choose "File – Open – Syntax" in order to read the file labels.sps. Choose "Run – All". As can be seen in the syntax file, FullText has deleted the "s" at the end of the words. The aim is to remove the plural forms, but this may have no use when analyzing a word/document occurrence matrix. By comparing to the original words in the file WRDFRQ.txt (which was generated by FrqList) the labels in the variable view of SPSS can be manually adapted. This is only necessary if one wants to use the words as labels; for example, in a table of the SPSS output. When visualizing the word/document occurrence matrix, as we explain below, the words can be adapted for use in Pajek at a later stage.

4.2.1. Factor Analysis

In order to analyze the word/document occurrence matrix in terms of its latent structure, one may wish to conduct a factor analysis in SPSS. The factor analysis can demonstrate which words belong to which components. Prior to the factor analysis one has to calculate the variance of the variables (the words from the matrix). Words with a variance of zero cannot be used in a factor analysis and therefore need to be left out of the process. (The variance can be computed in SPSS by choosing "Analyze–Descriptive Statistics–Descriptives", then selecting all the words into the right column and then ticking "Variance" under "Options".)

The next step is analyzing the data by means of a factor analysis. Choose "Analyze – Data Reduction – Factor" in SPSS. This step is visualized in Figure 5. Select all the variables in the left column, except the ones with a variance of zero, and select them to the right column. Then, under "Extraction", tick "Scree plot" and undo "Unrotated factor solution". Then, under "Rotation", tick "Varimax" and "Loading plot(s)" and

Figure 5. Factor analysis in SPSS

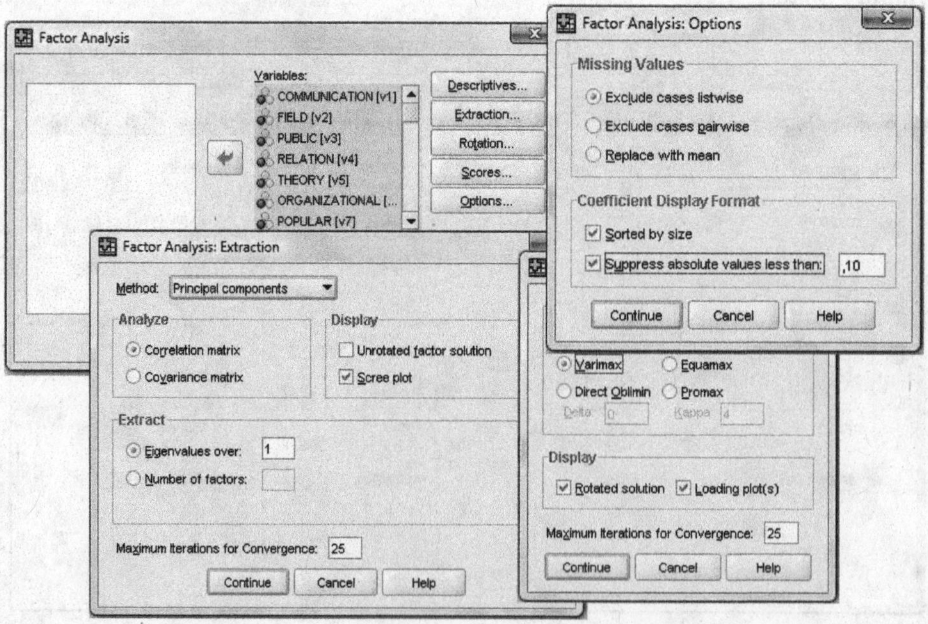

finally, under "Options", tick "Sorted by size" and "Suppress absolute values lower than", which is by default set at larger than .10.

Under Extraction it is additionally possible to manually choose the number of factors. When the output of the factor analysis produces too many factors, it may be advised to manually set the number of factors on, for example, six. More than six factors may be difficult to visualize and interpret through Pajek at a later stage.

The options are now set in order to conduct a factor analysis. SPSS produces several tables and figures in the output. The most relevant for our purpose is the Rotated Component Matrix. This matrix shows the number of components (factors) and the loading of the different words

on the components. At this stage, one can arrange the words under the different components, which can be used when visualizing the word/document occurrence matrix in the next stage. In Figure 6 an example of a few words are visualized with the arrangement under de different components. The various components can be considered as representations of different frames used in these texts. In the example in Figure 6, the texts are built around three different frames. How to use the output to visualize the word/document occurrence matrix will be discussed in the next section.

In addition to the positive factor loading, one may also wish to take into account that "level" has a negative loading (-.94) on Factor 3.

Figure 6. Output factor analysis in SPSS (an example with a limited number of words/variables)

Rotated Component Matrix^a

	Component		
	1	2	3
RESEARCH	,875	,436	-,209
FIELD	,780	,256	,572
WITHIN	,568	-,674	-,472
WELL	,568	-,674	-,472
LEVEL	,332		-,940
COMMUNICATION	-,147	,968	,202
APPLIED	,533	,843	
AREA	,483	,841	,243
PUBLIC	,345	,766	,542
THEORETIC	,345	,766	,542
RELATION	,345	,766	,542
TOOLS	,345	,766	,542
CONCEPTUAL	,345	,766	,542
DEVELOPED	,585	,734	-,344
CONCLUDES	-,332		,940
YEARS	,579		,811
ACROSS	,579		,811
APPLY	,579		,811
BASED	,579		,811
TRENDS	,579		,811
VISUAL	,324	-,860	,395
STUDIES	-,343	-,852	,395

Extraction Method: Principal Component Analysis.
Rotation Method: Varimax with Kaiser Normalization.

a. Rotation converged in 6 iterations.

Table 1. Output reliability analysis (Cronbach's α) in SPSS

Reliability Statistics	
Cronbach's Alpha	N of Items
.949	9

4.2.2. Cronbach's Alpha

Prior to the visualization of the matrix, one may wish to conduct a reliability analysis, by calculating Cronbach's alpha (α) for each frame (component). This measure controls after the factor analysis whether the frames form a reliable scale. First, one can determine which words belong to which frames by using the output of the factor analysis in SPSS, like the example in Figure 6.

The next step is the calculation of Cronbach's alpha in SPSS, by choosing "Analyze – Scale – Reliability Analysis". Select the words from the first frame into the right column and run the reliability analysis by choosing "OK". Table 1 shows the output of this analysis with Cronbach's alpha for the example from Figure 6, using the second frame which was composed of nine items (that is, words as variables).

In the example in Table 1, Cronbach's Alpha has a value of .95. In order to guarantee the internal consistency of the scale, Cronbach's Alpha needs to have a minimal value of .65.

4.3. Visualizing the Word/ Document Occurrence Matrix

In this section we explain how to visualize the word/document occurrence matrix by using Pajek[8] and the output of the factor analysis in SPSS. In order to visualize the output of FullText, one is advised to use the file cosine.dat, which was generated by FullText (see chapter 2).[9] In the first part of this section the drawing of the figure is discussed. After that we explain how the visualization can be informed by the output of the factor analysis in

SPSS. The final part of this section discusses the layout of the figure and how this can be changed.

Choose "File – Network – Read" to open the file cosine.dat in Pajek. To create a partitioned figure, one can choose "Net – Partitions – Core – All". To draw the Figure, choose "Draw – Draw partition". One can change the layout of the figure by choosing "Layout – Energy – Kamada-Kawai – Free". In this stage, one has created a figure which shows the different components with different colors, as can be seen in Figure 7. However, the algorithm used in Pajek for attributing the colors is different from the results of the factor analysis. We will change this below.

As noted above and shown again in Figure 7, FullText automatically removes an "s" at the end of a word. Also in Pajek it is possible to put back the "s", in case of an incorrect removal. To do so, close the Figure and choose "File – Partition – Edit" in Pajek. In this window one can change the words manually. After closing the window and drawing the partitioned figure again, the words are changed.[10]

The next step in visualizing the word/document occurrence matrix is the adjustment of the figure to the output of the factor analysis in SPSS, as discussed in the previous chapter. After the factor analysis in SPSS, each word was assigned to a specific frame. In the example, there were three different frames made visible in the output (Figure 6). In spite of the fact that Figure 7 also shows three frames in Pajek, there are differences between these frames and the frames from SPSS. These differences are being caused by the fact that Pajek uses the cosine matrix while SPSS uses the correlation matrix and performs an orthogonal rotation.

The visualization as shown in Figure 7 can be adjusted to the output of the factor analysis in SPSS. This adjustment can be done in the same way as the changing of the words in the previous section. By choosing "File – Partition – Edit", the frames can be reclassified by assigning the same numbers to words in the same frame.[11] After

Figure 7. Standard Pajek figure with different components

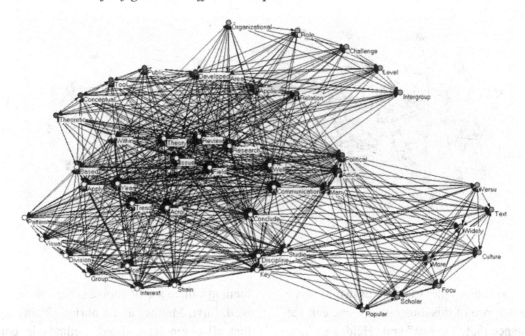

adjusting the figure from Figure 7 to the factor analysis in SPSS, a new figure can be drawn, which is shown in Figure 8.

The initial numbers, corresponding to the different frames, are provided by Pajek using another algorithm than factor analysis (the *k*-core algorithm). Nevertheless, the numbers are always one-to-one related to the colours of the vertices in the figure. As can be seen in Figures 8 and 9, it is difficult to read the words in the current layout of the figure. The different lines are also difficult to distinguish.

There are several options which can increase the readability of the figure. A few of these options are being introduced here. After following these steps, the figure will be better readable and interpretable. Table 2 provides an overview of the adjustment options in Pajek.

Figure 9 shows the same figure as in Figures 7 and 8 after passing through the preceding steps. The words can be read better and the differences in the loadings of the words can be interpreted.

A final option to complete the above figure is the addition of the frames to the figure (using Word

or a program like Paint). Through the different words it is possible to name the different frames. Figure 10 shows an example of this addition to the above figure.

4.4. The Discourse about "*Autopoiesis*" Visualized as an Example

In this section, a short illustration of the research methodology is provided by visualizing the international discourse on *autopoiesis*. The set of messages consists of nine newspaper articles from various English language newspapers harvested from LexisNexis.[12] The messages were saved as seperate text-files, and the output of the programs Frequency List (FrqList.exe), Full Text (FullText. exe) and SPSS were used to serve as input for Pajek. In Figure 11 the word/document occurrence matrix and the factor analysis are visualized using Pajek.

The visualization of the discourse on autopoiesis provides an illustration of the use of this research methodology. Although it is difficult to draw substantive conclusions based on the above

Figure 8. Pajek figure adjusted to factor analysis in SPSS

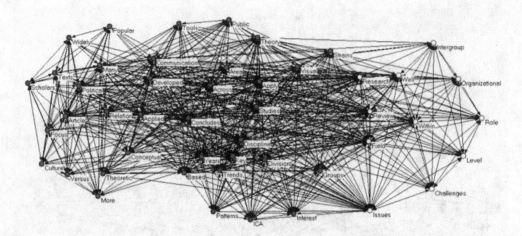

figure – as the sample was only drawn to serve for the purpose of this illustration – one can see for instance that "Derrida" and "Heidegger" are linked semantically via the concept of "Deconstruction." In the same manner it would be possible to study discourses on various concepts, by analyzing the visualizations as provided by Pajek.

5. LIMITATIONS

Although this method has the advantage of being more objective in frame extraction than other

methods, there are of course some limitations as well. First, Matthes and Kohring (2008) argued that all computer-assisted methods in content analysis assume that words and phrases have the same meaning within every context. A human coder could be better able to detect all the different meanings in a text and to provide an interpretation to the contexts of the words. As Simon (2001) also describes, the computer cannot understand human language with all its subtlety and complexiveness. Our methods, however, allow for further extension using, for example, factorial complexity as an indicator of words having different meanings

Figure 9. Pajek figure after changing the layout

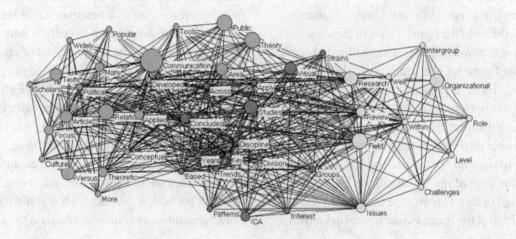

Table 2. Adjustment options in Pajek

Background The figure can be read best with a white background. To change the background, choose "Options – Colors – Background" and choose white as the background color.

Lines To make sure the different lines can be distinguished, it is possible to remove the lines with a value lower than for instance 0.2 (this depends on the figure, different values can be tried). To do so, close the figure, than choose "Net – Transform – Remove –Lines with value – lower than" and fill in the appropriate value. It is also possible to adjust the width of the lines to their values. In order to do so, draw the partitioned figure, then choose the option "Options – Lines – Different Widths". Since the cosine varies between zero and one, a value of 3 or 5 will provide differences.

Arrows The arrow heads are not adding anything to the figure, so they can be removed. To do so, choose "Options – Size – of Arrows" and fill in 0.

Font The size of the font can be changed through "Options – Size – of Font –Select". Use at least 12 for a PowerPoint presentation in order to make sure the words can be read. To make sure the words do not overlap each other, it is possible to drag the words a little into different directions.

Vertices The sizes of the vertices can be made proportional to the (logarithm of) the frequency of the words. In order to do so, choose "Options – Size – of Vertices defined in input file". To enlarge all the vertices, choose "Options – Size – of Vertices" and fill in the size. In Table 2, the vertices have been given the size of 10.

Colors To change the colors of the vertices choose "Options – Colors – Partition Colors – for Vertices". One can change the colors of the vertices, by clicking on the current color and then filling in the number of the wished color as seen on the color pallet. After that, click on OK and close the color pallet. Then click on one of the vertices you want to change and the entire frame will have the wished color. This can be done for each group of vertices. Make sure the colors are in different shades, in order to visually see the differences between the different frames.

in—translating between—different frames (Leydesdorff & Hellsten, 2005).

Second, one could argue that there is a problem of validity. Some words need to have a large frequency in order to occur in the analysis, in spite of being central to the content of the text

(Hertog & McLeod, 2001). This can further be elaborated in terms of various statistics, such as "term frequency-inverse document frequencies" (tf-idf; Salton & McGill, 1983) or the contribution of words (as variables) to the chi-square statistics of the word/document occurrence

Figure 10. Pajek figure after highlighting the different frames

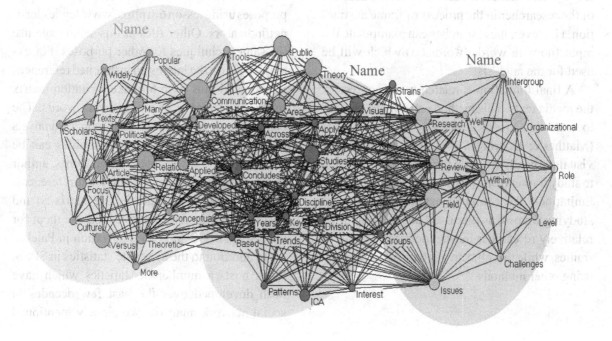

Figure 11. Visualization of the discourse on autopoiesis

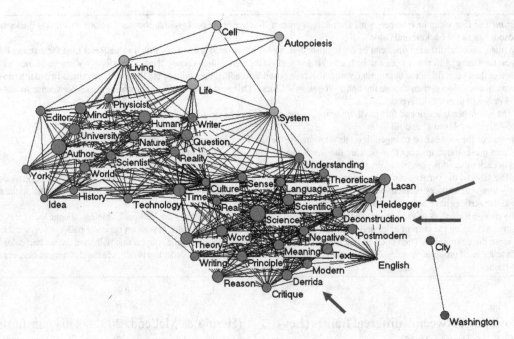

matrix. After running ti.exe or fulltext.exe, the file words.dbf contains additional information with these statistics (which are further explained at http://www.leydesdorff.net/software/ti/index. htm; Leydesdorff & Welbers, 2011). Again, this is a problem that occurs as a result of the absence of the researcher in the process of frame abstraction. However, the researcher can manipulate the input file with words (words.txt) which will be used for the analysis.

A final limitation is related to the sources of the media texts. This method can only be applied to texts that are electronically made available (Matthes & Kohring, 2008). As a result of this, visuals or handwritten texts cannot easily be used to study frames using this method. In spite of these limitations, the computer assisted approach of studying frames, as discussed above, provides a relatively researcher-independent assessment of frames, while this objective is hard to accomplish using other methods.

6. FUTURE RESEARCH DIRECTIONS

Our discussion has been oriented towards "getting started" with Pajek for the visualization of latent frames in textual messages. The resulting output can be further embellished for presentation purposes using lesson 6 at http://www.leydesdorff. net/indicators. Other files at this same page use the same techniques for other purposes. For example, one can be interested in the cited references in texts and thus wish to make a citation matrix instead of a matrix of co-occurring words. The basic scheme is that of textual units of analysis (messages) to which a set of variables can be attributed. These variables can be words, author names, institutional addresses, cited references, etc. One can then generate the file matrix.txt and cosine.dat as described above, and use them for analysis in SPSS and/or visualization in Pajek.

In addition to the available statistics in SPSS, Pajek hosts a number of statistics which have been developed over the past few decades in social network analysis. We already mentioned above the *k*-core algorithm which groups together nodes (vertices) which are interrelated with at least *k* neighbours. An introduction to these statistics is provided by: Hanneman, R. A., & Riddle, M. (2011). *Introduction to social network methods*. Riverside, CA: University of California, Riverside; available at http://faculty.ucr.edu/~hanneman/nettext/. An introduction to Pajek is provided by: De Nooy, W., Mrvar, A., & Batagelj, V. (2005). *Exploratory Social Network Analysis with Pajek*. New York: Cambridge University Press.

7. CONCLUSION

In our argument, semantics was considered as a property of language, whereas meaning is often defined in terms of use (Wittgenstein, 1953), that is, at the level of agency. Ever since the exploration of intersubjective "meaning" in different philosophies (e.g., Husserl, 1929; Mead, 1934), the focus in the measurement of meaning has gradually shifted to the intrinsic meaning of textual elements in discourses and texts, that is, to a more objective and supra-individual level (Luhmann, 2002). The pragmatic aspects of meaning can be measured using Osgood *et al.*'s (1957) Likert-scales and by asking respondents. Modeling the *dynamics* of meaning, however, requires further elaboration (cf. Leydesdorff, 2010a).

Our long-term purpose is modeling the dynamics of knowledge in scientific discourse. Knowledge can perhaps be considered as a meaning which is more codified than other meanings; it is generated when different meanings can further be compared and thus related (by an observer or in a discourse). As we noted above, meaning can be generated by an observer or in a discourse when different bits of (Shannon-type) information can be related and comparatively be selected. Thus, the selective operation can be considered as recursive. However, the generation of knowledge presumes the communication of meaning (Leydesdorff, 2011). As we

have shown, the analysis of the latter requires the progression from the network space to the vector space. The current contribution is made to support the user by facilitating this important step.

REFERENCES

Bullock, H., Fraser Wyche, K., & Williams, W. (2001). Media images of the poor. *Promoting Environmentalism, 57*(2), 229–246.

Burt, R. S. (1982). *Toward a structural theory of action*. New York, NY: Academic Press.

Burt, R. S. (1995). *Structural holes: The social structure of competition*. Cambridge, MA: Harvard University Press.

Callon, M., Courtial, J.-P., Turner, W. A., & Bauin, S. (1983). From translations to problematic networks: An introduction to co-word analysis. *Social Sciences Information. Information Sur les Sciences Sociales, 22*(2), 191–235. doi:10.1177/053901883022002003

Callon, M., Law, J., & Rip, A. (Eds.). (1986). *Mapping the dynamics of science and technology*. London, UK: Macmillan.

Danowski, J. A. (2007). *Frame change and phase shift detection using news story emotionality and semantic networks: A 25-month analysis of coverage of "Second Life"*. Paper presented at the Annual Meetings of the Association of Internet Researchers.

Danowski, J. A. (2009). Inferences from word networks in messages. In Krippendorff, K., & Bock, M. A. (Eds.), *The content analysis reader* (pp. 421–429). Los Angeles, CA: Sage.

De Boer, C., & Brennecke, S. (2003). *Media en publiek: theorieën over media-impact (vijfde, herziene druk)*. Amsterdam, The Netherlands: Boom.

De Nooy, W., Mrvar, A., & Batagelj, V. (2011). *Exploratory social network analysis with Pajek (2nd Edition)*. New York, NY: Cambridge University Press.

Edelman, G. M. (1989). *The remembered present: A biological theory of consciousness*. New York, NY: Basic Books.

Entman, R. M. (1993). Framing: Toward clarification of a fractured paradigm. *The Journal of Communication, 43*(4), 51–57. doi:10.1111/j.1460-2466.1993.tb01304.x

Fruchterman, T., & Reingold, E. (1991). Graph drawing by force-directed replacement. *Software, Practice & Experience, 21*, 1129–1166. doi:10.1002/spe.4380211102

Gamson, W. A. (1989). News as framing: "Comments on Graber. *The American Behavioral Scientist, 33*(2), 157–161. doi:10.1177/0002764289033002006

Giddens, A. (1984). *The constitution of society*. Cambridge, UK: Polity Press.

Goffman, E. (1974). *Frame analysis: An essay on the organization of experience*. New York, NY: Harper & Row.

Graff, G. (2002). The problem problem and other oddities of academic discourse. *Arts and Humanities in Higher Education, 1*(1), 27–42. doi:10.1177/1474022202001001003

Granovetter, M. S. (1973). The strength of weak ties. *American Journal of Sociology, 78*(6), 1360–1380. doi:10.1086/225469

Hanneman, R. A., & Riddle, M. (2005). *Introduction to social network methods*. Riverside, CA: University of California, Riverside. Retrieved from http://faculty.ucr.edu/~hanneman/nettext/

Hertog, J. K., & McLeod, D. M. (2001). A multi-perspectival approach to framing analysis: A field guide. In Reese, S. D., Gandy, O. H., & Grant, A. E. (Eds.), *Framing public life: Perspectives of media and our understanding of the social world* (pp. 139–161). Mahwah, NJ: Erlbaum.

Husserl, E. (1929). *Cartesianische Meditationen und Pariser Vorträge* [Cartesian meditations and the Paris lectures]. The Hague, The Netherlands: Martinus Nijhoff.

Kamada, T., & Kawai, S. (1989). An algorithm for drawing general undirected graphs. *Information Processing Letters, 31*(1), 7–15. doi:10.1016/0020-0190(89)90102-6

Krippendorff, K. (1980). *Content analysis: An introduction to its methodology*. Thousand Oaks, CA: Sage.

Krippendorff, K., & Bock, M. A. (2009). *The content analysis reader*. Los Angeles, CA: Sage.

Landauer, T. K., Foltz, P. W., & Laham, D. (1998). An introduction to latent semantic analysis. *Discourse Processes, 25*(2), 259–284. doi:10.1080/01638539809545028

Lazarsfeld, P. F., & Henry, N. W. (1968). *Latent structure analysis*. New York, NY: Houghton Mifflin.

Leydesdorff, L. (1997). Why words and co-words cannot map the development of the sciences. *Journal of the American Society for Information Science American Society for Information Science, 48*(5), 418–427. doi:10.1002/(SICI)1097-4571(199705)48:5<418::AID-ASI4>3.0.CO;2-Y

Leydesdorff, L. (2007). Scientific communication and cognitive codification: Social systems theory and the sociology of scientific knowledge. *European Journal of Social Theory, 10*(3), 375–388. doi:10.1177/1368431007080701

Leydesdorff, L. (2010a). The communication of meaning and the structuration of expectations: Giddens' "structuration theory" and Luhmann's "self-organization". *Journal of the American Society for Information Science and Technology, 61*(10), 2138–2150. doi:10.1002/asi.21381

Leydesdorff, L. (2010b). What can heterogeneity add to the scientometric map? Steps towards algorithmic historiography. In Akrich, M., Barthe, Y., Muniesa, F., & Mustar, P. (Eds.), *Débordements: Mélanges offerts à Michel Callon* (pp. 283–289). Paris, France: École Nationale Supérieure des Mines, Presses des Mines.

Leydesdorff, L. (2011). (in preparation). "Meaning" as a sociological concept: A review of the modeling, mapping, and simulation of the communication of knowledge and meaning. *Social Sciences Information. Information Sur les Sciences Sociales*. doi:10.1177/0539018411411021

Leydesdorff, L., & Hellsten, I. (2005). Metaphors and diaphors in science communication: Mapping the case of stem cell research. *Science Communication, 27*(1), 64–99. doi:10.1177/1075547005278346

Leydesdorff, L., & Schank, T. (2008). Dynamic animations of journal maps: Indicators of structural change and interdisciplinary developments. *Journal of the American Society for Information Science and Technology, 59*(11), 1810–1818. doi:10.1002/asi.20891

Leydesdorff, L., Schank, T., Scharnhorst, A., & De Nooy, W. (2008). Animating the development of social networks over time using a dynamic extension of multidimensional scaling. *El Profesional de la Información, 17*(6), 611–626. doi:10.3145/epi.2008.nov.04

Leydesdorff, L., & Vaughan, L. (2006). Co-occurrence matrices and their applications in information science: Extending ACA to the Web environment. *Journal of the American Society for Information Science and Technology, 57*(12), 1616–1628. doi:10.1002/asi.20335

Leydesdorff, L., & Welbers, K. (2011). (in press). The semantic mapping of words and co-words in contexts. *Journal of Informatrics*. doi:10.1016/j.joi.2011.01.008

Luhmann, N. (1984). *Soziale Systeme. Grundriß einer allgemeinen Theorie*. Frankfurt, Germany: Suhrkamp.

Luhmann, N. (1995). *Social systems*. Stanford, CA: Stanford University Press.

Luhmann, N. (2002). How can the mind participate in communication? In Rasch, W. (Ed.), *Theories of distinction: Redescribing the descriptions of modernity* (pp. 169–184). Stanford, CA: Stanford University Press.

Matthes, J., & Kohring, M. (2008). The content analysis of media frames: toward improving reliability and validity. *The Journal of Communication, 58*, 258–279. doi:10.1111/j.1460-2466.2008.00384.x

McCombs, M. E., & Shaw, D.-L. (1972). The agenda-setting function of mass media. *Public Opinion Quarterly, 36*(2), 176–187. doi:10.1086/267990

McCombs, M. F. (1997, August). *New frontiers in agenda-setting: Agendas of attributes and frames*. Paper presented at the annual convention of the Association for Education in Journalism and Mass Communication, Chicago.

McQuail, D. (2005). *McQuail's mass communication theory* (5th ed.). London, UK: Sage.

Mead, G. H. (1934). The point of view of social behaviourism. In Morris, C. H. (Ed.), *Mind, self, & society from the standpoint of a social behaviourist. Works of G. H. Mead* (*Vol. 1*, pp. 1–41). Chicago, IL: University of Chicago Press.

Osgood, C. E., Suci, G., & Tannenbaum, P. (1957). *The measurement of meaning*. Urbana, IL: University of Illinois Press.

Parsons, T. (1963a). On the concept of political power. *Proceedings of the American Philosophical Society, 107*(3), 232–262.

Parsons, T. (1963b). On the concept of influence. *Public Opinion Quarterly, 27*(Spring), 37–62. doi:10.1086/267148

Parsons, T. (1968). Interaction: I. Social interaction. In Sills, D. L. (Ed.), *The international encyclopedia of the social sciences* (*Vol. 7*, pp. 429–441). New York, NY: McGraw-Hill.

Salton, G., & McGill, M. J. (1983). *Introduction to modern information retrieval*. Auckland, Australia: McGraw-Hill.

Scheufele, D. A. (1999). Framing as a theory of media effects. *The Journal of Communication, 49*(1), 103–122. doi:10.1111/j.1460-2466.1999.tb02784.x

Simon, A. (2001). A unified method for analyzing media framing. In Hart, R. P., & Shaw, D. R. (Eds.), *Communication in U.S. elections: New agendas* (pp. 75–89). Lanham, MD: Rowman and Littlefield.

van Eck, N. J., Waltman, L., Dekker, R., & van den Berg, J. (2010). A comparison of two techniques for bibliometric mapping: Multidimensional scaling and VOS. *Journal of the American Society for Information Science and Technology, 61*(12), 2405–2416. doi:10.1002/asi.21421

Van Gorp, B. (2007). The constructionist approach to framing: Bringing culture back in. *The Journal of Communication, 57*, 60–78.

Von Foerster, H. (1982). *Observing systems* (with an introduction of Francisco Varela ed.). Seaside, CA: Intersystems Publications.

Wittgenstein, L. (1953). *Philosophical investigations*. New York, NY: Macmillan.

KEY TERMS AND DEFINITIONS

Codification: The process of stabilizing and/or refining the meaning of content in communication.

Discourse: The exchange of arguments in scholarly debate.

Frame: The latent meaning in a set of messages.

Meaning: The appreciation of the information content of messages by a receiving system.

Semantic Map: A graphical representation of the content of textual messages.

Sociocybernetics: The communication of meaning in social systems.

Vector Space: The positioning of relational information spans a vector space.

ENDNOTES

[1]   Corresponding author: loet@leydesdorff.net; http://www.leydesdorff.net. A previous version of this chapter appeared in the *Public Journal of Semiotics* 3(1) (2011) 28-50.

[2]   VosViewer, a visualization program available at http://www.vosviewer.org, reads Pajek files as input, but uses an algorithm akin to MDS (Van Eck *et al.*, 2010).

[3]   If one uses Word or WordPad, one should be careful to save the file as a so-called DOS plain text file. When prompted by Word, choose the option to add CR/LF to each line. (CR/LF is an old indication of Carriage returns and Line feeds, like using a typewriter.)

4   Sometimes, Windows adds the extension.txt automatically. One should take care not to save the files with twice the extension ".txt. txt". The programs assume only a single ".txt" and will otherwise lead to an error.

5   Sample files text1.txt, text2.txt, text3.txt, text4.txt can be found at http://www.ley-desdorff.net/software/fulltext/text1.txt, etc.

6   One can combine these files in Notepad or alternatively by opening a DOS box. In the DOS box, use "cd" for changing to the folder which contains the files and type: "copy text*.txt text.txt". Make sure to erase an older version of text.txt first.

7   Matrix.txt contains the same information as matrix.dbf. Matrix.dbf can directly be used with more than 256 variables in Excel 2007 and higher, but not in lower versions. In SPSS this depends on the version.

8   The latest version of Pajek can be downloaded at http://vlado.fmf.uni-lj.si/pub/networks/pajek/.

9   The cosine-normalized matrix can be compared to the Pearson correlation matrix which is used for the factor analysis, but without the normalization to the mean. Word-frequency distributions are usually not normally distributed and therefore this normalization to the mean is not considered useful for the visualization. The results of the factor analysis inform us about the latent dimensions which are made visible by the visualization as good as possible. Note that visualization is not an analytical technique.

10   Alternatively, one can change the words in the input file cosine.dat using an text editor such as Notepad.

11   In the Draw screen, Shift-Left click a vertex to increase its partition cluster number by one, Alt-Left click a vertex to decrease it by one.

12   The Washington Post (2), The Australian (1), Calgary Herald (1), The Herald (Glasgow) (1), The Independent Extra (1) The New York Times (1), The Observer (1), and Prince Rupert Daily News (Britisch Columbia) (1).

Chapter 17
System Approach to MIS and DSS and its Modeling within SD

Miroljub Kljajić
University of Maribor, Slovenia

Mirjana Kljajić Borštnar
University of Maribor, Slovenia

Andrej Škraba
University of Maribor, Slovenia

Davorin Kofjač
University of Maribor, Slovenia

ABSTRACT

In this chapter, the authors discuss system dynamics (SD) as a research methodology in Information Systems (IS). The goal is to demonstrate the usefulness of SD methodology in research and its implementation in IS and management Information Systems (MIS). The authors briefly discuss the fundamentals of SD methodology models and causal loop diagrams (CLD) as well as model validation. The usefulness of this transdisciplinary methodology has been demonstrated with the case of the quality of IS success and satisfaction. Some examples of modeling for public decision assessment of sustainable development as well as inventory control using SD have been demonstrated. The advantage of SD is in its natural language problem definition, which can be easily transformed into a directed graph that is convenient for qualitative and quantitative analysis in computer programs. SD enables studying the behavior of complex dynamic systems as the feedback processes of reinforcing and balancing loops.

INTRODUCTION

In this chapter, we discuss research methodology in information systems (IS) or, more precisely, in management information systems (MIS) within system dynamics (SD). IS is highly relevant and its problems are very complex; therefore, a variety of research methodologies addressing this field has been developed. This variety of approaches is conditioned by the context of the IS and the perspectives of the authors. IS plays the most important role in all living and technical systems. It provides communication among elements and

DOI: 10.4018/978-1-4666-0179-6.ch017

environments in the course of achieving goals, or maintains the reference values of the state variables. Without feedback and anticipative information, the functioning and developing of the systems would be impossible. However, depending of the nature of the systems, there are enormous differences among the types and complexities of IS.

In living systems (biological) or organizational systems (human-made), the main purpose of IS is to provide for the functioning of the system and, as such, it is an inseparable part of it. IS is a set of interrelated elements that can gather, store, process and retrieve information. IS consists of information inputs, state and outputs. Without this control, learning and adaptation are impossible. For research purposes, it should be considered as the part of the whole with the goal of providing functionality of the whole.

Without intending to have a deeper elaboration of the historical evolution of different IS at different phenomena, we would merely like to point out that all information systems are relations of special elements defining information subsystems with the purpose of providing communication within the system. When we refer to IS, we consider the information subsystems and research methodology that we used, and we have in mind the methodology that considers all relevant aspects of the whole system. For example, one of the established methodologies is the System Approach (SA). SA methodology was discussed in greater detail in (Ackoff, 1998, Kljajić & Farr, 2008).

The following text will be limited to the IS that is part of human-made organizational systems: enterprise, government organization, global organization, etc. The goal of IS in all these organizations is to provide control (management) of the system. Due to task and information processing ability, the IS in organizational systems have hierarchical structures, starting with Transaction Processing Systems, followed by MIS, Decision Support Systems (DSS) and ending with Executive Information Systems at the top of hierarchy

(Laudon & Laudon, 1988). A similar classification can be found in (Ackoff, 1969): Data Processing, MIS, Decision-Making and Support System and Management System on the top. By analogy, a similar classification could be found in living systems: the central nervous systems with the brain at the top, followed by the spinal cord and with the peripheral nerve systems. Each of the levels has local tasks and autonomy in order to facilitate data processing but is harmonized with the whole IS and within its own system. With organizational systems, IS consists of ICT, Software and Specialists who take care of the good functioning of IS and users.

Our main attention will be devoted to the IS of organizational systems. Even within organizational systems, there is great diversity from small and medium-sized enterprises (SME), large enterprises, government as well as global internet-oriented IS. As the backbone of the systems, IS has impact on individuals, groups, organizations and markets (Georgantzasa & Katsamakas, 2008). The success of an organization is proportional to the quality of IS. Therefore, much research effort has been devoted to the research methodology of the development, maintenance, user acceptance of IS and user satisfaction with IS. However, thus far there are no commonly accepted methodologies to predict that success of IS development project. From the Web of Science (WoS Expanded, 2011) we found 21,280 articles with "information systems" in the title and 1,516 articles with Quality and Success of IS. When we looked for IS&MIS we found 2,150 articles, IS(s)&MIS=901, and IS&DSS=479.

Some of the most influential papers devoted to research methodology of IS are (Davis, 1989; Davis et al., 1989) and (DeLone & McLean, 1992, 2003). Davis described the method of the measurement "technology acceptance model" (TAM) for modeling user acceptance of information technology IT. TAM defines several variables (blocks) interconnected in causal order: external variables influence on Perceived Usefulness and

Perceived Ease of Use, while Output from both blocks influence the Attitude Toward Using and later on the block Behavior Intention to Use and the Actual System Use; Perceived Ease of Use influences the Perceived Usefulness and later the Behavioral Intention to Use. This model represents a process-oriented causal order without the feedback loop.

DeLone and McLean (DeLone & McLean, 1992, 2003) investigated the model of IS Success. For that purpose, they defined variables that measure the success of IS System Quality (technical part of the system), Information Quality (information product), Use, User Satisfaction, Individual impact, and Organizational Impact. The method of both mentioned models are in a way complementary, enabling empirical research of the main attributes of IS quality: technology acceptance and user satisfaction. Seddon (Seddon, 1997) enhanced and respecified DeLone and McLean's model in the sense of interaction among the attributes within IS Success and Use. Ten years later, DeLone and McLean (DeLone & McLean, 2003) updated and enhanced their model of measuring of IS success with greater precision of each attribute. In their updated model, they added Service Quality in addition to Information and System Quality as the consequence of e-commerce and the internet. In their model, they introduced Net Benefits as a consequence of IS and its influence (feedback) on Intention to Use and User Satisfaction. Later, the model was the basis for several empirical research projects in real cases (Roldán & Leal, 2010) as well as for system dynamics application for IS success (Wang & Liu, 2005). Wang and Liu merged Davis and DeLone's and McLean's model and interpreted it within SD with promising results.

Although the system dynamics (SD) modeling method (Forrester, 1958, 1961, 1987, 1992) was promising in dealing with IS research questions, there is a quite modest amount of articles using SD methods in research of IS comparing to others methodology.

From (WOS Expanded, 2011) on the topics IS published in the System Dynamics Review, the official journal of System Dynamics, for 2009 we found only six papers published in a special issue "Information Systems Research with System Dynamics" (SDR, 2008), while for the 10 last years, we found 27 articles. This is too few, in our opinion, for one of the most powerful transdisciplinary methodologies. Certainly, this number should be a higher, because we performed this search only in the official Journal of System Dynamics. An excellent survey of IS research using methodology of SD can be found in (Georgantzasa & Katsamakas, 2008).

The goal of this chapter is to highlight the present state and perspectives of the theory and practice of decision assessments in enterprises, and other complex systems, based on SD and simulation models. In the following section on the general approach to system modeling paradigm, we discuss the principle of SD and CLD within general system theory and its appropriateness for research methodology in IS. The final section will deal with IS and DSS as a main part of MIS. Some examples from the authors and from the literature of development of DSS based on SD and simulation, and its success will be demonstrated.

SYSTEM DYNAMICS FUNDAMENTALS

Abstract Concept of System and Modeling Paradigm

In order to clarify previous statements that IS is an inseparable part of the system and that it could be described from different perspectives, we will start with definition of the systems. The word "system" is derived from ancient Greek and means a whole that consists of elements and is greater than the sum of its elements. An element is the smallest part of the whole, necessary for system description, which cannot or will not be divided any further. From a formal perspective (Mesarović & Takahara, 1989), a system is defined by the pair

$$S = (E, R) \qquad (1)$$

in which $E_i \in E \subset U$, $i = 1, 2,...,n$ represent the set of elements and $R \subseteq E \times E$ the binary relation between the elements, and U the universal set. Each element $E_i \in E$ can be further set as well and $R_{j_j} \in R$, $j = 1, 2,...m$ define different relations between the elements. For example, the relation Rj for each j =1, 2, 3,..., m reflects different connections among systems elements from energetic, material, production, electrical, chemical or informational aspects, etc. In concrete analysis, such a procedure is inductive and represents the abstract model of a real system.

In general, three classes of complex systems can be identified: Natural Systems, Biological Systems (living systems) and Organizational Systems (human systems). All have certain structural similarities; however, there are huge differences in our understanding of their behavior. We will consider Organizational Systems as complex because of the different relations among subsystems, such as: psychological, social, political, material, financial, informational, etc. Their structure and functioning change because of the changing relations among participants and the environment, due to changes in information technology. In this case, the information-based decision represents the prevalent force of development.

From the research perspective, human activity intended to gather new knowledge can be considered from two aspects: the subject of the research itself (process) and the methodology using different methods, tools and techniques for process analyses (Mingers, 2008).

There are three main concepts in a modeling approach to real world (Myers, 2009):

a)   Positivistic, which supposes that (1) the external world exists independently of the observer, (2) this world is not directly observable, and (3) for its representation, we set up simplified models;

b)   Interpretative, which starts with the assumption that social reality is a social construct and its understanding and interpretation is only possible through language, consciousness and shared meanings; and

c)   Critical researchers assume that social reality (realized reality) is historically constituted and that it is produced and reproduced by people. This paradigm can be stated (Kljajić, 1998, Lazanski & Kljajić, 2006) with the triad (O, S, M), in which O represents the real object; S represents the observer (subject) and M the model of the object as the consequence of observer knowledge, intention, interest etc.

The relation between the observer S and the object O is of essential significance. The observer is a person with all his cognitive qualities, while the object of research is the manifested world, which exists by itself, regardless of how it can be described. The third article of the triad, M, is the successive one and represents a model or a picture of the analyzed system, O. The relation $O \leftrightarrow S$ reflects human experiences of concrete reality. This cognitive consciousness represents our mental model. The relationship $M \leftrightarrow S$ represents the problem of knowledge presentation, i.e. the translation of the mental model into the actual model. The $O \leftrightarrow M$ relation represents the phase of model validation or proof of correspondence between theory and practice, which renders possible the generalization of experiences into rules and laws. The $S \rightarrow O \rightarrow M$ relationship is nothing else but the active relation of the subject in the phase of the object's cognition. The $M \rightarrow O \rightarrow S$ relation is nothing more than the process of learning and generalization. A theory is an intellectual construct enabling us to give a more generalized form to the phenomena of the research and direct results of the experiment. In the cognitive process, the value standpoints of subject S_v are far more important to us in relation to the object of research in the modeling process and represents key problems at model validation.

System Dynamics Conception

The fundamentals of System Dynamics were defined by J. Forrester in the mid-1950s (Forrester, 1958) as the method for modeling of industrial dynamics. At the beginning of the 1980s, the dawn of the information era, the method was renamed "System Dynamics" (SD). The method is straightforward in its essence, based on the conservation of mass principle. Nevertheless, the genius of Forrester is that, as the pioneer of computer science, he noticed that the power of computers could be used in business systems, not only for collecting, processing and storing data, but also for strategic decision making. For this purpose, dynamic models of systems were needed. Consequently, the method of modeling was developed, which is clear, straightforward, user friendly and holistic. J. W. Forrester developed the methodology and simulation tool, i.e. the program. The idea of modeling is based on the supposition that every real system, including business systems, could be described by the system of equations, which is represented by the interconnected flows, or rates and storages. i.e. Levels:

$$S = (L_j, R_r, A_r)\, j = 1, 2,\dots,m;\, r = 1, 2,\dots,l \qquad (4)$$

Here L_j represents the set of Levels (stocks) and R_i the set of R (flows) and A_r the Auxiliary expression by which we can express arithmetic relation among L and R. Each level L or state element has its own input, i.e. input rate Rin and its own output rate, $Rout$.

The principle of conservation of mass for the above model could be described by the dynamics equation in the form of difference equation:

$$L(k + 1) = L(k) + \Delta t(R_{in}(k) - R_{out}(k))\ k = 0, 1, 2,\dots n \qquad (5)$$

where k represents discrete time, Δt is the time interval of computation. Each entrepreneur understands that the value of Level element $L(k+1)$ increases if $R_{in}(k) > R_{out}(k)$; it is unchanged if $R_{in}(k) = Rout(k)$, and decreases if $R_{in}(k) < R_{out}(k)$. For example, in Figure 2, square symbols represents Level elements (Population, Natural Resources, Environment Degradation) while circle symbol represents Rate laments (like; Regeneration, Consumption etc.). The clouds at the beginning and at the end represent the environment of the model. This is, therefore, our boundary of modeling of the addressed model. From a formal viewpoint, this method is indeed straightforward and clear, as well as understandable. In Table 1, possible meanings of L and R elements for different classes of systems is given.

The methodology of solving problems by the principles of System Dynamics is similar to the

Table 1. Describing different systems with level, rate and desired state

System	Level	Rate	Desired state
Population	Population	Birth, Death	Sustainable Growth
Warehouse	Inventory	Delivery, Consumption	Desired level of inventory
Cash balance	Cash	Income, Expenses	Positive level of cash
Room heating	Room temperature	Temperature input flux, Temperature loss	Desired room temperature
Knowledge	Knowledge level	Learning, Forgetting	Appropriate level of knowledge
Information system	Information system capacity	New technology, Technology decay	Adequate IS for controlling real system

methodology of the systems approach and could be concisely described by the following steps:

- Problem definition
- Determination of goals
- Concept of investigation
- Formulation of mathematical model
- Coding of computer program
- Model validation
- Experiment preparation (simulation scenarios)
- Simulation and analysis of results

When defining a problem, one addresses the parts with which one is not satisfied or those that demonstrate undesired dynamics. Usually, these are the values of Level elements of the addressed process, L, and the interconnections between them, R. The goal of the research is to determine the goal states that should be achieved. Here the question "How?" emerges. With the application of the dynamic hypothesis, the dynamics of the system are determined as the consequence of key feedback loops in the system. In this phase, with complex problems, the key role is played by the team with an interdisciplinary approach. State elements and their relations are nonetheless the main part of the analysis, which could be performed in several different ways. In the end, the validated model is the tool for the testing of the dynamic hypothesis at the different visions (scenarios). In order to address complex problems, one has to apply systematic and team approaches (Škraba et al., 2003, 2007) in the process of solution.

Causal Loop Diagrams CLD and SD Models

The determination of model structure and its parameters is the most important part of the assignment. There are several methods and tools to aid in the articulation of the model structure. One exceptionally practical one is the method of Causal Loop Diagrams; these are directed graphs

with polarity. Each Level and Rate element has a directed arrow assigned, so that one element represents the cause and the other the consequence. Directed arrows from cause to consequence have the "+" sign if the cause and consequence have the same direction and "−" if the opposite direction exists. Another very important aspect of the SD methodology is the feedback loop. When several arrows in the CLD return to one element, a closing path or a loop is created, which gives some feedback to the original element; therefore, it is called a feedback loop. There are two kinds of feedback loops: a positive feedback loop (reinforcing loop) and a negative feedback loop (balancing loop) Reinforcing loops tend to grow or decline without limits and make the system unstable. Balancing loops tend to adjust themselves to some intended value. Hence, they tend to stabilize the system and guide it to the goal.

If we compare Equation 1's definition of a general system with Equations 4's generalized SD model one, a logical equivalence between two definitions can be seen. However, Equation 4 represents a concrete model of some reality. If we connect elements E_i as a node (vertex) with R_j as set of arcs among nodes, we can obtain a graph of Equation 1. Similarly, if we connect elements L (node) by arcs R in Equation 4 (if we omit the set of auxiliary elements), we obtain CLD, which is a more abstract concept of SD. If we look again at Equation 1, the abstract relation $R_j, j = 1, 2,...,$ m, represents one of the j aspects of the system, i.e. from one discipline. However, SD can take all these aspects in natural way into account by means of the L and R elements. We can conclude that SD is indeed a transdisciplinary methodology useful for modeling complex systems, both qualitative and quantitative.

The following simplified case of a Causal Loop Diagram for a paradigm of sustainable development is shown in Figure 1. Here we consider the extent and growth of population as well as the exploration of natural resources. The higher extent of the population results in the higher usage of natural resources. The volume of natural resources is dependent on the intensity of regeneration. The higher volume of natural resources consequently provides better conditions for the development of the population, which positively influences the growth of the population. The important factor is the efficiency of the natural resource usage, which both negatively influences resource consumption and positively influences the population growth. In this case, the negative feedback loop is considered, which has the property to converge to the goal state, i.e. the reference value. In our case, the goal state is determined by the regeneration of the natural resources, which is the key message of the described structure. In this manner, one could conclude that the growth of the population over the longer time frame is not dependent on the volume of the natural resources stock, but rather on the regeneration of natural resources. Regeneration in the sense of System Dynamics is represented as the Rate element, i.e. the element that represents the change, rather than the stock.

In the model analysis, one has to start with the model equilibrium. Special care should be taken

for the definition of the user-defined functions that are applied in the model. Figure 2 shows a model of sustainable development, in which the regeneration is taken into account as the Rate element. The model has three (3) Level elements: Population, Natural Resources and Environment Degradation. The user-defined function "Limits of natural resources" is applied as the limiter of the consumption of population members in the case that the supply of natural resources would shrink below the normal level. This function also considers that (in the case of increased volume of natural resources above the normal level) the consumption would increase for a certain, rather small, part. The goal of the population development is determined by the volume of natural resources and the demand of natural resources with respect to population. The growth is therefore limited by the stock of natural resources and by the consumption "Per capita". The dynamic response of the system with regard to the goal is determined by the rate element "Regeneration", which could be dependent on the investment in new technology.

Figure 1. Causal loop diagram of population ~ Natural resources

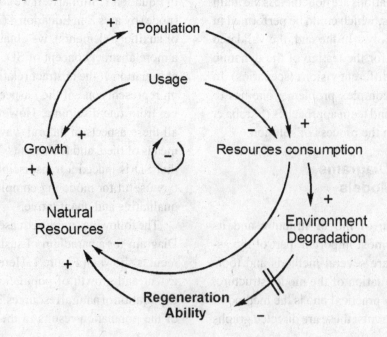

Figure 2. The model of sustainable development - Natural resources

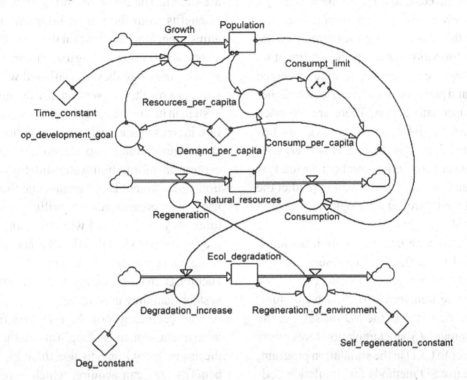

APPLICATIONS OF SD

Although System Dynamics methodology has been in use for more than 50 years, its application in the research of IS is rather uncommon and infrequent. Predominantly, it is used for the general business process, although it could also be used in analyzing the behavior of IS. Therefore, our goal is to demonstrate the usefulness of SD methodology in the research and implementation of DSS. As a methodology, applying SD in analyzing complex system behavior is very important from several reasons: it is *simple*, because it is based on the natural laws of Rate and Storage that describe relations between elements in quantitative/qualitative relations; it is *transparent*, because it allows unique discussion about elements relations defining problem; it is *coherent*, because it consists of simulation tools harmonized with methodology. The advantage of SD as a part of SA is in the fact that a problem defined in natural language can be easily transformed into a directed graph

convenient for qualitative and quantitative analysis in a computer program. In this case, the user can always check the validity of the stated problem and the model developed. SD enables studying the behavior of complex dynamic systems as a feedback process of reinforcing and balancing loops. As such, it provides testing of dynamic hypotheses about the anticipated properties of the IS: Life Cycle Development, Quality of Systems and IS Success and Satisfaction as well as assessment in the decision process.

Information System Technology Acceptance Model and User Satisfaction

In order to demonstrate the use of SD in specific aspects of IS, we will briefly discuss some examples of IS success. In (Wang and Liu, 2005), SD methodology was used to demonstrate IS success model and TAM. In Figure 3, there is an integrated model of TAM (Davis) and DeLone and

McLean's IS Success model (DeLone & McLean, 2003) in a new classical block-oriented process concept. In this model, we can see three external variables (information system quality, information quality and service quality) influencing perceived usefulness and perceived ease of use which further impact on user satisfaction. There are feedback loop from user satisfaction to perceived usefulness and perceived ease of use. However, with this model user satisfaction can be measured by statistical analysis but it is difficult to predict the behavior of the IS project development at certain requirements.

Figure 3 has a certain explanation behind it (Wang and Liu, 2005) and represents an extended model of integrated IS success, which could easily be transferred to CLD techniques, which is the first step to the SD model, i.e. the simulation model. (Some simulation tools allow direct transfer to CLD in the simulation program, while some use SD methods for simulation coding.) For the methodological perspective, see Section 3. The authors themselves prefer CLD and then the SD model. The advantage of SD methods lies in fact that it has richer structure than the process model. Within SD methodology, the relationship among the variables could be considered as qualitative or quantitative depending of the problem and the context.

Figure 4 shows the CLD of IS Success and TAM Implementation Issues. In Figure 4, two reinforcing loops, *R*, and one balancing loop, *B*, which is dominating the behaviors of the system,

are shown. The first reinforcing loop, *R1*, named "Benefits from the use of information systems adjustment loop" means that the more the users in an organization are willing to use their information system, the more they are satisfied with the system. As a result, the users can use the information system in more effective and efficient ways and in turn increase the actual task completion rate. The second reinforcing loop, *R2*, named "User's perception on information system quality and system usage adjustment loop" means that the more the users in an organization are willing to use IS, the more they are satisfied with them and the more they will start to feel that the IS is becoming more useful and easier to use. As a result, the users will become even more willing to use the information system than they used to be.

The balancing loop *B1* ("IS benefits and IS investment adjustment loop") means that the more the users are willing to use their IS, the more benefits they can acquire, which is reflected in the increase in actual completion rate. When the users obtain higher benefits from IS, the gap between the expected and actual task completion rate (performance ratio) will decrease. As a result, the users will have the perception that the IS is good for them and that this kind of performance of the information system will last even though the organization did not do anything afterwards. This perception will lead to the perception that there is no need to continue to invest, or devote more effort to the information system, since it is functioning fairly well. As a result, the users will

Figure 3. Integrated IS success model redrawn from (Wang and Yueh, 2005) with permission

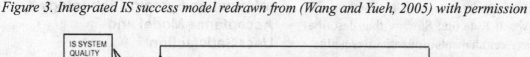
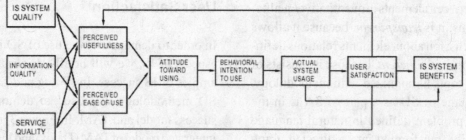

Figure 4. CLD of IS success and TAM redrawn from (Wang and Yueh, 2005) with permission

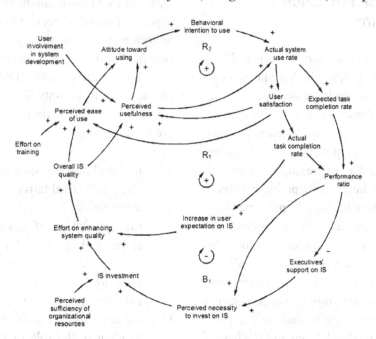

become less willing to use the information system than they used to be.

It is obvious that such presentations of TAM and IS success are more convenient for analysis. Moreover, the authors added the external variables "Users involvement in system development" (which is very important and known as "User-driven development") and "Effort of training". The authors (Wang & Liu, 2005) further discuss *R* and *B* loops according existing MIS theory and goal. The next step is the SD model, model validation and simulation (according to the previously described methodology).

The following examples were recently published in a special issue of SDR and represent obvious applications of SD methodology in the research of different aspect of IS behavior, its success and satisfaction. In their article (Luna-Reyes et al., 2008), the authors (based on empirical evidence) developed a model of the role of knowledge sharing in building trust during the requirements analysis of a complex IS project. In (Otto & Simon, 2008), dynamic perspectives on social characteristics and sustainability in online

community networks were analyzed. Successful networks include those whose participants are engaged in open source software development; the case of Wikipedia was used as the model. Dutta and Roy (2008) analyzed relevant issues of the dynamics of organizational information security. In (Pavlov et al., 2008), an SD model of message-based communication in which the information processing capacity of message recipients is limited was developed. The authors showed that message filtering can increase the flow of useful and valuable communication. Finally, in (Kanungo & Jain, 2008) the authors modeled the relations among variables that affect email use and users' productivity, using system dynamics.

All the above-mentioned cases highlight the usefulness of SD methodology for the systems approach for research in IS and represent deep analyses and clear solutions to some important cases in IS. Our motivations were to bring attention to IS researchers for usefulness of SD methodology for more intensive applications in the area of IS.

Simulation Based Decision Support Systems

A simulation-based *decision support system (DSS)* is an important part of MIS, which supports business or organizational decision assessment. The simulation model is used as an explanatory tool for better understanding of the decision process and/or for defining and understanding learning processes. The advantage of the simulation model as a part of DSS is in the fact that a problem defined in natural language can be easily transformed into a directed graph convenient for qualitative and quantitative analysis in computer programs. In this case, the user can always check the validity of the stated problem within a certain theory and further its translation to computer programming. This is especially important in cases of complex problems in which feedback loops and stochastic relations are present, regardless of the process being a continuous or discrete event. Big picture presentations and animation of simulated process make this technique flexible and transparent for testing a system's performance in all phases of system design and deployment. This has made it possible to examine the projected performance of systems through wide-ranging investigations of design and environmental assumptions very early in the development process, when key resources are committed. Simulation, together with the Systems Approach, has become ever more central to the development of complex systems. Human knowledge and the simulation methodology combined in a decision support system offer new levels of quality in decision making and research.

In the following sections, we will demonstrate two characteristic cases realized in SD for users' assessment in the decision process.

Case 1: System Dynamics Model for the Public Decisions Support

The SD model for public decision support in the Canary Islands, particularly ones related to stra-

tegic issues, involves qualitative and quantitative aspects of social systems. Quantitative variables are often crucial for strategic decisions. In addition, qualitative information is provided by a social actor and decision maker (DM) with an implicit character of uncertainty (Legna & Rivero, 2001; Legna 2002). The main pillars of our approach are the following:

- the building of qualitative models that integrate qualitative and quantitative information;
- the application of system dynamics that is particularly useful in determining the interrelations between the subsystems, building scenarios and running strategic simulations;
- the analysis of the leading forces that help to identify the role of the variables, their leverage potential and, consequently, to highlight key areas of the social system to implement policies.

This approach is based on the building of qualitative models and the application of system dynamics for the development of a simulation model. Variables were identified that affect the sustainable improvement of the quality of life in the Canary Islands. The relationships between the variables are expressed as an influence square Matrix M with dimension $n = 53 \times 53$, of which 12 are exogenous. Consequently, it has 41 state variables. Each element of M in this study may take values between 0 and 3. If $m_{ij} = 0$, changes in variable V_i do not affect V_j. If a_{ij} takes a value between 1 and 3, it means that the changes in variable "i" produce changes in "j" proportional to prescribed gain. These relationships are represented as: $V_j = f(V_1, V_2, V_3,..., V_{j-1})$. This function means that changes in the variables V_i ($i = 1,...,i-1$) will produce changes in the variable V_i. In this paper, the functions are expressed in a Matrix M, where each column represents a function Matrix M gives important information about the Canary

Islands' social and economic system. More about the influence matrix can be found in (Kljajić et al., 2002). We will apply the analysis of "Motricité et Dépendance" to identify both the indirect effects and the roles. The literature about this analysis is extensive, especially in France; for instance, see Roubelat (1993).

The Relationship between Influence Matrix and CLD Suitable for SD Modeling

To move to a quantitative model capable of cause-consequence analysis of decision makers' impacts on the long-term behavior, the influence matrix must be transformed to SD methodology. In this way, a direct connection between scenario planning (as a consequence of DM) and variable behavior is possible. Fifty-three variables are a rather demanding problem, especially with regards to model validation. In this case, it is necessary to specify the initial value of variables, parameters and other functions necessary for model implementation. Therefore, we will develop a procedure of influence matrix transformation into a Causal Loop Diagram (CLD). The influence diagram is obtained from the influence matrix. The variables v_i in influence Matrix M represent nodes of the graph and the value of the coefficient of Matrix M a_{ij} represents a gain of a directed branch. A different weight in the coefficient matrix represents the gain of a certain element in the system. By definition, it is assumed that the node (vertex) or variables belong to a certain entity in the system. Variable relevance in the systems will be estimated with a matrix. From this point, the transformation to SD methodology is merely the next step. Variables, which represent entities, have cumulative L or flow R properties suitable for system dynamics modeling. To perform the transformation, the influence Matrix M could be decomposed. In our case, we split the influence matrix into several sub-matrixes. In order to facilitate matrix decomposition, it is desirable to aggregate the variables

in a natural order. Several similar variables were mapped in one, e.g. population, ecology, industry etc. Subjective mapping is defined by an aggregation function $f(V_j)$: $V \rightarrow X_i$, $j = 1,...,53$, $i = 1,...5$ which gives us the following subsets:

$$X_1 = \{V_{48}, V_{30}, V_{33}\}$$

$$X_2 = \{V_{36}, V_{27}, V_{38}, V_{35}\}$$

$$X_3 = \{V_8, V_{11}, V_{10}, V_{12}, V_9, V_4, V_3, V_5, V_{37}, V_{32}, V_2, V_6\}$$

$$X_4 = \{V_{22}, V_{28}, V_{29}, V_{49}, V_{24}, V_{25}, V_{52}\}$$

$$X_5 = \{V_{26}, V_{18}, V_{19}, V_{20}, V_{21}, V_{40}, V_{42}, V_{53}\}$$

As a result of mapping, we obtained the aggregated connection matrix C:

$$C = \begin{array}{c} \\ X_1 \\ X_2 \\ X_3 \\ X_4 \\ X_5 \end{array} \begin{array}{ccccc} X_1 & X_2 & X_3 & X_4 & X_5 \\ \begin{bmatrix} 0 & 0 & C_{13} & C_{14} & C_{15} \\ 0 & 0 & 0 & C_{24} & C_{25} \\ C_{31} & C_{32} & 0 & C_{34} & C_{35} \\ C_{41} & C_{42} & C_{43} & 0 & C_{45} \\ C_{51} & C_{52} & C_{53} & C_{54} & 0 \end{bmatrix} \end{array}$$

In matrix C, the variables describe the following subsystems: X_1 = R&D, X_2 = Ecology, X_3 = Population, X_4 = GDP, X_5 = Economy. C_{ij} represents the sub-matrix of the connection between sub-systems X_i and X_j. The elements of the matrix under the main diagonal represent the feedback connections. If sub-systems X_i ; $i = 1,2,...,5$ are represented as the nodes of the graph and C_{ij} ; $i = 1,2,...,5$; $j = 1,2,...,5$; $i \neq j$ represent the branch of the directed graph, we can represent the matrix C as the influence diagram or influence graph, see Figure 5.

This graph is identical to matrix M but yet convenient for modeling in SD. The diagram represents a high level of abstraction convenient for further decentralized modeling. Next, we will

Figure 5. Graph of the aggregated system

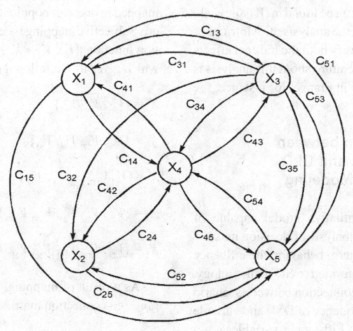

analyze the interconnection between the main variables relevant for the causal loop diagram CLD as shown in Figure 6. Feedback loops and interactions of particular subsystems are shown in the causal loop diagram. The locations, which are defined with variables, represent the system state element, while arrows show the direction of influence between a particular pair of elements. In the simulation process, an expert group in the form of a suggested policy heuristically determines key parameters. The causal loop diagram in Figure 6 represents interactions in the context of regional development and its influence on regional prosperity and quality of life.

The structural analysis of the system is of great significance since mental models of various kinds can be captured using the proposed methodology. For example, if Gross Domestic Product increases, the Investments in Education and R&D production increase above what they would have been and vice versa; therefore, the arrowhead is marked with the "+" symbol. If the Investments in Education and R&D production increase, the Economic volume increases above what it would

have been, which is also marked with the "+" symbol. If the Population increases, the Quality of Environment decreases and the cause effect is marked with the "−" symbol. All other causal connections are marked in the same manner. After the aggregation of variables, i.e. the joining of similarities, the next step is the determination of levels and rates according to system dynamics methodology.

With the proposed methodology, the system can be entirely determined by the System Dynamics models that form the general simulation model for the regional development of the considered case. Such decomposition allows for a multi-level approach in modeling, which facilitates the process of model validation. System Dynamics simulation models provide a basis for designing more effective industrial and economic systems in terms of material, energy and other aspects, such as ecology (Forrester, 1973). The combination of System Dynamics, expert systems and interactive experimentation based on business scenarios aids in the process of creating a regional policy. A preliminary sub-model was developed

Figure 6. Causal loop diagram of the Canary Islands case

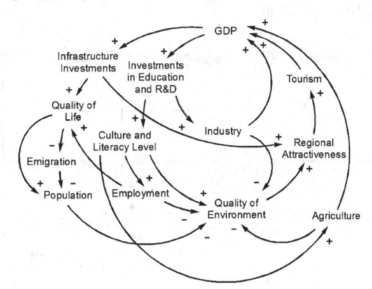

Case 2: SD Simulation Based Inventory Control

for population dynamics, which incorporated 150 parameters (Kljajić et al., 2003). The model enables changes for the different population variables that are relevant for decision makers. Users have the opportunity to actively participate in the decision process by defining relevant criteria and their importance, in spite of the large number of different simulation scenarios. The decision process is clear and creative. Later developments in the field consider group model building (Vennix, 1996) and the application of System Dynamics models. The preliminary model is built using the Powersim simulation tool (www.powersim.com), which provides results for the real application of the organizational strategy. Simulation also enables the inner view of system behavior for the selected scenario. The system makes it possible to analyze different situations, which is the basis for achieving the consistent formulation of a policy. The building of the model is still in progress (Legna & González, 2005).

The basic concept of inventory control with simulation is presented in Figure 7. Inputs into the simulation model are the data of production plan, inventory level, vendor's backlog, and simulation parameters. The simulation run is based on the data and inventory control algorithms, producing several inventory control policies. Now, we have to assess each policy and choose the one that produces the best result with regard of criteria function. The order policy was achieved with a user-friendly simulation algorithm, which was developed through SD problem formulation.

In our case, a single-vendor single-buyer model with backorders is assumed due to simplicity. The detailed inventory control model, developed according to SD, is described in (Kofjač et al., 2009).

Formally, from the control aspect, our inventory optimization problem (Kofjač et al., 2009) can be described with the following equation:

Figure 7. Block model of the inventory control model with simulation-based inventory control algorithms (Adapted from Kofjač & Kljajić, 2010)

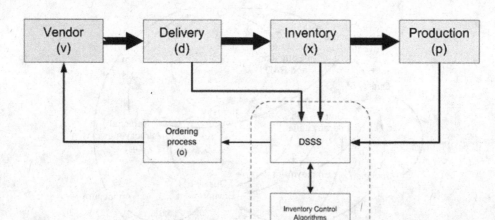

$$x(k+1) = x(k) + d(k) - p(k),\ k = 0,1,2,..$$
$$v(k+1) = v(k) + o(k) - d(k),\ k = 0,1,2,...$$
$$x(0) = x_0,\ v(0) = v_0$$

$$(6)$$

where $x(k)$, $v(k)$ represents inventory and vendors backlog, $d(k)$ stochastic item delivery, $p(k)$ stochastic production process, $o(k)$ order or control variables at k, and x_0, v_0 the initial inventory and backlog at $k = 0$. The demand of production is sporadic. Due to stochastic demand and lead times, the expected value $EV(x(k + 1))$ is estimated with the Monte Carlo simulation. Usually, only statistical data about delivery is available. Hence, the delivery function $d(k) = f(o(k - \tau))$ can be represented by a stochastic exponential delay function. To compensate for the stochastic delivery delay, the order placement policy $o(k)$ must be defined as:

$$o(k) = \gamma(x(k),\ d(k - \tau_d),\ p(k + \tau_r),\ p(k + \tau_p),\ u,\ x_{min})$$
$$(7)$$

where $p(k + \tau_r)$ represents a production plan prediction in the time interval $[k,\ k+\tau_r)$, $p(k + \tau_p)$ represents a production plan prediction in the time interval $[k+\tau_r,\ k+\tau_p]$, u uncertainty factor that impacts ordering quantity, and x_{min} safety stock. If we substitute o(k) in Equation 6 with the expression from Equation 7, we obtain a *delayed-advanced difference equation*, which is difficult to solve in a such a way as to minimize some criteria function and determine control variable *o(k)*. Instead, we used simulation technique combined with a heuristic.

The total cost function c is defined by:

$$\min_{o \in O} c = \sum_{k=0}^{m} (x(k)(c_c + c_p) \\ + d(k)(c_t(w) + c_v) + c_o o(k) + c_m p(k))$$
$$(8)$$

in which m represents the number of simulation steps, w transport weight, c_c cost of capital, c_p cost of physical storage, c_t transportation cost depending on shipment lot size, c_o fixed ordering costs, c_v cost of taking over products from the vendor, and c_m cost of manipulation while transferring items from inventory into the production process. It is necessary to find a replenishment policy $o(k)$ that minimizes the total cost function c, subject to

$$x_{min} \le x(k) \le x_{max}$$
$$(9)$$

The main advantage of such a model is in its increased man-machine interconnection, where a computer is capable of executing several simulation runs in a short period of time using different "what-if" scenarios. The manager then chooses the most appropriate scenario and modifies it if needed, allowing the process of inventory control to be faster and better. In comparison to the other methods, with such a dynamic analysis of the considered system, behavior is the main advantage of testing the strategy with the aid of simulation scenarios. The user interface plays a very important role in the DSS. The user interface must provide all the necessary information to the user in order to improve his decision making process. Furthermore, it must be intelligent and dynamic; otherwise, the user will not show

any enthusiasm to use the DSS regardless of the good performance of the simulation model and optimization algorithms. An efficient user interface will enable users to integrate their own ideas and decisions, thus guiding them through critical situations (Marinho et al., 1999).

An example of the prototype DSS user interface is shown in Figure 8. This screen appears after the initial screen (not shown in the picture), which gives the manager an initial overview of each ordering policy (algorithm) with regard of number of stockouts, minimal and maximal inventory level, and total cost. The selected algorithms can be analyzed in detail as shown in Figure 8. The manager can select two algorithms (represented by a brighter and darker lines in the graphs) and compare them with regard to ordering

Figure 8. An example of the user interface screen for the inventory control optimization

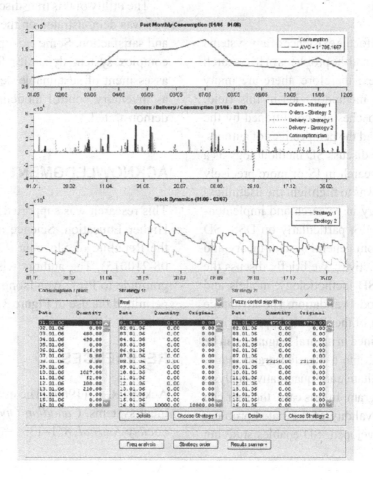

and inventory dynamics (the middle and the bottom graph), whereas the upper graph represents the historic data on demand dynamics, which is the same for both algorithms. The tables at the bottom are the upper three graphs represented numerically. Such an analysis allows in-depth insight into the reasons for the performance of each ordering policy. Moreover, the user interface provides the manager with more functionalities, which are not shown here: a) each algorithm can be evaluated financially, with the impact of each cost is shown in detail, b) the user interface enables frequency analysis for the ordering quantities and the intervals between two consecutive orders, c) the manager can setup his own ordering policy, rerun the simulation and compare the results with built-in algorithms.

CONCLUSION

The relevance of IS for the existence of any systems is highly important, and the problems of IS research are highly complex; therefore, there are many different research methodologies in this field. A variety of approaches are conditioned by the context of the IS and the perspectives of authors. In this chapter, we discuss SD methodology as a proper tool for research in IS or more precisely in MIS. Our goal was to highlight the usefulness of SD methodology in research and implementation in IS and MIS, particularly on DSS. SD was considered from general system theory and cybernetics perspectives. We briefly discuss the fundamentals of SD methodology, models and CLD, as well as model validation. The advantage of the SD as a part of the System Approach is in that a problem defined in natural language can be easily transformed into a directed graph that is convenient for qualitative and quantitative analysis in a computer program. In this case, the user can always check the validity of the stated problem and the model developed. SD enables studying the behavior of complex dynamic systems as a feedback process of reinforcing and balancing loops. As such, it provides testing of dynamic hypotheses about anticipated property of the IS: Life Cycle Development, Quality of Systems and Information System Success. As a methodology, applying SD in analyzing complex system behavior is very important from several reasons: it is *simple*, because it is based on natural laws of Rate and Storage that describes relations between elements in quantitative/qualitative relation; *transparent*, because it allows unique discussion about elements relations defining problem; and *coherent*, because it consists of simulation tools harmonized with methodology and the problem to be solved. SD is a transdisciplinary methodology, because it provides complex problem solving from different perspectives in interconnection with R and L elements.

The utility of this transdisciplinary methodology was demonstrated on the case of IS success and satisfaction. Some examples of modeling of complex system dynamics for public decision assessment of sustainable development as well as inventory control modeling using SD were demonstrated.

ACKNOWLEDGMENT

This research was supported by the Ministry of Higher Education, Science and Technology of the Republic of Slovenia (Contract No. 1000-08-210015). The authors wish to express their gratitude to Prof. Wei-Tsong Wang who kindly permitted the use of Figure 3 and Figure 4.

REFERENCES

Ackoff, R. L. (1969). The evolution of management systems. *Canadian Operational Research Society Journal, 8*, 1–13.

Ackoff, R. L. (1998). *Ackoff's best: His classic writings on management*. New York, NY: John Wiley & Sons.

Davis, F. D. (1989). Perceived usefulness, perceived ease of use, and user acceptance of information technology. *Management Information Systems Quarterly*, *13*, 319–339. doi:10.2307/249008

Davis, F. D., Bagozzi, R. P., & Warshaw, P. R. (1989). User acceptance of computer technology: A comparison of two theoretical models. *Management Science*, *35*, 982–1003. doi:10.1287/mnsc.35.8.982

DeLone, W. H., & McLean, E. R. (1992). Information systems success: The quest for the dependent variable. *Information Systems Research*, *3*, 60–95. doi:10.1287/isre.3.1.60

DeLone, W. H., & McLean, E. R. (2003). The DeLone and McLean Model of Information Systems success: A ten-year update. *Journal of Management Information Systems*, *19*(4), 9–30.

Dutta, A., & Roy, R. (2008). Dynamics of organizational information Security. *System Dynamics Review*, *24*(3), 349–375. doi:10.1002/sdr.405

Forrester, J. W. (1958). Industrial dynamics-A major breakthrough for decision makers. *Harvard Business Review*, *36*(4), 37–66.

Forrester, J. W. (1973). *Industrial dynamics*. Cambridge, MA: MIT Press.

Forrester, J. W. (1992). Policies, decisions and information sources for modeling. *European Journal of Operational Research*, *59*(1), 42–63. doi:10.1016/0377-2217(92)90006-U

Georgantzasa, N. C., & Katsamakasb, E. G. (2008). Information systems research with system dynamics. *System Dynamics Review*, *24*(3), 247–264. doi:10.1002/sdr.420

Kanungo, S., & Jain, V. (2008). Modeling email use: A case of email system transition. *System Dynamics Review*, *24*(3), 299–319. doi:10.1002/sdr.406

Kljajić, M. (1998). Modeling and understanding the complex system within cybernetics. In M. J. Ramaekers, (Ed.). *15th International Congress on Cybernetics* (pp. 864-869). Namur, Belgium: Association International de Cybernetique.

Kljajić, M., & Farr, J. (2010). Importance of systems engineering in the development of information systems. In Paradise, D. (Ed.), *Emerging systems approaches in information technologies: concepts, theories, and applications* (pp. 51–66). Hershey, PA: Information Science Reference. doi:10.4018/978-1-60566-976-2.ch004

Kljajić, M., Legna, V. C., & Škraba, A. (2002). System dynamics model development of the Canary Islands for supporting strategic public decisions. In P. I. Davidsen, E. Mollona, V. G. Diker, R. S. Langer, & J. I. Rowe (Eds.), *Proceedings of the 20th International Conference of the System Dynamics Society*. Albany, NY: System Dynamics Society.

Kljajić, M., Legna, V. C., Škraba, A., & Peternel, J. (2003). Simulation model of the Canary Islands for public decision support - Preliminary results. In R. L. Eberlein, V. G. Diker, R. S. Langer, & J. I. Rowe (Ed.), *Proceedings of the 21st International Conference of the System Dynamics Society*. Albany, NY: The System Dynamics Society.

Kofjač, D., & Kljajić, M. (2010). Decision support simulation system for inventory control with stochastic variables. In: M. Kljajić & G. E. Lasker (Eds.). *Advances in simulation-based decision support: Proceedings of the 22nd International Conference on Systems Research, Informatics and Cybernetics* (pp. 6 -10). Tecumseh, Canada: The International Institute for Advanced Studies in Systems Research and Cybernetics.

Kofjač, D., Kljajić, M., & Rejec, V. (2009). The anticipative concept in warehouse optimization using simulation in an uncertain environment. *European Journal of Operational Research*, *193*(3), 660–669. doi:10.1016/j.ejor.2007.06.055

Laudon, K. C., & Laudon, J. P. (1988). *Management Information Systems* (2nd ed.). New York, NY: Macmillan.

Lazanski, T. J., & Kljajić, M. (2006). Systems approach to complex systems modeling with special regards to tourism. *Kybernetes, 35*(7-8), 1048–1058. doi:10.1108/03684920610684779

Legna, V. C. (2002). *Bases para la promoción del desarrollo social y creación de una red sindical de intercambiode información y de formación*. Estudio de Canarias. European Trade Union Confederation.

Legna, V. C., & González, C. S. (2005). An intelligent decision support system (IDSS) for public decisions using system dynamics and case based reasoning (CBR). *Organizacija, 38*(9), 530–535.

Legna, V. C., & Rivero, C. J. L. (2001). *Las particularidades de las Regiones Ultraperiféricas y la necesidad de instrumentos específicos. Especial referencia a Canarias* (Document elaborated for the Canarian Government). La Laguna, Canary Islands: University of La Laguna.

Luna-Reyes, L. F., Black, L. J., Cresswell, A. M., & Pardo, T. A. (2008). Knowledge sharing and trust in collaborative requirements analysis. *System Dynamics Review, 24*(3), 265–297. doi:10.1002/sdr.404

Marinho, J., Braganca, A., & Ramos, C. (1999). Decision support system for dynamic production scheduling. In C. Ramos & R. Sharma (Eds.), *Proceedings of the 1999 IEEE International Symposium on Assembly and Task Planning* (pp. 424-429). Evanston, IL: IEEE Robotics & Automation Society.

Mesarović, M. D., & Takahara, Y. (1989). *Abstract systems theory*. Berlin, Germany: Springer-Verlag. doi:10.1007/BFb0042462

Mingers, J. (2008). Pluralism, realism, and truth: The keys to knowledge in Information Systems research. *International Journal of Information Technologies and Systems Approach, 1*(1), 79–90. doi:10.4018/jitsa.2008010106

Myers, M. (2009). *Qualitative research in business & management*. London, UK: Sage Publications.

Otto, P., & Simon, M. (2008). Dynamic perspectives on social characteristics and sustainability in online community networks. *System Dynamics Review, 24*(3), 321–347. doi:10.1002/sdr.403

Pavlov, O. V., Plice, R. K., & Melville, N. P. (2008). A communication model with limited information-processing capacity of recipients. *System Dynamics Review, 24*(3), 377–405. doi:10.1002/sdr.407

Roldán, J. L., & Leal, A. (2003). A validation test of an adaptation of the DeLone and McLean's model in the Spanish EIS field. In Cano, J. J. (Ed.), *Critical reflections on information systems: A systemic approach* (pp. 66–84). Hershey, PA: IGI Publishing. doi:10.4018/978-1-59140-040-0.ch004

Saad, N., & Kadirkamanathan, V. (2006). A DES approach for the contextual load modelling of supply chain system for instability analysis. *Simulation Modelling Practice and Theory, 4*(5), 541–563. doi:10.1016/j.simpat.2005.09.002

Seddon, P. B. (1997). A respecification and extension of the DeLone and McLean model of IS success. *Information Systems Research, 8*(3), 240–253. doi:10.1287/isre.8.3.240

Škraba, A., Kljajić, M., & Kljajić Borštnar, M. (2007). The role of information feedback in the management group decision-making process applying system dynamics models. *Group Decision and Negotiation, 16*(1), 77–95. doi:10.1007/s10726-006-9035-9

Škraba, A., Kljajić, M., & Leskovar, R. (2003). Group exploration of system dynamics models – Is there a place for a feedback loop in the decision process? *System Dynamics Review, 19*(3), 243–263. doi:10.1002/sdr.274

Vennix, J. A. M. (1996). *Group model building: Facilitating team learning using system dynamics.* Chichester, UK: John Wiley & Sons.

Wang, W. T., & Liu, C. Y. (2005). The application of the technology acceptance model: A new way to evaluate Information System success. In J. D. Sterman, N. P. Repenning, R. S. Langer, J. I. Rowe, & J. M. Yanni (Eds.), *Proceedings of the 23th International Conference of the System Dynamics Society.* Albany, NY: System Dynamics Society.

WOS Expanded. (2011). Retrieved February 2, 2011, from http://wos.izum.si/CIW.cgi

ADDITIONAL READING

Abdel-Hamid, T. K., & Madnick, S. (1989a). Lessons learned from modeling the dynamics of software development. *Communications of the ACM, 32*(12), 1426–1438. doi:10.1145/76380.76383

Abdel-Hamid, T. K., & Madnick, S. (1989b). Software productivity: potential, actual and perceived. *System Dynamics Review, 5*(2), 93–113. doi:10.1002/sdr.4260050202

Agarwal, A., Shankar, R., & Mandal, P. (2006). Effectiveness of information systems in supply chain performance: a system dynamics study. *International Journal of Information Systems and Change Management, 1*(3), 241–261. doi:10.1504/IJISCM.2006.011198

Forrester, J. W. (1994, Summer-Fall). System dynamics, systems thinking, and soft OR. *System Dynamics Review, 10*(2-3), 245–256. doi:10.1002/sdr.4260100211

Madachy, R. (2008). *Software Process Dynamics.* New York: Wiley-IEEE Press. doi:10.1002/9780470192719

Sterman, J. D. (2000). *Business Dynamics: Systems Thinking and Modeling for a Complex World.* Chicago: Irwin/McGraw-Hill.

KEY TERMS AND DEFINITIONS

Critical Researchers: Assume that social reality (realized reality) is historically constituted and that it is produced and reproduced by people.

Decision Support Systems: Is a computer-based information system that supports business or organizational decision-making activities.

Interpretivism: Starts with the assumption that social reality is a social construct and its understanding and interpretation is only possible trough language, consciousness and shared meanings.

Positivism: Is scientific method, which supposes that (1) the external world exists independently of the observer, (2) this world is not directly observable, and (3) for its representation, we set up simplified models.

Simulation Based Decision Support Systems: Represents model driven DSS used as an explanatory tool for a better understanding of the decision process and/or for defining and understanding learning processes.

System Dynamics: Is a computer-based approach to complex policy analysis and design for decision-making assessments.

Chapter 18
Project Contexts and the Possibilities for Mixing Software Development and Systems Approaches

D. Petkov
Eastern Connecticut State University, USA

A. Singh
Durban University of Technology, South Africa

S. Alter
University of San Francisco, USA

O. Petkova
Central Connecticut State University, USA

J. Wing
Durban University of Technology, South Africa

T. Andrew
Durban University of Technology, South Africa

K. Sewchurran
University of Cape Town, South Africa

ABSTRACT

It is widely agreed that no single approach for software or systems development addresses all problems and contexts. This chapter summarizes three software development and systems approaches that are often viewed as somewhat unrelated: soft system methodology (SSM), work system method (WSM), and agile development. Next it presents a framework linking stakeholder interests and problem contexts known as the System of Systems Methodologies (SOSM) from Jackson and Keys (1984) and frameworks from Bustard and Kennan (2005) and Alter and Browne (2005) for visualizing various Information Systems (IS) contexts. It uses SOSM to position and explore alternative sets of IS project contexts described by Bustard and Kennan (2005) and Alter and Browne (2005) using their own frameworks. Comparison of these contexts in relation to SOSM leads to observations about the suitability of SSM, WSM, and agile development in different project contexts. Contributions of this research include identifying and comparing alternative contexts for software and system development and identifying possibilities for including within one project combinations of methodologies that are often viewed as unrelated.

DOI: 10.4018/978-1-4666-0179-6.ch018

INTRODUCTION

In a recent interview (see Lane et al., 2008, p.101) Boehm underscored the role of the systems approach in addressing challenges in information systems (IS), software engineering and systems engineering and the importance of a more holistic approach to software development. Systems approaches such as Checkland's Soft Systems Methodology (SSM) (see Mingers & White, 2010; Checkland, 1999) have influenced information systems in the past. The use of SSM in combination with traditional IS development methods has been explored by Stowell (1995), Mingers and White (2010) and others. However, following Mingers and White (2010) and Jackson (2006), we recognize that the complexity of problem situations in software development rarely can be addressed by a single whole systems approach. Possibilities for combining SSM with other systems methods or with software approaches like agile methods raise a number of unanswered theoretical and practical questions.

Meanwhile the Work System Method (WSM) (see Alter 2006, 2010) emerged over the last decade as a new systems approach within the field of Information Systems. WSM is a rigorous but not technically complicated attempt to bring together systems thinking with the needs of software requirements analysis. It is gaining wider acceptance within the IS research community (see Petkov et al. (in press)). However, to the best of our knowledge its application in conjunction with the increasingly popular agile software approaches or Soft Systems Methodology has not been discussed in the literature, even though aspects of WSM have been applied in projects performed by student programmers in several academic settings using somewhat agile methods in relation to needs of real world clients.

This paper's goal is to explore the nature of software project contexts within the System of Systems Methodologies (SOSM), a well known framework in the field of Systems Thinking (for more details see Jackson, 2003) and the positioning of SSM, WSM and agile software development approaches within SOSM. Thus it potentially provides insights about the applicability and limitations of each of those methods, and also ways in which they might be used together within a single project.

The current research is motivated by the possibility that agile development, SSM, and WSM might be used together in the same project under some circumstances. This paper's goal is to provide insights about the applicability and limitations of each of those methods, and also on potential ways in which they might be used together within a single project.

Methodologically this research is based on applying elements from the body of knowledge of systems thinking applied to software development. We analyze SSM, the Work System Method and Agile Development Methods with respect to their positioning within the System of Systems Methodologies (SOSM), an "ideal-type" grid of problem contexts proposed originally in the systems literature in 1984 by Jackson and Keys (see Jackson, 2003). The latter is a tested framework for relating particular systems approaches to certain problem contexts (Jackson, 2003). We map project contexts onto the SOSM after an analysis of the software development contexts discussed by Bustard and Keenan (2005) and the typology of systems analysis and design (SA&D) contexts proposed by Alter and Browne (2005).

This paper contributes to systems theory by positioning SSM, WSM, and Agile Methods in relation to problem contexts mapped in the dimensions of the System of Systems Methodologies. The practical contribution to software development involves exploring the mapping of software development contexts in the SOSM and suggesting possibilities for mixing the above methodologies in particular project contexts. These contributions provide support for possible tailoring of software development processes for particular project contexts, thereby extending the work by Bustard and Keenan and also by Alter and Browne on developing a typology of software development contexts. The next section explores the main concepts in SSM, WSM, and Agile Software Development Methods.

THREE METHODOLOGIES RELATED TO SOFTWARE AND SYSTEM DEVELOPMENT

We look at three software and system development methodologies in turn: SSM, WSM, and agile development. Throughout this section remember a distinction between software development and system development. Software development is literally about developing software. System development can be construed in a broader way to mean the development and implementation of human activity systems (Checkland, 1999) or IT-reliant work systems (Alter, 2006, 2008) that contain human participants, and therefore are not purely technical artifacts. The distinction between systems as socio-technical systems and systems as completely automated technical systems is sometimes overlooked in discussions of analysis and design.

Soft Systems Methodology and Software Development

Stowell (1995) presents a detailed picture of the multifaceted role of SSM in Information Systems development. Checkland and Holwell (1998, p.155) distinguish SSM from information systems development methodologies, claiming that SSM is a "more general approach to managing or problem solving whose application area includes the problems commonly associated with information provision". The relationship between SSM and Information Systems was investigated in Mingers (1995), Mingers and White (2010) and elsewhere.

The relevance of SSM to the field of Information Systems has been explored in three directions.

One was to extend the standard SSM method to specify the information requirements of the system as specified originally by Wilson in 1984 (see Wilson, 1990). The second is through the linking of SSM analysis to the subsequent data and functional modeling of a software system applying the Unified Modeling Language (UML) or structured design methods. This is probably the most often pursued direction in the research on SSM applications in software development with a considerable number of publications (for further reviews see Mingers (1995) and Sewchurran and Petkov (2007)). A third line of research was the development of specific methodologies for building IS, such as the Multiview approach described in Wood-Harper, Antill and Avison (1985).

SSM can be characterized as an interpretive systems approach in which culture and politics play an important role. Its foundations are probably analyzed best in Jackson (2003). The world is taken to be complex, messy, and necessarily viewed from diverse perspectives. To cope with such diversity, a process of inquiry should be organized as a learning system, which is an inherent characteristic of SSM. Of concern in SSM are both technical aspects of a problem situation as well as cultural values, beliefs and interests. It accepts the need to accommodate multiple perceptions of reality. SSM supports the development of understanding of these perceptions, values, beliefs, and interests so that one could anticipate and control outcomes from a situation.

SSM has evolved over time. Initially, in 1981, Checkland proposed a seven stage model of SSM (see Checkland, 1999) which is not shown here for space reasons. According to (Checkland, 1999), it is still useful to teach the methodology and some of its techniques listed here:

- *Rich pictures*, showing structure, processes and relationships between structure and processes within a complex messy problem;

- *CATWOE analysis* which involves identifying the clients, actors, transformations, worldview (or Weltanschauung), owners and the environment of the systemic inquiry
- *Root definitions* of relevant systems needed for the situation.
- *Conceptual models* seeking improvement in the problem, based on the root definitions.

The seven stage model of SSM (known as SSM Mode 1) can be used iteratively until there is an understanding and consensus on the complexities. From experience gained in using SSM Mode 1, a more flexible model known as SSM Mode 2 emerged in the late 1980s and was published in Checkland and Scholes (1990). It focuses on both the technical analysis (which was the scope of the original SSM approach) and on a cultural and political analysis. Summarizing the recent understanding of SSM for gaining insight into a situation of concern, Checkland and Winter (2006, p.1436) mention the "four ways of doing this that emerged:

- Represent the situation in Rich Pictures (Checkland and Scholes, 1990, pp. 44-47);
- Carry out an analysis of the social characteristics of the situation ('Analysis Two': Checkland and Scholes, 1990, pp. 44-50; Checkland, 1999, pp. 16-19);
- Carry out an analysis of the disposition of power in the situation ('Analysis Three': Checkland and Scholes, 1990, pp. 44-51; Checkland, 1999, pp. 19-20);
- Carry out an analysis of the intervention itself ('Analysis One': Checkland & Scholes, 1990, pp. 44-48; Checkland, 1999, pp. 19-20".

Checkland and Winter (2006, p. 1435) explore for the first time two different uses of Analysis One (or the technical analysis) "within any SSM-based intervention, one devoted to the perceived content of the problematical situation (SSMc) and one devoted to the intellectual process of the intervention itself (SSMp)." Another thought provoking set of related ideas about the different ways of using SSM was presented earlier in Rose (1997).

The complexities of the relationship between the social, organizational, and cultural context and the information system can be addressed through SSM, which facilitates a learning process that allows its users to develop a more comprehensive understanding of the situation under study. The emphasis is on understanding as many aspects of the environment as possible in (Checkland, 1999). That learning process leads to the gradual development of a more comprehensive understanding of the situation, whereby stakeholders can reach agreements about which changes are needed and are acceptable to all stakeholders. Often SSM can be combined with other approaches in order to gain understanding of these complex situations. For example, Petkov et al. (2007) dealt with theoretical and practical issues in mixing SSM and other systems approaches in three large projects following the principles of Multimethodology by Mingers (2001). The variations in the process frameworks in the same interventions and possible implications for practice were explored in Petkov, Petkova, Andrew and Nepal (2008).

Holwell (2000) concludes that many published cases of SSM usage reveal misunderstandings of the methodology, contradictions and gaps. These may be attributed to the complexity of applying SSM in practice. SSM was also the subject of serious critique about whether it really supports human participation and on other issues (for a summary see Jackson (2003, chapter 10)). A problem linked to the goal of this research was raised by Mingers (1995) who noted that there would be no easy way to link SSM and IS because they embodied different and conflicting epistemologies. The latter criticism however does not apply to the methodology we review next.

The Work System Method

According to Alter (2006), WSM provides a rigorous but non-technical approach that any manager or business professional can use to visualize and analyze systems related problems and opportunities. Alter (2006, 2008) stresses that the emphasis is on developing an understanding about work systems. A work system is a system in which human participants and/or machines perform work using information, technology, and other resources to produce products and/or services for internal or external customers. Alter (2006, 2008, 2009) notes that information systems in general are a special case of work systems in general. An information system is a work system in which all of the work is devoted to processing information. There are many situations in which the information system is the work system of interest, e.g., information systems devoted to data analysis, use of e-commerce websites, and use of search engines. In many other situations, the information system is part of or overlaps with a separate work system, e.g., manufacturing work systems, customer service work systems, and package delivery work systems. Totally automated work systems are another special case, such as totally automated manufacturing cells. Almost all work systems in modern businesses rely on computerized information systems, and therefore can be described as IT-reliant work systems.

The work system method (see Alter 2006) is based on two major frameworks: *the work system framework* and the *work system life cycle model*. The work system framework is a model for organizing an initial understanding of how a particular work system operates and what it accomplishes at a particular point in time. The work system framework consists of nine elements that are part of even a basic understanding of work system: customers, products and services, processes and activities, participants, information, technologies, environment, infrastructure, strategies. Detailed definitions of the elements of the work system

framework are presented in Alter (2006, 2008). The analysis of the initial problem situation is captured through the AS IS work system model (known also as snapshot) of the system while the recommendations for improvement are reflected in the TO BE version of the snapshot. These features make the WSM suitable for business reengineering and for IS strategic planning.

Another useful technique in WSM is the work system life cycle model which is a dynamic view of how work systems change over time through iterations that may combine planned change (explicit projects with initiation, development, implementation phases) and unplanned change (incremental adaptations and experimentation). (Alter, 2006, 2008, 2009)

Alter (2006) introduces a three step process for the analysis of a work system:

- *Identify the system and problems*: identify the work system that has the problems or opportunities that launched the analysis. The work system's size and scope are determined based on the purpose of the analysis.
- *Analyze the system and identify possibilities*: understand current problems, opportunities, and issues in more depth, and find possibilities for improving the work system.
- *Recommend and justify changes*: specify proposed changes and justify the recommendation.

A very useful feature of WSM is the ability to conduct the analysis of a work system at different levels of detail depending on the actual purpose and granularity of analysis. Accordingly, various work system analysis templates have encouraged work system analysis at different levels of detail (e.g., a new work system analysis template used in Truex et al. (2010)). At the simplest level, rough definitions of the work system and the problem of concern are clarified to make sure that any proposed changes in the work system actually address the main issues. At a more detailed level, a number of specific prompting questions for each of the three steps of the analysis are explored. Those questions provide deeper information and perspectives on the problem situation. Drilling down further, diverse techniques such as check-lists, diagrams, and analysis of relevant data can provide finer understanding of the problem situation at a specialist level. More details and examples of applying WSM analysis at different levels during the three process steps (as defined earlier) are provided in Alter (2006).

A recent extension of work system theory is the work system metamodel first presented in Alter (2010) as a way to bridge the chasm between sociotechnical and technical thinking about systems in organizations. By default, work systems are assumed to be sociotechnical systems with human participants. However, successive decomposition of sociotechnical systems during the process of analysis usually reveals subsystems that are totally automated work systems, i.e., work systems having no human participants even though they are created, maintained, and used by other work systems that have human participants. The metamodel creates a bridge between the summary description of a work system at the level of the work system framework and the more detailed models of the subsystems that are developed during systems analysis and design by IT professionals and other technical experts. (Alter, 2010). The most detailed analysis of the role of the WSM in bridging the gap between sociotechnical and technical views of systems from a theoretical point of view is presented in Alter (2010). In terms of philosophical underpinnings, WSM is based broadly on pragmatism (e.g., see Lee & Nickerson, 2010). Further theoretical analysis of the epistemology of WSM, while desired, is beyond the scope of this paper. Further details on other recent developments in WSM research and its applications can be found in Petkov et al. (in press).

Agile Software Development Approaches

Pfleeger and Atlee (2010, p. 65) suggest that agile software development practices were introduced during the 1990s by a group of proponents who felt that classical software engineering approaches are incapable of flexibility. Agile development models are evolutionary, in that the requirements evolve during implementation. Agile development is best suited to small application projects that are conducted in the presence of a knowledgeable customer or user who has a clear understanding of the needs to be satisfied by the software system that is being built. There are several variations on the agile theme, but most agile process models emphasize the following (Koch (2005); Cockburn (2007); Conboy (2009); Fairley (2009)):

1. continuously involving a representative customer/user;
2. developing test cases and test scenarios before implementing the next version of the product;
3. implementing and testing the resulting version;
4. demonstrating each version of the evolving product to the customer;
5. eliciting the next requirement(s) from the customer; and
6. periodic delivery into the operational environment.

Beck (1999) indicates that agile software development activities place much less emphasis on detailed upfront plans of activities in comparison with classical software development methodologies. Van Vliet (2008) suggests that an agile approach allows for the development team to adapt to changes with minimal cost in terms of effort. For example, practices such as refactoring (Beck 1999) provide a mechanism to potentially improve the design of a software component toward the end of development. Software tends to be delivered in increments and integrated after each delivery cycle (Beck 1999) which allows the client to see the software system evolving and to make recommendations as their understandings change with each incremental improvement in the partially completed software.

Boehm (2002, p. 5) stresses that agile approaches call for smaller development teams which appear to be more productive due to greater efficiency in communication. Despite claims that agile methods are more effective, there are unresolved issues. Despite the widespread use and adoption of agile approaches, little research has been conducted concerning the ways in which design decisions are reached. To achieve and sustain effective communication within agile teams, Mora, Gelman, Forgionne, Petkov and Cano (2007) call for more research into this issue.

A perceived difficulty in maintaining consistent design knowledge is raised by Ko, Myers, Coblenz and Aaung (2006) who conclude that the only manner in which developers could keep design decisions synchronized is through frequent informal communication. Based on their findings, design modeling techniques such as UML are considered untrustworthy and costly in terms of effort.

Whitehead (2007) stresses the apparent inadequacy of tools and methodologies used to support collaboration among a group of software developers. He asserts that these need to be more focused toward the entire software project and move away from focusing at individual activities at a time. Sommerville (2011) points out difficulties in finding suitable agile team members because many developers have inadequate communication skills. Boehm (2002) argues that it is not necessarily a highly skilled team that makes agile approaches successful but rather the preservation and communication of the tacit knowledge embodied within the development team. Cockburn (2007, p. 11) refers to this as "common touch points" which relates to the ease at which team members can communicate on the project.

It appears that classical or plan-driven approaches are not able to cope with the rapid pace of change of business. Boehm and Turner (2004) feel that key weaknesses of plan driven approaches are that they encourage a "mechanical" process and a "checklist mentality" with more effort allocated to documentation than code production. Conboy (2009) identifies weaknesses of agile approaches that tends to lead to difficulty in practice, such as inadequate conceptual knowledge, inadequate theoretical underpinnings, lack of a widely agreed upon definition, and loosely defined application principles. Boehm and Turner (2004) note that both classical and agile software development approaches have inherent weaknesses and they suggest that a mixture of both should be utilized for software projects. They propose that this mixture or balance should be decided upon after considering the attributes of the software project and conducting a risk analysis. Their suggestion leads us to the topic explored next, the idea of analyzing problem contexts as a justification for mixing of software and system development approaches within particular projects.

THREE FRAMEWORKS FOR IDENTIFYING CONTEXTS OF SYSTEMS AND SOFTWARE DEVELOPMENT

This section reviews three alternative frameworks for characterizing the context of an information systems project. These frameworks include the System of Systems Methodologies (SOSM) from Jackson and Keys (1984) and frameworks from Bustard and Kennan (2005) and Alter and Browne (2005). Ideally, the formulation of a business process model for a specific project should be tailored to the specific context of a problem situation. Our mapping of different project contexts in the SOSM will be discussed in the next section.

System of Systems Methodologies

The System of Systems Methodologies, proposed by Jackson and Keys in 1984 is a grid of problem contexts (for an adapted version of it see Figure 1). According to Jackson (2003, p. 19) the SOSM is only dealing with ideal-type forms of problem contexts viewed "as logical extremes that can be used to construct abstract models of general realities". SOSM was used by Jackson and Keys to classify systems methodologies according to their assumptions about problem situations (see Jackson, 2003, p. 24).

The vertical axis relates to the complexity of the problem situation while the horizontal axis reflects the nature of values/interests of the stakeholders. People are considered to be in a unitary relationship if they share values and interests; in a pluralist relationship if their values and interests diverge but they have enough in common to make it worthwhile for them to remain members of the coalition that constitutes the organization; and in a conflictual or coercive relationship if their interests diverge irreconcilably (see Jackson, 2003, pp. 23-24).

We will use the SOSM later in the paper. To explore project contexts further, we will summarize two other frameworks in the IS literature for characterizing system or software development contexts.

Bustard and Keenan (2005): Choosing a Systems Analysis Strategy

Bustard and Keenan (2005) suggest that the most general approach to software process design involves blending of ideas from best practice and local experience. According to them the choice of a systems analysis strategy sets the context for subsequent design of the development process. They consider as one dimension of analyzing project contexts the relationship between a computing system and its environment. They suggest as a second dimension the evolution of a computing system in time. Bustard and Keenan (2005) identify four different possible starting positions for analysis:

- *bottom-up*, focusing on the computing system to be produced;
- *top-down*, starting with an environment analysis;
- *goal-oriented*, developing a vision of what the computing system (and its aligned environment) could or should become;
- *problem-oriented*, focusing on current shortcomings (or opportunities) and determining how they could be addressed.

Figure 1. Grid of problem contexts in the system of systems methodology (adopted from Jackson, 2003)

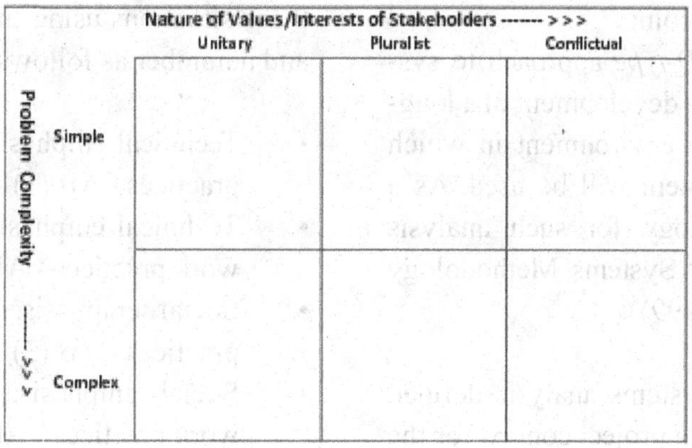

Each of the starting positions corresponds with one of four paths to systems analysis (A, B.C and D) that are further elaborated by Bustard and Keenan (2005):

- The focus in the *A-type* approach to systems analysis is the definition of a computing system to meet immediate needs. Such systems are assumed to be well defined against standard specifications or are not expected to evolve (for example, computer games) or that the computing systems are in use and no changes have happened since the original analysis was conducted.

- The initial focus in the *B-type* approach to systems analysis is the understanding of the current environment in which a computing system is to be developed or enhanced. *B-type* analysis is appropriate when a problem situation needs to be examined but future development is either obvious or of low importance. *B-type* analysis can be interpreted as the *A-type* approach, with a preceding environment analysis. Noting that this strategy for systems analysis matches the general systems approach, they stress the importance of considering the environment before development, even in situations that appear familiar to the developers.

- The focus in the *C-type* approach to systems analysis is the development of a long-term vision of what the software system could or should become.

- The focus in the *D-type* approach to systems analysis is the development of a long-term vision of the environment in which the computing system will be used. As a suitable methodology for such analysis they point to Soft Systems Methodology (see Checkland (1999)).

Each approach to systems analysis defined above can be viewed as a project context for the purposes of the current research. Bustard and Keenan (2005) indicate that agile development approaches are most obviously suitable for A-type contexts but they claim (without empirical evidence) that all four contexts might be addressed potentially with 'agile' methods. To be successful in any of the four contexts, the techniques used must be compatible with the agile philosophy of 'just enough' process to achieve the desired effect. Note also that the four contexts defined by Bustard and Keenan (2005) correspond to the extremes of the factors mentioned but there are many intermediate situations between these extremes according to them. In Figure 2 we will refer to the four contexts discussed in Bustard and Keenan (2005) as BK (A), BK (B), BK (C) and BK (D).

Alter and Browne (2005): The Range and Scope of Systems Analysis and Design Contexts

Another framework of Systems Analysis and Design (SA&D) problem contexts is introduced by Alter and Browne (2005). The first of its two dimensions is the focus of SA&D efforts (referring to the relative weight of social emphasis versus technical emphasis in the project). The second dimension is the extent of change in work practices, ranging from a goal of fixing the technology but not changing existing work practices through a goal of achieving significant changes in work practices. We will introduce codes for these situations using the initials of the authors and a number as follows:

- Technical emphasis, little change of work practices - AB (1)
- Technical emphasis, significant change in work practices - AB (2)
- Social emphasis, little change of work practices - AB (3)
- Social emphasis, significant change in work practices - AB (4)

Figure 2. Mapping of software and system project contexts defined by Bustard and Keenan (2005) and Alter and Brown (2005) in the system of systems methodology (SOSM)

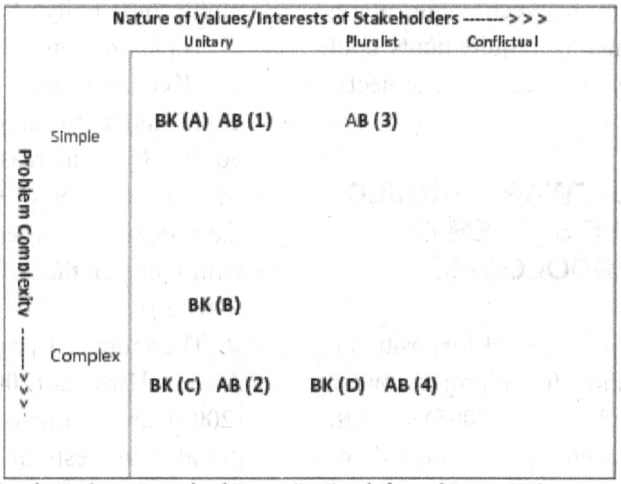

Note: BK and AB refers to Bustard and Keenan (2005) and Alter and Browne 2005

Alter and Browne (2005, p. 984) use their framework to identify six realistic project situations that are mapped along the two dimensions in a continuum and not as extreme cases:

1. SA&D for software or hardware maintenance.
2. SA&D projects for software or hardware upgrades lie at an intermediate position between focusing on work practices and focusing on technology, although the primary focus is still on the technology.
3. SA&D for monitoring and patching existing practices via process improvement and Six Sigma focuses more on work practices than on technology.
4. SA&D for the creation or major modification of IT-enabled work systems may involve the creation of new software.
5. SA&D for the creation or major modification of IT-enabled work systems may involve the configuration and installation of commercial application software.
6. SA&D for organizational change or reengineering brings the most direct focus on work practices.

Alter and Browne (2005) provide a detailed step by step business process view of SA&D work practices and various other research issues spanning systems analysis efforts organized along the elements of the work system framework. They outline research directions for each of the six distinct project situations.

Both Bustard and Keenan (2005) and Alter and Browne (2005) are interested in formulating system or software development process models that correspond to the nature of a specific problem situation. Both papers define somewhat similar role for Soft Systems Methodology. Thus Bustard and Keenan (2005) discuss the relevance of SSM to their type D problem context associated with development of long term vision for the environment of a computing system. Along similar lines, Alter and Browne (2005) discuss the relevance of several methodologies for one of their six project contexts (AB (4)), which is related to organizational analysis, socio technical analysis and change management. Those methodologies include Mumford's ETHICS, Checkland's Soft Systems Methodology, Multiview by Avison and Wood-Harper and Alter's WSM. Arguing that all these approaches deemphasize production of precise documentation that can be used immediately by programmers, Alter and Browne (2005, p. 994) suggest that better links between organizational analysis and programming requirements could improve the effectiveness of software projects.

MAPPING OF SOFTWARE PROJECT CONTEXTS IN THE SYSTEM OF SYSTEMS METHODOLOGIES

Figure 2 uses the SOSM framework for positioning each of the coded situations for the project contexts defined by Bustard and Keenan (2005) and Alter and Browne (2005). An immediate observation is that there may be fundamental differences between system projects for changing work systems and software projects that focus more on creating or modifying software. In relation to system thinking and systems analysis, this raises questions about whether systems thinking related to sociotechnical systems is essentially similar or different from systems thinking related to technical systems, a topic that is beyond this paper's scope. Software development projects may be either characterized as simple or complex (e.g. AB (1) or BK (A) versus complex (e.g. AB (2), AB (4), or BK (D).

Ideally, a software project should be characterized with unitary interests of its stakeholders or at least should have an overarching goal uniting those stakeholders with different, pluralist vested interests. It is extremely difficult to maintain communication and trust in projects with coercive/conflictual values and interests. Such project situations are rare though they deserve further research. Hence for practical reasons we consider that more complicated project situations in the IT industry are most often characterized as complex and pluralist.

The four project contexts defined by Alter and Browne (2005) were mapped onto SOSM under the generally accepted assumption that more human involvement (or social emphasis) contributes to the increase in pluralism in the interests of the stakeholders. The other assumption is that more changes in work practices contribute to an increase of the complexity of a project.

Three problem situations defined by Bustard and Keenan (2005) fall under the category of unitary situations in SOSM. They are only distinguished by an increase of their complexity when an understanding of the current environment of the system is considered (BK (B)) or when a long term focus on the software system is considered (BK (C)).

Therefore, all project contexts discussed by Alter and Browne (2005) and Bustard and Keenan (2005) are characterized by either unitary or pluralist interests of the stakeholders involved. The suggested mapping of the software project contexts explored by Alter and Browne (2005) and Bustard and Keenan (2005) onto the SOSM allows a comparison of those independently defined situations along the same dimensions (complexity and diversity of stakeholder interests). This leads to the next step in our analysis, the comparison of SSM, WSM and Agile Software Methods in terms of their ability to serve specific software project contexts in the SOSM.

EVALUATION OF THE SUITABILITY OF SSM, WSM AND AGILE METHODS FOR SPECIFIC PROJECT SITUATIONS

According to Jackson (2003, p. 21) approaches dealing with problems of unitary context but with increasing complexity down the vertical axis of the SOSM were trying "to identify those key mechanisms or structures that govern the behavior of the elements or subsystems and, therefore, are fundamental to system behavior". Jackson (2003, p. 22) notes that when moving horizontally towards pluralist problem contexts, "attention had to be given to ensuring sufficient accommodation between different and sometimes conflicting world views during the methodological process".

We need to stress that following Jackson's articulation of the role of SOSM mentioned earlier, we do not suggest that real life problem situations fit exactly within any of the six combinations of the two states of complexity and the three types of interests of the stakeholders in SOSM shown in Figure 1. This leads to the conclusion that the typologies of problem contexts developed by Bustard and Keenan (2005) and Alter and Browne (2005) which we mapped into the SOSM are useful primarily for exploring the diversity of problem contexts. In reality, a particular project context may evolve with respect to its complexity or with respect to changes in the diversity of the viewpoints of the stakeholders depending on the degree of accommodation of different viewpoints that was achieved.

Jackson (2003) positions SSM as suitable for contexts that are pluralist in nature and being either simple or complex. As mentioned earlier, Alter and Browne (2005) relate one of their typical project contexts (AB (4)) to SSM and WSM among others. Based on similar reasoning, Bustard and Keenan (2005) discuss the relevance of SSM to their type D problem context (DK (D)), which is associated with development of long term vision

for the environment of a computing system. Hence we position SSM in the area of complex-pluralist problem contexts (see Figure 3 where the methodologies are shown in larger font). Using our previous argument we may conclude that SSM will be suitable also for simple pluralist contexts and for both simple and complex unitary contexts.

On the basis of its socio-technical nature, WSM can be positioned on the border between simple and complex situations when the interests of the participants are pluralist in nature. In addition, the techniques of WSM analyses (see Alter, 2006) potentially support insights involving unitary (both simple and complex) and simple-pluralist project contexts. The discussion so far in this section can be illustrated with Figure 3.

By analogy to the previous argument we may conclude that Agile Software Development Methods might be suitable on their own for unitary project contexts described previously as BK (C), BK (B) and BK (A) and AB (1). There is nothing however in practice to prevent developers to use them for simple pluralist project contexts. However, if used alone that approach may not fully contribute to a better understanding of the problem situation unless developers mix Agile

Figure 3. Positioning of SSM, WSM, and agile software development methods related to the software project contexts defined by Bustard and Keenan (2005) and Alter and Browne (2005) in the system of systems methodology (SOSM)

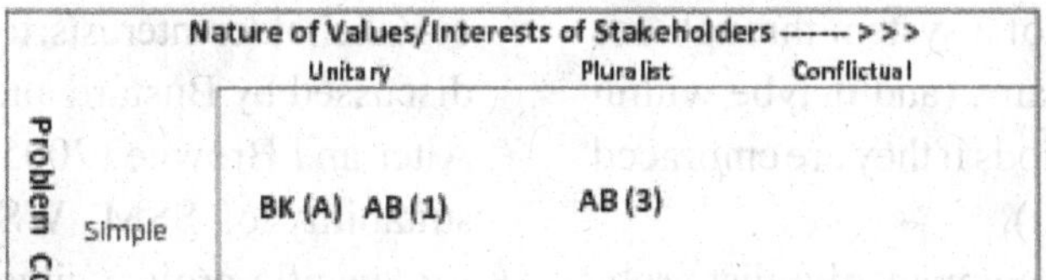

Note: BK and AB refers to Bustard and Keenan (2005) and Alter and Browne 2005

Methods with WSM and/or SSM. In a similar way, we claim that Agile Methods may provide good results for addressing complex pluralist project contexts only if mixed with soft systems methodology.

An existing criticism of Soft Systems Methodology is that no reasoning is provided on how applying SSM might lead to a data model or a functional process model in a particular software development methodology (see Mingers, 1995). The implication is that the role of SSM in software development has been stronger in sense making about the software project context and in guiding the methodology for the intervention along the suggestions in Rose (1997). This leads to the conclusion that in software development SSM was more successfully applied to the intellectual process of the intervention itself (or SSMp in the terminology of Checkland and Winter (2005)) than for revealing the content of a software development project (SSMc).

In contrast, the Work System Method snapshot (see Alter, 2006) summarizes work processes (activities) that are later reflected in use cases. Therefore one may conclude that the WSM provides a better way to transition from the stage of sense making about a problem to the subsequent step of modeling the functional requirements of a system. The implication is that we may combine SSM in software development practice with the Work System Method for better capturing of the functional requirements of a system through use cases or data flow diagrams (and maybe within the context of Agile Methods if they are embraced by the development team).

When using WSM in complex pluralist problem situations, an analyst may consider augmenting existing techniques within WSM with elements of SSM such as Rich Pictures in order to deal more effectively with the plurality of stakeholder interests and the related cultural and political aspects of the problem and better support for the intellectual processes in a software project itself (or SSMp in the terminology of Checkland and Winter (2005)). This is in line with the suggestion in Alter (2006) that other techniques should be used in conjunction with WSM whenever appropriate.

We would like to stress Jackson's (2003, p. 24) advice is that "there is no intention to pigeon-hole methodologies". This may be interpreted as a warning against assuming that if the three software methodologies discussed in the paper are usually associated with a particular type of context they cannot be used in other type of contexts as well. However, we may note that each methodology becomes less effective in situations with greater complexity or greater diversity of stakeholder interests than the typical position for it in the SOSM following the analysis in this paper. This implies that a particular methodology might be better suited for contexts above or to the left of their suggested position in the SOSM when applied on its own or in combinations with other systems development methodologies. This conclusion has practical implications on the possibilities for mixing methodologies in the same project context.

CONCLUSION

The paper provided a review of the development and of some research issues in soft systems methodology, the work system method and agile software development. We used the two dimensions of SOSM, system complexity and diversity of stakeholder interests, to map the project contexts discussed by Bustard and Keenan (2005) and by Alter and Browne (2005). Then we explored the suitability of SSM, WSM and Agile Methods for specific project situations along those same dimensions. These results constitute our theoretical contribution to systems thinking applied to software development. This paper's main practical contribution is its suggestions concerning the project contexts in SOSM would be suitable for mixing the above mentioned methodologies in software development practice. These contributions support better tailoring of software development processes for particular project contexts.

A potential limitation of this paper is its conceptual nature. However it creates the preconditions for future practical implementation and testing of these ideas through developing philosophically justified and relevant practical frameworks for combining aspects of SSM, WSM and Agile Methods in the context of software projects along the principles of multimethodology (see Mingers, 2001; Jackson, 2006; Petkov et al., 2007 and Petkov et al, 2008). That is the scope of two projects currently under way involving several of the authors. This research is a step towards developing a better understanding of diverse theoretical and practical aspects of the combined use of SSM, WSM and Agile methods in software development.

REFERENCES

Alter, S. (2006). *The work system method: Connecting people, processes, and IT for business results*. Larkspur, CA: Work System Press.

Alter, S. (2007). Service system fundamentals: Work system, value chain, and life cycle. *IBM Systems Journal*, *47*(1), 71–85. doi:10.1147/sj.471.0071

Alter, S. (2008). Defining Information Systems as work systems: Implications for the IS field. *European Journal of Information Systems*, *17*(5), 448–469. doi:10.1057/ejis.2008.37

Alter, S. (2009, August). *Project collaboration, not just user participation*, Paper presented at the Fifteenth Americas Conference on Information Systems, San Francisco, CA.

Alter, S. (2010, December). *Bridging the chasm between sociotechnical and technical views of systems in organizations*. Paper presented at the 31st International Conference on Information Systems, Saint Louis, MO.

Alter, S., & Browne, G. (2005). A broad view of systems analysis and design: Implications for research. *Communications of the Association for Information Systems*, *16*(50), 981–999.

Beck, K. (1999). Embracing change with extreme programming. *IEEE Computer*, *32*(10), 70–77. doi:10.1109/2.796139

Boehm, B. (2002). Get ready for agile methods, with care. *IEEE Computer*, *35*(1), 64–69. doi:10.1109/2.976920

Boehm, B., & Turner, R. (2004). *Balancing agility and discipline. A guide for the perplexed*. Boston, MA: Addison-Wesley.

Bustard, D. W., & Keenan, F. M. (2005, April). *Strategies for systems analysis: Groundwork for process tailoring*. Paper presented at the 12th Annual IEEE International Conference and Workshop on the Engineering of Computer Based Systems, Greenbelt, MD.

Checkland, P. (1999). *Systems thinking, systems practice. Includes a 30 year retrospective*. Chichester, UK: Wiley.

Checkland, P., & Holwell, S. (1998). *Information, systems and Information Systems*. Chichester, UK: Wiley. Checkland, P., & Winter, M. (2006). Process and content: Two ways of using SSM. *The Journal of the Operational Research Society*, *57*, 1435–1441. doi:10.1057/palgrave.jors.2602118

Checkland, P., & Scholes, J. (1990). *Soft systems methodology in action*. Chichester, UK: Wiley.

Cockburn, A. (2007). *Agile software development. The cooperative game* (2nd ed.). Boston, MA: Pearson.

Conboy, K. (2009). Agility from first principles: Reconstructing the concept of agility in Information Systems development. *Information Systems Research*, *20*(3), 329–354. doi:10.1287/isre.1090.0236

Fairley, R. (2009). *Managing and leading software projects* (2nd ed.). Hoboken, NJ: John Wiley and Sons Inc. doi:10.1002/9780470405697

Highsmith, J. (2002). *Agile software development ecosystems*. Indianapolis, IN: Addison-Wesley.

Holwell, S. (2000). Soft systems methodology: Other voices. *Systemic Practice and Action Research, 13*(6), 25. doi:10.1023/A:1026479529130

Jackson, M. C. (2003). *Systems thinking: Creative holism for managers*. Chichester, UK: Wiley.

Jackson, M. C. (2006). Creative holism: A critical systems approach to complex problem situations. *Systems Research and Behavioral Science, 23*(5), 647–657. doi:10.1002/sres.799

Jackson, M. C., & Keys, P. (1984). Towards a system of systems methodologies. *The Journal of the Operational Research Society, 35*, 473–486.

Ko, A. J., Myers, B. A., Coblenz, M. J., & Aung, H. H. (2006). An exploratory study of how developers seek, relate, and collect relevant information during software maintenance tasks. *IEEE Transactions on Software Engineering, 32*(12), 971–987. doi:10.1109/TSE.2006.116

Koch, A. S. (2005). *Agile software development*. Boston, MA: Artech House.

Lane, J. A., Petkov, D., & Mora, M. (2008). Software engineering and the systems approach: A conversation with Barry Boehm. *International Journal of Information Technologies and Systems Approach, 1*(2), 99–103. doi:10.4018/jitsa.2008070107

Lee, A. S., & Nickerson, J. V. (2010). Theory as a case of design: Lessons for design from the philosophy of science. In R. H. Sprague (Ed.), *The 43rd Hawaii International Conference on System Sciences* (pp. 1–8). Los Alamitos, CA: IEEE Computer Society Press.

Mingers, J. (1995). Using soft systems methodology in the design of information systems. In Stowell, F. (Ed.), *Information Systems provision: The contribution of soft systems methodology* (pp. 18–50). London, UK: McGraw-Hill.

Mingers, J. (2001). Multimethodology - Mixing and matching methods. In Rosenhead, J., & Mingers, J. (Eds.), *Rational analysis for a problematic world revisited: Problem structuring methods for complexity, uncertainty and conflict* (pp. 297–308). Chichester, UK: Wiley.

Mingers, J., & White, L. (2010). A review of the recent contributions of systems thinking to operational research and management science. *European Journal of Operational Research, 207*(3), 11–47. doi:10.1016/j.ejor.2009.12.019

Mora, M., Gelman, O., Forgionne, G., Petkov, D., & Cano, J. (2007). Integrating the fragmented pieces of IS research paradigms and frameworks: A systems approach. *Information Resources Management Journal, 20*(2), 1–22. doi:10.4018/irmj.2007040101

Petkov, D., Edgar-Neville, D., Madachy, R., & O'Connor, R. (2008). Information Systems, software engineering and Systems thinking – Challenges and opportunities. *International Journal of Information Technologies and Systems Approach, 1*(1), 62–78. doi:10.4018/jitsa.2008010105

Petkov, D., Petkova, O., Andrew, T., & Nepal, T. (2007). Mixing multiple criteria decision making with soft systems thinking techniques for decision support in complex situations. *Decision Support Systems, 43*, 1615–1629. doi:10.1016/j.dss.2006.03.006

Petkov, D., Petkova, O., Andrew, T., & Nepal, T. (2008). On the process of combining soft systems methodologies and other approaches in systemic interventions. *Journal of Organizational Transformation and Social Change, 5*(3), 291–303. doi:10.1386/jots.5.3.291_1

Petkov, D., Petkova, O., Sewchurran, K., Andrew, T., & Misra, R. (in press). The work system method as an approach for teaching and researching information systems. In Dwivedi, Y. K., Wade, M. R., & Schneberger, S. L. (Eds.), *Information Systems theory: Explaining and predicting our digital society*. doi:10.1007/978-1-4419-9707-4_21

Pfleeger, S. L., & Atlee, J. M. (2010). *Software engineering: Theory and practice* (4th ed.). Cranbury, NJ: Pearson.

Rose, J. (1997). Soft systems methodology as a social science tool. *Systems Research and Behavioral Science, 14*(4), 249–258. doi:10.1002/(SICI)1099-1743(199707/08)14:4<249::AID-SRES119>3.0.CO;2-S

Sewchurran, K., & Petkov, D. (2007). A systemic framework for business process modeling combining soft systems methodology and UML. *Information Resources Management Journal, 20*(3), 46–62. doi:10.4018/irmj.2007070104

Sommerville, I. (2011). *Software engineering* (9th ed.). Boston, MA: Pearson.

Stowell, F. (Ed.). (1995). *Information Systems provision - The contribution of soft systems methodology*. London, UK: McGraw-Hill Publishing Co.

Truex, D., Alter, S., & Long, C. (2010, June). *Systems analysis for everyone else: Business professionals through a systems analysis method that fits their needs*. Paper presented at the 18th European Conference on Information Systems, Pretoria, South Africa.

Van Vliet, H. (2008). *Software engineering* (3rd ed.). Hoboken, NJ: John Wiley and Sons Inc.

Whitehead, J. (2007). Collaboration in software engineering: A roadmap. *Future of Software Engineering, 2007*, 214–225. doi:10.1109/FOSE.2007.4

Chapter 19

Selecting Strategies and Approaches in Systems Engineering:
Applying the Descriptive Research Method

Moti Frank
Holon Institute of Technology, Israel

ABSTRACT

This chapter presents a method of applying the principles of the descriptive research method to studies aimed at ascertaining the data needed for making a recommendation in regard to what strategy or approach should be chosen in a certain development stage of future projects. The idea is to use data extracted from already-finished projects to make decisions related to similar projects in their early stages. First, the method is briefly described; next, two case studies that illustrate the method are presented. The method is based on isolating an independent variable, which can be development strategy, integration approach or any other strategy or approach, and deciding which attribute of the independent variable is preferable with respect to the dependent variable, project success, measured by the extent of meeting the requirements, planned budget, planned schedule, and customer satisfaction.

INTRODUCTION

Systems engineers are often required to make decisions about which approach or strategy should be applied at a certain development stage of a new system or product. In other words, the question is: What strategy or implementation approach is preferred over all other available and relevant approaches or strategies? This chapter presents a method for applying the principles of the *descriptive research method* to studies aimed at ascertaining the data needed for making a recommendation in regard to which strategy or approach should be chosen at certain development stages of future projects. The idea is to use data

DOI: 10.4018/978-1-4666-0179-6.ch019

extracted from already-finished projects to make decisions related to similar projects in their early stages. First, the method is briefly described, after which two case studies illustrating the method are presented.

A *descriptive study* is a statistical study used to identify patterns or trends in a situation, but not the causal linkages among its different elements (Business Dictionary, 2011). Tsang (1997) makes a distinction between the *descriptive* and *prescriptive* approaches. In the former, judgment and evaluation are suspended; in the latter not only are they undertaken, but the best practices are put forward to the reader. It seems that there is currently a growing dichotomy between the two streams of research. The descriptive stream deals with the question: How does an organization learn? Alternatively, the prescriptive stream asks: How should an organization learn?

According to Sekaran (2000), *descriptive studies* are undertaken in order to ascertain, and be able to describe, the characteristics of the variables of interest in a situation or in a given research problem. They describe relevant aspects of the phenomena of interest from an individual, organizational, industry-oriented or other perspective. Quite frequently, descriptive studies are undertaken in organizations to learn about the various aspects of a problem under investigation. The goal of a descriptive study is to provide the researcher with a profile or describe relevant aspects of the phenomena of interest. In many cases, such information may be vital before even considering certain corrective steps. Descriptive studies which present data in a meaningful form might help to (1) understand the characteristics of a group in a given situation; (2) think systematically about aspects in a given situation; (3) offer ideas for further examination and research, and (4) help make certain simple decisions about the issue.

Decision analysis is a method used to identify the best option from a set of alternatives, under uncertainty, using the possible outcomes of each alternative and their probabilities of occurrence to

calculate the expected value of the outcome (IN-COSE, 2010). Real world decisions often involve a high degree of ambiguity, conflicting goals due to multiple objectives, complex trade-offs, more than one decision maker, or several sequential decisions. It is in these types of situations where decision analysis is most valuable (Skinner, 2001).

At first glance, the method presented in this chapter has a similar purpose to that of a trade study – to select the most cost-effective alternative from a set of alternatives that may solve a given problem. According to the FAA (2006), a *trade study* is the activity of a multidisciplinary team to identify the most balanced technical solutions among a set of proposed viable solutions. According to INCOSE (2010), a trade study describes a process that compares the appropriateness of different technical solutions. However, this chapter does not deal with trade studies. The difference is that the method presented in the next section aims at analyzing systems projects in which the development phase has been completed. The results of this analysis may serve as lessons learned regarding the strategy or approach to be implemented in future projects that will be performed in similar contexts.

THE METHOD

The main goal of the study method presented in this chapter is to cope with questions such as: Given that there are several strategies or approaches, all of which can be implemented at a certain development stage of a given systems project, which is the preferred approach? How should a decision be made regarding the strategy or approach that is most appropriate for a certain decision gate, taking into account the project's unique characteristics, context and circumstances? What are the implications of choosing a specific approach or strategy in relation to meeting the requirements, and the planned budget and time? According to this study method, projects in which the development phase has already been finished should be analyzed in such a way that the results could serve as lessons learned regarding the preferred strategy or approach that should be taken in a current project in its early stages.

In order to study these sorts of questions, it is proposed to conduct a controlled experiment (i.e. Kirk, 1995). A *controlled experiment* generally compares the results obtained from an experimental sample against a control sample, which is practically identical to the experimental sample, except for the single variable whose effect is being tested. In the method presented in this chapter, the single independent variable is the 'strategy' or 'approach'. The attributes of the independent variable are the various strategies or approaches. The dependent variable can be the *extent of the project's success*, which may be defined as meeting the project's requirements, planned budget, planned time, and customer satisfaction.

For this purpose, it is necessary to examine several groups of similar projects, where in each group of projects one of the examined approaches is implemented. If 'project success' is the dependent variable, then all variables affecting project success should be practically identical, except for the tested variable that has to be isolated (the strategy/approach).

Usually, there are many factors affecting project success. In most cases, it is enough to limit the examination, for factors affecting projects success, to the top ten critical success factors (in addition to the tested variable – strategy/approach).

Literature review (e.g. Pinto & Slevin, 1988; Holland & Light, 1999; Nah & Lau, 2001) reveals that the top ten factors for ensuring project success are:

1. Clearly defined objectives and requirements
2. Top management support and involvement
3. Proper planning
4. Vendor and customer involvement and partnership
5. Appropriate staff selection and training
6. The existence of the required technology
7. Customer and end user satisfaction
8. Good control, monitoring and feedback
9. High levels of communication
10. Proper risk management

In analyzing the data collected during the study, it is necessary to ensure that all of these ten factors are practically identical in all examined projects. In addition to the ten factors, sometimes it is also necessary to compare the examined projects in relation to the overall budget and the extent of the project's complexity; that is, number of interfaces, interface types and configuration items.

Then, a comparison between the project groups should be carried out. The dependent variable is 'project success'. *Project success* means different things to different people. The literature mentions different ways of determining project success. The most common approach focuses on the 'Iron-Triangle', which is meeting cost, time and quality objectives. However, additional measures of project success can be found in the literature. Examples of such measures include: stakeholder satisfaction, performance of the end product, benefits to the project team and more. The focus of the method presented in this chapter is on the Iron-Triangle. Specifically, this means that the measures of project success are meeting the time, cost and quality objectives. A fourth measure has been added in the two case studies presented later – *customer satisfaction*. The method uses these measures because they are related to the end product, and in most cases senior management and customers are both interested in these four measures.

Thus, the extent of meeting the requirements, budget overrun, time overrun, and customer satisfaction should be analyzed and compared. Data might be collected by reviewing the official projects' documents, by interviewing the project managers, and by mining data from the company's central database. It is a good practice to present the data in a table, such as Table 1.

Table 1. Template for presenting projects' data (system level)

Project#	1	2	3		N
Strategy/Approach					
Number of requirements (sys. level)					
Number of realized requirements					
Number of changes in sys.-level req.					
Planned man-hours					
Actual man-hours					
Planned budget [K$]					
Actual cost [K$]					
Planned schedule [mo.]					
Actual Schedule [mo.]					
Man-hours Overrun [%]					
Budget Overrun [%]					
Time Overrun [%]					

Notes: *Man-hours*: A *man-hour* is the amount of work performed by an average worker in one hour. Man-hours do not take employees' work breaks into account; they only count hours of pure labor.

Planned schedule: The total man-hours plus break times, including daily breaks, weekends and holidays.

Overrun [%]: 100*(actual-planned)/planned

Sometimes, the conclusions can be simply deduced by looking at the data presented in the Table. For example, sometimes it is clear that in a group of projects in which one of the approaches was applied there were serious budget and time overrun - much more than in the other projects. However, at times it is difficult to make a first-glance decision regarding the most cost-effective project. In such cases, it is a good practice to use the Analytic Hierarchy Process (AHP) technique as a decision-making aid. The AHP was developed by Saaty in the 1970s (Saaty, 2000). It is a structured technique used for comparing alternatives and finding the alternative that best suits a pre-defined goal. First, a hierarchy of criteria has to be built. AHP suggests calculating the priorities by pairwise comparisons – to compare the nodes,

two by two, with respect to their contribution to the nodes above them. The criteria are then compared to one another, two at a time, to calculate the weight of each. Then, for each criterion, the alternatives are compared two at a time, to calculate the relative priorities (scores) for each alternative per each criterion.

The obtained final priorities had to be analyzed by performing a sensitivity analysis. This kind of analysis examines how the output of a mathematical model changes, due to different sources of variation in the model's input (Saltelli, 2008). By using commercial spreadsheet software, variations of five percent and ten percent should be applied to the various weights. The values of the final priorities might be slightly changed, but the rating should remain the same.

CASE STUDY 1: IMPLICATIONS OF PRESSURE FOR SHORTENING THE TIME TO MARKET (TTM) IN DEFENSE PROJECTS

Background

In recent years, government and prime contractors have been expressing a growing demand, requesting that their defense R&D contractors shorten the Time To Market (TTM). This case study aimed at investigating whether developing systems according to the principles of fast approaches is always preferable to traditional approaches. Does working according to a fast approach ultimately shorten TTM? And if so, what are the implications of achieving this goal in relation to meeting the requirements and the planned budget?

Systems engineering offers fast, as well as, traditional (step-by-step) development approaches. In software engineering, the fast approaches are often called "agile" (i.e. Cockburn, 2001; Larman & Basili, 2003); however, in recent years this term has been used to label hardware-software embedded projects in which a fast development approach is taken (i.e. Hallberg, Andorsson & Olvander, 2010). The most common traditional, step-by-step development strategies are the *Waterfall model* and *Vee-model* approaches, while the most common agile strategies are the *Spiral model* and *Prototyp*ing *model* (i.e. Alavi, 1984; Gull et al., 2009).

The *Waterfall model* (i.e. Royce, 1970; Eisner, 2008) is a sequential process of activities and phases. The progress is seen as flowing downwards like a waterfall through the phases of the system's life cycle. According to this model, moving to the next phase is occurs only when its preceding phase has been completed, verified, and validated.

The *Vee model* (i.e. Forsberg & Mooz, 1991; Defense Acquisition University, 2001) describes the systems development life cycle. The left side of the V represents the design stages – need approval, concept of operation, requirement analysis, decomposition of requirements, creation of system specifications, preliminary and detailed design. The right side of the V represents integration of parts, testing, verification and validation.

The essential concept of the Spiral Model is to minimize risks by the repeated use of *prototypes* and other means. Unlike other models, at every stage risk analysis is performed. The Spiral Model works by building progressively more complete versions of the software by starting at the center of the spiral and working outwards. With each loop of the spiral, the customer evaluates the work and suggestions are made for its modification. Additionally, with each loop of the spiral, a risk analysis is performed, which results in a 'go / no-go' decision. If the risks are determined to be too great, then the project is terminated. Thus, the Spiral Model addresses the problem of requirements engineering through the development of prototypes, and also addresses the need for risk management by performing a risk analysis at each step of the life cycle (Bohem, 1986; Balci et al., 2010). Each iteration is comprised of a requirement analysis, risk analysis, developing or upgrading

a prototype, simulating and testing the prototype and planning the next iteration, if needed.

The Prototyping Model is a systems development method in which a prototype (an early approximation of a final system or product) is built, tested, and then reworked, as necessary, until an acceptable prototype is finally achieved from which the complete system or product can now be developed. This model works best in scenarios where not all of the project requirements are known in detail ahead of time. It is an iterative, trial-and-error process that takes place between the developers and the users (Alavi, 1984; Gull et al., 2009).

The leading principle as regards the former strategies (the Waterfall and Vee models) is that before moving on to the next stage, all development activities in the previous stage must first be completed, verified and validated. On the other hand, using the latter strategies (the Spiral and Prototype models), the development progress is achieved through repeated cycles (iterations) and in smaller portions at a time (incremental); sometimes moving on to the next stage, even if all of the data is still not available, and not all the activities of the previous stage have been completed. This is a sort of trial-and-error process, involving the use of numerous models, simulations, mockups and preliminary prototypes.

Method and Findings

The study plan was designed according to the principles of a controlled experiment. For this purpose, two groups of similar projects were examined. All projects were aimed at developing or upgrading armored fighting vehicle (AFV) systems. Three projects dealt with developing a tailored system. The traditional, step-by-step, development strategy was chosen for these projects, and traditional systems engineering processes were applied including requirements' management, preliminary design, conceptual analysis, architecture synthesis, integration, verification, validation, operational tests, risk analysis, configuration management, and more. For the other three projects, fast development strategies were chosen. In these projects, the requirements were unclear or dynamic so a prototype was built, tested, and then reworked as necessary, until an acceptable prototype was finally achieved from which the complete system could then be developed. Thus, the independent variable had two attributes – (1) the traditional development approach and (2) the rapid development approach.

In this type of study, all variables affecting project success should be practically identical, except for the tested variable, which in this case was the development strategy. There are usually many factors affecting project success. In the current study, the examination had been limited to the top ten critical success factors. By analyzing the raw data collected in the interviews, it was found that all of these ten factors were practically identical in all of the examined projects.

A comparison between the two project groups was carried out. The extent of meeting the re-

quirements, budget overrun, time overrun, and customer satisfaction was analyzed and compared. The reason for comparing these measures and not other measures of project success was explained earlier (see the fifth paragraph of the Method section). Data was collected by reviewing the official projects' documents, by interviewing the project managers, and by mining data from the division's central database. The data analysis strategy used for analyzing the qualitative raw data was 'content analysis': defining the analysis units, determining categories (outstanding repeated elements), and examining the categories' frequencies. The results are presented in the following Table:

The findings of this case study clearly show that the agile approach is not always preferable to the traditional approach. Pushing for a shorter TTM eventually caused serious budget and time overrun problems in the three 'fast' projects, much more than in the 'traditional' projects.

Thus, from a long-term point of view, it is recommended that in projects in which shortening the TTM is a must, a mixed approach should be

Table 2. Case study 1: A comparison of the projects

Project#	A	B	C	D	E	F
Group 1: Traditional 2: Fast	1	1	1	2	2	2
Development strategy	V Model	V Model	V Model	Prototype	Prototype	Spiral
Number of requirements (sys. level)	208	103	128	36	57	78
Number of realized requirements	204	98	121	34	53	75
Number of changes in sys.-level req.	6	9	15	3	5	10
Planned schedule [mo.]	22	14	12	4	12	6
Actual Schedule [mo.]	26	20	14	7	32	9
Man-hours Overrun [%]	29	27	37	88	121	100
Budget Overrun [%]	49	25	37	57	135	107
Time Overrun [%]	18	43	17	75	167	50

taken. This means managing the design process based on a traditional strategy, while combining elements of the agile approach, such as building a prototype as soon as possible, testing it, and then modifying it, as needed. Another way to consider the issue is to manage the design process based on the agile approach, while combining elements of the traditional approach, such as conducting rigorous tests at the end of each step.

CASE STUDY 2: CHOOSING THE APPROPRIATE INTEGRATION APPROACH IN LARGE-SCALE SYSTEMS DEVELOPMENT PROJECTS

Background

This case study deals with the integration process in projects that develop systems according to systems engineering principles and practices. It is aimed at identifying the preferred integration approach for projects in which customer satisfaction is a major goal. *Systems integration* means different things to different people (Nilsson et al., 1990). For the sake of this case study, the INCOSE (2010) definition was adopted: "The purpose of the *integration process* is to assemble a system (by progressively combining system elements) that is consistent with the architectural design. This process is iterated with the *verification and validation processes* as appropriate". The integration process includes activities to perform the integration of system elements (hardware/physical, software, human and procedures) and the demonstration of end-to-end operation (system build). The integration process addresses both the internal interfaces among the elements comprising the system and the external interfaces between the system and other systems.

When discussing integration approaches relevant to the kind of systems projects discussed in this case study, the various approaches found in the literature can be classified into three groups – hardware-assisted versus software only, bottom-up versus top-down, and hierarchial versus functional approaches. However, the case study presented here focuses on the latter – hierarchial and functional approaches.

In systems engineering, the term 'hierarchial integration' relates to a process in which the integration steps follow the physical hierarchy of the system. This approach is commonly used when high risk is involved with the development of the various parts of the system. Functional integration is the process of integrating sub-systems according to their functionality by creating functional entities. This is a process in which the integration steps follow functions of the system. This approach is commonly used when high risk is involved with some functions of the system. Partial functioning of the whole system is obtained at an early stage of the integration process. The classification to *hierarchial* and *functional* is not dichotomous. Project managers often choose the integrated approach, which combines the hierarchial and functional approaches. An *integrated approach* means that part of the integration paths are performed according to the principles of the hierarchial approach, while the other part of the integration paths are performed according to the functional approach depending on needs, context, and available infrastructures, resources and parts. Indeed, this case study compares two integration strategies – the hierarchial and integrated approaches.

Method and Findings

The current study's aim was to investigate whether there is a relation between the integration approach and project success. The independent variable was *the integration approach*. This variable had two attributes – the hierarchial approach and the integrated approach. The dependent variable was *project success*, which was measured by the extent of meeting the requirements, project budget overrun, integration time overrun, and customer satisfaction at the end of the project.

The study plan was designed according to the principles of a controlled experiment. For this purpose, two groups of projects, two projects in each group, were thoroughly examined. The objective of all four projects was to develop electronics-software embedded systems. In the first group, the integration strategy was the hierarchial approach, while the strategy in the second group was the integrated approach. Data was collected by reviewing the official projects' documents, by interviewing engineers and managers who were involved with the projects' integration processes, by questionnaires, and by mining data from the company's central database. The data analysis strategy used for analyzing the qualitative raw data was 'content analysis': defining the analysis units, determining categories (outstanding repeated elements), and examining the categories' frequencies. The reliability of the questionnaire was checked by comparing the assessment of two experts regarding the clarity of each item, while the validity was based on content validity and checked by comparing the assessment of two experts regarding the content of each item. By analyzing the data, it was found that all top ten projects' critical success factors, the extent of project complexity, and the overall budget were practically identical for all examined projects.

A comparison between the two project groups was then carried out. The extent of meeting the requirements, project budget overrun, integration time overrun, and customer satisfaction were analyzed and compared. The reason for comparing these measures and not other measures of project success was explained earlier (see the fifth paragraph of the Method section). A summary of the results are presented in the following Table:

As mentioned above, the main objective of this case study was to make a decision regarding the preferred integration approach (hierarchial or integrated). When looking at the findings presented in Table 3, it is difficult to make a first-glance decision regarding the most cost-effective project. Therefore, the Analytic Hierarchy Process (AHP) technique was used for making this decision. In our case, the goal is to find the most cost-effective integration approach. First, we had to find the most cost-effective project (out of the four projects), and because the integration approach of each project was identified earlier, we could made a decision regarding the most cost-effective integration approach.

First, a hierarchy of criteria has to be built. In our case, the hierarchy is relatively simple; it is built from four criteria (sometimes called *factors*) – performance/meeting the requirements (percentage of successful realized requirements), meeting the planned budget, meeting the planned integration time, and customer satisfaction. The AHP hierarchy for our case is shown in Figure 1. The

Table 3. Case study 2: A comparison of the projects

Project#		A	B	C	D
	Integration Approach (independent variable)	Hierarchial	Integrated	Hierarchial	Integrated
Performance: Percentage of Successfully Realized Requirements		96	99	100	100
Budget Overrun		13%	15%	4.16% Under estimated budget	30%
Integration Time Overrun		50%	30%	50%	0
Customer Satisfaction (1-5 Scale)		5	3	5	3

Figure 1. The AHP hierarchy

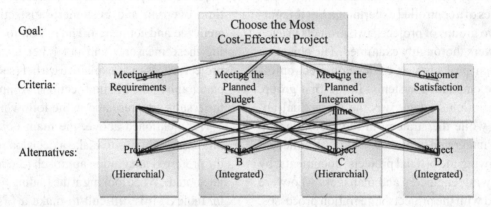

Table 4. AHP's fundamental scale for pairwise comparisons

Intensity of Importance	Definition
1	Equal importance
3	Moderate importance
5	Strong importance
7	Very strong importance
9	Extreme importance

goal of this decision is selecting the most cost-effective project from the four projects.

The next step is to determine the relative weight ('priorities' in AHP language) of each criterion ('factors' or 'nodes' in AHP language). AHP suggests calculating the priorities by pairwise comparisons – to compare the nodes, two by two, with respect to their contribution to the nodes above

them. AHP usually uses a 1-9 scale for comparing pairs. The fundamental scale for pairwise comparisons is presented in Table 4.

In our case, the alternatives were first compared in regard to their strengths in meeting each of the criteria. Then, the criteria were compared with respect to their importance to reaching the goal. It should be noted that regarding the criteria pairwise comparisons with respect to the goal, the top management, at the time of the study presented here, stressed the importance of customer satisfaction. In other words, at that time the customer satisfaction was considered to be more important compared to meeting the requirements, planned budget, and planned time of the project. Consequently, the weight of the customer satisfaction criterion was found to be the highest – 0.474. The whole AHP process will not be presented in this

Table 5. The priorities of the alternatives with respect to the goal

	Perfor.	Budget	Time	Satis.	Perfor.	Budget	Time	Satis.	Final Priorities
Weights	0.097	0.247	0.182	0.474	**Weighted Priorities=Priorities*Weights**				
Project A (Hierarchial)	0.048	0.190	0.0575	0.417	0.0047	0.047	0.011	0.198	0.26
Project B (Integrated)	0.165	0.109	0.212	0.083	0.016	0.027	0.038	0.039	0.12
Project C (Hierarchial)	0.393	0.653	0.0575	0.417	0.038	0.161	0.011	0.198	**0.41**
Project D (Integrated)	0.393	0.048	0.673	0.083	0.038	0.012	0.122	0.039	0.21

chapter; only the final results are presented – see Table 5.

We can see that Project C, with a priority of 0.41, is by far the most cost-effective project. Project A, with a priority of 0.26, is second. The integration approach in both Projects A and C was the hierarchial approach. The conclusion is that, particularly when customer satisfaction is determined as a major goal, the hierarchial integration approach is preferable to the integrated approach with respect to project success (as measured by meeting the requirements, planned budget, planned schedule, and customer expectations). Since the integrated approach combines principles of both hierarchial and functional approaches, it can be carefully concluded that in this case study, the hierarchial approach was found preferable to the functional approach.

CONCLUSION

This chapter presents a method of applying the principles of the *descriptive research method* to studies aimed at ascertaining the data needed for making a recommendation in regard to what strategy or approach should be chosen at a certain development stage of future projects.

The method aims at analyzing systems projects in which the development phase has been finished. The idea is that the results of this analysis may serve as lessons learned regarding the strategy or approach to be implemented in future similar projects. The method involves examining several groups of similar projects, where in each group of projects one of the examined approaches is implemented. If 'project success' is the dependent variable, then all variables affecting project success should be practically identical, except for the tested (independent) variable that has to be isolated.

Two case studies illustrating the method are presented at the end of the chapter. In the first case study, the independent variable is the 'development approach' which has two attributes – (1) the traditional development approach and (2) the rapid development approach. In the second case study, the independent variable is the 'integration approach' which has two attributes – (1) the hierarchial approach and (2) the integrated approach. In both cases, the dependent variable is 'project success'. The measures of project success in both cases are meeting the time, cost and quality objectives, and customer satisfaction.

In both cases, a comparison between the project groups has been carried out. The extent of meeting the requirements, budget overrun, time overrun, and customer satisfaction have been analyzed and compared. Data was collected by reviewing the official project documents, by interviewing project managers, and by mining data from the company's central database. Next, the collected data was carefully analyzed. In the first case study, the conclusion was that pushing for a shorter Time To Market eventually caused serious budget and time overrun problems. In the second case study, the conclusion was that when customer satisfaction is determined as a major goal, the hierarchial integration approach is preferable to the integrated approach with respect to project success.

Thus, it was demonstrated that the method enables choosing a development approach or integration strategy for future systems projects based on data that has been extracted from already-finished projects. Although the proposed method has been applied to the two case studies presented in this chapter, it can be carefully concluded that the method is applicable to any new system or product development stage in which an approach or strategic direction should be chosen.

REFERENCES

Alavi, M. (1984). An assessment of the prototyping approach to information systems development. *Communications of the ACM, 27*(6), 556–563. doi:10.1145/358080.358095

Balci, O., Gilley, W. S., Adams, R. J., Tunar, E., & Barnette, N. D. (2010). *Animations to assist learning some key computer science topics, software engineering, the spiral model*. Department of Computer Science, Virginia Tech. Retrieved May 26, 2011, from http://courses.cs.vt.edu/ csonline/ SE/ Lessons/ Spiral/ index.html

Boehm, B. (1986). A spiral model of software development and enhancement. *ACM SIGSOFT Software Engineering Notes, 11*(4), 14-24. Retrieved May 26, 2011, from http://delivery. acm.org/ 10.1145/ 20000/ 12948/ p14-boehm. pdf?key1 =12948&key2 =1109403921&coll =DL&dl =ACM&CFID =3425753&CFTOKEN =44820182

Business Dictionary. (2011). *Definition of descriptive study*. Retrieved May 26, 2011, from http://www.businessdictionary.com/ definition / descriptive-study.html

Cockburn, A. (2001). *Agile software development*. Boston, MA: Addison-Wesley.

Defense Acquisition University. (2001). *Systems engineering fundamentals*. Fort Belvoir, VA: Defense Acquisition University Press.

Eisner, H. (2008). *Essentials of project and system engineering management* (3rd ed.). Indianapolis, IN: Wiley.

Forsberg, K., & Mooz, H. (1991). The relationship of systems engineering to the project cycle. *Proceedings of the First Annual Symposium of the National Council on Systems Engineering (NCOSE)*, Chattanooga, TN, 21-23 October, 1991. Retrieved May 26, 2011, from http://www.csm. com /repository/ model/ rep/o/pdf/ Relationship% 20of% 20SE% 20to% 20Proj% 20Cycle.pdf

Gull, H., Azam, F., Butt, W. H., & Iqbal, S. Z. (2009). A new divided and conquer software process model. *World Academy of Science. Engineering and Technology, 60*, 255–260.

Hallberg, N., Andorsson, R., & Olvander, C. (2010). Agile architecture framework for model driven development of C^2 systems. *Systems Engineering, 13*(2), 175–185.

Holland, C. R., & Light, B. (1999). A critical success factors model for ERP implementation. *IEEE Transactions on Software Engineering, 16*(3), 30–36.

INCOSE. (2010). *Systems engineering handbook (version 3.2)*. Seattle, WA: International Council on Systems Engineering.

Kirk, R. E. (1995). *Experimental design: Procedures for behavioral sciences*. St. Paul, MN: Brooks/Cole Publishing Co.

Larman, C., & Basili, V. R. (2003). Iterative and incremental development: A brief history. *Computer, 36*(6), 47–56. doi:10.1109/MC.2003.1204375

Nah, F. F., & Lau, J. L. (2001). Critical factors for successful implementation of enterprise systems. *Business Process Management Journal, 7*(3), 285–296. doi:10.1108/14637150110392782

Nilsson, E. G., Nordhagen, E. K., & Oftedal, G. (1990). Aspects of systems integration. *Proceedings of the First International Conference on Systems Integration*, (pp. 434-443).

Pinto, J. K., & Slevin, D. P. (1988). Project success: Definitions and measurement techniques. *Project Management Journal, 19*(3), 67–73.

Royce, W. (1970). Managing the development of large software systems. *Proceedings of the IEEE WESCON* (Western Electronics Show and Convention), Los Angeles CA, August 1970, pp. 1-9. Retrieved May 26, 2011, from http://www. cs.umd.edu/ class/ spring2003/ cmsc838p/ Process/ waterfall.pdf

Saaty, T. L. (2000). *Fundamentals of decision making with the analytic hierarchy process*. Pittsburgh, PA: RWS Publications.

Sekaran, U. (2000). *Research methods for business: A skill building approach* (3rd ed.). New York, NY: John Wiley and Sons.

Sherrell, L. B., & Chen, L. (2001). The W life cycle model and associated methodology for corporate web site development. *Communications of the Association for Information Systems, 5*(7), 1–38.

Skinner, D. C. (2001). *Introduction to decision analysis* (2nd ed.). Gainsville, FL: Probabilistic Publishing.

Tsang, E. W. K. (1997). Organizational learning and the learning organization: A dichotomy between descriptive and prescriptive research. *Human Relations, 50*(1), 73–89. doi:10.1177/001872679705000104

ADDITIONAL READING

Abrahamsson, P., Warsta, J., Siponen, M. T., & Ronkainen, J. (2003). New directions on agile methods: A comparative analysis. *Proc. of the 25th International Conference on Software Engineering (ICSE)*. Portland OR, 3-10 May 2003, 244-254.

Boehm, B., & Turner, R. (2004). *Balancing Agility and Discipline*. Boston, MA: Addison-Wesley.

Brown, S. R., & Melamed, L. E. (1990). *Experimental Design and Analysis*. Newbury Park, CA: Sage Publications.

Chua, D. K., Kog, Y. C., & Loh, P. K. (1999). Critical success factors for different project objectives. *Journal of Construction Engineering and Management, 125*(3), 142–150. doi:10.1061/(ASCE)0733-9364(1999)125:3(142)

Davis, A. M., Bersoff, E. H., & Comer, E. R. (1988). A Strategy for Comparing Alternative Software Development Life Cycle Models. *IEEE Transactions on Software Engineering, 14*(10), 1453–1461. doi:10.1109/32.6190

Dvir, D., Raz, T., & Shenhar, A. (2003). An empirical analysis of the relationship between project planning and project success. *International Journal of Project Management, 21*(2), 89–95. doi:10.1016/S0263-7863(02)00012-1

FAA. (2006). Trade studies. *System Engineering Manual (Version 3.1, Section 4.6)*. Washington, DC.: Federal Aviation Administration.

FHWA. (2005). Clarus Concept of Operations. Publication No. FHWA-JPO-05-072, Federal Highway Administration. Retrieved May 26, 2011, from http://en.wikipedia.org/wiki/V-Model

Grover, V., Cheon, M. J., & Teng, T. C. (1994). A descriptive study on the outsourcing of information systems functions. *Information and Management, 27*(1), 33-44. Retrieved May 26, 2011, from http://www.sciencedirect.com/ science/ article/ pii/ 0378720694901007

Kiem, M. L., Wing, R. R., McGuire, M. T., Seagle, H. M., & Hill, J. O. (1997). A descriptive study of individuals successful at long-term maintenance of substantial weight loss. American Journal of Clinical Nutrition, 66, 239-246. Retrieved May 26, 2011, from http://www.ajcn.org/ content/ 66/ 2/ 239.full.pdf

NASA. (2004). The Standard Waterfall Model for Systems Development. Retrieved May 26, 2011, from http://web.archive.org/ web/ 20050310133243/http:// asd-www.larc.nasa.gov/ barkstrom/ public/ The_ Standard_ Waterfall_ Model_ For_ Systems_ Development.htm

Nelson, H. C., Nute, T., & Rodjak, D. J. (1996). Applying the spiral model: A case study in small project management. *Software Process: Improvement and Practice Journal, 2*(4), 239–251. doi:10.1002/(SICI)1099-1670(199612)2:4<239::AID-SPIP55>3.0.CO;2-V

TechTarget. (2011). Prototyping model. Retrieved May 26, 2011, from http://searchcio-midmarket. techtarget.com/ definition/ Prototyping-Model

Tripp, S., & Bichelmeyer, B. (1990). Rapid prototyping: An alternative instructional design strategy. *Educational Technology Research and Development*, *38*(1), 31–44. doi:10.1007/BF02298246

KEY TERMS AND DEFINITIONS

Analytic Hierarchy Process (AHP): A structured technique for comparing alternatives and finding the alternative that best suits a pre-defined goal.

Controlled Experiment: A study which generally compares the results obtained from an experimental sample against a control sample, which is practically identical to the experimental sample, except for the one single variable whose effect is being tested (Kirk, 1995).

Decision Analysis: A method of identifying the best option from a set of alternatives, under uncertainty, using the possible outcomes of each alternative and their probabilities of occurrence to calculate the expected value of the outcome (INCOSE, 2010).

Descriptive Research Method: *Descriptive study* is a study used to identify patterns or trends in a situation, but not the causal linkages among

its different elements (Business Dictionary, 2011). It is undertaken in order to ascertain and be able to describe the characteristics of the variables of interest in a situation or in a given research problem (Sekaran, 2000).

The Prototyping Model: Model in which a prototype is built, tested, and then reworked as necessary until an acceptable prototype is finally achieved from which the complete system or product can now be developed (Alavi, 1984; Gull et al., 2009).

The Spiral Model: Model that works by building progressively more complete versions of the software by starting at the center of the spiral and working outwards. With each loop of the spiral, the customer evaluates the work and suggestions are made for its modification. With each loop of the spiral, a risk analysis is performed.

The Vee Model: Model for describing the systems development life cycle. The left side of the V represents the design stages and the right side of the V represents integration of parts, testing, verification and validation.

The Waterfall Model: A sequential process of activities and phases. The progress is seen as flowing downwards like a waterfall through the phases of the system's life cycle.

Chapter 20
Engineering Design as Research

Timothy L. J. Ferris
Defence and Systems Institute, University of South Australia, Australia

ABSTRACT

Research is defined as an activity that creates new knowledge. This is often misunderstood in the engineering community as necessarily requiring a scientific contribution that advances the theory of some matter related to engineering materials or processes. Consequently, typical engineering research projects investigate physical phenomena thought likely to be interesting in potential applications or to describe the characteristics of processes used in engineering work. The results of such projects provide a fragmented, abstracted view of the phenomena investigated, which is difficult to use in engineering decision making related to contextualised situations. This chapter shows how the actual design of engineered artefacts is research because it provides knowledge of the impact of the integration of various elements of existing knowledge, which demonstrates the properties of the designs achieved through the design work and leads to discovery of solutions to the various challenges of integration discovered through the project which attempts to achieve the integration.

INTRODUCTION

Research is defined as an activity which develops new knowledge (Department of Education Training and Youth Affairs, 2001). A major challenge we have in understanding the nature of research is our preconceptions concerning the nature of knowledge, since the creation of knowledge is the objective of all research activities. In this chapter we introduce the particularly important issue of engineering activity and the act of design itself as research, that is, as methods of creating new knowledge. This is distinct from performing investigations about the engineering and design processes as an observer of those processes with the purpose of better understanding the processes. The idea of engineering activity and design being a research methodology requires explanation because it is quite different to the usual interpretation of research in engineering.

It is usually expected that the knowledge that is developed in processes to which we assign the

DOI: 10.4018/978-1-4666-0179-6.ch020

name 'research' is objective and generalizable to a wide range of problems. This understanding is derived from the idea of research as implemented in the natural sciences and fields inspired by their methods, in which the goal is to find out knowledge about the phenomenon or situation which is the subject of the work, and the work is regarded as completed when a sufficiently good theory or explanation of the situation is determined.

The idea of research concerning the discovery of generalizable knowledge about the subject matter of the investigation is prevalent in engineering related research conducted in universities, by both faculty and graduate students, and in the regulations for research degrees in engineering and in the engineering research journals published in recent decades. The engineering research journals of the 1950's, particularly prior to the changes in the US education and research system that followed Sputnik, reflected a different vision of the nature of engineering research and its relation to the achievement of engineering design. The latter will be discussed later in this chapter.

The idea of generalizability of knowledge relates to the manner in which it can be applied to situations other than the narrow set of situations in which the observations were made (Lee & Baskerville, 2003). Generalizability can be established in several ways and can have different meanings dependant on the manner in which it is achieved. The natural sciences use statistical analysis of observations to determine the confidence that can be established that the null hypothesis is not wrongly rejected, and so seek to establish results as being universally applicable across all analogous cases. Fields which accept interpretivist views of knowledge may be satisfied with developing knowledge that is true within the bounds of the situation of observation, without demanding that the knowledge obtained be demonstrated for a broader range of situations (Lee & Baskerville, 2003). In general, the notion of generalizability demands the assumption that the matter of observation is uniform across the

range of the generalization so that the observed sample represents a wider space (Lee & Baskerville, 2003).

When we look for objective, generalisable knowledge about subject matter we narrow our view of the nature of knowledge through the Positivist lens to concerning knowledge about external things. This is not the only view of knowledge which exists, and unnecessarily constrains research since it excludes the development of knowledge of other kinds.

KNOWLEDGE

We present now a discussion of the nature of knowledge which is necessary to develop a top-down approach to the evaluation of methods of research. We review some recent distinctions in the description of knowledge.

"Know that" is a formulation used to describe declarative knowledge, following Gilbert Ryle's distinction between "knowing that" and "knowing how" (Ryle, 1948). This distinction has been noted as significant in engineering, where both kinds of knowledge are required (Bucciarelli, 2003). Declarative knowledge is a kind that can be articulated in words or mathematics that represent ideas concerning the nature and relations of things. As such, declarative knowledge is a form of knowledge which it is fairly easy to teach and learn because it is possible to reduce the teaching or learning to recitation of the representation of the knowledge. The recitative character of declarative knowledge is discussed by Biggs (Biggs, 1999). Declarative knowledge is any knowledge which can be formulated in statements which convey the knowledge itself, whether that knowledge is generalizable across a wide range of cases or of limited applicability.

"Know how" is Ryle's formulation to describe the capacity to perform a function. This capacity is quite distinct from the capacity to describe the area of knowledge related to the function or the relevant theory. Biggs (1999) describes this kind of knowledge as "functional". Functional knowledge emphasizes the person's capacity to perform a function, not to articulate description of what is known. Functional knowledge does not preclude the ability to articulate what is known, but emphasizes ability to perform an act. The distinctive feature of functional knowledge is the knower's orientation to doing a function rather than describing something. Should someone articulate functional knowledge into a description it would be possible for another person to learn the description as declarative knowledge, which that person could recite, but not be able to perform appropriately.

A third kind of knowledge is named "knowing" in Nissen (2006), and by Biggs (1999) as "procedural knowledge", or "skill". The emphasis in this kind is on ability to choose and perform some action in an appropriate and effective manner. Nissen says that knowing how to ride a bicycle is demonstrated by mounting and actually riding a bicycle. The only test of "knowing" is a practical test in which the candidate must perform the action. Ability to articulate anything about the matter of action or a theory about the action is irrelevant to "knowing". "Knowing" contrasts with "know how", where the emphasis is on ability to perform a function, because "knowing" is usually associated with skills such as ability to discern when a particular action is apposite. The difference between "know how" to ride a bicycle and "knowing" how to ride a bicycle is that in the "know how" formulation the knower is able to perform the set-piece tasks associated with riding a bicycle, but may not yet be ready to integrate all the tasks into safe riding of a bicycle on a roadway with traffic. The "knowing" formulation refers to the more advanced achievement of being able to integrate all the set-piece tasks into effective and safe cycling in a normal situation.

The three kinds of knowledge span from the ability to abstract, describe and theorize about subject matter, through applied knowledge which enables performance of functions, to practical ability to perform whole and complex activities. These kinds of knowledge form identifiable points in the characterization of knowledge. Any particular knowledge held by a particular person will have its own combination of abstract theorizing and ability to act, and so could be described as belonging at a particular point along a continuum. Identification of the three kinds of knowledge is useful for theorizing about the nature of knowledge, and research.

Research is an activity which creates new knowledge, which could be of any kind. The new knowledge may be in an abstracted, declarative, form, or may be embedded in the capacity of a person to act appropriately as either functional or procedural knowledge. In describing research as means to produce new knowledge, it is important that the new knowledge be new to everyone. However, the knowledge advance may be of any size, including very small, and may be situationally constrained.

RESEARCH METHODS

At least some academic research degree regulations in engineering demand that the research work not apply "the normal engineering method"[1]. These regulations presume that there is clear agreement as to what constitutes a normal engineering method. There are two grounds for scepticism that there is a clearly agreed engineering method. These grounds are that:

1. There is very little teaching of method in engineering programs beyond quite rudimentary descriptions of things such as the project life-cycle. That is, descriptions of the engineering method omit detailed explanation of how the creative work of engineering which synthesises solutions to problems is actually done. This knowledge is the purview of Design Studies, which itself reflects

diversity of views about what constitutes the design process (Dorst, 2008; Gregor & Jones, 2007; March & Smith, 1995; Walls, Widmeyer, & El-Sawy, 1992).

2. Engineers, in general, discuss methodology very little. The engineering culture emphasises investigation of the technologies and principles which are applied in the technologies but says little about either how the principles are discovered or applied to achieve engineering outcomes. The measure of a good engineer is one who can successfully achieve challenging objectives (Hopkins, 1954).

Engineers tend to be a pragmatic lot who get on and do the work without extended discussions of the methods and principles upon which the work is based. Individual engineers develop a good pragmatic understanding of methods applicable to the kind of work that they do, largely through experience, including observation of the effectiveness of methods which they have attempted to use. This is an approach to knowledge consistent with the approach discussed above under the name "knowing".

The words from the research degree regulations "not apply the normal engineering method" are often interpreted to mean that design cannot be research because design is considered to be a normal engineering activity and therefore excluded. Design is a significant part of engineering work and the design of almost any product, from the simplest to the most complex, is the result of an engineering design activity.

We need to explore this issue. Design concerns development of situated knowledge. The outcome of design is knowledge which is specific to the particular need addressed by the project. The situated knowledge developed by design is specific to the particular solution which is offered. The knowledge that we developed through the design process is specific to the choice of technology and the system architecture selected and

provides "proof by construction" that the design idea is valid and effective (Hevner, March, Park, & Ram, 2004). The action of design always, but specifically including the case of design of novel or innovative products, demands rigor in the use of the underlying principles to posit an appropriate design and in the evaluation of the results achieved (Hevner, et al., 2004).

To posit design as a research methodology challenges the tacit idea, held particularly strongly in the natural sciences because of their Positivist conceptualisation of knowledge and therefore significantly influencing many engineers, that knowledge created through research should be generalizable to all cases (Lee & Baskerville, 2003). The knowledge developed in a particular design project is specific to the particular design implemented through the project and the context in which, and for which, it is tested. That is, a design project produces distinctly situated knowledge of what is apposite in constrained circumstances.

Various authors have written about research methodologies which are suitable for use, or which are commonly used, in particular disciplines. These works are often designed as texts for research methods courses. Such courses are usually designed to provide students with instruction in how to conduct activities in the discipline in which they are studying a research degree. Research methods courses which teach one, or a very few research methods, leave students with the impression that proper research must be done using one of the methods described in the course.

Engineering should not be approached as a field which permits only a few particular research methods. This is because the core concern of engineering is the development of suitable solutions to address needs. Therefore methods of research in engineering need to include methods which can explore the scientific phenomena which may be applied in a solution, but also need to be inclusive of research methods which can explore the nature of the need to be addressed and the effectiveness of any proposed solution to be a solution to the need which has been presented, and could explore the methods for doing engineering work (Ferris, 2009). The evidence provided by the content of mainstream engineering research journals shows that much of the engineering research publication since the 1960s has been constrained to discovery about scientific principles which may be useful in future engineering projects. This is evidenced by the focus of journals being mainly centred on technology areas, with only a few, less well-known, journals addressing niche areas. In the next section we discuss a different interpretation of engineering research evidenced in engineering journals during the 1950s.

ENGINEERING JOURNALS IN THE 1950S

We turn attention now to the content of engineering journals published in the 1950s because a significant number of papers emphasizing the whole of product system level of development were published during that decade. This section of the chapter is supported by a detailed analysis by the author (Ferris, 2007a, 2007b, 2008). In the context of the present work the point to be drawn from the history of the 1950s publications was the recognition of the achievement of a significant engineering design providing a product or system as being, itself, a research product and worthy of publication in an engineering research venue. This recognition and emphasis receded with the changes in education and engineering research following Sputnik.

Two important trends influencing the understanding of research in engineering occurred during the 1950s. Before the 1950s engineering was taught in institutions with names such as "Institute of Technology", and was only just entering into institutions known as universities. During the 1950s the professional standing of engineering was growing based on the obvious benefits of the rigorous application of complex scientific methods

to the achievement of engineering objectives. This shifted the standing of engineering from being concerned with the instantiation of things in workshops and factories, with all the associated connotations of dirty hands, to a field in which there was obvious benefit to be obtained through the application of advanced scientific theory, with the connotations of dealing with generalizable knowledge. This difference was important in the transition of engineering to become recognised as having a proper place in the university. The new view of engineering more closely aligned with concepts associated with the Platonic ideal associated with most of the other professions based on university education. The transition was supported by the obvious advances in engineering which had occurred during World War II as a result of fundamental scientific research into matters enabling the development of technologies which had made a significant difference in the war effort.

Universities were seen as the highest place of learning in most fields. So, during the 1950s when the physical sciences had already been accepted as legitimate fields of university activity, fields such as engineering were trying to be recognised as acceptable. The claim for engineering to enter the university was based on the demonstrable importance of application oriented scientific research in the advancement of engineering achievement of significant new technologies. Application oriented scientific research is research focused on the development of knowledge of the scientific principles associated with particular phenomena which are expected to be useful in applications in the foreseeable future. The pathway to be accepted into the university as a suitable field relied on a field demonstrating credentials as suitably "scientific". The claim to be scientific was supported by following something that appeared to be "the scientific method" in research and teaching in the manner used in the natural sciences. The focus of the natural sciences is to explain how and why things are as they are (March & Smith, 1995) which contrasts with the fundamental concern of engineering with the properties of artificial things (Simon, 1996). The matter of the scientific method will be discussed in a later section of this chapter.

Engineering journals report research related to engineering. Since the 1960s the majority of articles in the majority of engineering journals have reported investigations of particular situations or phenomena which appear to be potentially interesting in the possible engineering of solutions to needs. In this sense the work belongs in engineering journals, which properly contain research which is of interest to those who intend to make artificial things to have a planned effect.

However, the approach to investigation, as reported in most engineering journal articles, is largely abstraction from the context of a solution to a complete need to provide characterisations of particular phenomena, materials or components which may be useful in future engineering work. The post 1960s engineering research paper style is to present the research issue in an abstracted manner, as an issue separated from the practical context which motivated, or any practical application of, the work. In some fields the motivation of projects is to refine the theory which is already in the literature but without the refinement being called for by those who practice in the field.

The research methods which are used include empirical methods in which tests of real instances of the subject matter are performed to build conclusions and simulation and modelling studies in which the properties of a model of a scenario are investigated. Modelling and simulation research can be very valuable because it enables the exploration of the characteristics of a wide range of cases cheaply and conveniently. The value depends on whether the subject matter is amenable to physical investigation or can only be investigated through simulation. In either case the knowledge developed is of a "know that" kind that concerns the properties of the abstraction investigated rather than the behaviour of the subject matter in the context of a real instance.

Another notable change in engineering research papers commencing in the 1960s has been a shift in the balance of authorship of research papers to the university sector from the engineering practitioner sector. This change is associated with the change of subject matter because practising engineer's concerns are with finding means to address needs rather than describing abstractions of things which might be useful in some future engineering project.

In the 1950s the engineering journal literature was rather more diverse. There was greater diversity of authorship, including a significant proportion authored by practicing engineers, and diversity in the classes of subject matter. There were a reasonable number of papers discussing advances in engineering science but there were a large proportion of papers which discussed the development of solutions to particular needs. Some of these papers described solutions to needs addressed by engineers in their engineering work, that is the papers presented theoretical frameworks for particular kinds of analysis that addressed particular practical design needs. For example, the early volumes of *IRE Transactions on Reliability* outlined the theory of reliability as required by engineers who needed to do reliability analysis as part of their design activity. There were also many papers which described the implementation of product or system designs. These papers were written in a manner that would help other engineers confronting related problems to recognise the important issues and approaches to solutions which had been demonstrated successful by somebody else.

Of the two classes paper identified in the 1950s the former class, the theoretical and empirical contributions related to understanding of engineering relevant phenomena are fairly closely aligned to the papers published more recently. However, even here there is a significant difference. The papers published in the 1950s generally provided a clear, brief, explanation of what need in the physical domain had prompted the work which was reported in the papers. The work was not reported in an abstract manner, largely separated from its contribution as part of the solution of a broader engineering problem.

The papers describing the design of complete products and systems are a genre which has become rare in the engineering research literature. The papers describing the design of complete products and systems describe the results of projects in which the act of design created new knowledge that was perceived as worthy of publication as a description of new knowledge. The concept of engineering design as research, creating new knowledge of significant value to the engineering community, in the act of successfully designing a novel solution to a need was accepted in the 1950s, and has since faded from the engineering community.

The difficulty with accepting design as research arose during the 1950s as the engineering community sought to gain university status and consequently shifted its concept of research to that which would produce knowledge of the "know that" kind. The change in the kind of knowledge sought in engineering research resulted from the Platonic ideal, resulting in knowledge of the abstraction of something, rather than the concrete instantiated form of the subject matter, was seen as necessary to gaining a place within universities. The result has been an emphasis on discovery of generalisable knowledge of the "know that" kind in engineering research. The effect has been to separate the academic and practice communities so that, whilst an engineering degree is a prerequisite for entry into either the academic or engineering practice communities the two communities and career paths then diverge.

1950'S EXAMPLES OF DESIGN AS RESEARCH

We now discuss three examples of papers demonstrating design as research dating from the 1950s.

These are only samples from amongst many available from the decade. The first of our studies concerns the development of a photographic data logger which included both time and magnitude grids (Riblet, 1956). This paper commences by reviewing existing data logging and plotting instruments, noting that there are two classes of recorders. The two classes are those that directly write on a paper chart, useful for low-frequency signals, and those producing a photographic record through reflecting a light beam from a mirror, capable of responding high-frequency signals. The latter class do not include calibrated taxis and grids for the timescale and magnitude resulting in a very slow process of reducing data to a usable form.

The authors introduced their project objectives. They set out to develop equipment which could simultaneously plot a function on the time grid and make the chart produced in the data plotter the final data form. Their product simultaneously plotted the function being measured; the time grid; and a magnitude grid. They recognised that achieving these objectives would require design of three significant elements. After describing the goal the paper describes the design solutions for each of these major elements. The description was a verbal description of the elements as built and the rationale applied in the design. The paper concludes with an evaluation of the instrument developed in terms of the quality of the plots produced and an evaluation of the labour saved.

The second study concerns the development of a plasmatron tube (Johnson & Webster, 1952). Existing vacuum and gas tubes provided either high impedance, continuously controllable, low current or low impedance, uncontrolled, high current operation. The absence of a tube type capable of providing low impedance, high and controllable current operation presented a difficulty for designers in certain applications.

The tube designed was described using words to explain the principal by which worked, photographs to show its physical construction and test results. In addition the authors presented formulae which would assist in design of the components to achieve desired performance and a theoretical description of how the tube performed. The paper provided the information necessary for another engineer to design a similar product and the principal performance characteristics graphs to enable readers to understand its performance characteristics. This paper showed the design of a novel component type with the information necessary for users to use it or for others to design similar components.

The third case concerns the design of a very high power pulsed magnetron tube (Okress, Gleason, White, & Hayter, 1957). These authors provide detail of the electrical characteristics of the tube which they were required to build, noting that the specified parameters were very ambitious. The authors identified a number of major technical challenges. The technical challenges included achieving the required performance and achieving reliability that would make the component useful. The work commenced in 1946 and design was completed in 1953 with the paper being published in 1957, including an account of the reliability achieved.

The methods of addressing the technical problems resulted in development of appropriate materials. The paper describes the scientific experiments performed to demonstrate the suitability for purpose of the materials found. A further problem identified and solved was the difficulty of manufacture of such a large tube.

It is clear that the product was very challenging. The purpose was not explained but much else about the design was described. The performance and test results for the completed tube were provided showing successful completion of the project. What is significant is that this paper shows how the authors successfully satisfied their objective and solved a number of significantly challenging problems.

Each of the three papers discussed in this section demonstrated the successful design of a product which was inherently very challenging showing how such a design project can satisfy a novel need in a suitable way and how design activity may demand discovery of various kinds of solution to many distinct needs. The solution of the various needs that together comprise the project may involve a variety of research methods and lead to discoveries of various kinds.

DESIGN AS RESEARCH METHOD

The idea of the scientific method of how scientists proceed with research is a myth concerning how observations are transformed into knowledge. The common descriptions of the scientific method start with the proposal of an hypothesis which will be tested through the collection of appropriate empirical data. By nature of the case the empirical observations can only refute the hypothesis but can never prove it. This situation leads to several problems:

1. Often the research question is distorted so that the researcher can create an hypothesis which can be tested given the resources available.
2. Often the researcher's belief about the situation is reconstructed as a null hypothesis so that when the null hypothesis is refuted the researcher feels justified in asserting that their belief about the subject matter is supported.
3. The method, as described, does not provide an explanation of how the researcher can develop knowledge in a field which does not already have a body of work which can be used to construct formal hypotheses.
4. The result of such research is conclusions about particular hypotheses which represent abstractions from the context in which the observed phenomena exists or any situation in which the knowledge might be useful. The objective of such research is the development

of knowledge for its intrinsic value, not its instrumental value.

The result of research performed using an hypothesis testing approach is the creation of scientific knowledge describing certain aspects of the matters which are being investigated. This knowledge is often obtained in a situation where the researcher's objective is to obtain information about a situation which appears interesting for the intrinsic value of the knowledge sought. The impact of orientation to the intrinsic value of the knowledge is that the questions asked and the termination point of the research project are determined based on the expected achievement of the knowledge which is perceived to have an intrinsic value. The consequence is that the knowledge obtained may not be relevant to any application. The problem of distortion of the research questions in order to have questions which are amenable to answer by the standard method frequently results in good work which is difficult to apply.

The nature of the research process discussed above is that it provides knowledge about questions which are abstracted from their context. Abstraction is often necessary in order to construct the problem in a form which can be addressed using this approach. However, abstraction by its nature removes the matter of investigation from its context resulting in knowledge which is largely context independent. The difficulty of abstracted context independent knowledge is that it is difficult to integrate such knowledge into an arrangement which applies that knowledge to achieve a desired outcome. The difficulty in applying scientifically derived knowledge to achieve a desired outcome is a consequence of the different kinds of knowledge, as discussed above.

Scientifically derived knowledge concerns the development of a generally valid theory which explains the observations. As such it concerns knowledge of the "know that" kind. That is, scientifically derived knowledge is concerned with

description of things, transforming our awareness of those things from perception of the state of nature to description of a theory that explains the state of nature. The description of the theory is, inherently, and explicit articulated form. When someone desires to use knowledge and to integrate elements of knowledge to create some meaningful product the knowledge required is not just of the "know that" form describing the elements which must be integrated. The act of integrating the fragments of knowledge to achieve a useful outcome is an act of constructing knowledge in either the "know how" or "knowing" forms. The dynamism of the knowledge created in the act of application to the solution of a need occurs because in the act of integration of the elements of knowledge that described the abstracted phenomenon of the elements are transformed from knowledge about abstraction is to means to achieve an end.

We consider now the fundamental difference between science and engineering. Science seeks knowledge which enables the description of a state of affairs which already exists. Engineering is concerned with action which leads to desired outcomes. Engineering has two foci of action: the design of the product system itself; and the engineering organization and process which achieves the production focus. In relation to the engineering process some perform research of a prescriptive kind, as described by a number of design scientists, whose interest is to determine the processes that would be prescribed in order to achieve a desirable design (March & Smith, 1995; Walls, et al., 1992). In the development of a prescriptive theory, that is a theory which is designed to instruct future action, the researcher must be careful to consider the impact of the context in the situations observed, which are used to develop the theory, so that that context does not produce inappropriate prescription for other contexts (Dorst, 2008).

In relate to the former objective of engineering, the development of suitable solutions to needs, leads to work continuing until the need is satisfced

(Simon, 1996). If the need is routine we may be able to rely on precedence to guide a new design. If the need is very ambitious we might need to perform fundamental research to discover methods to solve the problem. In the case of routine design there is little that is particularly new that is discovered in the design process, since the design space is constrained to lead to an incremental variation of existing methods to achieve a suitable solution. In the case of design of novel products and systems there will be many discoveries made as the engineer seeks to integrate existing related knowledge of the various elements into a solution to the need. Another difference between science and engineering is that engineering is concerned with achieving a sufficient solution, which satisfices the need, rather than the completely satisfying theory sought by the scientist.

The engineer's goal is to make something which is useful. Usefulness is the characteristic that determines if an engineered product is successful and, by extension, the success of the engineer (Hopkins, 1954). To be useful a product must suit its purpose and intended situation of deployment, its *sitz im leben*.

To satisfy the opposite for the intended *sitz im leben* evaluation criterion the engineer may need to do significant research to develop understanding of the need. This requires significant care to ensure that the questions asked in the investigation do not lead to a particular set of findings which lead ultimately to the circular reasoning that the investigator finds what they presumed to be present by the nature of the question which they asked (Dobson, 2001) The process of designing a novel product, or a product using a different technology than has previously been used, to address that need will produce significant new knowledge of how that need can be addressed. Therefore, design is a means of creating new knowledge concerning the problem space and means of addressing the problem, and so a methodology for research.

The differences between engineering and science imply different epistemologies and possibly different ontologies. Both believe that there is a real world with which practitioners interact. Neither the engineer nor the scientist is a post-modernist, but rather both are significantly influenced by Positivist reasoning. As such both believe we can observe the world and make real observations and that multiple people could make the same observation. Both are Critical Realists who believe that observations are affected by the circumstances in which they are done but both believe that the object which prompted an observation is real and that differences in what is seen are the result of perturbations caused by the observation situation and differences of view point experienced by different observers. Recognition of this problem has led physical scientists and engineers to develop methods to compensate for variations of observation caused by the point of view. Both the scientist and engineer are positivists because they believe that there is real stuff.

The difference between the positions taken by the scientist and engineer is that a scientist is concerned with creating universally true knowledge and, in contrast, the engineer's concern is the delivery of apposite satisficing solutions to needs, which results in the engineer having a distinctly specific view of knowledge and discovery. To this end it is necessary for the engineer to have case specific knowledge. The engineer needs both general scientific knowledge and case specific knowledge. The engineer will also use phenomenological knowledge, that is knowledge which describes something repeatable may be useful even in the absence of a substantial theory to explain the observations. A lot of successful engineering work has been based on phenomenological knowledge, such as the engineering work based on graphical representations of relationships of variables where the relationship was too complex to express mathematically or numerically at the time the engineering work was done.

KNOWLEDGE DEVELOPED THROUGH DESIGN

Design and construction of a solution to a need demonstrates that it is possible to achieve a solution to address the need. That knowledge, alone, is not very exciting and would not be a satisfactory finding of a research project because it provides no foundation for further action. What is exciting as research is the development of understanding of how the need was addressed so that in future similar, but different, cases we have knowledge that will guide our approach. In this, useful research through the activity of design develops a theory which links design requirements with the solution developed and the method of developing the design (Markus, Majchrzak, & Gasser, 2002). Contrary to Hickey (1960), who asserted that "engineering answers the hypothesis that it is possible to build something", the purpose of engineering design is not to answer the hypothesis that it is possible to build a solution to the particular need, it is about coming up with an apposite satisficing solution to that need.

The engineer's goal is to produce a suitable solution to the need. Design based research determines the characteristics of a suitable solution, and carries through at least one design to a state in which it satisfices the need. Design based research in engineering concerns understanding what constitutes a suitable solution and determining whatever is needed to achieve such a solution. Hickey's view is a force-fit of an engineering activity into a scientific conceptualisation of research, which is inappropriate. It is notable that Hickey's view was published in 1960, when engineers were seeking to present and promote engineering as "scientific".

A point of difference between the design based research methodology and the scientific methodology is that design produces an instance of a solution to the need. That is, design produces a specific instantiation related to a specific problem. It is a reasonable to expect that there might have been other ways to address the need. And, we cannot prove that the solution offered is the best solution but rather, only an effective or satisficing solution. In contrast a scientist seeks to demonstrate that knowledge created is true, and so aims to make absolute assertions. Consequently, scientists are dissatisfied with the need to specify caveats on the quality or generalizability of the knowledge that they obtain.

Whilst the scientist cannot prove that the knowledge created is true their intention is to create universally applicable knowledge. In contrast the engineer's solution is never claimed to be universally desirable nor the best possible solution, but rather the best that the engineer was able to produce in the circumstances. Design yields background knowledge about components, materials and their behaviour which impact the product, but may also be useful in other cases.

CONCLUSION

Research is generally recognised as an activity which creates new knowledge. The discussion in this chapter has concerned the manner in which the action of designing novel engineering solutions to needs is a research process, contrary to much popular opinion. This chapter has examined the underlying conceptualisation of research embodied in the form of research which has become common in engineering since the 1960s, which is a form of research similar to that performed in the various science disciplines, and largely based on Positivist principles.

Underlying the conceptualisation of research is the question of what is seen as constituting knowledge. Research methods associated with the development of objective and generalizable knowledge are designed to produce scientific type understanding of extant things. This contrasts with the fundamental nature of engineering which concerns the development of solutions to needs. Therefore engineering has three levels of specificity. The need is specific and must be appropriately understood. The architectural approach to the design of a solution presents decisions about specific methods of instantiation of a solution to the need. The third layer of specificity in engineering design is the particular design which is used to realise the architectural approach which has been decided for the solution. Each of these three specific matters results in discovery related to specific ways of achieving solutions to the needs. The effectiveness of solutions which are offered may be evaluated but it is not possible to determine if any solution which is offered is the best possible solution or the best solution that could have been offered at a time or the best solution that could have been offered for a certain resource expenditure or according to some other measure of desirability. All that can be determined is that the solution satisfices the need when evaluated across the range of criteria determined as appropriate evaluation criteria. Therefore the kind of knowledge created by design as a research methodology is fundamentally different than the kind of knowledge created by science oriented research methodologies.

The knowledge created by science oriented research methodologies is desired for the intrinsic value it is believed to have. The knowledge is expected to be objective and generalizable and will be of some explicitly expressible form, consistent with the "know that" conceptualisation of knowledge. The knowledge created by the design methodology is desired for its instrumental value; the ability to achieve a solution to a problem that it enables. Knowledge generated through design is specific to the need addressed and the design approach used. The knowledge generated through design is of the "know how" form and may contribute to knowledge of the "knowing" form as experience with a number of design projects enables an engineer to develop better judgement about appropriate design strategies. The knowledge developed through design includes knowledge related to the achievement of the product which is designed and may contribute to knowledge of the design process as means for the performance of future design projects.

REFERENCES

Biggs, J. (1999). *Teaching for quality learning at university: What the student does*. Buckingham, UK: Society for Research into Higher Education, Open University Press.

Bucciarelli, L. L. (2003). *Engineering philosophy*. Delft, The Netherlands: DUP Satellite.

Department of Education Training and Youth Affairs. (2001). *Factors associated with completion of research higher degrees*. Department of Education Training and Youth Affairs.

Dobson, P. J. (2001). The philosophy of critical realism - An opportunity for information systems research. *Information Systems Frontiers*, *3*(2), 199–210. doi:10.1023/A:1011495424958

Dorst, K. (2008). Design research: A revolution-waiting-to-happen. *Design Research*, *29*(1), 4–11.

Ferris, T. L. J. (2007a). *Some early history of systems engineering - 1950's in IRE publications (part 1): The problem*. 17th International Symposium Systems Engineering: key to intelligent enterprises. San Diego, CA: International Council on Systems Engineering.

Ferris, T. L. J. (2007b). *Some early history of systems engineering - 1950's in IRE publications (part 2): The solution*. 17th International Symposium Systems Engineering: Key to intelligent enterprises. San Diego, CA: International Council on Systems Engineering.

Ferris, T. L. J. (2008). *Early history of systems engineering (Part 3) – 1950's in various engineering sources*. INCOSE International Symposium 2008. Utrecht, The Netherlands: International Council on Systems Engineering.

Ferris, T. L. J. (2009). *On the methods of research for systems engineering.* 7th Annual Conference on Systems Engineering Research. Loughborough, UK.

Gregor, S., & Jones, D. (2007). The anatomy of a design theory. *Journal of the Association for Information Systems, 8*(5), 312–335.

Hevner, A. R., March, S. T., Park, J., & Ram, S. (2004). Design science in Information Systems research. *Management Information Systems Quarterly, 28*(1), 75–105.

Hickey, A. E. Jr. (1960). The systems approach: Can engineers use the scientific method? *IRE Transactions on Engineering Management, 7*(2), 72–80. doi:10.1109/IRET-EM.1960.5007541

Hopkins, M. (1954). Human relations in engineering management. *Transactions of the IRE Professional Group on Engineering Management, 2*, 16–27. doi:10.1109/TPGEM.1954.5010170

Johnson, E. O., & Webster, W. M. (1952). The plasmatron: A continuously controllable gas-discharge developmental tube. *Proceedings of the IRE, 40*(6), 645–659. doi:10.1109/JRPROC.1952.274057

Lee, A. S., & Baskerville, R. L. (2003). Generalizing generalizability in Information Systems research. *Information Systems Research, 14*(3), 221–242. doi:10.1287/isre.14.3.221.16560

March, S. T., & Smith, G. F. (1995). Design and natural science research on Information Technology. *Decision Support Systems, 15*, 251–266. doi:10.1016/0167-9236(94)00041-2

Markus, M.-L., Majchrzak, A., & Gasser, L. (2002). A design theory for systems that support emergent knowledge processes. *Management Information Systems Quarterly, 26*(3), 179–212.

Nissen, M. E. (2006). *Harnessing knowledge dynamics: Principled organizational knowing & learning.* Hershey, PA: IGI Global.

Okress, E. C., Gleason, C. H., White, R. A., & Hayter, W. R. (1957). Design and performance of a high power pulsed magnetron. *IRE Transactions on Electron Devices, 4*(2), 161–171. doi:10.1109/T-ED.1957.14222

Riblet, H. B. (1956). A simplified automatic data plotter. *IRE Transactions on Instrumentation, 5*, 34–43. doi:10.1109/IRE-I.1956.5006999

Ryle, G. (1948). Knowing how and knowing that. *Proceedings of the Aristotelian Society,* (p. 46).

Simon, H. A. (1996). *The sciences of the artificial.* Cambridge, MA: The MIT Press.

Walls, J. G., Widmeyer, G. R., & El-Sawy, O. A. (1992). Building an Information System design theory for vigilent EIS. *Information Systems Research, 3*(1), 36–59. doi:10.1287/isre.3.1.36

KEY TERMS AND DEFINITIONS

Design: A human activity which combines existing knowledge and things to generate an output which is desired.

Engineering: A human activity centred on providing appropriate solutions to needs.

Know How: A form of knowledge which concerns being able to do particular itemised actions.

Know That: A form of knowledge which can be explicitly stated, and so can be learned and taught in the form of those statements.

Knowing: A form of knowledge related to the fluent and appropriate performance of action.

Knowledge: That which one has a suitable foundation for being assured is a true or appropriate description or method of interacting with the world or a part thereof.

Research: A human activity which creates new knowledge.

Science: A human activity centred on seeking to understand observed phenomena, things and situations with the purpose of providing accuratedescriptions and explanatory theories ofthe things observed.

Sitz im Leben: Situation in life, following usage in Theology which originated with Hermann Günkel.

ENDNOTE

[1] This was stated in the Master of Engineering by Research and Ph.D. regulations of the University of Adelaide in the late 1970s.

Chapter 21
Validation and Design Science Research in Information Systems

Rafael A. Gonzalez
Javeriana University, Colombia

Henk G. Sol
University of Groningen, The Netherlands

ABSTRACT

Validation within design science research in Information Systems (DSRIS) is much debated. The relationship of validation to artifact evaluation is still not clear. This chapter aims at elucidating several components of DSRIS in relation to validation. The role of theory and theorizing are an important starting point, because there is no agreement as to what types of theory should be produced. Moreover, if there is a theoretical contribution, then there needs to be clear guidance as to how the designed artifact and its evaluation are related to the theory and its validation. The epistemological underpinnings of DSRIS are also open to different alternatives, including positivism, interpretivism, and pragmatism, which affect the way that the validation strategy is conceived, and later on, accepted or rejected. The type of reasoning guiding a DSRIS endeavor, whether deductive, inductive, or abductive, should also be considered as it determines the fundamental logic behind any research validation. Once those choices are in place, artifact evaluation may be carried out, depending on the type of artifact and the type of technique available. Finally, the theoretical contribution may be validated from a formative (process-oriented) or summative (product-oriented) perspective.

INTRODUCTION

For researchers in computer science and information systems, carrying out their work and presenting their results in a scientific way has been a long-

standing concern. A significant contribution in this sense was submitted by Denning *et al.* (1989) as the result of the Task Force on the Core of Computer Science, which precisely stems from the question "Is computer science a science?" They presented the computer science (CS) discipline as resting on three paradigms: theory (rooted in mathemat-

DOI: 10.4018/978-1-4666-0179-6.ch021

ics), abstraction (rooted in the scientific method) and design (rooted in engineering). As such, they determine CS as sitting at the crossroads between those processes and thus being inherently, yet not totally, scientific. In fact, more recently, Denning (2005) still poses the original question in the title of a paper which establishes CS as a science, but with a credibility problem; in other words, CS as a science is seen as a work in progress. From an information systems perspective, around the same time as the Denning *et al.* paper, Nunamaker *et al.* (1990) contributed an influential paper concerned with a similar question. They support systems development as a research methodology in its own right, providing the process and the criteria required for this purpose. In their view, systems development results in an artifact that is the proof of concept for fundamental (design-oriented) research as well as potentially the focus of further (behavioral-oriented) research. Some years ago, a contribution by Hevner *et al.* followed a similar approach in presenting their proposal for a design science in information systems research (Hevner & March, 2003; Hevner, March, Park, & Ram, 2004). This will be the focus of the present chapter with an emphasis on the logic and process of validation within such a framework.

Design science seeks to create innovations that define the ideas, practices, technical capabilities, and products through which the analysis, design, implementation, management, and use of information systems can be effectively and efficiently accomplished (Hevner, March, Park, & Ram, 2004). As such, a design science research in information systems (DSRIS) contribution requires identifying a relevant organizational information and communication technology (ICT) problem, demonstrating that no solution exists, developing an ICT artifact that addresses this problem, rigorously evaluating the artifact, articulating the contribution to the ICT knowledge-base and to practice, and explaining the implications for ICT management and practice (March & Storey, 2008).

The genesis of design science may be placed in Herbert Simon's The Sciences of the Artificial (first published in 1969) in which he stated the difference between natural science, concerned with how things are, and design science, concerned with how things ought to be (Simon, 1996, p. 114). Following Simon's problem-solving tradition, design science was introduced to information systems researchers most clearly by March and Smith (1995) – notwithstanding the aforementioned related contributions by Denning *et al.* and Nunamaker *et al.* which do not explicitly use the term "design science" – who presented it as prescriptive research aimed at improving ICT performance, as opposed to natural science, corresponding to descriptive research aimed at understanding the nature of ICT. An important point was that information systems research should actually integrate both perspectives, an argument that came back on Hevner *et al.* (2004), establishing DSRIS as an adequate way of carrying out research with both relevance and rigor. This 2004 paper was the main thrust behind a strong DSRIS movement in the information systems and computer science fields, which has resulted in numerous journal special issues, a special conference (DESRIST), a book (Hevner & Chatterjee, 2010) and a rapidly increasing number of research articles claiming to use design science. This growth is probably due to the fact that design science research has been carried out for some time now, but without a common vocabulary and without widespread acceptance from publications emphasizing more traditional research approaches. With a DSRIS framework in place and an increasing openness from several publication targets, it is now possible to present the results of DSRIS in a more straightforward manner and without the need to force what is essentially the design of an artifact as the result of a kind of research that does not fit its nature. Nonetheless, in this short time of almost exponential growth many issues remain open to discussion, including agreement on the ontological and epistemological foundations of design science, the relationship between artifact evaluation and theory validation, as well as explicit guidelines for carrying out DSRIS projects (Gonzalez, 2009; Piirainen, Gonzalez, & Kolfschoten, 2010).

This chapter is aimed at contributing to the discussion on precisely those issues, taking into consideration the fact that they are related to each other. The main objective is to provide a framework for deciding, structuring and presenting DSRIS contributions which explicitly declare an onto-epistemological grounding and which also make clear how the artifact will be evaluated and how the resulting theory (if any) will be validated. By specifying the philosophical underpinnings of a DSRIS project, the researcher(s) is (are) able to clearly position the role of theory and theorizing within their research and the ensuing validation approach. Having determined whether indeed there is to be a theoretical contribution – some authors claim that DSRIS is not at all about theory development, notably the 1995 account of design science (March & Smith, 1995) – the researcher(s) must explicitly declare the kind of theory referred to. In addition, there should be recognition of the kind of reasoning which guides the DSRIS process (inductive, abductive or deductive). Those elements offer sufficient backing to the strategy used to validate the theoretical contribution, the specific technique(s) employed and the relationship with the evaluation of the artifact in order to guarantee consistency.

While specific guidelines or procedural recommendations for carrying out DSRIS are also open to discussion, they are beyond the scope of this chapter. However, it seems reasonable to expect that the choices made in terms of epistemology, theory and validation have an impact on the structure and ordering of DSRIS stages. Moreover, given the iterative nature of most design activities, Hevner's (2007) cyclical approach is likely to best embody the design science vision of integrating both relevance and rigor, as seen in Figure 1. Through three DSR cycles (rigor, relevance and design), the *Environment* (the ap-

plication domain and the problems or opportunities therein) and the *Knowledge Base* (theories and methods, experience and meta-artifacts) can be integrated into a main *Design Cycle* where an artifact is built and evaluated, founded on the *Knowledge Base* and aimed at solving a relevant problem in the *Environment* (Hevner & Chatterjee, 2010, pp. 16-19). The specific ordering and relationship between the cycles will depend on the intent and extent of the DSRIS project – for further methodological guidance see (Peffers, Tuunanen, Rothenberger, & Chatterjee, 2007). Typically, though, a problem will motivate the start of a DSRIS project, given that design science is issue-driven, rather than theory-driven (Klabbers, 2006). As such, the *Relevance Cycle* will often set the stage for the rest of the cycles. The *Rigor Cycle* will be subsequently or simultaneously executed in order to gather a necessary and sufficient set of theories, methods or models which are applicable to the problem at hand. Finally, the *Design Cycle* will proceed between building and evaluating the artifact thoroughly before field testing it in the application domain. As a result, some form of knowledge contribution will be added to the knowledge base. It will always be possible to reiterate a cycle or go back to other cycles as the design progresses (for instance to refine requirements or to find new theoretical grounding for an emergent design issue). In fact, all three cycle are typically connected to each other and it would be simplistic to expect that they can be carried out in sequence.

The structure of this chapter is as follows. The Background section present the epistemology, type of reasoning and theory development choices open to design science research. Epistemology may be positivist, interpretive or pragmatist. The type of reasoning may be inductive, deductive, abductive or inductive-hypothetical. Theory development may be non-existent or aimed at producing different kinds of theory, including: conceptual, prescriptive, descriptive, predictive, intermediate (with respect to the artifact created)

Figure 1. Design science research cycles, adapted from (Hevner, 2007; Hevner & Chatterjee, 2010, p. 16)

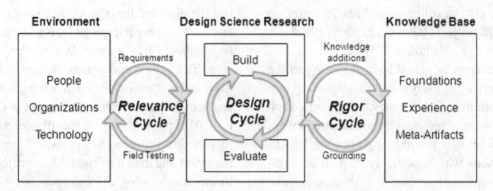

or meta-theoretical. The subsequent section, Evaluating Artifacts and Validating Theory in Design Science Research, presents the different options and techniques for evaluating and validating design science research contributions. Evaluation techniques may be based on the type of artifact (constructs, models, methods or instantiations) or on the type of technique (feature-based, theoretical, empirical, based on acceptance or done through simulation, among others). Validation may be formative (aimed at the process) or summative (aimed at the product). After presenting those components, the chapter goes on to present some Limitations and then the corresponding Future Research Directions to deal with those limitations. We then offer a concluding section, followed by a list of references, additional reading material and some key definitions.

BACKGROUND

Epistemology of Design Science Research

The epistemological underpinnings of any research approach constitute the philosophical basis which establishes the worldview held by the researchers and the main assumptions behind the research method. In information systems research, there has been a long-standing discussion

surrounding the epistemological alternatives open to different kinds of research problems, researchers and institutions. Typically, these choices stem from the classical division of positivism vs. interpretivism or include a third "critical" alternative (Klein & Myers, 1999). This epistemological openness has been both a feature and a source of confusion within the information systems field, but is a natural consequence of a discipline which combines computer science, organizational theory, psychology, and economy, among others. This generates both an ample richness for designing ICT systems in a real organizational environment where people are part of the system, but also generates potential inconsistencies and often results in researchers neglecting or not explicitly declaring their epistemological assumptions.

DSRIS is not exempt from this epistemological openness (Niehaves, 2007). On the one hand, it is rooted in information systems, which means that it inherits some of the open issues from information systems research – despite the fact that it also aims at solving a critical one: the imbalance between rigor and relevance in information systems research; see, for example (Benbasat & Zmud, 1999). On the other hand, DSRIS also comes from a problem-solving tradition which relates it to additional disciplines, such as architecture, industrial design and management (Cross, 2001). This stretches the philosophical background of DSRIS even more, but it is a crucial aspect of design that it be open to multiple theories and disciplines, as this enables the creative design process to apply knowledge from different fields into solving a problem.

Nonetheless, the epistemological choices related to a specific DSRIS research project are still necessary in order to guarantee rigor and consistency across the design science effort and in order to clearly separate it from a normal (non-scientific) design activity. Three epistemological choices are thus available for researchers to guide their DSR projects: positivism, interpretivism and pragmatism.

Positivism assumes that "the truth is out there" and that it can be reached through the methods of science (Wynn, 2001). It claims that the social world can be described by law-like generalizations stemming from collection of value-free facts (Chen & Hirschheim, 2004). It aims at verifiability or falsification of theories and believes in causality, supported by a quantitative-empirical methodological approach (Hirschheim, 1992). Positivist research can be identified by the presence of: hypotheses, propositions, models, quantitative variables and statistic inference of "objective" data (Klein & Myers, 1999). Extreme positivism in information systems research sees technology as neutral, believes in rational management, ignores power relations and conflict, sees organizations as individual closed entities and focuses on the business environment (Mitev, 2000). It would be hard to associate DSRIS with positivism as a whole, given that positivism theoretically excludes the researcher influence from the research process, while a design science approach must of necessity include the researcher / designer as a reflective practitioner. However, Niehaves (2007) has pointed out that some accounts of DSRIS do follow some of the language and premises of positivism.

Interpretivism argues that both the researcher and the human actors in the phenomenon under study interpret the situation (Nandhakumar & Jones, 1997). Instead of generalization it aims at in-depth understanding (Chen & Hirschheim,

2004). Interpretive research is identified with the presence of participant's perspectives as primary sources of information analyzed against cultural or contextual circumstances (Klein & Myers, 1999). Interpretivism sees organizations as social (conversational) processes in which the world is interpreted in a particular way, which legitimates shared actions and establishes shared norms (Checkland & Holwell, 1998). Interpretive approaches aim at understanding the information systems context and the way in which actors draw on and interpret elements of context; furthermore, they question the utility of generalizations, emphasizing the insight obtained with descriptive efforts (Mitev, 2000). *Constructivism* may be seen as a subset of interpretivism insofar as it is grounded on the same philosophical underpinnings, namely phenomenology and hermeneutics, and both crucially hold that the inquirer and the phenomenon under inquiry are inseparable, as opposed to positivism which holds the view of an independent observer. Accordingly, constructivism can also be considered as a relevant choice for a DSRIS epistemology. While constructivism has not been strongly or widely suggested as an epistemological alternative for DSRIS yet, it has been proposed as an adequate epistemology for organizational design science that can bridge the gap between rigor and relevance (Avenier, 2010). In this proposal constructivism is seen as good fit with Simon's sciences of the artificial and as such most of the arguments hold equally for DSRIS.

Pragmatism is a key contribution of American philosophy, pioneered by C.S. Peirce, William James and John Dewey (James, 2000, p. xiv in the introduction by Giles Gunn). Strictly speaking, pragmatism is not just epistemological in scope, but it does hold a particular theory of knowledge and truth. Some hold pragmatism to be aligned with positivism, but while in both cases facts are given prominence as a source of knowledge, the distinction between a language of observation and a language of theory was strongly rejected by James (Houser & Kloesel, 1992, p. xxxiv).

Moreover, Peirce's development of abductive reasoning (discussed in the next subsection) also places pragmatism further from positivism, especially due to the active role of the researcher, as opposed to the positivist requirement of an independent researcher which reduces his or her influence on the process of achieving knowledge (Niehaves, 2007). Essentially, pragmatism places the weight of truth on the consequences of beliefs, where beliefs are progressively attained, for instance, through the method of science (Peirce, 1992a). This stems from the understanding that our beliefs guide our desires and shape our actions. In other words, ideas are related to the effects they have on the real world: effects (actions), beliefs (conceptions) and the objects they refer to are inseparable. This is often reduced to the famous statement that Peirce used to characterize his early notion of pragmatism: "Consider what effects, which might conceivably have practical bearings, we conceive the object of our conception to have. Then our conception of these effects is the whole of our conception of the object." (Peirce, 1992b, p. 132). This would seem to fit the design science aim towards utility; given the strong claim that truth is utility or "what works in practice" (March & Smith, 1995). However, some claim that rather than linking truth to utility, design science artifacts have no truth, only utility and hence pragmatism would not be appropriate (Hevner *et al.*, 2004). This is precisely why we need to also consider the type of reasoning and the role of theory behind a DSRIS project.

Type of Reasoning in Design Science

The reasoning behind scientific inquiry has been classically divided into deduction and induction, based on the type of logic behind the reasoning process. Roughly, *deductivereasoning* refers to a "top down" process where the researcher starts from general theoretical propositions that are narrowed down to testable hypotheses which are then confirmed or falsified through observation (experimentation). The opposite approach, *inductivereasoning*, starts from a set of observations from which patterns are extracted to formulate tentative hypotheses that are tested and generalized into theoretical propositions.

With those two alternatives, design science research may include either, both or neither type of reasoning. First of all, one needs to consider whether there will indeed be any hypothesis testing at all. This is related to the role of theorizing and the kind of theory aimed for, as discussed in the next section. From a radical design-centered perspective, the creation of the artifact should suffice as long as the artifact is useful for solving a problem in a novel way, and provided that the researcher documents the process and the product as a contribution to current (information systems) design knowledge. This suggests that the type of reasoning may be focused on the creative design process without concerning itself with whether it is inductive or deductive, given that design does not follow a strictly unique logical process and is considered rather as iterative.

Simon had already pointed out that the dichotomy between induction and deduction gave only partial views of the scientific enterprise (Simon, Langley, & Bradshaw, 1981). Data, for example, may be gathered without clear theoretical preconceptions or theory derived from other theory. By understanding scientific discovery as problem-solving, Simon distinguished between expert problem-solving in a well-understood domain vis-à-vis novice problem-solving in a novel domain. While the first case is closer to how "normal science" works like, design science is closer to the latter, implying the use of "weak methods" out of necessity: "strong methods" are simply not available, by definition, when entirely new territory is to be explored (*ibid.* 1981). We have already established that design science is different from normal behavioral science precisely because it is concerned with how things ought to be, so it is to be expected that weaker methods are employed and that clear-cut uses of induction or deduction are hard to integrate into a DSRIS project. Moreover, there is an ideal connection between the process of design and that of innovation within DSRIS: innovation understood as a process of *counterinductive* decision-making, precisely because the resulting decision goes against what is to be expected; it changes expectations, it changes the existing structure (Luhmann, 1997, p. 89).

Accordingly, besides induction or deduction, Peirce was a proponent of *abduction* as a more powerful alternative. Rather than focusing on deduction as opposed to induction, Peirce found that since they are both error-prone, the principle of self-correction and growth holds equally; the really crucial factor is that there be a "hearty and active desire to learn what is true" (Peirce, 1998a). Essentially, Peirce argued that the focus on deduction / induction confused the actual logic of science. Hypothesis testing, at the most, corrects the value of a ratio or modifies a hypothesis in a way already contemplated as possible (Peirce, 1998b). Deduction, starting from known premises, is weaker at generating new ideas. According to Peirce, the only way to actually generate significant new knowledge is the generation of the hypothesis itself, something which precedes the induction process and which he termed abduction. While induction seeks for facts, abduction seeks a theory and this search is part of a mental process of revision of the belief system that a researcher holds. Abduction is then nothing but guessing, yet informed guessing animated by hope (*ibid.* 1998b). It should be noted, however, that these strong claims are not meant to do away with either induction or deduction, but rather to point out that to generate interesting or relevant hypotheses a social human process is required. Indeed, Simon *et al.* (1981) report on two software programs (AM and BACON) which use heuristics to either generate concepts from existing concepts (deduction) or generate new laws from analyzing existing data (induction). Similar efforts have been presented more recently, demonstrating that it is possible to "automate" the induction or deduction process,

at the same time highlighting the role of human intervention in generating meaningful hypothesis rather than just new hypotheses. As a result, the point is not to replace induction or deduction with abduction, but to recognize the importance of abduction as an integral (preceding) part of the two basic types of reasoning. It is not surprising then that DSRIS, given the already mentioned creative process involved, has already been associated with abduction (Kuechler & Vaishnavi, 2008).

There is a fourth alternative, which also departs from the division between induction and deduction, but goes further in widening the focus and serves as a framework to consider all types of reasoning together, given the likelihood that a design process employs all of them. Rather than placing the weight of scientific discovery solely on the logic of reasoning of the scientist, it considers it as a result of communicative scientific activity. This is the *Singerian form of inquiry*, or Singerian inquiring systems, as discussed in (Churchman, 1971, pp. 186-205). This strategy centers around the design problem of revision: when, how and why do we revise a system of beliefs or hypotheses? In Leibnizian (deductive) inquiring systems, revision depends on the relative weights of competing 'fact nets'. In Lockean (inductive) inquiring systems, revision is based upon consensus between 'reasonable men'. In Kantian inquiring systems, the scientific community shares a common a priori mode of shaping and interpreting empirical data; revision consists in self-examining the appropriateness of a specific representation as imposed on the data, in order to reach a minimal set of assertions that are absolutely necessary in order for the inquiring system to be capable of receiving inputs (*ibid.* 1971, pp. 133-134). Hegelian inquiring systems encourage conflict as a source of revision (as opposed to Locke); once the community has arrived at a shared world view (*Weltanschauung*) then a counter-*Weltanschauung* should be created. This means that when data and hypothesis are finally mutually compatible, it is time to "rock the boat" and encourage a revolution that departs from this *status quo* in order for the opposing views to dialectically reach a revision. With Singer, rather than attempting to force a specific "logical reconstruction" of science, the argument is that scientists use the whole scope of inquiry to aid in the design task. One process through which this holistic inquiry is achieved is "sweeping-in" which consists in bringing concepts and variables into the existing model to overcome inconsistencies in readings. A crucial aspect of this sweeping-in lies in its endlessness, because rather than aiming at agreement it aims at intensifying disputes (as in Hegel). However, the process is not capriciously endless, but anchored in a deep ethical understanding of science. This ethical underpinnings mean that the inquiring systems have the following set of principles: (1) the purpose is creating knowledge; (2) the measure of its performance is societal; (3) the client is mankind; (4) knowledge should go outward to be useful for all society; (5) the inquiring system needs a cooperative environment; (6) the decision-makers are ideally everyone; (7) the designers are ideally everyone. In addition, the assertions of the inquiring system should be stated in the imperative, so rather than "is", they should be stated in "ought" form. It is clear then that the Singerian inquiring systems (as discussed by Churchman) are deeply connected to design and problem-solving as a holistic, participative inter-disciplinary activity.

A specific "modelcycle" for Singerian inquiring systems is the *inductive-hypothetic* strategy (Sol, 1982), where artifacts are designed as prescriptive conceptual models that are to be validated or theories that can be refuted or hypotheses/propositions that can be rejected. The main characteristics of the inductive-hypothetic strategy are: (1) specification and testing of premises in an inductive way, by emphasizing the conceptualization and problem specification activities; (2) emphasis on an interdisciplinary approach; (3) enabling the generation of alternatives for solving the problem; (4) the analysis and synthesis activi-

ties are interdependent. The inductive-hypothetic strategy cycles through theory and practice by iteratively going through the construction of descriptive empirical models, to descriptive conceptual models, to prescriptive conceptual models and finally to prescriptive empirical models upon which the validation and evaluation is carried out. It should be noted that the inductive-hypothetic approach, based on Singerian inquiring systems, may also be placed as closely related to pragmatism, at least when we consider that Singer also belonged to the pragmatist group of philosophers led by James and Peirce. Nonetheless, Churchman's emphasis in using Singer's model is that it views pragmatism from an ethical point of view, taking responsibility for the consequences of the scientific inquiry.

Theory Development in Design Science

In abductive reasoning, we seek for theory; yet, design science is more issue-driven than theory-driven (Klabbers, 2006). Accordingly, researchers in design science need to make an explicit claim regarding the role that theory and theorizing have within their project. March and Smith (1995) originally and explicitly excluded theory development from design science, meaning that there should be *no theoretical contribution* (at least in the traditional sense of theory development). Despite this strong assertion, several other authors have become concerned with this exclusion as it may render the scientific claims of DSRIS weakened, placing the emphasis on design and not on science. Indeed, they propose that theorizing should be an intricate part of DSRIS as it is in other scientific inquiries (Gregor, 2009; Kuechler & Vaishnavi, 2008; Markus, Majchrzak, & Gasser, 2002; Walls, Widmeyer, & El Sawy, 1992). Furthermore, theory development already has a place within design science outside the information systems (IS) discipline (Friedman, 2003) or is seen as a necessary result of information systems research, regardless of whether it is based on natural science, social science or design science (Gregor, 2006). Having explicitly declared the aim to build, develop or extend theory, the researcher then needs to specify which type of theory will be contributed.

The choice regarding the type of theory to be developed may or may not be linked to the epistemological foundations of the research project. According to Iivari (2007), the type of theory produced should determine the epistemology that underlies design science research. Gregor (2006), however, has strongly argued that the type of theory produced by information systems research should not depend on the underlying paradigm; for her, theory is independent from specific ontological or epistemological choices. Broadly, the types of theory that can be attained through DSRIS are: conceptual, descriptive or prescriptive (Iivari, 2007). For Iivari, *conceptual theory* should express the essences of a particular research territory along with their relationships. This may take the form of taxonomies, typologies or conceptual frameworks which have "no truth value" given that they do not originate from or become validated through observations but rather are derived from existing concepts. *Descriptive theory* in the context of information systems is aimed at understanding the nature of information technology (March & Smith, 1995). Because descriptive theory is obtained through observational facts (whose empirical regularities are transformed into hypotheses and theories) then this type of theory does have truth value (Iivari, 2007). *Prescriptive theory* in DSR may be obtained through a knowledge-using (rather than producing) activity aimed at improving ICT performance (March & Smith, 1995). As such, it is concerned with how things ought to be in order to attain some utilitarian ends and results in design process and design product knowledge. Since the emphasis is on (potential future) utility, it has no truth value (Iivari, 2007; March & Smith, 1995). It is this kind of theory which has probably received the most support within the DSRIS community.

Prescriptive design theories were actually one of the first strong contributions to DSRIS, through the work of (Walls *et al.*, 1992) and later (Markus *et al.*, 2002). A prescriptive design theory in their framework is based on theoretical underpinnings which say how a design process can be carried out effective and feasibly and whose purpose is achievement of goals. As such, they are composed of design product knowledge and design process knowledge. The design product knowledge is composed of meta-requirements (a class of goals to which the theory applies), meta-design (a class of artifacts hypothesized to meet the meta-requirements), kernel theories (founding premises which govern the design requirements), and testable design product hypotheses (which are used to verify whether indeed the meta-design satisfies the meta-requirements). The design process knowledge follows a similar construction aimed at the method for producing the artifact: the design method itself, the kernel theories which govern the design process, and testable design process hypotheses (does the method actually conduce to an artifact consistent with the meta-design). Again, the idea is that the theory can be validated with respect to utility, not with respect to truth. It should be noted, however, that one of the main guiding principles of DSRIS is that it should combine relevance and rigor and in that same sense, from a pragmatist viewpoint, truth and utility go hand in hand (Hevner *et al.*, 2004).

Moreover, a design theory need not be prescriptive. Venable (2006) suggests that utility-based design theories should actually be through of as *predictive utility theories*. They should be predictive about the utility of applying the meta-design to solve the meta-requirements. This also simplifies the Walls *et al.* model by excluding kernel theories, testable design hypothesis and design methods. Instead, they link the problem space and the solution space through a predictive hypothesis that asserts the potential utility of the theory. Thus, utility is stated (and evaluated against) criteria of efficacy, effectiveness and perhaps elegance or ethicality; also, the cost and practicality may be evaluated with respect to alternative means. In this kind of theory, the link between utility and truth is expressed in terms of the truthfulness that the theory has in representing the utility of the type of solution for solving the problems inherent to a particular class of requirements.

Some will be concerned with the fact that evaluation or validation sits at the design / requirements level, while the theory is expressed at the meta-requirements / meta-design level. In an extreme case, this would result in *domain-independent design theories* (Käkölä & Taalas, 2008). Yet, given the emphasis that is placed on (potential) utility – and thus real world problem-solving, the only way that such theories can be examined for validity and utility is through applying specific domain-knowledge and creating domain-specific design theory in the evaluation or redesign of real information systems inside specific organizations.

One last option for placing the theoretical contribution within DSRIS is to describe it in design science terms to begin with. Design science research creates artifacts that can solve real-world problems; these artifacts can be: constructs, models, methods or instantiations (Hevner *et al.*, 2004; March & Smith, 1995). For Winter (2008), although theory building is not design science research, *theories as a fifth kind of 'intermediate' artifact* need to be included into DSRIS. In this view the theory specifies cause-effect relationships that bridge the constructs (concepts) to the models and methods, where the latter focus on means-ends relationships. Accordingly, while the models and methods suggest the mechanisms through which a specific end (or set of ends) is attained, the theory articulates the conceptual cause-effect relationships behind those mechanisms in order to be able to test the theoretical premises as regular hypotheses. Gregor and Jones (2007) take a *meta-theoretical view of design theory*, where the artifacts themselves (save for the instantiations) make up the theoretical contribution in DSRIS. Constructs, models and

methods are actually theoretical in nature and it is only the instantiations which correspond to the material artifact as such. In this last view, it is not necessary to come up with a specific kind of theory in which to fit the knowledge contributions of DSRIS; rather, the non-material results (constructs, models, principles and methods) embody the theoretical contribution. However, this kind of design theory still needs to be presented in a specific form, made up of eight components: purpose and scope, constructs, principles of form and function (models), artifact mutability (changes in the artifact anticipated in the theory), testable propositions, justificatory knowledge, principles of implementation (methods) and an expository instantiation (prototype). It should be noted that this type of theory does include a kernel theory (justificatory knowledge) and does include claims to truth (testable propositions).

EVALUATING ARTIFACTS AND VALIDATING THEORY IN DESIGN SCIENCE RESEARCH

The agreement is that DSRIS should produce an artifact (or a set of artifacts) and that it should be thoroughly evaluated before attempting to implement it in the real-world environment where the problem needs to be solved. If we compare two key contributions to DSRIS, on the one hand, March and Smith (1995) attach the activities of *discovery* (generating or proposing scientific claims) and *justification* (testing scientific claims for validity) to natural science and present them as separate from (but parallel to) the activities of *building* (constructing an artifact for a specific purpose) and *evaluation* (determining how well the artifact performs) attached to design science. On the other hand, this distinction was revised by Hevner *et al.* (2004) in order to support the claim that information systems research should involving the two complementary paradigms of behavioral science (rooted in natural science).

In this account the activities of building and evaluating (an artifact) were merged with those of developing and justifying (theory) – indeed this is presented as *Develop / Build* and *Justify / Evaluate*. This helps state the case in favor of research which is both relevant and rigorous, but may also leave behind lack of clarity with regards to how theory development and validation should be seen in DSRIS. Actually, and perhaps as a consequence of this potential confusion, the most recent version of Hevner and Chaterjee's (2010) framework now only include the *Build / Design* and *Evaluate* activities (Develop and Justify are no longer present), as seen in Figure 1. However, if there is going to be some theory development as part of the inquiry, then this raises the question of how to articulate the relationship between artifact evaluation and theory validation.

Artifact Evaluation

Design science produces artifacts to attain goals (Simon, 1996, p. 114). As such, the resulting artifacts are assessed against criteria of value or utility (March & Smith, 1995). This assessment is based on rigorous evaluation of the artifact, understood as the process of determining how well the artifact performs, which requires development of metrics and measurement of the artifact according to such metrics. Furthermore, metrics should depend upon specific assessment criteria corresponding to the resulting type of artifact, as can be seen in Table 1. The evaluation criteria offered here are quite generic and need to be operationalized for the target artifact in order to be measurable. If we refer back to the DSRIS framework on Figure 1, these criteria should be applied within the *Evaluate* activity of the *Design Cycle*. However, "Instantiations" are artifacts realized within the environment, and as such embody the transition from the *Design* into the *Environment*. Accordingly, evaluation in this case belongs to *Field Testing* within the *Relevance Cycle* (see Figure 1), since efficiency, effectiveness and impact are all context-dependent

and can only be fully assessed after the instantiation has been deployed. Nonetheless, it is also possible (desirable) to test those same features in advance (e.g. in the lab) with the caveat that they are only estimates or predictions of potential efficiency, potential effectiveness or potential impact. As we will see shortly, simulation and the technology acceptance model are two examples of techniques that can be employed to determine these potential effects prior to deployment of the instantiated artifact in the real-world environment. In any case, whether it is through field testing, lab testing or potential user assessments, it is to be expected that the results of the evaluation bring up defects or shortcomings that can be corrected by iterating back to the *Design Cycle*. In fact, all cycles in DSRIS are open-ended, because even if the artifact passes an acceptance criteria test, its use will end up modifying the environment and will possibly result in new opportunities or gaps for the future (hence in new requirements within the *Relevance Cycle*).

Stemming from March and Smith's initial considerations, Cleven, Gubler, & Hüner (2009) came up with a more complete overview of artifact evaluation alternatives that should guide researchers in determining the appropriate evaluation configuration, depending not only on (1) the type of artifact, but also on (2) the approach (qualitative vs. quantitative), (3) the artifact focus (technical, organizational or strategic), (4) the underlying epistemology (positivism, vs. interpretivism), (5) the function of the artifact (knowledge, control, development or legitimization), (6) the method (action research, case study, field experiment, formal proofs, controlled experiment, prototype or survey), (7) the object (whether it is to evaluate the product or the process), (8) the ontology (realism vs. nominalism), (9) the perspective (economic, deployment, engineering or epistemological), (10) the position (external or internal), (11) the reference point (artifact against research gap, artifact against real world, or research gap against real world) and, finally, on (12) the

Table 1. Evaluation criteria against the type of artifact designed, based on (March & Smith, 1995)

Type of artifact	Evaluation criteria
Constructs: concepts that form the vocabulary of a domain	Completeness, simplicity, understandability, ease of use
Models: sets of propositions or statements expressing relationships among constructs	Fidelity, completeness, level of detail, robustness, ease of use
Methods: sets of steps used to perform a task	Operationality, efficiency, generality, ease of use
Instantiations: realizations of an artifact in its environment	Efficiency, effectiveness, impact

time that the evaluation takes place (*ex ante* or *ex post*). This framework does not mention "validation" and "theory" is understood as a fifth type of artifact, as in Winter (2008). This suggests that theory is amenable to evaluation using the same twelve dimensions. It should be noted that Cleven *et al.* uses Peffers *et al.* (2007) as the methodological framework for DSRIS, rather than the one shown in Figure 1. The main difference is that the latter is less prescriptive and more conceptually oriented towards presenting the pillars of DSRIS (rigor, relevance and design) and their cyclical nature, while in Peffers *et al*, specific activities are presented in a sequence (with iterations to previous steps in a fashion akin to traditional systems development lifecycles). Although one of the dimensions in Celeven *et al.*'s framework asks whether the evaluation takes place in *ex ante* or *ex post* mode, Peffers *et al.* explicitly place evaluation after a demonstration of the artifact in a specific context. Cleven *et al.* note this by allowing *ex ante* evaluation to be part of the design activity (for instance aiding the selection among candidate artifacts) or by allowing the demonstration to also be part of the evaluation (for instance when the evaluation method is case study). On the one hand, this agrees with the view that evaluation or validation are not a one-time, single-point effort, but rather a continued concern to build trust, transparency and legitimacy. On the other hand, it also places Celeven *et al.*'s contribution as suited for assessing DSRIS contributions, even more than artifacts themselves. In other words, this framework may aid an evaluator of a DSRIS project determine whether

all the dimensions are explicit and whether the evaluation strategy fits with that specific configuration, as can be illustrated by Cleven *et al.* when they apply their framework to characterize published DSRIS papers.

With regards to more specific methods or instruments for artifact evaluation, Siau and Rossi (2008) have come up with a survey of existing evaluation techniques which are classified in terms of an underlying ontology (realism vs. nominalism) and epistemology (positivism vs. interpretivism), as well as depending on whether they are based on feature comparison, theoretical and conceptual investigation, or empirical evaluation, as shown in Table 2. This contribution is more instrumental in determining specific evaluation techniques that fit with a specific onto-epistemology. Feature comparison is typically aimed at comparing an instantiated artifact to other previous instantiations in order to determine improvements. Theoretical and conceptual investigation techniques offer analytical tools for evaluating artifacts with different levels of formalism and empirical evaluation requires empirical data to support the assessment. Seen from the point of view of the framework in Figure 1, feature comparison is a technique that may be applied in any of the cycles, or indeed across them. At the *Relevance Cycle* one would identify the artifacts that already exist in the environment and indeed the features that are susceptible of improvement. In the *Rigor Cycle* one would identify comparable artifacts in other environments and theoretical contributions that help in defining and classifying the features to compare. Most techniques then would be applied

Table 2. Artifact evaluation techniques, based on (Siau & Rossi, 2008)

Category	Evaluation technique	Onto-epistemology
Feature comparison	Feature checklist	Realist-interpretive
Theoretical and conceptual investigation	Metamodelling	Realist-positivist
	Metric analysis	Realist-positivist
	Paradigmatic analysis	Realist-positivist
	Contingency identification	Realist-positivist
	Ontological evaluation	Realist-positivist
	Cognitive evaluation	Nominalist-interpretive
Empirical evaluation	Survey	Nominalist-positivst
	Lab experiment	Realist-positivist
	Field experiment	Realist-positivist
	Case study	Nominalist-interpretive
	Action research	Nominalist-interpretive
	Verbal protocol	Nominalist-interpretive

in the *Design Cycle* (within the *Evaluate* activity) against the comparable artifacts and features identified in the *Rigor* and *Relevance* cycles. However, field experiments, case studies and action research (as well as some surveys) may be applied in the *Field Testing* transition between *Design* and *Environment*.

It should be noted that both Cleven *et al.* and Siau and Rossi exclude pragmatism (as an onto-epistemological alternative) from their frameworks. More importantly, Siau and Rossi's framework has not been produced within a DSRIS perspective; indeed, as the evaluation techniques show, it can be part of a completely different research approach. In addition, as Cleven *et al.* point out, Siau and Rossi focus on modeling methods; this in effect means that they are only considering one type of artifact. Nonetheless, by considering both contributions, a researcher in information system has a good overview of the evaluation techniques available and a starting framework for selecting which one is more appropriate for the project at hand.

Perhaps surprisingly, neither Cleven *et al.* nor Siau and Rossi consider the *technology acceptance model* (TAM) within their frameworks. TAM is a widely used evaluation model to assess potential user acceptance of information systems (Davis, Bagozzi, & Warshaw, 1989). The main premise behind (the original) TAM is that *perceived usefulness* and *perceived ease of use* are of primary relevance for user acceptance of an information system. This model has been revised recently to include the factors that precede or influence this initial perception: experience, voluntariness, subjective norms, image, job relevance, output quality and result demonstrability (Legris, 2003). As can be seen, both variations of TAM place the focus on the user, not on the artifact. This might explain why neither Cleven *et al.* nor Siau and Rossi include it; this emphasis on user acceptance can be best understood as stemming from a pragmatist epistemology placing utility above other considerations – indeed, the goal in this case is to establish the utility of the artifact not its internal features or claims to truth, because the object is to solve a real-world problem. It should come as no surprise then that many DSRIS contributions are actually evaluated using TAM, rather than the other evaluation techniques available (Donaldson & Golding, 2009; Purao & Storey, 2008).

Another widely used method for evaluating artifacts for potential utility is *simulation*. By systematically exposing the artifact to a simulated environment, it is possible to experimentally assess its (potential) utility. On the one hand, simulation may be used to measure performance and compare the results to existing artifacts or the current situation in the real-world environment (see for example Chang, 2008). On the other hand, simulation may be applied to evaluate the value of an artifact based on historical (or artificial) data. In this case, the artifact should be a prototype whose inputs are taken from the simulation and the outputs compared to historical data in order to empirically determine the prototype's ability to behave according to the proposed hypothetical expectations (see for example Muntermann, 2009). In both cases, evaluation is of the *ex ante* type (which is also the case in TAM) and can only provide evidence with respect to potential utility or value. This, however, fits with the premise that DSRIS artifacts be evaluated thoroughly in lab conditions before being released to the environment (Hevner, 2007). Furthermore, one could argue that actual implementation exceeds the realm of DSRIS and may be a task for consultants or spin-offs and where actual acceptance and usage may be conditioned by other factors not directly related to the artifact or the theory (like managerial support, resource availability or change management, among others).

Besides the aforementioned evaluation techniques, there are many other (mostly deterministic) metrics or models that may contribute to evaluating IS artifacts. In the information systems field, several options are available for assessing the impact of an IS in financial or economic terms, focusing on the bottom-line that the IS helps modify. Satisfaction metrics (of employees, users, managers or clients) can also be used to assess the effect of an IS. Performance improvement is another classic approach to ICT / IS evaluation and it may be focused at the technical level, at individual performance or at firm-wide performance.

A more qualitative approach focuses on IS success / failure studies, where several variables or dimensions are studied in order to determine the factors that determine an IS success or failure. In broader terms, ICT may be measured with respect to the contribution it makes to a community or to society at large, for example by using ICT development indexes as a source for assessing this impact. In general, it should be pointed out that the verification and validation techniques from systems and software engineering are applicable to most ICT artifacts and as such should be considered part of the catalogue of options for evaluating artifacts (especially models). Given the wide array of alternatives, a full account exceeds the aims of this chapter; however, in the additional reading section some of the most relevant techniques are offered.

Validation

The process of justifying or validating a theoretical contribution typically means the testing of the scientific claims embedded in the theory for validity (March & Smith, 1995). This still leaves open the question of what validity is, of course, which is most commonly understood as correspondence to truth or reality, and as we have established, this depends on the underlying ontological and epistemological assumptions. The correspondence to truth or reality, however, is not final or definitive. The "truth" of a theory is determined within a paradigmatic context which changes once the theory is unable to answer new questions emerging from the observation or interaction with a dynamic reality. Lee and Hubona (2009) state that theories are not proven true, only provisionally valid, or in Popper's terms corroborated or confirmed (until, and if, falsified). Additionally, we must once again point at the particular character of design science, where rather than describing or predicting reality, the aim is changing reality – solving problems is changing actual situations into desired situations, hence Simon's claim that design is counterinductive.

In the context of information systems research, Lee and Hubona (2009) have presented two basic types of validity: summative and formative. Summative validity is equated to the empirical testing of a theory against consistency with observed evidence. It is an attribute of the sum result of the theory development process, i.e. of the theory itself. Formative validation is an attribute of the process used in building the theory. Hence, a theory reaches this type of validity by following accepted procedures. It should be noted that a theory may thus have one kind of validity, but not the other; for example, in the *Design Cycle* of DSRIS, a researcher may employ tried and tested methods, but this does not automatically mean that the resulting artifact (even if it is of a theoretical nature) will pass an empirical test. This suggests that theory validation should include both types of validity.

In DSRIS, *formative validity* starts with transparency. Iivari (2007) has explicitly cited transparency as a validation component in constructive research. Such transparency in DSRIS should explicitly uncover and describe: (1) the provenance of the practical problem (*Relevance Cycle*); (2) comparable artifacts studied (*Rigor Cycle*); (3) metaphors or analogies employed (*Rigor Cycle*); and (4) kernel theories (*Rigor Cycle*). In addition, it is expected that the researcher /designer also describe the methods and procedures employed in building and evaluating the artifact (*Design Cycle*). This should be aligned with Peirce's (1992a) statement that the premises behind inquiry should be free from doubt. Or in Lakatos (1978) terms, that the "hard core" behind the research be constituted by common ideas that are shielded from falsification attempts by a "protective belt" of auxiliary hypotheses. In the case of DSRIS, the "hard core" corresponds to the "kernel theory" on which the design is based and the "protective belt" would constitute the new insight provided by the design which is fed back into the knowledge base as a theoretical contribution subject to (in this case summative) validation / falsification.

Typically, in DSRIS *summative validity* is achieved through artifact evaluation. March and Smith's contribution, for example, is rooted in the belief that reality cannot be directly apprehended (we can only access perceptions and representations); thus, the effectiveness of theories can only be proven through practical applications. This is similar to the claim that domain-independent design theories cannot be assessed directly and must use domain-depend knowledge in the creation of a domain-specific theory which is used to develop a real system that is amenable to assessment (Käkölä & Taalas, 2008). Walls *et al.* (1992) also take this path when they argue that even if a design theory has passed tests of explanatory or predictive power, they must also pass the test of practice. These understandings of validation are epistemologically placed in the same vein as pragmatism. In this view, evaluation of the resulting artifact corresponds to validation of the truthfulness of the design theory that it embodies or materializes (Venable, 2006; Walls *et al.*, 1992). In Lee and Hubona's terms, this means using formal logic of the *modus tollens* (denying the consequent) type: if the artifact does not solve the problem, then the theory is not true.

Within the field of organizational design, or management science in general, design science has also been gaining credence out of a long-standing tradition parallel to that of information systems – i.e. pursuing a balance between rigor and relevance through design. In Avenier (2010) a constructivist view of design science places "fit" and "work" as more appropriate criteria for theory validation, than "truth" as in positivist research. The legitimacy of knowledge is then of an epistemic and a pragmatic nature, which may be seen as corresponding to formative and summative validity respectively. *Epistemic legitimization* is achieved through reflectivity, following the principles of ethics, explicitness and *ostinato rigore*. Ethical considerations are usually addressed through participative design and evaluation methods (see Churchman's account of Singerian inquiring systems earlier in this chapter). Explicitness is similar to what we have already discussed as transparency above and may be aided by thick description and audits. Finally, *ostinato rigore* is evidently addressing the rigor of the research (indeed the very nature of the *Rigor Cycle* shown in Figure 1) by pointing out the continued effort towards rigor. This cyclical nature means that rigor is seen as an elusive goal which needs to be revised constantly through, for example, triangulation, negative case analysis, and member checks.

Pragmatic legitimization is akin to summative validation, and for achieving either the reader is referred back to the artifact evaluation section. Indeed, this is the bridge between artifact evaluation and theory validation which must be complemented by formative validation as discussed above. According to Avenier (2010), the idea behind pragmatic legitimization is that, on the one hand, putting knowledge into use is the main goal of knowledge generation on design science. On the other hand, since generic knowledge cannot be applied as such, it needs contextualization and interpretation according to practitioners' intentions and on the conditions of the environment (*ibid.*). From the constructivist perspective, the emphasis is placed on "activation" rather than application, since activation implies a cognitive action of integration into one's thought process as a means of reflecting upon the problem situation, enabling future reactivation, in line with Simon's problem-solving view.

On a final note, validation should always be considered as provisional. Moreover, validation should not be thought of as a binary attribute of the theory, but rather as an evolutionary goal, aiming at perfectibility. Both Popper and Peirce were proponents of this kind of understanding of scientific inquiry, which in time, should be expected to produce ever more accurate (or useful) models of reality. This means that part of the validation process should be an explicit declaration of the limitations, resistance or uncertainties remaining in the theoretical contribution, which should be used as input for further design cycles.

LIMITATIONS OF THIS CHAPTER

In this chapter we have presented a framework for establishing the provenance and dimensions of evaluation and validation in the context of DSRIS. This should help researchers (especially budding ones) to consider the different aspects that are involved in determining an evaluation and validation strategy. The different components that should be considered may not necessarily be articulated in the linear way in which this chapter must, of necessity, present them. For instance, it is not necessarily the case that a research project starts out by defining or declaring its epistemology and follows through with a corresponding logic of reasoning. Often – as discussed when presenting abduction earlier – the process is not straightforward nor done in a "pure" fashion. Design involves iteration, correction, revision and crucially it involves the use of multiple disciplines, perspectives and existing artifacts in order to come up with a specific creative solution to a problem. As such, it is very difficult to prescribe a particular way of going through the different choices that a researcher should make when defining his or her evaluation and validation strategy.

Furthermore, given the complexity and number of concepts and techniques presented, it is not possible to discuss each one in detail or present practical guidance on how to accomplish them in a methodical fashion. For each of the dimensions there may be other alternatives that could be open to the researcher – for example, a critical epistemology in addition to positivism, interpretivism and pragmatism. Furthermore, a researcher needs to take into consideration several factors that influence the choices. Such factors include: the institutional background where the research is being carried out, the limitations imposed by the application domain, the researcher's own background and preferences, the requirements and constraints that may be imposed from the outside (for example, from a funding agency, form a publication outlet, from the way of working of a particular research group) and the resources available to carry out the evaluation and validation (the effort required, the level of engagement needed from the researcher, the time to process the results, and the instruments and resources required to actually apply the specific techniques, among others).

An important question that is left open in this chapter is related to the key assumption that pragmatist validation holds when relating an artifact to the underlying theory used in designing it. On the one hand, artifacts are typically weakly connected to such theory (Iivari, 2007). What this suggests is that it may not be enough to evaluate or validate the artifact, because its acceptance or usefulness may not necessarily be an inherent property of the artifact and its theoretical premises, but rather the result of its configuration in a particular context (and as such, contextual factors should enter into the evaluation / validation effort). Conversely, if the artifact does not work or does not work as expected, this may suggest contextual limitations, rather than disconfirmation (Kuechler & Vaishnavi, 2008). On the other hand, even if we embrace a pragmatist model of validation and live with its limitations with respect to the connection of artifact to theory, there is a further question that is left open. If we say that the artifact has no truth, but only utility (March & Smith, 1995; Moody, 2003), then the epistemological connection between truth and utility is rendered meaningless. Perhaps, this "doing away" with truth might point us more towards constructivism that pragmatism, but this discussion is left out of this chapter.

Another discussion point is the debatable role that theorizing has within design science in terms of falsification or confirmation. Kuechler and Vaishnavi (2008) argue that in DSRIS the relation of a designed artifact to theory is extension and refinement, rather than disconfirmation. This may be aligned with the aforementioned notion of the Lakatos protective belt around a hard core, but it

also implies that many of the components presented in this chapter (which stem from the assumption that design theories can be validated through hypothesis testing) may not fit this understanding of theory development.

This chapter takes for granted that design is problem-solving in the Simonized sense. A simplistic view of this tradition emphasizes design as an engineering-style activity through which requirements are gathered, gaps are determined (as compared to state-of-the-art possibilities) and alternatives are generated and evaluated until a suitable solution is found which can be applied in the environment to satisfy the (typically business-related) requirements. This solution is not optimal, but "satisficing" in Simon's terms, given that human bounded rationality makes it impossible to find optimal solutions for complex situations which are intractable (the solution space is non-deterministic and finding the optimal solution is an "NP-hard" problem). Alternatively, some view design as a wider, more creative process in which problem-solving is crucial but not sufficient. Rather than focusing on finding satisficing solutions to deal with bounded rationality, Hatchuel (2001), for instance, has argued that design should be about expandable rationality because it refers to uncountable sets (the solution space is open). This shifts the design focus towards finding new concepts, new learning devices and new forms of social interaction, placing the emphasis on creative future-looking design, rather than backwards-looking requirements satisfaction. These are of course gross simplifications, but they do influence the way in which we view design and the relationship is has to the logic of reasoning / discovery and the corresponding validation strategy.

FUTURE RESEARCH DIRECTIONS

As a way to address the limitations in this chapter, we suggest a continued effort in answering the open questions that still remain. This may be a task for all information systems researchers in the sense that they should document and reflect upon their evaluation and validation choices more thoroughly, rather than presenting them as if they were a "necessary evil". Indeed, it may be only though a collaborative and widespread transparency that we can gather sufficient lessons learned to come up with a more mature classification, including: advantages and disadvantages, effort employed, and resources required. In the meantime, though, there are still many cases that are sufficiently rigorous as to use them in this sense. Accordingly, we plan to use a set of cases (mostly PhD theses) from many years of using design science research, as a starting point to illustrate the specific ways in which epistemological choices are made, the logic of reasoning employed, the evaluation carried out, the theoretical contributions articulated, and validity established. This should be conducive to a set of lessons or patterns that can form the basis for a more structured way of presenting our framework such as that it can provide more practical guidelines for researchers.

Furthermore, by comparing this set of cases to existing published research (that has declared using DSRIS) we plan to come up with a specific set of items or criteria that can be used in building a checklist of evaluation and validation in DSRIS. Such a checklist may be used as a self-assessment instrument to be employed by researchers in writing proposals, writing papers or checking the level of rigor in their projects; in the same vein, it can be used by editors, reviewers or evaluators as a template for evaluating papers or research proposals from a third party.

With respect to the underlying view of design (design-as-problem-solving vs. design-as-possibility) it is likely that an integrated view of both alternatives comes closer to the actual way in which design is or should be done. On the one hand, the (expandable rationality) "positive lens" is powerful in helping to articulate new visions for technology; on the other hand, unless these visions are tempered by (bounded rationality) analysis of downsides and risks, they could end up in disappointment (Carroll, Rosson, Farooq, & Xiao, 2009). In merging the two alternatives, we might avoid the over-simplistic consequences of artificially separating both views, as has been the case when placing too much emphasis in separating induction from deduction. A more integrated, holistic, multi-disciplinary approach could prove to be more useful. Such holistic approach may be achieved, for instance, through scenario analysis (Carroll *et al.*, 2009; Keen & Sol, 2008).

From a methodological perspective, one can view the DSRIS cycles of rigor, relevance and design (see Figure 1) as adjacent wheels (or gears, though these might be a too mechanistic metaphor), where the turning of one usually implies the turning of the others. For example, in field testing of an artifact one is clearly positioned within the *Environment* bringing the *Relevance Cycle* full circle. But in order to carry out the testing one usually needs a specific method and a set of concepts or models to represent and analyze the results; these come from the *Knowledge Base* and are thus applicable knowledge obtained in the *Rigor Cycle*. At the same time, however, the result of the field testing should be used as the basis for improvements in the design of the artifact, implying a parallel movement inside the *Design Cycle*. It is always possible to disengage one particular cycle from the other two for a period of time, but by nature any iteration within a cycle will often involve sidestepping into the other two. This is in line with modern iterative and agile systems development processes. This connection is amenable to further research and should contribute to filling the gap that some feel DSRIS still has in terms of specific methods for carrying out research projects.

CONCLUSION

This chapter discusses validation in relation to design science research in information systems. The contribution of the chapter is aimed at clarifying and providing a structure for the process of deciding, declaring and assessing a specific configuration of design science research, paying special attention to the consistency and coherence of evaluation and validation choices. Since there is still no generalized agreement on how validation and theorizing should be carried out within DSRIS, this contribution is helpful to researchers (especially younger ones), supervisors and evaluators of information systems research.

Specifically, this chapter is structured according to some components or dimensions which we consider necessary in order to plan and justify an evaluation and validation strategy. Although no specific order is suggested, there are clear pre-requisites and interrelations among these components. First, there are the epistemological foundations of the research, which may be positivist, interpretive or pragmatic. Second, we have presented four different choices in terms of the logic of reasoning and discovery: induction, deduction, abduction and the inductive-hypothetic modelcycle, stemming from Singerian inquiring systems. Third, we offer several options in terms of the kind of theory that may be developed through design science research: non-theoretical, conceptual, descriptive, prescriptive, predictive, as an intermediate artifact, or meta-theoretical.

Finally, we discuss evaluation and validation, offering a series of choices that should be connected to the previous foundations. With respect to artifact evaluation: it may be based on the type of artifact (whether it is a construct, a model, a method or an instantiation), it may be based on the type of technique (feature comparison, theoretical, or empirical) or it may be done through other popular models or methods, such as the technology acceptance model or through simulation. In terms of validation, we summarize the possibilities in terms of formative / epistemic validation (aimed at the process), or summative / pragmatic validation (aimed at the product). Because the main goal of design science research is the dual effort of creating a problem-solving artifact and making

a contribution to the knowledge base, then there should be logical consistency and coherence between validation and artifact evaluation. But this consistency is contingent on the choices regarding epistemology, reasoning and theory. Accordingly, mapping out and transparently declaring these elements should contribute to increased rigor, clarity and structure in design science research.

REFERENCES

Avenier, M.-J. (2010). Shaping a constructivist view of organizational design science. *Organization Studies*, *31*(9-10), 1229–1255. doi:10.1177/0170840610374395

Benbasat, I., & Zmud, R. W. (1999). Empirical research in Information Systems: The practice of relevance. *Management Information Systems Quarterly*, *23*(1), 3–16. doi:10.2307/249403

Carroll, J. M., Rosson, M. B., Farooq, U., & Xiao, L. (2009). Beyond being aware. *Information and Organization*, *19*(3), 162–185. doi:10.1016/j.infoandorg.2009.04.004

Chang, W.-L. (2008). A value-based pricing system for strategic co-branding goods. *Kybernetes*, *37*(7), 978–996. doi:10.1108/03684920810884360

Checkland, P., & Holwell, S. (1998). *Information, systems and Information Systems*. Chichester, UK: John Wiley & Sons.

Chen, W., & Hirschheim, R. (2004). A paradigmatic and methodological examination of Information Systems research from 1991 to 2001. *Information Systems Journal*, *14*(3), 197–235. doi:10.1111/j.1365-2575.2004.00173.x

Churchman, C. (1971). *The design of inquiring systems: Basic concepts of systems and organization*. New York, NY: Basic Books.

Cleven, A., Gubler, P., & Hüner, K. M. (2009). *Design alternatives for the evaluation of design science research artifacts.* Presented at the 4th International Conference on Design Science Research in Information Systems and Technology (DESRIST 2009), Philadelphia, PA.

Cross, N. (2001). Designerly ways of knowing: Design discipline versus design science. *Design Issues, 17*(3), 49–55. doi:10.1162/074793601750357196

Davis, F. D., Bagozzi, R. P., & Warshaw, P. R. (1989). User acceptance of computer technology: A comparison of two theoretical models. *Management Science, 35*(8), 982–1003. doi:10.1287/mnsc.35.8.982

Denning, P. J. (2005). Is computer science science? *Communications of the ACM, 48*(4), 27–31. doi:10.1145/1053291.1053309

Denning, P. J., Comer, D. E., Gries, D., Mulder, M. C., Tucker, A., Turner, A. J., & Young, P. R. (1989). Computing as a discipline. *Communications of the ACM, 32*(1), 9–23. doi:10.1145/63238.63239

Donaldson, O., & Golding, P. (2009). A design science approach for creating mobile applications. *ICIS 2009 Proceedings,* Paper 165.

Friedman, K. (2003). Theory construction in design research: Criteria, approaches, and methods. *Design Studies, 24*(6), 507–522. doi:10.1016/S0142-694X(03)00039-5

Gonzalez, R. A. (2009). Validation of crisis response simulation within the design science framework. *ICIS 2009 Proceedings,* Paper 87.

Gregor, S. (2006). The nature of theory in Information Systems. *Management Information Systems Quarterly, 30*(3), 611–642.

Gregor, S. (2009). *Building theory in the sciences of the artificial.* Presented at the 4th International Conference on Design Science Research in Information Systems and Technology (DESRIST 2009), Philadelphia, PA.

Gregor, S., & Jones, D. (2007). The anatomy of a design theory. *Journal of the Association for Information Systems, 8*(5), 312–335.

Hatchuel, A. (2001). Towards design theory and expandable rationality: The unfinished program of Herbert Simon. *Journal of Management and Governance, 5*(3), 260–273. doi:10.1023/A:1014044305704

Hevner, A. R. (2007). A three cycle view of design science research. *Scandinavian Journal of Information Systems, 19*(2), 39–64.

Hevner, A. R., & Chatterjee, S. (2010). *Design research in Information Systems: Theory and practice.* New York, NY: Springer.

Hevner, A. R., & March, S. T. (2003). The Information Systems research cycle. *Computer, 36*(11), 111–113. doi:10.1109/MC.2003.1244541

Hevner, A. R., March, S. T., Park, J., & Ram, S. (2004). Design science in information systems research. *Management Information Systems Quarterly, 28*(1), 75–105.

Hirschheim, R. (1992). Information Systems epistemology: An historical perspective. In Galliers, R. (Ed.), *Information Systems research: Issues, methods and practical guidelines.* Henley-on-Thames. UK: Alfred Waller Ltd.

Houser, N., & Kloesel, C. (Eds.). (1992). *The essential Peirce (Vol. 1).* Bloomington, IN: Indiana University Press.

Iivari, J. (2007). A paradigmatic analysis of Information Systems as a design science. *Scandinavian Journal of Information Systems, 19*(2), 39–64.

James, W. (2000). *Pragmatism and other writings.* New York, N Y: Penguin Books.

Käkölä, T., & Taalas, A. (2008). Validating the Information Systems design theory for dual Information Systems. *ICIS 2009 Proceedings,* Paper 119.

Keen, P. G. W., & Sol, H. G. (2008). *Decision enhancement services: Rehearsing the future for decisions that matter*. Amsterdam, The Netherlands: IOS Press.

Klabbers, J. H. G. (2006). A framework for artifact assessment and theory testing. *Simulation & Gaming, 37*(2), 155–173. doi:10.1177/1046878106287943

Klein, H. K., & Myers, M. D. (1999). A set of principles for conducting and evaluating interpretive field studies in Information Systems. *Management Information Systems Quarterly, 23*(1), 67–93. doi:10.2307/249410

Kuechler, B., & Vaishnavi, V. (2008). On theory development in design science research: Anatomy of a research project. *European Journal of Information Systems, 17*(5), 489–504. doi:10.1057/ejis.2008.40

Kuechler, W. L. Jr, & Vaishnavi, V. K. (2008). An expert system for dynamic re-coordination of distributed workflows. *Expert Systems with Applications, 34*(1), 551–563. doi:10.1016/j.eswa.2006.09.014

Lakatos, I. (1978). *The methodology of scientific research programmes: Philosophical papers*. Cambridge, UK: Cambridge University Press.

Lee, A. S., & Hubona, G. S. (2009). A scientific basis for rigor in Information Systems research. *Management Information Systems Quarterly, 33*(2), 237–262.

Legris, P. (2003). Why do people use Information Technology? A critical review of the technology acceptance model. *Information & Management, 40*(3), 191–204. doi:10.1016/S0378-7206(01)00143-4

Luhmann, N. (1997). *Organización y decisión. Autopoiesis, acción y entendimiento comunicativo*. Barcelona, Spain: Anthropos.

March, S. T., & Smith, G. F. (1995). Design and natural science research on Information Technology. *Decision Support Systems, 15*(4), 251–266. doi:10.1016/0167-9236(94)00041-2

Markus, M. L., Majchrzak, A., & Gasser, L. (2002). A design theory for systems that support emergent knowledge processes. *Management Information Systems Quarterly, 26*(3), 179–212.

Mitev, N. (2000). Toward social constructivist understandings of IS success and failure: introducing a new computerized reservation system. *ICIS 2000 Proceedings*, (pp. 84-93).

Moody, D. L. (2003). The method evaluation model: A theoretical model for validating Information Systems design methods. *ECIS 2003 Proceedings*, Paper 79.

Muntermann, J. (2009). Towards ubiquitous information supply for individual investors: A decision support system design. *Decision Support Systems, 47*(2), 82–92. doi:10.1016/j.dss.2009.01.003

Nandhakumar, J., & Jones, M. (1997). Too close for comfort? Distance and engagement in interpretive Information Systems research. *Information Systems Journal, 7*(2), 109–131. doi:10.1046/j.1365-2575.1997.00013.x

Niehaves, B. (2007). On epistemological pluralism in design science. *Scandinavian Journal of Information Systems, 19*(2), 93–104.

Nunamaker, J. F., Chen, M., & Purdin, T. D. M. (1990). Systems development in Information Systems research. *Journal of Management Information Systems, 7*(3), 89–106.

Peffers, K., Tuunanen, T., Rothenberger, M. A., & Chatterjee, S. (2007). A design science research methodology for Information Systems research. *Journal of Management Information Systems, 24*(3), 45–77. doi:10.2753/MIS0742-1222240302

Peirce, C. S. (1992a). The fixation of belief. In Houser, N., & Kloesel, C. (Eds.), *The essential Peirce* (*Vol. 1*, pp. 109–123). Bloomington, IN: Indiana University Press.

Peirce, C. S. (1992b). How to make our ideas clear. In Houser, N., & Kloesel, C. (Eds.), *The essential Peirce* (*Vol. 1*, pp. 124–141). Bloomington, IN: Indiana University Press.

Peirce, C. S. (1998a). The first rule of logic. In Peirce, C. (Ed.), *The essential Peirce* (*Vol. 2*, pp. 42–56). Bloomington, IN: Indiana University Press.

Peirce, C. S. (1998b). On the logic of drawing history from ancient documents, especially from testimonies. In Peirce, C. (Ed.), *The essential Peirce* (*Vol. 2*, pp. 75–114). Bloomington, IN: Indiana University Press.

Piirainen, K., Gonzalez, R. A., & Kolfschoten, G. (2010). Quo Vadis, design science? – A survey of literature. *Global Perspectives on Design Science Research, Lecture Notes in Computer Science* (vol. 6105, pp. 93-108-108). Berlin, Germany: Springer.

Purao, S., & Storey, V. C. (2008). Evaluating the adoption potential of design science efforts: The case of APSARA. *Decision Support Systems*, *44*(2), 369–381. doi:10.1016/j.dss.2007.04.007

Siau, K., & Rossi, M. (2008). Evaluation techniques for systems analysis and design modelling methods: A review and comparative analysis. *Information Systems Journal*, *21*(3), 249–268. doi:10.1111/j.1365-2575.2007.00255.x

Simon, H. A. (1996). *The sciences of the artificial* (3rd ed.). Cambridge, MA: MIT Press.

Simon, H. A., Langley, P. W., & Bradshaw, G. L. (1981). Scientific discovery as problem solving. *Synthese*, *47*(1), 1–27. doi:10.1007/BF01064262

Sol, H. G. (1982). *Simulation in Information Systems development*. Doctoral Dissertation. Rijksuniversiteit Groningen, Groningen.

Venable, J. R. (2006). *The role of theory and theorising in design science research*. Presented at the First International Conference on Design Science Research in Information Systems and Technology (DESRIST 2006), Claremont, CA.

Walls, J. G., Widmeyer, G. R., & El Sawy, O. A. (1992). Building an Information System design theory for vigilant EIS. *Information Systems Research*, *3*(1), 36–59. doi:10.1287/isre.3.1.36

Winter, R. (2008). Design science research in Europe. *European Journal of Information Systems*, *17*(5), 470–475. doi:10.1057/ejis.2008.44

Wynn, E. (2001). Möbius transitions in the dilemma of legitimacy. In Trauth, E. (Ed.), *Qualitative research in IS: Issues and trends*. Hershey, PA: Idea Group Publishing. doi:10.4018/978-1-930708-06-8.ch002

ADDITIONAL READING

Bartis, E., & Mitev, N. (2008). A multiple narrative approach to information systems failure: a successful system that failed. *European Journal of Information Systems*, *17*(2), 112–124. doi:10.1057/ejis.2008.3

Barzilai-Nahon, K. (2006). Gaps and Bits: Conceptualizing Measurements for Digital Divides. *The Information Society*, *22*(5), 269–278. doi:10.1080/01972240600903953

Baskerville, R. (2008). What design science is not. *European Journal of Information Systems*, *17*(5), 441–443. doi:10.1057/ejis.2008.45

Becker, J., & Niehaves, B. (2007). Epistemological perspectives on IS research: a framework for analysing and systematizing epistemological assumptions. *Information Systems Journal*, *17*(2), 197–214. doi:10.1111/j.1365-2575.2007.00234.x

Carlsson, S. A. (2006). Towards an Information Systems Design Research Framework: A Critical Realist Perspective. Presented at the First International Conference on Design Science Research in Information Systems and Technology (DESRIST 2006), Claremont, CA.

Cleven, A., Gubler, P., & Hüner, K. M. (2009). *Design alternatives for the evaluation of design science research artifacts*. Presented at the 4th International Conference on Design Science Research in Information Systems and Technology (DESRIST 2009), Philadelphia, PA.

Cross, N. (1993). Science and design methodology: A review. *Research in Engineering Design*, *5*(2), 63–69. doi:10.1007/BF02032575

Delone, W. H., & McLean, E. R. (2003). The DeLone and McLean Model of Information Systems Success: A Ten-Year Update. *Journal of Management Information Systems*, *19*(4), 9–30.

Dobson, P. J. (2001). The Philosophy of Critical Realism—An Opportunity for Information Systems Research. *Information Systems Frontiers*, 3(2), 199-210-210.

Dorst, K. (2008). Design research: a revolution-waiting-to-happen. *Design Studies*, *29*(1), 4–11.

Galliers, R. (1992). Choosing Information Systems Approaches. In Galliers, R. (Ed.), *Information Systems Research: issues, methods and practical guidelines*. Alfred Waller Ltd., Henley-on-Thames.

Gregg, D. G., Kulkarni, U. R., & Vinzé, A. S. (2001). Understanding the Philosophical Underpinnings of Software Engineering Research in Information Systems. *Information Systems Frontiers*, 3(2), 169-183-183.

Gurbaxani, V., & Whang, S. (1991, January). The impact of information systems on organizations and markets. *Communications of the ACM*, *34*(1), 59–73. doi:10.1145/99977.99990

Igbaria, M., & Tan, M. (1997). The consequences of information technology acceptance on subsequent individual performance. *Information & Management*, *32*(3), 113–121. doi:10.1016/S0378-7206(97)00006-2

Järvinen, P. (2007). Action Research is Similar to Design Science. *Quality & Quantity*, *41*, 37–54. doi:10.1007/s11135-005-5427-1

Kettani, D., Gurstein, M., Moulin, B., & El Mahdi, A. (2006). An Approach to the Assessment of Applied Information Systems with Particular Application to Community Based Systems. In On the Move to Meaningful Internet Systems 2006: OTM 2006 Workshops, *Lecture Notes in Computer Science* (Vol. 4277, pp. 301-310). Springer Berlin / Heidelberg.

Klein, E. E., & Herskovitz, P. J. (2007). Philosophy of science underpinnings of prototype validation: Popper vs. Quine. *Information Systems Journal*, *17*(1), 111–132. doi:10.1111/j.1365-2575.2006.00239.x

Kriz, W. C., & Hense, J. U. (2006). Theory-oriented evaluation for the design of and research in gaming and simulation. *Simulation & Gaming*, *37*(2), 268–283. doi:10.1177/1046878106287950

Martinsons, M., Davison, R., & Tse, D. (1999). The balanced scorecard: a foundation for the strategic management of information systems. *Decision Support Systems*, *25*(1), 71–88. doi:10.1016/S0167-9236(98)00086-4

McGrath, K. (2005). Doing critical research in information systems: a case of theory and practice not informing each other. *Information Systems Journal*, *15*, 85–101. doi:10.1111/j.1365-2575.2005.00187.x

Mingers, J. (2001). Combining IS Research Methods: Towards a Pluralist Methodology. *Information Systems Research*, *12*(3), 240–259. doi:10.1287/isre.12.3.240.9709

Petter, S., DeLone, W., & McLean, E. (2008). Measuring information systems success: models, dimensions, measures, and interrelationships. *European Journal of Information Systems*, *17*(3), 236–263. doi:10.1057/ejis.2008.15

Poston, R., & Grabski, S. (2001). Financial impacts of enterprise resource planning implementations. *International Journal of Accounting Information Systems*, *2*(4), 271–294. doi:10.1016/S1467-0895(01)00024-0

Saarinen, T. (1996). An expanded instrument for evaluating information system success. *Information & Management*, *31*(2), 103–118. doi:10.1016/S0378-7206(96)01075-0

Trauth, E. (2001). The Choice of Qualitative Methods in IS Research. In Trauth, E. (Ed.), *Qualitative Research in IS: issues and trends*. Hershey: Idea Group Publishing. doi:10.4018/9781930708068.ch001

van Aken, J. E. (2007). Design Science and Organization Development Interventions: Aligning Business and Humanistic Values. *The Journal of Applied Behavioral Science*, *43*(1), 67–88. doi:10.1177/0021886306297761

Wang, Y., & Liao, Y. (2008). Assessing eGovernment systems success: A validation of the DeLone and McLean model of information systems success. *Government Information Quarterly*, *25*(4), 717–733. doi:10.1016/j.giq.2007.06.002

KEY TERMS AND DEFINITIONS

Abduction: The process of reasoning through which a system of beliefs is modified in order to generate novel hypotheses that can then be tested (usually through a combination of induction and deduction).

Deduction: The process of reasoning through which existing theoretical propositions are narrowed down into testable hypothesis in order to produce new theoretical propositions.

Design Science Research: The process through which novel artifacts are built in order to solve a relevant problem in a rigorous fashion that can contribute to the existing body of knowledge.

Induction: The process of reasoning through which observations are generalized into hypothesis that can be tested.

Interpretivism: An epistemological approach in which models of reality are constructed intersubjectively in a specific context in order to produce in-depth understanding of a phenomena.

Positivism: An epistemological approach in which reality is assumed to be objectively and empirically amenable to study in order to produce (usually predictive) generalizations.

Pragmatism: A philosophical approach according to which the truth of a conception is directly related to the consequences or effects of this conception in reality.

Compilation of References

Aadne, J. H., Von Krogh, G., & Roos, J. (1996). Representationism: The traditional approach to cooperative strategies. In Von Krogh, G., & Roos, J. (Eds.), *Managing knowledge. Perspectives on cooperation and competition* (pp. 9–31). London, UK: Sage.

Abbott, A. (1995). Sequence analysis: New methods for old ideas. *Annual Review of Sociology, 21*, 93–113. doi:10.1146/annurev.so.21.080195.000521

Abrahamson, E. (1996). Management fashion, academic fashion, and enduring truths. *Academy of Management Review, 21*(3), 616–618.

Ackoff, R. (1960). Systems, organizations and interdisciplinary research. *General System Yearbook, 5*, 1–8.

Ackoff, R. (1971). Towards a system of systems concepts. *Management Science, 17*(11), 661–671. doi:10.1287/mnsc.17.11.661

Ackoff, R. L. (1969). The evolution of management systems. *Canadian Operational Research Society Journal, 8*, 1–13.

Ackoff, R. L. (1974). *Redesigning the future: A systems approach to societal problems.* New York, NY: John Wiley & Sons.

Ackoff, R. L. (1998). *Ackoff's best: His classic writings on management.* New York, NY: John Wiley & Sons.

Ackoff, R. L., & Emery, F. E. (1972). *On purposeful systems.* Chicago, IL: Aldine Atherton, Inc.

Ackoff, R., Gupta, S., & Minas, J. (1962). *Scientific method: Optimizing applied research decisions.* New York, NY: Wiley.

Adebesin, T. F., De Villiers, M. R., & Ssemugabi, S. (2009). Usability testing of e-learning: An approach incorporating co-discovery and think-aloud. *Proceedings of the 2009 Conference of the South African Computer Lecturers' Association, SACLA 2009* (pp. 6-15). ACM International Conference Proceedings Series.

Agrawal, V., & Haleem, A. (2002). Culture, environmental pressures, and the factors for successful implementation of business process engineering and computer based Information Systems. *Global Journal of Flexible Systems Management, 4*, 27–47.

Ahuja, M., & Thathcher, J. B. (2005). Moving beyond intentions and toward the theory of trying: Effects of work environment and gender on post-adoption Information Technology use. *Management Information Systems Quarterly, 29*(3), 427–459.

Al-Amoudi, I., & Willmott, H. (2011). Where constructionism and critical realism converge: Interrogating the domain of epistemological relativism. *Organization Studies, 32*(1), 27–46. doi:10.1177/0170840610394293

Alavi, M. (1984). An assessment of the prototyping approach to information systems development. *Communications of the ACM, 27*(6), 556–563. doi:10.1145/358080.358095

Alavi, M., & Carlson, P. (1992). A review of MIS research and disciplinary development. *Journal of Management Information Systems, 8*(4), 45–52.

Albert, S., & Whetten, D. A. (1985). Organizational identity. In Cummings, L. L., & Staw, B. M. (Eds.), *Research in organizational behavior* (*Vol. 7*, pp. 263–295). Greenwich, CT: JAI Press.

Albors, J., Ramos, J. C., & Hervas, J. L. (2008). New learning network paradigms: Communities of objectives, crowdsourcing, wikis and open source. *International Journal of Information Management, 28*, 194–202. doi:10.1016/j.ijinfomgt.2007.09.006

Aldrich, J. (1995). Correlations genuine and spurious in Pearson and Yule. *Statistical Science, 10*(4), 364–376.

Alexander, C., Ishikawa, S., & Silverstein, M. (1977). *A pattern language*. New York, NY: Oxford University Press.

Allen, N., Ingham, J., Johnson, B., Merante, J., Noveck, B. S., & Stock, W. ... Wong, C. (2008, June). *PeerToPatent first anniversary report*. The Center for Patent Innovations, New York Law School. Retrieved from http:// dotank.nyls.edu/ communitypatent/ P2Panniversaryreport. pdf

Allison, I., & Merali, Y. (2007). Software process improvement as emergent change: A structural analysis. *Information and Software Technology, 49*(6), 668–681. doi:10.1016/j.infsof.2007.02.003

Alonso, O., & Lease, M. (2011). Crowdsourcing 101: Putting the WSDM of crowds to work for you. In I. King, W. Nejdl & H. Li (Eds.), *Proceedings of the 4th ACM International Conference on Web Search and Data Mining (WSDM)*, (pp. 1-2). February 9-12, 2011, Hong Kong, China. Tutorial slides available, Retrieved February 14, 2011, from http://ir.ischool.utexas.edu/ wsdm2011_tutorial.pdf.

Alter, S. (2009, August). *Project collaboration, not just user participation*, Paper presented at the Fifteenth Americas Conference on Information Systems, San Francisco, CA.

Alter, S. (2010, December). *Bridging the chasm between sociotechnical and technical views of systems in organizations*. Paper presented at the 31st International Conference on Information Systems, Saint Louis, MO.

Alter, S. (2001). Recognizing the relevance of IS research and broadening the appeal and applicability of future publications. *Communications of the Association for Information Systems, 6*(1).

Alter, S. (2006). *The work system method: Connecting people, processes, and IT for business results*. Larkspur, CA: Work System Press.

Alter, S. (2007). Service system fundamentals: Work system, value chain, and life cycle. *IBM Systems Journal, 47*(1), 71–85. doi:10.1147/sj.471.0071

Alter, S. (2008). Defining Information Systems as work systems: Implications for the IS field. *European Journal of Information Systems, 17*(5), 448–469. doi:10.1057/ ejis.2008.37

Alter, S., & Browne, G. (2005). A broad view of systems analysis and design: Implications for research. *Communications of the Association for Information Systems, 16*(50), 981–999.

Amaravadi, C. S. (2001). Improving consumption. *Communications of the Association for Information Systems, 6*(1).

Amiel, T., & Reeves, T. C. (2008). Design-based research and educational technology: Rethinking technology and the research agenda. *Journal of Educational Technology & Society, 11*(4), 29–40.

Amin, A., & Cohendet, P. (2004). *Architectures of knowledge: firms, capabilities, and communities*. Oxford, UK: Oxford UP.

Anderson, J. C., & Gerbing, D. W. (1988). Structural equation modeling in practice: a review and recommended two-step approach. *Psychological Bulletin, 103*, 411–423. doi:10.1037/0033-2909.103.3.411

Applegate, L. M., & King, J. L. (1999). Rigor and relevance: Careers on the line. *Management Information Systems Quarterly, 23*(1), 17. doi:10.2307/249404

Arbuckle, J. L. (1989). AMOS: Analysis of moment structures. *The American Statistician, 43*, 66. doi:10.2307/2685178

Archak, N. (2010). Money, glory and entry deterrence: Analyzing strategic behavior of contestants in simultaneous crowdsourcing contests on TopCoder.com. *Proceedings of the 19th International Conference on World Wide Web*, (pp. 21-30).

Archer, M. (1995). *Realist social theory: The morphogenetic approach*. Cambridge, UK: Cambridge University Press. doi:10.1017/CBO9780511557675

Archer, M. (2003). *Structure, agency and the internal conversation*. Cambridge, UK: Cambridge University Press.

Arora, S., & Kumar, S. (2000). Reengineering: A focus on enterprise integration. *Interfaces*, *30*(5), 54–71. doi:10.1287/inte.30.5.54.11641

Ashby, R. W. (1956). *An introduction to cybernetics.* London, UK: Chapman.

Ashforth, B. E., & Mael, F. A. (1996). Organizational identity and strategy as a context for the individual. In Cummings, L. L., & Staw, B. M. (Eds.), *Research in organizational behavior* (*Vol. 13*, pp. 17–62). Greenwich, CT: JAI Press.

Avenier, M.-J. (2010). Shaping a constructivist view of organizational design science. *Organization Studies*, *31*(9-10), 1229–1255. doi:10.1177/0170840610374395

Avgerou, C. (2001). The significance of context in information systems and organizational change. *Information Systems Journal*, *11*(1), 43–63. doi:10.1046/j.1365-2575.2001.00095.x

Avison, D., & Fitzgerald, D. G. (1995). *Information Systems development.* London, UK: McGraw-Hill.

Ayim, M. (1982). *Peirce's view of the roles of reason and instinct in scientific inquiry.* Meerut, India: Anu Prakasan.

Bagozzi, R. P. (1994). Structural equation models in marketing research: Basic principles. In Bagozzi, R. P. (Ed.), *Principles of marketing research* (pp. 317–385). Oxford, UK: Blackwell.

Bagozzi, R. P. (2011). Measurement and meaning in information systems and organizational research: Methodological and philosophical foundations. *Management Information Systems Quarterly*, *35*(2), 261–292.

Baker, J., Burkman, J., & Jones, D. (2009). Using visual representations of data to enhance sensemaking in data exploration tasks. *Journal of the Association for Information Systems*, *10*(7), 533–559.

Balci, O., Gilley, W. S., Adams, R. J., Tunar, E., & Barnette, N. D. (2010). *Animations to assist learning some key computer science topics, software engineering, the spiral model.* Department of Computer Science, Virginia Tech. Retrieved May 26, 2011, from http://courses.cs.vt.edu/ csonline/ SE/ Lessons/ Spiral/ index.html

Balk, L. D., & Kedia, A. (2000). PPT: A COTS integration case study. *Proceeding of the 22nd International Conference on Software Engineering*, 2000, (pp. 42–49). ACM Press.

Bansler, J. P., & Havn, E. C. (2003). Building community knowledge systems: An empirical study of IT-support for sharing best practices among managers. *Knowledge and Process Management*, *10*(3), 156–163. doi:10.1002/kpm.178

Barabasi, A.-L. (2003). *Link*. Plume, Reissue edition.

Barab, S., & Squire, K. (2004). Design-based research: Putting a stake in the ground. *Journal of the Learning Sciences*, *13*(1), 1–14. doi:10.1207/s15327809jls1301_1

Barclay, D., Higgins, C., & Thompson, R. (1995). The partial least squares (PLS) approach to causal modelling: Personal computer adoption and use as an illustration. (Special Issue on Research Methodology). *Technology Studies*, *2*(2), 285–309.

Barnes, J. A. (1954). Class and committee in a Norwegian Island Parish. *Human Relations*, *n.d.*, 7.

Barnes, J. A. (1969). Group theory and social networks. *Sociology*, *n.d.*, 3.

Barroso, C., Cepeda, G., & Roldán, J. L. (2010). Applying maximum likelihood and PLS on different sample sizes: Studies on SERVQUAL model and employee behaviour model. In Esposito Vinzi, V., Chin, W. W., Henseler, J., & Wang, H. (Eds.), *Handbook of partial least squares: Concepts, methods and applications* (pp. 427–447). Berlin, Germany: Springer-Verlag. doi:10.1007/978-3-540-32827-8_20

Baskerville, R. L. (1999). Investigating Information Systems with action research. *Communications of the Association for Information Systems*, *2*(Article 19). Retrieved May 2006 from http://cais.isworld.org/articles/2-19/

Baskerville, R. L., & Myers, M. D. (2009). Fashion waves in information systems research and practice. *Management Information Systems Quarterly*, *33*(4), 647–662.

Baskerville, R. L., & Wood-Harper, A. T. (1996). A critical perspective on action research as a method for Information Systems research. *Journal of Information Technology*, *11*, 235–246. doi:10.1080/026839696345289

Baskerville, R., & Pries-Heje, J. (1999). Grounded action research: A method for understanding IT in practice. *Accounting. Management and Information Technologies, 9*, 1–23. doi:10.1016/S0959-8022(98)00017-4

Basri, S., & O'Connor, R. (2010b). *Organizational commitment towards software process improvement: An Irish Software VSEs case study.* 4th International Symposium on Information Technology 2010 (ITSim 2010), Kuala Lumpur, Malaysia.

Basri, S., & O'Connor, R. (2010a). Understanding the perception of very small software companies towards the adoption of process standards. In Riel, A. (Eds.), *Systems, Software and Services Process Improvement, CCIS* (Vol. 99, pp. 153–164). Springer-Verlag. doi:10.1007/978-3-642-15666-3_14

Bateson, G. (1972). *Steps to an ecology of mind: Collected essays in anthropology, psychiatry, evolution, and epistemology.* University of Chicago Press.

Bateson, G. (1980). *Mind and nature.* New York, NY: Bantam Books.

Battier, M., & Girieud, S. (2010). Technical innovations. *Communications and Strategies, 77*, 167–172.

Bavelas, A. (1948). A mathematical model for group structure. *Applied Anthropology, 7.*

Bavelas, A. (1950). Communication patterns in task-oriented groups. *Journal of the Acoustic Society of America, 22.*

Becker, D., & De Villiers, M. R. (2008). Iterative design and evaluation of an e-learning tutorial: A research-based approach. *South African Computer Journal, Special Edition, 42*, 38-46.

Beck, K. (1999). Embracing change with extreme programming. *IEEE Computer, 32*(10), 70–77. doi:10.1109/2.796139

Belsley, D. A. (1991). *Conditioning diagnostics: Collinearity and weak data in regression.* New York, NY: John Wiley & Sons.

Benbasat, I., Goldstein, D. K., & Mead, M. (1987). The case research strategy in studies of Information Systems. *Management Information Systems Quarterly, 11*(3), 369–385. doi:10.2307/248684

Benbasat, I., & Zmud, R. W. (1999). Empirical research in Information Systems: The practice of relevance. *Management Information Systems Quarterly, 23*(1), 3–16. doi:10.2307/249403

Bentler, P. M. (2006). *EQS 6 structural equations program manual.* Encino, CA: Multivariate Software. Retrieved from www.mvsoft.com

Bentler, P. M. (1985). *Theory and implementation of EQS, a structural equations program.* Los Angeles, CA: BMDP Statistical Software.

Bentler, P. M. (2000). Rites, wrong, and gold in model testing. *Structural Equation Modeling, 7*(1), 82–91. doi:10.1207/S15328007SEM0701_04

Bentler, P. M. (2007). Can scientifically useful hypotheses be tested with correlations? *The American Psychologist, 62*, 772–782. doi:10.1037/0003-066X.62.8.772

Bentler, P. M. (2009). Alpha, dimension-free, and model-based internal consistency reliability. *Psychometrika, 74*, 137–143. doi:10.1007/s11336-008-9100-1

Bentler, P. M., & deLeeuw, J. (2011). (in press). Factor analysis via components analysis. *Psychometrika.* doi:10.1007/s11336-011-9217-5

Bentler, P. M., & Satorra, A. (2010). Testing model nesting and equivalence. *Psychological Methods, 15*(2), 111–123. doi:10.1037/a0019625

Bentler, P. M., & Weeks, D. G. (1980). Linear structural equations with latent variables. *Psychometrika, 45*, 289–308. doi:10.1007/BF02293905

Bentler, P. M., & Wu, E. J. C. (2002). *EQS 6 for Windows user's guide.* Encino, CA: Multivariate Software.

Bhaskar, R. (1978). *A realist theory of science.* Sussex, UK: Harvester Press.

Bhaskar, R. (1979). *The possibility of naturalism.* Harvester Wheatsheaf, Hemel Hempstead.

Bhaskar, R. (2008). *A realist theory of science.* London, UK: Leeds Books.

Bhaskar, R., & Danermark, B. (2006). Metatheory, interdisciplinarity and disability research: A critical realist perspective. *Scandinavian Journal of Disability Research, 8*(4), 278–297. doi:10.1080/15017410600914329

Bhattacherjee, A. (2001). Understanding and evaluating relevance in IS research. *Communications of the Association for Information Systems*, 6(1).

Biggiero, L. (2010b). Knowledge redundancy, environmental shocks, and agents' opportunism. In J. Józefczyk & D. Orski (Eds.), Knowledge-based intelligent system advancements: Systemic and cybernetic approaches (pp. 252-282). Advances in Artificial Intelligence Technologies (AAIT). Hershey, PA: IGI Global Publishers. doi:10.4018/978-1-61692-811-7.ch013doi:10.4018/978-1-61692-811-7.ch013

Biggiero, L. (1997). Managerial action and observation: a view of relational complexity. *Systemica*, 12, 23–37.

Biggiero, L. (2001a). Are firms autopoietic systems? In van der Zouwen, G., & Geyer, F. (Eds.), *Sociocybernetics: Complexity, autopoiesis, and observation of social systems* (pp. 125–140). Westport, CT: Greenwood.

Biggiero, L. (2001b). Sources of complexity in human systems. *Nonlinear Dynamics and Chaos in Life Sciences*, 5, 3–19. doi:10.1023/A:1009515211632

Biggiero, L. (2009). Organizations as cognitive systems: is knowledge an emergent property of information networks? In Minati, G., Pessa, E., & Abram, M. (Eds.), *Emergence in systems* (pp. 697–712). Singapore: World Scientific. doi:10.1142/9789812793478_0045

Biggiero, L. (2010a). Exploration modes and its impact on industry profitability. The differentiated effects of internal and external ways to access market knowledge. In Faggini, M., & Vinci, P. (Eds.), *Decision theory and choice: A complexity approach* (pp. 83–115). Berlin, Germany: Springer. doi:10.1007/978-88-470-1778-8_5

Biggiero, L., & Sevi, E. (2009). Opportunism by cheating and its effects on industry profitability. The CIOPS model. *Computational & Mathematical Organization Theory*, 15, 191–236. doi:10.1007/s10588-009-9057-3

Biggs, J. (1999). *Teaching for quality learning at university: What the student does*. Buckingham, UK: Society for Research into Higher Education, Open University Press.

Bishop, M. (2009, May). *The total economic impact of InnoCentive challenges. Single company case study.* Forrester Consulting. Retrieved from http://www.economist.com/ businessfinance/ displaystory.cfm? story_id= 14460185

Bjornson, F. O., & Dingsoyr, T. (2005). Lecture Notes in Computer Science: *Vol. 3547. A study of a mentoring program for knowledge transfer in a small software consultancy company.* Berlin, Germany: Springer.

Blaikie, N. (1993). *Approaches to social enquiry.* Cambridge, UK: Polity Press.

Blanchard, A. L., & Markus, M. L. (2004, Winter). The experienced "sense" of a virtual community: Characteristics and processes. *The Data Base for Advances in Information Systems*, 35(1), 65–79.

Boehm, B. (1986). A spiral model of software development and enhancement. *ACM SIGSOFT Software Engineering Notes*, 11(4), 14-24. Retrieved May 26, 2011, from http://delivery.acm.org/ 10.1145/ 20000/ 12948/ p14-boehm.pdf?key1 =12948&key2 =1109403921&coll =DL&dl =ACM&CFID =3425753&CFTOKEN =44820182

Boehm, B. (2002). Get ready for agile methods, with care. *IEEE Computer*, 35(1), 64–69. doi:10.1109/2.976920

Boehm, B., & Turner, R. (2004). *Balancing agility and discipline. A guide for the perplexed.* Boston, MA: Addison-Wesley.

Boland, R. J., & Tenkasi, R. V. (1995). Perspective making and perspective taking in communities of knowing. *Organization Science*, 6, 350–372. doi:10.1287/orsc.6.4.350

Boland, R. J., Tenkasi, R. V., & Te'eni, D. (1994). Designing information technology to support distributed cognition. *Organization Science*, 5, 456–475. doi:10.1287/orsc.5.3.456

Bollen, K. A. (2011). Evaluating effect, composite, and causal indicators in structural equation models. *Management Information Systems Quarterly*, 35(2), 359–372.

Bollen, K., & Lennox, R. (1991). Conventional wisdom on measurement: A structural equation perspective. *Psychological Bulletin*, 110(2), 305–314. doi:10.1037/0033-2909.110.2.305

Bollobas, B. (1985). *Random graphs.* London, UK: Academic.

Bonabeau, E. (2009, Winter). Decision 2.0: The power of collective intelligence. *MIT Sloan Management Review*, 50(2), 45–52.

Borchers, A. S. (2001). Adding practitioner scholars to our faculties. *Communications of the Association for Information Systems, 6*(1).

Borgo, S., Carrara, M., Garbacz, P., & Vermaas, P. E. (2009). A formal ontological perspective on the behaviors and functions of technical artifacts. *Artificial Intelligence for Engineering Design, Analysis and Manufacturing, 23*(01), 3–21. doi:10.1017/S0890060409000079

Bornholdt, S., & Schuster, H. G. (Eds.). (2003). *Handbook of graphs and networks: From the genome to the Internet.* Weinheim, Germany: Wiley-VCH.

Bott, E. (1955). Urban families: Conjugal roles and social networks. *Human Relations, n.d.,* 8.

Bott, E. (1956). Urban families: The norms of conjugal roles. *Human Relations, n.d.,* 9.

Bott, E. (1957). *Family and social network.* London, UK: Tavistock.

Boulding, K. (1956). General systems theory – The skeleton of the science. *Management Science, 2*(3), 197–208. doi:10.1287/mnsc.2.3.197

Brabham, D. C. (2008a). Moving the crowd at iStockphoto: The composition of the crowd and the motivations for participation in a crowdsourcing application. *First Monday, 13*(6). Retrieved December 4, 2009, from http://www.uic.edu/ htbin/ cgiwrap/ bin/ ojs/ index.php/ fm/ article/ view/ 2159/1969

Brabham, D. C. (2009). *Moving the crowd at Threadless: Motivations for participation in a crowdsourcing application.* Paper presented at the Annual Meeting of the Association for Education in Journalism and Mass Communication, Boston, MA.

Brabham, D. C. (2008b). Crowdsourcing as a model for problem solving: An introduction and cases. *The International. Convergence (London), 14*(1), 75–90. doi:10.1177/1354856507084420

Brinkkemper, S., & Falkenberg, E. D. (1991). Three dichotomies in the Information System methodology. Informatiesystemen in beweging. *Some Reflections on the Namur Conference on Information Systems,* (p. 4). Namur University, Belgium.

Brown, R., Nerur, S., & Slinkman, C. (2004). Philosophical shifts in software development. In *Proceedings of the Tenth Americas Conference on Information Systems (AMCIS),* New York, NY, August 2004 (pp. 4136-4143). Retrieved August, 23, 2009, from http:// aisel.aisnet.org/ amcis2004/ 516

Brown, S. F. (2009). *Naivety in systems engineering research: Are we putting the methodological cart before the philosophical horse?* 7th Annual Conference on Systems Engineering Research, Loughborough University, UK.

Brown, A. L. (1992). Design experiments: Theoretical and methodological challenges in creating complex interventions in classroom settings. *Journal of the Learning Sciences, 2*(2), 141–178. doi:10.1207/s15327809jls0202_2

Brown, J. S., & Duguid, P. (1991). Organizational learning and communities of practice: Toward a unified view of working, learning and innovation. *Organization Science, 2*(1), 40–57. doi:10.1287/orsc.2.1.40

Brown, J. S., & Duguid, P. (1998). Organizing knowledge. *California Management Review, 40*(3), 90–111.

Brown, J. S., & Duguid, P. (2000). *The social life of information.* Boston, MA: Harvard Business School Press.

Brown, T. (2006). *Confirmatory factor analysis for applied research.* New York, NY: Guilford Press.

Bryde, D. (2005). Methods for managing different perspectives of project success. *British Journal of Management, 16,* 119–131. doi:10.1111/j.1467-8551.2005.00438.x

Bucciarelli, L. L. (2003). *Engineering philosophy.* Delft, The Netherlands: DUP Satellite.

Buchanan, D. A., & Bryman, A. (Eds.). (2009). *The SAGE handbook of organizational research methods.* London, UK: SAGE Publications.

Buchholz, W. (2006). Ontology. In D. Schwartz (Ed.), *Encyclopedia of knowledge management* (pp. 694-702). Hershey, PA: IGI (Idea Group).

Bullock, H. E., Harlow, L. L., & Mulaik, S. A. (1994). Causation issues in structural equation modeling research. *Structured Equation Modeling, 1*(3), 253–267. doi:10.1080/10705519409539977

Bullock, H., Fraser Wyche, K., & Williams, W. (2001). Media images of the poor. *Promoting Environmentalism, 57*(2), 229–246.

Burger-Helmchen, T., & Pénin, J. (unpublished). *The limits of crowdsourcing inventive activities: What do transaction cost theory and the evolutionary theories of the firm teach us?* Retrieved from http:// cournot.ustrasbg.fr/ users/ osi/ program/TBH_JP_crowdsouring%202010%20ENG.pdf

Burt, R. S. (1982). *Toward a structural theory of action.* New York, NY: Academic Press.

Burt, R. S. (1992). *Structural holes: The social structure of competition.* Massachusetts: Harvard University Press.

Business Dictionary. (2011). *Definition of descriptive study.* Retrieved May 26, 2011, from http://www.businessdictionary.com/ definition /descriptive-study.html

Bustard, D. W., & Keenan, F. M. (2005, April). *Strategies for systems analysis: Groundwork for process tailoring.* Paper presented at the 12th Annual IEEE International Conference and Workshop on the Engineering of Computer Based Systems, Greenbelt, MD.

Butler, T. (2003). From data to knowledge and back again: Understanding the limitations of KMS. *Knowledge and Process Management, 10*(3), 144–155. doi:10.1002/kpm.180

Buzan, B., Booth, K., & Smith, S. (1995). The level of analysis problem in international relations reconsidered. In *International relations theory today* (p. 367). College Park, PA: Penn State Press.

Bygstad, B. (2010). Generative mechanisms for innovation in information infrastructures. *Information and Organization, 20,* 156–168. doi:10.1016/j.infoandorg.2010.07.001

Byrne, B. M. (2006). *Structural equation modeling with EQS.* Mahwah, NJ: Lawrence Erlbaum Associates.

Calhoun, C. (1995). *Critical social theory: Culture, history, and the challenge of difference.* Oxford, UK: Blackwell.

Callon, M., Courtial, J.-P., Turner, W. A., & Bauin, S. (1983). From translations to problematic networks: An introduction to co-word analysis. *Social Sciences Information. Information Sur les Sciences Sociales, 22*(2), 191–235. doi:10.1177/053901883022002003

Callon, M., Law, J., & Rip, A. (Eds.). (1986). *Mapping the dynamics of science and technology.* London, UK: Macmillan.

Calvo-Mora, A., Leal, A., & Roldán, J. L. (2005). Relationships between the EFQM model criteria: A study in Spanish universities. *Total Quality Management & Business Excellence, 16,* 741–770. doi:10.1080/14783360500077708

Cameron, W. B. (1963). *Informal sociology: A casual introduction to sociological thinking.* New York City, NY: Random House.

Cantor, N. F., & Klein, P. L. (1969). *Seventeenth-century rationalism: Bacon and Descartes.* Waltham, MA: Blaisdell.

Carley, K. (1986). An approach for relating social structure to cognitive structure. *The Journal of Mathematical Sociology, 12,* 137–189. doi:10.1080/0022250X.1986.9990010

Carley, K. (1989). The value of cognitive foundations for dynamic social theory. *The Journal of Mathematical Sociology, 14,* 171–208. doi:10.1080/002225 0X.1989.9990049

Carley, K. M. (1999). On the evolution of social and organizational networks. *Research in the Sociology of Organizations, 16,* 3–30.

Carley, K. M. (2009). Computational modeling for reasoning about the social behavior of humans. *Computational & Mathematical Organization Theory, 15,* 47–59. doi:10.1007/s10588-008-9048-9

Carley, K. M., & Newell, A. (1994). The nature of the social agent. *The Journal of Mathematical Sociology, 19,* 221–262. doi:10.1080/0022250X.1994.9990145

Carley, K. M., & Prietula, M. (Eds.). (1994). *Computational organization theory.* Hillsdale, NJ: Lawrence Erlbaum Associates.

Carlsson, S. A. (2003). Advancing information systems evaluation (research): a critical realist approach. *Electronic Journal of Information Systems Evaluation, 6*(2), 11–20.

Carmines, E. G., & Zeller, R. A. (1979). *Reliability and validity assessment.* N. 07-017, Sage University Paper Series on Quantitative Applications in the Social Sciences. Beverly Hills, CA: Sage.

Carroll, J. M., Rosson, M. B., Farooq, U., & Xiao, L. (2009). Beyond being aware. *Information and Organization, 19*(3), 162–185. doi:10.1016/j.infoandorg.2009.04.004

Carter, B., & New, C. (Eds.). (2004). *Making realism work: Realist social theory and empirical research (critical realism: interventions)*. Oxfordshire, UK: Routledge.

Cartwright, D., & Zander, A. (Eds.). (1953). *Group dynamics*. London, UK: Tavistock.

Carvalho, L., Scott, L., & Jeffery, R. (2005). An exploratory study into the use of qualitative research methods in descriptive process modeling. *Information and Software Technology, 47*, 113–127. doi:10.1016/j.infsof.2004.06.005

Carver, J., & Basili, V. (2003). Identifying implicit process variables to support future empirical work. *Journal of the Brazilian Computer Society, November*.

Cassel, C., Hackl, P., & Westlund, A. H. (1999). Robustness of partial least-squares method for estimating latent variable quality structures. *Journal of Applied Statistics, 26*(4), 435–446. doi:10.1080/02664769922322

Castelfranchi, C., & Falcone, R. (2004). Founding autonomy: The dialectics between (social) environment and agent's architecture and powers. *Lecture Notes on Artificial Intelligence, 2969*, 40–54.

Casti, J. L. (1989). *Paradigms lost*. New York, NY: Avon Books.

Cenfetelli, R. T., & Bassellier, G. (2009). Interpretation of formative measurement in information systems research. *Management Information Systems Quarterly, 33*(4), 689–707.

Chalmers, A. (1999). *What is this thing called science?* (3rd ed.). Maidenhead, UK: Open University Press.

Chanal, V., & Caron-Fasan, M. L. (2008, May). *How to invent a new business model based on crowdsourcing: The Crowdspirit case*. Paper presented at the Conférence de l'Association Internationale de Management Stratégique, Nice.

Chandrasekaran, B. B., Josephson, J. R., & Benjamins, V. (1999). What are ontologies, and why do we need them? *IEEE Intelligent Systems & Their Applications, 14*(1), 20. doi:10.1109/5254.747902

Chang, W.-L. (2008). A value-based pricing system for strategic co-branding goods. *Kybernetes, 37*(7), 978–996. doi:10.1108/03684920810884360

Charette, R. N. (2005). Why software project fails. *IEEE Spectrum*, 42–49. Retrieved from www.spectrum.ieee.orgdoi:10.1109/MSPEC.2005.1502528

Charmaz, K. (2006). *Constructing grounded theory: A practical guide through qualitative analysis*. Thousand Oaks, CA: Sage Publication.

Charon, J. (1998). *Symbolic interactionism: An introduction, an interpretation, an integration*. Englewood Cliffs, NJ: Prentice Hall.

Checkland, P. (1981). *Systems thinking, systems practice*. Chichester, UK: Wiley.

Checkland, P. (1983). OR and the systems movement - Mappings and conflicts. *The Journal of the Operational Research Society, 34*(8), 661–675.

Checkland, P. (1999). *Systems thinking, systems practice. Includes a 30 year retrospective*. Chichester, UK: Wiley.

Checkland, P. (2000). Soft systems methodology: A thirty year retrospective. *Systems Research and Behavioral Science, 17*, S11–S58. doi:10.1002/1099-1743(200011)17:1+<::AID-SRES374>3.0.CO;2-O

Checkland, P., & Holwell, S. (1998). *Information, systems and Information Systems*. Chichester, UK: Wiley.
Checkland, P., & Winter, M. (2006). Process and content: Two ways of using SSM. *The Journal of the Operational Research Society, 57*, 1435–1441. doi:10.1057/palgrave.jors.2602118

Checkland, P., & Scholes, J. (1990). *Soft systems methodology in action*. Chichester, UK: Wiley.

Checkland, P., & Winter, M. (2006). Process and content: Two ways of using SSM. *The Journal of the Operational Research Society, 57*, 1435–1441. doi:10.1057/palgrave.jors.2602118

Chen, H. M., Kazman, R., & Garg, A. (2006). BITAM: An engineering principled method for managing misalignments between business and IT architectures. *Science of Computer Programming, 56*, 5–26.

Chen, W., & Hirschheim, R. (2004). A paradigmatic and methodological examination of Information Systems research from 1991 to 2001. *Information Systems Journal, 14*(3), 197–235. doi:10.1111/j.1365-2575.2004.00173.x

Chesbrough, H. W. (2003b, Spring). The era of open innovation. *MIT Sloan Management Review*, 35–41.

Chesbrough, H. W. (2003a). *Open innovation: The new imperative for creating and profiting from technology.* Boston, MA: Harvard Business School Publishing Corporation.

Chesbrough, H. W. (2006). *Open business models: How to thrive in the new innovation landscape.* Boston, MA: Harvard Business School Press.

Chia, R. (2003). Organization theory as a postmodern science. In Tsoukas, H., & Knudsen, C. (Eds.), *The Oxford Handbook of organization theory: meta-theoretical perspectives* (pp. 113–142). Oxford: Oxford UP.

Chilton, S. (2009). *Crowdsourcing is radically changing the geodata landscape: Case study of OpenStreetMap.* Paper presented at the 24th International Cartographic Conference.

Chi, M. T. H., Feltovich, P. J., & Glaser, R. (1981). Categorization and representation of physics problems by experts and novices. Pittsburgh, PA: Lawrence Erlbaum Associates. *Cognitive Science, 5*(2), 121–152. doi:10.1207/s15516709cog0502_2

Chin, W. W. (2001). *PLS-graph user's guide,* version 3.0. University of Houston, 2001

Chin, W. W. (2002). *Exploring some FAQs regarding PLS including to report results.* I Workshop on partial least squares methodology. Seville, Spain: University of Seville.

Chin, W. W. (1998). Issues and opinion on structural equation modeling. *Management Information Systems Quarterly, 22*(1), vii–xvi.

Chin, W. W. (1998b). The partial least squares approach to structural equation modelling. In Marcoulides, G. A. (Ed.), *Modern methods for business research* (pp. 295–336). Mahwah, NJ: Lawrence Erlbaum.

Chin, W. W. (2010). How to write up and report PLS analyses. In Esposito Vinzi, V., Chin, W. W., Henseler, J., & Wang, H. (Eds.), *Handbook of partial least squares: Concepts, methods and applications* (pp. 655–690). Berlin, Germany: Springer-Verlag. doi:10.1007/978-3-540-32827-8_29

Chin, W. W., & Newsted, P. R. (1999). Structural equation modeling analysis with small samples using partial least squares. In Hoyle, R. (Ed.), *Statistical strategies for small samples research* (pp. 307–341). Thousand Oaks, CA: Sage.

Chin, W. W., Peterson, R. A., & Brown, S. P. (2008). Structural equation modeling in marketing: Some practical reminders. *Journal of Marketing Theory and Practice, 16*(4), 287–298. doi:10.2753/MTP1069-6679160402

Chrissis, M. B., Konrad, M., & Shrum, S. (2003). *CMMI: Guidelines for process integration and product improvement.* Addison Wesley.

Christenson, D., & Walker, D. (2004). Understanding the role of "vision" in project success. *Project Management Journal, 35*(3), 39–52.

Churchman, C. (1971). *The design of inquiring systems: Basic concepts of systems and organization.* New York, NY: Basic Books.

Churchman, W. (1979). *Design of inquiring systems: Basic concepts of systems and organizations.* New York, NY: Basic Books.

Cleven, A., Gubler, P., & Hüner, K. M. (2009). *Design alternatives for the evaluation of design science research artifacts.* Presented at the 4th International Conference on Design Science Research in Information Systems and Technology (DESRIST 2009), Philadelphia, PA.

Cobb, P., Confrey, J., Disessa, A., Lehrer, R., & Schauble, L. (2003). Design experiments in educational research. *Educational Researcher, 32*(1), 9–13. doi:10.3102/0013189X032001009

Cockburn, A. (2001). *Agile software development.* Boston, MA: Addison-Wesley.

Cockburn, A. (2007). *Agile software development. The cooperative game* (2nd ed.). Boston, MA: Pearson.

Cockton, G. (2002). *My grounded design page*. Retrieved March 2011 from http://www.cet.sunderland.ac.uk/~cs0gco/grounded.htm

Cockton, G. (2004). *A tutorial: Grounded design and HCI. September 2004*. Pretoria, South Africa: University of South Africa.

Cocosila, M., Archer, N., & Yuan, Y. (2009). Early investigation of new information technology acceptance: A perceived risk - motivation model. *Communications of the Association for Information Systems, 25*(1).

Cohen, J. (1988). *Statistical power analysis for the behavioral sciences* (2nd ed.). Hillsdale, NJ: Erlbaum.

Cohen, L., Manion, L., & Morrison, K. (2005). *Research methods in education* (5th ed.). Abingdon, UK: Routledge Falmer.

Cohen, P. R. (1995). *Empirical methods for artificial intelligence*. Cambridge, MA: MIT Press.

Coleman, G., & O'Connor, R. (1997). Using grounded theory to understand software process improvement: A study of Irish software product companies. *Journal of Information and Software Technology, 49*(6), 531–694.

Collier, A. (1994). *Critical realism: An introduction to the philosophy of Roy Bhaskar*. London, UK: Verso.

Collins, A. (1992). Toward a design science of education. In Scanlon, E., & O'Shea, T. (Eds.), *New directions in educational technology*. Berlin, Germany: Springer-Verlag. doi:10.1007/978-3-642-77750-9_2

Collins, A., Joseph, D., & Bielaczyc, K. (2004). Design research: Theoretical and methodological issues. *Journal of the Learning Sciences, 13*(1), 15–42. doi:10.1207/s15327809jls1301_2

Collyer, M. (2000). Communication – The route to successful change management: Lessons from Guinness integrated business programme. *Supply Chain Management: an International Journal, 5*(5), 222–225. doi:10.1108/13598540010350556

Conboy, K. (2009). Agility from first principles: Reconstructing the concept of agility in Information Systems development. *Information Systems Research, 20*(3), 329–354. doi:10.1287/isre.1090.0236

Conlon, T. (2000). Visions of change: Information Technology, education and postmodernism. *British Journal of Educational Technology, 31*(2), 109–116. doi:10.1111/1467-8535.00141

Conradie, M. M., & de Villiers, M. R. (2004). Electronic assessment of free-text: a development research initiative. *South African Journal of Higher Education, 18*(2), 172–188. doi:10.4314/sajhe.v18i2.25462

Conte, R., Edmonds, B., Scott, M., & Sawyer, R. K. (2001). Sociology and social theory in agent-based social simulation: a symposium. *Computational & Mathematical Organization Theory, 7*, 183–205. doi:10.1023/A:1012919018402

Conte, R., & Paolucci, M. (2002). *Reputation in artificial societies: Social beliefs for social order*. Dordrecht, The Netherlands: Kluwer Academic Publishers.

Conte, R., & Turrini, P. (2006). Argyll-feet giants: a cognitive analysis of collective autonomy. *Cognitive Systems Research, 7*, 209–219. doi:10.1016/j.cogsys.2005.11.011

Cook, S. D. N., & Brown, J. S. (1999). Bridging epistemologies: the generative dance between organizational knowledge and organizational knowing. *Organization Science, 10*(4), 381–400. doi:10.1287/orsc.10.4.381

Cook, T. D., & Campbell, D. T. (1979). *Quasi experimentation: Design and analytical issues for field settings*. Chicago, IL: Rand McNally College.

Cornford, T., & Smithson, S. (2006). *Project research in information systems: A student's guide* (2nd ed.). London, UK: Palgrave.

Cotkin, G. (1996). Hyping the text: Hypertext, postmodernism, and the historian. *American Studies (Lawrence, Kan.), 37*(2), 103–116.

Council of Graduate Schools. (2008). *Ph.D. completion and attrition: Analysis of baseline program data from the Ph.D. completion project*. Washington, DC: Author.

Cowan, R. (2001). Expert systems: Aspect of and limitations to the codifiability of knowledge. *Research Policy, 30*(9), 1355–1372. doi:10.1016/S0048-7333(01)00156-1

Cowan, R., David, P., & Foray, D. (2000). The explicit economics of knowledge codification and tacitness. *Industrial and Corporate Change, n.d.*, 9.

Cowan, R., & Foray, D. (1997). The economics of codification and the diffusion of knowledge. *Industrial and Corporate Change, 6*, 592–622.

Craib, I. (1992). *Modern social theory: From Parsons to Habermas.* Hertfordshire, UK: Harvester Wheatsheaf.

Cresswell, A. M. (2001). Thoughts on relevance of IS research. *Communications of the Association for Information Systems, 6*(1).

Creswell, J. (1994). *Research design: Qualitative and quantitative approaches.* Thousand Oaks, CA: Sage Publication.

Creswell, J. W. (2009). *Research design: Qualitative, quantitative, and mixed method approaches* (3rd ed.). Los Angeles, CA: SAGE publications.

Creswell, J. W. (2011). *Educational research: Planning, conducting, and evaluating quantitative and qualitative research* (4th ed.). Sage Publishers.

Crombie, A. C. (1971). *Robert Grosseteste and the origins of experimental science, 1100-1700.* Oxford, UK: Clarendon Press.

Cross, N. (2001). Designerly ways of knowing: Design discipline versus design science. *Design Issues, 17*(3), 49–55. doi:10.1162/074793601750357196

Crotty, M. (1998). *The foundations of social research: Meaning and perspective in the research process.* St Leonards, Australia: Allen & Unwin.

Crowston, K. (2003). *Process as theory in information systems research.* Paper presented at the IFIP TC8 WG8. 2 International Working Conference on the Social and Organizational Perspective on Research and Practice in Information Technology, Aalborg, Denmark.

Crowston, K. (1997). A coordination theory approach to organizational process design. *Organization Science, 8*(2), 157–175. doi:10.1287/orsc.8.2.157

Crowston, K. (2003). A taxonomy of organizational dependencies and coordination mechanisms. In Malone, K. C. T. W., & Herman, G. A. (Eds.), *Organizing business knowledge: The MIT process handbook.* MIT Press.

Crowston, K. (2003a). Process as theory in information systems research. In Malone, T. W., Crowston, K., & Herman, G. A. (Eds.), *Organizing business knowledge: The MIT process handbook* (pp. 177–190). MIT Press.

Csemerly, P. (2006). *Weak links: Stabilizers of complex systems from proteins to social networks.* Berlin, Germany: Springer.

Cyert, R. M., & March, J. G. (1963). *Behavioral theory of the firm.* Oxford, UK: Blackwell.

Czarniawska, B. (1997). *Narrating the organization.* Chicago, IL: University of Chicago Press.

Czarniawska, B. (2003). The styles and the stylists of organization theory. In Tsoukas, H., & Knudsen, C. (Eds.), *The Oxford handbook of organization theory: Meta-theoretical perspectives* (pp. 237–262). Oxford, UK: Oxford UP. doi:10.1093/oxfordhb/9780199275250.003.0009

Czarniawska, B. (2008). *A theory of organizing.* Cheltenham, UK: Edward Elgar.

Damoradan, L., & Olphert, W. (2000). Barriers and facilitators to the use of knowledge management systems. *Behaviour & Information Technology, 19*(6), 405–413. doi:10.1080/014492900750052660

Danermark, B., Ekström, M., Jakobsen, L., & Karlsson, J. (2002). *Explaining society: Critical realism in the social sciences.* London, UK: Routledge.

Danowski, J. A. (2007). *Frame change and phase shift detection using news story emotionality and semantic networks: A 25-month analysis of coverage of "Second Life".* Paper presented at the Annual Meetings of the Association of Internet Researchers.

Danowski, J. A. (2009). Inferences from word networks in messages. In Krippendorff, K., & Bock, M. A. (Eds.), *The content analysis reader* (pp. 421–429). Los Angeles, CA: Sage.

Darke, P., Shanks, G., & Broadbent, M. (1998). Successfully completing case study research. *Information Systems Journal, 8*(4), 273–289. doi:10.1046/j.1365-2575.1998.00040.x

Datta, P., Walsh, K. R., & Terrell, D. (2002). The impact of demographics on choice of survey modes: Demographic distinctiveness between Web-based and telephone-based survey respondents. *Communications of the Association for Information System, 9*, article 13.

Davenport, T. (1997, April 15). Think tank – Storming the ivory tower. *CIO Magazine*.

Davenport, T. H., & Markus, M. L. (1999). Rigor vs. relevance revisited: Response to Benbasat and Zmud. *Management Information Systems Quarterly, 23*(1), 19–24. doi:10.2307/249405

Davidson-Reynolds, P. (1971). *Primer in theory construction*. Indianapolis, IN: Bobbs-Merrill.

Davis, F. D. (1989). Perceived usefulness, perceived ease of use and user acceptance of Information Technology. *Management Information Systems Quarterly, 13*(3), 319–342. doi:10.2307/249008

Davis, F. D. (1989). Perceived usefulness, perceived ease of use, and user acceptance of Information Technology. *Management Information Systems Quarterly, 13*(3), 319–340. doi:10.2307/249008

Davis, F. D. (1989). Perceived usefulness, perceived ease of use, and user acceptance of information technology. *Management Information Systems Quarterly, 13*, 319–339. doi:10.2307/249008

Davis, F. D., Bagozzi, R. P., & Warshaw, P. R. (1989). User acceptance of computer technology: A comparison of two theoretical models. *Management Science, 35*, 982–1003. doi:10.1287/mnsc.35.8.982

Davis, F. D., Bagozzi, R. P., & Warshaw, P. R. (1992). Extrinsic and intrinsic motivation to use computers in the workplace. *Journal of Applied Social Psychology, 22*, 1111–1132. doi:10.1111/j.1559-1816.1992.tb00945.x

Davis, J. P., Eisenhardt, K. M., & Bingham, C. B. (2007). Developing theory through virtual experiment methods. *Academy of Management Review, 32*(2), 480–499. doi:10.5465/AMR.2007.24351453

De Boer, C., & Brennecke, S. (2003). *Media en publiek: theorieën over media-impact (vijfde, herziene druk)*. Amsterdam, The Netherlands: Boom.

De Nooy, W., Mrvar, A., & Batagelj, V. (2005). *Exploratory social network analysis with Pajek*. New York, NY: Cambridge University Press.

De Villiers, M. R. (2004). Usability evaluation of an e-learning tutorial: Criteria, questions and case study. In: G. Marsden, P. Kotze, & A. Adesina-Ojo (Eds.), *Fulfilling the promise of ICT. Proceedings of SAICSIT 2004* (pp. 284-291). ACM International Conference Proceedings Series.

De Villiers, M. R. (2009). Applying controlled usability-testing technology to investigate learning behaviours of users interacting with e-learning tutorials. In T. Bastiaens *et al.* (Eds.), *Proceedings of World Conference on E-Learning in Corporate, Government, Healthcare, and Higher Education 2009* (pp. 2512-2521). Chesapeake, VA: AACE. Canada.

De Villiers, M. R. (2005). Interpretive research models for informatics: Action research, grounded theory, and the family of design and development research. *Alternation, 12*(2), 10–52.

De Villiers, M. R. (2005a). e-Learning artifacts: Are they based on learning theory? *Alternation, 12*(1b), 345–371.

De Villiers, M. R. (2005b). Interpretive research models for informatics: Action research, grounded theory, and the family of design- and development research. *Alternation, 12*(2), 10–52.

De Villiers, M. R. (2007). An action research approach to the design, development and evaluation of an interactive e-learning tutorial in a cognitive domain. *Journal of Information Technology Education, 6*, 455–479. Retrieved from http://jite.org/documents/Vol6/JITEv6p455-479deVilliers225.pdf

Deci, E. L., & Ryan, R. M. (1991). A motivational approach to self: Integration in personality. In R. Dienstbier (Ed.), *Nebraska Symposium on Motivation: Vol. 38. Perspectives on motivation* (pp. 237-288). Lincoln, NE: University of Nebraska Press.

Dede, C. (2005). Why design-based research is both important and difficult. *Educational Technology, 45*(1), 5–8.

Defense Acquisition University. (2001). *Systems engineering fundamentals*. Fort Belvoir, VA: Defense Acquisition University Press.

Dehmer, M., & Emmert-Streib, F. (Eds.). (2009). *Analysis of complex networks: From biology to linguistics*. Weinheim, Germany: Wiley-VCH.

DeLone, W. H., & McLean, E. R. (1992). Information systems success: The quest for the dependent variable. *Information Systems Research, 3,* 60–95. doi:10.1287/isre.3.1.60

DeLone, W. H., & McLean, E. R. (2003). The DeLone and McLean Model of Information Systems success: A ten-year update. *Journal of Management Information Systems, 19*(4), 9–30.

Denning, P. J. (2005). Is computer science science? *Communications of the ACM, 48*(4), 27–31. doi:10.1145/1053291.1053309

Denning, P. J., Comer, D. E., Gries, D., Mulder, M. C., Tucker, A., Turner, A. J., & Young, P. R. (1989). Computing as a discipline. *Communications of the ACM, 32*(1), 9–23. doi:10.1145/63238.63239

Dennis, A. R. (2001). Relevance in Information Systems research. *Communications of the Association for Information Systems, 6*(1).

Denzin, N. K., & Lincoln, Y. S. (2000). The discipline and practice of qualitative research. In *Handbook of qualitative research*. London, UK: Sage Publication.

Department of Education Training and Youth Affairs. (2001). *Factors associated with completion of research higher degrees*. Department of Education Training and Youth Affairs.

Derntl, M., & Motschnig-Pitrik, R. (2004). A pattern approach to person-centered e-learning based on theory-guided action research. *Proceedings of the Networked Learning Conference* 2004.

DeSanctis, G., & Poole, M. S. (1994). Capturing the complexity in advanced Technology Use: Adaptive structuration theory. *Organization Science, 5*(2), 121–147. doi:10.1287/orsc.5.2.121

Design Research in Information Systems (DRIS). (2006). Retrieved September 2006 from http://www.isworld.org/Researchdesign/drisISworld.htm

Design-Based Research Collective. (2003). Design-based research: An emerging paradigm for educational enquiry. *Educational Researcher, 32*(1), 5–8. doi:10.3102/0013189X032001005

Desouza, K. C., & Evaristo, J. R. (2006). Project management offices: A case of knowledge-based archetypes. *International Journal of Information Management, 26,* 414–423. doi:10.1016/j.ijinfomgt.2006.07.002

Devaraj, S., Fan, M., & Kohli, R. (2002). Antecedents of B2C channel satisfaction and preference: Validating e-commerce metrics. *Information Systems Research, 13*(3), 316–333. doi:10.1287/isre.13.3.316.77

Dholakia, U. M., Bagozzi, R. P., & Pearo, L. K. (2003). A social influence model of consumer participation in network- and small-group-based virtual communities. *International Journal of Research in Marketing, 21,* 241–263. doi:10.1016/j.ijresmar.2003.12.004

Di Gangi, P. M., & Wasko, M. (2009). Steal my idea! Organizational adoption of user innovations from a user innovation community: A case study of Dell IdeaStorm. *Decision Support Systems, 48,* 303–312. doi:10.1016/j.dss.2009.04.004

Diamanthopoulos, A., & Winklhofer, H. M. (2001). Index construction with formative indicators: An alternative to scale development. *JMR, Journal of Marketing Research, 38*(2), 269–277. doi:10.1509/jmkr.38.2.269.18845

Diamantopoulos, A. (2011). Incorporating formative measures into covariance-based structural equation models. *Management Information Systems Quarterly, 35*(2), 335–358.

Díaz-Casero, J. C., Hernández-Mogollón, R. M., & Roldán, J. L. (2011). (in press). A structural model of the antecedents to entrepreneurial capacity. *International Small Business Journal, 29.*

DiBona, A. Jr. (2000). Avoiding low-hanging fruit. *Knowledge and Process Management, 7*(1), 60–62. doi:10.1002/(SICI)1099-1441(200001/03)7:1<60::AID-KPM69>3.0.CO;2-9

Dick, B., Passfield, R., & Wildman, P. (1995). *A beginner's guide to action research*. Retrieved September 2006 from http://www.scu.edu.au/schools/gcm/ar/arp/guide.html

Dingsøyr, T., Djarraya, H. K., & Royrvik, E. (2005). Practical knowledge management tool use in a software consulting company. *Communications of the ACM, 48*(12), 97–103. doi:10.1145/1101779.1101783

Dobson, P. (2001). The philosophy of critical realism - An opportunity for Information Systems research. *Information Systems Frontiers*, (July): 2001.

Dobson, P. (2003). BPR versus outsourcing – Critical perspectives. *Journal of Systemic Practice and Action Research, 16*(3), 225–233. doi:10.1023/A:1023863906650

Dobson, P., Myles, J., & Jackson, P. (2007). Making the case for critical realism: Examining the implementation of automated performance management systems. *Information Resources Management Journal, 20*(2), 138–152. doi:10.4018/irmj.2007040109

Dodgson, M., Gann, D., & Salter, A. (2006). The role of technology in the shift towards open innovation: The case of Proctor & Gamble. *R & D Management, 36*(3), 333–346. doi:10.1111/j.1467-9310.2006.00429.x

Donaldson, O., & Golding, P. (2009). A design science approach for creating mobile applications. *ICIS 2009 Proceedings*, Paper 165.

Dooley, K. (2002). Virtual experiment research methods. In Baum, J. A. C. (Ed.), *Companion to organizations* (pp. 849–867). Oxford, UK: Blackwell.

Dorogovtsev, S. N., & Mendes, J. F. F. (2003). *Evolution of networks*. New York, NY: Oxford UP. doi:10.1093/acprof:oso/9780198515906.001.0001

Dorst, K. (2008). Design research: A revolution-waiting-to-happen. *Design Research, 29*(1), 4–11.

du Plooy, N. F. (2003). *The social responsibility of information systems developers*. IGI Publishing.

Du Poy, E., & Gitlin, L. N. (1998). *Introduction to research: Understanding and applying multiple strategies* (2nd ed.). St. Louis, MO: Mosby Inc.

Dubé, L., & Paré, G. (2003). Rigor in Information Systems positivist case research: Current practices, trends, and recommendations. *Management Information Systems Quarterly, 27*(4), 597–636.

Dubin, R. (1978). *Theory building*. New York, NY: Free Press.

Durmusoglu, S. S., & Barczak, G. (2011). The use of Information Technology tools in new product development phases: Analysis of effects on new product innovativeness, quality, and market performance. *Industrial Marketing Management, 40*(2), 321–330. doi:10.1016/j.indmarman.2010.08.009

Dutta, A., & Roy, R. (2008). Dynamics of organizational information Security. *System Dynamics Review, 24*(3), 349–375. doi:10.1002/sdr.405

Easthope, A. (2001). Postmodernism and critical and cultural theory. In Sim, S. (Ed.), *The Routledge companion to postmodernism* (pp. 15–27). London, UK: Routledge.

Easton, G. (1995). Methodology and industrial networks. In Moller, K., & Wilson, D. T. (Eds.), *Business marketing: An interaction and network perspective* (pp. 411–491). Norwell, MA: Kluwer Academic Publishing. doi:10.1007/978-94-011-0645-0_15

Easton, G. (2010). Critical realism in case study research. *Industrial Marketing Management, 39*, 118–128. doi:10.1016/j.indmarman.2008.06.004

Edelman, G. M. (1989). *The remembered present: A biological theory of consciousness*. New York, NY: Basic Books.

Edwards, J. R., & Bagozzi, R. P. (2000). On the nature and direction of relationships between constructs and their measures. *Psychological Methods, 5*, 155–174. doi:10.1037/1082-989X.5.2.155

Efron, B., & Tibshirani, R. J. (1993). *An introduction to the bootstrap. Monographs on Statistics and Applied Probability, no. 57*. New York, NY: Chapman and Hall.

Eisenhardt, K. M. (1989). Building theories from case study research. *Academy of Management Review, 4*(4), 532–550.

Eisner, H. (2008). *Essentials of project and system engineering management* (3rd ed.). Indianapolis, IN: Wiley.

Elo, S., & Kyngäs, H. (2008). The qualitative content analysis process. *Journal of Advanced Nursing, 62*(1), 107–115. doi:10.1111/j.1365-2648.2007.04569.x

Entman, R. M. (1993). Framing: Toward clarification of a fractured paradigm. *The Journal of Communication, 43*(4), 51–57. doi:10.1111/j.1460-2466.1993.tb01304.x

Fairley, R. (2009). *Managing and leading software projects* (2nd ed.). Hoboken, NJ: John Wiley and Sons Inc. doi:10.1002/9780470405697

Falk, R. F., & Miller, N. B. (1992). *A primer for soft modeling*. Akron, OH: The University of Akron.

Fallman, D., & Gronlund, A. (2002). Rigor and relevance remodeled. *Proceedings of Information Systems Research in Scandinavia*, IRIS25, Bautahoj, Denmark, August 10-13.

Fann, K. T. (1970). *Peirce's theory of abduction*. The Hague, The Netherlands: Martinus Nijhoff. doi:10.1007/978-94-010-3163-9

Fantoni, G., Apreda, R., Valleri, P., Bonaccorsi, A., & Manteni, M. (2008). *IPR tracking system in collaborative environments*. Retrieved from http:// 74.125.155.132/scholar?q=cache: uPhWjfQFxXMJ:scholar.google.com/&hl=en&as_sdt= 800000000000

Feagin, J., Orum, A., & Sjoberg, G. (Eds.). (1991). *A case for case study*. Chapel Hill, NC: University of North Carolina Press.

Feldhay, R. (1998). The use and abuse of mathematical entities: Galileo and the Jesuits revisited. In Machamer, P. (Ed.), *The Cambridge companion to Galileo* (pp. 80–145). Cambridge, UK: Cambridge University Press. doi:10.1017/CCOL0521581788.004

Feller, J., Finnegan, P., Hayes, J., & O'Reilly, P. (2010). *Sustainable crowdsourcing*. Draft Working Paper of the O3C Business Models Project, University College Cork.

Feller, J., Finnegan, P., Hayes, J., & O'Reilly, P. (2009). Institutionalizing information asymmetry: Governance structures for open innovation. *Information Technology & People, 22*(4), 297–316. doi:10.1108/09593840911002423

Ferdinand, M., Zirpins, C., & Trastour, D. (2004, July 26-30). Lifting XML schema to OWL. In *Proceedings of the 4th International Web Engineering Conference. Lecture Notes in Computer Science, 3140*, 354–358. doi:10.1007/978-3-540-27834-4_44

Ferris, T. L. J. (2007a). *Some early history of systems engineering - 1950's in IRE publications (part 1): The problem*. 17th International Symposium Systems Engineering: key to intelligent enterprises. San Diego, CA: International Council on Systems Engineering.

Ferris, T. L. J. (2007b). *Some early history of systems engineering - 1950's in IRE publications (part 2): The solution*. 17th International Symposium Systems Engineering: Key to intelligent enterprises. San Diego, CA: International Council on Systems Engineering.

Ferris, T. L. J. (2008). *Early history of systems engineering (Part 3) – 1950's in various engineering sources*. INCOSE International Symposium 2008. Utrecht, The Netherlands: International Council on Systems Engineering.

Ferris, T. L. J. (2009). *On the methods of research for systems engineering*. 7th Annual Conference on Systems Engineering Research. Loughborough, UK.

Feyerabend, P. (1993). *Against the method: An outline of an anarchistic theory of perception*. London, UK: Verso.

Feyerabend, P. K. (1975). *Against method: Outline of an anarchistic theory of knowledge*. London, UK: New Left Books.

Finch, P. (2003). Applying the Sleving-Pinto project implementation profile to an Information System project. *Project Management Journal, 34*(3), 32–39.

Firat, A. F., & Dholakia, N. (2004/2005). Theoretical and philosophical implications of postmodern debates: Some challenges to modern marketing. *Marketing Theory, 6*(2), 123-162. Retrieved May 17, 2010, from http:// mtq.sagepub.com/ cgi/ content/ abstract/ 6/ 2/ 123

Fleetwood, S. (2005). Ontology in organization and management studies: A critical realist perspective. *Organization, 12*, 197-222.

Flood, R., & Room, N. (Eds.). (1996). *Critical systems thinking*. New York, NY: Plenum Press. doi:10.1007/b102400

Fogg, B. J., & Kameda, T. Boyd. J., Marshall, J., Seith, R., Sockol, M., & Trowbridge, T. (2002). Stanford-*Makovsky Web credibility study 2002: Investigating what makes Web sites credible today*. A research report by the Stanford Persuasive Technology Lab & Makovsky & Company. Stanford University.

Fonseca, F. (2007). The double role of ontologies in Information Science research. *Journal of the American Society for Information Science and Technology, 58*(6) 786-793. Preprint retrieved March 23, 2009, from http:// www.personal.psu.edu/ faculty/ f/ u/ fuf1/ publications/ Fonseca_ Ontologies_ double_ role_ JASIST_ 2006.pdf

Fonseca, F., & Martin, J. (2007). Learning the differences between ontologies and conceptual schemas through ontology-driven information systems. *Journal of the Association for Information Systems, 8*(2), 129-142 (Article 3). Retrieved November 24, 2009, from http:// aisel.aisnet. org/ jais/ vol8/ iss2/ 4

Fornell, C. (1982). A second generation of multivariate analysis: an overview. In Fornell, C. (Ed.), *A second generation of multivariate analysis* (*Vol. 1*, pp. 1–21). New York, NY: Praeger.

Fornell, C., & Bookstein, F. L. (1982). A comparative analysis of two structural equation models: Lisrel and PLS applied to market data. In Fornell, C. (Ed.), *A second generation of multivariate analysis* (*Vol. 1*, pp. 289–324). New York, NY: Praeger.

Fornell, C., & Cha, J. (1994). Partial least squares. In Bagozzi, R. (Ed.), *Advanced methods of marketing* (pp. 52–78). Cambridge, UK: Blackwell.

Fornell, C., & Larcker, D. F. (1981). Evaluating structural equation models with unobservable variables and measurement error. *JMR, Journal of Marketing Research, 18*, 39–50. doi:10.2307/3151312

Forrester, J. (1991). *Systems dynamics and the lessons of 35 years*. Technical Report D-4224-4. Retrieved from http://sysdyn.mit.edu/sd-group/home.html

Forrester, J. W. (1958). Industrial dynamics-A major breakthrough for decision makers. *Harvard Business Review, 36*(4), 37–66.

Forrester, J. W. (1973). *Industrial dynamics*. Cambridge, MA: MIT Press.

Forrester, J. W. (1992). Policies, decisions and information sources for modeling. *European Journal of Operational Research, 59*(1), 42–63. doi:10.1016/0377-2217(92)90006-U

Forsberg, K., & Mooz, H. (1991). The relationship of systems engineering to the project cycle. *Proceedings of the First Annual Symposium of the National Council on Systems Engineering (NCOSE)*, Chattanooga, TN, 21-23 October, 1991. Retrieved May 26, 2011, from http://www. csm.com /repository/ model/ rep/o/pdf/ Relationship% 20of% 20SE% 20to% 20Proj% 20Cycle.pdf

Frank, U. (2006). *Towards a pluralistic conception of research methods in Information Systems research*. ICB-Research Report No. 7. Institute for Computer Science and Business Information Systems, University Duisburg-Essen. Retrieved May 19, 2011, from http://www.icb. uni-due.de/fileadmin/ICB/research/research_reports/ ICBReport07.pdf

Franzoni, C. (2006). *Do scientists get fundamental research ideas by solving practical problems?* Paper presented at the 11th International J. A. Schumpeter Society Conference: Innovation, Competition and Growth: Schumpeterian Perspectives, Sophia-Antipolis. France.

Frazer, M. J., & Sleet, R. J. (1984). A study of students' attempts to solve chemical problems. *European Journal of Science Education, 6*(2), 141–152. doi:10.1080/0140528840060204

Friedman, K. (2003). Theory construction in design research: Criteria, approaches, and methods. *Design Studies, 24*(6), 507–522. doi:10.1016/S0142-694X(03)00039-5

Fruchterman, T., & Reingold, E. (1991). Graph drawing by force-directed replacement. *Software, Practice & Experience, 21*, 1129–1166. doi:10.1002/spe.4380211102

Fu, J. R. (2006). *VisualPLS – Partial least square (PLS) Regression – An enhanced GUI for Lvpls (PLS 1.8 PC) Version 1.04*. Taiwan, ROC: National Kaohsiung University of Applied Sciences.

Galliers, R., & Land, F. (1987). Choosing an appropriate Information Systems research methodology. *Communications of the ACM, 30*(11), 900–902. doi:10.1145/32206.315753

Gallivan, M., & Benbunan-Fich, R. (2005). A framework for analyzing levels of analysis issues in studies of e-collaboration. *IEEE Transactions on Professional Communication, 48*(1), 87–104.

Gallupe, B. (2001). Knowledge management systems: Surveying the landscape. *International Journal of Management Reviews, 3*(1), 61–77. doi:10.1111/1468-2370.00054

Gamson, W. A. (1989). News as framing: "Comments on Graber. *The American Behavioral Scientist, 33*(2), 157–161. doi:10.1177/0002764289033002006

Gargeya, V. B., & Brady, C. (2005). Success and failure factors of adopting SAP in ERP system implementation. *Business Process Management Journal, 11*(5), 501–516. doi:10.1108/14637150510619858

Garrett, J. E. (1978). Hans-Georg Gadamer on "fusion of horizons". *Man and World, 11*(3), 392–400. doi:10.1007/BF01251946

Gefen, D., Rigdon, E. E., & Straub, D. (2011). An updated and extension to SEM guidelines for administrative and social science research. *Management Information Systems Quarterly, 35*(2), iii–xiv.

Gefen, D., & Straub, D. (1997). Gender differences in the perception and use of e-mail: an extension to the technology acceptance model. *Management Information Systems Quarterly, 21*(4), 389–400. doi:10.2307/249720

Gefen, D., & Straub, D. (2005). A practical guide to factorial validity using PLS-Graph: Tutorial and annotated example. *Communications of the AIS, 16*, 91–109.

Gefen, D., Straub, D. W., & Boudreau, M. (2000). Structural equation modeling techniques and regression: Guidelines for research practice. *Communications of AIS, 4*(7), 1–77.

Gefen, D., Straub, D., & Boudreau, M. (2000). Structural equation modeling and regression: Guidelines for research practice. *Communications of the Association for Information Systems, 7*(7), 1–78.

Gelman, O., & Garcia, J. (1989). Formulation and axiomatization of the concept of general system. Mexican Institute of Planning and Systems Operation. *Outlet IMPOS, 19*(92), 1–81.

Génova, G. (1997). *Charles S. Peirce: La lógica del descubrimiento.* Pamplona, Spain: Servicio de Publicaciones de la Universidad de Navarra.

Génova, G. (2010). Is computer science truly scientific? Reflections on the (experimental) scientific method in computer science. *Communications of the ACM, 53*(7), 37–39.

Génova, G., González, M. R., & Fraga, A. (2007). Ethical education in software engineering: Responsibility in the production of complex systems. *Science and Engineering Ethics, 13*(4), 505–522. doi:10.1007/s11948-007-9017-6

Génova, G., Valiente, M. C., & Marrero, M. (2009). On the difference between analysis and design, and why it is relevant for the interpretation of models in Model Driven Engineering. *Journal of Object Technology, 8*(1), 107–127. doi:10.5381/jot.2009.8.1.c7

Georgantzasa, N. C., & Katsamakasb, E. G. (2008). Information systems research with system dynamics. *System Dynamics Review, 24*(3), 247–264. doi:10.1002/sdr.420

Gergen, K. (1999). *An invitation to social construction.* London, UK: Sage.

Gerow, J. E., Grover, V., Roberts, N., & Thatcher, J. B. (2010). The diffusion of second generation statistical techniques in Information Systems research from 1990–2008. (JITTA). *Journal of Information Technology Theory and Application, 11*(4), 5–28.

Geyer, F., & van der Zouwen, J. (Eds.). (1986). *Sociocybernetic paradoxes.* London, UK: Sage.

Giddens, A. (1979). *Central problems in social theory: Action, structure and contradiction in social analysis.* London, UK: Macmillan.

Giddens, A. (1984). *The constitution of society: Outline of the theory of structuration.* Cambridge, UK: Polity Press.

Gilbert, N. (2008). *Agent-based models.* London, UK: Sage.

Gilbert, N., & Terna, P. (2000). How to build and use agent-based models in social science. *Mind & Society., 1*, 57–72. doi:10.1007/BF02512229

Gilbert, N., & Troitzsch, K. G. (2005). *Simulation for the social scientist.* Buckingham, UK: Open University.

Gilchrist, A. (2003). Thesauri, taxonomies and ontologies – An etymological note. *The Journal of Documentation, 59*(1), 7–18. doi:10.1108/00220410310457984

Glaser, B. G. (1992). *Basics of Grounded Theory Analysis*. Mill Valley, CA: Sociology Press.

Glaser, B., & Strauss, A. (1967). *The discovery of grounded theory: Strategies for qualitative research*. Chicago, IL: Aldine.

Glass, R., Ramesh, V., & Vessey, I. (2004). An analysis of research in computing disciplines. *Communications of the ACM*, *47*(6), 89–94. doi:10.1145/990680.990686

Glass, R., Vessey, I., & Ramesh, V. (2002). Research in software engineering: An analysis of the literature. *Information and Software Technology*, *44*, 491–506. doi:10.1016/S0950-5849(02)00049-6

Goede, R., & de Villiers, C. (2003). The applicability of grounded theory as research methodology in studies on the use of methodologies in IS practices. *Proceedings of SAICSIT*, (pp. 208-217). South Africa.

Goffman, E. (1974). *Frame analysis: An essay on the organization of experience*. New York, NY: Harper & Row.

Gonzalez, R. A. (2009). Validation of crisis response simulation within the design science framework. *ICIS 2009 Proceedings*, Paper 87.

Gonzalez, R., & Dahanayake, A. (2007). A concept map of Information Systems research approaches. In M. Khosrow-Pour (Ed.), *Proceedings of the 2007 IRMA International Conference*, Vancouver, Canada, May 11-14, (pp. 845-848).

Goodhue, D., Lewis, W., & Thompson, R. (2006). PLS, small sample size, and statistical power in MIS research. In *HICSS '06: Proceedings of the 39th Annual Hawaii International Conference on System Sciences*, (pp. 202.2). Washington, DC: IEEE Computer Society, CD-ROM, 10 pages.

Goodman, L. E. (2003). *Islamic humanism*. Oxford, UK: Oxford University Press.

Goulding, C. (2002). *Grounded theory: A practical guide for management, business and market researchers*. Sage Publications.

Gowan, J. A. Jr, & Mathieu, R. G. (2005). The importance of management practices in IS project performance - An empirical study. *Journal of Enterprise Information Management*, *18*(2), 235–255. doi:10.1108/17410390510579936

Graaff, H. (2001). *Developing interactive systems - A perspective on supporting ill-structured work. PhD*. Delft University of Technology.

Graff, G. (2002). The problem problem and other oddities of academic discourse. *Arts and Humanities in Higher Education*, *1*(1), 27–42. doi:10.1177/1474022202001001003

Gramsci, A. (1971). *Prison notebooks*. London: Lawrence & Wishart.

Granovetter, M. S. (1973). The strength of weak ties. *American Journal of Sociology*, *78*(6), 1360–1380. doi:10.1086/225469

Grant, I. H. (2001a). Postmodernism and politics. In S. Sim (Ed.), (2001a), *The Routledge companion to postmodernism* (pp. 28-40). London, UK: Routledge.

Grant, I. H. (2001b). Postmodernism and science and technology. In S. Sim (Ed.), (2001a), *The Routledge companion to postmodernism* (pp. 65-77). London, UK: Routledge.

Gray, P. (2002). *Relevance as an "unfulfilled promise"*. Presentation at ICIS 2001 Panel.

Greenhill, A., & Fletcher, G. (2007a). Exploring events as an Information Systems research methodology. *International Journal of Technology and Human Interaction*, *3*(1), 1–16. doi:10.4018/jthi.2007010101

Greenhill, A., & Fletcher, G. (2007b). Postmodern methods in the context of human-computer interaction (guest editorial preface). *International Journal of Technology and Human Interaction*, *3*(1), i–v.

Green, M. C., & Brock, T. C. (1998). Trust, mood, and outcomes of friendship determine preferences for real versus ersatz social capital. *Political Psychology*, *19*(3), 527–544. doi:10.1111/0162-895X.00116

Green, S. B. (1991). How many subjects does it take to do a regression analysis. *Multivariate Behavioral Research*, *26*, 499–510. doi:10.1207/s15327906mbr2603_7

Gregor, S. (2009). *Building theory in the sciences of the artificial*. Presented at the 4th International Conference on Design Science Research in Information Systems and Technology (DESRIST 2009), Philadelphia, PA.

Gregor, S. (2006). The nature of theory in Information Systems. *Management Information Systems Quarterly, 30*(3), 611–642.

Gregor, S., & Jones, D. (2007). The anatomy of a design theory. *Journal of the Association for Information Systems, 8*(5), 312–335.

Guarino, N., Masolo, C., & Vetere, G. (1999). OntoSeek: Content-based access to the Web. *IEEE Intelligent Systems & Their Applications, 14*(3), 70–80. doi:10.1109/5254.769887

Guba, E. G., & Lincoln, Y. S. (1994). Competing paradigms in qualitative research. In Denzin, N. K., & Lincoln, Y. S. (Eds.), *Handbook of qualitative research*. London, UK: SAGE Publications.

Gull, H., Azam, F., Butt, W. H., & Iqbal, S. Z. (2009). A new divided and conquer software process model. *World Academy of Science. Engineering and Technology, 60*, 255–260.

Gumünden, H. G., Salomo, S., & Krieger, A. (2005). The influence of project autonomy on project success. *International Journal of Project Management, 23*, 366–373. doi:10.1016/j.ijproman.2005.03.004

Gush, K., & de Villiers, M. R. (2010). Application usage of unsupervised Digital Doorway computer kiosks in remote locations in South Africa. In P. Kotze, A. Gerber, A. van der Merwe, & N. Bidwell (Eds.), *Fountains of Computing Research, Proceedings of SAICSIT 2010 Annual Research Conference of the South African Institute of Computer Scientists and Information Technologists*. ACM International Conference Proceedings Series.

Gush, K., De Villiers, R., Smith, R., & Cambridge, G. (2011). Digital Doorways. In Steyn, J., van Belle, J.-P., & Mansilla, E. V. (Eds.), *ICTs for global development and sustainability: Practice and applications* (pp. 96–126). Hershey, PA: IGI Global.

Guttenplan, S. (Ed.). (1994). *A companion to the philosophy of mind*. Oxford, UK: Blackwell.

Haas, P. (1992). Introduction. epistemic communities and international policy coordination. *International Organization, 46*(01), 1–26. doi:10.1017/S0020818300001442

Habermas, J. (1972). *Knowledge and human interests*. London, UK: Heinenmann.

Hackett, J. (1997). Roger Bacon: His life, career, and works. In Hackett, J. (Ed.), *Roger Bacon and the sciences: Commemorative essays* (pp. 13–17). Leiden, The Netherlands: Brill.

Hackney, R., & Pillay, J. (2002). *Organisational mission statements: A postmodernist perspective on the management of the IS/IT function. Information Resources Management Journal, ITJ2204 (Jan.-Mar. 2002)*. Hershey, PA: Idea Group Publishing.

Hack, S., & Lane, R. (Eds.). (2006). *Pragmatism old and new: Selected writings*. Amherst, NY: Prometheus Books.

Hage, J. (1972). *Techniques and problems of theory construction in sociology*. New York, NY: John Wiley & Sons.

Hair, J. F., Ringle, C. M., & Sarstedt, M. (2011). PLS-SEM: Indeed a silver bullet. *Journal of Marketing Theory and Practice, 19*(2), 137–149. doi:10.2753/MTP1069-6679190202

Håkanson, L. (2005). Epistemic communities and cluster dynamics: On the role of knowledge in industrial districts. *Industry and Innovation, 12*(4), 433–463. doi:10.1080/13662710500362047

Halaweh, M., Fidler, C., & McRobb, S. (2008). *Integrating the grounded theory method and case study research methodology within IS research: A possible road map*. ICIS 2008.

Halinen, A., & Törnroos, J.-Å. (2005). Using case methods in the study of contemporary business networks. *Journal of Business Research, 58*(9), 2006. doi:10.1016/j.jbusres.2004.02.001

Hallberg, N., Andorsson, R., & Olvander, C. (2010). Agile architecture framework for model driven development of C^2 systems. *Systems Engineering, 13*(2), 175–185.

Hamming, R. W. (1980). The unreasonable effectiveness of mathematics. *The American Mathematical Monthly, 87*(2), 81–90. doi:10.2307/2321982

Hancock, G. R., & Mueller, R. O. (2006). *Structural equation modeling*. Greenwich, CT: Information Age Publishing.

Hanenberg, S. (2010). Faith, hope, and love: An essay on software science's neglect of human factors. In W. R. Cook, S. Clarke & M. C. Rinard (Eds.), *Proceedings of the 25th ACM Conference on Object-Oriented Programming, Systems, Languages, and Applications (OOPSLA)*, (pp. 933-946). October 17-21, 2010, Reno/Tahoe, Nevada, USA.

Hanneman, R. A., & Riddle, M. (2005). *Introduction to social network methods*. Riverside, CA: University of California, Riverside. Retrieved from http://faculty.ucr.edu/~hanneman/nettext/

Hansen, B., & Kautz, K. (2005). Grounded theory applied – Studying Information Systems development methodologies in practice. In *Proceedings of 38th Annual Hawaiian International Conference on Systems Sciences*, Big Island, HI.

Hanson, N. R. (1958). The logic of discovery. *The Journal of Philosophy, 55*(25), 1073–1089. doi:10.2307/2022541

Haraway, D. (1988). Situated knowledges: The science question in feminism and the privilege of partial perspective. *Feminist Studies, 14*, 575–599. doi:10.2307/3178066

Hardin, A. M., Chang, J. C., & Fuller, M. A. (2011). Formative measurement and academic research: In search of measurement theory. *Educational and Psychological Measurement, 71*(2), 270–284. doi:10.1177/0013164410370208

Hardin, A. M., Chang, J. C.-J., & Fuller, M. A. (2008). Formative vs. reflective measurement: Comment on Marakas, Johnson, and Clay (2007). *Journal of the Association for Information Systems, 9*(9), 519–534.

Harding, S. (2004). *The Feminist standpoint theory reader*. New York, NY: Routledge.

Harrison, C. (2004). Postmodern principles for responsive reading assessment. *Journal of Research in Reading, 27*(2), 163–173. doi:10.1111/j.1467-9817.2004.00224.x

Hars, A., & Ou, S. (2002, Spring). Working for free? Motivations for participation in open-source projects. *International Journal of Electronic Commerce, 6*(3), 25–39.

Hatchuel, A. (2001). Towards design theory and expandable rationality: The unfinished program of Herbert Simon. *Journal of Management and Governance, 5*(3), 260–273. doi:10.1023/A:1014044305704

Hatton, L. (1998). Does OO sync with how we think? *IEEE Software, 15*(3), 46–54. doi:10.1109/52.676735

Haugeland, J. (Ed.). (1981). *Mind design. Philosophy, psychology, artificial intelligence*. Cambridge, MA: The MIT Press.

Hau, K.-T., & Marsh, H. W. (2004). The use of item parcels in structural equation modeling: Non-normal data and small sample size. *The British Journal of Mathematical and Statistical Psychology, 57*, 327–351. doi:10.1111/j.2044-8317.2004.tb00142.x

Haythornthwaite, C. (2009a). *Online knowledge crowds and communities*. In International Conference on Knowledge Communities. Reno, NV: Center for Basque Studies.

Haythorn, W. (1994). What is object-oriented design? *Journal of Object-Oriented Programming, 7*(1), 67–78.

Hedström, P., & Swedberg, R. (1998). *Social mechanisms: An analytical approach to social theory*. Cambridge, UK: Cambridge University Press. doi:10.1017/CBO9780511663901

Hegselsmann, R., Mueller, U., & Troitzsch, K. G. (Eds.). (1996). *Modelling and simulation in the social sciences from the philosophy of sciences point of view*. Dordrecht, The Netherlands: Kluwer Academic.

Heims, S. J. (1981). *John von Neumann and Norbert Wiener*. Cambridge, UK: NUT Press.

Heims, S. J. (1991). *The cybernetics group*. Cambridge, UK: NHT Press.

Hekkala, R. (2007). Grounded theory – The two faces of the methodology and their manifestation in IS research. *Proceedings of the 30th Information Systems Research Seminar in Scandinavia IRIS,* 11-14 August, Tampere, Finland.

Henseler, J., Ringle, C. M., & Sinkovics, R. R. (2009). The use of partial least squares path modeling in international marketing. *Advances in International Marketing, 20*, 277–320.

Hershberger, S. (2003). The growth of structural equation modeling. *Structural Equation Modeling, 10*(1), 35–46. doi:10.1207/S15328007SEM1001_2

Hertog, J. K., & McLeod, D. M. (2001). A multiperspectival approach to framing analysis: A field guide. In Reese, S. D., Gandy, O. H., & Grant, A. E. (Eds.), *Framing public life: Perspectives of media and our understanding of the social world* (pp. 139–161). Mahwah, NJ: Erlbaum.

Hevner, A. R. (2007). A three cycle view of design science research. *Scandinavian Journal of Information Systems, 19*(2), 39–64.

Hevner, A. R., & Chatterjee, S. (2010). *Design research in Information Systems: Theory and practice*. New York, NY: Springer.

Hevner, A. R., & March, S. T. (2003). The Information Systems research cycle. *Computer, 36*(11), 111–113. doi:10.1109/MC.2003.1244541

Hevner, A. R., March, S. T., Park, J., & Ram, S. (2004). Design science in information systems research. *Management Information Systems Quarterly, 28*(1), 75–105.

Hevner, A., & Chatterjee, S. (2010). Design science research in Information Systems. *Integrated Series in Information Systems, 22*, 9–22. doi:10.1007/978-1-4419-5653-8_2

Hickey, A. E. Jr. (1960). The systems approach: Can engineers use the scientific method? *IRE Transactions on Engineering Management, 7*(2), 72–80. doi:10.1109/IRET-EM.1960.5007541

Highsmith, J. (2002). *Agile software development ecosystems*. Indianapolis, IN: Addison-Wesley.

Hirschheim, R., & Klein, H. K. (2000). Information Systems research at the crossroads: External versus internal views. In R. Baskerville, J. Stage & J De Gross (Eds.), *Proceedings of the IFIP TC8 WG 8.2 International Working Conference on the Social and Organizational Perspective on Research and Practice in Information Technology*. Boston, MA: Kluwer Academic Publishers.

Hirschheim, R. (1992). Information Systems epistemology: An historical perspective. In Galliers, R. (Ed.), *Information Systems research: Issues, methods and practical guidelines*. Henley-on-Thames. UK: Alfred Waller Ltd.

Hogg, M. A., & Terry, D. J. (2000). Social identity and self-categorization processes in organizational contexts. *Academy of Management Review, 25*, 121–140.

Hohmann, C. (2007). Emotional digitalization as technology of the postmodern: A reflexive examination from the view of the industry. *International Journal of Technology and Human Interaction, 3*(1), 17–29. doi:10.4018/jthi.2007010102

Holland, C. R., & Light, B. (1999). A critical success factors model for ERP implementation. *IEEE Transactions on Software Engineering, 16*(3), 30–36.

Holland, P. W. (1986). Statistics and causal inference. *Journal of the American Statistical Association, 81*(396), 945–960. doi:10.2307/2289064

Holwell, S. (2000). Soft systems methodology: Other voices. *Systemic Practice and Action Research, 13*(6), 25. doi:10.1023/A:1026479529130

Hopkins, M. (1954). Human relations in engineering management. *Transactions of the IRE Professional Group on Engineering Management, 2*, 16–27. doi:10.1109/TPGEM.1954.5010170

Horridge, M. (Ed.). (2009). *A practical guide to building OWL ontologies using Protégé 4 and CO-ODE tools, edition 1.2*. The University of Manchester. Retrieved August 23, 2009, from http:// owl.cs.manchester.ac.uk/ tutorials/ protegeowltutorial/ resources/ ProtegeOWLTutorialP4_v1_2. pdf

Houser, N., & Kloesel, C. (Eds.). (1992). *The essential Peirce (Vol. 1)*. Bloomington, IN: Indiana University Press.

Hoving, R. (2002). Commments on the presentations by Klein, Gray and Myers, discussion at ICIS 2001 Panel.

Howe, J. (2006). The rise of crowdsourcing. *Wired, 14*(6).

Howe, J. (2008). *Crowdsourcing: Why the power of the crowd is driving the future of business*. New York, NY: Crown Business.

Hsieh, H. F., & Shannon, S. E. (2005). Three approaches to qualitative content analysis. *Qualitative Health Research, 18*(6), 51–59.

Hughes, T. P. (1996). Technological momentum. In M. R. Smith & L. Marx (Eds.), Does technology drive history? The dilemma of technological determinism (pp. 101-113). The Massachusetts Institute of Technology Press.

Hui, B. S. (1982). On building partial least squares models with interdependent inner relations. In K. G. Jöreskog & H. Wold (Eds.), Systems under indirect observations: Causality, structure, prediction (Part 2, pp. 249-272). Amsterdam, The Netherlands: North-Holland.

Hu, L. T., & Bentler, P. M. (1998). Fit indices in covariance structure modeling. *Psychological Methods, 3*, 424–453. doi:10.1037/1082-989X.3.4.424

Hu, L., & Bentler, P. M. (1999). Cutoff criteria for fit indexes in covariance structure analysis: Conventional criteria versus new alternatives. *Structural Equation Modeling, 6*(1), 1–55. doi:10.1080/10705519909540118

Hu, L., Bentler, P. M., & Kano, Y. (1992). Can test statistics in covariance structure analysis be trusted? *Psychological Bulletin, 112*, 351–362. doi:10.1037/0033-2909.112.2.351

Husserl, E. (1929). *Cartesianische Meditationen und Pariser Vorträge*Cartesian meditations and the Paris lectures. The Hague, The Netherlands: Martinus Nijhoff.

Huston, L., & Sakkab, N. (2006, March). Connect and develop. Inside Procter & Gamble's new model for innovation. *Harvard Business Review.* Retrieved from http:// 74.125.155.132/ scholar?q=cache: nJm-mXaQ4Gj0J: scholar.google.com/ +harvard+business+ review+connect+ and+develop+P% 26G&hl=en&as_sdt=2000

Hythornthwaite, C. (2009b). Crowds and communities: Light and heavyweight models of peer production. Proceedings from the *42nd Hawaii International Conference on System Science,* (pp. 1-10).

IEEE. (2004). *Software engineering 2004. Curriculum guidelines for undergraduate degree programs in software engineering. The Joint Task Force on Computing Curricula.* IEEE Computer Society, Association for Computing Machinery.

IEEE. (2010). *ISO/IEC/IEEE international standard 24765-2010 systems and software engineering -- Vocabulary.* Retrieved February 21, 2011, from http://www.computer.org/sevocab

Iivari, J. (2007). A paradigmatic analysis of Information Systems as a design science. *Scandinavian Journal of Information Systems, 19*(2), 39–64.

INCOSE. (2010). *Systems engineering handbook (version 3.2).* Seattle, WA: International Council on Systems Engineering.

International Association for Ontology and its Applications. (2009). *Welcome to FOIS 2010.* Retrieved October 28, 2009, from http:// fois2010.mie. utoronto.ca/

International Standards Organization /IEC 15288. (2008). *Systems engineering – System life cycle processes.* Geneva, Switzerland: ISO/IEC.

International Standards Organization. (2002). *ISO/IEC 15288:2002 Information Technology – Systems life cycle processes.* Geneva, Switzerland: ISO/IEC.

International Standards Organization/IEEE. (2008). *ISO/IEC 12207 Std 12207-2008 Systems and software engineering - Software life cycle processes.* Geneva, Switzerland: ISO/IEC.

Isabella, L. A. (1990). Evolving interpretations as a change unfolds: How managers construe key organizational events. *Academy of Management Journal, 33*(1), 7–41. doi:10.2307/256350

Ives, M. (2005). Identifying the contextual elements of project management within organizations and their impact on project success. *Project Management Journal, 36*(1), 37–50.

Jackson, D., Gillaspy, J., & Purc-Stephenson, R. (2009). Reporting practices in confirmatory factor analysis: An overview and some recommendations. *Psychological Methods, 14*(1), 6–23. doi:10.1037/a0014694

Jackson, M. (1990). *Systems approaches to management.* New York, NY: Kluwer Academic.

Jackson, M. C. (2003). *Systems thinking: Creative holism for managers.* Chichester, UK: Wiley.

Jackson, M. C. (2006). Creative holism: A critical systems approach to complex problem situations. *Systems Research and Behavioral Science, 23*(5), 647–657. doi:10.1002/sres.799

Jackson, M. C., & Keys, P. (1984). Towards a system of systems methodologies. *The Journal of the Operational Research Society, 35*, 473–486.

James, W. (2000). *Pragmatism and other writings*. New York, N Y: Penguin Books.

Järvinen, P. (2000). Research questions guiding selection of an appropriate research method. In *Proceedings of the 8th European Conference on Information Systems*, Vienna, Austria, July 2-5, (pp. 124-131).

Jarvis, C. B., Mackenzie, S. B., & Podsakoff, P. M. (2003). A critical review of construct indicators and measurement model misspecification in marketing and consumer research. *The Journal of Consumer Research*, *30*(2), 199–218. doi:10.1086/376806

Jennex, M. E. (2001). Research relevance-You get what you reward. *Communications of the Association for Information Systems*, *6*(1).

Jeppesen, L. B., & Frederiksen, L. (2006, January-February). Why do users contribute to firm-based user communities? *Organization Science*, *17*(1), 45–63. doi:10.1287/orsc.1050.0156

Johnson, E. O., & Webster, W. M. (1952). The plasmatron: A continuously controllable gas-discharge developmental tube. *Proceedings of the IRE*, *40*(6), 645–659. doi:10.1109/JRPROC.1952.274057

Johnson, W. J., Leach, M. K., & Liu, A. H. (1999). Theory testing using case studies in business to business research. *Industrial Marketing Management*, *28*(3), 201–213. doi:10.1016/S0019-8501(98)00040-6

Johnstone, A. H. (1997). Chemistry teaching: Science or alchemy? *Journal of Chemical Education*, *74*(3), 262–268. doi:10.1021/ed074p262

Jones, S., & Hughes, J. (2004). An exploration of the use of grounded theory as a research approach in the field of IS evaluation. *Electronic Journal of Information System Evaluation, 6*(1).

Jones, M. R., & Karstęn, H. (2008). Giddens's structuration theory and Information Systems Research. *Management Information Systems Quarterly*, *32*(1).

Jonker, J., & Pennink, B. (2010). *The essence of research methodology. A precise guide for Masters and PhD students in Management Sciences*. Heidelberg, Germany: Springer.

Joo, J. (2011). Adoption of Semantic Web from the perspective of technology innovation: A grounded theory approach. *International Journal of Human-Computer Studies*, *69*, 139–154. doi:10.1016/j.ijhcs.2010.11.002

Joreskog, J., & Sorbom, D. (1984). *Lisrel VI: Analysis of linear structural relationships by maximum likelihood, instrument variables, and least squares methods*. Mooreville, IN: Scientific Software.

Jöreskog, K. G., & Wold, H. (1982). *Systems under indirect observation - Causality structure prediction*. Amsterdam, The Netherlands: North Holland.

Judd, C. M., Smith, E. R., & Kidder, L. H. (1991). *Research methods in social relations*. Harcourt Brace Jovanovich College Publishers, 1991.

Jugdev, K., & Muller, R. (2005). A retrospective look at our evolving understanding of project success. *Project Management Journal*, *36*(4), 19–31.

Juristo, N., & Moreno, A. M. (2001). *Basics of software engineering experimentation*. Dordrecht, The Netherlands: Kluwer.

Käkölä, T., & Taalas, A. (2008). Validating the Information Systems design theory for dual Information Systems. *ICIS 2009 Proceedings*, Paper 119.

Kamada, T., & Kawai, S. (1989). An algorithm for drawing general undirected graphs. *Information Processing Letters*, *31*(1), 7–15. doi:10.1016/0020-0190(89)90102-6

Kanungo, S., & Jain, V. (2008). Modeling email use: A case of email system transition. *System Dynamics Review*, *24*(3), 299–319. doi:10.1002/sdr.406

Kappleman, L. A., McKeeman, R., & Zhang, L. (2006). Early warning signs of IT project failure: The dominant dozen. *Information Systems Management*, *23*(4), 31–36. doi:10.1201/1078.10580530/46352.23.4.20060901/95110.4

Kapyla, J., & Mikkola, H. (2010). A critical look at critical realism: Some observations on the problems of the metatheory. *World Political Science Review*, *6*(1), 1–37. doi:10.2202/1935-6226.1088

Kasi, P. M. (2009). *Research what why and how? A treatise from researchers to researchers*. Indiana, USA: AuthorHouse.

Katzer, J., Cook, K. H., & Crouch, W. W. (1998). *Evaluating information. A guide for users of social sciences research* (4th ed.). Boston, MA: McGraw-Hill.

Katz, J. (1983). A theory of qualitative methodology: The social system of analytical fieldwork. In Emerson, R. (Ed.), *Contemporary field research: A collection of readings*. Boston, MA: Little Brown Company.

Kauffman, S. A. (1993). *The origins of order: Self-organization and selection in evolution*. New York, NY: Oxford UP.

Kauffman, S. A. (1995). *At home in the universe: the search for the laws of self-organization and complexity*. New York, NY: Oxford UP.

Kauffman, S. A. (2000). *Investigations*. New York, NY: Oxford UP.

Kavan, C. B. (1998). Profit through knowledge: The application of academic research to information technology. *Information Resources Management Journal, 11*(1), 17–22.

Keen, P. G. W. (1991). Relevance and rigor in Information Systems research: Improving quality, confidence, cohesion and impact. In Nissen, H. E., Heinz, K. L., & Hirschheim, R. (Eds.), *Information Systems research: Contemporary approaches and emergent traditions* (pp. 27–49). Amsterdam, The Netherlands: North-Holland.

Keen, P. G. W. (1997). *The process edge: Creating value when it counts*. Harvard Business School Press.

Keen, P. G. W., & Sol, H. G. (2008). *Decision enhancement services: Rehearsing the future for decisions that matter*. Amsterdam, The Netherlands: IOS Press.

Keil, M., Rai, A., Mann, J. E. C., & Zhang, G. P. (2003). Why software projects escalate: The importance of project management constructs. *IEEE Transactions on Engineering Management, 50*(3), 251–261. doi:10.1109/TEM.2003.817312

Keil, M., & Tiwana, A. (2005). *Beyond cost: The driver of COTS application value. IEEE Software, May/June*. IEEE Computer Society.

Kelly, A. E. (2003). Research as design. *Educational Researcher, 32*(1), 3–4. doi:10.3102/0013189X032001003

Kendra, K., & Taplin, L. (2004). Project success a cultural framework. *Project Management Journal, 35*(1), 30–45.

Kenny, D. (2006). Series Editor's note. In Brown, T. (Ed.), *Confirmatory factor analysis for applied research*. New York, NY: Guilford Press.

Kettunen, P. (2003). Managing embedded software project team knowledge. *Software. IEEE Proceedings, 150*(6), 359–366.

Khazanchi, D. (1996). A framework for the validation of IS concepts. *Proceedings of the 2nd Annual Association for Information Systems Americas Conference,* Phoenix, Arizona, (August 16-18) (pp. 755-757).

Kim, G., Shin, B., & Grover, V. (2010). Investigating two contradictory views of formative measurement in information systems research. *Management Information Systems Quarterly, 34*(2), 345–365.

Kim, K. H. (2005). The relation among fit indexes, power, and sample size in structural equation modeling. *Structural Equation Modeling, 12*(3), 368–390. doi:10.1207/s15328007sem1203_2

Kim, S. S. (2009). The integrative framework of technology use: An extension and test. *Management Information Systems Quarterly, 33*(3), 513–537.

King, A. (2010). The odd couple: Margaret Archer, Anthony Giddens and British social theory. *The British Journal of Sociology, 61*(Suppl 1), 253–260. doi:10.1111/j.1468-4446.2009.01288.x

Kirk, R. E. (1995). *Experimental design: Procedures for behavioral sciences*. St. Paul, MN: Brooks/Cole Publishing Co.

Kitchenham, B. (1996). *DESMET: A method for evaluating software engineering methods and tools*. Technical Report TR96-09. Department of Computer Science. University of Keele, Staffordshire. Retrieved February 7, 2011 from http://www.osel.co.uk/desmet.pdf

Kitchenham, B., Pretorius, R., Budgen, D., Brereton, O. P., Turner, M., Niazi, M., & Linkman, S. (2010). Systematic literature reviews in software engineering - A tertiary study. *Information and Software Technology, 52*, 792–805. doi:10.1016/j.infsof.2010.03.006

Kitzinger, J. (1995). Introducing focus groups. *British Medical Journal*, *311*, 299–302. doi:10.1136/bmj.311.7000.299

Klabbers, J. H. G. (2006). A framework for artifact assessment and theory testing. *Simulation & Gaming*, *37*(2), 155–173. doi:10.1177/1046878106287943

Kleemann, F., Voß, G. G., & Rieder, K. (2008, July). Un(der)paid innovators: The commercial utilization of consumer work through crowdsourcing. *Science. Technology & Innovation Studies*, *4*(1), 5–26.

Klein, H. (2002). *Relevance as a "subtle accomplishment"*. Presentation at ICIS 2001 Panel.

Kleinbaum, D. G., Kupper, L. L., & Muller, K. E. (1988). *Applied regression analysis and other multivariate analysis methods*. Boston, MA: PWS-Kent Publishing.

Klein, H. K., & Myers, M. (1999). A set of principles for conducting and evaluating interpretive field studies in information systems research. *Management Information Systems Quarterly*, *23*(1), 67–93. doi:10.2307/249410

Klein, H. K., & Myers, M. D. (1999). A set of principles for conducting and evaluating interpretive field studies in information systems. *Management Information Systems Quarterly*, *23*(1), 67–93. doi:10.2307/249410

Klein, H. K., & Myers, M. D. (1999). A set of principles for conducting and evaluating interpretive field studies in Information Systems. *Management Information Systems Quarterly*, *23*(1), 67–93. doi:10.2307/249410

Klein, K. J., Dansereau, F., & Hall, R. J. (1994). Levels issues in theory development, data collection, and analysis. *Academy of Management Review*, *19*(2), 195–229.

Kline, R. B. (1998). *Principles and practice of structural equation modeling* (2nd ed.). New York, NY: Guilford Press.

Kline, R. B. (2006). Formative measurement and feedback loops. In Hancock, G. R., & Mueller, R. O. (Eds.), *Structural equation modeling* (pp. 43–68). Greenwich, CT: Information Age Publishing Inc.

Kljajić, M. (1998). Modeling and understanding the complex system within cybernetics. In M. J. Ramaekers, (Ed.). *15th International Congress on Cybernetics* (pp. 864-869). Namur, Belgium: Association International de Cybernetique.

Kljajić, M., Legna, V. C., & Škraba, A. (2002). System dynamics model development of the Canary Islands for supporting strategic public decisions. In P. I. Davidsen, E. Mollona, V. G. Diker, R. S. Langer, & J. I. Rowe (Eds.), *Proceedings of the 20th International Conference of the System Dynamics Society*. Albany, NY: System Dynamics Society.

Kljajić, M., Legna, V. C., Škraba, A., & Peternel, J. (2003). Simulation model of the Canary Islands for public decision support - Preliminary results. In R. L. Eberlein, V. G. Diker, R. S. Langer, & J. I. Rowe (Ed.), *Proceedings of the 21st International Conference of the System Dynamics Society*. Albany, NY: The System Dynamics Society.

Kljajic, M., & Farr, J. (2008). The role of systems engineering in the development of Information Systems. *International Journal of Information Technologies and Systems Approach*, *1*(1), 49–61. doi:10.4018/jitsa.2008010104

Kljajić, M., & Farr, J. (2010). Importance of systems engineering in the development of information systems. In Paradise, D. (Ed.), *Emerging systems approaches in information technologies: concepts, theories, and applications* (pp. 51–66). Hershey, PA: Information Science Reference. doi:10.4018/978-1-60566-976-2.ch004

Knights, D. (1992). Changing space: the disruptive impact of a new epistemological location for the study of management. *Academy of Management Review*, *17*, 514–536.

Ko, A. J., Myers, B. A., Coblenz, M. J., & Aung, H. H. (2006). An exploratory study of how developers seek, relate, and collect relevant information during software maintenance tasks. *IEEE Transactions on Software Engineering*, *32*(12), 971–987. doi:10.1109/TSE.2006.116

Koch, A. S. (2005). *Agile software development*. Boston, MA: Artech House.

Kock, N. (2011). *WarpPLS 2.0 user manual*. ScriptWarp Systems™. Laredo, Texas USA. Retrieved May 27, 2011, from http://www.scriptwarp.com/warppls/UserManual_WarpPLS_V2.pdf

Kock, N. (2004). The three threats of action research: a discussion of methodological antidotes in the context of an information systems study. *Decision Support Systems*, *37*, 265–286. doi:10.1016/S0167-9236(03)00022-8

Kock, N., Gray, P., Hoving, R., Klein, H., Myers, M., & Rockart, J. (2002). IS research relevance revisited: Subtle accomplishment, unfulfilled promise, or serial hypocrisy? *Communications of the Association for Information Systems, 8*, 330–346.

Kofjač, D., & Kljajić, M. (2010). Decision support simulation system for inventory control with stochastic variables. In: M. Kljajić & G. E. Lasker (Eds.). *Advances in simulation-based decision support: Proceedings of the 22nd International Conference on Systems Research, Informatics and Cybernetics* (pp. 6 -10). Tecumseh, Canada: The International Institute for Advanced Studies in Systems Research and Cybernetics.

Kofjač, D., Kljajić, M., & Rejec, V. (2009). The anticipative concept in warehouse optimization using simulation in an uncertain environment. *European Journal of Operational Research, 193*(3), 660–669. doi:10.1016/j.ejor.2007.06.055

Kohlbacher, F. (2006). *The use of qualitative content analysis in case study research.* IN: Forum Qualitative Sozialforschung/Forum: Qualitative Social Research.

Kohli, R. (2001). Industry-academia interaction: Key to IT relevance. *Communications of the Association for Information Systems, 6*(1).

Konda, D. (2010). Knowledge management framework for system development projects: Integrated knowledge management framework for knowledge enablement of Information Systems development (ISD) projects. *LAP LAMBERT Academic Publishing., ISBN-10, 3838391004.*

Kothari, C. R. (2006). *Research methodology: Methods and techniques.* Delhi, India: New Age International Publishers.

Kozinets, R. F., Hemetsberger, A., & Schau, H. J. (2008, December). The wisdom of consumer crowds: Collective innovation in an age of networked marketing. *Journal of Macromarketing, 4*, 339–354. doi:10.1177/0276146708325382

Kraft, T. (2008). *Systematic and holistic IT project management approach for commercial software with case studies.* Doctoral Dissertation, Lawrence Technological University, Southfield, Michigan, USA.

Kraft, T., & Steenkamp, A. L. (2010). A holistic approach for understanding project management. *International Journal of Information Technologies and Systems Approach, 3*(2), 17–31. doi:10.4018/jitsa.2010070102

Kraut, R., Patterson, M., Lundmark, V., Kiesler, S., Mukopadhyay, T., & Scherlis, W. (1998). Internet paradox: A social technology that reduces social involvement and psychological well-being? *The American Psychologist, 53*(9), 1017–1031. doi:10.1037/0003-066X.53.9.1017

Krippendorff, K. (1980). *Content analysis: An introduction to its methodology.* Thousand Oaks, CA: Sage.

Krippendorff, K., & Bock, M. A. (2009). *The content analysis reader.* Los Angeles, CA: Sage.

Kroeze, J. H. (2009). Bootstrapping an XML schema of syntactic functions into a skeleton ontology. *South African Journal of Information Management (SAJIM), 11*(3). Retrieved February 27, 2011, from http:// www.sajim.co.za/ index.php/ SAJIM/ article/ view/ 410/ 399 or http:// hdl.handle.net/ 10394/ 2911

Kroeze, J. H. (2010). The mutualistic relationship between Information Systems and the Humanities (full paper, edited version of inaugural lecture). In K. R. Soliman (Ed.), *Knowledge Management and Innovation: A Business Competitive Edge Perspective, Proceedings of the 15th International Business Information Management Association Conference (15th IBIMA),* November 6-7, 2010, Cairo, Egypt (pp. 915-927). Retrieved February 27, 2011, from http:// hdl.handle.net/ 10394/ 3824

Kroeze, J. H., Lotriet, H. H., Mavetera, N., Pfaff, M. S., Postma, D. J. R., Sewchurran, K., & Topi, H. (2011). ECIS 2010 panel report: Humanities-enriched Information Systems. *Communications of the Association for Information Systems (CAIS), 28*(1), 373-392. Retrieved May, 26, 2011, from http:// aisel.aisnet.org/ cais/ vol28/ iss1/ 24

Krueger, R. A., & Casey, M. A. (2000). *Focus groups: A practical guide for applied research.* Sage Publications, 2000.

Kuechler, B., & Vaishnavi, V. (2008). On theory development in design science research: Anatomy of a research project. *European Journal of Information Systems, 17*(5), 489–504. doi:10.1057/ejis.2008.40

Kuechler, W. L. Jr, & Vaishnavi, V. K. (2008). An expert system for dynamic re-coordination of distributed workflows. *Expert Systems with Applications, 34*(1), 551–563. doi:10.1016/j.eswa.2006.09.014

Kuhn, T. (1974). *The structure of the scientific theories.* Chicago, IL: University of Chicago Press.

Kuhn, T. S. (1962). *The structure of scientific revolutions* (3rd ed.). Chicago, IL: University of Chicago Press.

Kvale, S. (2007). *Doing interviews: The Sage qualitative research kit.* Thousand Oaks, CA: Sage.

Kvale, S. (2007). *Doing interviews; The Sage qualitative research kit.* Thousand Oaks, CA: Sage.

Kvasny, L., Greenhill, A., & Trauth, E. M. (2005). Giving voice to Feminist projects in management information systems research. *International Journal of Technology and Human Interaction, 1*, 1–18. doi:10.4018/jthi.2005010101

Lakatos, I. (1978). *The methodology of scientific research programmes: Philosophical papers.* Cambridge, UK: Cambridge University Press.

Lakhani, K. R., & Wolf, R. G. (2003, September). *Why hackers do what they do: Understanding motivation effort in free/open source software projects.* MIT Sloan School of Management. Retrieved from http://ssrn.com/abstract= 443040

Lakhani, K. R., Jeppesen, L. B., Lohse, P. A., & Panetta, J. A. (2007, October). *The value of openness in scientific problem solving.* (Harvard Business School Working Paper 07-050).

Lakhani, K. R., & Panetta, J. A. (2007, Summer). The principles of distributed innovation. *Innovations*, n.d., 97–112. doi:10.1162/itgg.2007.2.3.97

Lambe, P. (2007). *Organising knowledge: Taxonomies, knowledge and organisational effectiveness.* Oxford, UK: Chandos.

Landauer, T. K., Foltz, P. W., & Laham, D. (1998). An introduction to latent semantic analysis. *Discourse Processes, 25*(2), 259–284. doi:10.1080/01638539809545028

Landsberger, H. A. (1958). *Hawthorne revisited.* Ithaca, NY: Cornell UP.

Lane, J. A., Petkov, D., & Mora, M. (2008). Software engineering and the systems approach: A conversation with Barry Boehm. *International Journal of Information Technologies and Systems Approach, 1*(2), 99–103. doi:10.4018/jitsa.2008070107

Lange, O. (1965). *Wholes and parts: A general theory of system behaviour.* New York, NY: Pergamon.

Langley, A. (1999). Strategies for theorizing from process data. *Academy of Management Review, 24*(4), 691–710.

Laporte, C. Y., Alexandre, S., & O'Connor, R. (2008). A software engineering lifecycle standard for very small enterprises. In O'Connor, R. V. (Eds.), *Proceedings of EuroSPI, CCIS* (*Vol. 16*, pp. 129–141). Springer-Verlag. doi:10.1007/978-3-540-85936-9_12

Larman, C., & Basili, V. R. (2003). Iterative and incremental development: A brief history. *Computer, 36*(6), 47–56. doi:10.1109/MC.2003.1204375

Laudan, L. (1990). *Science and relativism: Some key controversies in the philosophy of science.* Chicago, IL: University of Chicago Press.

Laudan, L. (1996). *Beyond positivism and relativism.* Boulder, CO: Westview Press.

Laudon, K. C., & Laudon, J. P. (1988). *Management Information Systems* (2nd ed.). New York, NY: Macmillan.

Lave, J. (1988). *Cognition in practice.* Cambridge, UK: Cambridge UP. doi:10.1017/CBO9780511609268

Lave, J., & Wenger, E. (1992). *Situated learning: Legitimate peripheral participation.* New York, NY: Cambridge UP.

Law, K. S., Wong, C. S., & Mobley, W. H. (1998). Toward a taxonomy of multidimensional constructs. *Academy of Management Review, 23*(4), 741–755.

Lawson, T. (1997). *Economics and reality.* London, UK: Routledge.

Lawson, T. (2003). Theorizing ontology. *Feminist Economics, 9*(1), 161–169. doi:10.1080/1354570032000063038

Lazanski, T. J., & Kljajić, M. (2006). Systems approach to complex systems modeling with special regards to tourism. *Kybernetes, 35*(7-8), 1048–1058. doi:10.1108/03684920610684779

Lazarsfeld, P. F., & Henry, N. W. (1968). *Latent structure analysis*. New York, NY: Houghton Mifflin.

Lee, A. S., & Nickerson, J. V. (2010). Theory as a case of design: Lessons for design from the philosophy of science. In R. H. Sprague (Ed.), *The 43rd Hawaii International Conference on System Sciences* (pp.1–8). Los Alamitos, CA: IEEE Computer Society Press.

Lee, A. S. (1989). A scientific methodology for MIS case studies. *Management Information Systems Quarterly, 13*(1), 33–52. doi:10.2307/248698

Lee, A. S. (1999). Rigor and relevance in MIS research: Beyond the approach of positivism alone. *Management Information Systems Quarterly, 23*(1). doi:10.2307/249407

Lee, A. S., & Baskerville, R. L. (2003). Generalizing generalizability in Information Systems research. *Information Systems Research, 14*(3), 221–242. doi:10.1287/isre.14.3.221.16560

Lee, A. S., & Hubona, G. S. (2009). A scientific basis for rigor in Information Systems research. *Management Information Systems Quarterly, 33*(2), 237–262.

Leech, N. L., & Onwuegbuzie, A. J. (Eds.). (2005). *Taking the "Q" out of research: Teaching research methodology courses without the divide between quantitative and qualitative paradigms*. Florida, USA: Springer.

Leedy, P. D., & Ormrod, J. E. (2001). *Practical research: Planning and design. Upper Saddle River, NJ: Merrill Prentice Hall. Lincoln, Y. S., & Guba, E. G. (1985). Naturalistic inquiry*. Newbury Park, CA: Sage Publications.

Legna, V. C., & Rivero, C. J. L. (2001). *Las particularidades de las Regiones Ultraperiféricas y la necesidad de instrumentos específicos. Especial referencia a Canarias* (Document elaborated for the Canarian Government). La Laguna, Canary Islands: University of La Laguna.

Legna, V. C. (2002). *Bases para la promoción del desarrollo social y creación de una red sindical de intercambio de información y de formación*. Estudio de Canarias. European Trade Union Confederation.

Legna, V. C., & González, C. S. (2005). An intelligent decision support system (IDSS) for public decisions using system dynamics and case based reasoning (CBR). *Organizacija, 38*(9), 530–535.

Legris, P. (2003). Why do people use Information Technology? A critical review of the technology acceptance model. *Information & Management, 40*(3), 191–204. doi:10.1016/S0378-7206(01)00143-4

Lending, D., & Wetherbe, J. (1992). Update on MIS research: A profile of leading journals and U.S. universities. *ACM SIGMIS Database, 23*(3), 5–11. doi:10.1145/146548.146549

Lewis, T. G. (2009). *Network science: Theory and practice*. Hoboken, NJ: Wiley.

Leydesdorff, L. (1997). Why words and co-words cannot map the development of the sciences. *Journal of the American Society for Information Science American Society for Information Science, 48*(5), 418–427. doi:10.1002/(SICI)1097-4571(199705)48:5<418::AID-ASI4>3.0.CO;2-Y

Leydesdorff, L. (2007). Scientific communication and cognitive codification: Social systems theory and the sociology of scientific knowledge. *European Journal of Social Theory, 10*(3), 375–388. doi:10.1177/1368431007080701

Leydesdorff, L. (2010a). The communication of meaning and the structuration of expectations: Giddens' "structuration theory" and Luhmann's "self-organization". *Journal of the American Society for Information Science and Technology, 61*(10), 2138–2150. doi:10.1002/asi.21381

Leydesdorff, L. (2010b). What can heterogeneity add to the scientometric map? Steps towards algorithmic historiography. In Akrich, M., Barthe, Y., Muniesa, F., & Mustar, P. (Eds.), *Débordements: Mélanges offerts à Michel Callon* (pp. 283–289). Paris, France: École Nationale Supérieure des Mines, Presses des Mines.

Leydesdorff, L. (2011). (in preparation). "Meaning" as a sociological concept: A review of the modeling, mapping, and simulation of the communication of knowledge and meaning. *Social Sciences Information. Information Sur les Sciences Sociales*. doi:10.1177/0539018411411021

Leydesdorff, L., & Hellsten, I. (2005). Metaphors and diaphors in science communication: Mapping the case of stem cell research. *Science Communication, 27*(1), 64–99. doi:10.1177/1075547005278346

Leydesdorff, L., & Schank, T. (2008). Dynamic animations of journal maps: Indicators of structural change and interdisciplinary developments. *Journal of the American Society for Information Science and Technology, 59*(11), 1810–1818. doi:10.1002/asi.20891

Leydesdorff, L., Schank, T., Scharnhorst, A., & De Nooy, W. (2008). Animating the development of social networks over time using a dynamic extension of multidimensional scaling. *El Profesional de la Información, 17*(6), 611–626. doi:10.3145/epi.2008.nov.04

Leydesdorff, L., & Vaughan, L. (2006). Co-occurrence matrices and their applications in information science: Extending ACA to the Web environment. *Journal of the American Society for Information Science and Technology, 57*(12), 1616–1628. doi:10.1002/asi.20335

Leydesdorff, L., & Welbers, K. (2011). (in press). The semantic mapping of words and co-words in contexts. *Journal of Informatrics.* doi:10.1016/j.joi.2011.01.008

Li, L., & Bentler, P. M. (2011). (in press). Quantified choice of root-mean-square errors of approximation for evaluation and power analysis of small differences between structural equation models. *Psychological Methods.* doi:10.1037/a0022657

Li, Y. (2005). *PLS-GUI – Graphic user interface for partial least squares (PLS-PC 1.8) – Version 2.0.1 beta.* Columbia, SC: University of South Carolina.

Locke, J. (1894). *An essay concerning human understanding* (Fraser, A. C., Ed.). *Vol. 1*). Oxford, UK: Clarendon.

Locke, L., Silverman, S., & Spirduso, W. (2004). *Reading and understanding research.* New York, NY: Sage Publications.

Lohmöller, J. B. (1984). *LVPLS 1.6 program manual: Latent variables path analysis with partial least-squares estimation.* Munich, Germany: University of the Federal Armed Forces.

Lohmöller, J. B. (1989). *Latent variables path modeling with partial least squares.* Heidelberg, Germany: Physica.

Luhmann, N. (1984). *Soziale Systeme.* Frankfurt, Germany: Suhrkamp.

Luhmann, N. (1986). The autopoiesis of social systems. In Geyer, F., & van der Zouwen, J. (Eds.), *Sociocybernetic paradoxes* (pp. 172–192). London, UK: Sage.

Luhmann, N. (1990). *Essays on self-reference.* New York, NY: Columbia UP.

Luhmann, N. (1995). *Social systems.* Stanford, CA: Stanford University Press.

Luhmann, N. (1997). *Organización y decisión. Autopoiesis, acción y entendimiento comunicativo.* Barcelona, Spain: Anthropos.

Luhmann, N. (2002). How can the mind participate in communication? In Rasch, W. (Ed.), *Theories of distinction: Redescribing the descriptions of modernity* (pp. 169–184). Stanford, CA: Stanford University Press.

Łukasiewicz, J. (1957). *Aristotle's syllogistic, from the standpoint of modern formal logic* (2nd ed.). Oxford, UK: Oxford University Press.

Luna-Reyes, L. F., Black, L. J., Cresswell, A. M., & Pardo, T. A. (2008). Knowledge sharing and trust in collaborative requirements analysis. *System Dynamics Review, 24*(3), 265–297. doi:10.1002/sdr.404

Lyytinen, K., & Robey, D. (1999). Learning failure in Information Systems development. *Information Systems Journal, 9*(2), 85–101. doi:10.1046/j.1365-2575.1999.00051.x

MacCallum, R. C., & Browne, M. W. (1993). The use of causal indicators in covariance structure models: Some practical issues. *Psychological Bulletin, 114*(3), 533–541. doi:10.1037/0033-2909.114.3.533

MacCallum, R. C., Browne, M. W., & Cai, L. (2006). Testing differences between nested covariance structure models: Power analysis and null hypotheses. *Psychological Methods, 11*, 19–35. doi:10.1037/1082-989X.11.1.19

MacCallum, R. C., Lee, T., & Browne, M. W. (2010). The issue of isopower in power analysis for tests of structural equation models. *Structural Equation Modeling, 17*, 23–41. doi:10.1080/10705510903438906

MacCallum, R., Browne, M., & Sugawara, H. (1996). Power analysis and determination of sample size for covariance structure modeling. *Psychological Methods, 3*(2), 131–149.

MacKenzie, S., Podsakoff, P., & Jarvis, C. (2005). The problem of measurement model misspecification in behavioral and organizational research and some recommended solutions. *The Journal of Applied Psychology, 90*(4), 710–730. doi:10.1037/0021-9010.90.4.710

Madon, S. (2005). Evaluating e-governance projects in India: A focus on micro-level implementation. In Howcroft, D., & Trauth, E. M. (Eds.), *Handbook of critical Information Systems research: Theory and application* (pp. 325–349). Cheltenham, UK: Edward Elgar Publishing Limited.

Magalhães, R. (2004). *Organizational knowledge and technology. An action-oriented perspective on organization and information systems*. Cheltenham, UK: Edgar Elgar.

Magid, L. (2009, February 17). Microlending: Do good, make money? In *CBSNEWS*. Retrieved September 5, 2009, from http:// www.cbsnews.com/ stories/ 2009/ 02/ 17/ scitech/ pcanswer/ main4808591.shtml

Majchrak, A., Beath, C., Lim, R., & Chin, W. W. (2005). Managing client dialogues during information systems design to facilitate client learning. *Management Information Systems Quarterly, 29*(4), 653–672.

Malone, T. W., Laubacher, R., & Dellarocas, C. (2009, February). *Harnessing crowds: Mapping the genome of collective intelligence* (Working paper no. 2009-001). MIT Center for Collective Intelligence, MIT website. Retrieved from http:cci.mit.edu/ publications/ CCIwp2009-01. pdf

Malone, T. W., & Crowston, K. (1994). The interdisciplinary study of coordination. *ACM Computing Surveys, 26*(1), 87–119. doi:10.1145/174666.174668

March, J. G., & Simon, H. A. (1958). *Organizations* (revised edition). New York, NY: Wiley.

March, S. T., & Smith, G. F. (1995). Design and natural science research on Information Technology. *Decision Support Systems, 15*(4), 251–266. doi:10.1016/0167-9236(94)00041-2

Marcoulides, G. A., Chin, W. W., & Saunders, C. (2009). A critical look at partial least squares modeling. *Management Information Systems Quarterly, 33*(1), 171–175.

Marcoulides, G. A., & Saunders, C. (2006). PLS: A silver bullet? *Management Information Systems Quarterly, 30*(2), iii–ix.

Marinho, J., Braganca, A., & Ramos, C. (1999). Decision support system for dynamic production scheduling. In C. Ramos & R. Sharma (Eds.), *Proceedings of the 1999 IEEE International Symposium on Assembly and Task Planning* (pp. 424-429). Evanston, IL: IEEE Robotics & Automation Society.

Markus, K. A. (2010). Structural equations and causal explanations: Some challenges for causal SEM. *Structural Equation Modeling, 17*, 654–676. doi:10.1080/1070551 1.2010.510068

Markus, M. L., Majchrzak, A., & Gasser, L. (2002). A design theory for systems that support emergent knowledge processes. *Management Information Systems Quarterly, 26*(3), 179–212.

Markus, M. L., & Robey, D. (1988). Information technology and organizational change: Causal structure in theory and research. *Management Science, 34*(5), 583–598. doi:10.1287/mnsc.34.5.583

Marshall, C., & Rossman, G. B. (1999). *Designing qualitative research* (3rd ed.). Thousand Oaks, CA: Sage.

Marsh, H. W., Hau, K.-T., Balla, J. R., & Grayson, D. (1998). Is more ever too much? The number of indicators per factor in confirmatory factor analysis. *Multivariate Behavioral Research, 33*, 181–220. doi:10.1207/ s15327906mbr3302_1

Martins, E. C., & Terblanche, F. (2003). Building organizational culture that stimulates creativity and innovation. *European Journal of Innovation Management, 6*(1), 64–74. doi:10.1108/14601060310456337

Masemola, S. S., & De Villiers, M. R. (2006). Towards a framework for usability testing of interactive e-learning applications in cognitive domains, illustrated by a case study. In J. Bishop & D. Kourie (Eds.), *Service-Oriented Software and Systems: Proceedings of SAICSIT 2006* (pp. 187-197). ACM International Conference Proceedings Series.

Mason, R. O. (1989). MIS experiments: A pragmatic perspective. In Benbasat, I. (Ed.), *The Information Systems research challenge: Experimental research methods* (*Vol. 2*, pp. 3–20). Harvard Business School Research Colloquium, Harvard Business School.

Mason, S. F. (1962). *A history of the sciences*. New York City, NY: Collier Books.

Mathiassen, L., Ngwenyama, O. K., & Aaen, I. (2005). Managing change in software process improvement. *Software IEEE, 22*(6), 84–91. doi:10.1109/MS.2005.159

Mathiassen, L., & Pourkomeylian, P. (2003). Managing knowledge in a software organization. *Journal of Knowledge Management, 7*(2), 63–80. doi:10.1108/13673270310477298

Mathieson, K., Peacock, E., & Chin, W. W. (2001). Extending the technology acceptance model: The influence of perceived user resources. *The Data Base for Advances in Information Systems, 32*, 86–112.

Mathieson, K., & Ryan, T. D. (2001). A broader view of relevance. *Communications of the Association for Information Systems, 6*(1).

Matthes, J., & Kohring, M. (2008). The content analysis of media frames: toward improving reliability and validity. *The Journal of Communication, 58*, 258–279. doi:10.1111/j.1460-2466.2008.00384.x

Maturana, H. R. (1975). The organization of the living: a theory of the living organization. *International Journal of Man-Machine Studies, 7*, 313–332. doi:10.1016/S0020-7373(75)80015-0

Maturana, H. R. (1978). Biology of language: The epistemology of reality. In Miller, G. A., & Lenneberg, E. (Eds.), *Psychology and biology of language and thought* (pp. 27–63). New York, NY: Academic Press.

Maturana, H. R. (1980). Autopoiesis: Reproduction, heredity and evolution. In Zeleny, M. (Ed.), *Autopoiesis, dissipative structures, and spontaneous social orders*. Boulder, CO: Westview Press.

Maturana, H. R. (1981). Autopoiesis. In Zeleny, M. (Ed.), *Autopoiesis: A theory of living organization*. New York, NY: North Holand.

Maturana, H. R., & Varela, F. J. (1987). *El arbol del conocimiento, (The tree of knowledge)*. Horticultural Hall, MA: Shambhala Pub.

Maturana, H., & Varela, F. (1980). *Autopoiesis and cognition*. Dordrecht, The Netherlands: Reidel.

Matusitz, J. (2008). Cyberterrorism: Postmodern state of chaos. *Information Security Journal: A Global Perspective, 17*(4), 179-187.

Mazlish, B. (1993). *The fourth discontinuity: The co-evolution of humans and machines*. New Haven, CT: Yale University Press.

McAfee, A. (2009). *Enterprise 2.0: New collaborative tools for your organization's toughest challenges*. Boston, MA: Harvard Business Press.

McCombs, M. F. (1997, August). *New frontiers in agenda-setting: Agendas of attributes and frames*. Paper presented at the annual convention of the Association for Education in Journalism and Mass Communication, Chicago.

McCombs, M. E., & Shaw, D. L. (1972). The agenda-setting function of mass media. *Public Opinion Quarterly, 36*(2), 176–187. doi:10.1086/267990

McCorduck, P. (1979). *Machines who think*. San Francisco, CA: Freeman.

McDonald, R. P., & Ho, R. M. (2002). Principles and practice in reporting structural equation analysis. *Psychological Methods, 7*, 64–82. doi:10.1037/1082-989X.7.1.64

McIntosh, P. (2010). *Action research and reflective practice*. London, UK: Routledge.

McQuail, D. (2005). *McQuail's mass communication theory* (5th ed.). London, UK: Sage.

Mead, G. H. (1934). The point of view of social behaviourism. In Morris, C. H. (Ed.), *Mind, self, & society from the standpoint of a social behaviourist. Works of G. H. Mead* (*Vol. 1*, pp. 1–41). Chicago, IL: University of Chicago Press.

Meel, J. W. (1994). *The dynamics of business engineering. PhD*. Delft University of Technology.

Melhart, B. (2000). Software engineering. In Ralston, A., Reilly, E. D., & Hemmendinger, D. (Eds.), *Encyclopedia of computer science*. New York, NY: Grove's Dictionaries, Inc.

Menand, L. (1997). *Pragmatism: A reader*. Vintage Press.

Merriam Webster Dictionary. (n.d.). *Definition of methodology*. Retrieved February 23, 2011, from http://www.merriam-webster.com/dictionary/methodology

Mertens, D. M. (1998). *Research methods in education and psychology: Integrating diversity with quantitative and qualitative approaches*. Thousand Oaks, CA: Sage Publications.

Mesarović, M. D., & Takahara, Y. (1989). *Abstract systems theory*. Berlin, Germany: Springer-Verlag. doi:10.1007/BFb0042462

Meyers, M. D., & Klein, H. K. (2011). A set of principles for conducting critical research in Information Systems. *Management Information Systems Quarterly, 35*(1), 1–21.

Miles, M. B., & Huberman, A. M. (1984). *Qualitative data analysis: A sourcebook of new methods*. Sage Publications.

Miles, M. B., & Huberman, A. M. (1994). *Qualitative data analysis: An expanded sourcebook*. London, UK: Sage Publications.

Miller, K., & Tsang, E. (2011). Testing management theories: Critical realist philosophy and research methods. *Strategic Management Journal, 32*(2), 139–158. doi:10.1002/smj.868

Milosevic, D., & Patanakul, P. (2004). Standard project management may increase development project success. *International Journal of Project Management, 23*, 181–192. doi:10.1016/j.ijproman.2004.11.002

Mingers, J. (2011a). *Explanatory mechanisms: The contribution of critical realism and systems thinking/cybernetics*. Working paper, Kent Business School. Retrieved from http:// kar.kent.ac.uk/ 26306/

Mingers, J. (2011b). *The contribution of systemic thought to critical realism*. Working paper, Kent Business School. Retrieved from http:// kar.kent.ac.uk/ 26306/

Mingers, J. (1995). *Self-producing systems. Implications and applications of autopoiesis*. New York, NY: Plenum Press.

Mingers, J. (1995). Using soft systems methodology in the design of information systems. In Stowell, F. (Ed.), *Information Systems provision: The contribution of soft systems methodology* (pp. 18–50). London, UK: McGraw-Hill.

Mingers, J. (2000). The contribution of critical realism as an underpinning philosophy for OR/MS and systems. *The Journal of the Operational Research Society, 51*(111), 1256–1270.

Mingers, J. (2001). Combining IS research methods: Towards a pluralist methodology. *Information Systems Research, 12*(3), 240–259. doi:10.1287/isre.12.3.240.9709

Mingers, J. (2001). Multimethodology - Mixing and matching methods. In Rosenhead, J., & Mingers, J. (Eds.), *Rational analysis for a problematic world revisited: Problem structuring methods for complexity, uncertainty and conflict* (pp. 297–308). Chichester, UK: Wiley.

Mingers, J. (2003). A classification of the philosophical assumptions of management science methodologies. *The Journal of the Operational Research Society, 54*(6), 559–570. doi:10.1057/palgrave.jors.2601436

Mingers, J. (2008). Pluralism, realism, and truth: The keys to knowledge in Information Systems research. *International Journal of Information Technologies and Systems Approach, 1*(1), 79–90. doi:10.4018/jitsa.2008010106

Mingers, J., & White, L. (2010). A review of the recent contributions of systems thinking to operational research and management science. *European Journal of Operational Research, 207*(3), 11–47. doi:10.1016/j.ejor.2009.12.019

Minsky, M. (1987). *The society of mind*. New York, NY: Simon & Schuster.

Mitev, N. (2000). Toward social constructivist understandings of IS success and failure: introducing a new computerized reservation system. *ICIS 2000 Proceedings*, (pp. 84-93).

Mitev, N. N. (2006). Postmodernism and criticality in Information Systems research: What critical management studies can contribute. *Social Science Computer Review, 24*(3), 310–325. doi:10.1177/0894439306287976

Mohr, L. B. (1982). *Explaining organizational behavior.* San Francisco, CA: Jossey-Bass.

Monecke, A. (2010). *semPLS - Structural equation modeling using partial least squares.* Retrieved May 27, 2011, from http://cran.r-project.org/web/packages/semPLS/semPLS.pdf

Monge, P. R. (1990). Theoretical and analytical issues in studying organizational processes. *Organization Science, 1*(4), 406–430. doi:10.1287/orsc.1.4.406

Monge, P. R., & Contractor, N. S. (2003). *Theories of communication networks.* Oxford, UK: Oxford UP.

Monod, E., & Boland, R. J. (2007). Special issue on philosophy and epistemology: A Peter Pan Syndrome? *Information Systems Journal, 17,* 133–141. doi:10.1111/j.1365-2575.2007.00231.x

Moody, D. L. (2003). The method evaluation model: A theoretical model for validating Information Systems design methods. *ECIS 2003 Proceedings,* Paper 79.

Moores, T. T., & Chang, J. C. J. (2006). Ethical decision making in software piracy: Initial development and test of four-component model. *Management Information Systems Quarterly, 30*(1), 167–180.

Mora, M., Gelman, O., Paradice, D., & Cervantes, F. (2008). The case for conceptual research in Information Systems. In *Proceedings of the International Conference on Information Resources Management (CONF-IRM),* paper 52, May 18-20, 2008, Niagara Falls, Ontario, Canada.

Mora, M., Gelman, O., Forgionne, G., Petkov, D., & Cano, J. (2007). Integrating the fragmented pieces of IS research paradigms and frameworks: A systems approach. *Information Resources Management Journal, 20*(2), 1–22. doi:10.4018/irmj.2007040101

Mora, M., Gelman, O., O'Connor, R., Alvarez, F., & Macías-Lúevano, J. (2008). A conceptual descriptive-comparative study of models and standards of processes in SE, SWE and IT disciplines using the theory of systems. *International Journal of Information Technologies and Systems Approach, 1*(2), 57–85. doi:10.4018/jitsa.2008070104

Morello, H. J. (2007, Winter). E-(re)volution: Zapatistas and the emancipatory Internet. *A Contra Corriente, 4*(2), 54-76.

Moreno, J. (1934). *Who shell survive?* New York, NY: Bacon Press.

Morén, S., & Blom, B. (2003). Explaining human change - On generative mechanisms in social work practice. *Journal of Critical Realism, 2*(1), 37–60.

Morris, P. W., & Jamieson, A. (2005). Moving from a corporate strategy to project strategy. *Project Management Journal, 36*(4), 5–18.

Morton, P. (2006). Using critical realism to explain strategic information systems planning. *Journal of Information Technology Theory and Application, 8*(1), 1–20.

Mouton, J. (2001). *How to succeed in your Masters and Doctoral studies – A South African guide and resource book.* Pretoria, South Africa: Van Schaik Publishers.

Muhr, T. (1997). *Atlas TI user's manual.* Berlin, Germany: Scientific Software Development.

Mulkay, M. J. (1977). Sociology of the scientific research community. In Spiegel-Rosing, I., & de Solla Price, D. (Eds.), *Science, technology and society. A cross-disciplinary perspective* (pp. 93–148). Sage Publications.

Muniz, A. M., & O'Guinn, T. C. (2001, March). Brand community. *The Journal of Consumer Research, 27,* 412–432. doi:10.1086/319618

Munkvold, B. E., & Khazanchi, D. (2001). Expanding the notion of relevance in IS research: A proposal and some recommendations. *Communications of the Association for Information Systems, 6*(1).

Muntermann, J. (2009). Towards ubiquitous information supply for individual investors: A decision support system design. *Decision Support Systems, 47*(2), 82–92. doi:10.1016/j.dss.2009.01.003

Murphy, J. (1988). Computerization, postmodern epistemology, and reading in the postmodern era. *Educational Theory, 38*(2), 175–182. doi:10.1111/j.1741-5446.1988.00175.x

Mutch, A. (1999). Critical realism, managers and information. *British Journal of Management, 10,* 323–333. doi:10.1111/1467-8551.00142

Mutch, A. (2010). Technology, organization, and structure—A morphogenetic approach. *Organization Science, 21*(2), 507–520. doi:10.1287/orsc.1090.0441

Myers, M. D. (2004). Qualitative research in Information Systems. *MIS Quarterly*, 21(2), 241-242. Retrieved May 2006 from http://www.qual.auckland.ac.nz/

Myers, D. M. (2009). *Qualitative research in business & management*. Los Angeles, CA: Sage.

Myers, M. D., & Klein, H. K. (2011). A set of principles for conducting critical research in information systems. *Management Information Systems Quarterly, 35*(1), 17–36.

Mylonopoulos, N., & Tsoukas, H., (2003). Technological and organizational issues in knowledge management. *Knowledge and Process Management, 10*(3), 139–143. doi:10.1002/kpm.174

Nah, F. F., & Lau, J. L. (2001). Critical factors for successful implementation of enterprise systems. *Business Process Management Journal, 7*(3), 285–296. doi:10.1108/14637150110392782

Nakhleh, M. B., & Mitchell, R. C. (1993). Concept-learning versus problem-solving: There is a difference. *Journal of Chemical Education, 70*(3), 190–192. doi:10.1021/ed070p190

Nambisan, S., & Sawhney, M. (2008). *The global brain. Your roadmap for innovating faster and smarter in a networked world*. New Jersey: Pearson Education.

Nandhakumar, J., & Jones, M. (1997). Too close for comfort? Distance and engagement in interpretive Information Systems research. *Information Systems Journal, 7*(2), 109–131. doi:10.1046/j.1365-2575.1997.00013.x

Nan, N. (2011). Capturing bottom-up information technology use processes: A complex adaptive systems model. *Management Information Systems Quarterly, 35*(2), 505–507.

National Institute for Health Research. (2009). *University of Leeds*. Leeds Teaching Hospital Trusts. Retrieved February 15, 2011, from http://www.rdinfo.org.uk/flowchart/flowchart.html

Nel, D. F. (2007). *IT as an agent of postmodernism*. Unpublished Master's mini-dissertation, University of Pretoria, South Africa. Retrieved September 30, 2009, from http://upetd.up.ac.za/ thesis/ available/ etd-07032008- 130105/

Newell, A., & Simon, H. A. (1972). *Human problem solving*. Englewood Cliffs, NJ: Prentice Hall.

Newell, S., Tansley, C., & Huang, J. (2004). Social capital and knowledge integration in an ERP project team: the importance of bridging and bonding. *British Journal of Management, 15*, 43–S57. doi:10.1111/j.1467-8551.2004.00405.x

Newman, M., Barabasi, A.-L., & Watts, D. J. (2006). *The structure and dynamics of networks*. Princeton UP.

Niehaves, B. (2007). On epistemological pluralism in design science. *Scandinavian Journal of Information Systems, 19*(2), 93–104.

Nielsen, J., & Mack, R. L. (Eds.). (1994). *Usability inspection methods*. New York City, NY: John Wiley & Sons.

Nilsson, E. G., Nordhagen, E. K., & Oftedal, G. (1990). Aspects of systems integration. *Proceedings of the First International Conference on Systems Integration*, (pp. 434-443).

Nissen, M. E. (2006). *Harnessing knowledge dynamics: Principled organizational knowing & learning*. Hershey, PA: IGI Global.

Noble, K. A. (1992). *An international prognostic study, based on an acquisition model, of the degree Philosophise Doctor (PhD)*. Ottawa, Canada: University of Ottawa.

Nonaka, I., & Nishiguchi, T. (Eds.). (2001). *Knowledge emergence: Social, technical, and evolutionary dimensions of knowledge creation*. Oxford, UK: Oxford UP.

Nonaka, I., & Takeuchi, H. (1995). *The knowledge-creating company*. New York, NY: Oxford UP.

Nonaka, I., Umemoto, K., & Sasaki, K. (1998). Three tales of knowledge-creating companies. In Von Krogh, G., Roos, J., & Kline, D. (Eds.), *Knowing in firms: Understanding, managing and measuring knowledge* (pp. 146–172). London, UK: Sage.

Nonaka, I., Von Krogh, G., & Voelpel, S. (2006). Organizational knowledge creation theory: Evolutionary paths and future advances. *Organization Studies, 27*(8), 1179–1208. doi:10.1177/0170840606066312

Nunamaker, J. F., Chen, M., & Purdin, T. D. M. (1991). Systems development in Information Systems research. *Journal of Management Information Systems, 7*(3), 89–106.

Nunnally, J., & Bernstein, I. (1994). *Psychometric theory* (3rd ed.). New York, NY: McGraw-Hill.

O'Boyle, E. H. Jr, & Williams, L. J. (2011). Decomposing model fit: Measurement vs. theory in organizational research using latent variables. *The Journal of Applied Psychology, 96*(1), 1–12. doi:10.1037/a0020539

O'Donovan, B., & Roode, D. (2002). A framework for understanding the emerging discipline of Information Systems. *Information Technology & People, 15*(1), 26–41. doi:10.1108/09593840210423217

Oates, B. J. (2006). *Researching Information Systems and competing.* London, UK: Sage Publication.

Oberski, D. L. (2011). *Measurement error in comparative surveys.* Ph.D. Dissertation, Tilburg University.

O'Connor, R., & Coleman, G. (2009). Ignoring 'best practice': Why Irish software SMEs are rejecting CMMI and ISO 9000. *Australasian Journal of Information Systems, 16*(1).

OGC. (2007). *The official introduction to the ITIL service lifecycle.* London, UK: TSO.

Ohno, T. (1988). *Toyota production system: Beyond large-scale production.* Productivity Press.

Okress, E. C., Gleason, C. H., White, R. A., & Hayter, W. R. (1957). Design and performance of a high power pulsed magnetron. *IRE Transactions on Electron Devices, 4*(2), 161–171. doi:10.1109/T-ED.1957.14222

Olfman, L. (2001). We are doing relevant IS research: It's the truth. *Communications of the Association for Information Systems, 6*(1).

Olivier, M. S. (2004). *Information Technology research: A practical guide for computer science and informatics* (2nd ed.). Pretoria, South Africa: Van Schaik Publishers.

Orlikowski, W. (1993). CASE tools as organizational change: Investigating incremental and radical changes in systems development. *Management Information Systems Quarterly, 17*(3), 309–340. doi:10.2307/249774

Orlikowski, W. J. (2002). Knowing in practice. enacting a collective capability in distributed organizing. *Organization Science, 13*(3), 249–273. doi:10.1287/orsc.13.3.249.2776

Orlikowski, W. J., & Barley, S. R. (2001). Technology and institutions: What can research on information technology and research on organizations learn from each other? *Management Information Systems Quarterly, 25*(2), 145–165. doi:10.2307/3250927

Orlikowski, W. J., & Baroudi, J. J. (1991). Studying information technology in organizations: research approaches and assumptions. *Information Systems Research, 2*(1), 1–28. doi:10.1287/isre.2.1.1

Osgood, C. E., Suci, G., & Tannenbaum, P. (1957). *The measurement of meaning.* Urbana, IL: University of Illinois Press.

Otto, P., & Simon, M. (2008). Dynamic perspectives on social characteristics and sustainability in online community networks. *System Dynamics Review, 24*(3), 321–347. doi:10.1002/sdr.403

Outhwaite, W. (1987). *New philosophies of social science: realism, hermeneutics, and critical theory.* New York, NY: St. Martin's Press.

Palvia, P., Leary, T., Pinjani, P., & Midha, V. (2004). A meta analysis of MIS research. *Americas Conference of Information Systems, AMCIS 2004 Proceedings.* Paper 527. Retrieved from tp://aisel.aisnet.org/amcis2004/527

Panchal, J. H., & Fathianathan, M. (2008). Product realization in the age of mass collaboration. In *Proceedings of ASME 2008 International Design Engineering Technical Conferences and Computers and Information in Engineering Conference.* Retrieved from http:// westinghouse. marc.gatech.edu/ Members/ jpanchal/ Publications/ DETC2008_49865_MassCollaboration.April.12.08.pdf

Pan, G. S. C. (2005). Case study: Information Systems project abandonment: A stakeholder analysis. *International Journal of Information Management, 25*, 173–184. doi:10.1016/j.ijinfomgt.2004.12.003

Paper, D. J. (2001). IS relevance: Are we asking the right questions? *Communications of the Association for Information Systems, 6*(1).

Paper, D., & Chang, R. D. (2005). The state of business process reengineering: A search for success factors. *Total Quality Management, 16*(1), 121–133. doi:10.1080/1478336042000309907

Parsons, T. (1963a). On the concept of political power. *Proceedings of the American Philosophical Society, 107*(3), 232–262.

Parsons, T. (1963b). On the concept of influence. *Public Opinion Quarterly, 27*(Spring), 37–62. doi:10.1086/267148

Parsons, T. (1968). Interaction: I. Social interaction. In Sills, D. L. (Ed.), *The international encyclopedia of the social sciences* (*Vol. 7*, pp. 429–441). New York, NY: McGraw-Hill.

Pather, S., & Remenyi, D. (2004). Some of the philosophical issues underpinning realism in Information Systems: From positivsim to critical realism. In G. Marsden, P. Kotzé & A. Adessina-Ojo (Eds.), *Fulfilling the Promise of ICT - Proceedings of SAICSIT 2004.* Pretoria.

Pather, S., & Remenyi, D. (2005). Some of the philosophical issues underpinning research in Information Systems. *Proceedings of the 2004 Annual Research Conference of the South African Institute of Computer Scientists and Information Technologists on IT Research in Developing Countries.*

Patomäki, H. (2002). *After international relations: critical realism and the (re)construction of world politics.* London, UK: Routledge.

Patton, M. Q. (2002). *Qualitative evaluation and research methods* (3rd ed.). Newbury Park, CA: Sage Publications, Inc.

Pavlov, O. V., Plice, R. K., & Melville, N. P. (2008). A communication model with limited information-processing capacity of recipients. *System Dynamics Review, 24*(3), 377–405. doi:10.1002/sdr.407

Pawson, R. (2000). Middle-range realism. *European Journal of Sociology, 41*(02), 283–325. doi:10.1017/S0003975600007050

Pawson, R., & Tilley, N. (2007). *Realistic evaluation.* London, UK: Sage Publications.

Peak, D., Guynes, & C. S., & Kroon, V. (2005). Information Technology alignment planning – A case study. *Information & Management, 42,* 635–649. doi:10.1016/j.im.2004.02.009

Pearl, J. (2000). *Causality: Models, reasoning, and inference.* Cambridge, UK: Cambridge University Press.

Peffers, K., Tuunanen, T., Rothenberger, M. A., & Chatterjee, S. (2007). A design science research methodology for Information Systems research. *Journal of Management Information Systems, 24*(3), 45–77. doi:10.2753/MIS0742-1222240302

Peirce, C. (1931-1958). *Collected papers of Charles Sanders Peirce* (8 Volumes). Cambridge, MA: Harvard University Press.

Peirce, C. S. (1867). On the natural classification of arguments. In C. Hartshorne, P. Weiss & A.W. Burks (Eds.), *The collected papers of Charles Sanders Peirce,* (vols. 1-8, pp. 461-516). Cambridge, MA: Harvard University Press, 1931-1958.

Peirce, C. S. (1877). Deduction, induction, hypothesis. In C. Hartshorne, P. Weiss & A.W. Burks (Eds.), *The collected papers of Charles Sanders Peirce,* (vols. 1-8, pp. 619-644). Cambridge, MA: Harvard University Press, 1931-1958.

Peirce, C. S. (1901). On the logic of drawing history from ancient documents especially from testimonies. In C. Hartshorne, P. Weiss & A.W. Burks (Eds.), *The Collected Papers of Charles Sanders Peirce,* (vols. 1-8, pp. 164-255). Cambridge, MA: Harvard University Press, 1931-1958.

Peirce, C. S. (1931). *Collected papers.* Cambridge, MA: Belknap Press. (reprinted 1958)

Peirce, C. S. (1992a). The fixation of belief. In Houser, N., & Kloesel, C. (Eds.), *The essential Peirce* (*Vol. 1*, pp. 109–123). Bloomington, IN: Indiana University Press.

Peirce, C. S. (1992b). How to make our ideas clear. In Houser, N., & Kloesel, C. (Eds.), *The essential Peirce* (*Vol. 1*, pp. 124–141). Bloomington, IN: Indiana University Press.

Peirce, C. S. (1998a). The first rule of logic. In Peirce, C. (Ed.), *The essential Peirce* (*Vol. 2*, pp. 42–56). Bloomington, IN: Indiana University Press.

Peirce, C. S. (1998b). On the logic of drawing history from ancient documents, especially from testimonies. In Peirce, C. (Ed.), *The essential Peirce* (*Vol. 2*, pp. 75–114). Bloomington, IN: Indiana University Press.

Pentland, B. T., Osborn, C. S., Wyner, G., & Luconi, F. (1999). *Useful descriptions of organizational processes: Collecting data for the process handbook*. Retrieved from http:// ccs.mit.edu/ papers/ pdf/ wp208.pdf

Pentland, O. C. S., Wyner, G., & Luconi, F. (1999). *Useful descriptions of organizational processes: Collecting data for the process handbook*. Retrieved from http:// ccs.mit. edu/ papers/ pdf/ wp208.pdf

Pentland. (1999). Building process theory with narrative: From description to explanation. *The Academy of Management Review, 24*(4), 711-724.

Peterson, M. F. (1998). Embedded organizational events: The units of process in organization science. *Organization Science, 9*(1), 16–33. doi:10.1287/orsc.9.1.16

Petkov, D., Edgar-Neville, D., Madachy, R., & O'Connor, R. (2008). Information Systems, software engineering and Systems thinking–Challenges and opportunities. *International Journal of Information Technologies and Systems Approach, 1*(1), 62–78. doi:10.4018/jitsa.2008010105

Petkov, D., Petkova, O., Andrew, T., & Nepal, T. (2007). Mixing multiple criteria decision making with soft systems thinking techniques for decision support in complex situations. *Decision Support Systems, 43*, 1615–1629. doi:10.1016/j.dss.2006.03.006

Petkov, D., Petkova, O., Andrew, T., & Nepal, T. (2008). On the process of combining soft systems methodologies and other approaches in systemic interventions. *Journal of Organizational Transformation and Social Change, 5*(3), 291–303. doi:10.1386/jots.5.3.291_1

Petkov, D., Petkova, O., Sewchurran, K., Andrew, T., & Misra, R. (in press). The work system method as an approach for teaching and researching information systems. In Dwivedi, Y. K., Wade, M. R., & Schneberger, S. L. (Eds.), *Information Systems theory: Explaining and predicting our digital society*. doi:10.1007/978-1-4419-9707-4_21

Petter, S., Straub, D. W., & Rai, A. (2007). Specifying formative constructs in information systems research. *Management Information Systems Quarterly, 31*(4), 623–656.

Pfleeger, S. L., & Atlee, J. M. (2010). *Software engineering: Theory and practice* (4th ed.). Cranbury, NJ: Pearson.

Phillips, E., & Pugh, D. S. (1994). *How to get a PhD: A handbook for students and their supervisors* (2nd ed.). Buckingham, UK: Open University Press.

Piirainen, K., Gonzalez, R. A., & Kolfschoten, G. (2010). Quo Vadis, design science? – A survey of literature. *Global Perspectives on Design Science Research, Lecture Notes in Computer Science* (vol. 6105, pp. 93-108-108). Berlin, Germany: Springer.

Pinto, J. K., & Slevin, D. P. (1988). Project success: Definitions and measurement techniques. *Project Management Journal, 19*(3), 67–73.

PMI. (2000). *A guide to the project management body of knowledge PMBOK*. Newtown Square, PA: Project Management Institute (PMI).

Poincaré, J. H. (1952). *Science and hypothesis*. New York City, NY: Dover.

Polanyi, M. (1958). *Personal knowledge: Towards a post-critical philosophy*. Chicago, IL: University of Chicago Press.

Popper, K. (2002). *The logic of scientific discovery*. London, UK: Routledge.

Popper, K. R. (1963). *Conjectures and refutations: The growth of scientific knowledge*. London, UK: Routledge.

Powell, R. A., & Single, H. M. (1996). Focus groups. *International Journal for Quality in Health Care, 8*, 499–504. doi:10.1093/intqhc/8.5.499

Power, N. (2002). *A grounded theory of requirements documentation in the practice of software development*. PhD Thesis, Dublin City University, Ireland

Prandelli, E., Sawhney, M., & Verona, G. (2008). *Collaborating with customers to innovate: Conceiving and marketing products in the networking age*. United Kingdom: Edward Elgar Publishing Limited.

Preece, J., Rogers, Y., & Sharp, H. (2007). *Interaction design: Beyond human-computer interaction.* John Wiley & Sons, Inc.

Preece, J., Rogers, Y., & Sharp, H. (2007). *Interaction design: Beyond human-computer interaction.* John Wiley and Sons, Inc.

Purao, S., & Storey, V. C. (2008). Evaluating the adoption potential of design science efforts: The case of APSARA. *Decision Support Systems, 44*(2), 369–381. doi:10.1016/j.dss.2007.04.007

Putnam, H. (1975). What is mathematical truth? *Historia Mathematica, 2*(4), 529–533. doi:10.1016/0315-0860(75)90116-0

Putnam, H. (1995). *Pragmatism.* Cambridge, MA: Blackwell.

Qureshi, I., & Compeau, D. (2009). Assessing between-group differences in Information Systems research: A comparison of covariance- and component-based SEM. *Management Information Systems Quarterly, 33*(1), 197–214.

R Development Core Team. (2007). *R: A language and environment for statistical computing.* Vienna, Austria: R Foundation for Statistical Computing. Retrieved May 27, 2011, from http://www.R-project.org

Raduescu, C., & Vessey, I. (2008). *Causality in critical realist research: An analysis of three explanatory frameworks.* Annual Conference of International Association for Critical Realism, London, United Kingdom, 1st January 2008-31st December 2008

Raykov, T., & Marcoulides, G. A. (2006). *A first course in structural modeling.* Mahwah, NJ: Lawrence Erlbaum Associates.

Raykov, T., & Marcoulides, G. A. (2006). Estimation of generalizability coefficients via a structural equation modeling approach to scale reliability evaluation. *International Journal of Testing, 6*(1), 81–95. doi:10.1207/s15327574ijt0601_5

RealInnovation.com. (2011). *Innovation - What is innovation?* Retrieved 10 June, 2011, from http://www.realinnovation.com/content/what_is_innovation.asp

Rechenmacher, H., & Van Der Merwe, C. H. J. (2005). The contribution of Wolfgang Richter to current developments in the study of Biblical Hebrew. *Journal of Semitic Studies, 50*(1), 59–82. doi:10.1093/jss/fgi004

Redman, L. V., & Mory, A. V. H. (1923). *The romance of research, 10.*

Reed, M. (2005a). Doing the loco-motion: Response to Contu and Willmott's commentary on 'The realist turn in organization and management studies'. *Journal of Management Studies, 42*(8), 1663–1673. doi:10.1111/j.1467-6486.2005.00561.x

Reed, M. (2005b). Reflections on the realist turn in organization and management studies. *Journal of Management Studies, 42*(8), 1621–1644. doi:10.1111/j.1467-6486.2005.00559.x

Reed, M. (2009). Critical Realism: Philosophy, method or philosophy in search of a method. In Buchanan, D., & Bryman, A. (Eds.), *The Sage handbook of organizational research methods* (pp. 430–448). Sage Publications.

Reeves, T. C. (2000). Socially responsible educational technology research. *Educational Technology, 40*(6), 19–28.

Reeves, T. C. (2006). Design research from a technology perspective. In Van Den Akker, J., Graemeijer, K., McKenney, S., & Nieveen, N. (Eds.), *Educational design research* (pp. 52–66). New York, NY: Routledge.

Reichwald, R., Seifert, S., Walcher, D., & Piller, F. (2004, January). Customers as part of value webs: Towards a framework for webbed customer innovation tools. *Proceedings from 37th Hawaii International Conference on System Sciences.* Retrieved from http://wwwkrcmar.in.tum.de/public/webcoach/wsw/attachments/WINserv_Arbeitsbericht_Value-webs.pdf

Reinartz, W., Haenlein, M., & Henseler, J. (2009). An empirical comparison of the efficacy of covariance-based and variance-based (SEM). *International Journal of Research in Marketing, 26*(4), 332–344. doi:10.1016/j.ijresmar.2009.08.001

Remenyi, D., Williams, B., Money, A., & Swartz, E. (1998). *Doing research in business and management.* Sage Publications.

Riblet, H. B. (1956). A simplified automatic data plotter. *IRE Transactions on Instrumentation*, *5*, 34–43. doi:10.1109/IRE-I.1956.5006999

Rigdon, E. (1996). *Methodological alternatives to SEM/CFA, from Ed Rigdon's structural equation modeling.* Retrieved on February 12, 2011, from http://www2.gsu.edu/~mkteer/relmeth.html

Rigdon, E. (1995). A necessary and sufficient identification rule for structural models estimated in practice. *Multivariate Behavioral Research*, *30*(3), 359–383. doi:10.1207/s15327906mbr3003_4

Rigdon, E. E., Ringle, C. M., & Sarstedt, M. (2010). Structural modeling of heterogeneous data with partial least squares. *Review of Marketing Research*, *7*, 255–296. doi:10.1108/S1548-6435(2010)0000007011

Ringle, C. M., Wende, S., & Will, A. (2005). *SmartPLS 2.0 (M3) beta.* Hamburg, Germany.

Ringle, C. M., Götz, O., Wetzels, M., & Wilson, B. (2009). *On the use of formative measurement specifications in structural equation modeling: A Monte Carlo simulation study to compare covariance– based and partial least squares model estimation methodologies.* Maastricht University, METEOR Research Memoranda RM/09/014.

Rivard, S., & Huff, S. L. (1988). Factors of success for end user computing. *Communications of the ACM*, *29*(5), 486–501.

Roach, D. W., & Bednar, D. A. (1997). The theory of logical types: A tool for understanding levels and types of change in organizations. *Human Relations*, *50*(6), 671–699. doi:10.1177/001872679705000603

Roberts, N., & Thatcher, J. B. (2009). Conceptualizing and testing formative constructs: Tutorial and annoted example. *The Data Base for Advances in Information Systems*, *40*(3), 9–39.

Robey, D., & Markus, M. L. (1998). Beyond rigor and relevance: Producing consumable research about information system. *Information Resources Management Journal*, *11*(1), 7–16.

Rockart, J. (2002a). *Comments on the presentations by Klein, Gary, and Myers, discussion at ICIS 2001 panel.*

Rockart, J. (2002b). Editor's comments. *MISQ Executive, 1*(1).

Rogers, E. M. (1962). *Diffusion of innovations.* Glencoe, IL: Free Press.

Roldán, J. L., & Leal, A. (2003). A validation test of an adaptation of the DeLone and McLean's model in the Spanish EIS field. In Cano, J. J. (Ed.), *Critical reflections on information systems: A systemic approach* (pp. 66–84). Hershey, PA: IGI Publishing. doi:10.4018/978-1-59140-040-0.ch004

Rollier, B. (2001). Information Systems research: Reversing the orientation. *Communications of the Association for Information Systems*, *6*(1).

Roode, D. (2003). Information Systems research: A matter of choice? *Editorial in South African Computer Journal*, *30*, 1–2.

Rorty, R. (1979). *Philosophy and the mirror of nature.* Princeton, NJ: Princeton UP.

Rorty, R. (1982). *Consequences of pragmatism.* Minneapolis, MN: University of Minnesota Press.

Rorty, R. (1991). *Objectivity, relativism and truth.* Cambridge, UK: Cambridge UP.

Rose, J. (2000). *Information systems development as action research - Soft systems methodology and structuration theory.* PhD thesis, Management School, Lancaster University, England.

Rose, J. (1997). Soft systems methodology as a social science tool. *Systems Research and Behavioral Science*, *14*(4), 249–258. doi:10.1002/(SICI)1099-1743(199707/08)14:4<249::AID-SRES119>3.0.CO;2-S

Ross, M. (2006). Integrating three level 2 CMMI process areas: Closing the loop on software project management. *Proceedings of the IEEE Aerospace Conference*, Paper 1410, (pp. 1-17).

Rousseau, D. M. (1985). Issues of level in organizational research: Multi-level and cross-level perspectives. *Research in Organizational Behavior*, *7*(1), 1–37.

Royce, W. (1970). Managing the development of large software systems. *Proceedings of the IEEE WESCON* (Western Electronics Show and Convention), Los Angeles CA, August 1970, pp. 1-9. Retrieved May 26, 2011, from http://www.cs.umd.edu/ class/ spring2003/ cmsc838p/ Process/ waterfall.pdf

Rozenes, S., Vitner, G., & Spraggett, S. (2006). Project control: Literature review. *Project Management Journal, 37*(4), 5–14.

Rudd, E. (1985). *A new look at post-graduate failure*. Guildford Surrey, UK: Society for Research into Higher Education.

Rudd, E., & Hatch, S. (1968). *Graduate study and after*. London, UK: Weidenfeld & Nicolson.

Russell, B. A. W. (1997). *Problems of philosophy*. Oxford, UK: Oxford University Press.

Russell, C. (2009). A systemic framework for managing e-learning adoption in campus universities: Individual strategies in context. *Association for Learning Technology Journal, (ALT-J). Research in Learning Technology, 17*(1), 3–19. doi:10.1080/09687760802649871

Rychlak, J. F. (1999). Social constructionism, postmodernism, and the computer model: Searching for human agency in the right places. *Journal of Mind and Behavior, 20*(4), 379–390.

Ryle, G. (1948). Knowing how and knowing that. *Proceedings of the Aristotelian Society,* (p. 46).

Saad, N., & Kadirkamanathan, V. (2006). A DES approach for the contextual load modelling of supply chain system for instability analysis. *Simulation Modelling Practice and Theory, 4*(5), 541–563. doi:10.1016/j.simpat.2005.09.002

Saaty, T. L. (2000). *Fundamentals of decision making with the analytic hierarchy process*. Pittsburgh, PA: RWS Publications.

Saliba, G. (2007). *Islamic science and the making of the European renaissance*. Cambridge, MA: MIT Press.

Salton, G., & McGill, M. J. (1983). *Introduction to modern information retrieval*. Auckland, Australia: McGraw-Hill.

Sammarra, A., & Biggiero, L. (2001). Identity and Identification in Industrial Districts. *Journal of Management and Governance, 5*, 61–82. doi:10.1023/A:1017937506664

Samuels, H. (2011). Basic steps in the research process. *Cambridge Rindge and Latin School Research Guide*. Retrieved February 15, 2011, from http://www.crlsresearchguide.org/

Sánchez, G., & Trinchera, L. (2010). *PLSPM – Partial least squares data analysis methods*. Retrieved May 27, 2011, from http://cran.r-project.org/web/packages/plspm/plspm.pdf

Sánchez-Franco, M. J., & Roldán, J. L. (2005). Web acceptance and usage model: A comparison between goal-directed and experiential Web users. *Internet Research, 15*(1), 21–48. doi:10.1108/10662240510577059

Sanders, G. L., & Courtney, J. F. (1985). A field study of organizational factors influencing DSS success. *Management Information Systems Quarterly, 9*, 77–93. doi:10.2307/249275

Saris, W. E., Satorra, A., & van der Veld, W. (2009). Testing structural equation models or detection of misspecifications? *Structural Equation Modeling, 16*(4), 1–24. doi:10.1080/10705510903203433

Sarker, S., Lau, F., & Sahay, S. (2001). Using an adapted grounded theory approach for inductive theory building about virtual team development. *The Data Base for Advances in Information Systems, 32*(1), 38–56.

Satorra, A., & Bentler, P. M. (2010). Ensuring positiveness of the scaled difference chi-square test statistic. *Psychometrika, 75*, 243–248. doi:10.1007/s11336-009-9135-y

Saunders, C. S. (1998). The role of business in IT research. *Information Resources Management Journal, 11*(1), 4–6.

Savalei, V., & Bentler, P. M. (2006). Structural equation modeling. In Grover, R., & Vriens, M. (Eds.), *The handbook of marketing research: Uses, misuses, and future advances* (pp. 330–364). Thousand Oaks, CA: Sage Publications.

Sawhney, M., Verona, G., & Prandelli, W. (2005, Autumn). Collaborating to create: The Internet as a platform for customer engagement in product innovation. *Journal of Interactive Marketing, 19*(4), 4–17. doi:10.1002/dir.20046

Sayer, A. (2000). *Realism and social science*. Sage.

Schauer, C. (2007). *Relevance and success of IS teaching and research: An analysis of the "relevance debate"*. ICB Research Report No. 19, University Duisburg-Essen, Institute for Computer Science and Business Information Systems.

Schenk, E. & Guittard, C. (2009). *Crowdsourcing: What can be outsourced to the crowd and why?* Manuscript. Retrieved from L'archive ouverte pluridiciplinaire database.

Scheufele, D. A. (1999). Framing as a theory of media effects. *The Journal of Communication, 49*(1), 103–122. doi:10.1111/j.1460-2466.1999.tb02784.x

Schlenoff, C., & Uschold, M. (2004, November 30). Knowledge engineering and ontologies for autonomous systems: 2004 AAAI Spring Symposium. *Robotics and Autonomous Systems, 49*, 1–5. doi:10.1016/j.robot.2004.08.004

Schneeweiss, H. (1990). Models with latent variables. In Brown, P. J., & Fuller, W. A. (Eds.), *Contemporary mathematics (Vol. 112*, pp. 33–39). Providence, RI: American Mathematical Society.

Schön, D. A. (1987). *Educating the reflective practitioner*. San Francisco, CA: Jossey-Bass Publishers.

Schultze, U. (2000). A confessional account of an ethnography about knowledge work. *Management Information Systems Quarterly, 24*(1), 3–39. doi:10.2307/3250978

Schulze, K., & Krömker, H. (2010). A framework to measure user experience of interactive online products. In Spink, A. J., Grieco, F., Krips, O. E., Loijens, L. W. S., Noldus, L. P. J. J., & Zimmerman, P. H. (Eds.), *Proceedings of Measuring Behaviour 2010*. Eindhoven, The Netherlands. doi:10.1145/1931344.1931358

Scott, J. (1991). *Social network analysis: A Handbook*. Newbury Park, CA: Sage.

Seaman, C., & Basili, V. (1997). An empirical study of communication in code inspections. In *Proceedings of the 19th International Conference on Software Engineering*, May, Boston, MA (pp. 17-23).

Searle, J. R. (1995). *The construction of social reality*. New York, NY: Free Press.

Seddon, P. B. (1997). A respecification and extension of the DeLone and McLean model of IS success. *Information Systems Research, 8*(3), 240–253. doi:10.1287/isre.8.3.240

Sein, M. K. (2001). The relevance of IS academic research: Not as good as it can get. *Communications of the Association for Information Systems, 6*(1).

Sekaran, U. (2000). *Research methods for business: A skill building approach* (3rd ed.). New York, NY: John Wiley and Sons.

Senn, J. (1998). The challenge of relating IS research to practice. *Information Resources Management Journal, 11*(1), 23–28.

Sewchurran, K., & Petkov, D. (2007). A systemic framework for business process modeling combining soft systems methodology and UML. *Information Resources Management Journal, 20*(3), 46–62. doi:10.4018/irmj.2007070104

Sewchurran, K., Smith, D., & Roode, D. (2010). Toward a regional ontology for Information Systems project management. *International Journal of Managing Projects in Business, 3*(4), 681–692. doi:10.1108/17538371011076118

Sharma, M. (2004). *Research methodology*. New Delhi, India: Anmol Publications.

Shavelson, R. J. (1972). Some aspects of the correspondence between content structure and cognitive structure in physics instruction. *Journal of Educational Psychology, 63*(3), 225–234. doi:10.1037/h0032652

Shaw, M. (2003). Writing good software engineering research papers. In *Proceedings of the 25th International Conference on Software Engineering*, (pp. 726-736). IEEE Computer Society.

Sherrell, L. B., & Chen, L. (2001). The W life cycle model and associated methodology for corporate web site development. *Communications of the Association for Information Systems, 5*(7), 1–38.

Shneiderman, B., & Plaisant, C. (2009). *Designing the user interface: Strategies for effective human-computer interaction* (5th ed.). Upper Saddle River, NJ: Pearson Addison-Wesley.

Siau, K., & Rossi, M. (2008). Evaluation techniques for systems analysis and design modelling methods: A review and comparative analysis. *Information Systems Journal, 21*(3), 249–268. doi:10.1111/j.1365-2575.2007.00255.x

Sichman, J. S., Conte, R., & Gilbert, N. (Eds.). (1998). *Multi-agent systems and agent-based simulation.* Berlin, Germany: Springer.

Sicilia, M. (2006). Metadata, semantics, and ontology: Providing meaning to information resources. *International Journal of Metadata. Semantics and Ontologies, 1*(1), 83–86. doi:10.1504/IJMSO.2006.008773

Silva, L., & Backhouse, J. (1997). Becoming part of the furniture: The institutionalisation of Information Systems. In Lee, A., Liebenau, J., & DeGross, J. I. (Eds.), *Proceedings of Information Systems and Qualitative Research.* Chapman and Hall.

Silverman, D. (2004). *Qualitative research: Theory, method and practice* (2nd ed.). Thousand Oaks, CA: Sage Publications.

Simon, A. (2001). A unified method for analyzing media framing. In Hart, R. P., & Shaw, D. R. (Eds.), *Communication in U.S. elections: New agendas* (pp. 75–89). Lanham, MD: Rowman and Littlefield.

Simon, H. A. (1954). Spurious correlation: A causal interpretation. *Journal of the American Statistical Association, 49*(267), 467–479. doi:10.2307/2281124

Simon, H. A. (1969). *The Sciences of the artificial.* Cambridge, MA: MIT Press.

Simon, H. A. (1977). *Models of discovery.* Dordrecht: Reidel.

Simon, H. A. (1981). *The sciences of the artificial* (2nd ed.). MIT Press.

Simon, H. A. (1996). *The sciences of the artificial* (3rd ed.). Cambridge, MA: MIT Press.

Simon, H. A. (1997). Models of bounded rationality: *Vol. 3. Empirically grounded economic reason.* NY: MIT Press.

Simon, H. A., Langley, P. W., & Bradshaw, G. L. (1981). Scientific discovery as problem solving. *Synthese, 47*(1), 1–27. doi:10.1007/BF01064262

Sim, S. (2001b). Postmodernism and philosophy. In Sim, S. (Ed.), *The Routledge companion to postmodernism* (pp. 3–14). London, UK: Routledge.

Sim, S. (Ed.). (2001a). *The Routledge companion to postmodernism.* London, UK: Routledge.

Singh, Y. K., & Bajpai, R. B. (2008). *Research methodology: Techniques and trends.* New Delhi, India: A P H Publishing Corporation.

Siraj, S. A., & Ullah, F. (2007, Dec.). Postmodernism and its insinuations on media and society. *The Journal of Development Communication, 18*(2), 1–10.

Skinner, D. C. (2001). *Introduction to decision analysis* (2nd ed.). Gainsville, FL: Probabilistic Publishing.

Škraba, A., Kljajić, M., & Kljajić Borštnar, M. (2007). The role of information feedback in the management group decision-making process applying system dynamics models. *Group Decision and Negotiation, 16*(1), 77–95. doi:10.1007/s10726-006-9035-9

Škraba, A., Kljajić, M., & Leskovar, R. (2003). Group exploration of system dynamics models – Is there a place for a feedback loop in the decision process? *System Dynamics Review, 19*(3), 243–263. doi:10.1002/sdr.274

Skyttner, L. (2006). *General systems theory: Problems, perspective, practice.* Hackensack, NJ: World Scientific Publishing Company. doi:10.1142/9789812774750

Smith, M. (2008). Testable theory development for small-N studies: Critical realism and middle-range theory. *CONF-IRM 2008 Proceedings.*

Smith, M. (2006). Overcoming theory-practice inconsistencies: Critical realism and Information Systems research. *Information and Organization, 16*(3), 191–211. doi:10.1016/j.infoandorg.2005.10.003

Smith, M. L. (2010). Testable theory development for small-n studies: Critical realism and middle-range theory. *International Journal of Information Technologies and Systems Approach, 3*(1), 41–56. doi:10.4018/jitsa.2010100203

Software Engineering Institute. (2002). *CMMI for systems engineering and software engineering.* (CMU/SEI-2002-TR-001). Retrieved from www.sei.edu

Sol, H. G. (1982). *Simulation in Information Systems development*. Doctoral Dissertation. Rijksuniversiteit Groningen, Groningen.

Solomon, E. (2001). The dynamics of corporate change: Managements evaluation of stakeholder characteristics. *Human Systems Management, 20*, 257–365.

Sommerville, I. (2011). *Software engineering* (9th ed.). Boston, MA: Pearson.

Sosik, J. J., Kahai, S. S., & Piovoso, M. J. (2009). Silver bullet or voodoo statistics? A primer for using the partial least squares data analytic technique in group and organization research. *Group & Organization Management, 34*(1), 5–36. doi:10.1177/1059601108329198

Spears, R., Postmes, T., Lea, M., & Wolbert, A. (2002). When are net effects gross products? The power of influence in computer-mediated communications. *The Journal of Social Issues, 58*(1), 91–107. doi:10.1111/1540-4560.00250

Speier, C., & Morris, M. (2003). The influence of query interface design on decision making performance. *Management Information Systems Quarterly, 27*(3), 397–423.

Squido Education Topics. (2011). *Creative thinking techniques - Enhance your creativity.* Retrieved February 1, 2011, from http://www.squidoo.com/creative-techniques

Squires, D. (1999). Educational software for constructivist learning environments: Subversive use and volatile design. *Educational Technology, 39*(3), 48–53.

Srivannaboon, S., & Milosevic, D. Z. (2006). A two-way influence between business strategy and project management. *International Journal of Project Management, 24*, 493–505. doi:10.1016/j.ijproman.2006.03.006

Stainton, R. S. (1984). Applicable systems thinking. *European Journal of Operational Research, 18*, 145–154. doi:10.1016/0377-2217(84)90180-2

Statistics Canada. (2000). Brain drain and brain gain: The migration of knowledge workers from and to Canada. *Education Quarterly Review, 6*, 8–35.

Steenkamp, A. L., & Konda, D (2003). Information Technology, the key enabler for knowledge management: A methodological approach. *International Journal of Knowledge, Culture and Change Management, 3.* Article: MC03-0070-2003.

Steenkamp, A. L., & McCord, S. A. (2007). Approach to teaching research methodology for Information Technology. *Journal of Information Systems Education; ABI/INFORM Global, 255.*

Steenkamp, A. L., & McCord, S. A. (2007). Teaching research methodology for Information Technology. *Journal of Information Systems Education, 18*(2).

Steiger, J. H. (1979). Factor indeterminacy in the 1930's and the 1970's – Some interesting parallels. *Psychometrika, 44*, 157–167. doi:10.1007/BF02293967

Steinbach, T. A., & Knight, L. V. (2006). The relevance of Information Systems research: Informing the IS practitioner community; informing ourselves. *Proceedings of the 2006 Informing Science and IT Education Joint Conference*, Salford, UK – June 25-28.

Stones, R. (1996). *Sociological reasoning: Towards a past-modern sociology.* MacMillan.

Stowell, F. (Ed.). (1995). *Information Systems provision - The contribution of soft systems methodology.* London, UK: McGraw-Hill Publishing Co.

Strang, K. D. (2007). Examining effective technology leadership traits and behaviors. *Computers in Human Behavior, 23*, 424–462. doi:10.1016/j.chb.2004.10.041

Straub, D., Ang, S., & Evaristo, R. (1994). Normative standards for IS research. *Database, 25*(1), 21–34.

Straub, D., Boudreau, M. C., & Gefen, D. (2004). Validation guidelines for IS positivist research. *Communications of the Association for Information Systems, 14*, 380–426.

Strauss, A. L., & Corbin, J. (1990). *Basics of qualitative research: Grounded theory procedures and techniques.* Newbury Park, CA: Sage.

Strauss, A., & Corbin, J. (1990). *Basics of qualitative research: Grounded theory procedures and techniques.* London, UK: SAGE Publication.

Strauss, A., & Corbin, J. (1998). *Basics of qualitative research techniques and procedures for developing grounded theory.* USA: Sage.

Strong, D. M., & Volkoff, O. (2010). Understanding organization–enterprise system fit: A path to theorizing the Information Technology artifact. *Management Information Systems Quarterly, 34*(4), 731–756.

Tan, B. C. Y., Smith, H. J., Keil, M., & Montealegre, R. (2003). Reporting bad news about software projects: Impact of organizational climate and information asymmetry in an individualistic and collectivistic culture. *IEEE Transactions on Engineering Management, 50*(1), 64–77. doi:10.1109/TEM.2002.808292

Tarnas, R. (1991). *The passion of the western mind: Understanding the ideas that have shaped our world view.* New York, NY: Ballantine Books.

Tashakkori, A., & Teddies, C. (1998). *Mix methodology: Combining quantitative and qualitative approaches. Applied Social Research Methods, 46.* Thousand Oaks, CA: Sage Publication.

Taylor, F. W. (1947). *Scientific management.* Harper & Brothers.

Taylor, H., Dillon, S., & Van Wingen, M. (2010). Focus and diversity in information systems research: Meeting the dual demands of a healthy applied discipline. *Management Information Systems Quarterly, 34*(4), 647–667.

Taylor, S. J., & Bordan, R. (1984). *Introduction to qualitative research method.* John Wiley & Sons.

Tegmark, M. (2008). The mathematical universe. *Foundations of Physics, 38*(2), 101–150. doi:10.1007/s10701-007-9186-9

Temme, D., Kreis, H., & Hildebrandt, L. (2010). A comparison of current PLS path modeling software: Features, ease-of-use, and performance. In Esposito Vinzi, V., Chin, W. W., Henseler, J., & Wang, H. (Eds.), *Handbook of partial least squares: Concepts, methods and applications* (pp. 737–756). Berlin, Germany: Springer-Verlag. doi:10.1007/978-3-540-32827-8_32

Templeton, T. F. (1994). *The focus group: A strategic guide to organizing, conducting and analyzing the focus group interview.* McGraw-Hill Professional Publishing, 1994.

Tenenhaus, M., Vinzi, V. E., Chatelin, Y.-M., & Lauro, C. (2005). PLS path modeling. *Computational Statistics & Data Analysis, 48*(1), 159–205. doi:10.1016/j.csda.2004.03.005

Tesch, D., Kloppenborg, T. J., & Stemmer, J. K. (2003). Project management learning - What the literature has to say. *Project Management Journal, 34*(4), 33–39.

The Basics of Effective Learning. (2011). *Cognitive structures: Ways to organize information for more effectively understanding and remembering.* Retrieved 8 June, 2011, from http://www.bucks.edu/~specpop/Elabqst.htm

Thompson, B. (2004). *Exploratory and confirmatory factor analysis.* Washington, DC: American Psychological Association. doi:10.1037/10694-000

Thornham, S. (2001). Postmodernism and feminism (or: repairing our own cars). In Sim, S. (Ed.), *The Routledge companion to postmodernism* (pp. 41–52). London, UK: Routledge.

Tichy, W. F. (1998). Should computer scientists experiment more? *IEEE Computer, 31*(5), 32–40. doi:10.1109/2.675631

Trauth, E. (2001). *Qualitative research in IS: Issues and trends.* Hershey, PA: Idea Group Publishing.

Trauth, E. M. (1997). Achieving the research goal with qualitative methods: Lessons learned along the way. In Lee, A. S., Liebenau, J., & DeGross, J. I. (Eds.), *Information Systems and qualitative research* (pp. 225–245). London, UK: Chapman & Hall.

Trauth, E. M. (2000). *The culture of an information economy: Influences and impacts in the Republic of Ireland.* Dordrecht, The Netherlands: Kluwer Academic Publishers.

Trauth, E. M. (2006). Theorizing gender and information technology research. In Trauth, E. M. (Ed.), *Encyclopedia of gender and Information Technology* (pp. 1154–1159). Hershey, PA: Idea Group Publishing. doi:10.4018/978-1-59140-815-4.ch182

Trauth, E. M. (2011). What can we learn from gender research? Seven lessons for business research methods. *Electronic Journal of Business Research Methods, 9*(1), 1–9.

Trauth, E. M., & Jessup, L. (2000). Understanding computer-mediated discussions: Positivist and interpretive analyses of group support system use. *Management Information Systems Quarterly, 24*(1), 43–79. doi:10.2307/3250979

Treiblmaier, H., Bentler, P. M., & Mair, P. (2011). Formative constructs implemented via common factors. *Structural Equation Modeling, 18*, 1–17. doi:10.1080/10705511.2011.532693

Trompette, P., Chanal, V., & Pelissier, C. (2008). Crowdsourcing as a way to access external knowledge for innovation: Control, incentive and coordination in hybrid forms of innovation. *Proceedings of the 24th EGOS Colloquium.*

Truex, D., Alter, S., & Long, C. (2010, June). *Systems analysis for everyone else: Business professionals through a systems analysis method that fits their needs.* Paper presented at the 18th European Conference on Information Systems, Pretoria, South Africa.

Tsang, E. W. K. (1997). Organizational learning and the learning organization: A dichotomy between descriptive and prescriptive research. *Human Relations, 50*(1), 73–89. doi:10.1177/001872679705000104

Tsoukas, H. (1996). The firm as a distributed knowledge system: A constructionist approach. *Strategic Management Journal, 17*, 11–25.

Tsoukas, H. (2005). *Complex knowledge. Studies in organizational epistemology.* Oxford, UK: Oxford UP.

Tsoukas, H., & Knudsen, C. (Eds.). (2003). *The Oxford handbook of organization theory.* Oxford, UK: Oxford UP.

Tsoukas, H., & Mylonopoulos, N. (2004). Introduction: Knowledge construction and creation in organizations. *British Journal of Management, 15*, S1–S8. doi:10.1111/j.1467-8551.2004.t01-2-00402.x

Tsoukas, H., & Vladimirou, E. (2001). What is organizational knowledge? *Journal of Management Studies, 38*, 973–993. doi:10.1111/1467-6486.00268

Tummarello, G., Morbidoni, C., Puliti, P., & Piazza, F. (2008). A proposal for textual encoding based on semantic web tools. *Online Information Review, 32*(4), 467-477. Retrieved August 23, 2009, from http:// www.emeraldinsight.com/ 1468-4527. htm

Tushman, M. L., & O'Reilly, C. A. (2002). *Winning through innovation: A practical guide to leading organizational change and renewal.* Boston, MA: Harvard Business School Press.

Un, C. A., & Cuervo-Cazurra, A. (2004). Strategies for knowledge creation in firms. *British Journal of Management, 15*, 27–S41. doi:10.1111/j.1467-8551.2004.00404.x

University of Oxford. (2011). *Bachelor and Masters Degree on Computer Science and Philosophy.* Retrieved February 7, 2011, from http://www.comlab.ox.ac.uk/admissions/ugrad/Computer_Science_and_Philosophy

Urbach, N., & Ahlemann, F. (2010). Structural equation modeling in information systems research using partial least squares. *Journal of Information Technology Theory and Application, 11*(2), 5–40.

Urquhart, C. (2001). An encounter with grounded theory: Tackling the practical and philosophical issues. In Trauth, E. M. (Ed.), *Qualitative research in Information Systems: Issues and trends* (pp. 104–140). Hershey, PA: Idea Group Publishing. doi:10.4018/978-1-930708-06-8.ch005

Urquhart, C. (2002). Regrounding grounded theory – Or reinforcing old prejudices? A brief reply to Bryant. *The Journal of Information Technology Theory and Application, 4*(3), 43–54.

Urquhart, C., Lehmann, H., & Myers, M. D. (2010). Putting the 'theory' back into grounded theory: Guidelines for grounded theory studies in information systems. *Information Systems Journal, 20*, 357–381. doi:10.1111/j.1365-2575.2009.00328.x

Valerdi, R., & Brown, S. (2010). *Towards a framework of research methodology choices in systems engineering.* 8th Conference on Systems Engineering Research March 17-19, 2010, Hoboken, NJ.

van de Ven, A. H., & Huber, G. P. (1990). Longitudinal field research methods for studying processes of organizational change. *Organization Science, 1*(3), 213–219. doi:10.1287/orsc.1.3.213

Van Den Akker, J. (2002). The added value of development research for educational development in developing countries. In K. Osaki, W. Ottevanger C. Uiso & J. van den Akker (Eds.), *Science education research and teacher development in Tanzania.* Amsterdam, The Netherlands: Vrije Universiteit, International Cooperation Center.

Van Den Akker, J. (1999). Principles and methods of development research. In van den Akker, J., Branch, R. M., Gustafson, K. L., Nieveen, N., & Plomp, T. (Eds.), *Design approaches and tools in education and training*. Dordrecht, The Netherlands: Kluwer Academic Publishers. doi:10.1007/978-94-011-4255-7_1

Van der Merwe, T. M., & de Villiers, M. R. (2011). The partial approach to grounded theory integrated with activity theory: A generic framework illustrated by a base study in an e-learning context. *Alternation, 18*, 2.

Van der Merwe, T. M., van der Merwe, A. J., & Venter, L. M. (2010). A model to direct online continuous professional development opportunities for mathematics teachers in the South African context of disparities. *African Journal of Mathematics. Science and Technology Education, 14*(3), 65–80.

van Eck, N. J., Waltman, L., Dekker, R., & van den Berg, J. (2010). A comparison of two techniques for bibliometric mapping: Multidimensional scaling and VOS. *Journal of the American Society for Information Science and Technology, 61*(12), 2405–2416. doi:10.1002/asi.21421

Van Gorp, B. (2007). The constructionist approach to framing: Bringing culture back in. *The Journal of Communication, 57*, 60–78.

Van Vliet, H. (2008). *Software engineering* (3rd ed.). Hoboken, NJ: John Wiley and Sons Inc.

Vandapalli, V., & Mone, M. A. (2000). Information Technology project outcomes: User participation structures and the impact of organizational behavior and human resource management issues. *Journal of Engineering and Technology Management, 17*, 127–151. doi:10.1016/S0923-4748(00)00018-7

Vannoy, S. A., & Salam, A. F. (2010). Managerial interpretations of the role of Information Systems in competitive actions and firm performance: A grounded theory investigation. *Information Systems Research, 21*(3), 496–515. doi:10.1287/isre.1100.0301

Varela, F. G., Maturana, H. R., & Uribe, R. (1974). Autopoiesis: The organization of living systems, its characterization and a model. *Bio Systems, 5*, 187–196. doi:10.1016/0303-2647(74)90031-8

Varela, F. J. (1979). *Principles of biological autonomy*. New York, NY: North Holland.

Varela, F. J. (1992). Whence perceptual meaning? A cartography of current ideas. In Varela, F., & Dupuy, J. (Eds.), *Understanding origins: Contemporary views on the origin of life, mind and society* (pp. 235–263). Dordrecht, The Netherlands: Kluwer Academic.

Varela, F. J. (1996). The early days of autopoiesis: Heinz and Chile. *Systems Research, 13*(3), 407–416. doi:10.1002/(SICI)1099-1735(199609)13:3<407::AID-SRES100>3.0.CO;2-1

Varela, F. J., Thompson, E., & Rosch, E. (1991). *The embodied mind. Cognitive science and human experience*. Cambridge, MA: MIT Press.

Venable, J. R. (2006). *The role of theory and theorising in design science research*. Presented at the First International Conference on Design Science Research in Information Systems and Technology (DESRIST 2006), Claremont, CA.

Venkatesh, V., & Davis, F. D. (2000). Theoretical extension of the technology acceptance model: Four longitudinal field studies. *Management Science, 46*(2), 186–204. doi:10.1287/mnsc.46.2.186.11926

Venkatesh, V., & Morris, M. (2000). Why don't men ever stop to ask for directions? Gender, social influence, and their role in technology acceptance and usage behavior. *Management Information Systems Quarterly, 24*(1), 115–139. doi:10.2307/3250981

Venkatesh, V., Morris, M. G., & Ackerman, P. L. (2000). A longitudinal field investigation of gender differences in individual technology adoption decision making processes. *Organizational Behavior and Human Decision Processes, 83*(1), 33–60. doi:10.1006/obhd.2000.2896

Venkatesh, V., Morris, M. G., Davis, G. B., & Davis, F. D. (2003). User acceptance of Information Technology: Toward a unified view. *Management Information Systems Quarterly, 27*(3), 425–478.

Vennix, J. A. M. (1996). *Group model building: Facilitating team learning using system dynamics*. Chichester, UK: John Wiley & Sons.

Vessey, I., & Galletta, D. (1991). Cognitive fit: An empirical study of information acquisition. *Information Systems Research, 2*(1), 63–84. doi:10.1287/isre.2.1.63

Vlaar, P. W. L., van Fenema, P. C., & Tiwari, V. (2008). Cocreating understanding and value in distributed work: How members of onsite and offshore vendor teams give, make, demand, and break sense. *Management Information Systems Quarterly, 32*(2), 227–255.

Voelker, M. (2006). Targeting excellence. *TechDecisions, 8*(3), 18–22.

Volkoff, O., Strong, D., & Elmes, M. (2007). Technological embeddedness and organizational change. *Organization Science, 18*(5), 832–848. doi:10.1287/orsc.1070.0288

von Bertalanffy, L. (1950). An outline of general systems theory. (reprinted in Bertalanffy (1968)). *The British Journal for the Philosophy of Science, 1*, 134–164. doi:10.1093/bjps/I.2.134

von Bertalanffy, L. (1968). *General systems theory – Foundations, developments, applications.* New York, NY: G. Brazillier.

von Foerster, H. (1982). *Observing systems.* Seaside, CA: Intersystems Publications.

von Foerster, H. (1984). Principles of self-organization in a socio-managerial context. In Ulrich, U., & Probst, G. J. B. (Eds.), *Self-organization and management of social systems* (pp. 2–24). New York, NY: Springer. doi:10.1007/978-3-642-69762-3_1

von Glasersfeld, E. (1995). *Radical constructivism: A way of knowing and learning.* London, UK: The Falmer Press. doi:10.4324/9780203454220

von Hippel, E. A. (2001, Summer). Learning from open-source software. *MIT Sloan Management Review*, 82-86.

von Hippel, E. A. (2005). *Democratizing innovation.* Cambridge, MA: MIT Press.

von Hippel, E. A., & von Krogh, G. (2003, April). Open source software and the "private collective" innovation model: Issues for organization science. *Organization Science, 14*(2), 209–223. doi:10.1287/orsc.14.2.209.14992

Von Krogh, G., & Roos, J. (Eds.). (1995). *Managing Knowledge. Perspectives on Cooperation and Competition.* London: Sage.

von Krogh, G., Roos, J., & Kline, D. (Eds.). (1998). *Knowing in firms: understanding, managing and measuring knowledge.* London, UK: Sage.

von Krogh, G., Roos, J., & Slocum, K. (1996). An essay on corporate epistemology. In von Krogh, G., & Roos, J. (Eds.), *Managing knowledge. Perspectives on cooperation and competition* (pp. 157–183). London, UK: Sage.

Vreede, G. J. (1995). *Facilitating organizational change: The participative application of dynamic modeling.* Delft University of Technology.

Wad, P. (2001). *Critical realism and comparative sociology.* IACR conference, Roskilde University, August, 2001.

Waldrop, M. (1987). *Man-made minds.* New York, NY: Walker.

Walls, J. G., Widmeyer, G. R., & El Sawy, O. A. (1992). Building an Information System design theory for vigilant EIS. *Information Systems Research, 3*(1), 36–59. doi:10.1287/isre.3.1.36

Walsham, G. (1995a). Interpretive case studies in IS research: Nature and method. *European Journal of Information Systems, 4*(2), 74–81. doi:10.1057/ejis.1995.9

Walsham, G. (1995b). The emergence of interpretivism in IS research. *Information Systems Research, 6*(4), 376–394. doi:10.1287/isre.6.4.376

Wang, M.-L., & Chen, C.-L. (2009). Action research into e-learning curriculum development for library and Information Science in Taiwan. *Proceedings of the Asia-Pacific Conference on Library and Information Education and Practice, 2009* (pp. 437-449).

Wang, W. T., & Liu, C. Y. (2005). The application of the technology acceptance model: A new way to evaluate Information System success. In J. D. Sterman, N. P. Repenning, R. S. Langer, J. I. Rowe, & J. M. Yanni (Eds.), *Proceedings of the 23th International Conference of the System Dynamics Society.* Albany, NY: System Dynamics Society.

Wang, F., & Hannafin, M. J. (2005). Design-based research and technology-enhanced learning environments. *Educational Technology Research and Development, 53*(4), 5–23. doi:10.1007/BF02504682

Wasko, M. M., & Faraj, S. (2000). "It is what one does": Why people participate and help others in electronic communities of practice. *The Journal of Strategic Information Systems, 9*, 155–173. doi:10.1016/S0963-8687(00)00045-7

Wasserman, S., & Faust, K. (1994). *Social network analysis: Methods and applications*. Cambridge, UK: Cambridge University Press.

Watson, H. J., & Huber, M. W. (2000). Innovative ways to connect information systems programs to the business community. *Communications of the AIS, 3*(11).

Watson, N. (2001). Postmodernism and lifestyles (or: you are what you buy). In S. Sim (Ed.), (2001a), *The Routledge companion to postmodernism* (pp. 53-64). London, UK: Routledge.

Watts, D. J. (2004a). Six degrees. Vintage, New edition.

Watts, D. J. (2003). *Small worlds: The dynamics of networks between order and randomness*. Princeton UP.

Watts, D. J. (2004b). The "new" science of networks. *Annual Review of Sociology, 30*, 243–270. doi:10.1146/annurev.soc.30.020404.104342

Watzlawick, P. (Ed.). (1984). *The invented reality*. New York, NY: Norton.

Webster, B. (2009, May). Facebook democracy in Iran. *PoliticsOnline*. Retrieved September 5, 2009, from http://www.politicsonline.com/ blog/ archives/ 2009/ 05/ facebook_ and_de. php

Webster, J., & Martocchio, J. (1992). Microcomputer playfulness: Development of a measure with workplace implications. *Management Information Systems Quarterly, 16*(2), 201–226. doi:10.2307/249576

Webster, L., & Mertova, P. (2007). *Using narrative inquiry as a research method: An introduction to using critical event narrative analysis in research on learning and teaching*. New York, NY: Routledge.

Weick, K. E. (1969). *The social psychology of organizing*. Newberry Award Records Inc.

Weick, K. E. (1995). *Sensemaking in organizations*. London, UK: Sage.

Wells, J. D. (1996). Postmodernism and Information Technology: Philosophical perspectives and pragmatic implications. In J. Carey (Ed.), *Proceedings of the Americas Conference on Information Systems*, Arizona State University, Phoenix, Arizona (pp. 602-604).

Wenger, E. (1998). *Communities of practice: Learning, meaning, and identity*. Cambridge, UK: Cambridge UP.

Wenger, E. C., & Snyder, W. M. (2000, January-February). Communities of practice: The organizational frontier. *Harvard Business Review, 78*(6), 139–146.

Werts, C. E., Linn, R. L., & Jöreskog, K. G. (1974). Interclass reliability estimates: testing structural assumptions. *Educational and Psychological Measurement, 34*, 25–33. doi:10.1177/001316447403400104

Westfall, R. (1999). An IS research relevancy manifesto. *Communications of the Association for Information Systems, 2*(1).

Westfall, R. D. (2001). Dare to be relevant. *Communications of the Association for Information Systems, 6*(1).

West, J., & Lakhani, K. R. (2008, April). Getting clear about communities in open innovation. *Industry and Innovation, 15*(2), 223–231. doi:10.1080/13662710802033734

Westland, J. C. (2010). Lower bounds on sample size in structural equation modeling. *Electronic Commerce Research and Applications, 9*, 476–487. doi:10.1016/j.elerap.2010.07.003

Weyl, H. (1959). Mathematics and the laws of nature. In Gordon, I., & Sorkin, S. (Eds.), *The armchair science reader* (pp. 300–303). New York City, NY: Simon and Schuster.

Wheaton, B. (1987). Assessment of fit in overidentified models with latent variables. *Sociological Methods & Research, 16*, 118–154. doi:10.1177/0049124187016001005

Wheaton, B., Muthén, B., Alwin, D., & Summers, G. (1977). Assessing reliability and stability in panel models. *Sociological Methodology, 8*, 84–136. doi:10.2307/270754

Whetten, D. A. (1989). What constitutes a theoretical contribution? *Academy of Management Review, 14*(4), 490–495.

White, D., & Fortune, J. (2002). Current practice in project management – An empirical study. *International Journal of Project Management*, 20.

Whitehead, J. (2007). Collaboration in software engineering: A roadmap. *Future of Software Engineering, 2007*, 214–225. doi:10.1109/FOSE.2007.4

Whitla, P. (2009, March). Crowdsourcing and its application in marketing activities. *Contemporary Management Research, 5*(1), 15–28.

Wicks, A. C., & Freeman, R. E. (1998). Organization studies and the new pragmatism: positivism, anti-positivism, and the search for ethics. *Organization Science, 9*(2), 123–140. doi:10.1287/orsc.9.2.123

Widdows, R., Hensler, T. A., & Wyncott, M. H. (1991). The focus group interview: A method for assessing user's evaluation of library service. *College & Research Libraries, 52*(4).

Wiertz, C., & de Ruyter, K. (2007). Beyond the call of duty: Why customers contribute to firm hosted commercial online communities. *Organization Studies, 28*(3), 347–376. doi:10.1177/0170840607076003

Wigner, E. (1960). The unreasonable effectiveness of mathematics in the natural sciences. *Communications on Pure and Applied Mathematics, 13*(1), 1–14. doi:10.1002/cpa.3160130102

Williams, L. J., & Holahan, P. J. (1994). Parsimony-based fit indices for multiple-indicator models: Do they work? *Structural Equation Modeling, 1*(2), 161–189. doi:10.1080/10705519409539970

Williams, L., Vandenberg, R. J., & Edwards, R. J. (2009). Structural equation modeling in management research: A guide for improved analysis. *The Academy of Management Annals, 3*(1), 543–604. doi:10.1080/19416520903065683

Winograd, T., & Flores, F. (1986). *Understanding computers and cognition. A new foundation for design*. NJ: Ablex Publishing Co.

Winter, R. (2008). Design science research in Europe. *European Journal of Information Systems, 17*(5), 470–475. doi:10.1057/ejis.2008.44

Wittgenstein, L. (1953). *Philosophical investigations*. New York, NY: Macmillan.

Wold, H. (1982). Soft modeling: The basic design and some extensions. In K. G. Jöreskog & H. Wold (Eds.) *Systems under indirect observations: Causality, structure, prediction* (Part 2, pp. 1-54). Amsterdam, The Netherlands: North-Holland.

Wold, H. (1979). *Model construction and evaluation when theoretical knowledge is scarce: An example of the use of partial least squares. Cahiers du Département D'Économétrie*. Genève: Faculté des Sciences Économiques et Sociales, Université de Genève.

Wold, H. (1980). Soft modeling: intermediate between traditional model building and data analysis. *Mathematical Statistics, 6*, 333–346.

Wold, H. (1985). Systems analysis by partial least squares. In Nijkamp, P., Leitner, H., & Wrigley, N. (Eds.), *Measuring the unmeasurable* (pp. 221–251). Dordrecht, The Netherlands: Martinus Nijhoff.

Wong, C. S., Law, K. S., & Huang, G. H. (2008). On the importance of conducting construct-level analysis for multidimensional constructs in theory development and testing. *Journal of Management, 34*, 744–764. doi:10.1177/0149206307312506

Wood-Harper, T. (1985). Research methods in Information Systems: Using action research. In Mumford, E. (Eds.), *Research methods in Information Systems*. North-Holland: Elsevier Science Publishers B.V.

Wood, T. M., & Zhu, W. (2006). *Measurement theory and practice in kinesiology*. Champaign, IL: Human Kinetics Publisher.

Wordnet. (2010). *WordNet search 3.1*. Princeton University.

WOS Expanded. (2011). Retrieved February 2, 2011, from http://wos.izum.si/CIW.cgi

Wuisman, J. (2005). The logic of scientific discovery in critical realist social scientific research. *Journal of Critical Realism, 4*(2), 366–394. doi:10.1163/157251305774356586

Wu, M. F., & Chang, P. L. (2011). Assessing mechanism for pre-development stage of new product development by stage-gate model. *African Journal of Business Management, 5*(6), 2445–2454.

Wu, W., & West, S. G. (2010). Sensitivity of fit indices to misspecification in growth curve models. *Multivariate Behavioral Research, 45*, 420–452. doi:10.1080/00273171.2010.483378

Wynn, E. (2001). Möbius transitions in the dilemma of legitimacy. In Trauth, E. (Ed.), *Qualitative research in IS: Issues and trends*. Hershey, PA: Idea Group Publishing. doi:10.4018/978-1-930708-06-8.ch002

Yanow, D. (1995). Writing organizational tales. *Organization Science, 6*, 225. doi:10.1287/orsc.6.2.225

Yanow, D. (2004). Translating local knowledge at organizational peripheries. *British Journal of Management, 15*, 9–S25. doi:10.1111/j.1467-8551.2004.t01-1-00403.x

Yin, R. (2009). *Case study research: Design and methods*, 4th ed. Applied Social Research Methods Series, vol. 5.

Yin, R. K. (2003). *Case study research: Design and methods* (3rd ed.). Thousand Oaks, CA: Sage.

Yolles, M. (2006). *Organizations as complex systems. An introduction to knowledge cybernetics*. Greenwich, CT: IAP.

Yuan, K. H. (2005). Fit indices versus test statistics. *Multivariate Behavioral Research, 40*(1), 115–148. doi:10.1207/s15327906mbr4001_5

Yuan, K.-H., & Bentler, P. M. (2004). On chi-square difference and Z-tests in mean and covariance structure analysis when the base model is misspecified. *Educational and Psychological Measurement, 64*, 737–757. doi:10.1177/0013164404264853

Yun, H., Xu, J., Xiong, J., & Wei, M. (2011). A knowledge engineering approach to develop domain ontology. *International Journal of Distance Education Technologies, 9*(1), 57–71. doi:10.4018/jdet.2011010104

Zeleny, M. (2000). Knowledge vs. information. In Zeleny, M. (Ed.), *The IEBM handbook of Information Technology in business* (pp. 162–168). Padstow, UK: Thomson Learning.

Zeleny, M. (2005). *Human systems management. Integrating knowledge, management and systems*. London, UK: World Scientific. doi:10.1142/9789812703538

Zmud, R. W. (1978). An empirical investigation of the dimensionality of the concept of information. *Decision Sciences, 9*, 187–195. doi:10.1111/j.1540-5915.1978.tb01378.x

Zuber-Skerrit, O. (1992). *Action research in higher education*. London, UK: Kogan Page.

Zúñiga, G. L. (2001). Ontology: Its transformation from philosophy to information systems. *Proceedings of the International Conference on Formal Ontology in Information Systems*, Ogunquit, Maine, US (pp. 187-197).

About the Contributors

Manuel Mora is a Full Professor of Information Systems in the Autonomous University of Aguascalientes (UAA), Mexico, since 1994. Dr. Mora holds a B.S. in Computer Systems Engineering (1984) and a M.Sc. in Artificial Intelligence (1989) from Monterrey Tech (ITESM), and an Eng.D. in Systems Engineering (2003) from the National Autonomous University of Mexico (UNAM). He has published around 50 research papers in international top conferences, books, and/or journals. Dr. Mora has co-edited two books on DMSS and i-DMSS, and serves in editorial review boards for several international journals. His current main research interests are: foundations of service systems, design and evaluation methodologies for DMSS, and foundations of research methods for systems engineering, software engineering, and IT underpinned in the systems approach.

Ovsei Gelman is a Senior Researcher at the Center of Applied Sciences and Technology Development (CCADET) of the National Autonomous University of Mexico (UNAM). He holds a BS, MS, and PhD in Physics and Mathematics from the University of Tbilisi, Georgia. In the last 35 years he has contributed to the advance of the systems science discipline and interdisciplinary research through the publication of approximately 250 research papers in books, national and international journals, and conference proceedings, as well as by the participation as an advisor in the Engineering Graduate Program at UNAM and by the consulting for governmental and private organizations.

Annette Steenkamp is Professor of Information Technology Management at the Lawrence Technological University, Southfield, Michigan, USA. She has a PhD in Computer Science, University of South Africa with specialization in Software Engineering, with Dr. Daniel Teichroew, University of Michigan as supervisor. Her academic career spans several generations of computing systems, during which she taught a range of subjects at the graduate and doctoral level in the fields of Software Engineering, Enterprise Architecture, System Process Improvement, Project Management, Quality Assurance, and Research Methodology. Her current research agenda include the fields of knowledge management, enterprise architecture, and systems life cycle management, and she is engaged in supervising a number of doctoral research projects. She has contributed a large body of journal articles and conference papers at national and international conferences, and is a sought after keynote speaker. She serves on several editorial review boards, including IJITSA (*International Journal of Information Technologies and the Systems Approach*).

Mahesh S. Raisinghani is an Associate Professor in the Executive MBA program at the TWU School of Management. Dr. Raisinghani was awarded the 2008 Excellence in Research & Scholarship award and the 2007 G. Ann Uhlir Endowed Fellowship in Higher Education Administration. He was also the recipient of TWU School of Management's 2005 Best Professor Award for the Most Innovative Teaching Methods; 2002 research award; 2001 King/Haggar Award for excellence in teaching, research, and service; and a 1999 UD-GSM Presidential Award. His research has been published in several academic journals and international/national conferences. Dr. Raisinghani serves on the board of the Global IT Management Association and on the education task force of the World Affairs Council-D/FW. He is included in the millennium edition of Who's Who in the World, Who's Who among Professionals, Who's Who among America's Teachers and Who's Who in Information Technology.

* * *

Steven Alter is a Professor in Information Systems at the University of San Francisco, USA. He is author of 6 books and many articles in journals and conference proceedings including *HBR, SMR, MISQ, EJIS, DSS, IBM Systems Journal, CAIS, IRMJ, JISE, ICIS, ECIS, AMCIS,* and *HICSS*. Most of his research concerns systems analysis and design methods for business professionals.

Theo Andrew is a Professor and Dean of the Faculty of Engineering and the Built Environment at the Durban University of Technology, South Africa. Theo is a Fellow of the South African Institute of Electrical Engineers (SAIEE), and served as its Vice-President. His papers have appeared in *Telecommunications Policy, Int. Journal on Technology Management, Decision Support Systems, IEE Eng. Scienceand Ed. J.*, and elsewhere.

Peter M. Bentler received his Ph.D. in Psychology from Stanford University. A former Chair of the Department of Psychology at UCLA, he is now Distinguished Professor of Psychology and Statistics. He has been an elected President of the Society of Multivariate Experimental Psychology (SMEP), the Psychometric Society, the Western Psychological Association, and the Division of Evaluation, Measurement and Statistics of the American Psychological Association. He received SMEP's 2005 Sells Award for Outstanding Career Contributions to Multivariate Experimental Psychology and, in 2007, was the recipient (with Karl Jöreskog) of the American Psychological Association's Distinguished Scientific Contribution Award for the Applications of Psychology.

Lucio Biggiero is a Professor of Organisation Science at the University of L'Aquila (L'Aquila, Italy); he has published papers in several journals, among which include: *Entrepreneurship & Regional Development; Human Systems Management; International Review of Sociology; Journal of Financial Decision Making; Journal of Management and Governance; Journal of Management Studies; Journal of Technology Transfer; Science and Public Policy; Systemica*. He is the director of the Knownetlab Research Group (www.knownetlab.it) and of the MEFOR section of CIRPS (http://www.cirps.it/). He applies the following advanced research methodologies to social and natural systems: agent-based simulation models; network analysis; NK-FL simulation modelling; outranking methods for multicriteria decision making; social network analysis.

Mirjana Kljajić Borštnar holds a Ph.D. in Organizational Science from the University of Maribor. Her research work covers expert systems, multi-criteria decision-making, and Information Systems development methods. She holds a position of Assistant Professor and is a member of Laboratory for Decision Processes and Knowledge-Based Systems. During her postgraduate studies, she participated in several EU and national funded projects covering decision support in global e-business environment and fostering innovation in SMEs. Her recent research work is focused on experiments with decision groups applying system dynamics simulators in experimental, real, and interactive learning environments.

Ruth de Villiers is a Research Professor in the School of Computing at the University of South Africa, a large open-distance learning institution. Ruth has PhD and Master's degrees in Information Systems and Computer-Integrated Education. She has taught Computer Science and Informatics for more than 25 years. Her main research interests are human-computer interaction and e-learning, which she has combined by undertaking research, development, and usability evaluation of various e-learning applications and environments, including systems crossing the Digital Divide. She has also published in the domain of meta-research, working on research designs and methodologies. Ruth supervises Master's and Doctoral students in the above fields.

Phil Dobson worked at a senior level for a number of large Australian mining companies before returning to academia in the mid 1980's. He has a particular interest in the underlying philosophies of Information Systems research and has completed a PhD in 2002, which examined the application of a critical realist approach to aspects of IS research. He is currently Senior Lecturer in the School of MIS at Edith Cowan University in Perth, Western Australia and has a particular interest in the philosophical basis of IS research and qualitative approaches. Current research projects involve using critical realism as a basis for understanding organizational workflows and in examining broadband adoption and usage.

Theresa M. Edgington received her PhD in Information Systems and MBA (concentration in Computer Science) from Arizona State University after a successful twenty-plus year IT career. She has utilized SEM as her primary research method since 2003. Her research interests include knowledge creation/innovation/identification/structure, organizational cognition/coordination, failure analysis, strategic management, systems analysis, and healthcare and IS coordination. Her research has appeared in academic journals including *MIS Quarterly, Communications of the ACM, Decision Support Systems, Journal of Information Systems Education, Journal of Information Technology Education, ACM e-Learning,* and academic conferences including ICIS, HICSS, INFORMS, and AMCIS, Academy of Management and SIG workshops, and at numerous industry conferences.

Mariki Eloff has a PhD in Computer Science and has 20 years lecturing experience. In her capacity as full Professor at Unisa she is a member of: College of Science, Engineering and Technology Executive and Research Committees, Disability Committee, and National Council for Persons with Physical Disabilities in South Africa. Furthermore, she received the Women in Research award for Research Leadership. She participated in a number of information security research projects and international conferences. She served as the South African representative on ISO (International Standards Organisation) and contributed to the development of computer and information security standards on an international level.

Lee B. Erickson is a PhD Candidate in the College of Information Sciences and Technology at The Pennsylvania State University focusing on the uses and impacts of social media in business contexts. Currently she is examining the uses of and impacts on companies leveraging social media to connect with diverse audiences as potential sources of innovative knowledge (often referred to as "crowdsourcing"). Erickson brings 25+ years of industry experience working with leading high-technology companies, venture capital firms, associations, and foundations nationwide to her academic research. She holds an MA in Educational Communications & Technology, from New York University and a BA in Education from Virginia Tech.

Moti Frank earned his B.Sc. in Electrical Engineering in 1981 and M.Sc in 1996 both from the *Technion* – Israel Institute of Technology - and worked for more than 20 years as an Electronics and Systems Engineer. He earned his Ph.D. degree in Industrial Engineering and Management and Education in Technology and Science in 1999 from the *Technion*. He is Professor of Systems Engineering in HIT, Holon Institute of Technology. His research interests are systems engineering, systems thinking, project management, and research methods. Currently he is a visiting faculty at the department of Systems Engineering and Operations Research in George Mason University, Fairfax, Virginia.

Timothy L.J. Ferris is the Associate Director: Teaching and Learning in the Defence and Systems Institute at the University of South Australia. He holds degrees in Engineering, Theology, and Higher Education, received from various Australian universities, including a PhD in Engineering from the University of South Australia. His major teaching and research work is in the area of research methods for engineering. His research interests also include the impact of ethnic culture on engineering practice and the underlying fundamentals of engineering.

Martha García-Murillo is Full Professor and Director of the Telecommunications and Network Management Master's program at the School of Information Studies at Syracuse University. She has an M.S. in Economics and a Ph.D. in Political Economy and Public Policy. She has been involved in research projects for the UN, US State Department, and other regional and international organizations. Her areas of research include institutional economics in the ICT sector, the impact of technology on regulation, factors that affect infrastructure deployment, institutional factors that can affect innovation, and ICT in Latin America and theory construction.

Gonzalo Génova has an MS degree in Telecommunication Engineering from the Polytechnic University of Madrid (1992), an MS degree in Philosophy from the University of Navarre (1996), and a PhD in Computer Engineering from the Carlos III University of Madrid. He is currently an Associate Professor of Software Engineering in the Department of Computer Science and Engineering at the Carlos III University of Madrid. His main research subjects, within the Knowledge Reuse Group and in close cooperation with The Reuse Company, are models and modeling languages in software engineering, requirements engineering, and philosophy of Information Systems.

Rafael A. González is a Systems Engineer from Javeriana University (Bogotá) with an MSc in Computer Science and a PhD in Systems Engeeineering (cum laude) from Delft University of Technology (The Netherlands). He has been Lecturer in the areas of Information Systems, Systems Thinking, and Software Engineering, as well as acting as IT consultant for the public and private sectors. His research interests are focused on development of Information Systems with a design science approach, centered on the issues of coordination, complexity and the interplay between ICT and society. His is currently Associate Professor of Information Systems at Javeriana University.

Ezgi Nur Gozen is a Ph.D. student in Information Science and Technology program at Syracuse University. She has an M.S. in Telecommunications and Network Management also from Syracuse University. She received a B.S. in Information Systems from Binghamton University, and a B.E. in Information Systems Engineering from Istanbul Technical University. She worked as a Graduate Research Assistant at Syracuse University on a project related to Internet congestion and business continuity. She also worked as a Faculty Assistant on several academic projects. Her research interests include digital divide and the impact of ICTs in society.

Miroljub Kljajić obtained his Ph.D. from the Faculty of Electrical Engineering, University of Ljubljana in 1974. Since 1976 he has been employed by the Faculty of Organizational Sciences in Kranj in the field of System Theory, Cybernetics, Computer Simulation, and Decision Theory. His main research field is methods of modeling and simulation of complex systems. He is author of the book Theory of Systems. He published over 200 scientific articles, from which, 29 are in JCR. For achievements in research and pedagogical work he obtained many national and international awards and recognitions. He obtained the rank of Emeritus Professor in 2010.

Theresa Kraft teaches Computer Science and Information Technology courses at the University of Michigan Flint. She received her Doctor of Management in Information Technology from Lawrence Technological University, Southfield, Michigan, USA. Her graduate studies include an MBA from the University of Detroit Mercy and a Master's of System Engineering from Rensselaer Polytechnic Institute. Her recent articles on project management have been published in the *Information Systems Education Journal* and the *Journal of Information Systems Applied Research*. She has comprehensive industry experience in manufacturing engineering, project management, and Information Technology.

Davorin Kofjač obtained his Ph.D. from the University of Maribor in the field of Information Systems Management with a thesis "Fuzzy Adaptive Algorithm for Inventory Control in Uncertain Environment." He was a young and a senior researcher at the University of Maribor, Faculty of Organizational Sciences at the Cybernetics and Decision Support Systems Laboratory. He was/is participating in many research projects in the field of operational research, decision support systems, modeling and simulation, and artificial intelligence. Currently, he is an Assistant Professor at the University of Maribor, Faculty of Organizational Sciences.

Damodar Konda is an accomplished IT Executive with over 25 years of professional experience with several multinational companies including GM and Indian Railways. He is currently working as Vice President, Global Business Applications at RGIS, LLC., Auburn Hills, MI, USA and leading the implementation of several mission-critical enterprise IT solutions globally for RGIS. His expertise includes leading enterprise change management, IT strategy and blueprint, establishment of system delivery processes and PMO, program management initiatives for global rollout of ERP, COTS, and Custom-built IT solutions. He has a Master's degree in Engineering from IIT Madras, India, MBA from SIU, Carbondale, IL, and a DMIT from LTU, Michigan, USA.

Jan H. Kroeze has PhDs in Semitic Languages and Information and Communication Technology. He is the Chair of Department in the School of Computing at Unisa. His research area is Humanities-enriched Information Systems, and he currently focuses on the philosophical and theoretical aspects of IS research. He is a collaborator on the editorial committee of *The Journal for Transdisciplinary Research in Southern Africa* and a member of various academic societies, and he serves on the SAICSIT council. He is also the editor of a new IBIMA journal, *Journal of Humanities and Information Systems.*

Loet Leydesdorff (Ph.D. Sociology, M.A. Philosophy, and M.Sc. Biochemistry) is Professor at the Amsterdam School of Communications Research (ASCoR) of the University of Amsterdam. He is Visiting Professor of the Institute of Scientific and Technical Information of China (ISTIC) in Beijing, Honorary Fellow of the Science and Technology Policy Research Unit (SPRU) of the University of Sussex, and at the Virtual Knowledge Studio of the Netherlands Royal Academy of Arts and Sciences. He has published extensively in systems theory, social network analysis, scientometrics, and the sociology of innovation (see for a list of publications at http://www.leydesdorff.net/list.htm). In 2006, he published The Knowledge-Based Economy: Modeled, Measured, Simulated (Boca Rotan, FL: Universal Publishers). Previous monographs are: A Sociological Theory of Communication: The Self-Organization of the Knowledge-Based Society (2001) and The Challenge of Scientometrics: The development, measurement, and self-organization of scientific communications (1995). With Henry Etzkowitz, he initiated a series of workshops, conferences, and special issues about the Triple Helix of University-Industry-Government Relations. He received the Derek de Solla Price Award for Scientometrics and Informetrics in 2003 and held "The City of Lausanne" Honor Chair at the School of Economics, Université de Lausanne, in 2005. In 2007, he was Vice-President of the 8th International Conference on Computing Anticipatory Systems (CASYS'07, Liège).

Juan Llorens received his MS degree in Industrial Engineering from the ICAI Polytechnic School at the UPC University in Madrid in 1986, Spain, and his PhD in Industrial Engineering and Robotics at the Carlos III University of Madrid, Spain in 1996. He joined the Carlos III University in 1992 where he is currently a Full Professor of the Department of Computer Science and Engineering. Dr. Llorens is the leader of the Knowledge Reuse Group within the University. His main research subject is information representation and processing for software reuse. Since 1998 he has split his educational activities between Carlos III University and the Högskolan på Åland (Mariehamn, Åland, Finland).

Jorge Morato is currently an Associate Professor of Information Science in the Department of Computer Science and Engineering at the Carlos III University of Madrid (Spain). He obtained a PhD in Library Science from the Carlos III University in 1999 on the subject of Knowledge Information Systems and its relationships with linguistics. From 1991-1999, he had grants or contracts from the Spanish National Research Council. His current research activity is centered on text mining, information extraction and pattern recognition, NLP, information retrieval, Web positioning, and knowledge organization systems. He has published mainly on semi-automatic construction of thesauri and ontologies, topic maps, and conceptual and contextualized retrieval of semantic documents.

Rory V. O'Connor is a Senior Lecturer in Software Engineering at Dublin City University and a Senior Researcher with Lero, The Irish Software Engineering Research Centre. He has previously held research positions at both the National Centre for Software Engineering and the Centre for Teaching Computing, and has also worked as a Software Engineer and Consultant for several European technology organizations. He is also Ireland's Head of delegation to ISO/IEC JCT1/SC7. His research interests are centered on the processes whereby software intensive systems are designed, implemented, and managed.

Doncho Petkov is a Professor of IS at Eastern Connecticut State University, USA. He is on the editorial boards of *Systems Research and Behavioral Science, Intl. Journal on IT and the Systems Approach*, and other journals. His publications have appeared in *The Journal of Systems and Software, Decision Support Systems, Telecommunications Policy, IRMJ, IJITSA, JITTA, Kybernetes*, and elsewhere.

Olga Petkova is a Professor in MIS at Central Connecticut State University, USA. Her publications are in software development productivity, systems thinking and IT education. They have appeared in *Decision Support Systems, JITTA, Journal of Informatics Education Research, JITCAR, South African Computing Journal*, and elsewhere.

José L. Roldán is Associate Professor of Management at the Faculty of Economics and Business Administration, University of Seville. His recent contributions have been published in *International Small Business Journal, Computers in Human Behavior, Handbook of Partial Least Squares, Industrial Marketing Management, International Journal of Technology Management*, and *Internet Research*. Currently he is on the editorial board of *The Database for Advances in Information Systems*, and was guest editor of *European Journal of Information Systems' Special Issue on Quantitative Research Methodology*. His research interests include social network sites and PLS methodology.

Manuel J. Sánchez-Franco is Professor in e-Business Management and Advertising Communication at the University of Seville (Spain). His current research interests are in the areas of electronic markets and online consumer behaviour. His recent works have been published – or forthcoming – in *Computers & Education, Journal of Interactive Marketing, Information and Management, Computers in Human Behavior, Online Information Review, Electronic Commerce Research and Applications, Behaviour & Information Technology, Internet Research, Service Industries Journal, Journal of Product and Brand Management, Journal of Brand Management, Revista Española de Pedagogía, Revista Española de Investigación de Marketing*, among others.

Kosheek Sewchurran is an Associate Professor in Information Systems at the University of Cape Town. He is a rated researcher by the National Research Foundation and serves the editorial boards of *International Journal of Managing Projects in Business* (IJMPiB) and *International Journal of Information Systems and the Systems Approach* (IJITSA).

Taryn Schwartzel works in the field of Technology Consulting at Accenture specializing in IT Strategy and Transformation. Taryn works across telecommunications, public services, financial services, energy, mining, and retail industries. She completed a MTech in 2009 at University of Johannesburg in Information Technology. Taryn is in the process of completing her PhD part time at the University of South Africa (Unisa) in the field of Information Systems. In 2002 she received an Orbicom Mandela Bursary sponsored by companies such as MTN, Orbicom, Pan Am Sat, Worldspace, Telemedia, and former President Nelson Mandela. Taryn has a keen interest for innovative technologies.

Alveen Singh is a PhD candidate in the Department of Information Technology at Durban University of Technology, South Africa. He received his Master's in Technology from Durban University of Technology. He is currently a Lecturer in the Department of Information Technology. His areas of teaching and research include software engineering, IT project management, and programming.

Andrej Škraba obtained his Ph.D. in the field of Organizational Sciences from the University of Maribor. He works as a Researcher and Assistant Professor at the Faculty of Organizational Sciences in the Cybernetics and DSS Laboratory. His research interests cover modeling and simulation, system dynamics, decision processes, and multiple criteria decision-making. His work has been published in the following journals: *Simulation, System Dynamics Review*, and *Group Decision and Negotiation*. In the course of post-doctoral studies he successfully completed three distance-learning courses on System Dynamics from MIT, Center for Advanced Educational Services and Worchester Polytechnic Institute.

Henk G. Sol is a Dutch Organizational Theorist and Professor of Business Engineering and ICT at the University of Groningen (UoG). His research focuses on the development of services enabled by ICT, management Information Systems, decision enhancement, and telematics. Prof. Sol received an M.A. and a PhD from the UoG. He was Founding Dean of the School for Engineering, Policy Analysis and Management at the TU Delft as well as of the Faculty of Economics and Business at UoG. He serves in several editorial boards and acts as a management consultant. Under his responsibility, over 70 PhD dissertations have been finished.

Eileen M. Trauth is Professor of Information Sciences and Technology at The Pennsylvania State University. Her research on human capital in the information economy includes investigations of skills and knowledge of IT professionals, economic development, gender diversity, globalization, and research methods. She has lectured and conducted research in several European countries, including Australia, New Zealand and South Africa. Trauth has published numerous scholarly articles and 9 books with grants from the National Science Foundation, Science Foundation Ireland and the Australian Research Council. She is recipient of a Fulbright Scholar Award (Ireland 1989) and the Fulbright Distinguished Chair in Gender Studies (Austria 2008).

Esther Vlieger follows a Research Master's in Communication Science at the University of Amsterdam. Her research interests are in the fields of Media, Journalism, and Political Communication. Since 2009, she has been research assistant of Professor Loet Leydesdorff. In her thesis – "The measurement of news frames by use of manual and automated content analysis; exploring the use of manually coded frame elements and computer-assisted semantic maps to study newsframes" – she explores new ways of measuring newsframes. She is currently working as a media analist at a media research organization, where she conducts quantitative and qualitative media analyses for clients from public and financial institutions.

Jeanette Wing is a PhD candidate in the Department of Information Technology, at the Durban University of Technology, South Africa. She is currently a Senior Lecturer in the Department of Information Technology in the areas of Programming and Software Engineering. Her major research interests include software engineering, requirements analysis, the influence of social systems on Information Systems, and its implications.

Index